Exploring Tech Careers

FOURTH EDITION

VOLUME 2

Ferguson
An imprint of Infobase Publishing

Exploring Tech Careers, Fourth Edition

Ferguson
An imprint of Infobase Publishing
132 West 31st Street
New York NY 10001

Exploring tech careers.—4th ed.
v. <2> p. cm.
Includes bibliographical references and index.
ISBN 0-8160-6447-4 (hc : alk. paper)
1. Technology—Vocational guidance.
T65.3.E95 2006
602.3—dc22 2005019101

Ferguson books are available at special discounts when purchased in bulk quantities for businesses, associations, institutions, or sales promotions. Please call our Special Sales Department in New York at (212) 967-8800 or (800) 322-8755.

You can find Ferguson on the World Wide Web at http://www.fergpubco.com

Text design by Mary Susan Ryan-Flynn
Cover design by Salvatore Luongo

Printed in the United States of America

VB MSRF 10 9 8 7 6 5 4 3 2 1

This book is printed on acid-free paper.

CONTENTS

Volume 1

Volume 2

INDUSTRIAL RADIOLOGICAL TECHNICIANS

Definition
Industrial radiological technicians work with materials that emit radiation in biomedical, biological, and industrial settings.

Alternative Job Titles
Hot-cell technicians
Industrial radiographers
Radioisotope production technicians

High School Subjects
Chemistry
English
Mathematics

Personal Skills
Following instructions
Mechanical/manipulation

Salary Range
$21,470 to $35,790 to $56,470

Minimum Educational Level
Associate's degree

Certification or Licensing
Required by certain states

Outlook
About as fast as the average

DOT
719

GOE
N/A

NOC
N/A

O*NET-SOC
N/A

It is slow going for Dave this morning. For 20 minutes he has painstakingly tried to perform what normally would be a simple task—twisting a lid back on a jar. The problem is, he cannot touch the glass jar or the metal lid with his hands. They are in a "hot cell," a laboratory room filled with radiation, and Dave is in the room next door, operating a remote-controlled, mechanical arm.

Frustrated, Dave takes a deep breath and makes another attempt. He positions the mechanical arm, grasps the round lid in his "hand," and brings it down over the jar. Persistently turning, releasing, and grasping, he finally manages to secure the lid and screw it tight. Dave lets out a laugh and comments, "Things like this can really drive you loony."

The jar is just one of the many items Dave has handled by remote control. As a hot-cell technician at a government research facility, he specializes in performing tests and other procedures on materials that have been exposed to radiation.

What Does an Industrial Radiological Technician Do?

Certain naturally occurring elements, such as radium and uranium, radiate energy that is dangerous, but it can also be put to use in many ways. X rays that provide pictures of broken bones, radiation therapy for cancer patients, and electricity generated at nuclear power plants are just a few examples. The practical application of radiation in its various forms is the job of the *industrial radiological technician*.

There is a wide range of career options for industrial radiological technicians. They can specialize in health and safety. They monitor radiation levels in laboratories, nuclear energy plants, particle accelerator complexes, and other settings where humans could be exposed. They design, test, manufacture, maintain, or sell nuclear instruments or equipment that controls the quality of X rays. Some technicians conduct research and test the effects of radiation on living things and inorganic materials. Many industrial radiological technicians are involved in nondestructive testing, a science that detects flaws in a material such as concrete without damaging it. The three most common careers for industrial radiological technicians are hot-cell technician, radioisotope production technician, and radiographer.

Hot-cell technicians work indirectly with materials that have been exposed to radiation and placed in a "hot cell," an enclosed room shielded with materials such as lead or concrete. The room is filled with nitrogen, and no one can enter without protective clothing.

Most of the work is done by technicians using a "master-slave manipulator," a mechanical device that acts like a pair of arms and hands inside the hot cell. The "master," or technician, manipulates the "slave" to grasp, move, cut, polish, and perform tests on materials being exposed to the radiation in the cell.

Hot-cell technicians work primarily with metallurgical materials. For example, a hot-cell technician might spend a great deal of time examining metal pins that have been used in the construction of nuclear reactors. The pins are removed from the nuclear facility and placed inside the hot cell where they are examined for flaws, cracks, or instabilities. The results of these tests are documented by the technician to help determine the life span of the pin, its safety, and its limitations.

Like hot-cell technicians, *radioisotope production technicians* use a process known as irradiation. An irradiated product is a naturally occurring element or chemical that has been placed inside a special container and bombarded with neutrons.

Radioisotope production technicians work in nuclear laboratories or other facilities that produce radioactive materials. Radioisotopes are the unstable form of an element that produces radiation. They are used for medical, biological, industrial, and other applications.

Radioisotope production technicians place materials in glass containers and prepare them for shipping to irradiation facilities. They replace the air in the container with an inert gas by using a vacuum pump that sucks out the oxygen, making sure that no chemical reactions can occur inside the container.

These technicians may also receive and treat irradiated materials on their way back from an irradiation facility. Using manipulators, the technician opens the containers and adds chemical solutions to the contents. The radioisotope production technician may perform tests on the radioactive material or ship it to a chemical laboratory for analysis. Once the product has been approved, the technician fills shipping containers and sends the radioisotopic material to those who use it.

One of the largest fields for industrial radiological technicians is that of radiography. *Radiographic technicians* take X rays, also called radiographs, of many kinds of industrial materials. Unlike the other professions discussed here, radiographic technicians, or *radiographers,* can be found in a wide variety of industries, not just those related to the use of nuclear power.

A radiograph is a picture taken by placing an object against a photographic plate and exposing it to radiation. The radiographer develops the film and examines it, looking for cracks or other flaws in the object that was photographed. The technician may write up the findings, verbally explain them to the client, or make recommendations for maintenance or repairs.

Radiographers examine many types of objects, such as metal castings, plastics, pipe welds, tubing, and poured concrete structures. Much of this work is done in a special lead- or concrete-encased room. The radiographer sets up the material, secures the room, and then takes the X rays from a different location to avoid being exposed to radiation. Sometimes the material to be X-rayed is so big the radiographer must set up the project in a location other than the shielded room. In that case, the technician takes extra precautions to secure the area by surrounding the material with lead plates and keeping it clear of people.

Lingo to Learn

Hardness testers Tools that use a solid force to test durability.

Light boxes Boxes that illuminate film for viewing.

Master-slave manipulator Remotely operated devices that act as the arms and hands of the person at the controls.

Micrometers Tools for measuring the thickness of an object.

Tensile testers Tools that grip and pull an object to test its breaking point.

Tomography A form of the CT scan used on materials such as ceramics and engine parts.

X-omat An automatic film processor.

What Is It Like to Be an Industrial Radiological Technician?

Dave is a senior hot-cell technician with Argonne National Laboratories, a government research facility that specializes in radiation technology. He works exclusively with materials inside a hot cell in a laboratory, a job that requires him to observe strict guidelines and safety regulations.

Dave does all his work with remote-controlled mechanical devices and manipulators. Occasionally, technicians are required to get a little closer to the cell than normal, putting their arms through special protective coverings like long gloves that extend into the cell. Using their own hands and not the more awkward "slave" hand, the technicians can accomplish a task in less time than it takes with a manipulator.

In some facilities a technician may put on a protective suit and go into the hot cell, but not at Argonne, where Dave works. "We're a research facility, and we take on 'dirty' jobs, jobs that other places might refuse. As a result, our cell is fairly contaminated. No one's been inside it for years," he says.

The cell is 50 feet wide and 75 feet long. Its atmosphere is nitrogen with high radiation. Every job Dave performs requires painstaking preparation. For special projects, he may need to build new devices. "Ninety percent of the tools we use, we make up ourselves, welding things together," he says.

A typical project for Dave is inspecting metal pins taken from nuclear reactors. He secures the pin inside the hot cell, then takes radiographic views of it, looking for possible flaws. It is critical for researchers to know what happens to the metal objects used in the construction of nuclear facilities. "They need to see what has happened to this pin while it was in the reactor," Dave says. "What is its life? Does it need to be replaced and how often?"

Like other industrial radiological technicians, Dave often does repetitious tasks, but he rarely finds work boring. It can be both physically and psychologically demanding, always keeping him on his toes. "Sometimes I spend all day running a tool over one object, mapping it, over and over again. And sometimes I do 20 little jobs in one day," Dave says.

One of Dave's co-workers at Argonne, Chuck Vulyak, also performs some repetitive tasks. As a radiographic technician, he uses radiation to make pictures on film, which he can analyze to detect flaws in a pipe weld, for example. When Chuck arrives for work each morning, he turns on the equipment, warming up the X-ray machines and X-omats. Depending on the machine, he may have to increase the temperature manually, turning dials and monitoring the heat levels. With everything in order, Chuck reads over the inspection forms to see what is in store for him that day. Today, the first order of business is to examine a pipe weld.

To Be a Successful Industrial Radiological Technician, You Should . . .

- have manual dexterity for performing intricate tasks
- be able to work well with others as part of a team
- have a lot of patience
- be able to communicate well both verbally and in writing
- be detail oriented and follow safety guidelines

The radiographer has different standards and rules that need to be followed for each project. Chuck looks at his orders, checking for acceptance criteria and the codes he will need to follow. Once he has determined at what angle the pipe weld should be photographed and how much exposure he will need, Chuck sets up metal identification markers that spell out what the object is. "There are usually about 45 to 60 minutes of setup involved in each shot," he says. "Preparation is very important."

After he gets the developed film from the developing machine or X-omat, Chuck places it on the light box and examines the weld for flaws. He fills out paperwork and may discuss his findings with the welding engineer or foreman. Because of his early job experience as a welder, Chuck has an advantage over some of his fellow radiographers. "Because of my background in welding, I can look at my own film and see just what needs to be done," he says.

There are days when Chuck may repeat the same process over and over again. Often, most of his work for the day can be accomplished in the radiography room, but there are times when the radiographers are needed at different sites. "That's where the long hours come in," says Chuck.

For those projects, safety requirements dictate that the area be clear of people. The radiographers wait until regular working hours are over, then put

In-depth

Nondestructive Testing Methods

Most of the work done by industrial radiological technicians consists of nondestructive testing to determine how radiation affects various materials. Nondestructive testing (NDT) can involve radiography, magnetic particles, ultrasonics, liquid penetrants, eddy currents, leaks, acoustic emissions, visual examination, microwaves, ultrasonic imaging, lasers, holography, liquid crystals, and infrared thermal testing techniques.

Radiography X rays are used to reveal flaws in a product or material.

Magnetic particle testing reveals imperfections in materials. The surface is dusted with iron particles and a magnetic field is introduced, causing the particles to gather at the flaw.

Ultrasonics testing transmits high frequency sound waves into the material to detect imperfections or changes in the material's properties.

In *liquid penetrant testing,* the test object is coated with an invisible fluorescent dye then exposed to a developer that draws the dye out of imperfections, thus exposing them to the eye.

In *eddy current testing,* electrical currents are sent through conductive material by a magnetic field. Interruptions in the flow of current show changes and flaws in the material.

in overtime at night and on weekends. "Most of the work is done in the lab. We usually leave by 5:00 P.M. When there's fieldwork, that's when we put in the long hours and the occasional Saturday," says Chuck.

Long hours are also a part of Dave's job as a hot-cell technician. He puts in six-day workweeks on a fairly regular basis. "It's not required by the company," says Dave. "But the overtime is good, and it shows you're a dedicated and dependable worker."

Do I Have What It Takes to Be an Industrial Radiological Technician?

Both Dave and Chuck work with hazardous materials every day. They spend a great deal of time following detailed safety regulations to protect themselves and their surroundings. Their movements need to be precise and safe at all times. "We have to be very safety conscious," says Dave. "On jobs outside our normal work, we assess hazards and plan for special equipment. You can't take the chance of anything happening."

There is also paperwork to complete for each project. A technician should be able to write well and communicate facts and findings clearly.

Dave and Chuck both stress the importance of good communication skills and the ability to work well with others. Cooperation is the key to these technicians' jobs. "It's a buddy system," says Chuck.

"One person watches the other's back. You can't do a lot of these jobs yourself," Dave points out. "You have to work in harmony with others."

The ability to think on your feet is also important. Working with radiation, adapting existing tools to a job, and creating new tools to serve a specific purpose are all part of the package. Creativity is the part of his job that Dave likes best. "There's always something new going on. Every day is different," he notes.

"I get to work on things that have never been done before," says Chuck, who occasionally assists engineers with research projects. The fact that most of the jobs industrial radiological technicians perform are related to research often makes the work more interesting.

Many people rely on these technicians to perform complex tasks with potentially dangerous materials. It is a hands-on job that requires diligence and skill. "You've got to like working with your hands," says

Dave. "This isn't a job where you sit in an office in a suit and tie, punching computer buttons."

How Do I Become an Industrial Radiological Technician?

Both Dave and Chuck Vulyak started their careers in different fields than the ones in which they now work. Previously, Dave had a job as a nuclear reactor operator. When the plant shut down, the hot-cell division of his company offered him a new job and training there. "They knew my work and said, 'Come on over,'" he recalls.

Like Dave, Chuck switched fields when his job ended. Fifteen years ago, he was a welder, but the company for which he worked went out of business. Chuck went back to school and trained to become an industrial radiographer.

Both Chuck and Dave were forced to adapt when their jobs fell prey to changing technology and cutbacks. Today, they say, people entering this field will see an increased emphasis on education as companies require more scholastic training than in the past.

EDUCATION

High School

A high school diploma or the General Equivalency Diploma (GED) is the first step toward a career as an industrial radiological technician. Students interested in any of the technician areas are encouraged to take classes in math and science since radiological technology is based on physical and mathematical principles. High school physics and chemistry are good basic courses to prepare you for later studies. Algebra and plane geometry are crucial for this field.

"Take as many math and science classes as you can," recommends Chuck Vulyak. Numbers and formulas are part of a day's work for these technicians. Often, you are required to read or compose charts and graphs based on numbers and you must be able to work easily with them.

Chuck also advises taking whatever shop classes are offered in high school. As a radiographer, he often has to x-ray automotive or engine parts. Auto shop offers the opportunity to familiarize yourself with the industrial materials used by many industrial radiological technicians. The same goes for metal shop. Dave spends a great deal of time examining metal pins and pipe welds in his role as a hot-cell technician. And according to Chuck, "The most x-rayed object in the world is the weld."

> **FYI**
>
> Industrial radiographers who extend their education to include medical and health-related applications of radiology can hold certifications in both areas, increasing career opportunities.

You should also study English and composition since communication skills are just as important as technical ones. Relaying information, writing clearly and concisely, and interacting with fellow workers are all part of the job.

Postsecondary Training

There are several ways to acquire the training to be an industrial radiological technician. The most common and increasingly accepted credential is a college degree. Many employers are satisfied with graduates of a two-year program, but students with four-year degrees are more often recruited, especially if the choice is between a candidate with a two-year degree and a candidate with a four-year degree.

College training programs come with a variety of names, such as radiation and nuclear technology, physical radiologic technology, applied sciences, and nondestructive testing. To prepare for the area in which you plan to specialize, consult your career guidance counselor.

Chuck Vulyak originally earned a two-year associate's degree in applied science from his local community college. He went on to earn a bachelor of science degree with a minor in business administration from a four-year university. He feels that his business background has increased his job skills and marketability and given him a better understanding of the job.

Most college programs begin by teaching the fundamentals of radiation, followed by classes in specialized areas, including radiation biology,

In-depth

History

During the 1880s and 1890s, scientists researching naturally occurring chemical elements began to suspect that certain elements radiated special forms of energy, either spontaneously or under the influence of specific stimuli. Early investigators included Wilhelm Roentgen, who discovered X rays in 1895; Henri Becquerel, who discovered radioactivity in uranium in 1896; and Pierre and Marie Curie, who discovered polonium and radium.

During the 20th century, investigation into the nature of radiation has led to various successful applications in many areas. Almost as soon as X rays were discovered, medical researchers began exploring their usefulness as a diagnostic tool, and as early as World War I, this new technology was widely used for locating bullets in wounded soldiers. In the 1940s, industrial applications, such as gamma ray and X ray inspection, were developed in the nondestructive testing field. Currently in the industry, radiology includes tomography, backscatter, gaging, and other radiation inspection methods.

From its earliest years, radiological technology has relied on skilled assistants both in the research and development field and in industries such as aerospace, construction, and petrochemicals. Today, as radiation technology is brought to a wider range of applications, qualified industrial radiological technicians are sought after in the nondestructive testing field.

radiation elements, and environmental radiation technology. Other courses include physics, chemistry, statistics, technical math, electronics, and technical writing. Chuck stresses the importance of writing classes to improve communication skills. Photography courses are also recommended for prospective radiographers.

If college does not seem to be the best route for you, you might be able to get technical training through on-the-job experience. Dave received all of his training as a hot-cell technician at the laboratory where he works, although he had previous experience as a nuclear reactor operator, and he does hold a two-year associate's degree in mechanical engineering. "These days, you need a two-year degree at the very least," he says.

The armed forces offer another training option. Service in any of the nuclear-related government programs, such as nuclear submarines and aircraft, is accepted by many employers instead of or in addition to some educational requirements.

CERTIFICATION OR LICENSING

Certification or licensing is sometimes required of industrial radiological technicians. The National Institute for Certification in Engineering Technologies (NICET) offers a general certification, and the American Society for Nondestructive Testing (ASNT) gives certification in all areas of the field.

After Dave completed his training as a hot-cell technician, he was certified by his employer. The training was done in compliance with guidelines from the U.S. Department of Defense.

Chuck Vulyak is certified in several areas of nondestructive testing, including industrial radiology. He took part in written and physical testing, meeting the requirements of the ASNT. In addition to being a radiologist, he is qualified as an ultrasonic inspection technician, eddy current inspection technician, and magnetic particle technician. He says certification requirements differ among employers. His company is diversified enough that he is able to use all his various skills on the job.

Certification is not the only credential you might need in this field. Many industrial radiological technicians need security clearance for their jobs. This is required by all federal and private industries that engage in projects involving national security. All employees are screened through the Nuclear

Regulatory Commission. Some projects may even require military clearance separate from or in addition to clearance by the Nuclear Regulatory Commission. Also, many employers now require drug testing of job applicants and random, follow-up testing of employees.

SCHOLARSHIPS AND GRANTS

When Chuck Vulyak decided to go back to school after the welding plant for which he worked closed down, he used his GI Bill to pay the expenses. After receiving his associate's degree, he landed his current job in radiography. While working full time, he completed two more years of school.

If you already have a job, you might not have to pay your own tuition. Often, employers will pay part or all of the educational expenses for their employees who attend school.

For information on other ways to pay for college, contact the Oak Ridge Institute for Science and Education (ORISE), which is affiliated with the U.S. Department of Energy. ORISE offers a wide variety of educational courses to familiarize students with the many forms of radiation technology. The Institute organizes tours, provides high school and college students with information, and even runs a summer camp for students interested in math and science. ORISE publishes a resource guide with scholarship and grant information for students interested in pursuing careers in related fields.

INTERNSHIPS AND VOLUNTEERSHIPS

Most nuclear or radiation facilities do not allow unauthorized personnel inside their grounds. You might be able to take a guided tour of some sites, though, to see what it would be like to work there. Some facilities that handle radioactive materials, such as nuclear power plants, have visitor centers and educational exhibits open to the public, which explain their operation and safety procedures.

Who Will Hire Me?

Industrial radiological technicians work in a variety of settings. Potential employers include nuclear materials handling and processing facilities, nondestructive testing firms, research laboratories, nuclear waste handling facilities, nuclear service firms, nuclear shipyards, chemical and petrochemical companies, radiopharmaceutical companies, and medical research and manufacturing facilities.

Recruiters from various businesses often contact students who are nearing graduation. Job placement offices in colleges and universities offer important services to both the job seeker and employer. Many technicians find their first jobs in this way.

Both Dave and Chuck Vulyak took a different route, locating their jobs through friends and contacts. "I knew someone who worked there and liked it. I just applied for a job when one opened up," says Dave.

Even though Dave started out with his present employer in a different field, he didn't mind switching to a hot-cell technician. The move was convenient, and he welcomed the opportunity to stay with the same employer. Many technicians will find that contacts and company loyalty will yield good jobs.

In the early 1990s most technicians worked in the aerospace industry. This focus has changed in response to recent trends, such as the closing of many government-contracted facilities, especially in California. Today, medical supply and pharmaceutical companies make up the largest group of employers. New opportunities are also expected to open up in nuclear waste handling facilities and private consulting firms.

FYI

The bronze Statue of Freedom, which stood above the United States Capitol dome for 130 years, was lowered from its perch in 1993 to undergo repairs, including an exhaustive battery of tests by radiographers. While police kept the crowds who gathered at a safe distance, crews of radiographers used direct-exposure radiography to determine the statue's iron content. The developed film revealed an iron skeleton within the statue's feather headdress and supplied a reason for the statue's frequent lightning strikes.

ADVANCEMENT POSSIBILITIES

Research technicians help develop new ideas and techniques in the radiation and nuclear field.

X-ray calibration technicians test equipment reliability, safety settings, and calibrations. They also evaluate field and filter performance.

Instrument design technicians help design and prepare specifications and testing of radiation equipment.

Customer service specialists sell, modify, install, and maintain customers' equipment.

To learn where jobs are, you can contact professional associations such as the ASNT. They publish trade magazines and have current job listings available to members. National laboratories, research institutions, colleges, universities, and large companies often post job listings within their facilities.

Where Can I Go from Here?

Career paths for industrial radiological technicians are usually very structured. An entry-level hot-cell technician starts as a junior technician, then proceeds through a series of levels, from level three to level one. Then, it is on to senior technician and finally chief technician.

Dave is a senior hot-cell technician but claims he has no goals of becoming chief technician. "There's too much paperwork involved in that job. I don't like to worry that much," he says. "What I'm doing now isn't too stressful."

Many technicians advance into supervisory roles within their fields, but this may mean leaving behind the hands-on work for which they train. While Dave is reluctant to do that, Chuck Vulyak welcomes the opportunity. He took business management classes in college and enjoys the responsibility he is often given.

Industrial radiological technicians can also become more involved in new technology and research as their careers progress. They can apply the skills they have learned to emerging technologies and help develop ways to improve those that already exist.

What Are the Salary Ranges?

According to the *Occupational Outlook Handbook*, science technicians, which includes nuclear technicians, had median annual salaries of $35,790 in 2003. Those in the lowest paid 10 percent earned $21,470 a year, while those in the highest paid 10 percent earned $56,470.

Salary.com reported earnings in 2005 for radiologic technicians working in medical facilities between $39,480 and $45,398 annually, and nondestructive testers earned salaries ranging from $53,478 to $62,655.

Some industrial radiological technicians earn overtime pay. In addition to salary, most employers offer benefits such as vacations, holidays, sick pay, health and medical insurance, and tuition reimbursement for continuing education.

What Is the Job Outlook?

Trying to predict the future of radiological and nuclear-related occupations is extremely difficult. Many of the larger employers, such as nuclear research facilities, are dependent on government funding and public support, both of which have decreased in recent years.

Nuclear power is a controversial topic. After the accidents at Three Mile Island and Chernobyl, questions arose about public safety and the proper disposal of nuclear waste. Many reactors were shut down, eliminating those jobs.

The future looks stable for some areas of specialization and less hopeful for others. Hot-cell technicians will likely experience a decline. Larry Niemark, a hot-cell supervisor at Argonne, says, "Hot-cell technicians are a dying breed." Each cell has a finite life span. When the interior of the cell becomes so contaminated it can no longer be used, it is filled with cement and sealed. It is not certain and perhaps unlikely that new cells will be built. While research will have to continue on materials inside nuclear reactors, whether closed or operational, the number of facilities doing this type of work will probably not increase.

Isotope production technicians may also experience a decline in the number of job opportunities. Many research facilities have closed these departments. As irradiation becomes more widely used in private industry, jobs may shift to these areas. Again, this process is new and controversial, and the job outlook will depend on government approval and public opinion.

The most stable area is expected to be radiography. With advanced technology and computer-related fields, this is the area of radiological sciences considered to be the safest and most effective. Industrial radiography is increasingly relied upon in an expanding number of industries.

How Do I Learn More?

PROFESSIONAL ORGANIZATIONS

The following are organizations that provide information about industrial radiological technician careers, accredited schools and scholarships, and possible employers:

American Nuclear Society
555 North Kensington Avenue
La Grange Park, IL 60526
708-352-6611
http://www.ans.org

American Society for Nondestructive Testing
PO Box 28518
1711 Arlingate Lane
Columbus, OH 43228-0518
800-222-2768
http://www.asnt.org

Oak Ridge Institute for Science and Education
PO Box 117
Oak Ridge, TN 37831-0117
865-576-3146
http://www.orau.gov/orise.htm

U.S. Nuclear Regulatory Commission
One White Flint North
11555 Rockville Pike
Rockville, MD 20852-2738
800-368-5642
http://www.nrc.gov

BIBLIOGRAPHY

The following is a sampling of materials relating to the professional concerns and development of industrial radiological technicians:

Bushong, Stewart C. *Radiologic Science for Technologists: Physics, Biology, and Protection.* 7th ed. St. Louis, Mo.: Mosby, 2001.

Gollnick, Daniel A. *Basic Radiation Protection Technology.* 4th ed. Altadena, Calif.: Pacific Radiation Corporation, 2000.

Halmshaw, R. *Industrial Radiology: Theory and Practice.* Norwell, Mass.: Chapman & Hall, 1995.

Walker, J. Samuel. *Permissible Dose: A History of Radiation Protection in the Twentieth Century.* Berkeley: University of California Press, 2000.

INDUSTRIAL SAFETY AND HEALTH TECHNICIANS

There is a forklift driver with a backache in Department 737, and it is Lawain's job to do something about it. According to the driver, his back is hurting chronically because the forklift does not have enough air in the tires.

Lawain talks with the supervisor and discovers that metal shavings from a nearby machine cover the floor in that area. If the forklift tires were fully inflated, they would puncture. The machine that produces the shavings needs to be realigned so that the metal shavings are caught before they escape onto the floor. It is not a dangerous situation, but it needs to be remedied.

Lawain brings the worker who filed the complaint and his supervisor together and tells them what needs to be done. "The forklift may cause you some discomfort until the machine is fixed," he says. "When the machine is fixed, inflate the tires to the normal level." The worker is satisfied, and work continues in Department 737.

Definition
Industrial safety and health technicians inspect machines, train workers in proper safety procedures, investigate accidents, and recommend changes in procedures to prevent accidents and illness.

Alternative Job Titles
Industrial hygiene technicians
Safety engineering assistants
Safety inspectors
Safety compliance officers

High School Subjects
English
Health

Personal Skills
Helping/teaching
Leadership/management

Salary Range
$26,480 to $48,330 to $74,520

Minimum Educational Level
Associate's degree

Certification or Licensing
Voluntary

Outlook
About as fast as the average

DOT
168

GOE
04.04.02

NOC
2263

O*NET-SOC
29-9012.00

What Does an Industrial Safety and Health Technician Do?

Accidents and illnesses are going to happen, but they happen less often if preventive measures are taken. *Industrial safety and health technicians* strive to reduce the number of workplace mishaps and health problems. They carry out the procedures and precautions designed by industrial safety engineers to make the workplace safer. Technicians often assist *industrial hygienists,* who hold at least a bachelor's degree.

There are actually two areas of specialization in this profession, but they so often overlap that they tend to be lumped together. The first, safety, deals with issues such as the proper ventilation of fumes and ensuring that workers place ladders so they will not fall. The second, industrial hygiene, is not about nagging people to brush their teeth or take a shower. Instead, it revolves around protecting workers from health hazards, such as noise from a jackhammer or exposure to chemicals. A third area, the environment, is less often combined with the first two; it encompasses questions about how to dispose of hazardous wastes, for example.

Industrial safety and health technicians have three major responsibilities. First, they make workers aware of hazards and teach them proper safety practices. Second, they inspect and study the workplace to detect potential hazards. Third, they write reports and keep records detailing what has been done to reduce or avoid accidents.

Because the majority of job-related accidents involve people who have been on the job six months or less, industrial safety and health technicians conduct seminars on safety for newly hired workers. The seminars generally include a tour of the work area, along with classroom instruction. Industrial safety and health technicians explain safeguards, safety rules, and potential hazards, and they point out posted warning signs. They may also explain the work rules regarding personal safety codes, such as where a person must wear a hard hat or safety glasses.

This initial contact with employees is important because it helps impress upon new employees the importance of safety in the workplace. The goal is to make every employee think about safety first, making the workplace safer for everyone.

Industrial safety and health technicians need to be aware of many different hazards in the workplace. For example, they watch for mechanical and electrical hazards. An unattended machine or an improperly grounded electrical wire could injure someone. Not so obvious, but possibly just as dangerous, are the fumes that the machines emit, which linger in the air. The technician must make sure that there is adequate ventilation. Other unseen hazards include noise and vibration.

Industrial safety and health technicians inspect safety equipment, such as fire extinguishers and first aid kits, to make sure they are effective and complete. Technicians also arrange for necessary repairs and keep inspection records on safety equipment.

Industrial safety and health technicians also write, file, and study reports. The Occupational Safety and Health Administration (OSHA) requires a report for all illnesses and injuries that are job related. Industrial safety and health technicians help investigate injuries and file follow-up reports to document that corrective action has been taken to prevent further injury. They read safety articles in trade journals and recommend ways to reduce the likelihood of accidents. They also make sure that instructions for operating and maintaining machines as well as posted emergency procedures are easy to understand and include updated information for new machines or safety policies.

Many of the tasks performed by an industrial safety and health technician are done in coordination with other departments within the company. New workers are trained with the help of the personnel department, and the accounting department oversees compensation given to an employee injured on the job.

Lingo to Learn

Accident An unplanned, uncontrolled, and unexpected event that results in—nearly, potentially, or really—injury or damage to property.

Industrial hygiene A profession that anticipates, recognizes, evaluates, and controls factors in the workplace that might damage a worker's health, cause discomfort, or decrease productivity.

Safety audit A tour of a facility, during which the technician observes any problems that could affect the workers' health and safety. The technician then explains to workers or management how to correct the problems and comply with regulations.

Work practice controls Steps taken to change the way in which tasks are performed. These measures are intended to reduce workers' risk of illness or injury.

Worksite analysis A visit to a workplace to note potential problems and identify and measure workers' exposure to harmful substances. The health and safety professional then conducts research, analyzes how the health of workers might be affected by a chemical or physical hazard, and recommends corrective action.

What Is It Like to Be an Industrial Safety and Health Technician?

"The biggest part of my job is relating to people and reminding them of the importance of safety," says Lawain Judisch. For example, he tries to make sure workers understand that machines are designed to operate safely, but they must be used correctly. Workers have a higher risk of injury if they take shortcuts.

Lawain also inspects machinery at the John Deere plant where he works as an industrial safety and health technician. "I feel that my presence on the shop floor is helpful. I want people to see me and think safety," he says. Because of his profession, Lawain is in the spotlight and must set a good example for other workers, following all safety procedures and wearing protective clothing when necessary.

To help everyone reach agreement on safety and health issues, Lawain talks to workers and persuades them to talk with their supervisors. "I'm a mediator of sorts," he explains. "Wage earners see issues from the standpoint of how it will affect them, and it's the supervisor's job to see issues based on how it will affect profitability for the company. My job is to remove the emotion and think about the facts and how the situation may jeopardize safety."

Like Lawain, most industrial safety and health technicians perform inspections and talk with workers on the floor of a factory or plant. They usually spend the rest of their time in an office where they file reports, study government regulations and new safety procedures, and learn tips from trade journals, such as *The Occupational Safety and Health Reporter.*

"It's hard to plan too far into the day," Lawain says. "Problems come up that demand my immediate attention."

Resolving health concerns and responding to emergencies is an important part of a safety and health professional's job, according to Vera Bolton, who is completing an eight-month combined internship and fellowship for Lockheed Martin Idaho Technologies. The internship is one of the final requirements for her bachelor's degree in safety and health.

To Be a Successful Industrial Safety and Health Technician, You Should . . .

- be a good listener
- be good at explaining procedures and policies to a wide variety of people
- have self-confidence and self-assurance to point out safety problems without taking negative reactions personally
- be able to set a perfect safety example
- be able to understand often complex technical documentation on equipment operation and safety and government rules and regulations

Vera is part of a team of about 30 certified industrial hygienists and several interns. It is her responsibility to recognize and evaluate hazards and help control the work site for about 7,000 employees at a federal nuclear facility. The workers handle potentially harmful asbestos and hazardous wastes. There is always construction and renovation in progress, and accidents could happen easily.

Vera monitors the workers and anything that might harm them. She takes samples to test for toxic substances in their bodies, and she checks the air quality, ventilation systems, and noise level. She also tries to prevent workers from endangering themselves; for instance, she might oversee how high an employee is allowed to climb on a large piece of equipment. She performs ergonomic studies, which might involve measuring a person and a piece of equipment and suggesting adjustments to eliminate injuries. For example, she might recommend raising a typist's chair to prevent carpal tunnel syndrome by placing the worker's wrists at the proper angle.

Another part of Vera's job is overseeing the application of plans already approved by the senior members of the health and safety team. For instance, a painter might ask her to check a spray booth and pumps that have just been set up. Vera would inspect the apparatus, calibrate the pumps, and write a report.

She spends a significant amount of time in her office, working at her computer and reading trade magazines to keep up with rapid changes in her field. There are always new regulations and new technologies to learn. "The versatility will always be there. It's a fascinating field. It's never boring," she says.

Do I Have What It Takes to Be an Industrial Safety and Health Technician?

To succeed as an industrial safety and health technician, you need to have an aptitude for analyzing possible hazards. You should be good at noticing details and remembering numerous regulations. Perhaps most importantly, you need to care about people and the environment.

"I chose the industrial hygiene field to go into due to the fact that I had a medical background for

15 years. I always had to work with people after they were injured," says Vera Bolton. A career that would help prevent sickness and injuries appealed to her.

Although Vera feels that her schooling has prepared her well for her profession, she has discovered that the job is so varied it is a challenge to stay on top of everything. She needs a broad range of knowledge about many things. One aspect of her job that has been particularly difficult is convincing people to perform their work in a safe manner.

"To get the normal worker to change his habits is one of the biggest challenges in my field. But they're really supportive of us," Vera remarks. She attributes the cooperative atmosphere at Lockheed to the corporation's managers, who place great emphasis on safety and health.

Not all workers immediately appreciate that industrial safety and health technicians are there to protect them, as Lawain Judisch has discovered at the John Deere plant. Some of the employees are paid extra money if they exceed their quotas and that tempts them to bend safety rules in the interest of getting more work done. "There is a tendency for workers to perceive me as a threat," Lawain admits. "I need to stress the importance of doing things safely, and I need to do it in a positive and friendly but firm way."

I need to stress the importance of doing things safely, and I need to do it in a positive and friendly but firm way.

When Lawain observes an employee breaking a rule, he lets the worker know this is an unsafe practice that must stop. If the worker continues, Lawain sometimes needs to issue a citation that could lead to disciplinary action against the worker. He needs to be self-confident enough to tell workers or managers things they might not want to hear, and he has to avoid taking negative reactions personally.

"I'm not going to win any popularity contests," he concedes. "If I'm doing my job right, I've got the wage earner mad at me half the time and management mad at me the other half."

How Do I Become an Industrial Safety and Health Technician?

The most common way to become an industrial safety and health technician is to graduate from a two-year industrial safety study program. Many community colleges and technical schools offer this type of educational program. On-the-job training is also valued by industrial engineers and employers. Some factory workers, like Lawain, become safety technicians after acquiring skills on the job.

EDUCATION

High School

"This is such a neat career. It's very exciting. I would have liked to have known about it in high school," says Marie Edson, an industrial hygienist in training who works for the Southern California Gas Company in Los Angeles.

Marie wishes she had taken more classes such as physics, biology, and chemistry in high school and as an undergraduate at college. Eventually she had to study those subjects for her master's degree, and because she had taken only sciences such as oceanography earlier, she had to complete the more difficult ones at the graduate level, which was much more demanding. "I recommend to every young person that I know, 'Take the hard stuff,' " she comments. "There are so many things you can do if you've taken those classes." For example, she says, science classes help prepare you for a career in engineering, chemistry, biology, or medicine.

It is also important to take English and speech classes because industrial safety and health technicians compile many reports, keep extensive records, and constantly communicate with others. Other recommended classes include algebra, calculus, trigonometry, computer science, psychology, mechanical drawing, and photography.

Postsecondary Training

Most employers hire only certified workers, and you cannot become certified without a degree. You can earn an associate's degree in two years to become an industrial safety and health technician, or you can earn a bachelor's degree in four years to become an industrial hygienist.

In-depth

A Brief History

Two hundred years ago, during the industrial revolution, workers were considered to be responsible for their own safety. Conditions were often quite dangerous, and many workers died on the job. The Chimney-Sweepers Act of 1788 and the English Factory Acts beginning in 1833 were among the first of a series of European laws aimed at protecting employees or compensating them for health problems associated with their jobs.

Things improved by the 20th century, when labor leaders and employers began a serious effort to prevent industrial accidents and diseases. Throughout the century, industrial safety engineers and industrial hygienists helped develop safety standards and practices. By 1948 all states had enacted industrial hygiene legislation. The Metallic and Nonmetallic Mines Safety Act of 1966 and the Federal Coal Mine Safety and Health Act of 1969 were landmark pieces of legislation intended to safeguard workers' health.

In 1970 the Occupational Safety and Health Act (OSHAct) made employers legally responsible for the safety and health of their workers. Many companies hired safety and health technicians to ensure compliance with the new legislation. Others enlisted the services of independent safety consulting firms.

As the demand for qualified technicians increased, technical institutes, technical colleges, community colleges, and some four-year colleges developed training programs. Many of these programs were launched during the 1980s and have become an important step in entering the profession.

According to the Occupational Safety and Health Administration (OSHA), workplace fatalities have been reduced by 60 percent since the organization's inception in 1971. In addition, on-the-job injuries and illnesses have been reduced by 40 percent. But problems still exist: OSHA reports that in 2003 there were 4.4 million work-related injuries and illnesses and 5,559 worker deaths among private industries. There were also 114 deaths among the self-employed and 61 workplace violence deaths.

Two-year programs combine classroom studies and laboratory experience. Course work typically includes safety and health regulations, safety planning, traffic safety, power sources and hazards, fire protection, noise control, chemical hazards, sanitation and public health, disaster preparedness, first aid, accident investigation, industrial economics, workers' compensation and insurance, technical reporting, algebra, physics, and chemistry.

Because few colleges offer an industrial hygiene major for undergraduates, it is common to earn a bachelor's degree in a science, such as biology, chemistry, or engineering, then advance by earning a master's or doctoral degree in industrial hygiene. According to the Board of Certified Safety Professionals (BCSP), 3 percent of those certified by BCSP hold associate's degrees, 48 percent hold bachelor's, 40 percent master's, and 3 percent doctoral degrees.

"With the background that I get from Montana College of Mineral Science and Technology, I'm ready to do what I do," Vera Bolton says. With her graduation from college only two months away, Vera is confident that she has received an excellent education and is prepared for her new career. She says the program of study was intense, but she enjoyed it, particularly the hazardous waste training, the experience in designing ventilation systems, and the chance to try various types of equipment. Vera plans to return to the Montana College of Mineral Science and Technology to pursue a master's degree.

CERTIFICATION OR LICENSING

There are no certification or licensing requirements to enter this field, but an increasing number of employers hire only certified applicants. The Occupational Safety and Health Administration and the American Society of Safety Engineers (ASSE) offer safety training programs and grant certificates of completion. The two main organizations that certify professionals in the field are BCSP, which offers certification for technicians and focuses on the safety aspect of the field, and the American Board of Industrial Hygiene (ABIH), which focuses on the hygiene aspect.

In general, an associate safety professional (ASP) is a technician who holds an associate's degree in safety or a bachelor's degree in any field and has passed the Safety Fundamentals Examination. A certified safety professional (CSP) typically holds an associate's degree in safety or a bachelor's degree in any field, has at least four years of experience, and has passed the Safety Fundamentals Examination and the Comprehensive Practice Examination.

An industrial hygiene technician holds a one- to three-year associate's degree and has passed a certificate program but is not certified. A certified occupational health and safety technologist (COHST) has at least five years of experience and has completed special studies or training. An industrial hygienist in training (IHIT) has a bachelor's degree and at least one year of experience and is temporarily certified. A certified industrial hygienist (CIH) has at least a bachelor's degree and five years of experience in the field and has become certified by passing a rigorous examination.

Continuing education is necessary to maintain certification. Marie Edson holds a master's degree and spends at least two weeks each year on continuing education. She must pass the certification examination every six years or lose her credentials and start at the bottom again. It is not easy to maintain the credentials, but the process is necessary to ensure that hygienists are familiar with the latest developments in their field.

INTERNSHIPS AND VOLUNTEERSHIPS

Vera Bolton's internship experience with Lockheed Martin Idaho Technologies has been even better than she expected; there is an air of camaraderie among the team of hygienists, and the company's managers have a supportive attitude. "It gives me hands-on experience in the industrial world. I would recommend any student doing [an internship with Lockheed], because the education you get here is wonderful," she says with enthusiasm. Vera gained additional on-the-job experience one summer when she worked at Rocky Mountain Laboratories in Hamilton, Montana, where she helped design and improve an inventory control system for more than 60 laboratories.

Who Will Hire Me?

Industrial safety and health technicians work for a variety of employers, including manufacturing, insurance, petrochemical, and hazardous waste companies. They are also employed by consulting firms, the government, public utilities, hospitals, research laboratories, and universities and colleges. The U.S. Occupational Safety and Health Administration (OSHA) employs a significant number of health and safety professionals, but only those with at least a bachelor's degree.

According to BCSP, 30 percent of its members are employed in manufacturing; 26 percent in insurance; and the remaining work in construction (4 percent); utilities (4 percent); for the government (9 percent); or for employers classified as other (27 percent), which may include those working as private consultants and in the petrochemical industry.

Some companies send recruiters to college campuses to hire new employees through the school's placement office as students near graduation. Sometimes an internship will lead to permanent employment.

It is not always easy to find a job in this field, however. Marie Edson says the best way to learn about job openings is by word of mouth since many positions are never advertised in newspapers. She recommends making friends in the field, especially by attending local meetings of the American Industrial Hygiene Association. "It's good to get in very closely with the associations," she advises. Marie also points out that most jobs in this field are in urban areas, since they tend to be concentrated in industrial settings; it is not realistic to plan to live in the country if you are in this profession.

ADVANCEMENT POSSIBILITIES

Industrial health engineers plan and coordinate private or government industrial health programs. They apply engineering principles and technology to analyze and control conditions that contribute to occupational hazards and diseases.

Industrial engineers plan the best way to use facilities, equipment, materials, and personnel to improve the efficiency of operations.

Safety engineers develop and implement safety programs to prevent or correct unsafe working conditions. The profession requires knowledge of industrial processes, mechanics, chemistry, psychology, and industrial health and safety laws.

Where Can I Go from Here?

Lawain started his career at the John Deere company as a fire inspector. As he gained experience and showed initiative, he became a safety technician for a few departments. Now he oversees the entire assembly division.

It is possible to advance by learning on the job and proving that you are a capable employee, but it is helpful to obtain additional education or certification. After they have gained a few years of on-the-job experience, many technicians earn a bachelor's degree and advance to industrial hygienist or take the examinations to become certified safety professionals.

Marie Edson is the supervisor's personal safety consultant for a company with about 300 employees. Immediately after earning her master's degree two years ago, Marie was able to jump past the technician level and into a management-level position. She is called an "industrial hygienist in training," because she has not yet gained the five years of experience required before she can take the examination to become a certified industrial hygienist.

Technicians who keep up with new developments in the field are most apt to receive raises and promotions to positions such as safety director, safety manager, or supervisor. In a large company, a supervisor might oversee many departments. Some safety professionals specialize in areas such as fire protection, design of engineering hazard controls, ergonomics, product safety, or environmental safety and health. Some people combine a knowledge of health and safety with expertise in some other field, such as management and business administration. With experience and a successful safety record, a technician could become a government inspector, be promoted to specialized safety consultant, or open a business as a private consultant.

What Are the Salary Ranges?

Industrial hygiene can be a lucrative field, particularly for someone with certification and advanced education. The U.S. Department of Labor reports annual salaries in 2003 for occupational health and safety technicians ranged from $26,480 to $74,520 with a median of $48,330.

According to a 2003 survey by the American Society of Safety Engineers, salaries averaged about $74,000 annually, and about half of respondents received an annual bonus of between $1,000 and $5,000. In this profession, education and experience pays. The ASSE reports that those with certification and 10 years of experience earned almost $10,000 more per year than an employee with only a high school diploma. Holding a bachelor's degree added about $12,000 to annual salaries, and a master's degree increased salaries about $20,000.

The BCSP reports that the average salary for certified safety professionals in 2004 was $85,000 annually. Entry-level CSPs earned between $25,000 and $40,000, while those with several years of experience had salaries from $50,000 to $70,000.

What Is the Job Outlook?

Many jobs for industrial safety and health technicians are generated as industries and insurance companies strive to make the workplace safer. In general, however, there are more jobs in this field when the government is regulating industry rigorously. During the 1980s, the federal government placed less emphasis on regulating industrial safety and health than it had in previous years. In such times, employment in the field is apt to increase slowly. Conversely, if the government passes new laws and spends more money on regulation, jobs in the field will be more plentiful.

The American Industrial Hygiene Association (AIHA) regularly conducts member surveys. The 2000 survey found that the number of women in the field has grown over the years: In 1994, 81 percent of the respondents were male; in 1997, 77 percent were male. That percentage dropped to 73 percent in 2000. Fifty-nine percent of the respondents anticipate that the best employment opportunities will be as generalists in environmental, health, safety, and industrial hygiene.

The U.S. Department of Labor projects that employment opportunities for health and safety specialists and technicians will grow about as fast as the average of all occupations through 2012.

How Do I Learn More?

PROFESSIONAL ORGANIZATIONS

The following are organizations that provide information on industrial safety and health technician careers, accredited schools and scholarships, certification, and employers:

American Board of Industrial Hygiene
6015 West St. Joseph, Suite 102
Lansing, MI 48917-3980
517-321-2638
abih@abih.org
http://www.abih.org

American Industrial Hygiene Association
2700 Prosperity Avenue, Suite 250
Fairfax, VA 22031
703-849-8888
http://www.aiha.org

Board of Certified Safety Professionals
208 Burwash Avenue
Savoy, Illinois 61874
217-359-9263
bcsp@bcsp.com
http://www.bcsp.com

National Institute for Occupational Safety and Health
200 Independence Avenue, SW, Room 715H
Washington, DC 20201
800-356-4674
http://www.cdc.gov/niosh

National Safety Council
1121 Spring Lake Drive
Itasca, IL 60143-3201
630-285-1121
http://www.nsc.org

Occupational Safety and Health Administration
200 Constitution Avenue, NW
Washington, DC 20210
202-219-8151
http://www.osha.gov

BIBLIOGRAPHY

The following is a sampling of materials relating to the professional concerns and development of industrial safety and health technicians:

Banerjee, Sanjoy. *Industrial Hazards and Plant Safety.* London: Taylor & Francis, 2003.

Plog, Barbara A. *Fundamentals of Industrial Hygiene.* 5th ed. Itasca, Ill.: National Safety Council, 2001.

Salvendy, Gavriel, ed. *Handbook of Industrial Engineering,* 3d ed. New York: John Wiley & Sons, 2001.

Wall, Darolyn K. *Industrial Hygiene Made Easy.* Orange Park, Fla.: Safetycertified.com, 2000.

INSTRUMENTATION TECHNICIANS

Chuck's schedule that morning looked fairly routine. He was going to complete some diagnostic testing on the manometers in Unit Two of the nuclear power plant where he worked. He knew something else would come up, but he had no idea that a serious malfunction in the equipment he maintained might threaten the safety of the entire plant.

The operator in the control room first called him around 10:00 A.M., but at the time, it did not sound like a priority. The gauges on the equipment were so sensitive, they often registered minor problems. Chuck told the control operator that he would investigate the malfunction later in the day.

As the morning wore on, however, the operator was becoming more concerned, and finally she realized she had a potentially dangerous problem on her hands. She called Chuck again at 11:30 A.M. This time it sounded urgent. There was a problem with one of the control rods in the reactor operator.

Chuck was not unusually concerned; he had dealt with many similar problems in the past. In fact, he enjoyed these challenges. Each time something like this happened, however, he knew that a great deal was riding on his ability to troubleshoot the problem and get it fixed immediately.

Definition
Instrumentation technicians inspect, test, repair, and adjust instruments that detect, measure, and record changes in industrial environments.

Alternative Job Titles
Calibration technicians
Electromechanical technicians
Instrumentation design technicians
Instrument repairers
Mechanical instrumentation technicians

High School Subjects
Chemistry
Computer science
Mathematics

Personal Skills
Mechanical/manipulative
Technical/scientific

Salary Range
$28,400 to $45,400 to $66,800

Minimum Educational Level
Associate's degree

Certification or Licensing
Voluntary

Outlook
About as fast as the average

DOT
003

GOE
02.08.04

NOC
2243

O*NET-SOC
17-3023.02, 17-3024.00

What Does an Instrumentation Technician Do?

When a household thermostat stops working, most homeowners have to bring in a specialist who is trained and knowledgeable in heating to make the necessary repairs. This is true with almost all of the major appliances and instruments found in a home. Similarly, businesses that rely on instruments require specialists called *instrumentation technicians* to maintain and repair them.

Instrumentation technicians install, operate, maintain, and repair all sorts of instruments. Depending on the industry in which they are employed, these technicians may work on altimeters, pressure gauges, radiation detection devices, speedometers, or even thermostats.

As part of their duties, instrumentation technicians work with three major categories of instruments. Pneumatic and electropneumatic equipment is run by, started with, or uses compressed air. This type of instrument includes pressure springs, diaphragms, bellows, and temperature and flow transmitters and receivers. Hydraulic instrumentation uses water pressure in much the same way and includes such devices as hydraulic valves, valve operators, and electrohydraulic equipment. Electrical and electronic instrumentation is run by electrical currents and electrical impulses, respectively. Electrical sensing elements and transducers, electronic recorders, electronic telemetering systems, and computers are all in this category.

In some industries technicians are in charge of a range of duties, working on equipment from each category, while in other industries they perform only one type of task on one type of equipment. The different levels of responsibility depend also on the technician's level of training and experience.

While some technicians specialize in a certain type of instrument, others specialize in a certain type of work. *Mechanical instrumentation technicians* deal mostly with mechanical functions, performing tests before instrument operation, doing calibrations during operation, rebuilding the equipment using standard replacement parts, interconnecting equipment following a blueprint, and completing routine repairs. They use simple tools, such as a screwdriver, wrench, pliers, electrical drill, and soldering iron. They must also be able to troubleshoot problems with various mechanisms.

Instrumentation repair technicians require a little more training than mechanical instrumentation technicians. When an instrument breaks down, they determine what caused the problem and perform the needed repairs. They usually work on individual pieces of equipment, not systems.

Troubleshooting instrumentation technicians determine the cause of a problem and perform corrections in instruments and control systems. They make adjustments, calibrate equipment, set up tests, diagnose malfunctions, and revise existing systems. Their work is performed either on site or at a workbench. This position requires more advanced training, including studies in mathematics, physics, and graphics.

Technicians who help design instruments are *assistant instrumentation design technicians* or *instrumentation design technicians*. They work under the supervision of design engineers. Although they are not responsible for the creative ideas in developing new instruments, they build models and prototypes, and they prepare freehand sketches, working drawings, and diagrams. These technicians also test new system designs, order parts, and make mock-ups of new systems.

Technicians in certain industries are required to be more specialized, but they all install, maintain, repair, and calibrate equipment. *Biomedical equipment technicians* work with instruments used during medical procedures. These technicians must consider the effects of the instruments on both the patient and the medical technician operating the equipment.

Calibration technicians, also known as *standards laboratory technicians*, work in the electronics, aircraft, and aerospace industries. They work with electrical, mechanical, and electronic instruments that measure and record voltage, heat, and magnetic resonance. The tools they use include micrometers, calipers, other precision instruments, jeweler's lathes, files, and soldering irons. Calibration technicians help engineers develop calibration standards, formulas for solving problems, and procedures for other technicians.

Nuclear instrumentation technicians work with instruments at nuclear power plants. These instruments control the various systems within the nuclear reactor, detect radiation, and sound alarms when equipment malfunctions.

What Is It Like to Be an Instrumentation Technician?

Chuck Feeney is an instrument maintenance supervisor for ComEd (formerly known as Commonwealth

Lingo to Learn

Altimeter An instrument used especially in aircraft for determining elevation, commonly by barometric sensing of pressure changes.

Calibrate To check, adjust, or systematically standardize the graduations of a quantitative measuring instrument.

Hydraulic Moved or operated by a fluid, especially water, under pressure.

Manometer An instrument for measuring the pressure of liquids and gases.

Pneumatic Run by or using compressed air; filled with compressed air.

Potentiometer An instrument for measuring an unknown voltage or potential difference by comparison to a standard voltage.

Oscilloscope An electronic instrument that translates an oscillating motion into a visual image on a viewscreen.

Voltmeter An instrument designed to measure electrical current or potential.

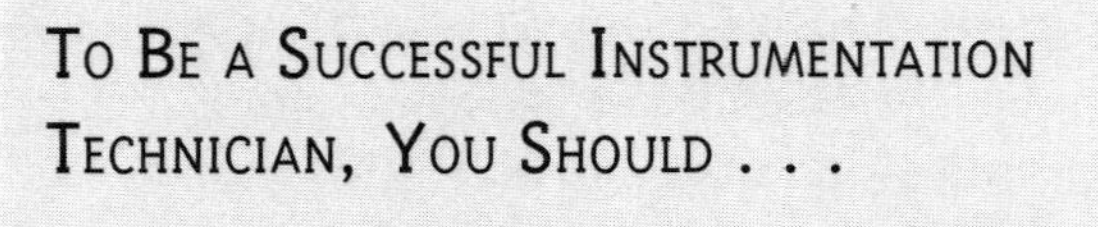

- like to work with mechanical or electrical tools or equipment
- understand and enjoy math and science
- possess an inquisitive mind and like to figure out puzzles
- get along well with other people

Edison) at the Zion, Illinois, nuclear power plant. He has been in the trade for over 30 years. His job involves the routine tasks performed by most instrumentation technicians, as well as specialized functions relating to the nuclear industry. It's up to him to make sure the equipment is operating safely and dependably, a vital function in a nuclear plant. Chuck's coworkers depend on him to help ensure that they won't be exposed to dangerous radiation. He also helps keep the plant operating efficiently.

For Chuck, each day brings different problems, since he works with many types of instruments, including basic temperature indicators, complex electrical "loops," mercury manometers, potentiometers, oscilloscopes, voltmeters, and watt meters. "Technicians have a wide range of responsibilities... [and] are expected to know a lot," he comments.

He replaces resistors on circuit boards, rewires electrical equipment, and adjusts mechanical and pneumatic instruments. He inspects meters, indicators, and gauges that detect fluctuations in the way the power plant's equipment is operating. He tests the accuracy of flowmeters, pressure gauges, and radiation counters and detectors. He calibrates equipment to specific standards and reports the results to the National Institute of Standards and Testing.

Chuck documents his work by preparing schematic drawings and sketches of changes he has made to the instruments. He records the names and numbers of all components he uses, and he keeps an inventory of parts on hand.

One of Chuck's most important duties is to run tests that indicate whether each instrument in the plant is functioning properly. He often works with engineers to design and develop these tests, install them, and use them to check the equipment. Sometimes he recommends that a method of testing or a piece of equipment used in testing be changed.

Chuck also interacts with the nuclear reactor operators who work in the plant's control room. They often let him know when equipment needs repair and work with him to coordinate the time of the repair, since the equipment might need to be shut down for servicing.

Chuck does not spend his day at a desk; he has rounds to make as he checks equipment and makes repairs. He has a personal workbench in a maintenance shop, a building separate from the main complex at the plant. Sometimes the maintenance room is busy, loud, and crowded. Chuck also spends time in the power plant's main control room, which is usually sterile and relatively quiet. In addition, he frequently works wherever the equipment is set up, which may be in a cramped, cold place or a cramped, hot place.

Depending on where they work, instrumentation technicians might have to wear hard hats and special radiation-resistant clothing. In that case they usually also carry badges or pocket monitors to measure their exposure to radiation. Some are allowed to wear standard work clothes, and others wear laboratory coats.

Whether a technician works at a power plant, an oil refinery, or the surgical room of a hospital, the basic skills of the trade are generally the same. A technician's duties may be mostly routine or frequently complicated and challenging. Whatever the particular situation, this is a career for people who can handle responsibility.

Do I Have What It Takes to Be an Instrumentation Technician?

An instrumentation technician needs an aptitude for science and mathematics and must be good at working with machinery. Patience and a calm manner are necessary for solving complex problems in a methodical way. It is important to be able to work in a disciplined, precise fashion, following procedures. On the other hand, instrumentation technicians often need to think quickly, using sound judgment and ingenuity in tense situations.

Chuck says the most stressful aspect of his job is the responsibility of working with equipment that could shut the plant down. Mistakes could cost the utility hundreds of thousands of dollars a day. "You have to be sure the repair is right the first time," he explains. "You can't be rushed, but you have to work in a timely manner." In most other industries instrumentation technicians commonly face that same pressure.

> You can't be rushed, but you have to work in a timely manner.

Chuck believes the most important personal quality for an instrumentation technician is an inquisitive mind. Troubleshooting is a big part of his job, and it is sometimes difficult to determine why a piece of equipment is not working. Chuck says a good technician "likes to know how something works, likes to figure out the puzzle."

Technicians also must be able to relate well to other people. "It's not a job for loners," Chuck says. He finds that he must communicate particularly well with the reactor operators in the control room, who work closely with him so much of the time.

Finally, Chuck has to consider the possibility that he could be exposed to radiation. "Training is supposed to help reduce the fear," he says, but some people continue to worry about it.

How Do I Become an Instrumentation Technician?

To enter this field, you need to have completed a two-year technical program or have a significant amount of experience in a related field. You can gain that experience through employment in an electronics firm, a manufacturing firm, or any job where you work with mechanical or electrical equipment.

The technicians Chuck supervises at Zion have a variety of technical backgrounds. One worked previously in air-conditioning and refrigeration, and one worked with robotics for a manufacturing firm. "People with experience in computerized processes or equipment are excellent candidates," Chuck says.

EDUCATION

High School

If you are interested in this career, you should take math and science courses, including algebra, geometry, physics, and chemistry. "I can't stress this enough," Chuck says. "This area seems to be the weakness in employees who have failed training. You have to be ready to learn on a technical level."

In addition, machine and electrical shop courses will help you become familiar with electrical, mechanical, and electronic technology. Classes in mechanical drawing and computer-aided design are beneficial. English and speech courses are also recommended to help you communicate on the job.

Postsecondary Training

Many junior or community colleges and technical schools have two-year programs geared toward instrumentation technology. Students may earn an associate's degree in electrical, mechanical, biomedical, nuclear, or instrument technology. They usually learn practical skills as well as theory. In these schools you would probably study courses such as mathematics, physics, electronic circuitry, computers, electronics, graphics, and technical writing. If you plan to advance in the field, it is wise to take classes in plant management, psychology, and industrial economics.

Chuck's employer, like many others, hires many graduates of schools that offer a thorough, technical education. Even if you graduated from one of these programs, though, you would probably have to take a long series of aptitude tests during the hiring process. The tests are designed to reveal your knowledge of industry standards and practices. New hires in the nuclear industry are also required to pass background checks.

Another excellent source of experience is the armed forces. Each service has its own training program. Veterans are usually well qualified for civilian technical positions.

Many companies offer a third option, internal training programs, which sometimes consist of both classroom study and on-the-job experience. New technicians in these programs usually work under the close supervision of senior technicians.

That is the case at the Zion nuclear plant, where new instrumentation technicians must complete two tracks of training. First, they serve as apprentices or trainees and learn about basic pneumatic and pressure instrumentation. The second track concentrates more on math, electronics, and component theory.

Throughout the training, which takes one to three years and consists of 16 modules of instruction, technicians must pass examinations. Upon completing the two tracks, they must pass a test on an interactive computer, troubleshooting various problems and recommending repairs.

Technicians who complete the initial training are eligible for promotion to the next level of responsibility, but their training doesn't stop there. All technicians are continually training to prepare for the next project or to master new technology.

CERTIFICATION OR LICENSING

Certification is not required for this trade, but if you graduate from a qualified technical program, you may be certified by the National Institute for the Certification of Engineering Technicians. If you join the Instrumentation, Systems and Automation Society of America (ISA) and other organizations specific to particular industries, you will receive educational resources and updates on new technology. ISA also publishes books, periodicals, and journals.

SCHOLARSHIPS AND GRANTS

Many two-year and technical schools offer scholarships for students in instrumentation technology programs. For details, inquire at the school's financial aid office. Professional organizations for specific industries can provide additional information.

INTERNSHIPS AND VOLUNTEERSHIPS

Some companies offer summer or internship employment that provides the chance to work in an industrial setting. You probably will not work directly on instrumentation in this type of job, but it can help you see if you have sufficient manual dexterity and an aptitude for a mechanical or technical career. This is also a good way to view the working conditions in a particular industry. To see if summer internships or part-time employment are available, contact the company's employment office.

LABOR UNIONS

Many instrumentation technicians are members of labor unions. The technicians at the ComEd nuclear plant belong to the International Brotherhood of Electrical Workers, which represents many employees in a broad range of industries. Other unions that represent instrumentation technicians include the Communications Workers of America; the International Association of Machinists and Aerospace Workers; the International Union of Electronic, Electrical, Salaried, Machine, and Furniture Workers; and the United Automobile, Aerospace and Agricultural Implement Workers of America.

Who Will Hire Me?

Like many people in the nuclear industry, Chuck began his career in the navy, where he served seven years as an instrumentation technician. He decided to seek employment in private industry, submitted a resume to ComEd, and has worked there for more than 21 years.

It is relatively easy to switch jobs in this field, since the basic principles of instrumentation maintenance and repair can be adapted to various industries. Businesses that employ instrumentation technicians include everything from oil refineries, chemical and industrial laboratories, and electronic firms to oceanographic research facilities, aircraft and aeronautics manufacturers, biomedical firms, and organizations involved in space exploration.

Manufacturing firms employ large numbers of instrumentation technicians to service their automated machinery. Automation is becoming more prevalent as computer-controlled machinery continues to replace manual labor. Many other industries are also becoming more dependent upon computerized equipment.

Openings are also common in various emerging fields. Instrumentation technicians are needed to service equipment used for air and water pollution control. There are jobs with organizations that use sensors and computers to diagnose medical conditions. Chemical and medical research organizations hire many technicians to maintain and operate equipment. Telecommunications companies are becoming more widespread and continue to hire many instrumentation technicians.

There will also be opportunities in education. Colleges and universities need qualified instructors, and so do outside consultants and businesses with internal training programs. These instructors need to be knowledgeable in both theory and practice.

Many graduates of technical programs find that employers are seeking them. Prospective employers often recruit from two-year and four-year technical schools; they frequently concentrate on schools that offer training in the specific type of skills the employer needs. The placement services division of the school is the place to learn about these positions. You can find other job openings in the classified advertising sections of newspapers, or you can submit a resume directly to businesses that need technicians to service their instruments.

Where Can I Go from Here?

The entry-level job for instrumentation technicians at the Zion nuclear plant is Instrument Mechanic B. Technicians spend a year or two at this level as they complete their training. Then they're eligible for promotion to Instrument Mechanic A, a position that involves supervising one or two Mechanic B workers and being in charge of designated projects each day.

Some technicians move from Mechanic B directly into supervisory jobs, but most continue training toward the third level, control systems technician, a position reserved for highly qualified workers with years of experience. Chuck says *control systems technicians* have the most stressful of the nonmanagement instrumentation positions because they work with the control systems at the nuclear reactor. That means their duties are more difficult, and if they make a mistake, it can be more dangerous.

Chuck was promoted from Mechanic B to supervisor. At the time, it appeared that no control systems technician opening would be available for several years.

Within the labor union, promotions into nonmanagement positions are based on seniority. In contrast, promotions into management are based on merit.

Advancement in most industries follows a similar track. Technicians with training and years of experience can be promoted to supervisor or manager. Some positions require specialized knowledge obtained only from years of experience. In certain industries, particularly manufacturing, instrumentation technicians with the appropriate skills can move into sales. A job in sales usually requires more general knowledge instead of skills specific to one area of expertise.

Advancement Possibilities

Electronics engineering managers direct and coordinate activities of the engineering department to design, manufacture, and test electronic components, products, and systems.

System development engineers plan and coordinate activities to provide for orderly development and improve operating efficiency of electric power systems.

Electrical engineers research, develop, design, and test electrical components, equipment, and systems, applying principles and techniques of electrical engineering.

Electronics engineers research, develop, design, and test electronic components, products, and systems for commercial, industrial, medical, military, and scientific applications, applying principles and techniques of electronic engineering.

What Are the Salary Ranges?

Because there is such a wide range of industries that employ instrumentation technicians, there is also a wide range of salaries. Location and level of experience also influence salaries.

According to the U.S. Department of Labor Occupational Information Network, calibration and instrumentation technicians had median annual earnings of $45,400 in 2003. Those in the lowest paid 10 percent earned $28,400, while those in the highest paid 10 percent earned $66,800.

A 2005 review of earnings nationwide by Salary.com found annual earnings for entry-level instrumentation and calibration technicians ranged from $22,651 to $39,979. Those with two to five years of experience earned between $38,855 and $51,264 with a median of $45,055.

Most union workers are paid extra money for overtime and receive bonuses for special circumstances such as working holidays. Typical company benefits include medical and life insurance, retirement benefits, paid holidays, sick leave, and vacation. Many companies also provide financial support for continuing education programs.

What Is the Job Outlook?

The demand for engineering technicians is expected to continue growing about as fast as the average for all occupations through 2012, according to the U.S. Department of Labor. Employment opportunities will be best for technicians who have completed formal, postsecondary training programs.

As industries become more automated, instrumentation technicians will be needed to install and service the new equipment. In addition, as the population continues to grow, more instrumentation will be needed to keep up with the demand for utilities, health and medical services, consumer products, and transportation.

The future of the nuclear industry is in question because of concerns about public health and safety, the effects on the environment, and waste disposal. Other industries, such as aeronautics, robotics, and electronics, will experience rapid growth. Organizations that monitor pollution in the land, air, and water will be hiring many technicians. Another expanding field, oceanography, includes opportunities to participate in the search for oil and minerals beneath the seas. Medical diagnosis is also expanding; for example, technicians will be needed to work on instruments that allow doctors to diagnose illness by using remote sensors and computers.

How Do I Learn More?

PROFESSIONAL ORGANIZATIONS

The following are organizations that provide information on instrumentation technician careers, accredited schools and scholarships, and employers. Specific industries may have additional professional associations.

American Nuclear Society
555 North Kensington Avenue
La Grange Park, IL 60526
708-352-6611
http://www.ans.org

The Association for Manufacturing Technology
7901 Westpark Drive
McLean, VA 22102-4206
703-893-2900
http://www.mfgtech.org

Association for the Advancement of Medical Instrumentation
1110 North Glebe Road, Suite 220
Arlington, VA 22201-4795
703-525-4890
http://www.aami.org

IEEE Instrument and Measurement Society
c/o Institute of Electrical and Electronics Engineers
1828 L Street, NW, Suite 1202
Washington, DC 20036-5104
202-785-0017
http://www.ieee.org

Instrumentation, Systems, and Automation Society
67 Alexander Drive
Research Triangle Park, NC 22709
info@isa.org
http://www.isa.org

Junior Engineering Technical Society
1420 King Street, Suite 405
Alexandria, VA 22314
703-548-5387
info@jets.org
http://www.jets.org

National Institute for Certification in Engineering Technologies
1420 King Street
Alexandria, VA 22314
888-476-4238
http://www.nicet.org

BIBLIOGRAPHY

The following is a sampling of materials relating to the professional concerns and development of instrumentation technicians:

Camenson, Blythe, and Jan Goldberg. *Real People Working in Mechanics, Installation, and Repair.* Lincolnwood, Ill.: VGM Career Horizons, 1999.

Careers in Focus: Technicians. 2d ed. New York: Facts On File, 2004.

Simons, Samuel. *Technician's Guide to Instrumentation.* Berne, N.Y.: Uhai Publishing, 2004.

LASER TECHNICIANS

Winding his way through the noisy machine shop at the diesel engine factory where he works, Bob Wire passes the usual heavy machinery. Grease streaks and metal machine shavings cover the floor. Pushing through a set of double doors, he enters an entirely different setting, one that seems more like a futuristic laboratory.

In fact, this part of the diesel engine factory is a laboratory, a laser laboratory. Computers and lasers are everywhere, some small, some as large as a closet. Workers in uniforms and white lab coats move about busily. A few stand in small groups, reviewing data, while others sit alone at computer terminals, programming in complicated sequences for the lasers to perform. Bob walks over to a computer terminal and gets ready to work his particular brand of wizardry with lasers.

The laser Bob operates is so precise it can inscribe a letter or number that the human eye cannot see. Should the engine that his company makes malfunction, the problem can easily be traced via the marking information that Bob records on each part. This information can include the date, time, and machine that produced the defective part, as well as the part's specifications. Having carefully programmed the computer and put on his safety glasses, Bob begins marking a new series of parts.

Definition
Laser technicians produce, test, service, operate, and install laser systems in industrial, medical, or research settings.

Alternative Job Titles
Industrial laser technicians
Medical laser specialists

High School Subjects
Mathematics
Technical/shop

Personal Skills
Mechanical/manipulative
Technical/scientific

Salary Range
$31,530 to $45,472 to $58,999

Minimum Educational Level
Associate's degree

Certification or Licensing
Voluntary

Outlook
Much faster than the average

DOT
019

GOE
N/A

NOC
2241

O*NET-SOC
N/A

What Does a Laser Technician Do?

Laser technicians help design, test, install, and repair laser systems and fiber optics equipment. Under the direction of engineers and scientists, they install and operate laser systems in a variety of industries and fields. Depending upon the type of laser system—gas or solid state—a laser technician generally works either with information systems or with robotics, manufacturing, or medical equipment.

Semiconductor laser systems are the most compact and reliable type. Technicians who work with these lasers mainly help design, test, install, and repair computers and telephone systems. Laser technicians who work with the more costly gas-type laser systems usually assist scientists, engineers, and doctors in the fields of robotics, material processing/manufacturing, and medical equipment and instruments.

Whether working on an information system or in a manufacturing plant, laser technicians clean and maintain lasers, perform tests and take measurements, gather data, make calculations, and prepare reports based on the data they have accumulated. They read and interpret shop drawings, diagrams, schematics, and sketches, whether their goal is to inscribe a part number on a bolt or fashion the blade on a fingernail-sized surgical instrument. Based on these drawings, laser technicians working in manufacturing, research, or design might then fabricate or direct the assembly of components.

Laser technicians help build devices such as solid-state lasers, which consist of a crystal rod in a flash tube, with mirrors positioned to direct the light precisely. Laser technicians may also repair lasers and

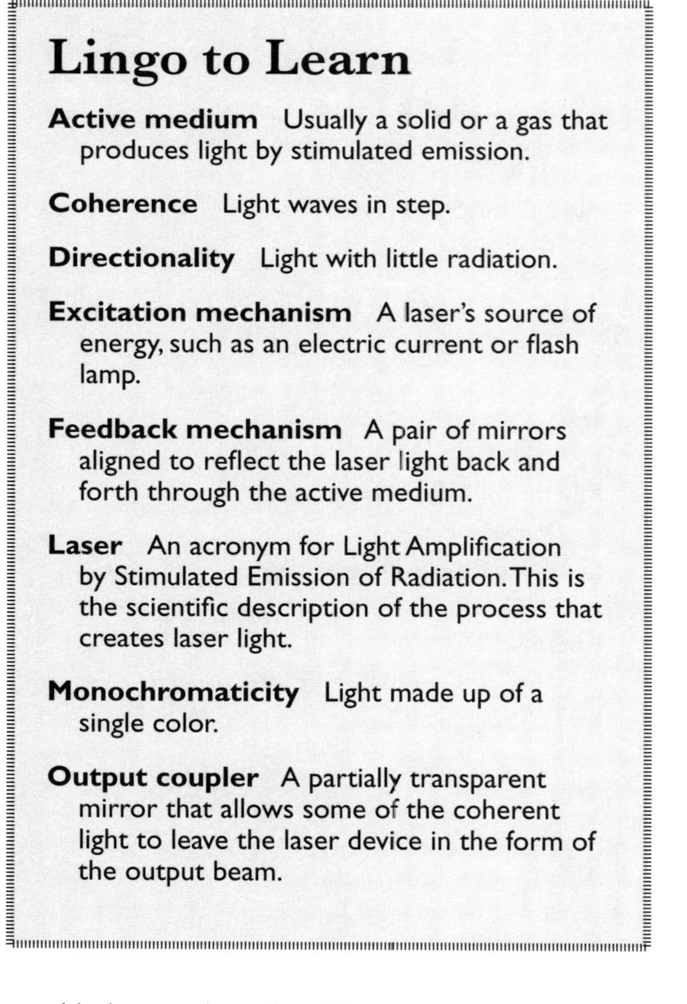

Lingo to Learn

Active medium Usually a solid or a gas that produces light by stimulated emission.

Coherence Light waves in step.

Directionality Light with little radiation.

Excitation mechanism A laser's source of energy, such as an electric current or flash lamp.

Feedback mechanism A pair of mirrors aligned to reflect the laser light back and forth through the active medium.

Laser An acronym for Light Amplification by Stimulated Emission of Radiation. This is the scientific description of the process that creates laser light.

Monochromaticity Light made up of a single color.

Output coupler A partially transparent mirror that allows some of the coherent light to leave the laser device in the form of the output beam.

troubleshoot technical problems. They use drawings, research data, and reports to communicate with co-workers such as engineers, doctors, scientists, and sales personnel.

Not all laser technicians perform all of the tasks described above. Their duties vary, depending on where they work and what positions they hold. For example, some technicians repair lasers and instruct different companies on their use, while others perform work for specific applications, such as optical surgery or for manufacturing machine parts. Laser technicians are employed in five broad categories: materials processing, communications, military, medical, and research.

Materials processing is the most diversified area of laser use and includes applications for machining, fabrication, testing, measurement, construction, excavation, and photo-optics. Lasers are used in communications to send light impulses through optical fibers. They are also used in this field for data storage and retrieval. Military and space projects use lasers for locating, tracking, ranging, and identifying targets, as well as for research and communication. Medical uses of lasers include surgical operations, ophthalmology, dermatology, and research.

Research and development of lasers is continuing in many areas. For instance, they might prove useful for producing inexpensive electricity through nuclear fusion. Laser technicians will help develop that type of technology.

What Is It Like to Be a Laser Technician?

Bob Wire is a laser technician for a leading Midwestern diesel engine manufacturer. He operates, repairs, maintains, and oversees the laser systems his company owns. He works with engineers, laboratory managers, and other technicians. Every day he uses laser technology to perform two major tasks: measuring and identifying mechanical parts.

Using a low-powered laser (with roughly the same wattage as that in the laser that scans the bar code on your groceries at the supermarket), Bob takes measurements of parts used in the manufacture of diesel engines. So precise are these measurements, Bob can verify the accuracy of the length or width of any given part down to 1/1000th of a millimeter. "That's in the micron range," Bob says.

To identify parts, Bob uses a marking laser. Much stronger than the one he uses to measure parts, the marking laser uses 50 watts, enough to cut through a thin piece of steel. "But I don't use it to cut," Bob says. "I use it to mark with a number or a letter each part that's inside an engine. I can laser in a little mark where even a jeweller couldn't get to."

Marking each component or piece is a crucial step in the manufacture of a product, especially in an engine. Marking is used to identify every component, Bob explains. The process helps technicians trace manufacturing problems to their source and also adds to the overall quality control of a product. "I keep a log of the parts and their numbers and characteristics. That way, should something happen, an engine breakdown, for example, every part is identified," he says.

"What continues to amaze me," he adds, "is how effective lasers are compared to conventional machinery." Bob remembers what it was like to do the same job without the help of lasers. "In the past, we used a sort of vibrating pen or an acid etch to record the part number. In addition to being illegible or next-to-impossible to read, those tools marred the finish of the product, and that was unacceptable in terms of the kind of quality we wanted. But that's all that was available. Now, with a laser, there is no heat distortion, no surface disfigurement."

On a typical day Bob might have a line meeting with the other members of his team, technicians who are all working on the same components, and then he begins the setup for marking parts. To do this, Bob writes a computer program for the type of marking he wants to make on a particular part or component. There are many factors to consider. "Using the x, y, and z axes, you program the location, where you want to inscribe the part number, plus other variables like duration, power, and speed," he explains. He enjoys this more than any other aspect of the job. "Setting up the program is the fun part. It's like writing a story and making 100 copies of it. Which is more fun: writing the story or standing at the copy machine making 100 copies? Writing the story is always more fun."

Bob began his career as a machinist and now works only with lasers and other technical equipment. "When I first started here, there were no computer numerical control machines, no lasers. Now there are computers every five feet, and several lasers," he says.

His background in conventional machining and tooling gives Bob an appreciation for the advantages of lasers in the manufacturing world. "We can do more work, and lasers create less strain on the parts. So the parts last longer, and our customers are more satisfied," he says.

Another technician who has witnessed significant changes with the advent of lasers is Tim Putnam, Director of Laser/Advanced Surgery at Saint Mary's Medical Center in Evansville, Indiana. "Fifteen years ago, if you walked into an operating room, it looked more like a carpenter's shop. There was hardly anything high tech in the room, with the exception of the anesthesia machine. The same operating room, today, looks more like people getting ready to launch the space shuttle," he says.

Increasingly, doctors and surgeons are turning to less invasive methods of surgery and other treatments to cure their patients' problems, and lasers are among the most promising solutions. Laser technicians working in the medical field support the surgeons and other physicians who use lasers and fiber optic equipment.

Before entering the medical field, Tim worked as a laser technician in several areas of expertise, including field service and research. "Working as a field service laser technician is very different from being a part of a team in an operating room," Tim says. "Laser technicians are the technical equipment experts during the operation and must respond quickly and efficiently to any problems."

As Tim explains it, the physician is the expert on the patient's needs, while the laser technician is the expert on technology. So, while the doctor is the only person who actually uses a laser instrument and has direct contact with the patient, the laser technician has to be there to make recommendations, to fine-tune the many attachments and machines, and to assist the physician if a technical problem occurs.

Just as a golfer uses many different clubs to hit the ball, depending upon the situation, a surgeon needs to choose various instruments for specific purposes. Not only do lasers have a multitude of functions, but there are many different ways to deliver a laser beam to a patient's body, and a surgeon might use several methods during one surgery.

For example, the surgeon could choose to deliver lasers through a microscope, through a fiber optic tube, or through a contact tip that transfers the energy to the patient's tissue in the form of heat. The surgeon knows what cut or excision to make; laser technicians simply advise how best to do it and what instrument to use. In addition, laser technicians help set up reflection devices, similar to mirrors, which are used to aim the laser beam in hard-to-reach spots.

To Be a Successful Laser Technician, You Should . . .

- be willing to learn new technology
- have manual dexterity and good hand-eye coordination
- be a problem solver
- have excellent computer skills
- be patient, careful, and consistent in your work
- be able to articulate your ideas and questions

An average day for Tim means checking the operating room schedule first thing in the morning to make certain that a laser technician and nurse are covering all of the laser/advanced surgery cases. "If they're not all covered," Tim says, "that's where I am all day—in surgery." Normally, he spends his day assisting in surgery, working with new instrumentation, handling administrative tasks, and reading up on new techniques and instruments.

Tim's hours are usually consistent, although he may be called in for an emergency surgery that requires his expertise. Bob consistently works five days a week, eight hours per day, unless a special project requires overtime. As a member of a labor union, Bob receives overtime pay at time and a half.

Do I Have What It Takes to Be a Laser Technician?

Working with lasers does not require much physical strength. It does require manual dexterity, hand-eye coordination, and the ability to work with deliberation. No matter what field you work in as a laser technician, you can expect some degree of stress, pressure, and even danger. For example, Tim says, "If equipment fails or a physician is using it incorrectly, it is the laser technician who has the responsibility to intercede—even during an operation—if the patient could be in jeopardy."

Tim has to work quietly and with little discussion while in surgery, but later, working with the same doctor on an experimental instrument, Tim might have to voice his opinion without feeling intimidated by the doctor. "A surgical team operates with very little conversation. Familiarity with procedures and with the physicians is necessary to respond to any situation that might occur with the equipment," Tim says. "The laser technician is a liaison between the physicians and the equipment."

Bob Wire experiences similar pressure in his position in manufacturing. He often works with machinery and parts that are highly specialized and expensive, and, as he says, "When you're working with lasers, there's no such thing as an eraser." As a result, laser technicians take safety precautions very seriously. "Lasers can be extremely dangerous," Bob says, "and, like guns, shouldn't be pointed unless you know what you're doing."

The work of many laser technicians becomes so routine that they might be tempted to ignore safety and procedural policies. "It would be real easy to get lazy about things when you're marking the same part all day," Bob says. "But I am always careful to wear my safety glasses and do everything right, every time." It is important for laser technicians to observe safety measures, such as wearing safety glasses. Many, like Bob, have their vision tested periodically by their employer to make sure that the laser is not harming their eyes.

Adding to the pressures of working in tense situations with potentially dangerous instruments is the industry-wide effort at cost-containment. Laser technology is incredibly expensive. Bob estimates that the laser with which he marks parts costs between $175,000 and $200,000. If a laser costs too much for the manufacturer to produce or for the consumer to buy, the company's sales and profits drop. To some degree, laser technicians are responsible for reducing costs without sacrificing quality. This can increase on-the-job stress.

Although the job may be somewhat stressful, the environment is usually pleasant. If you are working with lasers, you will probably be in a clean, quiet, temperature-controlled space. Lasers are expensive, and they are sensitive to dust and temperature, so they must be maintained with great care. Unlike the typical atmosphere of a factory, the surroundings in which Bob works are clean and bright with a low level of noise. "Some of our labs are kept 10 times more sanitary than a surgical lab," Bob says.

When he works in a laboratory or other area of the factory, Bob is a member of a team. Communication skills are important for a laser technician, especially when you are working with people from varying technological backgrounds. For example, Bob helps with projects from other departments at his manufacturing plant, including research and development. "I do work for the whole plant," Bob says. "In fact, I'd say the marking laser is rapidly becoming the most overused machine in the entire plant." In addition to the people he works with every day, Bob has to articulate his ideas and questions to clients who want custom parts machined and to research scientists who may or may not know much about lasers.

One positive result of working with people with different backgrounds is that problems are solved that otherwise might never have been addressed. As Tim Putnam has discovered, "Two people from two totally different fields talking to each other create breakthroughs." For example, he says, "I'm helping a doctor develop an instrument that will fit inside a tiny mass of tissue within the heart and deliver a charge. Before I spoke with the doctor, I had no idea that mass of tissue existed, let alone created problems for doctors. And without my special knowledge of lasers, the doctor might be searching for other, less successful solutions."

Communication skills also come in handy when Tim is trying to design a new part or tool. Tim has done a fair amount of design and fabricating and has even machined the parts himself. Both Bob and Tim believe that a good knowledge of diagrams and schematics is particularly helpful. "After speaking with the doctor and getting her feedback on how well the instrument worked," Tim explains, "I have to go back to the designer and manufacturer and be able to communicate the sort of modifications the doctor wants made."

Both Tim and Bob enjoy the challenges of being laser technicians but acknowledge that there can be some tedious aspects of the job. "When I worked as a field service representative, the job seemed that it was constantly changing for the first six to eight months," Tim says. "Then the problems started repeating themselves. After becoming familiar with the laser systems out there, the work and problem solving can become mundane. Major auto makers change their models every year, but people who invest in laser systems cannot usually afford to do that, so you're looking at the same system time after time."

Doing some tedious work, following directions, and working by a plan are all a part of a laser technician's job. "A person who enjoys working with models would have many of the characteristics of a good laser technician," Tim says. The satisfaction of completing a project, whether it is a model or a complicated laser surgery is the same. "Someone who is ready to work in a patient-care environment but who also has a handle on technology will do well," says Tim.

How Do I Become a Laser Technician?

Bob's company sent him through special training to become a laser technician. However, most laser technicians enter the field by attending a two-year program at a vocational, technical, or community college.

Tim Putnam received an associate's degree in lasers and optics from Vincennes University in Vincennes, Indiana. After graduating, he went to work in research at a hospital in Cincinnati, Ohio, where he received practical, on-the-job experience.

"A lot of the technology involving lasers was just blossoming when I began in research. I was lucky, in that sense, because it was an incredibly dynamic field then. It still is a very dynamic field, but recent pressures to keep the costs down for insurance purposes have made the field tighten up a bit, in terms of spending money on research," he explains.

FYI

Lasers have three special light properties: monochromacity, directionality, and coherence. Monochromacity is useful in photochemistry, atomic isotope separation, and spectroscopy. Directionality gives laser light the ability to travel great distances and remain intense, which makes the laser helpful for welding and drilling. The coherency of laser light helps surveyors to accurately measure distances and the military to track missiles.

EDUCATION

High School

Students should start preparing for this highly technical field while still in high school. Important classes include four years of English, two years of mathematics (including algebra), and at least one year of physical science (preferably physics) with laboratory instruction. Computer programming and applications, machine shop, basic electronics, and blueprint reading are also useful. Any classes that explore systems and the ways in which they work will help you understand lasers.

"Everything is computerized these days," Bob says. "You have to know how to 'talk' to each piece of equipment, and some high school shop classes are using the computerized machinery."

In-depth

Lasers and Medicine

The laser is a precisely controlled light beam that is narrowly focused and aimed at a minute target.

In each laser, various frequencies of light are converted into an intense beam of single wavelength, or color. The color determines how the beam will interact with particular kinds of tissue; it may be different for different kinds of surgery. Lasers may function continuously or in pulsed bursts. The type of laser determines the number of pulses per second, the duration of the pulses, and whether the light will be used to cut through tissue, vaporize it, or seal it.

Lasers take their names from the various substances that produce the beams. The carbon dioxide laser, with a wavelength in the far infrared spectrum, penetrates tissue to a depth of only one millimeter. Carbon dioxide's ability to turn the body's water content into steam allows it to sear, cook, or cut tissue to a precisely controlled depth, sealing blood vessels and nerve endings in a bloodless procedure. The carbon dioxide laser has been used widely to treat some types of cancer, gynecological disorders, and brain tumors.

The argon laser, functioning in the blue-green frequencies, reacts with the color red and will penetrate the skin until it comes in contact with blood. Because it readily coagulates blood in the operating area, the argon laser has been particularly useful in the fields of ophthalmology, plastic surgery, and dermatology.

The YAG laser, with a wavelength in the near infrared spectrum, is used to cook or vaporize tissue that will then be removed from the body. The most invasive of all surgical laser devices, the YAG laser can penetrate four to five millimeters.

Dye lasers can be tuned to react to different wavelengths of light, simply by adding or diluting tint.

The free-electron laser, also tunable, uses magnets to stimulate pulsed light from a stream of electrons.

The excimer laser breaks up inter-molecular bonds and decomposes matter, allowing precise surgery through holes so small no stitches are necessary. For example, patients undergoing excimer laser surgery to repair corneal damage do not experience the thermal effects or shock waves of conventional lasers. Without even touching the cornea, the excimer vaporizes with cool ultraviolet light the molecular links that bond the tissue.

Postsecondary Training

The best way to enter the field as a laser technician is to attend a two-year technical school or community college. Most of these programs feature intensive technical and scientific study, with more hours in a laboratory or work situation than in the actual classroom.

The first year of study includes courses in mathematics, physics, drafting or drawing, diagramming and sketching, basic electronics, electronic instrumentation and calibration, introduction to solid-state devices, electromechanical controls, introductory computer programming, and English composition. The second year of study includes an introduction to lasers, geometrical optics, digital circuits, microwaves, laser and electro-optic components, devices and measurements, vacuum techniques, communication skills, technical report writing, microcomputers, and computer hardware. Special projects are often a part of the second year and can help students narrow the field in which they plan to use their laser technician degree.

Further training after employment is almost always required. Employers usually pay for training to help laser technicians adapt their knowledge to specific positions.

CERTIFICATION OR LICENSING

There are no national certification or licensing requirements for laser technicians. Some laser technology college programs offer their own certification along with a degree. Security clearance may be required for military or government agency work. The National Council on Laser Excellence offers laser technicians several certification options, including certified laser repair technician (CLRT), certified laser operator/medical (CLO/M), and certified laser safety officer (CLSO). Certification is also available through the National Laser Institute.

ADVANCEMENT POSSIBILITIES

Supervisors and directors manage their departments or particular areas and supervise other technicians. They might also coordinate schedules, organize and hold meetings, and direct the training of new hires or the advanced training of current employees.

Consultants work closely with clients to define needs or problems, conduct studies and surveys to obtain data, and analyze data to advise or recommend solutions. They are responsible for updating their knowledge of laser theory, principles, and the technology of their specific disciplines or fields of specialization.

Vocational training instructors teach intermediate or advanced laser and fiber optics technology courses to students in public or private schools or industrial plants. Courses include safety practices and new advances in techniques and technology.

SCHOLARSHIPS AND GRANTS

Scholarships and grants may be available through technical or community colleges. There are no scholarships available through the national associations.

INTERNSHIPS AND VOLUNTEERSHIPS

Summer or part-time work in areas where lasers are used give you valuable contacts and information. For details, inquire at the personnel offices of manufacturing, industrial, medical, and construction organizations.

LABOR UNIONS

Most laser technicians who work in the manufacturing industry belong to a labor union. Those working in other industries usually do not.

Who Will Hire Me?

Many laser technicians graduating from a two-year school obtain their first jobs through interviews on campus. The Laser Institute of America also provides a list of potential employers.

Many colleges provide students with lists of companies and resume assistance. The colleges often work closely with industry, as in the case of Idaho State University's Laser Electro-Optics Program, which involves a Corporate Advisory Committee of six to 12 companies. This advisory committee is active in hiring graduates as well as in giving advice on the university's curriculum.

"For our students graduating with a technical degree, we feel that one of the main parts of our job is placement," says Dave Tyree, chairman of the laser department and an associate professor at Vincennes University in Vincennes, Indiana. Alumni of the college frequently help with placement. "Our first graduating class was in 1975, and whenever any of them needs to fill positions, they call us," Dave says.

Factories, hospitals, and research facilities are just some of the areas that employ laser technicians. "The field is very broad," Dave says. "Last year we placed students in the medical, research, and materials processing areas."

Tim Putnam has also noticed that laser technicians work in many different employment areas. "If I got together with the rest of my graduating class and talked about what we were doing, we'd have almost nothing in common," he comments.

Some companies offer their own training. Bob Wire developed his skills as a laser technician through such training. Most companies also offer additional training to those who already have a basic education in lasers or fiber optics.

The armed forces provide another entry for the laser technician. Military training is not always compatible with civilian requirements, however, so those entering the civilian field may need additional training.

Where Can I Go from Here?

There are many possibilities for advancement, although the primary ways are through on-the-job experience and by keeping up with technological changes and breakthroughs in the field.

After 10 years of experience as a laser technician, Tim Putnam still has technical duties in the surgical room, but he is now both a manager and director, responsible for supervising the department's caseload and personnel. He helps shape the future of laser surgery at Saint Mary's. "It is definitely possible to advance by learning all you can and getting all the experience you can," Tim says.

Many employers designate levels of employment according to experience, education, and job performance. By working through these levels, laser technicians can advance to supervisory or management positions.

Part of what Tim enjoys most about his work is that it allows him to wear several different hats, as technician, administrator, and perpetual student of new technology. "New instrumentation develops rapidly in this field. As best I can, I stay up to date." Constant training in safety and lasers is necessary for all types of laser technicians to keep up with the industry. Many companies pay for employee training, and several opportunities for continuing education are available through the Laser Institute of America.

Some laser technicians use their knowledge to become consultants or specialists for individual firms. Some move into sales or technical writing. Others teach for laser technician programs. With additional education, laser technicians can become laser or fiber optic engineers.

What Are the Salary Ranges?

Salaries for laser technicians vary in different parts of the country and for different educational backgrounds and applications. The laser program at Vincennes University advises students that they can expect starting salaries of between $18,500 and $32,000 a year. According to Salaryexpert.com, in 2005 the median annual salary for laser technicians was $45,472. The lowest paid average $31,530 annually, while the highest paid earned $58,999. Most laser technicians can expect a wide array of benefits including insurance, paid holidays and vacations, and retirement plans. Many employers offer opportunities for continuing education.

What Is the Job Outlook?

Vincennes University boasts nearly 100 percent placement for its laser technician graduates. "Last year," says Dave Tyree, "we had companies who could not fill all of the positions they had open, so this year they're back to hire our graduates."

Program directors advise their students to remain open to all offers. For the best entry-level jobs, graduates must sometimes relocate to another area.

Depending on the strength of the economy, laser technicians who want to work in research areas may have a greater challenge locating a position. One of the fastest growing areas for laser technicians is fiber-optic systems used in the communications field. Other strong areas include production, medicine, construction, defense, and entertainment. Clinics offering LASIK, a laser vision-correction surgery, are needing technicians to help provide the procedure to a growing number of patients. Eyecare professionals anticipate that within a few years, the annual rate of LASIK surgeries will increase from 1 million to 3 million.

How Do I Learn More?

PROFESSIONAL ORGANIZATIONS

The following organizations provide information on the industry, laser technician careers, accredited schools, and employers:

Aerospace Industries Association of America
1000 Wilson Boulevard, Suite 1700
Arlington, VA 22209-3901
703-358-1000
http://www.aia-aerospace.org

Institute of Electrical and Electronics Engineers
Lasers and Electro-Optical Society
445 Hoes Lane
Piscataway, NJ 08855-1331
Tel: 732-562-3892
http://www.i-leos.org

Junior Engineering Technical Society
1420 King Street, Suite 405
Alexandria, VA 22314
703-548-5387
http://www.jets.org

Laser Institute of America
13501 Ingenuity Drive, Suite 128
Orlando, FL 32826
800-345-2737
http://www.laserinstitute.org

National Council on Laser Excellence
PO Box 522379
Marathon Shores, FL 33052
866-252-0880
http://www.lasercertification.org

BIBLIOGRAPHY

The following is a sampling of materials relating to the professional concerns and development of laser technicians:

Bone, Jan, and Julie Rigby. *Opportunities in Laser Technology Careers*. Lincolnwood, Ill.: VGM Career Horizons, 2000.

Careers in Focus: Technicians. 2d ed. Chicago: Ferguson Publishing Company, 2004.

Hecht, Jeff. *The Laser Guidebook*. 2d ed. New York: McGraw-Hill, 1999.

Hitz, C. Breck et al. *Introduction to Laser Technology*. 3d ed. Piscataway, N.J.: Wiley-IEEE Press, 2001.

Petruzzellis, Thomas. *Optoelectronics, Fiber Optics, and Laser Cookbook*. New York: McGraw-Hill, 1997.

LIBRARY TECHNICIANS

"Attention to detail is very important," says Lori O'Hara, who has worked as a library technician for 17 years. With so much material, so much information available today, library patrons rely a great deal on library technicians to keep everything in order for easy access. "When you work in a library, everything has to be done right. If a book isn't shelved in the right place, then the next person who needs it won't be able to find it. Almost anything you do, if it's not done right, will cause your patron to suffer somewhere down the line."

Definition
Library technicians work in all aspects of library services, including circulation, reference, acquisitions, and shelving.

Alternative Job Titles
Library aides
Library assistants
Library associates
Library clerks
Library technical assistants

High School Subjects
English
Government
History

Personal Skills
Helping/teaching
Leadership/management

Salary Range
$14,700 to $24,900 to $40,100

Minimum Educational Level
Some postsecondary training

Certification or Licensing
Voluntary

Outlook
About as fast as the average

DOT
100

GOE
12.03.04

NOC
5211

O*NET-SOC
25-4031.00

What Does a Library Technician Do?

Libraries are centers of information. *Library technicians* assist librarians (or in some cases work independently) to help people access that information. There are usually three broad divisions within a library: technical services, user services, and administrative services. Most library technicians are familiar with the duties in each category.

In technical services, library technicians make certain the information is there for the user. They acquire, prepare, and organize materials for the library, including books, periodicals (magazines, journals, newsletters), recordings, video cassettes, or special collections, such as limited edition books. *Acquisitions technicians*, *classifiers*, and *catalogers* work behind the scenes to select, order, index, and describe books and other materials. Their work includes arranging for one library to borrow the materials of another library or for a library to display a special collection temporarily. Technicians also type book orders, label new books, make basic repairs to damaged books, place books on display shelves, maintain library equipment, and collect late fines for overdue books.

In user services, technicians help library patrons find the materials they need. *Reference library technicians* specialize in locating information. *Children's library technicians* and *young adult library technicians* specialize in getting children and young adults interested in books, reading, and learning by organizing summer reading programs, reading hours, and other fun activities. Technicians also operate and maintain audiovisual equipment and help library patrons use microfilm and microfiche readers, as well as computers.

In administrative services, library technicians are involved with the management of the library. They might help prepare budgets, coordinate the efforts of different departments, write policies and procedures, and develop the library's collection. Those with more responsibility supervise and coordinate staff members, recruit and supervise volunteers, organize fund-raising efforts, sit on community boards, and develop programs to promote reading and learning.

Lingo to Learn

Bibliographic records Documents that contain the information that uniquely identifies each work by author, title, subject, publisher, date of publication, edition number, and call number.

Bookmobile A trailer or truck that is driven by a "mobile" librarian into remote, rural areas to provide library materials.

Call number An identification code assigned to books and other items. The code makes these materials easy to locate, since they're stored in a specific order.

Circulate Loaning a book, or checking it out, to a patron. Materials, such as reference books, that are not allowed out on loan are called "noncirculating."

Folio An oversized book, usually shelved with other larger books.

Microfiche A flat sheet of film onto which information is reduced and stored. A special microfiche machine is needed to read the film.

The specifics of a library technician's job often depend on the type and size of the institution. An *academic library technician* works in a university or college library, handling reference materials and specialized journals and helping professors and students find materials for research. *School library technicians* and *school library media specialists* work with teachers and teacher-librarians to show students how to use the library. A library technician working in a small, branch library might handle a large number of tasks while a technician working for a large university library might specialize in one area and seldom, if ever, perform any other tasks.

Library technicians also work in special libraries maintained by government agencies, corporations, law firms, advertising agencies, museums, professional associations, medical centers, religious organizations, and research laboratories. Special libraries contain materials of special interest to the organizations that maintain them. For instance, a medical center might feature a library full of medical books and journals. Library technicians at special libraries organize bibliographies, prepare abstracts and indexes of periodicals, or research and analyze background information on issues important to the group.

Library technicians use computers to organize and access information. Many libraries are either linked to remote databases through their computers, or they maintain their own computerized databases. Library technicians develop and index databases and help users develop searching skills to access the information they need. *Automated system technicians* help plan and operate computer systems. *Information technicians* help design and develop information storage and retrieval systems. They also devise procedures for collecting, organizing, interpreting, and classifying information.

The computer age has changed the role of the library technician. In the past technicians functioned solely as the librarian's support staff. Now, computers enable many librarians to spend more time on acquisitions and administration, while technicians handle the technical and user service responsibilities. An increasing number of library technicians have the same responsibilities as a librarian and some have replaced librarians. This development is most common at institutions with limited funding.

What Is It Like to Be a Library Technician?

Lori O'Hara works at the Veterans Administration Medical Center in Grand Junction, Colorado. Among her responsibilities as a library technician is the supervision of volunteers. "We have people at our circulation desk, and people who take a book cart out to the wards," Lori says. "I don't actually sit at the circulation desk all day checking books in and out, but I'm in close proximity to the desk so I can make sure everything's okay." Lori trains new volunteers when necessary, but the library has a good reliable crew of about 13 volunteers that she can call upon. The library requires two or three volunteers to be there every day. "We probably have between 30 and 50 patrons through here a day," she says, "nothing like at a public or university library."

Despite the relatively low number of patrons, Lori is often busy dealing with specialized information. "Because we're a medical facility," she says, "we do computer searches and find out medical information for the physicians and nurses. We also help patients

To Be a Successful Library Technician, You Should . . .

- enjoy problem solving, working with people, and books
- be patient, analytical, detail oriented, and flexible
- be familiar and skilled with cataloging systems, computers, and the Internet
- be articulate and enjoy fielding questions and assisting with research
- not mind being interrupted during tasks

find patient education materials." The computer searches involve using databases, such as PubMed of the National Library of Medicine. "We also run the satellite network for education purposes. We're very involved with education, which may be out of scope for most library technicians. We get a calendar from the VA headquarters of all the satellite programs that are going to be brought into the VA nationwide. Then we downlink them into our facility. We let people know about it, advertise it."

Lori is also involved in book ordering. "Quarterly, we have a meeting, and we send out ads that we've gotten from different medical journals, and ads that come in from publishers. We send those out to all of the departments here at our hospital, and they send those back with their requests. We use something called the Brandon/Hill list of medical books for small libraries as a basis." Lori will call book jobbers (companies that consolidate multiple purchase orders) and look for the best prices. "We also have 140 journals which I subscribe to for the library." Once the books arrive, Lori prepares them for the shelves by putting in the cards and pockets, and applying the spine labels.

Lori enjoys the variety of the work. "Because I'm the only technician here, I get lots of different things to do. I don't sit for hours and hours doing the same thing."

The Internet has brought significant changes to libraries, simplifying many tasks and allowing the general public to conduct searches that once would have required the expertise of a librarian. Instead of thumbing through printed catalogs to order materials, a technician can now visit a publisher's Web page or consult an online list of books in print. The Internet also provides a convenient way to ask other library professionals for suggestions, discuss relationships with colleagues, list conferences, and quickly find materials such as specific books, songs, or poems. Unfortunately, information posted on the Internet is not always accurate, and the volume of it can be overwhelming. "Anybody who goes into library work really needs to know how to use the Internet," Lori says. "These days, a library is really an information management service more than anything else."

Do I Have What It Takes to Be a Library Technician?

A library technician should be tactful, patient, and able to do detailed, analytical work. Most library jobs require the flexibility to work on some weekends, holidays, and evenings. It is important to enjoy learning and helping others learn. The technician should be able to work with a range of people, including colleagues, children, senior citizens, business people, and the general public.

Cynthia Beuselinck, a library technician in Canada, feels the most important quality for a library technician is the ability to work well with people and enjoy helping them find the answers to their questions. "If you don't have good interpersonal skills, you can't cut it," she says.

A library technician also has to juggle many duties at once. "There are so many things to do, so many, many things," Cynthia emphasizes. "You have to break the tasks down into smaller tasks, if only to celebrate the smaller successes." Patience, flexibility, and being able to handle innumerable interruptions with grace are also important. "You have to expect that someone will interrupt you to ask a question," she says.

Although Cynthia generally enjoys her career, it is sometimes stressful. Low budgets and small staffs can make the job seem overwhelming, even unmanageable. There is also occasionally tension because some institutions are replacing librarians with library technicians in an effort to reduce costs. "I usually don't encounter resentment from librarians, but I can't say it's never happened. This new demand for technicians is good news for us, but I can understand the librarians' position. They've gone to school for six years, instead of two. They have more theory and more research behind them, and yet their jobs are disappearing, because it's cheaper to hire a technician," Cynthia remarks.

How Do I Become a Library Technician?

EDUCATION

High School

With only a high school diploma, you might find a job as a circulation clerk or a clerk-typist at a library, which would give you valuable experience and contacts, but you probably would not be able to advance without further training. Libraries encourage the public to be educated, and library employees are expected to be educated, too. A high school diploma is required for admission into most programs that train library technicians.

To prepare for a career in library science, it is best to have a broad education that includes some business, history, science, mathematics, and languages. Computer skills are essential, since libraries now feature access to the Internet and offer many products on CD-ROM. A technician is apt to work with databases, library automation systems, online library systems, online public access systems, and computerized circulation systems. A command of English and the ability to write well are important, and speech classes will help you articulate ideas. Literature classes are also helpful, but it might not be necessary to have a deep understanding of literature; a specialized library might focus on a topic such as business, law, corporate concerns, medicine, or science, and a knowledge in that particular area would be more important in that institution.

Postsecondary Training

Because of the lack of standardized certification requirements, there is some variation among libraries, but most employees in the United States who are called library technicians, library assistants, or library associates have about two years of postsecondary training. In the East most technicians hold an associate's degree in library science. Degrees in other fields are frequently accepted in the West. Technicians at this level do not just arrange books on the shelves; they perform more responsible tasks, such as entering data on computers, assisting patrons, and putting bar codes on the library's holdings.

"If a person is looking at this as their career for the next 10 to 15 years, or if they want this to be a terminal career, the best way to go would be the associate's degree in library media technology," says Margaret Barron, executive director of the Council on Library/Media Technicians (COLT). "That associate's degree doesn't have to be terminal. Many times, after completing two years of education, a person will decide to go on for a bachelor's."

Technicians with a four-year degree are often called paraprofessionals, although the term is also broadly applied to any technician. Paraprofessionals typically perform duties such as assisting librarians, conducting story hours and tours, compiling bibliographies, and performing literature searches.

Advanced education can be very important for library technicians and librarians, because they are expected to be able to answer questions from patrons. For example, you might need to know enough about chemistry to help someone conduct research for a professional journal. You would not have to be an expert on chemistry, but you would need to understand what the researcher needed and where to find it.

CERTIFICATION AND LICENSING

Certification is recommended but not required for library technicians. The credential now available for library technicians is the associate's degree that colleges award to students who complete a two-year program in library technology. Since these programs vary, the credential is not a consistent indicator of the technician's training and ability.

COLT is developing a national certification, though it is as yet uncertain when it will be available. Certification would standardize the requirements to enter the profession and would eliminate some confusion. For example, technicians with the same qualifications would all have the same job title instead of using a handful of titles interchangeably.

SCHOLARSHIPS AND GRANTS

There are few scholarships specifically for library technicians, but COLT is exploring offering scholarship opportunities in the future. Some organizations, such as the Medical Library Association, do administer scholarships, grants, and other awards for library

In-depth

The History of Libraries

Libraries have been around for more than 3,000 years. One of the most famous early libraries was located in Alexandria, Egypt; it was destroyed, along with a vast amount of irreplaceable information. The first public library was probably located in Athens, Greece, in about 500 B.C. During the Middle Ages, books became so rare and valuable that they were commonly chained to their shelves to prevent people from taking them.

After the invention of the printing press and movable type, more books and other publications were available, and more people learned to read. Libraries became increasingly popular, especially during the 1800s, when public education was being established in the United States. Andrew Carnegie and other wealthy philanthropists provided invaluable help to libraries by donating large sums of money for books and buildings to house them

The development of the Dewey Decimal System in 1876 and *Poole's Index to Periodical Literature* in 1882 enabled library patrons to use the holdings much more easily. The establishment of the American Library Association in 1876 is noted as the beginning of librarianship as a profession.

During the 20th century, the information explosion has placed an overwhelming number of publications and other materials at the disposal of the general public, and that flood of information has increased dramatically in the computer age. By some estimates, the amount of information published about most subjects doubles every decade or two. Since the 1940s, libraries have been training support staffs to help sort through this vast amount of information. Because of the high cost of operating such a program, many libraries have turned to community colleges and other postsecondary schools to train workers who can perform these increasingly complex duties.

The Web site of the Library of Congress (http://www.loc.gov) features a great deal of information, and not just about the library. In addition to access to catalogs and collections, the site also features a number of online exhibitions. Recently the site included exhibits about the designs of Frank Lloyd Wright, women journalists of World War II, historic comic strips, and the Dead Sea scrolls.

studies toward a master's degree. You can also apply for the general scholarships and grants offered by colleges and other schools. Some civic and community organizations offer general scholarships, and some local libraries offer awards specifically for students in library programs.

INTERNSHIPS AND VOLUNTEERSHIPS

Most internships for library personnel are tied to a master's program. Some libraries require only a high school diploma and offer on-the-job training for their employees, and others will hire employees who have experience but little education.

Who Will Hire Me?

As a technician, you might work in a library operated by a public or private school, a corporation, or the government; or you could be employed at a public library or a special library. Technicians also work as archivists in museums, as records managers or database specialists for businesses, or as self-employed computer and information consultants.

According to Cynthia, any company that needs someone with skills in gathering information could hire you. "The skills you learn and develop in technical school translate incredibly well to other careers, too, like sales and publishing," she says. "Look beyond the school library, for that matter, look beyond the library. The field is opening up dramatically."

Look beyond the school library, for that matter, look beyond the library. The field is opening up dramatically.

The best place to begin looking for a job is at the placement offices of schools that offer training for library technicians.The American Library Association provides a listing of jobs for library support staff. Jobs and related useful information are also listed in library magazines and journals such as *Library Mosaics*.

Jobs are available most often at larger libraries, where the turnover is higher than at smaller institutions. Sometimes you can leave a resume on file at a library's personnel office. Most libraries are government institutions, however, and it might be necessary to apply through a local Job Service or comply with other hiring procedures.

Where Can I Go from Here?

If you are hired as a technician at a library, your first duties will probably be at the circulation desk, checking materials in and out. After you gain some experience, you might move behind the scenes and focus on storing and verifying information, which involves a great deal of work on computers. Later, you might help with the library's budget. The most experienced technicians sometimes are promoted to supervisors where they oversee less experienced employees and manage the way an entire department operates.

To advance beyond the level of a technician and become a *librarian*, you need a master's degree. You might be given a great deal of responsibility without becoming a librarian, however, since the trend recently has been toward hiring more technicians.

Librarians tend to move from one facility to another as opportunities arise, but most technicians remain with one institution and work their way up. Though the needs of each library are unique, most institutions are looking for the same basic education and experience in technicians.

Advancement Possibilities

Coordinators of young adult/children's services select library materials, develop and sponsor educational programs aimed at encouraging children to read, educate parents on the importance of reading, and provide training and support for other children/young adult librarians.

Directors of serials departments acquire and take inventory of journals, magazines, newspapers, and other periodicals; negotiate the rates of purchase of these publications; and manage department staff members.

What Are the Salary Ranges?

According to the U.S Department of Labor *Occupational Outlook Handbook*, median annual earnings of library technicians were $24,900 in 2003. Technicians in the lowest paid 10 percent earned $14,700, while those in the highest paid 10 percent earned $40,100. Clerical library assistants earned between $13,120 and $32,420 with a median salary of $19,980 annually. The best-paid positions were with the federal government, which paid library technicians an average of $36,788 annually in 2003. A review of earnings nationwide by Salaryexpert.com found that library assistants earned between $24,466 and $44,668 annually in 2005, while library technical assistants earned between $16,803 and $33,660. Full-time technicians in large libraries may have benefits such as vacation pay, retirement, and health and life insurance.

What Is the Job Outlook?

The U.S. Department of Labor expects employment of library technicians to grow about as fast as the average through 2012. "There's been an increased interest in this field," says Margaret Barron of COLT, "because of computer technology. Many people with the associate's degree are also computer literate. Also, with the increased retirement of the professional librarian and the increase in the closings of library schools, we have all these vacancies that need to be filled. There's a shift in the internal duties and responsibilities because you don't have enough librarians to perform what we previously called 'librarian duties, responsibilities, and functions.'" As a result, technicians are brought into the workplace in order to free up those with professional degrees. "In many cases the professionals are providing leadership for several library entities within a regional area."

Also, technology is allowing support staffs to do more advanced work, such as working with computer databases. In addition, many patrons no longer need the level of knowledge a librarian can provide; they're conducting their own research on the Internet, for example, and need only be pointed in the right direction.

Technicians might find openings at public libraries and school libraries, because those institutions have been receiving fewer tax dollars from the government and will be apt to reduce their expenses by hiring fewer librarians.

How Do I Learn More?

PROFESSIONAL ORGANIZATIONS

The following organizations provide information on library technician careers, accredited schools and scholarships, and employment opportunities:

American Library Association
Library Careers
Office for Library Personnel Resources
50 East Huron Street
Chicago, IL 60611
800-545-2433
http://www.ala.org

Council on Library/Media Technicians
28262 Chardon Road, PMB 168
Wickliffe, OH 44092-2793
630-257-6541
http://colt.ucr.edu

Library of Congress
Employment Office
101 Independence Avenue, SE
Washington, DC 20540
202-707-5000
http://www.loc.gov

Medical Library Association
65 East Wacker Place, Suite 1900
Chicago, IL 60601-7245
312-419-9094
info@mlanet.org
http://www.mlanet.org

Smithsonian Institution Libraries
PO Box 37012, MRC 154
Washington, DC 20013-7012
202-633-2240
libmail@si.edu
http://www.sil.si.edu

Special Libraries Association
331 South Patrick Street
Alexandria, VA 22314-3501
703-647-4900
sla@sla.org
http://www.sla.org

BIBLIOGRAPHY

The following is a sampling of materials relating to the professional concerns and development of library technicians:

Eberts, Marjorie, and Margaret Gisler. *Careers for Bookworms and Other Literary Types.* 3d ed. New York: McGraw-Hill, 2002.

Kane, Laura Townsend. *Straight from the Stacks: A First-Hand Guide to Careers in Library and Information Science.* Chicago: American Library Association, 2003.

McCook, Kathleen De La Pena, and Margaret Myers. *Opportunities in Library and Information Science Careers.* Lincolnwood, Ill.: VGM Career Horizons, 2001.

Rubin, Richard. *Foundations of Library and Information Science.* New York: Neal-Schuman Publishers, 2000.

LICENSED PRACTICAL NURSES

Part of Debra McFadden's day as a licensed practical nurse (LPN) at a correctional facility may involve working the doctor's line, which means she sees patients who have requested to see the nurse because of illness. "It's like doing a kind of triage," she says. "We go in and assess them for these various ailments. If we want, we can have them go see the doctor. 'Doctor's line' is getting these people prepared to see the doctor, something like how an office nurse does."

Debra finds the work to be fast-paced and very educational. "You really do learn about the vast majority of illnesses," she says. "I never knew of all the different medications. It really is quite interesting."

Definition
Licensed practical nurses administer direct patient care under the supervision of physicians or registered nurses in hospitals, clinics, private homes, schools, and other similar settings.

Alternative Job Titles
Home health nurses
Vocational nurses

High School Subjects
Biology
Chemistry
Health

Personal Skills
Following instructions
Helping/teaching

Salary Range
$22,860 to $31,440 to $44,040

Minimum Educational Level
Some postsecondary training

Certification or Licensing
Required by all states

Outlook
About as fast as the average

DOT
075

GOE
14.07.01

NOC
3233

O*NET-SOC
29-2061.00

What Does a Licensed Practical Nurse Do?

Licensed practical nurses are trained to provide quality, cost-effective nursing care wherever patient care is needed. Work sites include hospitals, nursing homes and long-term care facilities, rehabilitation facilities, doctors' offices, health maintenance organizations (HMOs), clinics, schools, and private homes. LPNs may also be recruited as members of the military services. Their duties vary according to each state's Nurse Practice Act and the place of employment but generally involve basic patient care. The LPN might also participate in the planning, implementation, and evaluation of nursing care. LPNs provide for the emotional and physical comfort and safety of patients: observing, recording, and reporting to the appropriate people any changes in the patient's status. LPNs can also perform more specialized nursing functions, such as administering medications and therapeutic treatments, as well as assisting with rehabilitation.

In the hospital setting, LPNs usually work under the supervision of registered nurses (RNs), performing many basic nursing duties of bedside care, particularly those that are routine or performed regularly. They take vital signs, keeping checks on temperature, pulse, and blood pressure readings; prepare and administer prescribed medicines to patients (in most states); help prepare patients for examinations and operations; collect samples from patients for testing; and perform routine laboratory procedures, such as urinalysis. They also observe patients and report any adverse reactions to medications or treatments. One of an LPN's main functions is to ensure that patients are comfortable and that their personal hygiene needs are met. They are on hand to give alcohol rubs or massages or to help patients bathe or brush their teeth, and to respond to patients' calls and answer their questions. The LPN may work in any unit of the hospital, including intensive care, recovery, pediatrics, medical-surgical, and maternity, with varying duties according to the demands of the department. For

Lingo to Learn

Anatomy The science of the structure of the body and its organs.

Catheter A rubber, plastic, or glass tube used to insert into the bladder in order to withdraw urine; or a tube for passage into a structure for the purpose of injecting or withdrawing a fluid into or out of the body.

Charge nurse The nurse in charge of a particular floor or unit of a hospital, nursing home, or other health care setting.

Clinical rotation Time spent working on a floor or unit of a health care facility, usually as part of required training for medical health care professionals.

Geriatrics A branch of medicine that deals with the problems and diseases of old age and aging people.

Inpatient A hospital patient who receives lodging and food as well as treatment.

IV Abbreviation for intravenous—going into a vein.

Obstetrics The branch of medicine dealing with childbirth.

Occupational health nurse A nurse who provides nursing services to employees at their workplace.

Outpatient A patient who does not sleep overnight in a hospital, but who visits a clinic or dispensary connected with it for diagnosis or treatment.

Pediatrics A branch of medicine dealing with the development, care, and diseases of children.

Physiology The science dealing with the study of the function of tissues or organs.

Psychiatric nursing A nursing specialty that deals with psychiatry, that is, mental, emotional, or behavioral disorders of patients.

Public health nurse A nurse working for a community or government health organization stressing preventive medicine and social science.

Registered nurse A degreed nurse who has been licensed by a state authority after qualifying for registration.

instance, in the obstetrics department, an LPN helps in the delivery room and may feed and bathe newborns, as well as give basic care to recovering new mothers. Some LPNs direct nursing aides and orderlies and may also have clerical duties.

In nursing or retirement homes, LPNs often serve as *charge nurses,* taking over many of the responsibilities that RNs would have in a hospital setting. Because much of the care provided in nursing homes is of the routine variety, LPNs are used extensively and are often in charge of an entire floor, with responsibility for the hands-on care of many patients. In addition to providing routine bedside care, LPNs in nursing homes (fast becoming the largest employer of LPNs after hospitals) may also help to evaluate residents' needs, develop care treatment plans, and supervise nursing aides. In addition, they are charged with contacting doctors when necessary, completing any associated paperwork, and reporting to doctors or RNs on patients' status. Doctors and RNs often depend on detailed reporting from LPNs to accurately maintain patient records and treatment courses. LPNs frequently act as supervisors of nursing assistants in nursing homes.

LPNs working in clinics for physicians and dentists, including HMOs, help prepare patients for examination and even help the physician conduct the exam. They apply dressings, explain prescribed treatments or health measures, schedule appointments, keep records, and perform other clerical duties. LPNs who work in home health care as private duty nurses prepare meals for their patients, keep rooms orderly, and teach family members simple nursing tasks as part of patient care.

What Is It Like to Be a Licensed Practical Nurse?

Debra McFadden works as a licensed practical nurse in a county prison, where her primary responsibilities include leading the intake process to gather medical information on those people entering the system. Her day begins with preparing medications, then going into the cell block area and passing them out. "After that I go to the quarantine units," she says. "New people just coming in go to a quarantine unit until they've had their medical intake done. Basically, the intake process involves asking them health-related questions: illnesses, diagnoses, whether or not they're withdrawing from any drugs or alcohol. I take their vitals, and I give them a TB test. We also draw blood for syphilis testing."

The area of the jail in which Debra works is like a small hospital. "We have routine medication orders," she says, "and emergencies. Anything from somebody trying to clean out his ears with a Q-tip and getting it stuck, to overdose, broken bones, people attempting suicide. We have a medical unit for those who are in medical distress of any type. It all runs the gamut, from colds to HIV. We do have emergencies—guys getting into fights. It can sometimes be just like an ER, with somebody bleeding. Anybody in immediate distress, we have to send out. We also have a psych ward for those the psychiatrist is following closely, for those we are concerned about, or who have verbally stated that they were going to try to commit suicide."

Debra also prepares "rewrites" for people with long-standing illnesses such as cardiac problems or diabetes. "They get medication on a routine basis every day, but we're only allowed to have a 30-day order. So every 30 days we have to go back and do a rewrite—get the doctor to re-sign for those medications. A lot of times in nursing homes, the pharmacies just send you new med sheets. We have to do that ourselves, so we get the patient's chart out, write down all the medications they're getting on an ongoing basis, and the doctor signs off on that."

Most of Debra's patients are men, though there is also a small unit for women at the prison. Working in corrections requires that Debra be aware of certain aspects of the work not common to LPNs of other facilities. "You learn about the security issues," she says. "We have a lot of people who come in and are withdrawing from drugs. They try to manipulate you to get medications they don't really need." Though Debra hasn't had much problem with the transition into correctional nursing, she has watched some nurses leave the work. "Some people can't stand the sound of the door closing and locking. Some are very intimidated by the whole penal system. But it is an interesting option for nurses. Part of traditional nursing is working with people who are infirm and elderly; you have so much more with prison nursing. It covers everything."

Karen Hanson has worked as an LPN in different kinds of facilities, including long-term care. "You provide the best care possible," Karen says. "If they are an Alzheimer's patient, or forgetful, you reorient them to the time and place, and help them to maintain their sense of independence. It's not that they can't do for themselves; you just must remind them of how to do things."

Karen assures that her patients are without pain and that they're comfortable. "This includes medicating the patient as per doctor's orders; turning the patient if they're unable to do so on their own, to prevent the bedsores that can cause more pain and infection; cleaning the patient and providing proper skin care if they are incontinent of stool or urine. You have to assist them with eating. If they're not eating and they're losing weight, that opens the door for dehydration and infection."

Do I Have What It Takes to Be a Licensed Practical Nurse?

"In correctional nursing," Debra says, "you definitely have to know right from wrong. Most people get into nursing because of their compassion. You still must have that, but you must also not be gullible, you must know where to draw the line. Even though you may do much for a drug addicted person, that person may always want more."

Karen emphasizes patience. "In a long-term facility you really must care," she says. "The patients become like your family. You're with them all the time, and you assure that they're being taken care of. But you need to know how to let go, as well. You are usually with these patients until they pass on."

The patients become like your family. You're with them all the time, and you assure that they're being taken care of.

Licensed practical nurses, and virtually anyone opting for a career in patient care, should also possess physical and mental stamina and endurance. While LPNs should possess a compassionate nature, they sometimes need to be thick-skinned when it comes to occasional unkind treatment from others. Doctors, nurses, and others who supervise LPNs, particularly in a hospital setting, are often under a lot of pressure

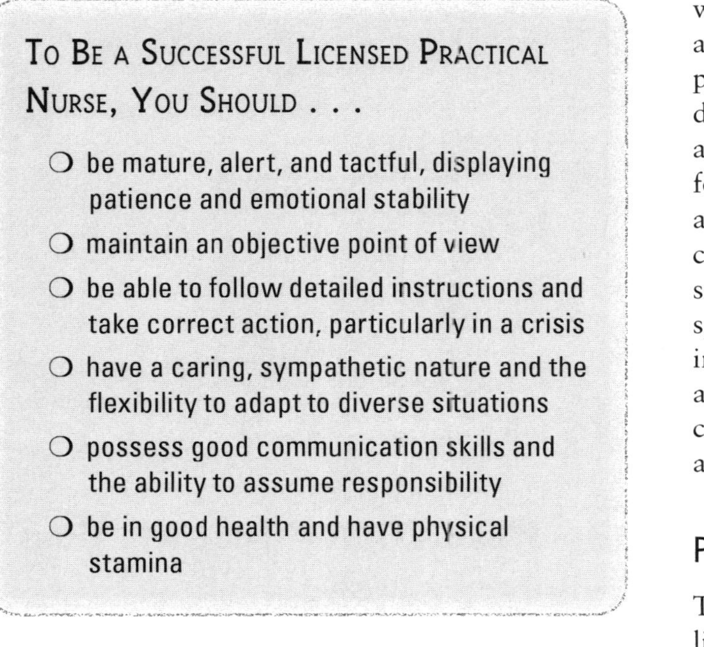

To Be a Successful Licensed Practical Nurse, You Should . . .

- be mature, alert, and tactful, displaying patience and emotional stability
- maintain an objective point of view
- be able to follow detailed instructions and take correct action, particularly in a crisis
- have a caring, sympathetic nature and the flexibility to adapt to diverse situations
- possess good communication skills and the ability to assume responsibility
- be in good health and have physical stamina

and may take their frustrations out on those standing shoulder to shoulder with them in providing patient care.

In any case, focusing on the higher goal of contributing to the health and well-being of people can counter the stresses of being on your feet all day or being the recipient of unkind remarks from anguished patients or overburdened and frustrated doctors or supervisors. These qualities, along with good communication skills and the ability to follow directions, will help LPNs achieve a workable balance in their chosen field.

How Do I Become a Licensed Practical Nurse?

EDUCATION

High School

To become an LPN, you must first complete an approved practical nursing program in your state. Nearly all states require a high school degree to enroll in the program. Several states in the country, however, require only that applicants complete one or two years of high school. And some high schools even offer a practical nursing program that is approved by a state board of nursing or other regulatory body.

Generally, students with a broad-based educational background and wide-ranging interests will be well prepared to adapt to the academic work and clinical practice required for the LPN training program. Although many practical nursing schools do not require specific high school courses for admission, high school students interested in more focused nursing career preparation will find science and mathematics courses helpful, including biology, chemistry, and physics. Because communication skills are critical to effective nursing, English and speech courses are also a good idea. But perhaps most important are the intangible benefits of possessing a caring, sympathetic nature, a sincere desire to contribute to the health and well-being of people, and the ability to follow oral and written directions.

Postsecondary Training

To be eligible to take the examination required for licensing, students must graduate from an approved school of practical nursing. (A correspondence course in practical nursing does not qualify you to take the state licensing examination.) The length of this program varies from state to state, depending on the individual state's admission requirements. Most programs run for 12 months, although some are as long as 18 months, and a few are less than a year. The trend now is toward an 18-month or two-year program leading to an associate's degree. The trend of expanded education speaks to the growing need for all nurses to have a broader base of knowledge. More complex technologies and the desire to minimize liability risks are reasons why. Many nursing students are opting for a four-year degree because of the accompanying increase in job status and opportunities.

LPN programs are generally offered through two-year colleges and vocational and technical schools. Some programs are offered in high schools, hospitals, and colleges and universities. Men and women 18 years of age or older are eligible to apply, and some programs actually have an upper age limit. Students go to school five days a week, for six to eight hours a day. Participation in a practical nursing program is a full-time commitment. Students who must work a part-time job while enrolled should consult the program director in advance to work out an arrangement.

Although practical nursing programs are no longer strictly hospital-based and contain more theory than clinical practice, they are generally affiliated with a hospital and include a clinical rotation along with classroom instruction. Classroom study covers basic nursing concepts, anatomy, physiology, medical-surgical nursing, pediatrics, obstetrics, psychiatric nursing, administration of drugs, nutrition, and first aid. Clinical practice usually takes place in a supervised hospital setting, but may include other settings as well. Students practice nursing techniques on mannequins before moving on to human patients. After successfully completing the program, students receive a diploma or certificate and may then sit for the state board licensing exam in the state where they plan to work.

Some schools have waiting lists for their practical nursing education programs. It is wise to plan early by obtaining and completing all application forms, beginning this process approximately one year ahead of intended enrollment. Interested students should write to several schools in the desired area and ask for their brochures, financial aid information, and application forms. Make sure the practical nursing program you select is approved by your state's board of nursing. For information on practical nursing education and accredited programs, see "How Do I Learn More?"

CERTIFICATION OR LICENSING

After graduating from an approved school of practical nursing, applicants must then pass an examination to become licensed. All states and the District of Columbia require practical nurses to be licensed and to renew that license every two years. The state board of nursing issues the practical nursing license (or the vocational nursing license in California and Texas) once the National Council Licensure Examination for Practical Nurses, a written exam, is passed. Legal minimum requirements for the license are set by each state through its board of nursing, so these may vary from state to state. LPNs in one state wishing to practice nursing in another state must apply to the board of nursing in that state. Although requirements vary slightly, it is generally not difficult to obtain another license and may not even require a written examination. Licensed practical nurses can identify themselves by putting the initials LPN or LVN (in Texas and California) after their names.

SCHOLARSHIPS AND GRANTS

Students interested in pursuing a scholarship should contact the counselor or program director working directly with the school or educational program where they are seeking entry. Applicants are urged to write for this information well in advance of starting the term.

LABOR UNIONS

Although hospitals often have unions that medical employees are eligible to join, LPNs don't necessarily benefit much from membership. Hospital unions often group professional employees with other employee groups whose interests do not converge with those of professional nurses. Consequently, union membership does not benefit those without the greatest voice. Membership with a professional association that has the interests and issues of the LPN at its core is often more beneficial.

Who Will Hire Me?

Newly licensed LPNs frequently step into part-time or full-time jobs with the hospitals where they did their training. Networking among staff may uncover other job leads worth exploring. While VA hospitals still employ a large number of LPNs, continued growth for LPNs working in hospitals generally is not expected to continue. This is due largely to the decreasing number of inpatients, which is related to cost concerns: It has become too costly for hospitals to care for patients for a prolonged recovery period.

According to the U.S. Department of Labor, the latest available statistics show the major employer of practical nurses still to be hospitals (28 percent), but nursing homes are quickly gaining on hospitals, employing about 26 percent of LPNs. Nursing homes will offer the most new jobs for LPNs as the number of aged and disabled persons in need of long-term care rises rapidly with the aging baby boomer population. Nursing homes will also be called on to care for the increasing number of convalescing patients who have been released from hospitals but are not recovered enough to go home.

Job seekers may apply at local employment agencies, although newspaper want ads may be the best avenue. Openings for LPNs are usually advertised in the classified section of the paper under headings such as "Nurses," "Licensed Practical Nurses," "LPNs," "Health Care," "Hospitals," "Private Duty," or "Temporary Nursing." LPNs can also apply directly to hospitals, public health agencies, or nursing homes.

FYI

Approximately 40 percent of LPNs use their practical nursing license as a stepping-stone to other health occupations with greater pay and more responsibilities.

Targeting a major hospital with acute care facilities may offer greater growth potential, and veteran's hospitals in particular use a large number of LPNs to meet their ongoing need for basic, hands-on patient care. Applicants can send their resumes, with a short cover letter, directly to the personnel directors of health care facilities. With the shortage of qualified people, calls for interviews should quickly follow. Nurses' associations and professional journals sometimes offer job leads and should be contacted individually (see "How Do I Learn More?").

Rapid growth for LPN employment is also expected in such residential care facilities as board and care homes and group homes for the mentally disabled. In-home health care will also have high demand. Those interested in private duty nursing may be able to sign up with a hospital registry or with a physician's office. Employment is projected to grow rapidly in physicians' offices and clinics as well, including HMOs. Again, newspaper want ads are a good place to begin the job search, along with employment agencies. Large cities generally have employment agencies that specialize in jobs in the health care industry.

Where Can I Go from Here?

Licensed practical nurses can advance to higher-paying careers as medical technicians and registered nurses, and many do. Forty percent, in fact, use their LPN designation as a stepping-stone to greater pay and more responsibilities. There are several ways for an LPN to climb the ladder. One is to locate similar positions in larger or more prestigious facilities where higher salaries are offered. It is also possible, by accumulating experience, to obtain supervisory duties over nursing assistants and nurses aides. Another way to advance is to complete the additional education (usually two years at a community college) necessary to become a registered nurse.

But regardless of specialty or career ambition, LPNs must keep their skills current; participation in ongoing self-education is critical to job performance and advancement. Participating in continuing education courses is a good way to stay current with the technological advances and growing complexity of patient care techniques and procedures. Some states even require a minimum number of continuing education hours before they will renew the practical nursing license every two years.

Continuing education programs may be sponsored by a variety of organizations, including community colleges, government agencies, vocational-technical institutes, private educational firms, and local, state, and national health associations. LPNs must assess the educational opportunities available in their communities and determine which are the most relevant for maintaining their practice skills.

Advancement Possibilities

Nurse anesthetists administer anesthesia to patients before and during surgery to desensitize them to pain, also working with pain management and respiratory management of patients.

Physician assistants provide health care services to patients under the direction and responsibility of a physician and may perform comprehensive physical examinations, compile patient medical data, administer or order diagnostic tests, and interpret test results.

Surgical technicians, also known as **operating room technicians,** perform any combination of tasks before, during, and after surgery, including arranging instruments and supplies in the operating room, maintaining supplies of fluids for use during an operation, handing instruments and supplies to the surgeon, and performing other tasks as directed by the surgeon during the operation.

Another method of improving skills and growing in the field is to take advantage of in-service educational programs that many employers are offering. These may include seminars, workshops, and clinical sessions on relevant work topics. Taking advantage of these in-house opportunities will help LPNs accumulate additional skills and may even lead to more specialized and higher-paying careers. Some hospitals offer programs that teach LPNs to do kidney dialysis or to work with patients in cardiac or intensive care units, which may lead to more specialized job titles.

What Are the Salary Ranges?

According to the *Occupational Outlook Handbook*, the median annual salary for LPNs was $31,440 in 2002. Those in the lowest 10 percent earned less than $22,860, while those in the highest paid 10 percent earned more than $44,040. Salaries also are determined by the place of employment. Licensed practical nurses working for home health care services earned an average annual salary of $32,850; in nursing care facilities, $32,220; hospitals, $30,310; and in physicians' offices, $28,710.

For accurate information on wage scales for LPNs in the community where you want to work, call a hospital in the area, ask for the personnel department, and inquire about salaries for newly licensed LPNs. Other sources include registries, long-term care facilities, or the visiting nurse associations, which can provide specific details on LPN wage scales.

What Is the Job Outlook?

The job outlook is good for LPNs and anyone choosing a medical health care profession. As the number of students graduating from practical nursing schools continues to rise, so does the demand for their services. The general growth in health care and the long-term health care needs of an aging population help ensure the continued need for LPNs and other health care professionals. The nursing workforce is also aging, and experts predict a severe shortage of registered nurses as they retire. LPNs will likely be needed to help deal with this shortage.

However, employment of LPNs is expected to increase only as fast as the average for all occupations through 2012, according to the U.S. Department of Labor. This is because hospital LPNs mostly work with inpatients, and the number of those patients is not expected to increase. Some in the medical field have been concerned that health maintenance organizations (HMOs) negatively affect nursing employment. Cost-cutting measures by HMOs result in fewer hospital patients and the replacement of registered nurses with unlicensed assistive personnel. In staff reductions, LPNs are believed to be more affected than registered nurses.

As mentioned previously, most new jobs for LPNs will be in nursing homes and long-term care facilities that cater to the growing aging population. These agencies will also house recovering patients released from hospitals but not yet well enough to return home. State and federal regulations on nursing homes are requiring them to hire more LPNs in lieu of other so-called "health aides," who may be given minimal training, are unlicensed, and often underqualified to administer patient care.

A similar demand for LPNs will occur in physicians' offices and clinics, including HMOs, concerned with liability issues. New rules and regulations set out by insurance companies shortening the length of stay allowed for patients in a facility will create a great demand for private duty nurses. Rapid growth is expected in board and care homes and group homes for the mentally disabled as well.

How Do I Learn More?

PROFESSIONAL ORGANIZATIONS

The following are organizations that provide information on licensed practical nursing careers, approved practical nursing programs, and employers:

National Association for Practical Nurse Education and Service Inc.
PO Box 25647
Alexandria, VA 22313
703-933-1003
http://www.napes.org

National Council of State Boards of Nursing
676 North St. Clair Street, Suite 550
Chicago, IL 60611-2921
http://www.ncsbn.org

National Federation of Licensed Practical Nurses
605 Poole Drive

Garner, NC 27529
919-779-0046
http://www.nflpn.org

National League for Nursing
61 Broadway
New York, NY 10006
http://www.nin.org

BIBLIOGRAPHY

The following is a sampling of materials relating to the professional concerns and development of licensed practical nurses:

Anderson, Mary Ann, and Susan Corwin Stolz. *To Be a Nurse: Personal/Vocational Relations for the LPN/VN*. Philadelphia: F. A. Davis & Company, 2000.

Duncan, Gena, and Rene DePew. *Transitioning from LPN/VN to RN: Moving Ahead in Your Career*. New York: Thomson Delmar Learning, 2004.

Hill, Signe S., and Helen A. Howlett. *Success in Practical Nursing: Personal and Vocational Issues from Student to Leader*. 5th ed. Philadelphia: W. B. Saunders, 2004.

Myers, Ehren. *LPN Notes: Nurse's Clinical Pocket Guide*. Philadelphia: F. A. Davis & Company, 2003.

MARINE SERVICES TECHNICIANS

Arthur Cook drives down the highway on a late spring morning towing a 24-foot cabin cruiser behind him on a hydraulic trailer. He has just picked up the boat from a customer for servicing to get it ready for the boating season. This customer, like dozens of others, wants the boat ready by Memorial Day weekend. Back at the Black River marina, Art uses the hydraulic trailer to shore the boat up on jack stands and cinder blocks.

But first Art takes a minute to enjoy the view of Black River before taking the boat into the shop's service bay. Here in eastern Michigan, boating season is getting into full swing, and by week's end he will have worked on more than 40 boats. Now that he is working between 60 and 65 hours a week, Art, a boating enthusiast himself, may not often get the chance to do much more than enjoy the view for a while. But that is all part of being a marine services technician. And there is always test-driving the boats to look forward to. For now, his top priority is to get started on the first of the day's many jobs.

Definition
Marine services technicians repair and maintain boats in a marine service facility.

Alternative Job Titles
Fiberglass repairers
Marine electronic technicians
Motorboat mechanics

High School Subjects
Mathematics
Technical/shop

Personal Skills
Following instructions
Mechanical/manipulative

Salary Range
$19,000 to $29,700 to $44,600

Educational Requirements
High school diploma; two-year postsecondary course recommended

Certification or Licensing
Required for those who test and repair marine radio transmitting equipment

Outlook
About as fast as the average

DOT
806

GOE
05.03.01

NOC
7335

O*NET-SOC
49-3051.00

What Does a Marine Services Technician Do?

According to *Boating Industry* magazine, Americans own more than 16 million boats. The people who inspect, maintain, and repair all these boats are called *marine services technicians*. They test and repair boats' engines, transmissions, and electrical, propulsion, and refrigeration systems. They also repair hulls, navigational equipment and other marine electronics, marine plumbing, and steering gear. Technicians work on everything from personal watercraft to yachts. The type of boats technicians work on and the kinds of repairs they do depend largely on the repair facility's geographic location. They may work on all the boat's systems and components or, increasingly, specialize in one area of repair.

Motorboat mechanics clean, lubricate, repair, and adjust the engines and electrical and mechanical equipment of inboard, outboard, and inboard/outboard marine engines. When necessary, they replace worn or defective parts such as spark plugs, ignition points, and valves. Routine maintenance is a major part of the mechanic's job and is critical because a breakdown may leave a boater stranded for hours in open water.

When breakdowns occur, mechanics diagnose mechanical, fuel, or electrical problems, starting with a description of the symptoms of the problem from the owner or service manager. Then, if possible, they operate the equipment to observe the symptoms. Mechanics may have to use special testing equipment such as engine analyzers, compression gauges, ammeters, and voltmeters to help them locate faulty parts. Mechanics may also use laptop or handheld computers for diagnostic testing. Mechanics may also have to disassemble components for further examination or refer to service manuals for detailed

Lingo to Learn

Ammeter An instrument used for measuring electric current.

Gyrocompass A type of compass using a continually spinning gyroscope so that the compass always points to the true north.

Inboard An engine that is permanently mounted inside the hull of a boat.

Inboard/outboard (I/O) An engine that is mounted inboard but the propeller fits on an assembly that resembles an outboard motor drive. Also called stern-drive. Found in most speedboats and in other boat types that have high-power requirements.

Ohmmeter An instrument for indicating electrical resistance.

Oscilloscope An electronic instrument that graphically displays an electrical signal as a glowing line on a fluorescent screen. The pattern on the screen is actually a rapidly moving point of light. The oscilloscope has become an indispensable tool of the electronic technician.

Outboard An engine mounted outside the hull of the boat, usually at the stern.

directions and specifications while performing repairs.

Many motorboat mechanics also install and repair electronics, sanitation, and air-conditioning systems. Mechanics in large shops may work only on motors and other running parts of the boat. They may specialize in either outboard or inboard motors. Most small boats have gasoline-powered outboard motors that can be taken off of the boat easily and brought in for repair. Inboard motors may be either gasoline- or diesel-powered and are not removed from inside the boat except for major repairs and overhauls.

Motorboat mechanics need an extensive set of hand tools, which are normally acquired gradually. Most mechanics have several thousand dollars invested in hand tools, which may include some specialty tools that can only be bought from boat manufacturers to work on their products. However, most expensive specialty tools are provided by the repair facility for their mechanics' use, as are power tools.

Marine electronics technicians specialize in the installation, maintenance, and repair of electronic safety and navigational equipment used in boats, such as radar, depth sounders, loran, autopilots, and gyrocompass systems. They install, repair, and calibrate equipment to make sure it functions properly. Like motorboat mechanics, they perform routine maintenance, checking, cleaning, repairing, or replacing defective parts to prevent problems.

When making repairs, they check for common causes of trouble such as loose connections and obviously defective components. If routine checks do not reveal the problem, they may refer to schematics and manufacturers' specifications that show connections and give instructions on how to locate the problem. Electronics technicians use small hand tools such as pliers, screwdrivers, and soldering irons to replace circuit boards and wiring. Other equipment they use includes voltmeters, ohmmeters, signal generators, ammeters, and oscilloscopes. Typically, electronics technicians supply their own hand tools at a cost of approximately $300 to $500, while their employers provide the testing equipment. Electronics technicians may be field repairers, going to the marina to make repairs, or bench repairers, working in the shop on equipment brought in by the customer, or both.

Other technicians only work on the hulls of boats. Wooden boats make up a very small portion of the repair business in most parts of the country. Technicians repair wooden hulls by cutting and shaping replacement wooden sections.

Most pleasure crafts are built of fiberglass. Fiberglass repairers may be able to reinforce or strengthen the damaged area. If it has to be replaced completely, technicians may grind the damaged piece with a sander or cut it away with a jigsaw and then replace the fiberglass section using resin-impregnated fiberglass cloth. They smooth the replaced sections with sanding equipment and paint the finished repair with a gel coat, then buff the new area for shine.

What Is It Like to Be a Marine Services Technician?

Arthur Cook has been a marine services technician for over five years. Most of that time he worked for a boat dealership. Now he works for Pro Marine, an independent repair shop, at one of their two locations. Pro Marine also has a mobile unit that travels to marinas without repair facilities, but most of Art's time is spent in the shop at the Black River marina.

Some mechanics, however, do much or most of their work outdoors in all weather. Matt Harvey is a former technician and previous owner of Pro Marine. Now a general manager of Marysville Marine Distributors' branch office near Nashville, Tennessee, he recalls repairing inboard engines on boats in their slips at marinas. "If it's 90 degrees that day and the boat doesn't have air-conditioning, you're working in a 90-degree hole. It can be uncomfortable."

To Be a Successful Marine Services Technician, You Should . . .

- have mechanical aptitude
- have good people skills
- be willing to work irregular, possibly long hours
- have problem-solving abilities
- like boats and working outdoors

If it's 90 degrees that day and the boat doesn't have air-conditioning, you're working in a 90-degree hole. It can be uncomfortable.

Technicians also "have to do a lot of squeezing and crawling around into sometimes tight, uncomfortable places to perform service repairs," says Matt. Art agrees, saying that sailboats have especially tight access to inboard engines.

The hours technicians work vary. In the summer they usually work considerably more than 40 hours, which often includes weekends. Holidays are an especially busy time. "There's a big cram the week before Memorial Day and the Fourth of July," Art says. In contrast, technicians may work less than 40 hours a week in the winter. Mechanics are usually laid off some portion of the winter, generally from four to eight weeks. Usually mechanics draw unemployment during that time.

The type of work mechanics do varies from season to season as well. In the summer, much of Art's time is spent changing oil and filters, greasing U joints, and performing other kinds of preventive maintenance. Now and then he installs navigational systems or draws diagrams of new parts for machine shops to follow when making the part. He also cleans engines, checks engine alignment, and starts the engines up to listen to them to help make sure they are running properly or to diagnose a problem. In order to run engines without doing damage, marine mechanics use test tanks or garden hoses. For small outboard motors that have been taken off the boat for servicing, a test tank, which is a large drum filled with water, is used to simulate running the motor on the boat. Another tool is a fixture provided by the manufacturer that allows the mechanic to put a garden hose attachment onto an outdrive or outboard in order to run the motor safely.

After Labor Day, Art's primary duty is winterizing boats. He drains water from engines, hot and cold water systems on boats that have heads (toilets) or kitchenettes, and air-conditioning units and puts in nontoxic antifreeze. This takes him through the first part of November, when he starts performing major repairs. Engine overhauls and other meticulous, time-consuming repairs that cannot be undertaken during the busy summer season are done, and problems that were discovered while the boats were being winterized are fixed. Art says this type of "heavy mechanical work" is what he enjoys most, and it keeps him busy through most of December. He does not work from about the week before Christmas through the end of February. When Art goes back to work, he finishes up any of the big jobs not completed, then it is time to get ready for "spring start-up" and the busy season once more.

Mechanics working indoors generally work in well-lighted, ventilated shops. Because there tends to be less grease and dirt on marine engines compared to car engines, it is cleaner than working as an auto mechanic; however, shops can be noisy when engines are being run. There is potential danger from operating power tools, and technicians working with fiberglass, resins, and other chemicals must wear gloves and masks and take other safety measures. Technicians may also suffer minor cuts, bumps, and bruises from using equipment or working in tight spaces.

FYI

According to *Marine Business Journal,* most of the men who responded to a tongue-in-cheek boat engine survey in *Sports Illustrated* said they would rather be stranded at sea with their mechanic than with their wife, supermodel Kathy Ireland, or their best friend.

Do I Have What It Takes to Be a Marine Services Technician?

Both Matt and Art agree that one of the most important qualities a technician needs is a pleasant, well-mannered personality. "People have boats to have fun, and when they have problems with their toys, they can be pretty irate," notes Matt. "Being able to work with people to solve their problems and asking the right questions to help determine the problem is important," he adds.

Since boating is a seasonal business, technicians must be able to adapt to the cyclical nature of the job. "Generally, repair facilities do between 60 to 70 percent of their business in just three months of the year," says Matt. "You work really hard. You put in a lot of hours and you're under a lot of pressure generally from the first of May to the first of August."

Technicians must be flexible in the type of work they do, because some repair facilities turn to repairing different types of equipment during the winter. Boatyards and marinas may repair snowmobiles, while marine electronics dealerships fix cellular phones, two-way radios, and other electronics. Employers may also ask technicians to help with landscaping, painting, stocking, and performing other general chores as an alternative to a layoff.

Particularly for motorboat technicians, the job can be physically demanding. While hydraulic lifting equipment is normally used, circumstances sometimes require one or more mechanics to lift heavy outdrives weighing as much as 180 pounds in order to take them on and off boats.

For electronics technicians, good eyesight and color vision are needed to inspect and work on small, delicate parts and printed circuit boards, and good hearing is necessary to detect malfunctions revealed by sound.

Most technicians will probably spend at least part of their time outdoors, so they should like working outdoors and driving boats, a requirement technicians do not mind meeting. "Generally, you get an opportunity to do some boating. A lot of people think, 'Oh, marine mechanic, all you do is drive boats all day long.' That's generally not what happens, but the majority of places I've worked at I've always had boats as a benefit, boats that were available to me to use on weekends," Matt says.

How Do I Become a Marine Services Technician?

Familiarity and experience with boats was an asset for Art. "I grew up on an island, Harson's Island, and I grew up around boats. I've liked boating all my life." His high school education included woodshop and plastics (fiberglass) shop, both of which proved to be helpful in his future career.

Art attended a vocational skill center for four hours a day his junior year, where he learned small-engine repair. As a senior he participated in a co-op training program, working at a boat dealership. After graduation he entered the marine engine technology program at Northwest Technical College Detroit Lakes, earning an associate's degree in applied science. Sending out resumes resulted in seven job interviews in two days. He accepted a job at a boat dealership, which he left after four years for his current job at Pro Marine.

Other marine services technicians get their start as general boatyard workers, cutting the grass, cleaning boat bottoms, and doing other odd jobs. Matt estimates as many as 60 to 80 percent of motorboat technicians get into the field this way. If they demonstrate ability and interest, they may be assigned to work with experienced mechanics and learn repair skills on the job. It is helpful if the aspiring technician already has a basic knowledge of small two- and four-cycle engines from having worked on cars, motorcycles, boats, or outdoor power equipment as a hobby.

Many marine electronics technicians start out in other areas of electronics repair. Many come into the field with electronics repair experience in computer and office machines, VCRs, stereos, satellite dishes, and home appliances, for example.

Fiberglass repairers usually acquire training on the job. Experience gained in plastics (fiberglass) shop classes is a plus, as is experience with auto body repair.

EDUCATION

High School

Most employers prefer to hire high school graduates, but some will hire applicants without a diploma if they have adequate reading, writing, and arithmetic skills and a good background in mechanics. Some boat dealers will hire students part-time and during the busy season to help assemble new equipment and make minor repairs.

If you are interested in a career as a marine services technician you should take classes in small-engine repair, auto mechanics, electronics, science, and business arithmetic. Electrical and machine shop as well as woodshop and plastics shop are also useful. Being able to communicate effectively with others, including service managers and customers, is also important. Thus you should develop your communication skills through English and writing courses.

Postsecondary Training

Postsecondary training, while not a requirement, can be very helpful. Basic mechanical and electronics skills can be acquired through vocational training in any number of technical schools or community colleges. Electronics training, which includes general mathematics, physics, electricity, schematic reading, and electronic and circuit theory, can also be obtained in the military services.

A very small number of programs designed specifically for marine technologies also exist. These specialized programs are of varying lengths, generally ranging from several weeks to two years. They are taught at a few public and private colleges, including technical colleges, community colleges, maritime academies, and marine institutes.

Subject matter taught varies, depending on the program's focus. Training ranges from education in hull and rigging maintenance, marine mechanics, and fiberglass construction and repair, to small vessels operation and boatbuilding, to marine business and management. Internships are available at some of these training facilities. Depending on the program, graduates are awarded either a diploma, an associate's degree in science or marine technology, a certificate of completion, or certification.

Art attended a technical college with a marine engine technology program, earning an associate's degree in applied science. Some of his technical classes included battery, charging, and starting systems; marine hydraulics; stern-drive engine and outboard engine theory and service; and electrical systems and fuel systems. General education courses included mathematics, fundamental physics, composition and literature, and interpersonal communications. One of Art's favorite projects was rebuilding a motor for a jet boat, an exercise that took about three weeks to pull the motor out, completely disassemble it, and put it back together again in good running condition.

Matt attended the same technical college as Art several years earlier. Although the marine engine technology program was a little different when Matt went through—being a one-year program at the time—they both describe the program as demanding, with much study and hands-on work. And they both believe their specialized training gave them a distinct advantage. "When I finished that one-year program, I was probably at the level of someone who's been in the business banging their head learning the hard way for about five years," Matt says.

After employment, new and experienced technicians alike are frequently sent to "factory schools," one- or two-week courses taught by boat motor and electronics manufacturers and distributors, designed to upgrade technicians' skills and provide information on repairing new models. They might also upgrade their skills by attending private trade and professional schools for short courses and seminars.

SCHOLARSHIPS AND GRANTS

State or regional associations may offer scholarships or be able to provide training information for their area. To find out if there is a marine association in your area, contact the Marine Retailers Association of America (MRAA).

CERTIFICATION OR LICENSING

Those who test and repair marine radio transmitting equipment must have a general radio-telephone operator license from the Federal Communications Commission.

Certification for technicians in the marine electronics industry is voluntary and is administered by the National Marine Electronics Association (NMEA). There are three grades of Certified Marine Electronic Technicians: basic certification (CMET) for technicians with one year of experience, advanced grade certification (ACMET) for those with three years of experience, and senior grade certification (SGMET) for those with 10 years of experience. The NMEA also offers an entry-level marine electronics installer (MEI) certification program.

Basic certification is by written examination and the employer's verification as to the technician's proficiency in the repair of basic radar, voice SSB, VHF, depth sounders, and autopilots. The higher degrees of certification are earned by meeting all previous grade requirements plus satisfactorily completing a factory training course or having the employer attest to the technician's proficiency in repairing advanced equipment.

Who Will Hire Me?

Most motorboat mechanics work near large bodies of water in the shops of boat dealers and marinas. According to Boating Industry, there are 10,000 marine retailers in the United States, nearly 80 percent of which also provide service on boats and motors. Nearly 3,000 of the retailers have on-the-water locations with marina facilities. In addition, there are approximately 1,500 boatyards with the equipment and ability to do extensive hull and engine repairs.

The largest marinas are found in coastal areas. Smaller marinas are found near lakes and water-recreation facilities. Coastal areas in New York, California, Texas, Florida, Washington, Massachusetts, and Louisiana have many shops with several mechanics. Few shops have more than 10 mechanics.

Most work that is available near small bodies of water is for mechanics who fix outboard motors. Near large bodies of water, both inboard and outboard motors are serviced and repaired. Some marinas operated by federal, state, and local governments also employ mechanics. Contact your state employment service for jobs at these marinas.

Some mechanics work for boat engine manufacturers making final adjustments and repairs to the motors when they come off the assembly line. Because the fishing portion of the marine industry is big business, factories also employ mechanics to provide on-site mechanical support to professional fishermen who use the manufacturer's products. These mechanics travel on the fishing circuit, going from tournament to tournament. Independent repair shops also hire mechanics, and a small number of mechanics work for boat rental firms and resorts.

Marine electronics manufacturers and retailers are the primary employers of marine electronics technicians. Most marinas and other boat repair facilities tend to hire mechanics who also know some electronics rather than hire electronics specialists.

The majority of fiberglass repairers work at specialty shops, although some larger marinas and shops may also employ these technicians. Marine services technicians of all kinds may also be self-employed.

Where Can I Go from Here?

Art already serves as the service manager in his one-man shop. He deals with customers directly, writing up work orders and calling customers to discuss problems and solutions. In the future he would like to get away from repair work and devote his time exclusively to managing.

Matt followed a career path that began with a promotion to service manager, overseeing about a dozen technicians. He then opened his own mobile marine repair facility and is currently a general manager for a marine distributor.

Mechanics could also become marina managers. Their technical background also makes them good candidates to become manufacturers' salespeople or field representatives.

Some technicians may become boat brokers, selling boats for commission much like a realtor sells houses. Unlike real estate agents, however, brokers do not need a license in most states. Florida, where there is a lot of boat-selling activity, is a key exception.

Dorman Burtch of the National Yacht Brokers advises those interested in boat brokering to spend

Advancement Possibilities

Hull inspectors inspect the construction of hulls, compartments, tanks, and decks of ships for conformance to plans and specifications.

Boat outfitting supervisors supervise and coordinate activities of workers engaged in outfitting and installing engines in fiberglass boats.

about four or five years at a new boat dealership first. You should also check with your state's Department of Business and Professional Regulations for possible licensing requirements.

Another advancement possibility for marine services technicians is to become a marine surveyor. Marine surveyors make value surveys to verify the condition and value of a boat. They are independent contractors used by insurance companies or lending institutions. Marine surveying is a growing field for which there is no federal or state regulation or licensing. However, most reputable surveyors are either accredited through the Society of Accredited Marine Surveyors or certified by the National Association of Marine Surveyors. The requirements for accreditation or certification differ somewhat between the two organizations, but in general include special schooling and/or training with a marine surveyor.

What Are the Salary Ranges?

Most mechanics are paid hourly, although some, like Art, are salaried. Other mechanics are paid a base salary plus commission, which is usually a percentage of the cost of labor or the parts used in the job. When mechanics work on a commission basis, their wages depend on how much work they are given and how fast they complete it. The more work they do, the more money they can make.

Technicians tend to receive few fringe benefits in small shops, but those employed in larger shops often receive paid vacations and sick leave and health insurance. Some employers also pay for work-related training and provide uniforms.

Earnings vary with geographic area, the skill level of the employee, his or her duties, and the size of the repair facility. According to the U.S. Department of Labor, the median annual earnings for small engine mechanics, which includes motorboat and marine equipment mechanics, were $29,700 in 2003. The lowest paid 10 percent earned about $19,000 a year, while the highest paid 10 percent earned $44,600. The middle 50 percent earned between $23,400 and $36,700 per year.

What Is the Job Outlook?

According to the U.S. Department of Labor, employment opportunities for small engine mechanics, including marine services technicians, is expected to grow about as fast as the average through 2012. The majority of job openings are expected to occur because many experienced motorboat mechanics leave each year to transfer to other occupations or retire.

As boat design and construction becomes more complicated and as more electronic parts are used, the outlook will be best for well-trained technicians. In addition, more mechanics may be required if the growing complexity of boat engines forces more consumers to turn to professional technicians for maintenance and repair services.

The 40-year-old and older age group is now the biggest buyer of motorboats and the most active boating participants. These potential buyers and their need for qualified boat mechanics will help expand employment opportunities in the field. Another demographic trend that will influence job opportunities is the shift of the population to the South and West, where warm-weather seasons are longer and thus attract more boating activity.

Like many other U.S. industries, U.S. boat manufacturers have become more globally oriented and have placed greater emphasis on exports. While the pleasure boat industry in most foreign markets is not as developed as in the U.S. market, it is likely U.S. manufacturers will continue to develop these markets and establish more distribution channels.

Legislation that could negatively impact the boating industry over the next few years includes state and federal laws that may require boat operator licenses and stricter emission standards and limit the area of use for pleasure boats. Some industry leaders fear licensing will discourage boat ownership, while meeting stricter environmental regulations will require major investments by marinas and many smaller operations may not survive.

States also will be searching for ways to offset shrinking federal support and may target boat users and products, applying user fees or other charges and taxes similar to the former luxury tax.

How Do I Learn More?

PROFESSIONAL ORGANIZATIONS

For information on industry trends, careers, accredited schools, and scholarships contact the following organizations:

Marine Retailers Association of America
PO Box 1127
Oak Park, IL 60304
708-763-9210
mraa@mraa.com
http://www.mraa.com

National Marine Electronics Association
Seven Riggs Avenue
Severna Park, MD 21146
410-975-9425
info@nmea.org
http://www.nmea.org

BIBLIOGRAPHY

The following is a sampling of materials relating to the professional concerns and development of marine services technicians:

Burr, William M., and William Burr Jr. *Boat Maintenance: The Essential Guide to Cleaning, Painting, and Cosmetics*. New York: McGraw-Hill, 2000.

Fleming, John. *Complete Guide to Diesel Marine Engines*. Enola, Pa.: Bristol Fashion Publications, 2000.

Sherman, Edwin R. *Powerboater's Guide to Electrical Systems: Maintenance, Troubleshooting, and Improvements*. Camden, Maine: International Marine, 2000.

Toghill, Jeff. *The Essential Boat Maintenance Manual*. Guilford, Ct.: Lyons Press, 2001.

MATHEMATICAL TECHNICIANS

San Francisco has suffered an earthquake, a big one. Bridges and roads have collapsed. Power lines are down, fires rage all over town, and the underground gas lines are in danger of rupturing. Damages need to be contained, but where to start?

Jaime Garces is working on the answer. She knows the layout of the city, where the roads are, what areas are in the most danger, and the best places to begin the cleanup. Months of study and research have led to this point.

No, San Francisco is not in ruins, at least not yet. The whole scenario is a mathematical model, put together by a research team that has spent months gathering data and studying the best ways to deal with a disaster of this kind. When the big one does hit, the city emergency workers hope to be ready.

Definition
Mathematical technicians use mathematical formulas, principles, and methods to solve technological problems in engineering and the physical sciences. They work in a variety of research and industrial settings.

Alternative Job Titles
Data reduction technicians
Mathematical support personnel

High School Subjects
Computer science
English
Mathematics

Personal Skills
Following instructions
Technical/scientific

Salary Range
$24,700 to $37,400 to $67,800+

Minimum Educational Requirements
Associate's degree

Certification or Licensing
None available

Outlook
More slowly than the average

DOT
020

GOE
02.06.02

NOC
2161

O*NET-SOC
15-2021.00

What Does a Mathematical Technician Do?

In this age of computer-generated data, industrial research and development often depend on professionals who know how to gather, read, analyze, and apply information and theoretical principals, such as mathematical formulas, to solve real-life problems. This endeavor, known as "applied mathematics," is the realm of *mathematical technicians*.

These technicians use mathematical formulas and principles to solve technological problems, especially in engineering and the physical sciences. They work on research projects designed to improve industrial processes, equipment, and products.

For example, the managers of an airline might want to streamline its service. They need to know what cities or areas need the most flights, at what times of day, the destinations of the flights, and what size planes will be needed for the expected number of passengers. A mathematical technician would compile all this data, using computers and mathematical formulas. From this analysis, the managers can determine what areas of service need to be kept, cut, or expanded.

Mathematical technicians select the most practical and accurate method of computing all the available data. They may use algebra, trigonometry, vector analysis, and calculus to simplify raw data into manageable terms. They also choose the most economical and reliable data-processing methods and equipment, sometimes modifying standard formulas for optimum effectiveness. They then analyze the processed data, compiling all their results, step by step.

Next, the technician transcribes the data into equations, flowcharts, graphs, or other media and tells the airline managers, for example, what the research has uncovered. Perhaps the company has a large number of passengers on one route but only on weekdays. On weekends the airline has the same size plane flying that route, but it is only half full. The technician's findings might cause the airline to use smaller planes on those days, saving money while still serving its customers.

Another type of applied mathematical problem is figuring out when most customers are patronizing retail stores, restaurants, banks, or gas stations. This helps managers determine how many employees to have on hand during these times.

Mathematical modeling is also used to establish prices and calculate profits. For example, if a fast food restaurant sells X amount of hamburgers, how much can it charge and still make a profit? The mathematical model takes into account the cost of producing burgers, the salary of the staff, and other expenses, and it determines how much each burger must cost to ensure that the restaurant will not lose money, referred to as "breaking even." From there, the mathematical model must determine how much higher than the break-even point the company can go. How much money can you charge for a burger, and how many people will buy it at that price?

Mathematical and computational analysis is also used to examine and solve problems of allocating food and natural resources. It helps sharpen search strategies for these resources, predict crop yields, raise productivity, and explore for oil and minerals.

Some mathematical technicians work for aircraft construction companies. They gather data on stress or metal fatigue, safety, and construction costs. In the auto industry, technicians work with engineers on projects such as layout or design features on cars or other vehicles.

What Is It Like to Be a Mathematical Technician?

Jaime Garces is part of a team of mathematicians and mathematical technicians who work for a consulting firm. A customer comes to her company with a problem or question, and the team looks for a solution by using applied mathematics. Mathematical problems can take an hour or a year to solve, depending on their complexity.

In the course of her work for a systems engineering company, Jaime spends much of her time gathering data for research. Her current assignment is to design plans for relief and cleanup after an earthquake or other disaster. For six months, she has been compiling information that applies to city planning. The computer is her greatest tool, helping her in every aspect of her job. Locating all the pertinent information is a time-consuming process. Jaime uses a computer network to conduct a search. Online word searches provide her with all the available written material in a particular area.

Part of Jaime's project involves examining gas lines and determining which are most in danger of breaking or are hardest to access, so repairs can be made. Eventually, Jaime and her co-workers will have information on all the elements that might be affected by a natural disaster in a populated area. Using mathematical formulas, they will project all the possible scenarios that could result from the disaster.

As a mathematical technician you might be assigned to analyze the effects of a new drug on a certain disease, or you might examine the aerodynamic qualities of an experimental airplane. Like Jaime, you would be apt to work with mathematicians, who would probably have somewhat more education and experience than you. Other coworkers might include engineers, computer scientists, physicists, and economists. Those professionals also use mathematics extensively, but they specialize in fields other than mathematics.

There are other professionals who specialize in a particular branch of mathematics. *Actuaries* calculate insurance rates and premiums. *Cryptanalysts* study and decode encryption systems (secret codes) that allow sensitive information to be transmitted with minimal fear that it will be read by unauthorized persons. Encryption is commonly used by the military, political entities, law enforcement agencies, and businesses.

Statisticians use numerical data for purposes such as predicting population growth or making economic forecasts. They frequently focus on one area of expertise, perhaps biology, economics, medicine, or psychology. Statisticians often conduct surveys to gather data. A statistician might, for example, oversee

Lingo to Learn

Linear programming A way to achieve an objective function to maximize or minimize something without violating any predetermined constraints.

Mathematical model A description of a real-world situation in mathematical terms to explain or predict behavior.

Network flow Determining how to best move from point A to point B.

Optimization Making a decision as efficiently as possible.

a team of workers who call 3,000 people at random to estimate the popularity of a television program.

Operations research analysts use mathematical principles to streamline the operation of a complex organization, such as an airline or a manufacturing plant. They typically develop a set of equations (known as a mathematical model) that shows how the organization functions. They assign numerical values to the various components of a problem, then substitute other numbers to see how changing that part would affect the rest of the equation. For example, the analyst might run a computer simulation that changed the shifts of certain hospital workers to determine whether the hospital would operate with greater efficiency if more workers were available during specified time periods.

Whatever the project, a mathematician or mathematical technician can expect to work under pressure sometimes to meet deadlines or to complete a rush request. Occasional overtime might be required, but usually these professionals work regular office hours. Their tools and equipment primarily consist of a computer and related programs. "Any technical job these days uses computers," says Jaime. "You have to know how to use them or be willing to learn."

Much of what Jaime does involves what she calls, "making order out of chaos." Her work takes a vast amount of information and tries to narrow things down, ultimately coming up with workable conclusions.

For Jaime, the best part of her work is the opportunity to be creative. "With math there's more than one way to approach a problem. Math is flexible and intuitive. You can come up with a wacky idea, try it, and see if it works," she says.

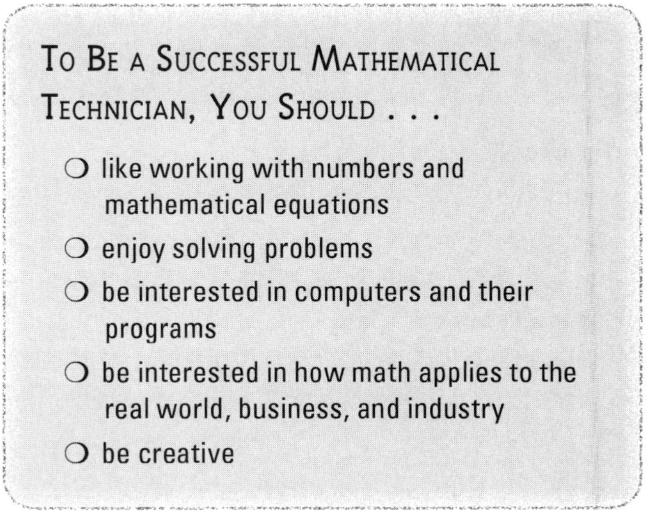
TO BE A SUCCESSFUL MATHEMATICAL TECHNICIAN, YOU SHOULD . . .

- like working with numbers and mathematical equations
- enjoy solving problems
- be interested in computers and their programs
- be interested in how math applies to the real world, business, and industry
- be creative

Do I Have What It Takes to Be a Mathematical Technician?

Mathematical technicians deal with complex formulas and equations in every aspect of their work. It is not enough to be good with numbers. Mathematical technicians should really enjoy math and all its applications.

When Jaime entered college, she was originally a biochemistry major. "I always enjoyed math and science, but biochem was too narrow," she says. "A neighbor recommended a book called *Chaos: Making a New Science*, by James Gleick. She said if I liked it, I would probably enjoy being a mathematician."

Jaime switched to a math major and was much happier. "It's still technical, but it gave me the tools to look at all kinds of problems in all different fields," she says. "I can dabble in different things."

Computers play a key role in Jaime's work. She recommends being familiar with their functions and says it is good to know programming languages, no matter how difficult or daunting they may be.

"Hopefully I'll never have to write in code," says Jaime. "But it's useful to understand them. I work with computer programmers, and for them to write the codes I need, I have to speak their language or the language of the program."

The large amount of research mathematical technicians do is time consuming. Diligence and attention to detail are critical in their work. Collecting and analyzing data can be tedious, so patience is definitely a virtue.

Communication skills are extremely important for people involved in all areas of mathematics. Data that has been gathered and analyzed is worthless if the mathematical technician cannot convey the results to others. Both oral and written skills are necessary.

How Do I Become a Mathematical Technician?

EDUCATION

High School

All the math courses available in high school are helpful in preparing for a career as a mathematical

In-depth

History

The history of mathematics begins with counting. Prehistoric people most likely used their fingers to count, keeping track of numbers with pebbles, knots on a cord, or some other basic method. About 3500 B.C., the Egyptians developed the decimal system, which has remained the basic form of counting.

The ancient Greeks concentrated on pure math, specifically geometry. About 300 B.C., Euclid wrote the influential book *Elements,* constructing a system of geometry that we use to this day. Other Greek contributions include the discovery of the number *pi* by Archimedes, Ptolemy's work on the *Almagest,* and the formulation of the Pythagorean theorem.

Arabic peoples made substantial contributions to mathematics between A.D. 825 and 1100. During that time, they introduced the study of algebra, discovered and applied the number zero, and made substantial contributions to trigonometry. So influential were the Arabic peoples that our number system today is based on Arabic numerals.

The Europeans continued to develop mathematical formulas during the Renaissance. It was not until the scientific revolution in the 1600s, however, that the study of mathematics blossomed. One of the greatest contributions to mathematics was Sir Isaac Newton's invention of calculus in the mid-1660s.

From the 1600s to the present day, such accomplishments as René Descarte's discovery of analytical geometry, Jakob Bernoulli's work with probability, George Boole's study of symbolic logic, and the manufacture of the computer have turned mathematics into a fundamental part of our lives.

With the advent of computers, the progression of mathematics has accelerated. Great minds can now work on theory, while computers deal with the dull computational tasks in a matter of minutes or seconds.

---

technician. If possible, you should take everything that is offered.

Algebra, geometry, trigonometry, and calculus are recommended. "Take calculus in high school if you have the option. That way, when you come in as a college freshman, it will be more of a review," says Jaime.

Some other areas of interest, such as business, earth science, psychology, or pre-medicine, can be combined with mathematics to help you focus your career. Take classes in fields that interest you and be sure to learn as much as possible about computers. Jaime advises, "Become familiar with all the different possible ways you can use a computer."

English and composition classes are important for mathematical technicians. Writing and speaking skills are crucial for most professions, even those that work with numbers.

Postsecondary Training

Mathematical technicians need two to four years of postsecondary training to work in their field. People who hold four-year college degrees are now increasingly sought by employers. That is the minimum qualification for a mathematician with a federal job; those in the private industry usually hold a master's or doctoral degree, as do operations research analysts. Statisticians typically hold at least a bachelor's degree.

Technicians can earn degrees in areas other than mathematics. Many colleges offer a four-year degree in engineering technology. These programs will teach you how to use mathematics and science in industrial research, production, or design.

Core college classes include calculus, advanced calculus, linear algebra, statistics, and computers. Technicians take courses in applied mathematics such as linear and nonlinear programming, graph theory, discreet optimization, and combinatorics. It is highly recommended that you also take courses in another discipline, such as engineering or computer science, which will give you a broader range of knowledge to offer an employer. This will also allow you to specialize in that area.

For Jaime, the most interesting classes were those that applied math to real-world problems. These optimization-type courses use math in a way that helps optimize a decision or decision-making process.

Jaime's least favorite classes were the theoretical ones, such as advanced linear algebra. "As I look back, I realize the basics you learn in algebra and some of the theory are important," she says. "But once you master the basics, you move on. Don't lose heart. The first classes you take are the least interesting. With introduction to applied mathematics, you get a feel for what's to come."

After college, continuing education is often available through programs sponsored by employers. Some industrial firms provide on-the-job training for technicians with a background in mathematics. Some will even subsidize study and continuing education for their workers.

SCHOLARSHIPS AND GRANTS

Mathematics is a very broad field, so students interested in a career as a mathematical technician have many options. Most scholarships and grants are sponsored by private industries. Mathematics is one of the fields in which the largest amount of financial aid is offered. The American Geological Institute, the American Institute of Aeronautics and Astronautics, and the Science Service are just a few of the many organizations that offer scholarships in math, science, and engineering. Write early for application requirements and deadlines.

INTERNSHIPS AND VOLUNTEERSHIPS

Mathematical technicians may find it difficult to find internships in their field. "There are a few out there, but mostly, they just don't exist," says Jaime. Students typically gain the necessary experience and training at school, not on the job.

"Maybe you can get a summer job, but employers are reluctant to do it," Jaime says. "I'd like to see that change. The only way to really understand the job is to actually do it."

Limited work opportunities for students in mathematics do exist. College placement offices can provide you with this information.

ADVANCEMENT POSSIBILITIES

Mathematicians conduct research in fundamental mathematics and in applying mathematical techniques to science, management, and other fields. They use mathematical methods to solve problems or direct others solving problems in various fields.

Operations research analysts examine management and operational problems and formulate mathematical or simulation models of problems to be solved by computers or other means.

Mathematics professors conduct college or university courses in mathematics for undergraduate or graduate students.

Who Will Hire Me?

As Jaime neared graduation from college, she set up job interviews through her school's placement office. She was hired after only three interviews and still works for that employer.

Employers often recruit from colleges and technical institutes. Public and private employment offices also have information on available jobs. Professional organizations often have publications that list job openings.

Government agencies have their own personnel offices, which may have information on positions with the federal government. The U.S. Department of Defense is the largest employer of mathematicians and related workers. Other potential employers include the National Aeronautics and Space Administration

FYI

Steps In Developing a Mathematical Model

1. Define the problems or questions to be solved.
2. List the parts of the situation being modeled and describe the relationships between them.
3. Use mathematical devices to specify the relationships.
4. Determine what is essential and what complicates the model beyond the point of possible analysis.
5. Evaluate the data needed in defining the mathematical relationships and in assessing how well the model matches the real-world situation.
6. Solve the equations representing the mathematical model.
7. Evaluate and interpret the results.

(NASA), the U.S. Department of Commerce, and the National Institute of Standards and Technology.

Many mathematicians work for the government, but mathematical technicians find jobs primarily in private industry. Aircraft and automobile manufacturers are some of the largest employers of these technicians. Private consulting firms represent a growing area of employment. Businesses of all kinds are increasingly relying upon the services of mathematical technicians to streamline their production methods and provide the most cost-efficient service possible.

"The driving force is the economic factor," Jaime points out. "As industries become more competitive, these services become more important. They need to maximize profit in real-world decisions."

Advancing technology has led to an increase of mathematical applications in all fields. The fastest growing job sector for mathematical technicians is in the computer and communications industries. As the world becomes more technologically oriented, industries are becoming more dependent on computers and other high-tech equipment. Mathematical technicians are an integral part of the workings of these companies.

"There are good jobs out there, but they won't fall in your lap," says Jaime.

Where Can I Go from Here?

"There are lots of different ways to use math to advance," says Jaime. "There are no set tracks to be on. It's not like being an accountant. It's wide open."

Jaime hopes to continue her education and get her master's degree in mathematics. "Somewhere down the line I'd like to teach at a university or college," she says. "It's the life I picture for myself." Many mathematicians become teachers. With a bachelor's degree that includes a teaching endorsement, you can become a mathematics instructor at an elementary or high school. With more advanced education you can become one of the 20,000 professors who teach mathematics at a college or university.

Another 16,000 mathematicians are employed in nonteaching positions. Many of them work for state or federal governments. About three out of four mathematicians in federal jobs work for the Department of Defense. Private industry also offers opportunities, most commonly in research and testing, educational services, security and commodity exchanges, management, and public relations. Mathematicians often find employment with drug manufacturers, banks, insurance companies, and public utilities. Job opportunities in the field of mathematics are increasing, and a working background as a mathematics technician is a good foundation for a successful career.

Technicians who pursue further studies and have a good work record can expect to advance in both job rank and pay. They may be promoted to supervisory positions where they lead teams of technicians, direct projects, and oversee the work of other technicians. Promotions go to technicians who have computer skills, technical expertise, and the ability to manage people and organize work.

What Are the Salary Ranges?

According to the U.S. Bureau of Labor Statistics, the median salary for mathematical technicians in 2003 was $37,400 a year. The lowest paid 10 percent earned about $24,700, and the highest paid 10 percent earned $67,800 annually. In 2003, operations research analysts had median salaries of $62,360. Mathematicians with federal jobs averaged $82,200 a year, and statisticians averaged $64,210. A review of annual salaries nationwide by Salary.com reported that in 2005 mathematical technicians earned between $39,658 and $48,121. Benefits typically include paid holidays and sick leave, health and life insurance, and a pension plan.

What Is the Job Outlook?

Employment opportunities for mathematical technicians are expected to increase slower than the average, through 2012, according to the U.S. Department of Labor. However, as automation increases and computer-related fields expand, jobs for technicians will be opening up.

Technicians are in high demand in transportation, communications, and computer industries. Applied mathematics is being used increasingly in numerous industries. Students with a bachelor's degree in mathematics will find entry-level positions and opportunities for professional growth.

If you have expertise in mathematics and in some other area, such as computer science or electrical engineering, you will have a much better probability of finding a good job. Many companies are no longer expanding their research and development departments, and some are cutting them back, but employers continue to hire mathematicians who have a broad education and multifaceted skills. More openings are expected in applied mathematics than in theoretical research.

How Do I Learn More?

PROFESSIONAL ORGANIZATIONS

The following organizations and associations provide information on mathematics technician careers, accredited schools, scholarships, and employers:

American Academy of Actuaries
1100 17th Street, NW, 17th Floor
Washington, DC 20036-4601
202-223-8196
http://www.actuary.org

American Geological Institute
4220 King Street
Alexandria, VA 22302-1502
703-379-2480
http://www.agiweb.org

American Institute of Aeronautics and Astronautics
2221 Rosecarns Avenue
El Segundo, CA 90245
310-643-7510
http://www.aiaa.org

American Mathematical Society
201 Charles Street
Providence, RI 02940-2294
800-321-4267
http://www.ams.org

American Statistical Association
1429 Duke Street
Alexandria, VA 22314-3415
888-231-3473
http://www.amstat.org

Association for Women in Mathematics
11240 Waples Mill Road, Suite 200
Fairfax, VA 22030
703-934-0163
awm@math.umd.edu
http://www.awm-math.org

Mathematical Association of America
1529 18th Street, NW
Washington, DC 20036-1358
800-741-9415
http://www.maa.org

Science Service
Westinghouse Science Scholarships and Awards
1719 N Street, NW
Washington, DC 20036
202-785-2255
http://www.sciserv.org

BIBLIOGRAPHY

The following is a sampling of materials relating to the professional concerns and development of mathematical technicians:

Burnett, Rebecca. *Careers for Number Crunchers and Other Quantitative Types.* 2d ed. New York: McGraw-Hill, 2002.

Dunham, William. *Journey through Genius: The Great Theorums of Mathematics.* New York: Penguin Putnam Inc., 1990.

Lambert, Stephen E., Ruth Decotis, and Julie Ann Degalan. *Great Jobs for Math Majors*. Lincolnwood, Ill.: NTC/Contemporary Publishing Group, 1998.

Sterrett, Andrew, ed. *101 Careers in Mathematics*. 2d ed. Washington, D.C.: The Mathematical Association of America, 2003.

MECHANICAL ENGINEERING TECHNICIANS

Definition
Mechanical engineering technicians work under the direction of mechanical engineers to design, build, maintain, and modify many kinds of machines, mechanical devices, and tools. They work in a wide range of industries and in a variety of specific jobs within every industry.

High School Subjects
English
Mathematics
Physics

Personal Skills
Mechanical/manipulative
Technical/scientific

Salary Range
$27,700 to $42,700 to $64,000

Minimum Educational Level
Associate's degree

Certification or Licensing
Voluntary

Outlook
About as fast as the average

DOT
007

GOE
02.08.04

NOC
2232

O*NET-SOC
17-3027.00

Tony Chavarria has worked as a mechanical engineering technician in a variety of areas, assisting in the production of anything from video games and slot machines to bedding and printing machines. His work has required a great deal of attention to detail, such as in adjusting slot machines to recognize coins from around the world, but he has also worked on large machinery.

"You have to be prepared to work beyond your normal duties," Tony says. "The job requires a lot of effort. With a smaller company, one mechanic may be responsible for a number of things. Once, I was working the job of three people: mechanic, shipper, and stocker." This involved building machines, preparing them for shipment, and keeping track of all stock, down to the screws, bolts, nuts, and wiring.

What Does a Mechanical Engineering Technician Do?

Mechanical engineering technicians are employed in a broad range of industries. Technicians may specialize in any one of many areas, including biomedical equipment, measurement and control, products manufacturing, solar energy, turbo machinery, energy resource technology, and engineering materials and technology.

Within each application, there are various aspects of the work with which the technician may be involved. One phase is research and development. In this area, the mechanical engineering technician assists an engineer or scientist in the design and development of a variety of products from ballpoints to sophisticated measuring devices. These technicians prepare rough sketches and layouts of the project being developed. In the design of an automobile engine, for example, mechanical engineering technicians prepare schematics that detail the fans, pistons, connecting rods, and flywheels to be used in the engine. To do so, they may work with CAD and other computer software. They estimate cost and operational qualities of each part, taking into account friction, stress, strain, and vibration. By performing these tasks, they free the engineer to accomplish other research assignments.

A second common type of work for mechanical engineering technicians is testing. For products such as engines, motors, or other moving devices, technicians may set up prototypes of the equipment to be tested and run performance tests. Some tests require one procedure to be done repeatedly, while others require that equipment be run over long periods of time to observe any changes in operation. Technicians collect and compile all necessary data from the testing procedures and prepare reports for the engineer or scientist.

In manufacturing, preparations must be made for a product's production. In this effort, mechanical engineering technicians assist in the product design by making final design layouts and detailed drawings of parts to be manufactured and of any special manufacturing equipment needed. Some test and inspect machines and equipment or work with engineers to eliminate production problems.

Other mechanical engineering technicians examine plans and drawings to determine what materials are needed and prepare lists of these materials, specifying quality, size, and strength. They also may estimate labor costs, equipment life, and plant space needed. After the product is manufactured, some mechanical engineering technicians may help solve storage and shipping problems, while others assist in customer relations when product installation is required.

Some engineering technicians work with tool designers. They help in preparing sketches of designs for cutting tools, jigs, special fixtures, and other devices used in mass production. Frequently, they redesign existing tools to improve their efficiency.

What Is It Like to Be a Mechanical Engineering Technician?

Tony Chavarria works as an electrical mechanical assembler, most recently in the printing industry. "The machines we built were specialized for the label and packaging industry, such as labels for bar codes," Tony says. "The machines can also print lottery tickets. The biggest machine I ever saw built was 300 feet long, at a cost of $10 million. It can print up to a million tickets in one roll."

Tony works closely with the machines to keep them operating. "In order to prevent rust in a machine, you accelerate the rust. There's a chemical process, in which we clean the part then we dip it into a tank with acids combined with water. This oxidizes the steel. After that, we dip it in water, then into sheet oil."

Once the parts have been prepared, Tony collects the parts and the drawings. "My company doesn't like to provide all the information, in order to keep design secrets. They give you only one view of your assembly. So the mechanic has to be smart and focused." Tony's section of the machine was to make holes in the paper, and required that he install nine gears.

"If you damage them," he says, "you damage them for good. You have to be very careful how you assemble, so that the gears don't rub against each other, so that they work with each other. You have to keep your ears open. You'll hear a noise if something is wrong."

Tony has also worked for an electronics company that produces video games, pinball machines, and slot machines for the casino industry. The company's market was Canada and overseas. "In the beginning, I was testing small printers, because some casinos don't pay off in cash; they print out paper receipts. One problem was that the printer kept getting jammed. I went in and tested, and found that the biggest problem was humidity. I could feel the wet ink on the paper. Humidity was making the paper weak, and the shape of the exit wasn't helping the paper along." Tony then assisted in the change of the design of the machine.

Tony has worked with mechanical engineers, electrical engineers, and software engineers. "These machines are operated by software," he says. "When I was doing testing, I was testing coin handling. Coin handling is how you're going to set the machine to recognize that the coin is a real quarter, a real nickel, the way it's going to be detected properly and counted properly in the machine. So I was testing coins, dollar

Lingo to Learn

Dynamics The velocities, accelerations, and resulting forces for a system in motion.

Fluid mechanics The study of pressure from fluid flow.

Kinematics How a mechanism behaves as it moves through a range of motion.

Nanotechnology Controlling individual atoms and molecules to create devices such as computer chips that are thousands of times smaller than what current technologies permit.

Schematic A diagram, plan, or drawing created and used by engineers.

Thermodynamics The science concerned with the relations between heat and mechanical energy or work, and the conversion of one into the other.

bills, testing coins from other countries, money from South Africa, from England, France, Czechoslovakia, Poland. Customers from those countries were buying our machines." Because of the differing weights and sizes of coins, the technicians had to measure each kind of coin, going into the thousandth of a gram, and enter the information into the computer program.

"The testing responsibilities were growing so much, that people were assigned to do the testing for me, and I then had to use my skills in computers. I had to create charts, because we were making around 5,000 machines for Canada, but the same model had to be customized for all the different customers." Software was a major element of the machines, so the coin handling had to be properly designed for the software to function properly. "As the coin travels, it has to be detected by the coin comparator. If it's okay, it travels through an infrared receiver and transmitter to be detected a second time. If the timing of the coin falling is incorrect, the machine automatically rejects the coin whether it's good or bad. It's just to protect the casino." In the testing process, a small South African coin caused many problems. "It would bounce too much. We had to narrow the metal where the coin was supposed to travel and do a lot of retesting."

While this required some intricate design work, Tony's responsibilities with a company that built machines for the bedding industry involved machinery that weighed up to five tons. "Every weekend we were shipping 10 to 50 machines," he says. "There I was an electrician. I was installing modules and motors."

One of the downsides to the work can be the moving of heavy equipment and the potential for accidents. "For instance, you have to split a machine at the time of shipping. The machine can weigh about 25,000 pounds, and the forklift is holding it six feet above me."

Do I Have What It Takes to Be a Mechanical Engineering Technician?

Technicians need mathematical and mechanical aptitude. They must understand abstract concepts and apply scientific principles to problems in the shop or laboratory, in both the design and the manufacturing process. They should be interested in people and machines and have the ability to carry out detailed work. They analyze sketches and drawings and need patience, perseverance, and resourcefulness. They also should have good communication skills as they can present both spoken and written reports. "You have to keep an open mind," Tony says, "and be ready to listen to others. You must remain aware that everyone has different experience in different areas."

To Be a Successful Mechanical Engineering Technician, You Should . . .

- have problem solving skills
- be detail oriented
- possess communication skills and enjoy working with others
- be able to understand and apply abstract concepts to real situations

Mechanical engineering technicians work in a variety of conditions depending on their field of specialization. Technicians who specialize in design may find that they spend most of their time at the drafting board or computer. Those who specialize in manufacturing may spend some time at a desk but also spend considerable time in manufacturing areas or shops.

Conditions also vary according to industry. Some industries require technicians to work in foundries, die-casting rooms, machine shops, assembly areas, or punch-press areas. Most of these areas, however, are well lighted, heated, and ventilated. Moreover, most industries employing mechanical engineering technicians have strong safety programs.

Mechanical engineering technicians are often called upon to exercise decision-making skills, to be responsible for valuable equipment, and to act as effective leaders. At other times they carry out routine, uncomplicated tasks. In some cases, they may coordinate the activities of others, while at other times they are the ones supervised. They must be able to respond well to both types of demands. In return for this flexibility and versatility, mechanical engineering technicians are usually highly respected by their employers and coworkers.

How Do I Become a Mechanical Engineering Technician?

EDUCATION

High School

Preparation for this career begins in high school. Although entrance requirements to associate programs vary somewhat from school to school, mathematics and physical science form the backbone of a good preparatory curriculum. Classes should include algebra, geometry, science, computer science, mechanical drawing, shop, and communications.

Postsecondary Training

Associate's degree or two-year mechanical technician programs are designed to prepare students for entry-level positions. Most programs accredited by the Accreditation Board for Engineering and Technology (ABET) offer one year of a basic program with a chance to specialize in the second year. The first year of the program generally consists of courses in college algebra and trigonometry, science, and communication skills. Other classes introduce students to the manufacturing processes, drafting, and language of the industry.

The second year's courses focus on mechanical technology. These include fluid mechanics, thermodynamics, tool and machine design, instruments and controls, production technology, electricity, and electronics. Many schools allow their students to choose a major in the second year of the program, which provides training for a specific area of work in the manufacturing industry.

CERTIFICATION OR LICENSING

Many mechanical engineering technicians choose to become certified by the National Institute for Certification in Engineering Technologies (NICET). To become certified, you must combine a specific amount of job-related experience with a written examination. Certifications are offered at several levels of expertise. Such certification is generally voluntary, although obtaining certification shows a high level of commitment and dedication that employers find highly desirable.

Mechanical engineering technicians are encouraged to become affiliated with professional groups, such as the American Society of Certified Engineering Technicians (ASCET), that offer continuing education sessions for members. Some

In-depth

History

Mechanical engineering dates back to ancient times, when it was used almost exclusively for military purposes. Perhaps the Romans were the first to use the science for nonmilitary projects, such as aqueducts, roads, and bridges, although many, if not most, of these structures were built to advance military objectives.

With the advent of the industrial revolution and the use of machines for manufacturing, mechanical engineering technology took a giant step forward. One of the most important figures in this revolution was Eli Whitney. Having received a government contract in 1798 to produce 15,000 muskets, he hired not gunsmiths but mechanics. At that time, all articles, including muskets, were built one by one by individual craft workers. No two muskets were ever alike.

Whitney took a different approach. For two years after receiving the contract, he focused on developing and building special-purpose machines and then trained mechanics to make specific parts of the gun. When he was finished, Whitney had invented new machine tools and attachments, such as the milling machine and jig, made real the concept of interchangeable parts, and paved the way for the modern manufacturing assembly line.

mechanical engineering technicians may be required to belong to unions.

Who Will Hire Me?

To familiarize yourself with the work, you may be able to obtain part-time or summer work in a machine shop or factory. This type of work usually consists of sweeping floors and clearing out machine tools, but it offers an opportunity to view the field firsthand and also demonstrates interest to future employers. Field trips to industrial laboratories, drafting studios, or manufacturing facilities can offer overall views of this type of work. Hobbies like automobile repair, model making, and electronic kit assembling can also be helpful. Finally, any high school student interested in the engineering field should consider joining the Junior Engineering Technical Society (JETS).

Many engineering technicians work in durable goods manufacturing, primarily making electrical and electronic machinery and equipment, industrial machinery and equipment, instruments and related products, and transportation equipment. A sizable percentage of work is in service industries, mostly in engineering and business services companies that do contract work for government, manufacturing, and other organizations.

The federal government employs engineering technicians in the departments of Defense, Transportation, Agriculture, and Interior as well as the Tennessee Valley Authority and the National Aeronautics and Space Administration. State and municipal governments also have engineering technicians working for them.

Where Can I Go from Here?

As mechanical engineering technicians remain with a company, they become more valuable to the employer. Opportunities for advancement are available to those who are willing to accept greater responsibilities either by specializing in a specific field, taking on more technically complex assignments, or by assuming supervisory duties. Some technicians advance by moving into technical sales or customer relations. Mechanical technicians who further their education may choose to become tool designers or mechanical engineers.

Advancement Possibilities

Mechanical engineers plan and design tools, engines, machines, and other mechanical systems that produce, transmit, or use power. They may work in design, testing, robotics, transportation, or bioengineering, or other areas.

Technical writers express technical and scientific ideas in easy-to-understand language.

Technical editors revise written text to correct any errors and make it read smoothly and clearly. They also coordinate the activities of writers, illustrators, and other staff in preparing material for publication.

What Are the Salary Ranges?

According to the U.S. Department of Labor Occupational Information Network, median annual earnings for mechanical engineering technicians were $42,700 in 2003. Those in the lowest paid 10 percent made $27,700, while those in the highest paid 10 percent earned $64,000. The middle 50 percent had annual earnings of between $34,200 and $53,000.

These salaries are based upon the standard workweek. Overtime or premium time pay may be earned for work beyond regular daytime hours or workweek. Other benefits, depending on the company and union agreements, include paid vacation days, insurance, retirement plans, profit sharing, and tuition-reimbursement plans.

What Is the Job Outlook?

Job opportunities for mechanical engineering technicians are expected to grow as fast as the average through 2012, according to the U.S. Department of Labor. Manufacturing companies will be looking for more ways to apply the advances in mechanical technology to their operations. Opportunities will be best for technicians who are skilled in new manufacturing concepts, materials, and designs. Many job openings also will be created by people retiring or leaving the field.

However, the employment outlook for engineering technicians is influenced by the economy. Hiring will fluctuate with the ups and downs of the nation's overall economic situation. Technicians whose jobs are defense-related may experience fewer opportunities because of defense cutbacks.

How Do I Learn More?

PROFESSIONAL ORGANIZATIONS

For information on the profession of mechanical engineering, colleges and universities offering accredited programs in engineering technology, and certification, contact the following organizations:

Accreditation Board for Engineering and Technology Inc.
111 Market Place, Suite 1050
Baltimore, MD 21202-4012
410-347-7700
http://www.abet.org

American Society of Certified Engineering Technicians
PO Box 1348
Flowery Branch, GA 30542
770-967-9137
http://www.ascet.org

American Society of Mechanical Engineers
3 Park Avenue
New York, NY 10016
800-843-2763
http://www.asme.org

National Institute for Certification in Engineering Technologies
1420 King Street
Alexandria, VA 22314-2794
888-476-4238
http://www.nicet.org

Junior Engineering Technical Society
1420 King Street
Alexandria, VA 22314
703-548-0769
info@jets.org
http://www.jets.org

BIBLIOGRAPHY

Baine, Celeste. *Is There an Engineer Inside You?: A Comprehensive Guide to Career Decisions in Engineering.* 3d ed. Farmerville, La.: Bonamy Publishing, 2004.

Careers in Focus: Technicians. 2d ed. New York: Facts On File, 2004.

Garner, Geraldine. *Careers in Engineering.* 2d ed. New York: McGraw-Hill, 2002.

Kreith, Frank, ed. *The CRC Handbook of Mechanical Engineering.* 2d ed. Boca Raton, Fla.: CRC Press, 2004.

MEDICAL ASSISTANTS

Around 3:00 in the afternoon, Donna Bolton, CMA (certified medical assistant) greets Marie and begins to prepare her for a treadmill test. Eighty-three-year-old Marie had called the Kalispell Diagnostic Clinic first thing that morning. She'd been feeling tired lately, run-down, and barely had the motivation to get out and sell her Avon products. She thought something might be wrong with her heart.

Donna took Marie's call when it came in. Experience had taught Donna not to mess around with heart complaints. "Have you had any shortness of breath, dizzy spells, or pains up and down your arms or in your chest?" she asked Marie.

"No," Marie answered slowly. "I'm just tired."

"Better come right in," Donna told her, checking the appointment log. "We can see you this afternoon." After hanging up, Donna discussed Marie's call with the doctor, who prescribed a treadmill test for Marie.

Now Donna weighs Marie, takes her blood pressure and temperature, and then prepares her skin for the electrodes soon to be attached to her chest. She tells her patient about the test, explaining to her how to walk on the machine and to be sure and let the doctor know right away if she feels dizzy or has any arm or chest pain. After a few minutes, the doctor enters the room to monitor Marie's test, and Donna stays to assist. "Marie stayed on the treadmill for a full five minutes, and her heart was strong the whole time," Donna says. "She did great. She's tired because she's 83. Sometimes, it's hard to accept that you're slowing down."

Definition
Medical assistants help physicians keep their offices and clinics running smoothly. They maintain medical records, assist with the examination and treatment of patients, and perform routine office duties so doctors can spend more time working directly with patients.

High School Subjects
Biology
Computer science
Health
Mathematics

Personal Skills
Helping/teaching
Technical/scientific

Salary Range
$25,064 to $27,363 to $30,239+

Minimum Educational Requirements
Some postsecondary training

Certification or Licensing
Voluntary

Outlook
Much faster than the average

DOT
079

GOE
14.02.01

NOC
6631

O*NET-SOC
31-9092.00

What Does a Medical Assistant Do?

Medical assistants are trained to do both clerical and clinical duties. Often, depending on the size of the office, they do both. The larger the office, the greater the chance the medical assistant will specialize in one type of work. In smaller offices or clinics with only one doctor and one registered nurse, for example, the medical assistant may find herself, or himself, doing everything it takes to run the practice, from making appointments to greeting patients to billing them.

The clinical duties of a medical assistant are those tasks that are patient-centered. Assistants take the medical histories of patients and records them in patient files. They find out what a patient's current symptoms are and determines what concerns to share with the doctor. Assistants help physicians by preparing patients for examination and treatment. They may check and record a patient's blood pressure, pulse, and temperature. Medical assistants help with the preparation of diagnostic tests and procedures, including educating the patient about what to expect during the test. They also educate patients about medication, special diets, and instructions about their treatments. Assistants prepare patients for X rays, electrocardiograms (ECGs), and treadmill tests; some may administer ECGs. Assistants can

Lingo to Learn

Aseptic technique Any procedure used to prevent microorganisms from contaminating equipment, rooms, or people.

Dialysis A process that is used to purify the blood of persons whose kidneys have stopped functioning.

Electrocardiogram (ECG) This test registers, in wave patterns, the electrical currents from heart muscle contractions.

Lavage The French term for washing, especially the therapeutic washing out of an organ. An ear lavage washes out the ears with very warm water, usually to dissolve excessive wax buildup that could be causing pain and hearing loss.

Medical transcription A typed record of a physician's dictated material concerning a patient's medical record.

Physician assistant A person who is certified to diagnose, treat, and prescribe medication under the direct supervision of a licensed physician.

Vitals These are the signs of life. To take someone's vitals is to measure blood pressure, temperature, respiratory rate, and pulse.

give injections, apply or change dressings, remove sutures, draw blood, and collect specimens for laboratory tests, such as Pap smears.

"Injections," says Donna, "are one of the most controversial procedures. Some states restrict medical assistants from giving injections, other states allow it. Here in Montana, CMAs can give injections. In other states, only a registered nurse or doctor can." Other procedures are likewise prohibited in some states and allowed in others. Invasive procedures, such as setting up intravenous tubes, are the most controversial. "We definitely don't put patients through dialysis in this state, either," says Donna.

Medical assistants are usually the ones who prepare the examination rooms for patients, keeping them clean and orderly. After each examination, they straighten up the room, dispose of the used linen and medical supplies, then restock the room. They sterilize the instruments and equipment used during examinations, and order new supplies and keep track of inventory.

An assistant's administrative duties vary depending on how many other employees staff the office. Medical assistants type case histories and surgery reports and keep patients' files, X rays, and other medical records up to date. This includes the financial records, too, preparing and sending the bills and receiving payment when it comes in. Assistants answer the phone, greet patients, fill out insurance forms, schedule appointments, take care of correspondence, and arrange for patients to be admitted to hospitals for treatment and tests when necessary. They call in prescriptions to pharmacies and authorize drug refills as instructed by the doctor. Assistants do many of these tasks by computer. Some offices have medical secretaries and medical receptionists who perform these administrative duties, but they rarely do the clinical tasks of a medical assistant.

Medical assistants can specialize in specific medical fields. *Ophthalmic medical assistants* help ophthalmologists with eye exams and treatments. They give eye drops and use special equipment to test eyesight and check for disease. They show patients how to use eye dressings, protective shields, and safety patches and how to use and care for contact lenses. They maintain and sterilize the optical and surgical equipment and could assist during eye surgery. An *optometric assistant* prepares patients for examination and helps them select their eyewear. A *chiropractic medical assistant* works with patients with muscular and skeletal problems. And a *podiatric medical assistant* exposes and develops X rays, makes castings of feet, and assists podiatrists in surgery.

What Is It Like to Be a Medical Assistant?

"I walked in the door this morning and was handed a chart before I even got my coat off," says Donna. "I had to phone in a prescription for a patient who called, checking it with the doctor first." After that was done, Donna sat down with the doctor to discuss a few problems that had cropped up. "I didn't get a chance to talk with her the day before, so I wanted to do it first thing." By that time, the first patient of the day had arrived for a treadmill test, and Donna needed to prep him and get all of his information into the computer.

Donna works in a large and busy practice. There are six doctors, five certified medical assistants, and one registered nurse (RN). Two of the medical assistants are *coders*. They handle the billing, and one does strictly office billing while the other does hospital billing. One CMA is the *records clerk,* gathering all the patient's information such as previous tests, X rays, and hospital stays. The other two medical assistants, Donna included, are clinical. "We do everything you've ever been to a doctor's office for," says Donna.

After the morning's treadmill test, Donna noticed a Holter Monitor scheduled before lunch. "A Holter Monitor runs off batteries and is designed to give us a true picture of what is happening with the heart," Donna explains. It is the size of a large calculator, a box about six inches by three inches, that fits into a pouch with a strap that goes over the shoulder. It monitors the heart through electrodes. "Each electrode has a little pad that sticks to your skin. Conducting gel is in the pad, and the gel picks up the electricity your heart puts out," says Donna. "We give people a diary to record the times they feel dizzy or have pain in the chest or arms, anything irregular. When they feel this, they push a button on the monitor. We later read the printout and the diary to get a truly accurate picture of what's going on." Doctors may order the monitor kept on for 24 to 48 hours, depending on the patient's situation. "I get them hooked up properly, educate them about the diary and using the monitor correctly, and chart the visit. The doctor reads and interprets the printout."

After lunch, Donna calls in all her prescriptions. As the afternoon's patients come in, Donna grabs their chart, greets them, and shows them into an examination room where she learns the reason for their visit. She charts this information and passes it on to the doctor, saving the doctor valuable time to work directly with the patient. Donna then preps the patients for the doctor's exam, taking their vitals and weighing them.

One patient needed an ear lavage (washing). "I normally do several ear lavages a day," says Donna. She usually has several ECGs (electrocardiograms) to do in a day as well, but this particular day there weren't any scheduled. "It's just as well," says Donna, "because we have four men from the fire department coming in unexpectedly for routine treadmill tests. They needed to have it done today for their certification, and they're all due after three o'clock. The rest of the day is going to be busy." Most of Donna's days are. "I'm never bored," says Donna. "I'm a people person and I love working with the patients. I make them feel more comfortable, and it's gratifying."

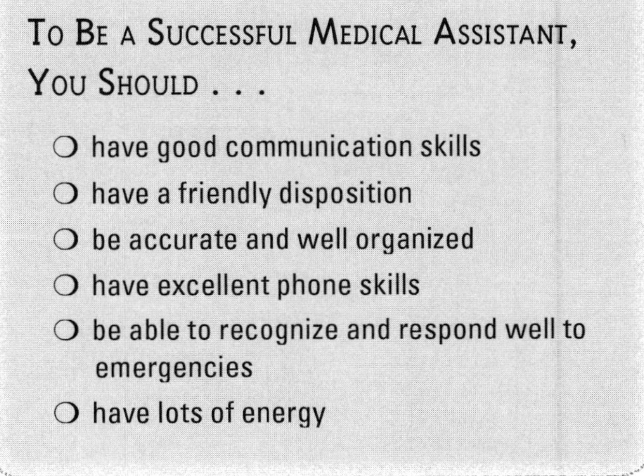
To Be a Successful Medical Assistant, You Should . . .

- have good communication skills
- have a friendly disposition
- be accurate and well organized
- have excellent phone skills
- be able to recognize and respond well to emergencies
- have lots of energy

Donna works a 40-hour week, 8:00 A.M. to 5:00 P.M., Monday through Friday. "If you want to be in the medical profession, this is a nice schedule if you have a family," says Donna. "Nursing shifts in hospitals are long, late hours that make it hard to spend time with your children."

Do I Have What It Takes to Be a Medical Assistant?

"We're there for the patient," says Donna. "Above all, a medical assistant must be able to work well with people." Good medical assistants have patience, a friendly disposition, and empathy and compassion for all people. They recognize and respect cultural diversity. Putting patients at ease is essential. "You can't shy away from people," says Donna.

Medical assistants must be able to explain complicated procedures and doctors' instructions to patients as well as explain patients' symptoms to doctors. "Medical assistants are the go-between, the liaison, for patient and doctor," says Donna. Assistants are responsible to keep accurate records and charts of everything that happens to a patient. Therefore, good communication skills, both verbal and written, are important. This includes phone skills. Medical assistants spend a lot of time on the phone, talking with patients and making appointments, calling in prescriptions, and collaborating with hospital and laboratory staff. Assistants should be able to recognize and respond to emergency situations and think well on their feet. Donna never hesitates to bring someone in if they have an ear infection. "You don't mess around with ear infections. You could end up with a ruptured eardrum."

Medical assistants are the go-between, the liaison, for patient and doctor.

Medical assistants should have solid organ-izational skills. They are called upon to perform many different tasks, and they must know how to prioritize and manage their time effectively. They are required to have a neat appearance and be professional at all times. Respecting patient confidentiality, following instructions, and complying with complicated policies and procedures are all part of the professional conduct of a medical assistant.

Donna believes medical assistants need to have lots of energy and be able to deal with tragic situations. "You have to leave your patients' problems at the office. You can't take it home with you," says Donna. "If you do, you won't last long as a medical assistant. You'll go crazy."

How Do I Become a Medical Assistant?

Donna was planning to be a registered nurse when she met her future husband, "a handsome Marine who swept me off my feet." Donna married in the 1950s, and her husband was shipped off first to Korea, then later Vietnam. "I began to think that I needed a career so I could support myself and my children, in case something happened to my husband. The possibilities were very real." Donna saw an ad on television for a medical assisting program. "It looked like a solid career choice. It was faster than becoming a nurse, two years as opposed to four, and I liked the hours better." Donna has never been sorry. "For 10 years we moved all over the place, and I was never without a job."

EDUCATION

High School

Most medical practices and clinics will not hire a medical assistant without a high school diploma or its equivalent. Some medical assistants are trained on the job, but this is becoming less common than it was in the past.

If you are interested in becoming a medical assistant, you should take health, biology, computer science, and business courses. Because being a medical assistant is a combination of administrative and clinical work, it is important to have a background in both. Bookkeeping, typing, and other office practices are essential to learn. Most of your record keeping will be done by computer, so don't neglect computer science, either. Advanced math classes, especially algebra, are also important. If you decide to enter into a two-year CMA program or move into nursing or some other related job, you'll have the required math and science.

High school is a good time to begin volunteering in the medical profession. Working in hospitals, nursing homes, and other health care facilities is one way to determine if the medical field is right for you. Another way is to join clubs or organizations, such as Future Nurses of America.

Postsecondary Training

The majority of doctors' offices and other health care facilities prefer medical assistants to complete a two-

FYI

In a dialysis machine, blood is circulated on one side of a porous layer of tissue while dialysis fluid—containing matter necessary to the body and closely matching the composition of blood—is circulated on the other. Waste products such as urea, the main solid component of urine, are diffused through the tissue into the dialysis fluid and are discarded, while the diffusion of substances needed by the body is prevented.

year associate's degree program or some other formal training program. Two agencies recognized by the U.S. Department of Labor accredit medical assisting training programs: the Commission on Accreditation of Allied Health Education Programs (CAAHEP) and the Accrediting Bureau of Health Education Schools (ABHES). In 2002 there were about 665 accredited medical assisting programs recognized by either of these two boards. The Committee on Accreditation for Ophthalmic Medical Personnel accredited 14 programs in ophthalmic medical assisting. South Dakota is the only state that requires medical assistants to be graduated from an accredited medical assisting program.

Formal training to become a medical assistant is available at trade schools, community colleges, junior colleges, and universities, and can last anywhere from nine months to two years. A two-year associate's degree can be applied to a nursing degree if you want to continue on someday. In medical assisting programs, you do course work in biology, anatomy, physiology, and medical terminology. You learn all nine systems of the body as well as how to draw blood, take vitals, expose and develop X rays, and administer an ECG and other medical tests and procedures. "Medical assistants work with all the instruments, learning their names and how to use them," says Donna. For the administrative end of the job, you study computer science, record keeping, transcribing and typing, and other office procedures.

During your formal training, you also do what is called an externship, working three months in the field practicing a variety of clinical and administrative duties. Schools usually help arrange a student's externship with nearby health care facilities, doctors' offices, and clinics. Although you're not graded, the facility where you work sends in a report on how well you did. According to Donna, a well-rounded externship is crucial. The CAAHEP requires it for certification, and future employers look closely at it. "It may be your only experience out in the field before your first job, so it counts a lot," says Donna.

For more information about CAAHEP-accredited programs and a list of ABHES-accredited programs, write The American Association of Medical Assistants (AAMA) or the Accrediting Bureau of Health Education Schools (see "How Do I Learn More?").

CERTIFICATION OR LICENSING

Although there is no required state or national licensing or certification for medical assistants, there is voluntary certification. And some states require medical assistants to receive additional training or certification for specified tasks, such as exposing and developing X rays. The American Association of Medical Assistants awards the Certified Medical Assistant (CMA) credential, and the American Medical Technologists awards the Registered Medical Assistant (RMA) credential. The Joint Commission on Allied Health Personnel in Ophthalmology awards the Certified Ophthalmic Assistant, and the American Society of Podiatric Medical Assistants awards the Podiatric Medical Assistant Certified credential.

The CMA national certification exam is given twice a year, in January and June, to students who graduate from a CAAHEP-accredited medical assisting program. The exam consists of 300 questions covering clinical, administrative, and general material. In order to retain your certification, you must have 60 hours of

In-depth

History

In 1903, the first practical electrocardiograph (ECG) for measuring the activity of the heart was developed by W. Einthoven. The electrocardiograph is the instrument that records the electrical output occurring during a heartbeat, and the electrocardiogram is what registers the wave patterns of the heart on a light-sensitive film recording. Deviations in the normal height, form, or duration of the wave pattern indicate specific disorders, and the ECG is an important aid in diagnosing heart disease.

The ECG is also referred to as an EKG after its European spelling. In 1923, Einthoven was awarded the Nobel Prize in medicine for his efforts.

continuing education credits, or take a recertification exam every five years. The RMA is given to students who graduated from an ABHES-accredited program. RMA recipients automatically become members of the American Medical Technologists association and must pay yearly dues to renew their certification. Annual continuing education credits are voluntary but recommended.

Donna, who is a Montana state representative for the AAMA, believes being a member of a professional medical assisting organization offers medical assistants a great support system. "If your right to practice is being questioned, the help you receive is invaluable," says Donna. "Being a member gives you the opportunity to communicate with others in your field at the local, state, and national level." In addition to a bimonthly publication titled *PMA* (Professional Medical Assistant), members of the AAMA can attend an annual convention with continuing education credits available. They also have access to a toll-free information line.

SCHOLARSHIPS AND GRANTS

The AAMA offers the Maxine Williams scholarship once a year to a medical assisting student attending a CAAHEP-accredited school. The scholarship is for $1,000. To apply, call or write the AAMA (see "How Do I Learn More?").

To receive financial assistance to attend a school with a postsecondary medical assisting training program, contact the school's financial aid office for information about the availability of grants and scholarships.

INTERNSHIPS AND VOLUNTEERSHIPS

The externship done in conjunction with medical assisting training programs is a nonpaid learning experience considered part of your overall course work.

Volunteering in a hospital, clinic, or other health care facility is a good way to see if being a medical assistant is right for you. Many facilities offer volunteer opportunities and welcome the extra help and personal touch that volunteers bring. Donna suggests volunteering with children, too, to test your ability to be a medical assistant, as many practices are exclusively pediatric or serve children. To explore these opportunities, contact hospitals, nursing and residential care facilities, child care centers, and state and county health services near you for more information about their volunteer programs.

Who Will Hire Me?

Most jobs for medical assistants are found in immediate care facilities, such as physicians' offices. Sixty percent of all medical assistants work in private doctors' offices, and another 14 percent work in public and private hospitals, including inpatient and outpatient facilities. About 10 percent work for other heath care facilities such as optometrists' and chiropractors' offices. The remainder work in medical facilities like nursing homes and physical therapy practices or for ambulatory health care services, public and private educational services, and medical and diagnostic laboratories.

If you're in a postsecondary medical assisting training program, your supervised clinical experience may lead you to a job. In fact, students are often asked to stay on and are offered permanent positions when their externship is over. "That's how I got my first job in California," says Donna. School career placement offices usually list jobs available in the field, and high school guidance counselors may also have information about possible job openings. Calling local doctors' offices and health care facilities, checking out the want ads, and registering with state employment agencies are all good methods of finding out about medical assisting positions near you.

For information about career opportunities in medical assisting, you can write the American Association of Medical Assistants and the American Medical Technologists. For information about careers in ophthalmology, write the Joint Commission on Allied Health Personnel in Ophthalmology.

Where Can I Go from Here?

Donna has been a medical assistant for more than 29 years and still loves it. "It's where I belong," says Donna, "although working with children is not my forte. I could never stand to stick them and hear them cry." Donna plans to retire in just a few years.

Although Donna is content where she is, many medical assistants must change occupations in order to advance. Medical assistants can move into

Advancement Possibilities

Nurses care for the sick and injured and help individuals achieve health and prevent disease.

Advanced practice nurses are nurses with training beyond that required to have the RN designation. They handle many of the duties previously restricted to the physician.

Physician assistants practice medicine under the supervision of licensed doctors, providing various health care services.

managerial or administrative positions without further education, and as more clinics and group practices open up, the need for office managers will increase. These positions could easily go to experienced, well-qualified medical assistants.

As with most jobs on the market today, the better your computer skills, the greater your chances of moving into a management position. Teaching medical assisting courses at a training program is also a possibility for advancement that may appeal to you. However, if you think you may someday want to advance into an occupation with more clinical responsibilities, such as nursing or physician assisting, or a more technical position such as respiratory therapist and technician, you will need to return to school. Donna believes being a medical assistant gives you the background to go just about anywhere in the medical field.

What Are the Salary Ranges?

The earnings of medical assistants vary widely, depending on experience, skill level, and location. According to the *Occupational Outlook Handbook*, median annual earnings for medical assistants were $23,940 in 2002. The highest paid 10 percent earned more than $34,130 a year, while the lowest paid 10 percent earned less than $17,640. In 2002, medical assistants earned the following median annual salaries by industry: offices and clinics of medical doctors, $24,260; offices of other health practitioners, $21,620; hospitals, $24,460; and outpatient care centers, $23,980.

Salary.com reports that nationwide in 2005 the median earnings of medical assistants were $27,363 annually. The lowest paid earned on average $25,064 per year, and the highest paid earned $30,239.

Whether or not a medical assistant receives health insurance benefits, a pension plan, and paid vacation and sick leave is usually up to the individual employer. Some doctors' offices and clinics have excellent benefit packages for medical assistants; others tend to hire part-time employees who are excluded from the benefits package.

What Is the Job Outlook?

Job prospects for medical assistants look particularly good in the years to come. Jobs in all areas of medical assisting are expected to increase much faster than the average for all other occupations as the health care industry grows to meet the needs of a large population of elderly people.

According to the U.S. Department of Labor, medical assisting is expected to be the fastest growing occupation through 2012. Employment opportunities will be the best for medical assistants who have completed formal training, particularly for those with certification. It predicts that employment will grow by 58 percent from 1998 to 2008. Employment will be driven by the number of new clinics, group practices like the one where Donna works, and health care facilities that need a higher proportion of support staff to run efficiently. The more flexible you are as a medical assistant, able to handle both clinical and administrative duties, and the better trained you are, the more likely you will be to find a job.

How Do I Learn More?

PROFESSIONAL ORGANIZATIONS

The following organizations provide information on career opportunities, medical assisting certification and certification exams, accredited schools and training programs, and medical assisting programs in ophthalmology:

Accrediting Bureau of Health Education Schools
7777 Leesburg Pike, Suite 314 N

Falls Church, VA 22043
703-917-9503
info@abhes.org
http://www.abhes.org

American Association of Medical Assistants
20 North Wacker Drive, Suite 1575
Chicago, IL 60606
312-899-1500
http://www.aama-ntl.org

American Medical Technologists
710 Higgins Road
Park Ridge, IL 60068
800-275-1268
http://www.amt1.com

Joint Commission on Allied Health Personnel in Ophthalmology
2025 Woodlane Drive
St. Paul, MN 55125-2998
800-284-3937
jcahpo@jcahpo.org
http://www.jcahpo.org

BIBLIOGRAPHY

The following is a sampling of materials relating to the professional concerns of medical assistants:

Clement, J. E. *Review Questions for the Medical Assistant Examination.* Boca Raton, Fla.: CRC Press, 2001.

Hosley, Julie B. *Lippincott's Pocket Guide to Medical Assisting.* Philadelphia: Lippincott Williams & Wilkins, 1998.

Lindh, Wilburta et al. *Delmar's Comprehensive Medical Assisting.* 2d ed. Albany, N.Y.: Thomson Delmar Learning, 2001.

Palko, Tom, and Hilda Palko. *Prentice Hall Health Question and Answer Review for the Medical Assistant.* 7th ed. Appleton & Lange Review Series. Upper Saddle River, N.J.: Prentice Hall, 2004.

Sacks, Terence J. *Opportunities in Physician Assistant Careers.* Rev. ed. Lincolnwood, Ill.: VGM Career Horizons, 2002.

MEDICAL RECORD TECHNICIANS

The intensive care unit of Saint Patrick Hospital is crowded with doctors, nurses, and visitors as Susan Lucchesi examines a patient's medical chart and writes in her notepad every diagnosis, procedure, and comment that has been added since she reviewed the data two days ago. She jots down a few questions that come to mind, points of clarification that she will call to the attention of the attending physicians.

After discussing the chart with one of the nurses, she adds another comment to her notes. Although the patients in intensive care probably have no idea who she is, and she might not recognize their faces, she's familiar with each of them, because she studies their charts regularly. As a records technician she makes sure that the details of their stay at the hospital are documented with impeccable thoroughness and accuracy.

When she returns to her quiet, pleasant office in the medical records department, she enters information from her notes into the hospital's computer system, prints it, keeps a copy for the patient's medical records folder, writes out her questions for the doctors, attaches them to a second copy of the printout, and sends it back to intensive care for the doctors to review. She'll repeat the procedure every two or three days until the patient is moved to another department, where a different medical record technician will take over.

Definition
Medical record technicians compile, code, and maintain medical records to document patient diagnoses and treatments. They also tabulate and analyze data from the records to assemble reports.

Alternative Job Titles
Certified coding specialists
Health information technicians
Medical records clerks

High School Subjects
Biology
English

Personal Skills
Following instructions
Technical/scientific

Salary Range
$27,190 to $30,332 to $33,346+

Minimum Educational Level
Some postsecondary training

Certification or Licensing
Recommended

Outlook
Much faster than the average

DOT
079

GOE
09.07.02

NOC
1413

O*NET-SOC
29-2071.00

What Does a Medical Record Technician Do?

If you've ever spent time in a hospital, either as a patient or visitor, you may remember the steady parade of nurses and doctors in and out of the patients' rooms for one thing or another. They might check body temperature, blood pressure, heart rate, or frequency of labor pains, give medication, check incisions, or test range of motion in a damaged limb. They're always writing on that little chart at the foot of the bed, generating an amazing amount of data for each patient at every hospital. If you've wondered what happens to all that information when the patient goes home, you have wondered about the job of the *medical record technician*.

An individual's medical record consists of all the information noted by any health care workers who have dealt with the patient. Along with the patient's medical history, it may include admission date, diagnoses, progress notes, surgical procedures, X rays, lab reports, prescribed medications or treatments, and discharge assessment. Medical record technicians assemble and organize records, make sure they're accurate, and prepare them for the use of doctors, insurance companies, or other authorized agencies or individuals. The technician also may compile statistical reports from groups of records. Hospital administrators, public health agencies, health program planners, and others use these reports to analyze trends and patterns or to see if a treatment is effective.

In smaller organizations, with fewer records to manage, the technician may work in all areas of the medical records department. In larger institutions there may be separate departments for each phase of the work, with each technician having very specific responsibilities.

Technicians who specialize in assigning a numerical code to every diagnosis and procedure are called *medical record coders* or *coder/abstractors*. To determine the correct codes, these technicians use specialized computer software, a coding reference guide, medical dictionaries, and the *Physician's Desk Reference*. Most hospitals in the United States use a nationally accepted coding system, which makes the data easier to handle and analyze in the records department and by organizations that pool information from many institutions. A coded record can be cross-referenced and sorted by its various components, such as physician, patient, diagnosis, or treatment. The technician may also assign the patient to a diagnosis-related grouping (DRG), which helps the Medicare system and insurance companies determine the amount to reimburse the hospital for the patient's stay. At some institutions patients are assigned to DRGs by technicians who specialize in using computers to analyze patients' charts.

In larger facilities some records technicians work in a release-of-information department that does nothing but release medical records to doctors, insurance agencies, state and federal organizations, law enforcement agencies, attorneys, and the patients themselves. These technicians prepare and release information for authorized use only. Maintaining confidentiality of patient records is a priority, not only for this department but for all medical records technicians.

Finally, the medical record must be filed away for storage and easy retrieval, either on computer, paper, or microfilm. In some institutions the medical record technicians supervise other personnel, such as *medical records clerks*, who perform the storage and retrieval work.

Most medical record technicians have more advanced training than medical records clerks, but not all have passed certification exams. Those who hold an associate's degree and certification are called *accredited records technicians*. They ensure the accuracy of medical records, create disease registries for research, and submit data to insurance companies, which then reimburse the health care facility.

Registered records administrators hold a bachelor's degree and certification. They are managers who also interpret data, do research and statistical reports, and ensure the privacy of health information.

Certified coding specialists have taken seminars or college classes in coding, along with on-the-job experience, and they are certified. The credential, *certified coding specialist physician-based,* is for technicians who specialize in coding for physician services in facilities other than hospitals.

What Is It Like to Be a Medical Record Technician?

As a medical records coder at Saint Patrick Hospital in Missoula, Montana, Susan Lucchesi spends most of the day at her computer in the medical records department assigning a numerical code to each diagnosis and procedure on patients' charts. She works in cooperation with a team of coders, a transcriptionist, and the clerks in the office next door; the clerks maintain an entire room full of records documented on paper, neatly stored in filing cabinets. "We all help each other out. We work together, and no one person gets the credit for anything. We're a very close team," she says.

Like many technicians in her field, Susan used to see little of the doctors, nurses, and other health care professionals who perform the work summarized in the medical charts. Thanks to a new program at the hospital, however, Susan now spends a few hours each day reviewing charts in the intensive care unit. The other coders on her team have different departments to visit; Susan has the option of covering the intensive care unit for one year and then rotating to another department.

It's almost like you're trying to solve a puzzle.

She still communicates with doctors by notes, e-mail, and phone calls from the medical records department, but she has enjoyed the chance to see how the intensive care unit operates. "I've made a lot of friends with doctors and nurses on my floor. That's been a learning experience," she says.

By tracking each patient's progress and assigning codes that help identify the main reason the person was admitted for treatment, Susan helps the doctors zero in on the patient's most pressing health problems and possible remedies. "It's almost like you're trying to solve a puzzle," she says. "There's a lot more to it than you'd think."

Some medical record technicians are more involved in following up after the patient has been discharged and the paperwork has been done. Terri Young works in the release-of-information department in another hospital. She also works as part of a team that processes many requests for medical information every day. One technician mans the special phone line, known as the "stat line," which receives calls mainly from emergency rooms. Information for those calls may be given over the telephone or by fax after the technician has verified the patient's name and birth date; all other requests must be in writing and include either the patient's authorization or a court order.

Requests are logged into the computer and prioritized. Terri's hospital strives to send out the information within two weeks of receiving it, but medical requests always receive priority over insurance requests. For each request, Terri gets the patient's medical record number from the computer, uses it to locate the chart, looks for the requested information in her records, and locates any specialized information in other areas of the hospital, such as the X-ray department. When she has found everything to complete the request, she fills out a worksheet, indicating what items need to be copied, and turns the file over to a medical record clerk.

Other technicians in the medical records department perform other duties. There are coding and abstracting technicians, most of whom have taken special training in coding. They spend their days almost exclusively at computer terminals. "You have to be able to concentrate," says Terri. "You have to be able to sit and sit and keep your mind on what you're doing."

There's a data entry team, the first technicians to work with patient records. They visit each floor of the hospital daily, pick up the charts for patients discharged the day before, assemble each chart in a specific order, and enter the information into the hospital's computer system.

There's a chart analysis team, which puts each patient's diagnoses in the correct time sequence and uses a computer software package to assign the patient to one of hundreds of diagnosis-related groupings. The groupings determine how much the hospital will be reimbursed by Medicare and insurance companies for the patient's stay. Accuracy is essential for the chart analysis team. Terri explains, "Medicare is so picky that if diagnoses aren't sequenced properly, it may make thousands of dollars difference in what they pay."

Because the hospital's records department never closes, some of the technicians work second and third shifts, as well as some weekends and holidays. Terri works Monday through Friday, 7:00 A.M. until 4:00 P.M. The 40-hour workweek is standard for most medical record technicians.

Lingo to Learn

Abstracting Removing pertinent information from a patient's medical record for use in a larger study or survey.

Coding In medical records, assigning numbers for systematic classification.

CPT (Common Procedural Terminology) The numerical classification system used in the medical records field to code procedures and treatments.

DRG (Diagnosis-Related Grouping) A system used by Medicare and many insurance companies to classify medical patients' care and treatment.

ICD (International Classification of Diseases) The numerical classification system used in the medical records field to code diagnoses.

Source-oriented chart order A system of organizing patient charts by grouping information into sections based on different health care departments, such as nursing, radiology, or attending physician.

Stat Immediately.

Terminal Digit Order A numerical filing method emphasizing the last two digits, which is the most effective use of filing space, as well as the most effective method of insuring patient privacy.

Transcription Making written copies of orally dictated material.

To Be a Successful Medical Record Technician, You Should . . .

- be extremely thorough and detail oriented
- feel confident in dealing with medical staff, administrators, and insurance agencies
- be able to concentrate for long periods of time
- be able to handle a heavy workload
- feel comfortable working with computers

Do I Have What It Takes to Be a Medical Record Technician?

The medical record technician is responsible for keeping accurate records for the benefit of the hospital, the physician, and the patient. Sloppy work could cause serious problems; the hospital might not receive proper payment, and inaccuracies in the records could affect the patient's health care in the future. The technician must develop precise and fastidious work habits to ensure as complete and correct a job as possible. Susan says a medical record technician should be detail oriented, interested in medicine, and adaptable. "It can be stressful sometimes," she adds. "There are so many federal regulations."

The technician needs to handle heavy workloads, pressure to get things done rapidly, and constant interruption. "It's stressful," Terri Young says, "because people want things immediately. They don't take no for an answer." The phone rings constantly, she says, with requests to have records retrieved, prepared, copied, and faxed. It is also important for the technician to be able to deal with sometimes trying personalities. "Doctors get frustrated," Terri says, "and tempers flare at you, even if it's not your fault." She adds that technicians need to react in a professional manner and avoid taking things personally.

What Terri likes most about her job is that it is challenging. She enjoys the detailed work and the opportunity for growth. "I have learned a great deal by working here," she says. She has worked in several different capacities since she started in the medical records department. The department itself has become more computerized and automated. Terri agrees with Susan that being adaptable to change is very important for a technician.

She also thinks it is important to have a strong interest in the medical field. "I think that a lot of people have a desire to work in the medical field, but they don't want to deal with the actual patients," she says. "This job would fulfill that need." Discretion and tact are also a must, Terri cautions. Medical records are confidential, and maintaining a patient's privacy is an important aspect of this job. "If it's in a file, it's confidential, no matter what," says Terri. "You have to remember that you heard it here, not on the street corner."

How Do I Become a Medical Record Technician?

Susan became interested in the medical records profession soon after she left high school. She heard that job openings were plentiful in this occupation, so she enrolled in a two-year medical records program at a vocational school. After earning an associate's degree, she completed several internships, which gave her experience in various aspects of the profession.

To prepare for a career in medical records, Susan recommends taking high school classes in computers, anatomy, physiology, medical terminology, and pharmacology. She didn't take specific preparatory classes in high school, because at that time she hadn't decided what career she wanted to pursue, but her classes in biology, chemistry, and computers proved helpful.

Terri Young became interested in health information management because two of her older cousins were record technicians. "They just loved it," she says. "They were always talking about their jobs." Terri decided when she was still in high school that she wanted to be a medical record technician. She earned an associate's degree from a junior college that offered an accredited program, then took the test to become accredited. She says her classes were challenging and enjoyable, good preparation for the examination.

EDUCATION

High School

Students contemplating a career in medical records should take as many high school English classes as possible, because technicians need both written and verbal communication skills to prepare reports and communicate with other health care personnel. Basic math or business math is very desirable because statistical skills are important in some job functions. Biology courses help by familiarizing the student with the terminology that medical record technicians use. Other science courses, computer training, typing, and office procedures are also helpful.

Postsecondary Training

Most employers prefer to hire medical record technicians who have completed a two-year associate's degree program accredited by the American Medical Association's Commission on Accreditation of Allied Health Education Programs (CAAEHP) and the American Health Information Management Association (AHIMA). There are approximately 175 of these accredited programs available throughout the United States, mostly offered in junior and community colleges. They usually include classroom instruction in such subjects as anatomy, physiology, medical terminology, medical record science, word processing, medical aspects of record keeping, statistics, computers in health care, personnel supervision, business management, English, and office skills.

In addition to classroom instruction, the student is given supervised clinical experience in the medical records departments of local health care facilities. This provides you with practical experience in performing many of the functions learned in the classroom and with the opportunity to interact with health care professionals.

CERTIFICATION OR LICENSING

Medical record technicians who have completed an accredited training program are eligible to take a national qualifying examination to earn the credential of Registered Health Information Technician (RHIT). Most health care institutions prefer to hire individuals with an RHIT credential as it signifies that they have met the standards established by the AHIMA as the mark of a qualified health professional.

Technicians who have achieved the RHIT credential are required to obtain 20 hours of continuing education credits every two years in order to retain their RHIT status. These credits may be obtained by attending educational programs, participating in further academic study, or pursuing independent study activities approved by the AHIMA.

AHIMA also offers the following certifications for technicians who complete advanced education and pass a national certification examination: Registered Health Information Administrator, Certified Coding Specialist, and Certified Coding Specialist-Physician Based.

SCHOLARSHIPS AND GRANTS

AHIMA has a foundation that offers scholarships and loans to health information management students. Undergraduate applicants may qualify for loans up to $2,000. The foundation also bestows a number of scholarships, ranging in amount from $1,000 to $5,000. For details, contact AHIMA (see "How Do I Learn More?").

Who Will Hire Me?

When Terri Young graduated from her two-year college program, she put together a resume and started looking for a job. She responded to an ad in her hometown newspaper for a medical record technician's position at the local hospital. After two interviews and a nerve-wracking two weeks, she was offered the job. Her first duty was to transfer some of the older records to microfilm for storage. "I worked way in the back," she says, "and never even saw any current records at first."

About 37 percent of medical record technicians in the United States worked in hospitals in 2002, according to the U.S. Department of Labor. Most of the others work in other health care settings, such as nursing homes, group medical practices, health maintenance organizations, outpatient clinics, surgery centers, or veterinary hospitals. There are also technicians who work for insurance companies and accounting and law firms that deal with health care issues. Public health care departments also use medical record technicians to help collect and research data from health care institutions.

If you are graduating from an associate's degree program, your school placement office might help you find a job. You may also want to apply directly to the personnel departments of local hospitals, nursing homes, and outpatient clinics. Checking newspaper classified ads is also a good idea, since they often list medical record technicians' job openings.

Some publications geared specifically to the health information management field carry classified advertising, including job listings. Also, the American Health Information Management Association (AHIMA) offers a resume referral service to its members. The technician can send the AHIMA office a resume, which will be kept on file and faxed to employers who have notified AHIMA of job opportunities (see "How Do I Learn More?").

Where Can I Go from Here?

"The jobs are there, everywhere," says Susan. "You can go overseas. You could go to Saudi Arabia for a year, or Hawaii. There's a lot you can do with this degree."

She explains that medical record technicians have the option of working for companies that assign them to temporary jobs almost anywhere in the nation or in other countries, with travel and lodging allowances included. Some technicians work as consultants, teaching other technicians how to do coding and other tasks that require specialized skills. Others are assigned to temporary, contract jobs. Some freelance or work as independent contractors, typically coding records on a hospital's computer system.

Susan has worked at Saint Patrick Hospital for more than a year and says the hospital's progressive medical records department offers her an excellent opportunity to learn the latest technology, a real advantage if she ever wants to make a career move elsewhere. "This is my first real coding job," she comments. "I really like it. I could leave here and get a job almost anywhere."

In contrast, Terri has spent over seven years in the medical records department of her hospital and has worked in almost every phase of the record-keeping process. She feels she may have exhausted the new frontiers available within the department and is currently taking classes in transcription. She plans to run a doctors' transcription service from her home eventually.

For the technician who works in a large health care facility, advancement may mean becoming a *section supervisor* and overseeing the work of the others in the section. Another way to climb the ladder is to specialize in an area such as coding.

Better advancement and higher pay are possible for the technician who goes back to school. Those with a bachelor's degree in medical record administration, along with AHIMA accreditation, can become department directors or assistant department directors. Because of the shortage of medical record administrators, hospitals often make it easy for technicians to get their bachelor's degree by giving them financial aid and time off to go to class.

What Are the Salary Ranges?

According to a 2000 membership survey by the American Health Information Management Association (AHIMA), 67 percent responding earned between $20,000 and $39,000 annually. A little over 11 percent of the respondents earned between $40,000 and $49,000, while 6.7 percent earned between $50,000 and $74,999. The *Occupational Outlook Handbook* reports that health information technicians had median annual earnings of $23,890 in 2002. Those in the middle 50 percent earned between $19,550 and $30,600 annually. The lowest paid 10 percent earned less than $16,460, and the highest paid 10 percent earned more than $38,640. A review of medical records technicians' earnings in 2005 by Salary.com found that the median earnings nationwide were $30,332. The lowest paid earned $27,190, while the highest paid earned $33,346.

Most full-time positions in health information management include a benefits package. Health care insurance, paid vacations and holidays, pension plans, and sick leave are commonly offered.

What Is the Job Outlook?

Employment prospects for medical record technicians are excellent. The U.S. Department of Labor predicts that employment in this field will grow by 44 percent in the next decade. The demand for well-trained medical record technicians will grow rapidly and will continue to exceed the supply. This expectation is related to the health care needs of a population that is both growing and aging and the trend toward more technologically sophisticated medicine and greater use of diagnostic procedures. It is also related to the increased requirements of regulatory bodies that scrutinize both costs and quality of care of health care providers.

Advancement Possibilities

Tumor registrars compile and maintain records of patients who have cancer to provide information to physicians and for research studies.

Medical record administrators plan, develop, and administer health information management systems for health care facilities; develop procedures for documenting, storing, retrieving, and processing patient information; supervise staffs; and analyze patient data.

Utilization-review coordinators analyze patient records to determine legitimacy of treatment and the patient's hospital stay to comply with government and insurance reimbursement policies. They also review applications for patient admission, abstract data from records, maintain statistics, and determine patient review dates.

Medical billing service owners use special software to help doctors and other health care professionals get payment for services. They send bills to patients, private insurance companies, Medicare, and other insurers. Most billers work from their home offices, though some work in the offices of doctors and clinics.

Because of the fear of medical malpractice lawsuits, doctors and other health care providers are documenting their diagnoses and treatments in greater detail. Also, because of the high cost of health care, insurance companies, government agencies, and courts are examining medical records with a more critical eye. These factors combine to ensure a healthy job outlook for medical record technicians.

Technicians with associate's degrees and RHIT status will have the best prospects, and the importance of such qualifications is likely to increase.

How Do I Learn More?

PROFESSIONAL ORGANIZATIONS

For information on earnings, careers in health information management, and RHIT accreditation, contact

American Health Information Management Association
233 North Michigan Avenue, Suite 2150
Chicago, IL 60601-5800
312-233-1100
info@ahima.org
http://www.ahima.org

For a list of schools offering accredited programs in health information management, contact

Commission on Accreditation of Allied Health Education Programs
American Medical Association
35 East Wacker Drive, Suite 1970
Chicago, IL 60601-2208
312-553-9355
caahep@caahep.org
http://www.caahep.org

BIBLIOGRAPHY

The following is a sampling of materials relating to the professional concerns and development of medical record technicians:

Careers in Focus: Medical Technicians. 4th ed. New York: Facts On File, 2004.

Goldberg, Jan. *Medical Record Technician (Careers Without College)*. Mankato, Minn.: Capstone Press, 1999.

McMiller, Kathryn. *Being a Medical Records Clerk/Health Information Clerk*. 3d ed. New York: Prentice Hall, 2003.

Rudman, Jack. *AMRA Medical Record Technician National Registration Examination*. Susosett, N.Y.: National Learning Corporation, 1997.

MEDICAL TECHNOLOGISTS

Reflecting on his 52-year career as a medical technologist and the importance of the profession, Patrick Cuviello says, "My personal feeling is that physicians can't practice medicine without the lab. Technologists help physicians either confirm a patient's diagnosis or help make the diagnosis." He continues, "It takes a special person to go into any medical profession, and medical technologist is as much a profession as nursing, pharmacy, or medical doctors."

Definition
Medical technologists are health professionals who perform laboratory tests to help physicians detect, diagnose, and treat diseases in patients.

Alternative Job Titles
Clinical laboratory technologist

High School Subjects
Biology
Chemistry

Personal Skills
Helping/teaching
Technical/scientific

Salary Range
$31,400 to $44,400 to $60,800

Minimum Educational Requirements
Bachelor's degree

Certification or Licensing
Recommended (certification)
Required by some states (licensing)

Outlook
About as fast as the average

DOT
078

GOE
14.05.01

NOC
3219

O*NET-SOC
29-2011.00

What Does a Medical Technologist Do?

Working under the direction of laboratory managers and pathologists, *medical technologists* perform a variety of laboratory tests that help physicians detect, diagnose, and treat diseases in their patients.

Medical technologists typically work in five major areas: blood banking, chemistry, hematology, immunology, and microbiology. Regardless of their area of work, medical technologists ensure the quality of laboratory tests performed for diagnosis of disease. They also may be responsible for interpreting the test data and results and reporting that information to a patient's physician. Many technologists assist physicians when they compare lab test results with clinical data to recommend a proper course of additional tests or series of tests.

Which duties are assigned to medical technologists is usually determined by the setting in which they work. Those employed by small labs usually conduct a large variety of tests, such as blood counts, urinalyses, and chemical analyses of blood and body fluids. Microscopes are used to study body fluids and tissue samples to determine the presence of bacteria, fungi, and other organisms. On occasion technologists prepare slides from tissue samples and body cells to check for the presence of diseases such as cancer.

Depending on the laboratory's needs, a medical technologist also may be responsible for operating sophisticated medical instruments and equipment, conducting research, and performing minor repairs to the instruments and equipment used in testing.

Unlike their counterparts in small labs who perform a range of tests and complete a variety of duties, medical technologists employed by large laboratories typically specialize in just one area of testing.

What Is It Like to Be a Medical Technologist?

Patrick has been a certified medical technologist with the American Medical Technologists (AMT) for 52 years. Although he has retired from his work in a hospital laboratory, he remains active in the profession, working as an adjunct professor in the medical laboratory technology department of Navarro College in Corsicana, Texas, where he teaches future medical

To Be a Successful Medical Technologist, You Should . . .

- be accurate and patient
- be able to work under pressure
- get along with people and work well as part of a team
- have good manual dexterity
- have good eyesight

technicians. He is also chairman of the AMT Education, Qualification, and Standards Committee, and he is president of the AMT Institute for Education.

When he was a practicing medical technologist, Patrick says, "I was a lab director and had an office in the hospital, but I also did bench work. I ran tests in the lab, all of the blood tests, chemical analysis, microbiology to find the type of infection and bacteria causing the problem and the proper antibiotics to treat it, blood matching for transfusions."

As part of his job, Patrick said he had direct contact with patients and physicians. He also worked closely with each department of the hospital, including with nurses and pharmacists.

Patrick says the work was rewarding and gave him a sense of accomplishment knowing he was helping people. "I enjoyed working with patients and doctors, knowing I was part of the team that helped get patients back to health."

The most difficult aspect of the job for Patrick was accepting that there were patients who could not be helped. "The hard part is knowing the [medical] team has done all it can and the patient doesn't recover."

Do I Have What It Takes to Be a Medical Technologist?

Patrick says that a good medical technologist "first must be dedicated. This isn't an 8 to 5 job." You must be willing to work the necessary hours to provide good patient care. "You also must be compassionate and able to relate to the patients," he continues, "and you have to be honest, sincere, able to get along well with people, and be able to work as part of a team."

Because accurate test results are critical to positive outcomes in patient care, a good medical technologist must possess the skills of accuracy, patience, and an ability to work well under pressure. Technologists should be able to communicate with other members of the medical team, including doctors, nurses, and pharmacists. And because technologists' work involves testing tissue, blood, and other body fluids you need to be comfortable handling those things.

The course of study to be a medical technologist can be difficult and demanding, so those planning to pursue a career in this profession should have above average scholastic abilities.

How Do I Become a Medical Technologist?

"I earned a bachelor's degree in biology with a split minor in chemistry and English," Patrick says, "Then I did two years of additional training after college in a veterans hospital and got a master's degree in biology: zoology and botany."

Lingo to Learn

Andrology A branch of medicine that studies male diseases, especially those affecting reproduction.

Bacteriology A science that studies bacteria as it relates to medicine, industry, and agriculture.

Embryology The branch of biology that studies embryos and their development.

Hematology A science that studies the blood and blood-forming organs.

Immunohematology The branch of immunology (the study of the immune systems) concerned with the immunologic properties of blood.

Microbiology The branch of biology that studies microscopic life forms.

Virology The study of viruses and viral diseases.

In-depth

History

The history of clinical laboratory work and of medicine are intertwined. In the late 19th century, medical specialties such as bacteriology were developing rapidly, creating a need for people to work in laboratories full time. To meet the growing demand for laboratory workers, in the early 20th century physicians began training their assistants to perform some of the more frequently used lab procedures. Because the quality of the work by assistants varied greatly, in the 1930s efforts were made to develop standardized training programs for medical technologists. Since that time, medical laboratory technologists have become an important part of the health care system. It is estimated that approximately 150,000 medical technologists were employed in the United States in 2002 and that number is expected to grow to 178,900 by 2012.

EDUCATION

High School

If you are interested in a career as a medical technologist you should take college preparatory classes while in high school. Science courses that include laboratory work such as biology and chemistry will be beneficial. Also take algebra, calculus, and other math courses, and computer science classes. Courses in English will help develop your research and writing skills.

Postsecondary Training

A number of colleges and universities offer bachelor's degree programs in medical technology and clinical laboratory science. The first two or three years of a typical program will include studies in chemistry, biology, math, physiology, psychology, English, and statistics. The final year, studies are focused on the specific skills of medical technologists. During this time you will take classes such as immunohematology, clinical chemistry, and virology. You will also complete an internship in a medical center or hospital laboratory affiliated with the program to gain hands-on experience. Courses in management, business, and computer science may be part of the program as well.

A list of schools in the United States offering accredited programs for medical technologists is available from the National Accrediting Agency for Clinical Laboratory Sciences (NAACLS).

CERTIFICATION OR LICENSING

Some states and Puerto Rico require that medical technologists be licensed or registered. Because requirements vary by state and other states may adopt new licensing laws you need to check with your state's department of health or occupational licensing board for information about your area.

Whether or not the state where you practice requires licensing, certification is highly recommended for those who wish to advance in this profession. Also, some employers will not hire medical technologists who are not certified.

For certification as a medical technologist (MT) candidates must meet educational and experience requirements and pass exams. Organizations that certify medical technologists include the Board of Registry of the American Society for Clinical Pathology (ASCP), the American Medical Technologists (AMT), and the American Association of Bioanalysts (AAB). Certification as a clinical laboratory scientist (CLS) is offered by the National Credentialing Agency for Laboratory Personnel.

SCHOLARSHIPS AND GRANTS

Scholarships are offered by numerous professional organizations for qualified students enrolled in accredited medical technologist or clinical labortory programs. Among the organizations that offer scholarships are the American Association for Clinical Chemistry (AACC), which awards fifty $1,000 scholarships annually, and the AMT, which grants five $500 scholarships each year. A list of organizations that award scholarships also is available from the American Society for Clinical Laboratory Science (ASCLS) and the NAACLS. Information about federal student assistance programs, including scholarships and loans, is available from the U.S. Department of Health and Human Services at http://bhpr.hrsa.gov/dsa.

INTERNSHIPS AND VOLUNTEERSHIPS

Medical technologists are required to complete a one-year internship as part of their education, which are arranged by the schools. Volunteering in a hospital or medical facility, while you may not be in a laboratory analyzing samples, will give you an opportunity to experience what it is like to work in that environment.

Because some people are uncomfortable handling blood and other body fluids as required by the job, Patrick strongly advises anyone considering a career as a medical technologist "to go to a hospital or clinical lab and observe to be sure you want to be in this profession. See first hand what is done and be sure this is for you." He also suggests attending job fairs and talking with people who are working as medical technologists.

Who Will Hire Me?

Although most medical technologists work in hospitals, other employers include clinics, physicians' offices, pharmaceutical laboratories, public health agencies, and research institutions. The federal government hires medical technologists to work in Veterans Affair hospitals or for the U.S. public health service.

Medical technologists also may choose to concentrate in specific areas such as veterinary science, epidemiology study and application, or diagnostic equipment research. Technologists may find work in crime labs, as sales representatives for pharmaceutical companies, and as teachers in colleges.

"With the changes in science and the development of the equipment used, individuals with training can work in many fields. There are many opportunities besides hospitals and clinics," Patrick says.

Most colleges and universities offer placement services for graduates, and professional organizations typically maintain a list of job openings. Trade journals are also a resource for finding employment opportunities.

Patrick says that internships completed by students may lead to jobs as well. "Often internships can lead to positions in that hospital or clinic because they know the student's work and he's trained already."

ADVANCEMENT OPPORTUNITIES

Chemistry or **biochemistry technologists** test samples of blood, urine, gastric juices, and spinal fluid to detect the presence of chemicals, drugs, and poisons. They also check the levels of substances made by the body such as sugar, albumin, and acetone. The information gathered is used to diagnose diabetes and other metabolic diseases.

Microbiology or **bacteriology technologists** test specimens for the presence of microorganism, including viruses, fungi, bacteria, and parasites. The results of the tests help determine the proper treatment of a condition in a patient.

Clinical laboratory directors usually hold an M.D., Ph.D., or D.O. They oversee the laboratory or laboratory department and supervise the staff of medical technologists. Directors also assign job duties, hire and fire staff, and establish the laboratory work rules and standards.

Clinical laboratory and **medical technology supervisors** manage the laboratory staff on a day-to-day basis by assigning work schedules and projects, reviewing staff work and lab results, and may assist in staff training and continuing education.

Chief medical technologists supervise the work of the entire laboratory operations, assigns duties, and reviews reports and analyses.

Where Can I Go from Here?

Medical technologists may advance their careers by obtaining advanced degrees and specializing in one area of expertise. For example, a medical technologist who gains advanced skills and specializes in cell marker technology, biogenetics, or product development will probably receive a higher salary and greater job responsibilities.

Experienced medical technologists with certification and additional training may advance to a supervisory position. Advancement opportunities for supervisory positions such as chief medical technologist are best in large hospitals or large independent laboratories.

What Are the Salary Ranges?

According to the U.S. Department of Labor, in 2003 the median annual salary for medical and clinical laboratory technologists was $44,400, with the middle 50 percent earning between $37,800 and $53,000. The lowest paid 10 percent earned $31,400 annually, and the highest paid earned more than $60,800.

Benefits vary by employer, but most provide paid vacation time, sick leave, and health insurance.

What Is the Job Outlook?

Employment is expected to grow about as fast as the average for all occupations through 2012 despite fewer job openings for medical technologists in hospital laboratories, according to the U.S. Department of Labor. Demand for laboratory tests will increase as new tests are introduced. Employment opportunities are expected to grow in medical and diagnostic laboratories, physicians' offices, ambulatory health care centers, and blood and organ banks.

Patrick Cuviello says that during his long career as a medical technologist "there has always been a shortage of technologists," which concurs with a 2002 survey by the American Society of Clinical Pathologists that reported nearly half of all labs with openings for medical technologists were having difficulty filling the positions.

How Do I Learn More?

PROFESSIONAL ORGANIZATIONS

For information about medical and clinical laboratory technologist careers, employment opportunities, accredited schools, and certification contact the following organizations:

American Association for Clinical Chemistry
2101 L Street, Suite 202
Washington, DC 20037-1558
800-892-1400
info@aacc.org
http://www.aacc.org

American Association of Bioanalysts
906 Olive Street, Suite 1200
St. Louis, MO 63101-1434
314-241-1445
aab@aab.org
http://www.aab.org

American Medical Technologists
710 Higgins Road
Park Ridge, IL 60068
800-275-1268
http://www.amt1.com

American Society for Clinical Laboratory Science
6701 Democracy Boulevard, Suite 300
Bethesda, MD 20817
301-657-2768
http://www.ascls.org

American Society for Clinical Pathology
2100 West Harrison Street
Chicago, IL 60612
312-738-1336
info@ascp.org
http://www.ascp.org

National Accrediting Agency for Clinical Laboratory Sciences
8410 West Bryn Mawr Avenue, Suite 670
Chicago, IL 60631
773-714-8880
info@naacls.org
http://www.naacls.org

National Credentialing Agency for Laboratory Personnel
PO Box 15945-289
Lenexa, KS 66285
913-438-5110, ext. 4647
nca-info@goamp.com
http://www.nca-info.org

BIBLIOGRAPHY

The following is a list of materials with information relevant to the profession of medical technologist:

Chaskey, Cheryl R. et al. *Opportunities in Clinical Laboratory Science Careers.* New York: McGraw-Hill, 2002.

Graves, Linda. *Case Studies in Clinical Laboratory Science*. Paramus, N.J.: Prentice Hall, 2002.

Nicoll, Diana et al. *Pocket Guide to Diagnostic Tests*. 4th ed. New York: McGraw-Hill, 2004.

Polansky, Valerie Dietz. *Medical Laboratory Technology: Pearls of Wisdom*. 2d ed. Lincoln, Neb.: Boston Medical Publishing, 2002.

Springhouse. *Diagnostic Tests: A Prescriber's Guide to Test Selection and Interpretation*. Philadelphia: Lippincott Williams & Wilkins, 2003.

MICROELECTRONICS TECHNICIANS

Definition
Microelectronics technicians assist in the development, construction, and testing of microchips and electronic instruments using microchips.

Alternative Job Title
Electronics technicians
Semiconductor processors and technicians

High School Subjects
Computer science
English
Mathematics

Personal Skills
Mechanical/manipulative
Technical/scientific

Salary Range
$19,430 to $27,480 to $40,770+

Minimum Educational Level
Some postsecondary training

Certification or Licensing
Voluntary

Outlook
Decline

DOT
590

GOE
N/A

NOC
9483

O*NET-SOC
N/A

As a microelectronics technician, Devin Burdge tests SD-RAM memory chips produced by IBM. Though he doesn't make improvements to the chips, he does help to identify any problems with the design. "Very rarely do you get a chip that is perfect," he says. "Fairly recently we had a design that was not working properly. We were able to internally probe points on the chip." This involved the use of a microscope that allows for the testing of a chip while it is still on the wafer (the original disk from which individual chips will be cut). "We looked at the signals, and working with one of the designers, we were able to find the problem. They went back and redesigned the tool that actually prints the image onto the wafer as the circuit is being built. Usually any repairs like that are done by the design team, with a little bit of help from us to characterize the fail."

What Does a Microelectronics Technician Do?

Today, nearly every area of industry, manufacturing, entertainment, health care, and communications uses electronics to improve the quality of people's lives. The book you are reading, for example, was created by people using electronic equipment, from the writing of each article, to the design, layout, and production of the book itself.

The earliest electronic systems depended on electron vacuum tubes to conduct current. But these devices were too bulky and too slow for many of their desired tasks. In the early 1950s, the introduction of microelectronics, that is, the design and production of integrated circuits and products using integrated circuits, allowed engineers and scientists to design faster and smaller electronic devices. Initially developed for military equipment and space technology, integrated circuits have made possible such everyday products as personal computers, microwave ovens, and DVD players and are found in nearly every electronic product that people use today.

This reliance on technology has created a need for skilled personnel to design, construct, test, and repair electronic components and products. The increased use of microelectronics has created a corresponding demand for technicians specially trained to assist in the design and development of new applications of electronics technology.

Microelectronics technicians typically work closely with electronics engineers, who design the components, to build, test, and prepare the component or product for large-scale manufacture. Usually microelectronics technicians work with microchips, which contain tiny electronic systems called integrated circuits. A microchip may be smaller than a fingernail but contain many thousands of electronic components, including transistors, resistors, and capacitors, that have been arranged to perform specific functions. The microelectronics technician works with the engineer to design and develop components that require the integrated operation of several or many different types of chips.

Microelectronics technicians generally work from a schematic received from the design engineer. The schematic contains a list of the parts that will be needed to construct the component and the layout for the technician to follow. The technician gathers the parts and prepares the materials to be used. Following the schematic, the technician constructs the component and then uses a variety of sophisticated, highly sensitive equipment to test the component's performance. One such test measures the component's "burn-in time." During this test the component is kept in continuous operation for a long period of time, and the component and its various features are subjected to a variety of tests to be certain the component will stand up to extended use.

If the component fails to function according to its required specifications, the microelectronics technician must be able to troubleshoot the design, locating where the component has failed and replacing one part for a new or different part. Test results are reported to the engineering staff, and the technician may be required to help evaluate the results and prepare reports based on these evaluations. In many situations, the microelectronics technician works closely with the engineer to solve any problems arising in the component's operation and design.

After the testing period, the microelectronics technician is often responsible for assisting in the technical writing of the component's specifications. These specifications are used for integrating the component into new or redesigned products, or for developing the process for the component's large-scale manufacture. The microelectronics technician helps develop the production system for the component and also writes reports on the component's functions, uses, and performance.

Microelectronics technicians perform many of the same functions of *electronics technicians* or *semiconductor technicians,* but generally work only in the development laboratory. More experienced technicians may assume greater responsibilities and work even more closely with the engineering staff to develop layout and assembly procedures. They use their own knowledge of microelectronics to suggest changes in circuitry or installation, often with an eye on simplifying the assembly or maintenance requirements. After making any changes, they test the performance of the component, analyze the results, and suggest and perform further modifications to the component's design. Technicians may fabricate new parts using various machine tools, supervise the installation of the new component, or become involved in training and supervising other technical personnel.

Some microelectronics technicians specialize in the fabrication and testing of semiconductors and integrated circuits. These technicians are usually called *semiconductor development technicians.* They are involved in the development of prototype chips, following the direction of engineering staff, and perform the various steps required for making and testing new integrated circuits.

Lingo to Learn

Capacitor An element in an electrical circuit used to store a charge temporarily.

Conductor A substance that conducts an electrical charge.

Insulator A material that does not conduct electricity.

Integrated circuit A tiny chip of material imprinted or etched with many interconnected electronic components.

Microchip, or chip A tiny slice of semiconducting material processed to hold specific electrical properties in order to be developed into an integrated circuit. Also refers to an integrated circuit.

Resistor A device that provides resistance, used to control electric current.

Schematic A diagram that provides structural and/or procedural information on the construction of an electrical or mechanical system.

Semiconductor The basic component of microchips. A solid, crystalline substance (especially silicon in electronics) with conducting properties between true conductors and insulators.

Transistor A small, electronic device used in a circuit as a switch, detector, or an amplifier.

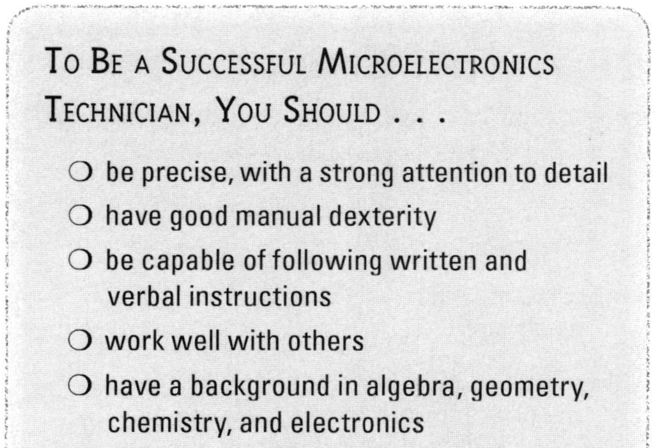

To Be a Successful Microelectronics Technician, You Should . . .

- be precise, with a strong attention to detail
- have good manual dexterity
- be capable of following written and verbal instructions
- work well with others
- have a background in algebra, geometry, chemistry, and electronics
- have good communications skills, including writing and reading comprehension

What Is It Like to Be a Microelectronics Technician?

Devin Burdge works in a laboratory at IBM, assisting in the design of SD-RAM memory chips. "When my department gets a new design," Devin says, "we debug the design, verify it, and make sure it does what we designed it to do. Once we get the design up and running, we start cutting wafers up and building chips and modules out of them." The technicians rely on a series of tests that have been developed by IBM to assure that the product is functioning. "Sometimes the product doesn't pass these tests. In that case, it would come back to us and we're responsible for figuring out why it's not passing the test, what kind of problems with the chip are causing it to fail all these tests."

Devin explains that redundancies are built into every SD-RAM chip. "So if you have cells that are not working properly, or a column or rows that aren't working properly, you can fuse the chip to use some of these redundant columns or rows. A lot of times you're using redundant rows and columns to make a flawed chip a perfect chip that can be sold. When we get chips that are failing, we characterize the fail, then design a test that will allow us to capture the fail during the build process so we can repair the fail with some of the redundancy that's built into the chip."

Devin uses "bench testers" that are run through PCs. "A lot of times we're sitting in a chair at a PC, writing programs, running programs." These bench testers run programs that put chips through a series of tests. Devin also uses basic test equipment like digital multimeters. "Many of the fails in chips can be caused by extreme heat or cold, so we also have equipment that allows us to heat or cool the chip anywhere from 125 degrees all the way down to minus 15."

Devin must also work at a probing station when doing wafer work. "A wafer can have 200 to 400 chips on it," he says, "depending on the size of the chip. We have probing stations with a microscope that allow us to test a chip while it's still on the wafer. We have tools that allow us to manipulate a microscopic probe to hit internal parts of the chip so that we can look at different signals and see when they might be turning on or off. Much of the time, that will give us an idea why a chip may be failing." In characterizing a fail, Devin is often responsible for writing reports and presenting them to managers.

Though Devin spends some time in an office, most of his time is spent in the lab. He usually works with one other technician, while five or six engineers work in another section of the lab. He works a regular eight-hour workday.

"What I do is very relaxed," Devin says. "You're not constantly rushed. The management at IBM allows you to perform at your own level."

Do I Have What It Takes to Be a Microelectronics Technician?

Testing must be performed with a high degree of precision. When assembling a new component, for example, the microelectronics technician must follow the design engineer's specifications and instructions exactly. Similar diligence and attention to detail are necessary when following the different procedures for testing the new components. "You need to have good reasoning skills," he says, "a good ability to hunt down a problem. It's a lot of diagnostic work."

You should also be capable of learning on the job and of developing an understanding of some complex systems. "The chips themselves are very complicated," Devin says. "It takes two or three years to get a good grasp on what's going on and a definite understanding of how the chips work. It may be disheartening to go into a job wanting to do good work right away, and to find out you don't know what you're doing."

How Do I Become a Microelectronics Technician?

Devin pursued training in electronics after tiring of his previous career in the automotive business. "I was leaning toward computers and programming, the technology industry," he says. He completed a two-year associate's degree program in electronics through the ITT Institute. Continuing education isn't required by his employer, but it is offered. "You're always learning something," he says, "whether it's a new piece of test equipment or a new technology."

You need to have good reasoning skills, a good ability to hunt down a problem. It's a lot of diagnostic work.

FYI

Microelectronics are used in a variety of applications, including

- radar
- microwave technology
- radio
- television
- computers
- calculators
- X rays
- stereos
- compact disc players
- robotics
- space technology
- weapons systems

EDUCATION

High School

High school students interested in microelectronics can begin their preparation by taking courses such as algebra and geometry. If you have taken science courses, especially chemistry and physics, you will have a better chance to enter an apprenticeship program and will be more prepared for postsecondary educational programs. A knowledge of proper grammar and spelling is necessary for writing reports, and you should also develop your reading comprehension. Industrial classes, such as metalworking, wood shop, auto shop, and machine shop, and similar courses in plastics, electronics, and construction techniques, will be helpful in your future career. Another area of study for the prospective microelectronics technician is computers, and you would do well to seek experience in computer technology.

Postsecondary Training

Few employers will hire people for microelectronics technician positions who do not have advanced training. Although some low-skilled workers may advance into technician jobs, employers generally prefer to hire people with higher education. Technician and associate's degree programs are available at many community colleges and at public and private vocational training centers and schools. Many technical schools will be located where the microelectronics industry is particularly active. These schools will often have programs tailored specifically for the needs of companies in their area. Community colleges offer a greater degree of flexibility in that they are able to keep up with the rapid advances and changes in technology and can redesign their courses and programs to meet new requirements. You can expect to study in such areas as mathematics, including algebra, geometry, and calculus, physics, and electronic engineering technology. You may take classes in semiconductor devices, digital electronics, and microelectronics manufacturing. Many schools will require you to take courses in English composition, as well as fulfill other course requirements in the humanities and social sciences.

Another method of entry are three- and four-year apprenticeship programs. These programs generally involve on-the-job training by the employer. You can locate apprenticeship opportunities through your high school guidance office, in listings in local newspapers, or by contacting local manufacturers.

Military service is also an excellent method for beginning an electronics career. The military is one of the largest users of electronics technology and offers training and educational programs to enlisted personnel in many areas of electronics.

Finally, the rapid advancements in microelectronics may make it desirable or even necessary for microelectronics technicians to continue to take courses, receive training, and study various trade journals throughout their careers.

CERTIFICATION OR LICENSING

Certification is not mandatory in most areas of electronics (although technicians working with radio-transmitting devices are required to be licensed by the Federal Communications Commission), but voluntary certification may prove useful in locating work and in increasing your pay and responsibilities. The International Society of Certified Electronics Technicians (ISCET) offers certification testing to technicians with four years of experience and/or schooling, as well as associate level testing of basic electronics for beginning technicians. The ISCET also offers a variety of study and training material to help prepare for the certification tests. Certification is also available from the Electronics Technicians Association International (ETA) and the National Institute for Certification in Engineering Technologies (NICET), which offers four levels of technician certification in electrical/electronics engineering technology.

Who Will Hire Me?

Devin got his first job simply by surfing for listings on the Internet. "I applied for the position online through IBM's Web page," he says.

Microelectronics technicians are employed in a variety of industries, especially those that make use of computer and electronics technologies. Many jobs will be found in those parts of the country where the electronics industry is most heavily concentrated, especially in California, Texas, and Massachusetts. In addition, manufacturers in a wide variety of industries that utilize electronic components, either in their products or in their manufacturing processes, also have need for skilled microelectronics technicians and related personnel.

Some schools may provide job placement services to students completing their degree program or offer on-the-job training as a part of the program. Many companies recruit new hires directly on campus. Newspapers, trade journals, and employment offices are also good sources when looking for job leads.

FYI

According to the Semiconductor Industry Association (SIA), annual industry sales of chips exceeded $200 billion for the first time in 2000. The industry has had a compound annual growth rate of 17 percent over the past 40 years. Much of this growth is explained by the demand for data networking, broadband, wireless, optoelectronics, and personal computers. In 2003 the semiconductor industry manufactured 90 million transistors for every person on Earth and that number is expected to increase to 1 billion transistors per person by 2010.

Where Can I Go from Here?

Microelectronics technicians who choose to continue their education can expect to increase their responsibilities and be eligible to advance to supervisory and managerial positions.

Microelectronics technicians may also choose to enter other, more demanding areas of microelectronics, such as semiconductor development and engineering. Additional education may be necessary; engineers will be required to hold at least a four-year degree in electronics engineering. Continuing educational efforts will help the microelectronics technician keep up with advances in the field.

What Are the Salary Ranges?

According to the *Occupational Outlook Handbook*, the median salary for semiconductor technicians and processors in 2003 was $27,480. The highest paid 10 percent earned $40,770, and the lowest paid 10 percent earned $19,430. The U.S. Department of Labor Occupational Information Network reports that the median annual earnings for electronics engineering technicians were $48,000 in 2003. Those in the top paid 10 percent earned $66,800 annually, while the lowest paid 10 percent earned $28,000. Microelectronics technicians generally work a 40-hour week, although they may be assigned to different shifts or be required to work weekends and holidays. Overtime and holiday pay can usually be expected in such circumstances. Benefits will vary from company to company and according to geographic region.

What Is the Job Outlook?

Jobs opportunities for semiconductor technicians and processors are expected to be on the decline through 2012. This is due to companies importing computer chips and increased automation of fabrication plants. In addition, many domestic companies are moving their fabrication plants overseas where costs are lower. However, electronics and the use of electronics technology will become more and more important to every aspect of people's lives. According to the Semiconductor Industry Association (SIA) the semiconductor industry employs a domestic workforce of approximately 226,000, and there are approximately 70 fabrication facilities in the United States.

Because of the high demand for electronics such as cell phones, game consoles, and handheld computers, the industry has seen shortages of semiconductor chips. Not only are more people purchasing such items, but they're also upgrading more frequently as products improve and prices drop. The job outlook is best for microelectronics technicians with some postsecondary training in electronics or semiconductor technology.

Advancement Possibilities

Electronics engineers research, develop, design, and test electronic components, products, and systems for commercial, industrial, medical, military, and scientific applications.

Electronics test engineers plan, develop, and conduct tests on electronic components, products, and systems, applying knowledge and principles of electronic theory, testing methodology and procedures, and electronics engineering.

Supervisors of electronics processing supervise and coordinate activities of workers engaged in processing electronic components and parts, such as printed circuit boards, electron tubes, and semiconductor devices.

How Do I Learn More?

PROFESSIONAL ORGANIZATIONS

The following organizations can provide news on the latest technology and industry trends, information about education and certification, and employment opportunities:

Electronic Industries Alliance
2500 Wilson Boulevard
Arlington, VA 22201-3834
703-907-7500
http://www.eia.org

Electronics Technicians Association International
Five Depot Street
Greencastle, IN 46135
800-288-3824
eta@eta-i.org
http://www.eta-i.org

Institute of Electrical and Electronics Engineers
Three Park Avenue, 17th Floor
New York, New York 10016-5997
212-419-7900
http://www.ieee.org

International Society of Certified Electronics Technicians
3608 Pershing Avenue
Fort Worth, TX 76109-4527
800-946-0201
info@iscet.org
http://www.iscet.org

National Institute for Certification in Engineering Technologies
1420 King Street
Alexandria, VA 22314-2794
888-476-4238
http://www.nicet.org

Semiconductor Equipment and Material International
3081 Zanker Road
San Jose, CA 95134
408-943-6900
semihq@semi.org
http://wps2a.semi.org/wps/portal

Semiconductor Industry Association
181 Metro Drive, Suite 450
San Jose, CA 95110
408-436-6600
mailbox@sia-online.org
http://www.sia-online.org

BIBLIOGRAPHY

The following is a sampling of materials relating to the professional concerns and development of microelectronics technicians:

Careers in Focus: Technicians. 2d ed. New York: Facts On File, 2004.

Emko, Tod. *Vault Guide to Technology Careers.* New York: Vault Inc., 2004.

Farr, J. Michael. *America's Top Computer and Technical Jobs: Detailed Information on 87 Major Jobs at All Levels of Education and Training.* Indianapolis, Ind.: Jist Publishing, 2002.

Leaver, Keith. *Microelectronic Devices.* River Edge, N.J.: World Scientific, 1997.

Sedra, Adel S., and Kenneth C. Smith. *Microelectronic Circuits.* 5th ed. New York: Oxford University Press, 2003.

Smith, Kenneth C. *Laboratory Explorations for Microelectronic Circuits,* 4th ed. New York: Oxford University Press, 1998.

MORTUARY COSMETOLOGISTS

A baby girl has passed away and mortuary cosmetologist Linda Worthey has the important and sensitive task of preparing the baby for viewing by her parents and loved ones.

"The death of a baby or child is not the natural order of life and, so for me, it is more difficult emotionally," she explains.

Linda gently massages baby lotion on the baby, sprinkles on baby powder, fastens on a diaper, and finally slips the pink dress that her family has provided over her head. She applies minimum cosmetics to the face of the tiny infant. When her work is done, Linda walks to the visitation room to meet the parents of the baby girl. The room has been set up with a rocking chair, a children's lamp, and bassinet before the family arrived.

Linda explains to the family what to expect, specific details on how their baby will look and feel when they caress her. She answers their questions and then excuses herself to get their daughter. Linda wraps the baby in a blanket, walks back to the visitation room, and places her in the waiting arms of the parents.

"It was a very emotional reunion for them," Linda explains later, "and I know it is always comforting for parents to know that we treat their baby or child as if it were our very own."

Definition

A mortuary cosmetologist is a licensed cosmetologist who performs a variety of cosmetic services to prepare a deceased person for funeral services. Mortuary cosmetologists are trained to use products to style or alter the hair, face, or nails to prepare a deceased person for viewing and/or burial.

Alternative Job Title

Desairologists

High School Subjects

Art
Chemistry

Personal Skills

Artistic
Leadership/management

Salary Range

$12,670 to $19,300 to $34,920+

Minimum Educational Level

Some postsecondary training

Certification or Licensing

Required by all states

Outlook

Faster than the average

DOT

339

GOE

N/A

NOC

N/A

O*NET-SOC

39-5012.00

What Does a Mortuary Cosmetologist Do?

Making the deceased appear as they did in life—the way their families want them to be remembered—is no small task. Occasionally, *mortuary cosmetologists*, or *desairologists*, are asked to perform cosmetic services on a person they knew, often a client. But more frequently, mortuary cosmetologists work from a photograph provided by the family. Each situation is different—the quality of the photograph, difficulty of the hairstyle requested, conditions of death such as illness or trauma, and chemicals used in preparation of the body can all make the mortuary cosmetologist's job easier or more difficult.

Sterilizing and embalming chemicals used by funeral home personnel add to the dehydration process that occurs on a body, making the hair very dry and brittle. Also, the hair of decedents who were on medication before their deaths can be very thin and fall out easily when the cosmetologist attempts to cut or style it. In addition to these factors, the simple fact that the person who is being styled is in a horizontal rather than vertical position can be a challenge to a beginning mortuary cosmetologist.

As with most health care and funeral professionals, the initial experience dealing with the deceased usually evokes uneasiness. However, as mortuary cosmetologists gain more experience, the knowledge of the comfort they may provide to a grieving family generally helps offset their own discomfort. Also with experience comes a natural focus on the task at

Lingo to Learn

Catafalque The stand which supports the casket during a funeral service.

Chapel The room of a funeral home in which the service is held.

Embalming Temporarily disinfecting and preserving a dead body by circulating chemicals through the veins, capillaries, and arteries.

Mortuary A funeral home.

Preparation room The area within the funeral home where embalming takes place.

Restorative art Using wax, plaster, and other substances to restore distorted features.

hand. Most mortuary cosmetologists are too busy to dwell on morbid thoughts; rather, their focus is on doing their job well for the sake of the family and the memory of the deceased. In general, mortuary cosmetologists do not handle the deceased beyond the preparations they are asked to make to the hair, face, or nails.

Requests for desairology services for deceased men are infrequent. On occasion, mortuary cosmetologists may be requested for a deceased man, based on the family's request or a trauma or illness requiring camouflage makeup. Because the pores open after death, a transparent makeup is applied to the deceased—men and women alike—in preparation for viewing. This makeup is generally applied by the mortuary cosmetologist.

Most jobs are paid on a commission or per-case basis. In many cases, the funeral home bills the deceased's family for all services provided, even if the funeral home didn't directly provide them—including cosmetology services—so the family has just one bill to worry about. This also is done because the Federal Trade Commission requires funeral homes to disclose their fees to consumers on a general price list. The list includes the category "Other Preparation of Body," which means any preparation made to make the body presentable, including dressing, placing in casket, hair cutting, styling, and makeup.

Mortuary cosmetologists find clients in many different ways. If a mortuary cosmetologist has a relationship with a funeral home, the funeral home director may recommend him or her to a client who inquires about such services. Other clients may hear about a mortuary cosmetologist from their own beauticians, who may not provide such services. Also, mortuary cosmetologists seeking clients may find that listing their services in the yellow pages under funeral services is helpful, as well as leaving their business cards with salons who don't have their own mortuary cosmetologist on staff. Mortuary cosmetologists often do other work, and common places of employment include salons, malls, department stores, cruise ships, nursing homes, beauty supply stores, and cosmetic counters.

Cosmetic procedures are generally done in a well-ventilated, sterile preparation room. Mortuary cosmetologists generally are not left alone with the deceased; a member of the funeral home staff will generally greet the cosmetologist and be present throughout the services if the cosmetologist desires. Mortuary cosmetologists often perform cosmetic procedures to a body on a dressing table. This arrangement makes it easier for a cosmetologist to apply cosmetics and nail polish, as well as style hair.

Morticians, of course, work all hours. Their work depends basically on a person's time of death. Mortuary cosmetologists, on the other hand, may take an occasional call at an odd hour, but generally perform their services at their earliest convenience. A cosmetologist usually has only a day's notice of services needed at a mortuary but can perform cosmetic services during day or evening hours, whatever is convenient.

Many mortuary cosmetologists provide services to several funeral homes, especially in more rural areas, where there are fewer people who specialize in such work. In larger cities, one or two large funeral homes that see a high volume may provide enough business for a mortuary cosmetologist to make a part-time or even full-time income.

What Is It Like to Be a Mortuary Cosmetologist?

Linda Worthey has worked as an office manager and mortuary cosmetologist for Horan & McConaty Funeral Service in the Denver area for over four years.

She appreciates being able to assist with the grieving process, to bring comfort to families, knowing "that I do my part to help a family get through what may be one of the most difficult times they will ever experience," she says.

Linda's day begins at 7:30 A.M. "The mortuary preparation/care department manager assists me in determining the order of the persons that I care for depending on their promise time [the time that families wish to view their loved one; mortuary cosmetologists complete their work one hour in advance of this time]. In most cases, the deceased are already dressed and waiting for me to begin. The first thing that I do is review paperwork to see if a photo was provided to assist me, and if any special instructions were provided by the family. In some cases, the family will provide cosmetics, nail polish, and fragrances. If I do not receive complete instructions from a family, I contact the arranger that met with the family or the family directly and request more information."

Once this work is done, Linda sets up her work area and begins to work on her client. She styles the client's hair, applies cosmetics to exposed areas (areas not covered by clothing), and applies nail color. "In some cases," Linda says, "a haircut, trim, or application of color is required. I also do some limited restoration work. I use wax for minor restoration work; anything major is handled by a licensed embalmer."

Linda is responsible for a number of secondary duties. She must complete a care center prep sheet for each patient. This internal form details the cosmetic work she did on the client. "The more detailed it is, the better," she says, since other workers may need to refer to it if a question arises. Linda's duties also include an occasional trip to a beauty supply house to pick up supplies. "I also pitch in by helping with laundry and other tasks."

Linda's workload varies. She has worked on as few as one person in a day and more than eight on her busiest days. Her work is subject to the choices of the families—some arrange morning or afternoon viewings, while others prefer evening viewings.

Do I Have What It Takes to Be a Mortuary Cosmetologist?

Cosmetology can be a physically and mentally demanding occupation, and the same applies to mortuary cosmetology. Cosmetologists are on their feet much of the day and their work is very "hands-on." Physical endurance in the shoulders and arms, and finger dexterity are important attributes. Much of a cosmetologist's time is spent shampooing, cutting, and styling. Aching shoulders, arms, and even backs are some of the physical challenges cosmetologists may have to face at some time in their careers. A more serious concern for cosmetologists is carpal tunnel syndrome, which occurs when damage is done to nerves in the wrist because of repetitive hand motion.

Other helpful attributes for a cosmetologist include a sense of form and balance, a willingness to keep up with the latest fashions and techniques, and a strong business sense, since many cosmetologists work for themselves or manage shops.

According to Linda, the most important personal traits for a successful mortuary cosmetologist are "dependability, a superior work-ethic, an ability to view and touch a person that is deceased, and most importantly, compassion!" She explains, "This is not my 'job,' but my ministry. If there comes a time that I can't view it as such, I will seek other opportunities."

To Be a Successful Mortuary Cosmetologist, You Should . . .

- be patient, compassionate, and flexible
- pay close attention to details
- be artistic and creative
- enjoy "hands on" work and have good manual dexterity

How Do I Become a Mortuary Cosmetologist?

Linda attended State Beauty School in Colorado Springs, Colorado. After she earned her state license to practice cosmetology, Linda joined the military. After she was discharged, she worked at various jobs. Although she didn't practice cosmetology during those years, she did keep her license current. It was not until she began work at Horan & McConaty

Funeral Service that she began to specialize in mortuary cosmetology via on-the-job training.

EDUCATION

High School

People outside the field of cosmetology are often surprised at the diverse subjects that cosmetology students must learn. High school classes that are part of a college preparatory curriculum are also helpful to students who plan to pursue a career in cosmetology. Tough academic subjects such as physics, chemistry, geometry, and biology provide background that high school students will find valuable years down the road—both in cosmetology school, when they learn specifically how those disciplines apply to their trade, and as practicing cosmetologists, when they use their knowledge to solve problems independently.

At a high school in South Garland, Texas—one of the few high schools in the United States that offers cosmetology programs as part of their vocational curriculum—students study bacteriology to properly sanitize equipment, electricity to clear up skin disorders, and geometry to cut hair with precision.

Of course, classes such as English and oral communications are also helpful to cosmetologists, who deal with a wide variety of people. Students planning to pursue a career in cosmetology should keep in mind that most cosmetology schools require a high school diploma or general equivalency diploma and set a minimum age of 16.

Linda recommends that high school students take speech courses to be able to talk sensitively to the families of the deceased. "Taking a speech class," Linda says, "will benefit anybody in whatever job they do."

Postsecondary Training

Cosmetology schools, still popularly known as beauty schools, prepare students for different careers in cosmetology. Cosmetology school generally requires 1,000 to 1,500 hours of training, which generally can be completed in a year. Many schools have classes starting throughout the year. According to the National Accrediting Commission of Cosmetology Arts and Sciences (NACCAS), no beauty schools currently offer specific program sequences for mortuary cosmetologists. Many schools offer classes on mortuary services as part of their cosmetology curriculum or as part of a funeral services program, but states don't require special licensing for mortuary cosmetologists beyond the standard cosmetology license.

> **FYI**
>
> One commonly held belief about the human body is that the hair and nails continue to grow after death. Actually, the skin around the hair follicles and nail cuticles begins to shrink because of dehydration caused by death and the embalming process. Thus the embedded portions of the hair and nails are exposed, giving the impression that they have grown.

Cosmetology schools offer training that leads to licenses in cosmetology (the full range of beauty services, including hair, skin, and nails), esthetics (which is limited to skin care, facial hair removal, and makeup), or nail technology (which is limited to care for the nails and cuticles on the hands and feet). Students of cosmetology can expect their curriculum to include classes in hair cutting and styling, permanent waves, tinting, eyebrow arching, facials, corrective makeup, manicuring, and pedicuring. These classes generally have students practice their new skills on mannequins or observe demonstrations. As students advance in their skills, they often practice on each other. Theory classes may include state law, chemistry, salon business management, and sterilization and sanitation.

There are cosmetology schools in every state. According to NACCAS, there were approximately 1,000 accredited schools in 2005 serving over 100,000 students. As a rule, general cosmetology internships are part of postsecondary schooling, although they usually are not called internships. Students advance to hands-on training only after they have completed the classroom and theoretical courses. Many cosmetology schools operate their own salons and offer discounted cosmetology services to the public, provided by cosmetology students in a supervised setting. Students observe and perform a specific type and number of procedures on clients to fulfill requirements of the school and the state they wish to practice in.

In addition to passing a written exam, most states require a minimum number of hours of training on live subjects. During school "in-salon training," cosmetologists can expect to work at least 100 hours per month. Situations vary, but many cosmetologists-in-training receive a percentage of the fee for their work. Instructors, in addition to supervising techniques, use this time to give hints on building clientele, such as handing out business cards and explaining other services to the client. This practical experience is vital to launching a successful cosmetology career.

CERTIFICATION OR LICENSING

All 50 states require cosmetologists to be licensed. A person must be licensed as a funeral director or embalmer (except for Colorado, the only state without a funeral home license requirement) to perform cosmetic services on the deceased. In many funeral homes, unless the family requests special services or a certain cosmetologist, funeral home personnel do the necessary cosmetic preparations. Most mortuary schools require a class on restorative art that includes basic hair styling and makeup techniques. Restorative art also covers more difficult body preparation work for bodies that have suffered a trauma, such as makeup to camouflage bruises and scrapes or techniques to rebuild a nose.

Only those who have completed the recommended training are permitted to apply for a cosmetology license. Although requirements vary by state, each state requires an application, generally with a minimal fee, and passage of a written examination. The exam determines the applicant's knowledge of pertinent areas such as product chemistry, sanitary rules and regulations, sanitary procedures, chemical service procedures, knowledge of the anatomy of the skin, provisions and requirements of the state in which they wish to practice, and knowledge of labor and compensation laws.

FYI

The mortuary cosmetologist's role is the last part of the lengthy process of preparing remains for viewing. Before the cosmetologist arrives at the funeral home the deceased is prepared for embalming: The funeral home personnel remove the clothing, inventory and/or secure jewelry, and set the mouth and limbs of the deceased.

- The body is embalmed: A formaldehyde solution is pumped into the carotid artery, while the blood is drained from the jugular vein. After this step (arterial embalming), the internal organs are treated (cavity embalming).
- The deceased is thoroughly washed, including the hair and fingernails, and any necessary shaving is completed.
- The deceased is dressed, cosmetics are applied, hair is styled, and the deceased is placed in a casket (this is usually done by funeral home personnel, not the cosmetologist).

Who Will Hire Me?

Linda Worthey was initially hired as an office manager at Horan & McConaty Funeral Service. "A few months after I started," Linda says, "a dear friend of mine died and I requested to care for her. It was such an honor to be able to give my friend this last gift. After that, I approached the preparation/care department manager about filling in as needed on the weekends, was trained, and have been doing it [mortuary cosmetology] on-call for over four years now."

Mortuary cosmetologists are rarely employed directly by funeral homes, particularly on a full-time basis. Since this area of cosmetology is relatively new, there generally is not yet a strong enough demand for these services to support full-time mortuary cosmetologists. Most are cosmetologists—either self-employed or employed by a salon—who provide mortuary services on a freelance basis. Funeral directors and embalmers are also allowed to provide cosmetic services to the deceased. The

Advancement Possibilities

Funeral directors arrange and direct funeral services.

Funeral home owners are usually licensed funeral directors and embalmers who perform those functions in addition to running a business.Related jobs

The U.S. Department of Labor classifies mortuary cosmetologists under the heading *Barbering, Cosmetology, and Related Service Occupations.* Also under this heading are people who perform electrolysis and give therapeutic massage. Other related jobs incude **beauty consultants, beauty supply distributors, electrolysis technicians, makeup specialists, audio and television stylists,** and **wig specialists.**

outlook for mortuary cosmetology is very good due to the expected increase in the death rate during the coming decades and the growing awareness of and desire for these services. Those who aggressively market themselves to local funeral homes have the best chance of building a full-time career in mortuary cosmetology.

Where Can I Go from Here?

A January 1998 article in the salon trade magazine *Techniques* discussed growth areas in the field of cosmetology, including mortuary cosmetology. The article noted that desairology may not hold the glamour of other cosmetology specialties, such as a stage or film artist, but it offers additional attractions, such as the opportunity to perform humanitarian services. Mortuary cosmetologists who make funeral homes, salons, and the general public aware of the valuable service they provide can help their businesses grow. Mortuary cosmetologists who build a reputation for providing a valuable service can carve a niche for themselves in their area. Becoming a funeral home's or salon's designated desairologist can lead to steady work, which because of its specialized nature, generally pays more than regular cosmetology services.

What Are the Salary Ranges?

The nature of the field of mortuary cosmetology, and indeed the field of cosmetology in general, is that earnings grow only as clientele increases. In any aspect of cosmetology, that means low earnings and hard work in the beginning. As cosmetologists develop client loyalty, their earnings will rise. In the mortuary cosmetologist's case, proving the value of one's services to a funeral home or a salon is the key to higher earnings.

Mortuary cosmetologists charge more for their services to funeral homes than services in a salon. For example, a haircut and style may cost $10 to $20 in many areas. In the same area, a cut and style done on a visit to a funeral home will bring $30 to $40 because it is a specialized service. However, anyone planning to enter the field should remember it is a relatively new and highly specialized career and demand is still somewhat limited. Mortuary cosmetology is not well known to the general public, and with the higher earnings comes the responsibility of marketing one's services to generate business.

The median annual salary of all full-time cosmetologists, both veterans and newcomers alike, was $19,300 in 2003, according to the *Occupational Outlook Handbook*. However, the number of clients and cost of living in a geographic area have an effect on earnings. Those in the lowest paid 10 percent percent earned $12,670 annually, and the top paid 10 percent earned $34,920.

A 2005 review of salaries nationwide by Salary.com found that hairstylists had median annual earnings of $20,777, with the lowest paid earning $17,252, and the highest paid earning $25,512.

What Is the Job Outlook?

The rate of growth for mortuary cosmetology is dependent on two factors: how well those in the cosmetology industry market their services and the age of the population and number of deaths. According to statistics compiled by the National Funeral Directors Association, the death rate per thousand in the U.S. population is expected to increase significantly, from a projected rate of 8.82 deaths per thousand in 2000 to 10.24 deaths per thousand in 2020, and 13.67 per thousand in 2050. As the large baby boomer population ages, all careers that provide services to the elderly population are expected to experience growth that is faster than the average for all other occupations.

Another factor affecting the funeral industry is an increase in the number of cremations. According to the Cremation Association of North America, this number is increasing because of environmental concerns, diminishing religious restrictions, and the lesser expense of preparation. The Association predicts that by 2010 the rate of cremation will reach 42 percent of all deaths, compared to 23.6 percent in 1997. Percentages are lower in smaller communities and regions such as the Midwest and the South where there is more emphasis on tradition. Even in cases of cremation, however, families often opt for traditional services and viewings of the body before cremation, so the services of licensed cosmetologists will still be required.

How Do I Learn More?

PROFESSIONAL ORGANIZATIONS

There are currently no national organizations with a focus on mortuary cosmetology. Funeral organizations such as the National Funeral Directors Association or a state funeral directors association can provide information on "restorative art," the preparation of the deceased for funeral services. The National Accrediting Commission of Cosmetology Arts and Sciences sets the standards for cosmetology schools nationwide and can provide statistics, information on individual schools, and career information. A cosmetology school in your area is a good place to start. Most have brochures that outline their courses, requirements, and costs. State regulatory agencies offer information on licensing and other requirements for each state.

National Accrediting Commission of Cosmetology Arts and Sciences
4401 Ford Avenue, Suite 1300
Alexandria, VA 222303
703-600-7600
http://www.naccas.org

National Funeral Directors Association
13625 Bishop's Drive
Brookfield, WI 53005
262-789-1880
nfda@nfda.org
http://www.nfda.org

BIBLIOGRAPHY

The following is a sampling of materials relating to the professional concerns and development of mortuary cosmetologists:

Charest-Papagno, Noella. *Desairology: Hairstyling of the Deceased*. Hollywood, Fla.: JJ Publishing, 1996

——— *Handbook of Desairology for Cosmetologists Servicing Funeral Homes*. 3d ed. Hollywood, Fla.: JJ Publishing, 1996.

Sacks, Terence J. *Opportunities in Funeral Service Careers*. Lincolnwood, Ill.: VGM Career Horizons, 1997.

Szabo, John F. *Mortuary Science: A Sourcebook*. Lanham, Md.: Scarecrow Press, 2003.

MUSEUM TECHNICIANS

How do you build a museum display that will allow visitors to observe a giant colony of ants living behind large, glass windows and still protect the ants from the killing heat of the desert sun?

For Peter Oftedahl, such a question is all in a day's work. As a museum technician, he designs and constructs the exhibit cases and displays that house collections at the Arizona-Sonora Desert Museum, a combination natural history museum and zoological garden that contains artifacts and animals native to southern Arizona.

Peter mulls over his problem. The glass windows are necessary, because museum visitors must be able to see deep inside the burrow where the harvester ants live. Unfortunately, unless Peter can design a cooling system, the glass will also warm the soil to such an intense temperature that the ants would soon die.

After considering various options, Peter arrives at an inventive solution. Instead of using natural soil inside the display, he'll fill it with an artificial soil made from gypsum cement. And to keep the gypsum cool, he'll install copper tubing through which he can pump cold water. As a final precaution, instead of using regular window glass in the frame, he'll use a specially designed thermal glass that will reflect away much of the damaging and dangerous sunlight, yet still allow museum visitors a close-up view of the ants and their activities.

Definition
Museum technicians help clean, repair, and prepare objects to be displayed in museums. They also build and set up museum displays, including electrical and audiovisual components.

Alternative Job Title
Museum exhibit technicians

High School Subjects
Art
Earth science
History
Technical/shop

Personal Skills
Mechanical/manipulative
Technical/scientific

Salary Range
$20,600 to $36,160 to $66,600

Minimum Educational Level
Some postsecondary training

Certification or Licensing
None

Outlook
About as fast as the average

DOT
102

GOE
12.03.04

NOC
5212

O*NET-SOC
25-4013.00

What Does a Museum Technician Do?

When we go to a museum, most often what we notice are the artifacts or art objects on display. We are awed by the size of the dinosaur skeleton, intrigued by the mummy in a gold sarcophagus, stunned by the beauty of a rare diamond or painting. What we are less likely to notice is how the object or artifact we have admired has been displayed.

The job of the *museum technician* is to create exhibits and displays for a museum's collections. Sometimes it involves the construction of a simple wood and glass display case. It might require the manufacture and installation of special mounting brackets to secure a large, heavy object, such as a dinosaur skeleton. A museum technician might also help rearrange all the exhibits in an entire wing of the museum.

In every instance, the museum technician has two primary responsibilities. The first is to design and construct displays and exhibits that will give viewers an up-close look at a museum's collections. The other responsibility is to protect the artifact or art object. Rare and expensive gemstones must be displayed in ways that will eliminate the possibility of their theft. Fragile or sensitive artifacts might require special dehumidifiers and temperature regulators in their display cases to protect them from environmental damage.

Museum technicians are members of a team of professionals who care for a museum's artifacts and other holdings. Museum technicians work in the museum's collections or exhibits department, designing and building displays and exhibit cases according to plans developed by curators. The job requires skill with hand tools and power tools, such as table saws, sanders, welding equipment, and drill presses. In addition to knowing carpentry skills, museum technicians commonly install plumbing, electrical wiring and lighting fixtures, speakers for interactive exhibits, and other audiovisual equipment. They may specialize as exhibit carpenters or electricians, sound technicians, or graphic artists who make sketches and signs. Sometimes they help curators conduct research related to the museum's holdings or they catalog, label, and file documents.

Museum technicians may also help prepare specimens and arrange them in the museum's exhibits. That might mean using an electric drill to remove bits of stone from the fossilized spine of a woolly mammoth, recreating a missing part of the backbone with modeling clay, or using plaster and glue to make a duplicate of the fossil. The technician might help assemble the skeleton of a saber-toothed tiger and build a mount to hold it in a lifelike position.

Curators oversee collections in museums, zoos, botanical gardens, nature centers, state parks, aquariums, and historic sites. Most hold a master's or doctoral degree and are specialists in the care and preservation of a specific type of artifact, realia, or art object. Many curators have worked their way up to this position after gaining experience in the field as museum technicians.

Conservators coordinate the activities of workers who examine, repair, and display museum holdings. They perform historical research on objects, determine each item's condition, perform any necessary repairs, and generally preserve the holdings in the best possible condition. Conservators usually hold a master's degree in conservation or a related field, along with significant on-the-job experience.

Conservation technicians care for art objects in a museum's collections. They restore art objects to their original or natural appearance. They might also repair damaged art objects and prepare them for display.

Lingo to Learn

Archaeology The scientific study of material remains of past human life and activities.

Artifact Objects created by humans, usually for practical purposes, that are used for study, display, or educational materials. This includes pottery, jewelry, and other objects found in archaeological digs.

Controlled environment An area where relative humidity, light sources, and temperature are observed and regulated.

Dig The site of an archaeological excavation, or unearthing, of historical treasures.

Exhibition A presentation of objects and information.

Fabrication The preparation of mounting and other materials used to display or store objects.

Mount A bracket or support used to display objects safely in an exhibit.

Paleontology A science dealing with fossil remains of life from past geological periods.

Realia Something found in nature, used for display purposes or educational materials, such as feathers or animal skins.

Zoological garden A park or garden where wild animals are kept for exhibition.

What Is It Like to Be a Museum Technician?

The Arizona-Sonora Desert Museum's unique blend of artifacts and living animals presents many unusual challenges for a museum technician. One day Peter might design and construct a display for an inanimate object, such as a mineral, in the museum's Earth Science Center. Another day he might build a display that will house a living animal, as he did for the harvester ants.

A typical day for Peter begins at 8:00 A.M. and ends at 4:30 P.M. During the summer months, when the temperatures can hover near 110 degrees, Peter works from 7:00 in the morning to 3:30 in the afternoon.

To Be a Successful Museum Technician, You Should . . .

- enjoy building and constructing things
- work well with people
- be skilled at problem solving
- have good carpentry skills
- be able to work around fragile and valuable objects

His day usually begins with a tour of the museum's 35 acres of exhibits. Peter examines all exhibits, both indoors and outdoors, to see if they require any maintenance. The problems he encounters most often are burned-out light bulbs in display cases. In the museum's Earth Science Center, there are several projectors and other audiovisual equipment that often need minor maintenance.

Most of the museum's display cases are very small to leave plenty of room for viewers to walk past. "That means I have to crawl into some pretty tight places to service some of the displays. You get dirty," says Peter.

After he has completed his rounds, Peter returns to his workshop in the museum's exhibits office. There he goes over the list of projects requiring the construction of display cases. Peter notes the special features that the museum's exhibits curator needs to have incorporated into each display. These requirements may include materials from which the display should be constructed, whether the artifact will be displayed in a case, on a platform, or mounted to a wall, and whether humidity or temperature regulators should be installed. Peter spends up to six hours of his eight-hour day working on display cases, using a table saw, drill press, sanders, and various hand tools.

In addition to maintaining and fabricating the museum's exhibits, Peter also helps the museum's graphics department develop signs for the exhibits. In the intense Arizona sun, the signage at the outdoor exhibits can bleach out in a matter of weeks. Peter has helped make the signs last longer by placing them between sheets of acrylic.

Peter not only constructs exhibits, sometimes he has to take them apart. Recently, when one of the museum's wolf spiders died, Peter had to open the display case and carefully remove the deceased specimen without disturbing the habitat within the display case.

Do I Have What It Takes to Be a Museum Technician?

Museum technicians are responsible for ensuring that artifacts and art objects are displayed in ways that will both serve the public and protect the objects on display. Since these objects can be priceless works of art or irreplaceable historical artifacts, the museum technician has a weighty and often stressful responsibility.

To do well at this job, you should be creative and able to do moderate lifting and carrying. You will be climbing ladders and working in cramped spaces. At times the work is demanding.

Because many museums have strict financial restraints and cannot afford to have large exhibits departments, museum technicians may find there is more work to do than can be accomplished in a day. "Without a doubt the hardest part of the job is trying to get everything done," says Peter. "It can get very frustrating."

. . . what you find are people who work for the love of the field. They have a real enthusiasm for their work.

However, as Peter can attest, many museum technicians find the rewards of the career outweigh those few complaints. Peter says that one of the greatest rewards of being a museum technician is the opportunity to work on many types of projects. "I love the variety of the work," he says. "You're always faced with problems and have to come up with creative solutions to those problems."

Peter has also found that he enjoys working with curators and other museum employees who pull together as a team to keep the museum operating smoothly. "I've found through my experience that I really like museum people," says Peter. "In general, museums don't pay a lot, so what you find are people who work for the love of the field. They have a real enthusiasm for their work."

How Do I Become a Museum Technician?

Peter has always liked museums. As a child growing up in Detroit, Michigan, he would spend hours at the city's museums gazing at the fossils and other artifacts on display. After graduating from high school he attended the University of Arizona and received a bachelor of science degree in geology. As he neared completion of his degree, Peter decided that he really was not enthused about the job opportunities available to geology majors. Instead of pursuing those limited options, he enrolled in the university's graduate school and worked toward a master's degree in anthropology with a minor in museum studies.

As part of his graduate school requirements, Peter served an internship with a museum in Tucson. It was during this internship that he became interested in how artifacts were displayed and how to construct exhibits.

Peter worked as a museum technician at a facility operated by the Arizona Historical Society, then several years ago, he accepted his current job as a museum technician at the Arizona-Sonora Desert Museum in Tucson.

Peter's educational background is a little unusual because he attended a graduate program before becoming a museum technician. You might be able to find a job in this field if you have only a high school diploma, but two to four years of training at a college or technical-vocational school is necessary for most positions. Any experience you gain as a volunteer, intern, or apprentice will improve your chances of being employed in this competitive occupation.

In-depth

The Legacy of America's Earliest Museums

The first museums in the United States were usually operated by individuals or families. The owner typically performed many tasks, including designing exhibits, preparing specimens, and publicizing the facility.

The first natural history museum in postcolonial North America was the Philadelphia Museum, owned by Charles Willson Peale, who used his skills in saddle making, painting, and taxidermy to construct lifelike displays of mounted specimens against painted backdrops. Peale first exhibited his animal specimens in open displays that allowed visitors to step in close enough to touch them. To protect the exhibits, Peale later built display cases and placed the most valuable specimens in more secure rooms of their own.

Museums today still employ Peale's strategies for displaying their holdings, but many are moving toward a more hands-on experience for visitors.

In some activity centers, also called "junior museums," visitors may observe specimens being prepared, touch items in the displays, and use interactive computer exhibits.

EDUCATION

High School

Shop and vocational courses are recommended to anyone considering a career as a museum technician. These courses can introduce you to many of the tools that museum technicians use when fabricating exhibits. Courses in the natural sciences, mathematics, electronics, electrical wiring, and history are recommended. Because museum technicians have to communicate with other museum professionals on a daily basis, courses in English are also advisable.

Postsecondary Training

There are several colleges and universities that offer programs in the conservation and restoration of artifacts and art objects. These programs can last from six months to two years, and students are often required to work in museums as interns to gain on-the-job experience. A bachelor's degree and studies in archaeology, geology, and paleontology are usually required for technicians who work with fossils. Courses in graphic design, drafting, and engineering are also helpful.

Advancement Possibilities

Conservators coordinate the activities of museum technicians engaged in examination, repair, and conservation of art objects.

Conservation technicians work under the supervision of conservators and complete maintenance work on the collection.

Curators direct and coordinate the activities of workers at exhibiting institutions, such as museums, botanical gardens, arboretums, and art galleries.

Exhibit designers plan, develop, and produce physical displays for exhibitions at museums and similar institutions.

Graphic designers are practical artists whose creations are intended to express ideas, convey information, or draw attention to a product.

Museum registrars keep records of how and where objects in the museum's collections were obtained, their condition, and their location. They also oversee movement, packing, and shipping of objects to conform to insurance regulations.

Museum teachers provide information, share insight, and offer explanations of exhibits.

Continuing education is necessary to keep abreast of new developments in the profession. Historical, archival, and museum associations offer this training through conferences and workshops.

INTERNSHIPS AND VOLUNTEERSHIPS

Competition for museum jobs is always intense, and this increases the importance of gaining work experience as an intern or volunteer. Most museums rely on volunteer workers because of strict financial limitations. Many postsecondary training programs in museum studies require students to complete an internship with a museum. On-the-job experience will help you learn how a museum operates, observe museum technicians at work, and make contacts who can improve your chances of being offered a job. Interns and volunteers who prove their worth and dedication are often hired when paid positions open up.

Who Will Hire Me?

As the position's title implies, museum technicians usually work in our nation's museums. They are most often employed in a museum's collections or exhibits department, which will vary in size and number of employees according to the size of the institution.

The largest employers in the museum industry are art and history museums. Other types of museums and related institutions that employ museum technicians include children's museums, clothing or costume museums, gem and mineral museums, aquariums, zoos, botanical gardens, and living historical sites and farms. Museum technicians may also be employed by private companies that museums hire to install exhibits.

Where Can I Go from Here?

Peter is happy with his current position and employer and hopes to continue working at the Arizona-Sonora Desert Museum. A museum technician's advancement depends greatly upon the size of the museum he or she works for. Larger museums may employ 10 to 20 museum technicians and will therefore have greater opportunities for advancement into supervisory positions than will a museum that employs only one or two museum technicians.

Typically, museums promote current employees into more advanced positions based upon an employee's level of seniority. Often, positions are organized into grades, and advancement to a higher grade requires an employee to have acquired a certain number of years' experience at a lower grade. With each grade an employee advances, there is usually an increase in responsibilities and salary.

Experienced museum technicians can specialize as graphic artists, exhibit designers, art conservators, or restorers. They may also become conservation technicians. With further education, a museum technician might also find employment as a *curator.* Curators tend to have completed a graduate school program and have developed an expertise in a specialized area. They develop plans for displaying and caring for a museum's collections. They also coordinate tours and lectures to educate the public, conduct research, and acquire items for the museum's holdings.

What Are the Salary Ranges?

Salary ranges for museum technicians vary widely from region to region and from museum to museum. Some larger museums, such as the Smithsonian Institution, may have the financial resources to pay their museum technicians more than what technicians would earn at small, local museums that do not receive much funding.

The U.S. Department of Labor reports that the median annual earnings for museum technicians, archivists, and curators were $36,160 in 2003. The lowest paid 10 percent earned $20,600, while the highest paid 10 percent earned $66,600 annually. Those in the middle 50 percent earned between $27,320 and $49,180. Medical and dental insurance, paid vacations and sick leave, and retirement plans vary according to each employer's benefit policies.

What Is the Job Outlook?

Employment opportunities for people who work at museums are expected to increase at a rate about as fast as the average for all occupations through 2012. According to the U.S. Department of Labor *Occupational Outlook Handbook*, archivists, curators, and museum technicians held about 22,000 jobs in 2002. Competition for positions with museums is expected to increase, because many people find the idea of working at a museum an attractive one. Unfortunately, there are a limited number of positions, and vacancies in those positions usually attract a large number of qualified candidates.

Some museums are now saving money by hiring independent, privately owned companies to design and set up exhibits. The number of people employed by these companies has been increasing. Opportunities at federally funded museums have been decreasing.

How Do I Learn More?

PROFESSIONAL ORGANIZATIONS

The following organizations can provider information on careers, accreditation, training and educational programs, conservation specialties, workshops, and publications:

American Association of Museums
1575 Eye Street, NW, Suite 400
Washington, DC 20005
202-289-1818
http://www.aam-us.org

American Institute for Conservation of Historic and Artistic Works
1717 K Street, NW, Suite 200
Washington, DC 20006
202-452-9545
info@aic-faic.org
http://aic.stanford.edu

Intermuseum Conservation Association
2915 Detroit Avenue
Cleveland, OH 44113
216-658-8700
http://www.ica-artconservation.org

International Planetarium Association
PO Box 1812
Greenville, NC 27835
252-328-6218
http://www.ips-planetarium.org

BIBLIOGRAPHY

The following is a sampling of materials related to the professional concerns and development of museum technicians:

Bates, G.W. *Museum Jobs from A-Z: What They Are, How to Prepare, and Where to Find Them.* Jacksonville, Fla.: Batax Museum Publishing, 1994.

Burcaw, George Ellis. *Introduction to Museum Work.* Walnut Creek, Calif.: AltaMira Press, 1997.

Camenson, Blythe. *Opportunities in Museum Careers.* Lincolnwood, Ill.: VGM Career Horizons, 1996.

Careers in Museums: A Variety of Vocations. Washington, D.C.: American Association of Museums, 1994.

Danilov, Victor J. *Museum Careers and Training.* Westport, Conn.: Greenwood Publishing, 1994.

Glaser, Jane R., and Artemis A. Zenetou. *Museums: A Place to Work: Planning Museum Careers.* New York: Routledge, 1996.

MUSIC RECORDING TECHNICIANS

A large window overlooks the main recording room where a group of musicians are busy setting up their equipment. "That guitar sounds horrible," Chris says, speaking into a microphone. "Turn the gain down a bit and add some more treble." He pauses and smiles. "Well, I don't know. Is that the sort of muddy sound you're after? You should listen to it in here. It sounds pretty ugly." He holds the headphones to his ears with one hand and studies for a moment the countless dials, levers, and lights on the control console. He turns a dial. "Hold on a minute, it's the mic, I think. Did someone move it?"

In the recording room he places his hands on his hips and surveys the setup. "We need to move these amps farther apart, and put another barrier between them, they're bleeding too much into each other." He slides a large carpeted makeshift wall in front of one of the guitar amplifiers and adjusts the microphone. "Now please, nobody move this mic. Play that riff again," he says to the guitarist, and walks back to the control room.

Definition
Music recording technicians work with musicians in a controlled studio to record music. They adjust microphones and recording levels to manipulate sounds or entire tracks to musicians' specifications.

Alternative Job Titles
Audio recording engineers
Music recording engineers
Recording studio engineers/technicians
Sound mixers
Sound engineer technicians

High School Subjects
Computer science
Music
Technical/shop

Personal Skills
Mechanical/manipulative
Technical/scientific

Salary Range
$15,480 to $33,430 to $71,930+

Minimum Educational Requirements
High school diploma; two-year degree or apprenticeship recommended

Certification or Licensing
Recommended

Outlook
Little change or more slowly than the average

DOT
194

GOE
01.08.01

NOC
5225

O*NET-SOC
27-4014.00

What Does a Music Recording Technician Do?

No matter how technically proficient the musicians are, and no matter how good the song is, if it is not recorded properly, to the potential of the musicians, the song can end up sounding boring, lifeless, even bad. For many popular recordings today, the *music recording technician* (also frequently called *engineer*) is often, if he or she does the job well, an additional member of the band. Recording technicians play a very significant role in how the end product sounds. They have control of every sound, every level, every intensity of the final recording, and when all is said and done, they can be responsible, in many ways, for the success of the recording.

Ultimately, of course, it is the music that counts, and how the musicians and producers direct the recording technician to work. However, if a trumpeter says he wants a particular sound from his instrument, or a guitarist needs that extra fullness, or a producer wants a livelier mood in the mix, it is up to the recording technician to find that sound, that feeling, or intensity. They must be the interpreter between the musician as artist and the recording technology, and when the languages don't translate literally, they must come up with close approximations.

Music recording technicians work in specially designed, soundproof studios. Generally, the technician sits in the control room where the recording and mixing equipment is located and directs the musicians who are in a separate room (or often in separate rooms), all visible from the control room through soundproof glass. The musicians and technician wear headphones and can all talk to each other through microphones. Before recording actually begins, the technician must place microphones in precise locations near either the amplifiers or individual instruments. Correct placement of the microphone is a crucial element in getting the "right" sound.

Depending on what sort of band is recording and how many instruments are involved, the technician will either record each instrument separately or all at once for a more raw, "live" sound. Often the first instrument recorded in popular music is the drums. This is the foundation for the song and the most difficult instrument to record because of the many different drums and sound levels needed to be "mic-ed" for a good mix.

Music recording technicians are responsible for setting up the musicians in the studio and "mic-ing" their instruments for the desired sound. Often each musician will record in separate rooms. It is the duty of the technician to find the right level of each instrument as it relates to the other instruments. The guitar and bass, for example, may sound at the right mix, but when the drums begin they get drowned out. Light indicators on the control console aid the technician in determining the appropriate levels.

Recording technicians often record the same song several times. They listen for flaws in the mix and extraneous sounds such as hissing or popping. The source of such flaws must be pinpointed and eliminated. In each recording the technician is listening for imperfections in the mix, sound, or playing. At the end of a take the technician will have several versions of the track to work with. When establishing the final mix, the producer and musicians may decide, for example, that on take three they like a particular part of the song better than on the overall best take. In this case the engineer must edit the take with computer editing devices by combining the good parts from one take with the good parts of another.

Recording technicians are also responsible for setting up studio times for musicians. They must keep a thorough account of who is coming in when (making certain times do not conflict), what sort of band is recording, what specific equipment they will be needing, and any other special arrangements needed to make the session run smoothly. They make sure the studio is stocked with the right working accessory equipment: chords, cables, microphones, amplifiers, tapes, tuners, effect pedals, etc. When needed, some technicians may perform maintenance and minor repairs on musicians' more sophisticated equipment.

Lingo to Learn

Amplifier A device employing speakers and transistors (or electron tubes) used to increase volume of instruments and voice.

Control room An acoustically isolated room in a recording studio where the recording and mixing equipment is located.

Equalizer An electronic device that allows control and manipulation of recorded or amplified tones.

Microphone ("mic") A device that translates sound waves (usually from a voice or instrument) into electric currents for the purpose of transmitting or recording.

Mixing board A device that receives numerous microphone or amplifier inputs in order to control the volume or tonal quality of the sounds before their output is transmitted to the recorder.

Recorder Any number of devices that record either on recording tape or digitally the output from the mixing board.

What Is It Like to Be a Music Recording Technician?

Glamour aside in the music business, a recording studio can be a pretty stressful work environment. There is often a lot of pressure, both on the musicians and on the recording technician, to produce. After a six-month internship at a recording studio in Los Angeles, Chris Garibaldi found a job as a recording technician at a small, though constantly busy, independent recording studio in Chicago. "There are bands in here all the time," Chris says. "When time is tight, and time is money, you can feel the tension some times."

Chris is one of three main recording engineers. They usually work separately on different projects, but do occasionally help each other out with special

A music recording technician works at a mixing desk in a sound recording studio. *(Maximilian Stock Ltd. / Photo Researchers Inc.)*

problems. During Chris's shift he has an intern or a part-timer as an assistant who helps with some of the more routine aspects of the job.

When time is tight, and time is money, you can feel the tension sometimes.

Before an actual session, Chris will meet with the band and producer (if there is one) to discuss the recording. "Often bands bring in demo tapes they've recorded on four-track recorders. It's helpful," Chris says, "especially if I've never heard them before." During these presession meetings, it is important for Chris to find out exactly how many instruments will be in the main band and what extra instrumentation will be used in the mix. He needs to know how many microphones he will need and any other special equipment, such as amplifiers, special percussion instruments, or even a piano. It is important for Chris to know beforehand what instrumentation is in the band, because he needs to plan in advance exactly how he will go about recording each instrument. "This way I can get right to work and not fiddle around wasting anyone's time trying to figure out the best way to mic and record say, an acoustic bass, or set of bongos and a cello."

When the band arrives at the studio for session time, Chris directs each musician where to set up his or her equipment. Once the musicians are in place, Chris works on microphone placement. He has each musician play a typical piece of what they are about to record, and listens to the sound and volume in the control room through a set of headphones, adjusting the levels accordingly as he goes along. When necessary, he adjusts the microphone for the "right" sound. "Sometimes you just move the mic back a foot and two inches to the left and it solves all of your problems," he says.

When everything is in place, and all the volumes and levels are set, Chris has the musicians "make a take." With all of the instruments playing at once, different adjustments might need to be made or unforeseen problems might occur. While the band is playing, Chris wears headphones and listens carefully to every aspect of the playing. He experiments with different recording levels and instrument effects and listens for unwanted sounds.

The hours Chris works often depend on the musicians he is recording. "I've begun a session at four in the afternoon and worked until four in the morning with bands. It's the bands that book the time, and they're charged by the hour. I'm really at their whims. It wouldn't be fair for me to say I've got to go home just when the band finds the sound or groove they've been after." Even when everything is set up perfectly and everyone is happy with their sound, they still run into problems beyond Chris's control. "Musicians get into the studio and they suddenly can't play their instruments anymore," Chris says, laughing. "Put a mic in front of a guitar player when he's got a solo and he'll screw it up time after time." Once Chris has everything on his end in order, he simply has to wait for the musicians to get it right. "It gets frustrating at times," he admits.

After the recording Chris spends time with the band and producers "mixing down" the takes for a final cut. This entails coordinating the sound levels for each instrument according to suggestions from both the musician and the producer. Most of the equipment Chris uses for the mixing is highly technical, computerized machines. "Everything these days in recording is moving away from analog and into the realm of computerized digital recording," Chris says. "My advice to anyone starting in this business is to become very familiar and comfortable using computers and music software. That's the future."

To Be a Successful Music Recording Technician, You Should . . .

- enjoy music
- be comfortable working with "difficult" egos and personalities
- be patient and have excellent troubleshooting skills
- have a good ear
- be creative and willing to experiment

Do I Have What It Takes to Be a Music Recording Technician?

One of Chris's biggest challenges is staying patient. He often works with musicians and producers who have "inflated egos." "I really hate it when a producer asks me to do something really simple and then proceeds to show me how to do it. I know my job, and if I want his assistance I'll ask for it. But I have to put up with it. I want their business. I want them coming back to use our studio and not one down the street." Another problem Chris admits having a difficult time handling is the often arrogant attitude of some of the musicians. "Some of these guys have no idea what the recording process is all about, and when I don't give them the sound they want immediately they get these condescending attitudes. Really though, it's a small problem; most musicians I work with are very understanding. It's just a problem of dealing appropriately with the bad eggs."

Today's modern recording studio is filled with high tech, extremely expensive machinery that requires care and caution when using. Recording technicians need to feel comfortable with a variety of different electronic equipment. This equipment often must be moved or adjusted to fit in with specific situations. The technician should have a solid understanding of electronics when rewiring or moving such equipment.

During a typical recording session, a recording technician will run into any number of problems. "There's always something wrong," Chris says. "No session ever runs 100 percent smoothly. Sometimes it's the simplest thing, like a cord is bad, but other times it's a major problem, like my console is smoking." Technicians need to be resourceful problem solvers. When the pressure is on, they need to keep a level head. "When I've been here all night with a band working out sound problems, or what have you, and the producer is breathing down my neck, I need to be sure that I'm ready to record when they're ready."

How Do I Become a Music Recording Technician?

To land a job in this highly competitive field, technicians need to show dedication and demonstrate

In-depth

An Early History of Sound Recording

In the span of less than a century, the diverse history of sound recording made possible the job of the music recording technician. Today's high tech computer-aided mixing boards, MIDI machines, and digital recording devices ultimately owe their eminence to the recently obsolete playback medium: the record, or, as it was originally called, the phonograph. The history of music recording begins (mechanical devices aside) with the phonograph.

In 1877, when Thomas A. Edison spoke "Mary had a little lamb" into a device that, in reaction to the vibrations of his voice, cut fine grooves with a stylus in tinfoil, he became the first person to record the human voice. Edison wrapped tinfoil around a cylinder, which in turn he rotated as sounds were recorded (spoken) through a diaphragm. To play back the sound, the stylus was repositioned on the groove at a lighter pressure, and the cylinder rotated. The phonograph was born.

In 1885 two Americans, Chichester Bell and Charles Summer Tainter, applied for a patent on a sound recording device that was a slight improvement over Edison's. Instead of tinfoil, which produced very poor sound quality, they coated the cylinder with wax. This resulted in much better sound reproduction.

Emile Berliner made a significant advancement in sound reproduction in 1887 with his gramophone. Berliner didn't like the awkwardness of the cylinder, so he made his recordings on flat disks. Disks proved to be much more practical for storage and mass production. Instead of wax, Berliner used zinc coated in a fatty substance. Edison's cylinder phonographs were soon abandoned, but the term hung on in describing either device.

The method of recording on Berliner's disks was called acoustic recording. Horns of various diameters were placed near what was being recorded. Once the recording was made, levels could not be adjusted, that was what the diameter of the horn determined. When recording multiple-piece bands, and especially with orchestras, finding the right acoustics (how many horns to use and where to place them) for a good recording became a grueling, time-consuming task.

For the next 38 years, sound was recorded acoustically and was the topic of much research and debate.

To improve and increase the sound quality of orchestral instruments on recordings, sound boxes were used (devices that were actually attached to the instrument, usually on violins and violas). It wasn't until 1925, with the introduction of the microphone, that music recording entered a new and groundbreaking era.

their ability to provide reliable, consistent work. They need to be on top of the current technology, trends, and techniques in recording. Technicians should know who's who in the business and establish as many contacts as possible early on. The best way to do all of this is to pursue a formal education in audio. "There's of course a certain amount of luck in it," Chris admits. "A lot of getting a job in this business is being at the right place at the right time."

EDUCATION

High School

Unlike many of the musicians they may work with, music recording technicians will need a strong, well-rounded education to achieve success. High school is where many of the basic fundamental skills needed to be successful in any field can first be learned and explored. In the glamorous arena of music recording, jobs are very competitive. To stay on top of what is new and what is in demand, music recording technicians will need to be educated about the latest technologies. Most technical schools and workshops that offer such learning programs will require a high school diploma for admittance.

Technology in audio fields is continually becoming more computerized. In most of today's modern recording studios, technicians use computers to aid them in the mixing process, editing, sound manipulation, and countless other applications. Students should take as many computer classes and workshops as their high school offers. A strong background in mathematics and physics will be very helpful in many of the problem-solving aspects of music recording. "Complex math problems are not an uncommon sight at serious recording studios," Chris says. "We need to calculate things more often than you might think, and it's not just x plus y equals z; they get pretty hairy."

Music recording technicians should have a thorough understanding of music, both as a creative process and as a science. School bands and orchestras provide great environments to learn not only how to play an instrument but also how instruments work together and how music is composed. High school classes in music theory will help students learn the more technical approach to music. An understanding of exactly what it is the musicians are doing will be the key to working efficiently and professionally with them.

Postsecondary Training

After high school there are three basic levels of postsecondary education depending on the time, energy, and money you are willing to invest. This is the most important time of an aspiring music recording technician's education, when he or she is first introduced to many of the highly technical aspects of the field, when contacts are first established, and when mistakes can be made.

The most basic level of education is enrollment in seminars and workshops. This may be the best way to determine if the music recording business is right for you before you invest time and money in broader training. These programs are generally intended to introduce new technologies in the audio field. A seminar can last from a couple of hours to several weeks. Many workshops are geared toward introducing a certain aspect of recording such as mixing, editing, or music production.

FYI

There are many extra perks to being a music recording technician: You may just find yourself working with some of your favorite musicians and bands, and getting the much sought after backstage passes to sold out shows.

Students looking for a more comprehensive course of study in specific areas of the recording industry can enroll in trade school programs. Depending on the curriculum, these programs can take from several weeks to a year to complete. In order to cover as much information as possible, trade school courses are often taught at an intensive level. Some typical trade school subjects include studio engineering, disc cutting, record production, music marketing, MIDI studies, and electronic music recording. Upon completion of many of these programs, students are awarded a certificate or diploma.

The most complete level of postsecondary education is a two- or four-year degree from a university. At a university, students will find an ideal learning environment complete with state-of-the-art equipment and a teaching staff of knowledgeable professionals in the industry. Universities incorporate music, music technology, and music business in a comprehensive curriculum that will prepare their graduates to be highly competitive in the industry. Chris received a certificate from the two-year program at UCLA Extension. "I had a lot of experience from an internship I did and two different workshops, but I knew that if I wanted to be competitive, I should have a certificate or a diploma," he says.

SCHOLARSHIPS AND GRANTS

With some four-year university programs costing as much as $45,000, scholarships and grants offer the only realistic way for many students to attend the programs of their choice. There are two main sources for grants and scholarships: individual universities and professional trade associations. In either case, there will be stiff competition.

Although all of the scholarships and grants available from professional trade associations are not directly related to music recording, many are related to the study of audio and should not be overlooked by students who are solely interested in recording. These grants will get you into the school and broaden your expertise, making you more attractive to prospective employers. A sampling of some trade associations that offer grants are the Audio Engineering Society (AES), offering grants for graduate studies; the Broadcast Education Association (BEA), offering scholarships for study in broadcasting and radio; the Down Beat Student Music Awards, offering scholarship money in 17 different categories, including live and studio recording, music composition, and music performance; the National Foundation for the Advancement of the Arts, offering graduating high school seniors scholarships to pursue their education in the arts; and the National Systems Contractors Association offering scholarships to students who study the more technical electronics end of audio.

INTERNSHIPS AND VOLUNTEERSHIPS

Finding a job as a music recording technician will be difficult if you have not gained practical experience interning. To a prospective employer, an internship listed on a resume says that you have seen what really goes on in a studio, you have real experience outside of academic studio training, and that you are responsible and can hold a job. Interning provides you with the opportunity to make connections, obtain letters of reference, and possibly even land a job at the studio where you intern.

Most universities and colleges offer internships to their senior year students; some may even require an internship to graduate. The university or college usually has a relationship with a local recording studio. A student will earn credit hours working (usually unpaid) for a semester at the studio.

The NSCA offers an apprenticeship training program for electronic systems technicians in 10 states: Michigan, Ohio, Indiana, Illinois, Wisconsin, Minnesota, Iowa, Missouri, Kansas, and Nebraska.

Professional trade associations also support internships for their members by either matching students with employers or funding internship expenses. A National Directory of Internships is available from the National Society for Experiential Education.

National Society for Experiential Education
515 King Street, Suite 420
Alexandria, VA 22314
703-706-9552
info@nsee.org

Who Will Hire Me?

During your final semester of study, you should be on the job hunt. Take advantage of any placement services your university or college offers while you still have easy access. Your main objective is to land a job at a recording studio, and one specifically that specializes in the music you enjoy. Recording studios will record any line-up of musicians playing any style of music, but most studios have a reputation for recording a certain kind of music. If you dislike country music, chances are you will be miserable with a job at a studio in Nashville, no matter how much you enjoy your work. Look on the inner sleeve of your favorite records and CDs; it usually says where it was recorded. This will help in pinpointing studios where you may want to seek a position.

Chris spent time during his final semester of study at UCLA Extension researching where he would like to work. "I knew that I wanted a job in either Chicago, New York, or Minneapolis," Chris says. "I'm into rock, jazz, and newer, original music, so I began to pinpoint the studios that cater to these sorts of bands." By the end of his training, Chris had a list of a dozen studios in the three cities in which he wanted to work. Through his boss at the studio in Los Angeles where he interned, Chris learned the names of people who ran some of the studios on his list, made calls to these studios, and then sent them his resume. "I was surprised that my boss knew of these studios and the names of their owners. I've learned that this is a pretty tight industry."

As with most fields today, word of mouth and having good connections play very significant roles in finding a job. Although some studios will place ads in newspapers and trade magazines, the majority of jobs never need to be advertised. Why spend money on an ad when a studio manager simply has to let it be known that a position is available? The music recording community is relatively small, and word travels fast when a good job is open. In addition to having a steady stream of qualified resumes to study, a studio manager also has old interns to consider who could fill the job. Keeping good relations with your intern employer and your instructors will prove very instrumental when looking for your first job. If they do not know of any immediate openings, they may be able to refer you to somebody who does. Stay in touch after your internship and graduation.

Recording studios are generally located in larger metropolitan areas. The cities with the largest concentration of studios are Los Angeles, New York, Chicago, and Nashville. Where there is a music scene, there will be recording studios.

Where Can I Go from Here?

After you establish yourself as a dependable and resourceful recording technician, your immediate advancement possibilities are as either a *project manager* or *studio manager*. As project manager you will be responsible for every stage of a particular recording session, such as the recording of a major label band's new CD. As studio manager you will supervise project managers, new hires, and interns, as well as work on recordings. Studio managers are responsible for keeping the studio's equipment up to date with the current trends in recording technology, as well as making sure their employees are aware of new recording techniques.

Music recording technicians also commonly advance to producer. Music producers are hired by bands and record labels to manage the recording of a band's music. They, in conjunction with the musicians, have a vision of what the final recording should sound like and are in many ways responsible for the overall sound of the end product. Producers must be well versed in the work of music recording technicians, and many of them begin their careers in the recording industry.

Technicians will find other advancement possibilities in the fields of radio and television, where technicians oversee the sound of live or recorded broadcast programming. Positions in radio and television generally pay more, but there tends to be more stress on the job due to the fact that many programs are done live and often require split-second decision making.

What Are the Salary Ranges?

Nationwide, earnings of music recording technicians are about the same, except in Los Angeles and Nashville where salaries are generally higher. According to The Recording Workshop, a school in Ohio that offers training in recording engineering, while a few audio recording engineers make exceptionally high annual salaries, most earn a "middle-class income." As sound engineering technicians gain experience and prove themselves reliable through successful completion of projects, their median earnings can range between $24,600 and $56,100 a year. The high end for music recording technicians at managerial levels at busy, state-of-the-art studios can be as much as $84,800 a year.

According to the U.S. Department of Labor, the median income for broadcast and sound technicians, including audio recording technicians, was approximately $33,430 in 2003. At the low end of the scale, about 10 percent of these workers made around $15,480. The highest paid 10 percent made around $71,930 or more.

Freelance technicians can set their fees according to what the market is willing to pay. For their time alone, freelancers charge between $35 and $65 an hour. "I knew a freelance engineer in L.A.," Chris says, "who everybody wanted to record with. He really enjoyed recording little no-name garage bands and he'd charge them $35 an hour for his time. But when a band had a big time major label behind them flipping the bill, he'd charge $350 an hour. That's how he made his living."

What Is the Job Outlook?

Because the music recording industry is relatively small, jobs are very competitive and can take up to a year to find. The *Occupational Outlook Handbook* reports that employment of sound engineer technicians is expected to grow about as fast as the average through 2012. Computer automated recording programming is making the job of sound engineer technicians much easier, freeing them from many of the more mundane and difficult tasks, which in turn means technicians will need less help and the job will be done quicker.

Yet, it is exactly this new technology that makes the future of jobs in the recording industry so uncertain. "This field is changing fast," Chris exclaims. "Some of the newer machines out there are just amazing in what they can do. Everything is so computerized." For this reason, many people in the industry expect the job availability to grow. Freeing up time with effective computerized recording "gadgets" means that more

Advancement Possibilities

Project managers are responsible for every stage of a particular recording session and oversee the entire project.

Studio managers supervise project managers, new hires, and interns, as well as work on recordings. They are responsible for keeping the studio's equipment and technicians up to date on the latest technology trends.

Producers manage the recording of a band's music, helping them find their individual "sound" and presenting them in their best light.

bands will be able to be booked, which means more studio hours, and finally more workers. "Things are in the air. It's really a very exciting time," Chris says.

As long as music is a popular form of entertainment, there will be a need for music recording technicians. New music, bands, and ensembles are springing up continually. Musicians, as a way of spreading their music and promoting themselves, need to record. Whether they are associated with a record label or are an independent band trying to make their name known, they will inevitably book time in a recording studio.

The one main worry for the music recording industry is, again, technology. As new computerized recording devices become cheaper and more accessible, many computer-literate musicians may decide to record themselves at home. With the computers doing most of the grunt work, and allowing complete control and manipulation of sound, some of these home recordings can sound just as good as a studio recording.

How Do I Learn More?

PROFESSIONAL ORGANIZATIONS

The following organizations provide information on music recording technician careers, accredited school, and employers:

Audio Engineering Society
60 East 42nd Street, Room 2520
New York, NY 10165-2520
212-661-8528
HQ@aes.org
http://www.aes.org

Broadcast Education Association
1771 N Street, NW
Washington, DC 20036-2891
888-380-7222
beainfo@beaweb.org
http://www.beaweb.org

National Foundation for the Advancement of the Arts
444 Brickell Avenue, P-14
Miami, FL 33131
800-970-2787
http://www.nfaa.org

National Systems Contractors Association
625 First Street, SE, Suite 420
Cedar Rapids, IA 52401
800-446-6722
http://www.nsca.org

Recording Industry Association of America
1330 Connecticut Avenue, NW, Suite 300
Washington, DC 20036
202-775-0101
http://www.riaa.com

Society of Professional Audio Recording Services
Nine Music Square, S, Suite 222
Nashville, TN 37203
800-771-7727
http://www.spars.com

BIBLIOGRAPHY

The following is a sampling of materials relating to the professional concerns and development of music recording technicians:

Ballora, Mark. *Essentials of Music Technology*. Paramus, N.J.: Prentice Hall, 2002.

Burgess, Richard James. *The Art of Music Production*. London: Music Sales Corp., 2002.

Careers in Focus: Arts and Entertainment. Chicago: Ferguson Publishing Company, 1998.

Huber, David Miles, and Robert E. Runstein. *Modern Recording Techniques*, 5th ed. Woburn, Mass.: Focal Press, 2001.

Katz, Bob. *Mastering Audio: The Art and Science*. Woburn, Mass.: Focal Press, 2002.

Massey, Howard. *Behind the Glass: Top Record Producers Tell How They Craft the Hits*. Gilroy, Calif.: Miller Freeman Books, 2000.

NONDESTRUCTIVE TESTERS

The work of a nondestructive tester might take him or her to the cramped, hot, and dirty boiler rooms of ships crossing the ocean, where tests are performed in transit to make sure the boiler pipes are holding up well.

Or to the high-rise construction site of a commercial building, where the tester may hang off a 40-story frame to inspect the integrity of the steel.

Or to offshore drilling platforms in the Atlantic or Pacific, where the tester may don scuba gear, dive underwater, and perform tests on the parts of the drilling structure that are beneath the water.

Or to the Indianapolis Motor Speedway, to test race car parts to ensure the drivers' safety.

Or to the Alaskan pipelines, working as part of a team to test the integrity of the pipes.

Or to the service facilities of a passenger airline, in order to run service tests on commercial aircraft and ensure reliability while the aircraft is in operation.

Nondestructive testers also work with painting forgery specialists, using technology to help determine, for example, if a painting is a real van Gogh or a clever fake. They go to archaeological dig sites to examine the bones or artifacts found. And they work in labs, checking the integrity of metals, plastics, ceramics, and other materials used in various manufacturing processes.

In short, under the fairly dry title of nondestructive testing lies a whole world of tests designed to meet hundreds of different testing needs.

Definition
Nondestructive testers use special testing methods to check parts or materials for cracks, flaws, or other problems without damaging them. Tests may be run during the design process and later to ensure that designs are effective.

Alternative Job Titles
Inspectors
Testers

High School Subjects
Mathematics
Physics
Technical/shop

Personal Skills
Mechanical/manipulative
Technical/scientific

Salary Range
$17,160 to $28,200 to $50,520+

Minimum Educational Level
Some postsecondary training

Certification or Licensing
Voluntary

Outlook
More slowly than the average

DOT
750

GOE
08.02.03

NOC
9423

O*NET-SOC
51-9061.01

What Does a Nondestructive Tester Do?

Nondestructive testers primarily check the quality of metal and nonmetal parts and materials to make sure these articles meet performance specifications or pass quality control standards, all without destroying the article itself. Nondestructive testing (NDT) may be used in the specialized applications already mentioned, like checking paintings to see if they are forgeries, or in routine applications, such as in industrial manufacturing processes as a means for checking quality control.

Using any of a wide range of tests, which may involve, for example, examining the article using X-ray photography, submerging the article in water to check for leaks, or creating a magnetic field on the article to check for surface flaws, nondestructive testers can determine whether the article has a defect, crack, or other flaw that might hinder performance or even endanger the people using the article.

Although each type of test works differently and is useful for different types of materials or components, all of the tests provide some type of visual evidence of existing flaws. This is known as the indication. For example, radiographic tests produce an X-ray film, with defects showing up as light areas on the film; flaws in ultrasonic testing are revealed through

Lingo to Learn

Calibration Comparing a measuring device against an equal or better standard.

Cold shut A discontinuity in metal created by poor joining of molten material due to temperature differences.

Computer modeling and simulation In NDT, a method of testing parts or components using a computer model to check the part in action under given conditions.

Die casting A process of molding metal into a specific shape.

Discontinuity A break or interruption (such as a crack or flaw) in the normal physical structure of an article.

Forging The stage of metal manufacturing when the raw metal, still very hot and soft from the refining stage, is hammered or pressed into the needed shape.

Forging burst A break caused by forging metal at the wrong temperature (for example, under heating it).

Hot tears Ragged cracks in metal created when sections of cast metal shrink unequally.

Indication Visual evidence of flaws, such as an accumulation of magnetic particles or the light spots on radiographic film.

Nonmetallic inclusions Pockets of slag (impure, nonmetal material) that form in metal as the metal is being processed and can cause cracks or tears after the metal is formed, weakening it.

Slag Impure materials left from the processing of metal.

Smelting A process of melting, or fusing, metal.

a reading on a CRT screen; surface flaws show up in magnetic particle testing through a very visible buildup of colored magnetic particles. Nondestructive testers are trained not only to run the tests but also to understand what the different types of indications mean: how serious the flaw is, for example, or whether there's a problem in the manufacturing process that should be checked and corrected.

Nondestructive testing not only helps to locate flaws or defects that might result in the failure of a product or service but also can be used to check the dimensions of a component or structure, examine its physical or structural properties, or otherwise quantify different things about an article that need to be known to ensure quality control and reliability.

Nondestructive testing is used in a variety of industries and research facilities that require quality control testing, but primarily in the aerospace, airframe, automotive, marine, railroad, chemical, petroleum, electronics, nuclear, materials-joining, ordnance, and utilities industries.

The tests may be performed just once, or at several stages during the making of the article, during the production of a component or product that uses the article, or even after the article has been in use for a while. For example, in metal making, nondestructive testing may be performed during the metal casting, forging, welding, and machining stages. Then, if the metal making process has produced, say, steel to be used in the construction of a commercial high-rise building, a nondestructive tester also might test the steel frame as the building is going up. Later, after the building has been up for a few years, a nondestructive tester might run tests on the steel to see how well it is holding up.

There are two major benefits of nondestructive testing. First, it can be far less expensive than destructive, or operational, testing. Second, it allows a manufacturer to test 100 percent of the parts or materials it produces as they come out of production and before they are shipped out the door.

Unlike destructive testing, which might involve twisting, bending, or breaking the item—even blowing it up—to see how well it performs under stress, with nondestructive testing, the article can still be sold and used. Testing has not changed the article's performance capabilities, altered its physical makeup, or otherwise damaged it.

Testing, and testing everything, is increasingly a requirement in the quality-control-obsessed U.S. manufacturing industry. This is much easier to achieve with nondestructive testing. Even if their customers do not require it, 100 percent testing through nondestructive testing may still be a good idea to protect the manufacturer in case of accusations that there were flaws. "With all the lawsuits and liabilities out there, I'd think the customer would want to test

100 percent of parts," says Stan Stypka, engineer with InterTech Development Co., a designer and manufacturer of automated leak-testing equipment.

A lot of work has gone into developing and perfecting different nondestructive testing methods in the past 50 years, in part due to the needs of the aviation and nuclear energy industries, where the slightest flaw in a part that goes into a plane or a nuclear reactor could spell disaster for many people. There are now numerous variations on the different tests developed for these and other industries.

To understand how a part or component may be flawed in a way that the naked eye cannot see, consider what happens in metal manufacturing. In the process of smelting and forming the metal, certain impure nonmetal materials are left over. This material is called slag. Though metal manufacturers try to get rid of slag, some can get into the pure metal by accident. Pockets of slag in the metal, known as nonmetallic inclusions, are trouble. They can cause ragged cracks or tears in metal after it is formed, weakening the material and raising the risk that it will not perform as expected.

This is actually just one of a number of problems that may occur in metal manufacturing. Gas may get trapped in the metal during the process, causing the metal to become too porous; seams or cracks may form when the metal cools; or problems may be introduced during the forging process. Forging is the stage of metal manufacturing when the raw metal, still very hot and soft from the refining stage, is hammered or pressed into the needed shape. Several different kinds of problems can occur at this stage. For example, if the metal is forged at the wrong temperature, ruptures or other flaws can form.

In the past, the metal might have been tested simply by looking at it or by performing some type of sound test. A worker would strike the iron casting or other article with an iron bar and determine from the resulting sound whether there were any problems with the metal: cracks, pockets, etc. If this sounds a little iffy, it was. But designers back then used to compensate for probable flawed materials by doubling up on materials, having extra supports, or otherwise overdesigning in case the materials used had problems.

Of course, this was not very cost-effective. Today, across a broad range of industries, the emphasis is on increasing the strength of the part or component while at the same time reducing its weight. For example, an airplane should be light, fast, sleekly designed, yet all of the thousands of parts and components that go into it should be as reliable and risk-free as possible.

The type of nondestructive test used depends on a number of factors, including the type of material or part to be tested; the environment in which the part will be used, especially if there will be extremes of temperature; types of pressures the part will experience; whether the flaw is expected to be inside the article or on its surface; how much time and money the manufacturer can spend; and skill level of the people running the tests. It costs more to run some tests than others, and it may not be worth it to use the more expensive test if the part itself is relatively inexpensive.

Putting the nondestructive tests into broad categories, they include (1) those that use radiological methods, such as X rays, gamma rays, or neutron beams; (2) those that use sound or vibration methods, such as ultrasonic and mechanical impedance measurements; (3) those that use electrical and magnetic methods, such as eddy current, magnetic flux leakage (including magnetic particle inspection), and microwave testing; (4) those that use sight-assisted methods, such as interferometry, holography, and methods that use a dye that penetrates the material to be tested; and (5) those that use thermal methods, such as infrared radiation or thermal paint tests.

Again, the type of testing used depends partly on the material to be tested. For example, in nondestructive testing of metals, X-ray testing (radiographic testing) involves making an X-ray film of the article and may be used to reveal internal cracks, pockets or voids, inclusion of impurities, porosity, or other problems. Any flaws are recorded on the X-ray film.

Eddy current testing may be used to find flaws or check how well a material conducts electricity. It may be used, for example, on wire, tubing, areas of sheet metal, or other material. With this type of testing, an electrical current is shot onto the article to be tested to create "eddy currents" on the surface of the article. Special readers check to see if the path of this current veers from the way it should go, which may indicate that the article being tested has a surface flaw.

Microwave testing involves inducing microwaves into the test piece to find and record the presence of large flaws. It might be used on plastics, ceramics, or other materials and may be able to check moisture content, thickness, and other qualities. It cannot be used on metals, because the microwaves cannot penetrate the metal.

Magnetic particle testing reveals problems by detecting changes in the magnetic field of very small magnetic particles applied to the item to be tested. It can help detect very tiny problems with the surfaces of materials that X rays or other types of testing may not be able to spot.

Ultrasonic testing uses ultrasound waves to penetrate the item being tested. Surface problems or problems at the subsurface level can be detected, and an image of the problem is projected on an oscilloscope screen. This type of testing also can be used to measure the thickness of a material.

Dye-penetrant testing is used to test surface problems on solid objects. The test object is covered with dye that is attracted to the flaws on the surface. These flaws are magnified when the right type of light is directed at the object.

Another type of nondestructive testing is leak testing. In a simple version of this, known as bubble testing, the article is submerged in water. The operator waits until the water stills and then checks for bubbles coming out from the part. The presence or absence of bubbles arising in the water may indicate a flaw in the article's composition.

Each type of testing has its strengths and limitations. Often, one limiting factor is cost. The more complex test methods—ultrasonic, eddy current, and others—can be expensive and may require a fairly sophisticated, well-trained operator to run and interpret the tests. Still, continuous improvements have increased the cost-effective use of nondestructive testing. Frequently, two or more tests are done to make a complete check of the article.

Often, nondestructive testing is taken into consideration during the design of a part or component. The designer's job may include deciding which test method is best and most cost-effective for meeting the standards for that type of part. Designers will generally write their testing specifications to an accepted standard, such as those from the American Society for Testing Materials (ASTM International).

Designers may need to envision how the part they are designing will be used, what stresses it will undergo, and what the weather may be like when the part is being used.

They also may need to consider what type of testing equipment is available, how the equipment will be calibrated, what the minimum standards for quality can be (for example, small cracks or flaws may be okay), who is qualified to perform the tests, and what computer hardware or software, if any, is needed.

Computer modeling may be used to help the designer determine what tests are required, and the designer may note the type of test required on the engineering drawings: "PT" for liquid penetration testing, for example, or "RT" for radiographic testing. Designers have to plan carefully; they don't want testing to be cost-prohibitive.

In some cases, nondestructive testing is needed not only during the design and manufacturing processes but also while the part, component, or material is being used. Parts may need to be tested if they are routinely put under heavy stresses, for example, or are subjected to hard wear, corrosion, or fatigue.

Such service tests are commonly required for aircraft, to name an obvious example. Periodically, aircraft are pulled out of service to undergo tests to check for wear and tear on important parts. Service testing also is useful for the equipment used at nuclear reactor sites, in chemical processing operations, in offshore fuel operations, and in other applications.

A complementary field, nondestructive evaluation (NDE), may be called on to evaluate the findings of service tests. NDE may make use of sophisticated calculations like finite element analysis.

What Is It Like to Be a Nondestructive Tester?

Paul Haack has been in the nondestructive testing field for more than 15 years, including nine years as a technician. He supervises nondestructive testing technicians at the Elk Grove Village, Illinois, facility of MQS, a 60-year-old commercial nondestructive testing lab with 28 operations throughout the country. MQS stands for Magnaflux Quality Services; at one point, this was the testing arm of Magnaflux, the country's largest maker of nondestructive testing equipment and supplies. MQS was recently acquired by C.B. Non-Destructive Testing Ltd. and is now part of that company, which was founded in 1984.

Tests performed under Paul's supervision include radiographic, ultrasonic, liquid penetrant, magnetic particle, eddy current, and visual tests for a variety of companies all over the world, either in-house in MQS's labs or on-site at the customer's facility. "Our customers are in the aircraft, automotive, construction, utility [for work with gas pipelines], railroad, manufacturing, process safety management, and many other industries," says Paul. "About the only type of testing we don't do is that related to the building of houses, which has special problems from a liability standpoint. But all in all, we really do a wide variety of testing."

Each day in the life of a nondestructive testing technician is different. "It's all over the place," Paul says. "Right now, about 80 percent of our testing is at the customer's facility; a technician may go there every day and perform tests all day long, like for a petrochemical, refinery, or nuclear reactor operation; or a technician may just go and do a single test per day for the company. Often, the company will have a special 'quarantine' area set aside for the testing, or a testing room; or the technicians will simply do it in the middle of the plant. It changes all the time. The technicians have to be flexible."

Paul describes the steps for one type of nondestructive testing, magnetic particle (MP) testing. "The magnetic particles are extremely small, finely divided particles, about a micron in size, like talcum powder," he says.

First, the particles have to be applied to the item being tested. "In wet fluorescent testing [a version of MP testing], these particles may be mixed with mineral water and sprayed on the article using an aerosol can," says Paul. "Or, the article may be placed in a bath, and the wet particles pumped into the bath with a hose. In dry fluorescent testing, the dry particles may be applied to the article to be tested with a puffer ball."

Second, after the magnetic particles are applied to the item to be tested, a magnetic field is induced in the article by applying a certain amperage level to the article. If there is a discontinuity on the surface of the article being tested, the magnetic particles will be drawn to that discontinuity. In wet fluorescent testing, a black light is shone on the article, and the particles surrounding the discontinuity may show up as a bright fluorescent green or yellow area. In dry powder testing, the buildup of dry particles may show as a contrasting color such as red, black, or yellow. Finally, the operator evaluates the seriousness of the flaw and decides whether to accept or reject the article.

"How long a specific test takes varies widely," says Paul. "It depends on the parts being tested, what they're looking for, the amperage level required, and so forth."

The magnetic particles used in the MP tests are specifically manufactured for this purpose. "We test the particles after we buy them to make sure they're of good quality," says Paul. "We also preclean the parts to be tested; they can't have any grease, rust, or dirt on them." He adds that both steps help to ensure the integrity of the test.

Of course, an industrial manufacturer may perform its own nondestructive testing instead of or in addition to using an outside service like C.B. Nondestructive Testing Ltd.

George Strabel, coordinator of nondestructive testing for Howmet Castings Corporation, a producer of airfoils among other products, says nondestructive testing methods used by the company include digital radiography. "In general, everything we make is x-rayed," he says. This includes everything from full airfoil assemblies to small structural castings. X-ray testing allows the company to examine the inside of a part or component to check for flaws that can't be found in surface testing, such as magnetic particle testing.

Typically, groups of airfoils or castings are grouped up and x-rayed in batches rather than one at a time, he explains. "It's not a one-at-a-time activity," he says. "That would slow the manufacturing operation down too much." If Howmet is testing small airfoils, for example, batches of 10 or 15 might be x-rayed all at once, using a camera that looks much like the ones used in a hospital.

"It may take a few minutes to lay out the articles, a few minutes to shoot them, a cycle of five to 10 minutes to develop the film," says George. An operator then examines the developed film to see if any defects are visible. "An experienced reader may be able to read and evaluate the film in seconds," he adds.

Smaller parts like the castings may be x-rayed in larger batches, such as 20 at a time. Depending on the customer's requirements and other factors, more than one shot may be taken. "For castings, we might do in excess of 100 shots; for the airfoils, we may make two or three shots showing different views," says George.

There are specific standards across the aerospace industry for the qualifications needed to be in charge of the X-ray testing, to be one of the people who works under the supervisor, and so forth, says George. Also, he adds, "If you want to do business in the aerospace industry, your nondestructive testing operation will be certified by an outside agency that will inspect your facility." For example, there is a group within the National Aerospace and Defense Contractors Accreditation Program that oversees the auditing and certification of nondestructive testing facilities and personnel. "You're audited to conformance to

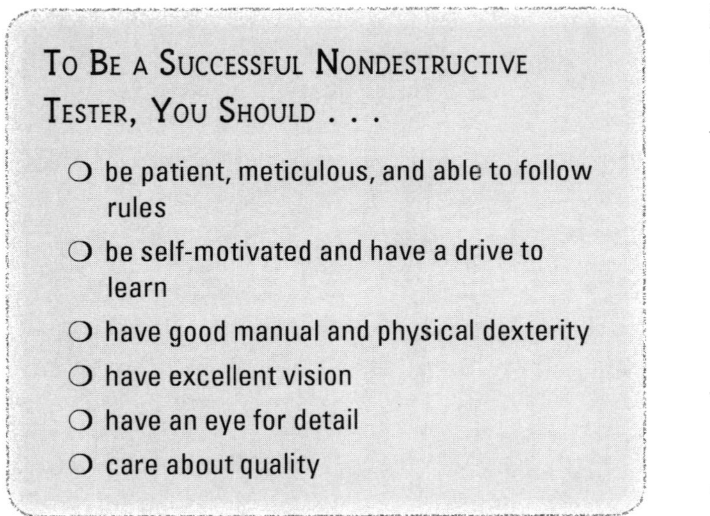

To Be a Successful Nondestructive Tester, You Should . . .

- be patient, meticulous, and able to follow rules
- be self-motivated and have a drive to learn
- have good manual and physical dexterity
- have excellent vision
- have an eye for detail
- care about quality

the basic steps for testing, to traceability to standards (primarily standards from the American Society for Test Manufacturers [ASTM] or Society of Automotive Engineers [SAE], for example)," he says.

These standards cover a wide variety of mechanical aspects, such as dimensional restrictions, stress rupture, creep rupture, fatigue properties, tensile properties for alloys after they're cast; they also cover things like microstructural standards, porosity, and other factors. Department of Defense (DOD), Federal Aviation Administration (FAA), or other standards also are widely used in nondestructive testing.

The customer specifies the standard to be met, such as "ASTM Standard Number X," letting the manufacturer know that the hardness has to meet a specific ASTM standard for hardness or whatever parameter the customer requires.

Do I Have What It Takes to Be a Nondestructive Tester?

Patience, good physical dexterity, excellent vision, and an eye for detail all are excellent traits to have for those who work in nondestructive testing.

"Patience is definitely a plus," agrees George Strabel. "You have to be meticulous," he says. "You can't short-circuit the procedures; you have to follow a lot of rules and regulations. The customer has reasons for wanting the tests performed the way they do, and you have to do them that way, even if it doesn't always make sense to you." There also can be pressure from "customers who want it yesterday," he says. "Not everyone has the fortitude for this type of work."

> You have to be meticulous. You can't short-circuit the procedures; you have to follow a lot of rules and regulations.

Self-motivation also is important, says George. "If you want to get beyond the 'grunt stage,' where you're just positioning the products to be tested, for example, you also have to undergo a lot of training."

On the upside, adds Paul Haack, "There are a lot of opportunities for travel, both nationally and internationally. Nondestructive testing can get you into a lot of heavy technical situations, if you're interested in that. For example, I recently just toured one of the new 777 jets—it was great—and a lot of interesting locations, like Argonne National Laboratories. If you pick up things quickly, you can advance quickly, increasing your level of responsibility and your level of pay. Also, because of the demands for testing, you have the opportunity to freelance, to work for yourself and go where you are needed," he adds.

How Do I Become a Nondestructive Tester?

Paul worked as a nondestructive test technician for nine years before landing the job as supervisor at MQS more than six years ago. George worked in the research end of nondestructive testing for 17 years before joining Howmet as its nondestructive testing consultant/coordinator about two decades ago.

Paul began his career by taking a course of study in nondestructive testing at a vo-tech college. His school's nondestructive testing program, like many such vo-tech courses of study, gave him initial training in a variety of nondestructive testing methods. "It was valuable," says Paul. "But I've learned just as much or more on the job as I did in school. Classroom studies are good for teaching you things like the equations necessary for some of the tests. But particularly with some methods, like ultrasonic testing, the classroom training doesn't always teach you how to evaluate the findings." This type of knowledge may be best picked up on the job in specific test situations, with a veteran explaining what the different indications may mean, he says.

EDUCATION

High School

While opportunities may be found for people who haven't graduated from high school, "A high school diploma or equivalent typically is the minimum requirement for certification," says Paul.

Physics, math (algebra, geometry), and metal shop are good classes to take while still in high school. The math is helpful for the calculations you will need to make as part of some of the testing procedures. "It's basically high level algebra and geometry," says Paul. Geometry is used in determining things like the depth of material, for example; radiographic tests may require you to figure exposure times or radiation doses needed; magnetic particle tests may require you to determine appropriate current levels.

Although some nondestructive testing is automated, many positions require the operators to assess, evaluate, and make decisions that can affect the reliability and quality of a product or service. They may need to understand the composition of the material being tested, physical properties, and other sophisticated concepts. Visual testing, for example, can be highly sophisticated. "It requires knowledge of welding processes, pumps, valves, bolting, welding inspection, pressure vessels, and more," says Paul.

Postsecondary Training

Most of the technicians supervised by Paul have an associate's degree from a vocational-technical college, says Paul, who adds that there are a number of nondestructive testing programs at vocational-technical schools around the country. Nondestructive testing is a definitely a field where receiving more training and postsecondary schooling offers greater opportunities for advancement. There is continual improvement and refinement in understanding of materials, processes, and nondestructive testing methods; therefore, it is critical to receive ongoing training if you are going to stay on top of the field.

CERTIFICATION OR LICENSING

Personnel and the nondestructive testing facilities themselves may be certified from one of many formal bodies. Individual companies determine the final certification criteria for their employees and operations, based on the industries they serve and their customers' requirements. Certification is usually earned through a combination of formal training and testing and attainment of a certain number of hours of on-the-job experience. At many companies, earning certification is necessary to advance and it is not uncommon to earn certification in two or more types of nondestructive testing. "Most of the technicians here are cross-certified in more than one type of test," says Paul Haack.

Certification is available through the American Society for Nondestructive Testing (ASNT) in any of nine different types of nondestructive testing methods. Certification is earned by taking a written test. ASNT also has written guidelines for recommended schooling and on-the-job training hours for each certification type. Under ASNT guidelines, it is possible to move right into Level II work without going through Level I first if you have enough schooling and time on the job. At Level III certification, more formal schooling is usually necessary.

Who Will Hire Me?

Nondestructive testing work is found in industry, including the aerospace, airframe, automotive, marine, railroad, chemical, petroleum, electronics, nuclear, materials-joining, ordnance, and utilities industries. Other options are to work in commercial labs like C.B. Non-Destructive Testing, which does nondestructive testing for many different companies; for a consulting firm, which may help different companies determine what type of testing they need or help them design the specific testing system and procedures; government agencies; and research institutes. Opportunities in sales, education, and other related areas also can be found.

Another possibility is to work for the companies that design and manufacture test equipment. InterTech Development Company in suburban Chicago, for example, designs and builds in-line and standalone leak testing systems for automotive and other industrial supply companies.

In-depth

Leak Testing in Action

Leak testing may involve submerging a part in water and seeing if there is a leak. However, this leaves the parts wet, and a manufacturer working under a tight schedule may not be able to afford to take the time needed to let the parts dry before they can be shipped to the customer. Therefore, some types of leak tests use gas instead of water.

Let's take a look at how this might work. One die casting and fabricating company supplies transmission valve bodies, differential clutch housings, extension housings for transmissions, air-conditioning cylinders, and other die-cast parts to auto companies like Ford and Chrysler. Under the terms of its contract with the automakers, the die casting company has to test every part that comes off the production line to be sure the parts come up to the automakers' quality control standards. Transmission extension housings, for example, are leak-tested to a level of 3 standard cubic centimeters per minute to be sure that transmission oil will not leak from the housing when someone is using the car. The housings, which look like heavy metal road cones, are pulled off the production line and brought to a test station. They're secured onto the table with a clamp, sealed, and then filled with gas. Then, a special detector checks to see if the pressure in the part is decaying; if so, there's a leak. If a leak is bad enough, the part is pulled and tossed in the reject bin. If the part passes, it can be shipped to the customer, immediately, if necessary.

There are also specialists in particular types of nondestructive testing who go where they are needed in the field: to the pipelines in Alaska, for example, or to the oil rig operations in the ocean. These are the freelancers mentioned earlier by Paul, who adds that freelance work is available at both the technician and project manager levels.

Those who attend a vo-tech college for nondestructive testing can get assistance from the job placement office to land their first position. To learn of opportunities, job seekers also can contact professional organizations like ASNT, ITEA, ASTM, and others. Most of these organizations also have professional journals that include information on local chapters, member companies, and suppliers, all potential sources of job information or opportunities.

Where Can I Go from Here?

Because nondestructive testers work with standards, one possibility is to move into higher-level standards work. This type of knowledge and expertise may be applicable across a wide range of industries. For example, *standards engineers* may determine the engineering and technical limitations and applications for materials, processes, methods, or other areas for use by designers of machines and equipment in the aircraft, automobile, space vehicle, or other manufacturing industries.

Within nondestructive testing itself, technicians may rise to the level of foreman/chief technician or supervisor, quality control specialist, engineer, or scientist. They may move into sales or education or become independent contractors/consultants. Because of the variety and widespread use of nondestructive testing, this is an occupation that seems to hold people for many years.

Of course, this experience may not be gained all at the same place. Paul Haack says the average length of time that a technician stays with a company is about two years. Of course, some companies hold workers longer.

What Are the Salary Ranges?

According to the U.S. Department of Labor, the median earnings in 2003 for quality control inspectors, which also includes testers, sorters, samplers, and weighers, were $28,200. Those in the lowest paid 10 percent earned $17,160, and the highest paid 10 percent earned $50,520. The middle 50 percent earned salaries between $21,570 and $37,810.

What Is the Job Outlook?

Some in the industry believe that nondestructive testing may have peaked, primarily because of cutbacks in aerospace and military operations. Also, there have been many improvements and new technologies, such as infrared testing and robotics testing. Some of these would eliminate the operator. Also expected to impact the industry are medical diagnostics and treatment, technology transfer, miniaturization, and wireless communication. The requirements of the industry are driven by a need for instruments and methods of lower cost and greater user friendliness, reliability, and speed. the U.S. Department of Labor projects that job growth in this field will be more slowly than the average for all professions through 2012.

"Here at Howmet, nondestructive testing is a given," says George. "However, in general, there is a move to reduce the amount of nondestructive testing in many operations. Many people look at it as a cost and seek to reduce nondestructive testing to reduce costs." If a process is robust enough, he adds (that is, if it is well proven already), they may be able to reduce the nondestructive testing without suffering a loss of quality.

Many people in nondestructive testing emphasize the importance of gaining an understanding of and training in a variety of testing methods. Because test methods and applications are continuously evolving, it is also important to stay up to date on cutting edge nondestructive testing technologies. Both of these strategies will help keep people in the nondestructive testing field more marketable in the years to come.

How Do I Learn More?

PROFESSIONAL ORGANIZATIONS

The following organizations provide industry news and information on nondestructive testing technician careers, accredited schools and scholarships, and employers:

American Society for Testing and Materials (ASTM International)
100 Barr Harbor Drive
West Conshohocken, PA 19428-2959
610-832-9585
http://www.astm.org

American Society for Nondestructive Testing
PO Box 28518
1711 Arlingate Lane
Columbus, OH 43228-0518
800-222-2768
http://www.asnt.org

International Testing and Evaluation Association
4400 Fair Lakes Court, Suite 104
Fairfax, VA 22033-3899
703-631-6220
itea@itea.org
http://www.itea.org

NDT Personnel
135 Beaver Street, Suite 19
Waltham, MA 02452
800-736-3841
http://www.ndt.org

BIBLIOGRAPHY

The following is a sampling of materials relating to the professional concerns and development of nondestructive testers:

McBride, Don, and Don E. Bray. *Nondestructive Testing Techniques*. New York: John Wiley & Sons, 1992.

Mix, Paul E. *Introduction to Nondestructive Testing: A Training Guide*. New York: John Wiley & Sons, 2005.

Pyzdek, Thomas. *Handbook for Quality Technicians and Mechanical Inspectors*. Tucson: Quality Publishing, 2000.

Shull, Peter J., ed. *Nondestructive Evaluation: Theory, Techniques, and Applications*. New York: Marcel Dekker, 2002.

NUCLEAR MEDICINE TECHNOLOGISTS

Definition
Nuclear medicine technologists work with patients and physicians to diagnose and treat certain conditions with radioactive drugs. They prepare and administer dosages, operate cameras that record images of the drug as it passes through or stays in parts of the body, and keep careful records for review by the supervising physician.

High School Subjects
Biology
Chemistry
Mathematics
Physics

Personal Skills
Helping/teaching
Technical/scientific

Salary Range
$44,234 to $47,472 to $51,038+

Minimum Educational Requirements
Some postsecondary training

Certification or Licensing
Required by certain states; recommended in all other states

Outlook
Faster than the average

DOT
078

GOE
14.05.01

NOC
3215

O*NET-SOC
29-2033.00

The patient, Mrs. Kelly, had been experiencing a great deal of back pain and fatigue lately. Her doctor had referred her to have a diagnostic test conducted. As the nuclear medicine technologist who runs the test, Tim Dunn takes it upon himself to familiarize himself with each patient's medical history prior to the visit. By the time he introduces himself to Mrs. Kelly, he is already aware that her right breast was removed for cancer three years ago. His concern, and her doctor's, is that the cancer might have spread to her bones now.

When he enters the waiting room, he says, "Good morning, Mrs. Kelly. My name's Tim, and I'll be running your tests. How are you feeling today?" Mrs. Kelly acknowledges that she's been in some pain lately and worries it could be something serious.

Tim nods and says, "These tests are a good way to find out why your back hurts. I'm going to inject a radioactive substance into your bloodstream to see how your bones absorb it. It won't hurt, and it'll only expose you to about the same amount of radiation as an X ray."

He gives her the injection and explains that since it takes the substance some time to be absorbed, he'd like her to come back in two hours for the actual test. When she returns, he greets her and takes her into the room where the test will be conducted. "If you could just take off your watch and earrings, then lie down and relax on the table," he says.

The test, which involves shooting images of her whole body with a gamma scintillation camera, takes about 45 minutes. After the test, Tim prints several images out on film for the nuclear medicine physician to review. But by this time, Tim suspects what the physician will later confirm. Mrs. Kelly's breast cancer has spread into her lower spine. This diagnosis will be relayed to her oncologist (a cancer specialist), who will discuss treatment options with Mrs. Kelly.

What Does a Nuclear Medicine Technologist Do?

Radiation has long been used to diagnose and treat many illnesses. Doctors use radiography (X-ray imaging) to penetrate the soft tissues of the body to reveal on film a crack in a bone, for example, or a mass in an organ. Nuclear medicine technology is also used to diagnose and treat illness and disease, but, unlike radiography, with nuclear technology a patient is given radioactive drugs, either by injection or by drinking liquid or taking a pill. The progress of the radioactive substance through the body is recorded by special cameras or scanners, and the functions of body systems are thus documented.

Nuclear medicine imaging is used to diagnose several types of diseases and disorders of major organs such as the bones, heart, brain, lungs, liver, and kidneys. Sometimes the technology is used on specimens from a patient, such as blood or urine, to detect and measure small amounts of hormones or drugs. At other times, the technology is used for therapy. For example, nuclear medicine can be used to destroy abnormal thyroid tissue that has migrated throughout the body. In some instances, radioactive strontium is administered to ease the pain of terminally ill patients with bone cancer.

Under the direction of physicians, *nuclear medicine technologists* are responsible for patient care. They prepare dosages of radioactive drugs to give to patients, explain procedures to patients and reassure them that the procedures are safe, position patients for imaging, and operate the gamma-ray-detection equipment and scanner. They make sure the images of the target organ are clear and understandable and then process the images. Technologists sometimes have to rescan certain areas to get a better diagnosis. Nuclear medicine technologists also work in the lab, applying radioactive drugs to specimens from patients to detect certain drugs or hormones. In a clinical study, for instance, it is important for researchers to be able to assess the behavior of a radioactive substance inside the body.

Radioactive substances are under the control of either the federal Nuclear Regulatory Commission or a state agency, depending on where the hospital or clinic is located. Because they work with radioactive substances, nuclear medical technologists must follow strict procedures and keep complete and accurate records. Technologists are responsible for the inventory, storage, and use of these substances, and the correct disposal of radioactive waste. The technologists are exposed to very little radiation themselves and use lead shields to reduce their risk. As an added precaution, they also wear badges that measure radiation while they are in a radiation area.

A nuclear medicine technologist must also perform significant administrative duties, which include keeping records of patients and the scanned images, keeping track of the radioactive drugs received into the office and used for patients, and overseeing other staff members. Some technologists are responsible for scheduling and assigning tasks for other colleagues.

Lingo to Learn

Cancer A general term for many diseases that are characterized by uncontrolled, abnormal growth of cells, which can spread through the bloodstream to other parts of the body.

Gamma camera The equipment used to produce a nuclear medicine image.

Gamma ray Electromagnetic radiation put out by an element going through radioactive decay, having the energy of thousands or even millions of electron volts.

In vitro Procedures done in a test tube.

In vivo Procedures in which trace amounts of pharmaceuticals are given directly to the patient. The majority of nuclear medicine tests are in vivo.

Nuclear medicine The area of medical technology and knowledge based on using radioactive elements to identify and treat certain diseases.

Planar This is a two-dimensional view of the specific organ being imaged by nuclear medicine.

Radiation The energy that is emitted from atomic elements when their nuclei break up.

Radioimmunoassay An in vitro procedure that measures the levels of hormones, vitamins, and drugs in a patient's blood.

Radionuclides Unstable atoms that emit radiation spontaneously. They are used in radiopharmaceuticals to diagnose and treat disease.

Radiopharmaceutical The basic radioactively tagged compound needed to produce nuclear medicine images. Also known as tracer or radionuclide.

What Is It Like to Be a Nuclear Medicine Technologist?

Nuclear medicine technologists usually work in hospitals, although employment in clinics and outpatient facilities is becoming more common. They work closely with other professionals in the field, especially radiologic (X-ray) technicians and nuclear medicine physicians.

Tim Dunn works at Maine Medical Center, the largest hospital in his state. Since most nuclear medicine tests are done during the day, Tim usually works Monday through Friday, from about 8:00 A.M. until 5:00 P.M. At some hospitals and clinics, nuclear medicine technologists are scheduled for night and weekend hours as well. In addition, technologists are often on call for evening and weekend emergencies on a rotating basis with their colleagues.

According to Tim, patients with potential recurrences of cancer make up the majority of his caseload. He also sees a number of people who are referred by cardiologists. These patients need cardiac function tests to determine how their heart muscles are working. In such a test, the patient is asked to walk and run on a treadmill to the point of exhaustion. Tim then asks the patient to lie on a stretcher, and he injects a radioactive substance into the bloodstream. Next, Tim takes sequential pictures of the heart as the substance passes through blood vessels. After 45 minutes, the patient can leave the hospital but is asked to return in three hours so that Tim can take more pictures of the heart in a resting state.

Other common nuclear medicine applications include diagnosis and treatment of hyperthyroidism (Graves' Disease), bone scans for orthopedic injuries, lung scans for blood clots, and liver and gall bladder procedures to diagnose abnormal function or blockages. Nuclear medicine technologists also work with a number of pediatric patients. Children commonly undergo procedures to evaluate bone pain, injuries, infection, and kidney and bladder function.

Tim has been at this job for more than three years. "You set your own schedule," he says. "You need to know how long each test takes, how often the images must be recorded, and so on, so that you can make the most efficient use of your time." Tim is especially careful to allow enough time in his schedule to thoroughly explain the procedures to the patients and answer any questions.

He notes that his job can also be physically demanding at times. "You have to be physically fit. You're on your feet most of the time. Sometimes, if you can't get an orderly, you have to lift patients up onto the table."

Depending upon the size of the hospital or clinic, a nuclear medicine technologist may also handle tasks that are not directly related to patient care. For instance, each morning when Tim arrives at the hospital, he performs a quality-control test on his equipment cameras that takes about 30 minutes. Other aspects of the job include recording pertinent information about each test in the patients' medical records and maintaining a record of the radioactive drugs administered every day. Tim notes that in his particular hospital, nuclear medicine technologists are not required to handle much of this paperwork. "I'm lucky to be in a big hospital, since we have a unit secretary who does the everyday tasks," he says.

A nuclear medicine technologist must be prepared for emergencies as well. "Just last Monday," says Tim, "another technologist came running into my room and said that her heart patient had just arrested [had a heart attack] right after his stress test. I called in a code and started CPR [cardiopulmonary resuscitation]. Someone else gave him the oxygen bag. When the code team got there they said I was doing just fine, so I kept it up until they got the paddles on him. Whew! I don't want to do that every day. The guy's fine, just got out of surgery with a triple bypass. Boy, I'm glad I insisted I learn CPR!"

Do I Have What It Takes to Be a Nuclear Medicine Technologist?

Nuclear medicine technologists must be good with people. "First of all," Tim says, "patients are worried about their diagnosis. Some of them suspect that their cancer may have come back or that their heart is in bad shape. You have to be compassionate about their illness and the pain and fear they are experiencing. Then too, you have the 'nuclear' tag. You need to reassure people that they won't be harmed by radioactivity."

"I was a high school hockey player and can't stress enough the importance of being on a team. You have to work together with the doctors and other technologists. You need to be able to communicate clearly. Part of this is keeping up with your paperwork so that every member of the team understands what tests the patient had, what the results were, and so forth."

Nuclear medicine technologists must also be able to grasp and explain scientific concepts. In order to work well with other medical professionals, it's especially important to have a solid understanding of biology, physics, anatomy, and physiology.

In some hospitals, nuclear medicine technologists must concoct radioactive drugs out of the raw materials. They need to have good attention to detail, be able to follow procedures, and have math skills adequate enough to understand the relationship of the patient's weight to drug dosage.

A familiarity with computers and an ability to do visual analysis (that is, to see certain patterns) are important as well. "I never thought that the art history course I loved in college would be so useful," states Tim.

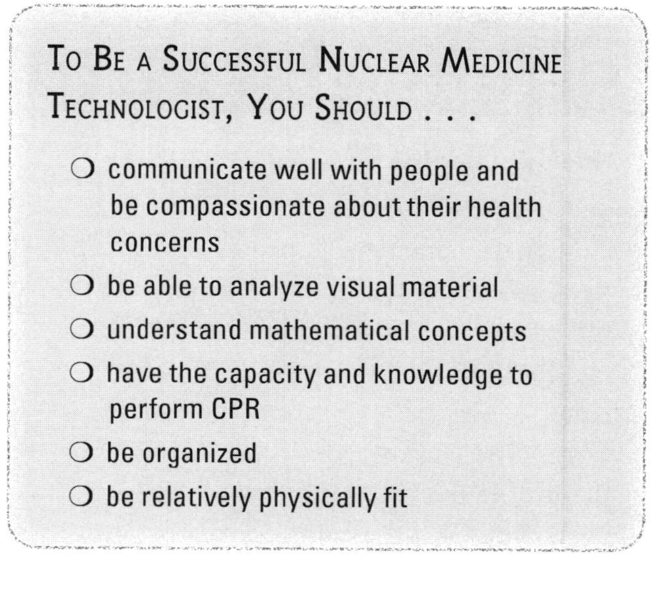

To Be a Successful Nuclear Medicine Technologist, You Should . . .

- communicate well with people and be compassionate about their health concerns
- be able to analyze visual material
- understand mathematical concepts
- have the capacity and knowledge to perform CPR
- be organized
- be relatively physically fit

How Do I Become a Nuclear Medicine Technologist?

After earning a bachelor's degree in biology, Tim briefly considered getting his master's degree so that he could work in that field. "Then I heard that a fellow graduate had become a [nuclear medicine] technologist," he explains. "Soon after that, I was waiting tables and found out that the wife of one of the regular customers was a nuclear medicine technologist. On her suggestion I toured a local hospital, liked it, and applied to their program."

EDUCATION

High School

All programs in nuclear medicine technology require a high school diploma. High school courses in biology, physics, chemistry, and algebra will help prepare you for the postsecondary training program. As in Tim Dunn's case, having been involved in a team sport is surprisingly helpful. And, as with many careers, volunteer work (in this case, perhaps in social service) provides valuable learning experiences.

Postsecondary Training

There are several ways to become a nuclear medicine technologist, depending on your prior education and previous medical work experience. Some training programs are based in hospitals, some are offered in technical colleges, and some are a part of four-year colleges. Students can earn either a certificate, an associate's degree, or a bachelor's degree in nuclear medicine technology. All programs that are accredited by the Joint Review Committee on Nuclear Medicine Technology (JRCNMT) prepare students for entry-level positions in hospitals and clinics.

There are 98 JRCNMT-accredited programs nationwide that offer instruction and clinical internship in nuclear medicine technology. These programs can be found mostly on the East Coast, in the Midwest, and on the West Coast. Most programs are open to a small number of students per year (six to 24), although some are larger. They range in length from one to four years, depending on the qualifications of the student entering.

The curriculum includes courses in anatomy, physiology, nuclear physics, mathematics, chemistry, and computer science. Students also study psychology and sociology, medical terminology, and medical ethics. Advanced courses cover how to use the cameras, the nature of radioactive drugs, and federal laws and procedures on handling radioactive materials.

Students usually spend time in hospitals while they are completing their academic course work. This clinical training allows them to practice imaging techniques with patients and to gain experience doing laboratory work. According to Tim, it is very important to make sure there is enough clinical training in a program. "I've seen some recent graduates who are really not well prepared to deal with patients."

Training programs in nuclear medicine technology can be rigorous, and because of the small number of openings in each program, competition to gain admittance is stiff. By talking with program directors at several schools about what the academic expectations are, you will be better prepared to choose the right program for your skills and aptitudes.

CERTIFICATION OR LICENSING

In some instances, completion of a training program is enough to be hired for an entry-level position.

In-depth

Nuclear Imaging

Nuclear imaging is one way of diagnosing problems not easily detected by X rays. In nuclear imaging, the patient swallows, inhales, or is instilled or injected with a radioactive isotope, which acts like a marker or tracer. The isotope goes directly to where the problem is and is then located by a special camera that produces an image.

Two uses of nuclear imaging are the bone scan and the bone density test. These tests are more sensitive than X rays and can often identify a problem months before it shows up on the X ray. They are used when the X rays come back normal, but symptoms persist.

In the bone scan, the patient receives an injection of a bone-seeking nuclide in a vein. Scanning begins two to four hours later. Images are taken of either the entire body or just the concerned part. Injuries, infections, and tumors can all be located with this technique.

The bone density test is used to diagnose osteoporosis, the decrease in bone density that is the major cause of fractures in the elderly. The patient lies on a table while two L-shaped devices (an emitter above the table and a detector below the table) pass over him or her. The emitter emits energy and the detector detects it. Because the energy has to go through the patient's body before it is detected by the detector, the amount that the body absorbs is an indication of the patient's bone density. This procedure is formally called absorptiometry.

However, the majority of positions are open only to those who become certified or registered by either the Nuclear Medicine Technology Certification Board (NMTCB) or the American Registry of Radiologic Technologists (ARRT). The certification exams are offered two or three times a year by the NMTCB and the ARRT at locations across the country. The tests measure a candidate's knowledge of radiation safety, instrumentation, clinical procedures, and radiopharmacy. The tests can be taken three times. Any candidate who fails the third time has to complete more course work and can retake the tests. Those who pass certification exams may use the title of either certified nuclear medical technologist (CNMT) or radiologic technologist in nuclear medicine (RTN), depending on the certifying organization.

Many states require state licensure as well as national certification. These states will accept national certification from either the NMTCB or the ARRT. To maintain a license, the technologist must take a certain number of hours of CEUs (continuing education units). For example, Tim has to take 24 credits every two years. These courses are available in daylong workshops as well as in weekend programs. Sometimes, continuing education courses on new diagnostic techniques and tools are offered by pharmaceutical companies right at the hospital.

SCHOLARSHIPS AND GRANTS

You can contact the NMTCB to get a comprehensive list of accredited training programs, many of which offer scholarships. Better yet, visit their Web site where you'll find links to financial aid information at various schools. Individual schools also have their own financial aid programs, so you should talk with a counselor in the financial aid office of wherever you are applying. Stipends (which are living expense allowances given with scholarships) are offered in a small number of institutions.

INTERNSHIPS AND VOLUNTEERSHIPS

Volunteering in a hospital or clinic is a good way to see if you enjoy working with patients. Many facilities offer volunteer opportunities and welcome the extra help that volunteers bring. To explore these opportunities, contact hospital cancer centers, nursing homes, and research facilities near you for more information about their volunteer programs.

Who Will Hire Me?

Hospitals are still the primary employer of nuclear medicine technologists, although clinics, doctors' offices, and research institutions employ 20 percent of them.

Various regional nuclear medicine journals advertise job openings, as do publications geared toward radiologic and nuclear medicine technologists. Some colleges have placement services, and students who have trained in a hospital program may find work at that hospital.

Tim got his job indirectly because of his excellent performance as a student. "One of my fellow students heard that there was an opening here and he applied. The hospital asked the director of my program for a recommendation for this person, which the director felt he was not in position to give. However, he warmly recommended me instead. I came to interview, and here I am."

In-depth

Female Role Model

Manya (Marie) Sklodowska is part of the history of nuclear technology and medicine. Manya learned to read at the age of four and had a remarkable memory. When she was 16 she won a gold medal and many other awards from the Russian school she attended in her native Poland. She became a teacher and also took part in the "floating university," which was forbidden by the Russians who had control of Poland at the time; she secretly read in Polish to women workers.

Manya, a brilliant scientist, eventually went to Paris, and her marriage to Pierre Curie began a partnership that would lead them to major scientific discoveries. Marie Curie coined the term radioactivity, which is the phenomenon that occurs when invisible radiation is emitted from the atoms of certain elements, such as radium. In 1911 she was awarded the Nobel Prize in chemistry for her work in isolating pure radium, which kills diseased cells.

Where Can I Go from Here?

Staff technologists who do well in their jobs and who have education beyond the associate's degree may advance to *supervisor*, then to *chief technologist*, and on to *department director*. More experienced technologists may also have the opportunity to instruct others in nuclear medicine technology.

Technologists who work in larger hospitals might decide to specialize in a clinical area such as nuclear cardiology or computer analysis. As mentioned earlier, some technologists leave patient care altogether to take jobs in research laboratories. Here, they conduct research aimed at improving laboratory conditions or imaging techniques. Other technologists shift into sales careers for medical equipment or radiopharmaceutical firms. Those who enjoy hands-on training might become *applications specialists* and travel around the country helping hospital staffs learn to use new computer imaging equipment. Still another advancement possibility is to become a *radiation safety officer* for a federal or state regulatory agency.

Jobs related to nuclear medicine technologists include radiologic technologists. The jobs are similar in that both operate diagnostic imaging equipment. The U.S. Department of Labor classifies nuclear medicine technologists under the headings *Occupations in Medical and Dental Technology* (DOT) and *Nursing, Therapy, and Specialized Teaching Services: Therapy and Rehabilitation* (GOE). Other medical and dental technology occupations include biochemistry technologist, cytogenetic technologist, medical radiation dosimetrist, radiologic technologist, Holter scanning technician, and radiation therapy technologist. Those working in therapy and rehabilitation include dialysis technicians, respiratory therapists, and occupational therapists.

What Are the Salary Ranges?

The American Society of Radiologic Technologists reports that the average annual salary for nuclear

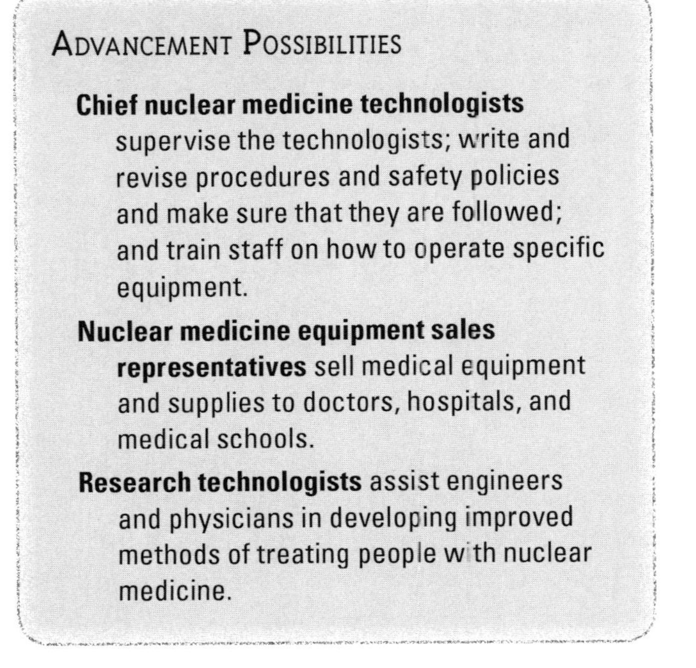
ADVANCEMENT POSSIBILITIES

Chief nuclear medicine technologists supervise the technologists; write and revise procedures and safety policies and make sure that they are followed; and train staff on how to operate specific equipment.

Nuclear medicine equipment sales representatives sell medical equipment and supplies to doctors, hospitals, and medical schools.

Research technologists assist engineers and physicians in developing improved methods of treating people with nuclear medicine.

medicine technologists was $65,401 per year in 2004. Technologists with three or more years of experience earned an average of $78,210. Those working in hospitals earned $79,709; in outpatient imaging facilties, $69,995; and in clinics or physicians' offices, $63,400. According to Salary.com, in 2005 the median earnings nationwide for nuclear medicine technologists were $47,472. The lowest paid earned $44,234, and the highest paid earned $51,038. Typical benefits for hospital workers include health insurance, paid vacations and sick leave, and pension plans.

What Is the Job Outlook?

Employment of nuclear medicine technologists is expected to grow faster than the average through 2012, according to the U.S. Department of Labor. In 2002, 17,000 nuclear medicine technologists were employed nationwide. Because the field is relatively small, there is little job turnover each year. The increase in jobs will come from rising numbers of middle-aged and elderly people, the chief users of all diagnostic procedures, including nuclear medicine tests. Thanks to advances in technology, nuclear medicine can be used for an increasing number of diagnostic procedures. For instance, certain radiopharmaceuticals can now detect cancer at an earlier stage than before and without the need for surgery. Nuclear medicine techniques are also used increasingly by cardiologists in order to visualize how effectively the heart is pumping blood.

However, some of the most promising technological advances are prohibitively expensive for hospitals and for patients. Hospitals that wish to use such procedures will have to weigh the cost of equipment against the potential reimbursement and the number of users. These cost considerations will impact how quickly revolutions in research can be put to common use by nuclear medicine technologists.

Other factors could also cause job opportunities in nuclear medicine technology to level off. In an effort to lower labor costs, many hospitals have begun to merge nuclear medicine and radiologic technology departments. Therefore, job opportunities will be best for those trained to perform both nuclear medicine and radiologic procedures. In addition, noninvasive imaging technologies (those that don't involve penetration of the skin, as with injections), such as magnetic resonance imaging (MRI), may supplant nuclear medicine for certain tests because they don't involve radioactivity.

How Do I Learn More?

PROFESSIONAL ORGANIZATIONS

The following organizations provide information on nuclear medicine technologist careers, accredited schools, and employers:

American Registry of Radiologic Technologists
1255 Northland Drive
St. Paul, MN 55120-1155
612-687-0048
http://www.arrt.org

FYI

The U.S. Food and Drug Administration initiated withdrawal of the exemption it granted to radiopharmaceuticals and began regulating them as drugs in 1970, and in 1971 the American Medical Association officially recognized nuclear medicine as a medical specialty.

American Society of Radiologic Technologists
15000 Central Avenue SE
Albuquerque, NM 87123-3917
800-444-2778
http://www.asrt.org

Joint Review Committee on Educational Programs in Nuclear Medicine Technology
One Second Avenue East, Suite C
Polson, MT 59860-2320
406-883-0003
jrcnmt@centurytel.net

Nuclear Medicine Technology Certification Board
2970 Clairmont Road, Suite 935
Atlanta, GA 30329
404-315-1739
board@nmtcb.org
http://www.nmtcb.org

Society of Nuclear Medicine
1850 Samuel Morse Drive
Reston, VA 20190
703-708-9000
http://www.interactive.snm.org

BIBLIOGRAPHY

The following is a sampling of materials related to the professional concerns and development of nuclear medicine technologists:

Careers in Focus: Medical Technicians. 4th ed. New York: Facts On File, 2004.

Damp, Dennis V. *Health Care Job Explosion: High Growth Health Care Careers and Job Locator*. 3d ed. Moon Township, Pa.: Bookhaven Press, 2001.

Field, Shelly. *Career Opportunities in Health Care*. 2d ed. New York: Facts On File, 2002.

Foss, Anna M. Gallo. *Review Questions for Nuclear Medicine: The Technology Registry Examination*. New York: Parthenon Publishing Group, 1997.

Karni, Karen R. *Opportunities in Medical Technology Careers*. Lincolnwood, Ill.: VGM Career Horizons, 1996.

Ramesh, Chandra. *Nuclear Medicine Physics: The Basics*. New York: Lippincott Williams and Wilkins, 1998.

NUCLEAR REACTOR OPERATORS

Definition
Nuclear reactor operators are responsible for the continuous and safe operation of a nuclear reactor.

Alternative Job Titles
Control operators
Power plant operators
Station reactor operators
Turbine operators

High School Subjects
Chemistry
Computer science
Mathematics
Physics
Technical/shop

Personal Skills
Following instructions
Technical/scientific

Salary Range
$49,000 to $63,300 to $83,200+

Minimum Educational Requirements
High school diploma; up to four years of specialized, formal training

Certification or Licensing
Required

Outlook
Decline

DOT
015, 952

GOE
02.05.01

NOC
7352

O*NET-SOC
19-4051.01, 51-8011.00

It is 2:00 A.M. on a Thursday morning and Ivy Netzel has just completed "taking rounds," one of four that are completed every 24 hours. All of the meters on her control board are within the required parameters. She has written down all of the temperature, pressure, and flow readings, and all the equipment in the unit is functioning properly.

It is time for a fresh cup of coffee when suddenly a flashing annunciator goes off, along with an audible alarm indicating the first sign of trouble with a steam generator. It looks as if a tube has ruptured, a serious event in a nuclear reactor.

As it turns out, this problem is actually just a "spurious trip": a false alarm. Ivy, however, has to treat the alarm as a real emergency. According to coworkers and the unit supervisor, Ivy has reacted calmly and professionally during the entire event. Her training has paid off.

What Does a Nuclear Reactor Operator Do?

The *nuclear reactor operator* (NRO) can be thought of as the nuclear station's driver, in that the NRO controls all of the machines that are used to generate power at the station. He or she is responsible for making sure that the station continues running safely and continuously. Most nuclear power plants consist of more than one nuclear reactor unit. Each NRO is responsible for only one of the units.

NROs work in the station control room, monitoring meters and gauges. They read and interpret instruments that record the performance of every valve, pump, compressor, switch, and water treatment system in the reactor unit. When necessary, they make adjustments to fission rate, pressure, and water temperature and the flow rate of the various pieces of equipment to ensure safe and efficient operation.

The NRO is also responsible for coordinating and operating activities performed by personnel in the "field," which are those people working at the site of the equipment. This work can include anything from turning a valve to bringing a piece of equipment in and out of service. All requests for action on any of the machines must go through and be approved by the NRO.

Most units run at 100 percent power, but occasionally power demand will require changes to the unit's output. When that happens, the NRO makes adjustments to the turbine to change output. These adjustments are done at the direction of the *utilities load dispatcher.*

In addition to monitoring the instruments in the control room, the NRO is responsible for running periodic tests on each piece of equipment. These tests include pressure readings, flow readings, and vibration analysis. Sometimes the tests require the NRO to perform "out-of-services," bringing a piece of equipment out of service to perform tests that cannot be done while the equipment is operating. The NRO must also perform logic testing on the electrical components to check the built-in safeguards.

One of the tasks the NRO has to perform is "refueling" the reactor unit, sometimes called an "outage." This procedure is performed every 12 to 18 months. During the refueling, the turbine is brought "offline," or shut down. It is allowed to cool and depressurize. The unit is opened, and any repairs, testing, and preventive maintenance that cannot be done when the unit is operating are taken care of. Depleted nuclear fuel is exchanged for new fuel. Once complete, the unit is repressurized and reheated, then brought back online, or restarted.

Although the NRO performs a great deal of scheduled monitoring, maintenance, and testing, there are also times when he or she must deal with emergencies. Often these "emergencies" are false alarms caused by actions in the field. The NRO, however, has to treat each incident as a real emergency.

Lingo to Learn

Containment A structure that houses the nuclear reactor and isolates the reaction from the balance of the power plant.

Control rods Devices containing material that absorbs radioactive particles within the reactor to moderate the nuclear fission chain reaction process.

Coolant A fluid that draws off heat by circulating through a machine.

Fission A nuclear reaction in which an atomic nucleus splits into fragments, usually two, with the evolution of approximately 100 million to several hundred million electron volts of energy.

Nuclear reaction A chain reaction in which the energized subatomic particles of split atomic nuclei collide with and split other atomic nuclei.

Radiation The propagating waves or particles, such as light, sound, radiant heat, or particles, emitted as a consequence of a nuclear reaction.

Reactor A device in which a nuclear chain reaction is initiated and controlled, with the consequent production of heat.

What Is It Like to Be a Nuclear Reactor Operator?

Ivy Netzel was a licensed nuclear reactor operator for Commonwealth Edison (CECO) at the Zion, Illinois, nuclear power plant. Ivy worked in that position for two and a half years before moving on to work for CECO as an independent safety engineer.

When Ivy first started at the Zion plant, she worked in Systems Engineering, where she monitored and maintained specific electrical systems within the plant. She worked in this department for four and a half years before moving into operations as an NRO.

Operations employees at Zion work in rotating 12-hour shifts, beginning at 7:00 A.M. and 7:00 P.M. The rotating shift is on a five-week schedule. Ivy explains that the schedule begins with four days on the job, three days off, three nights on, seven days off, four nights on, three days off, three days on, one day off, four eight-hour days in training, and then the weekend off. The schedule starts all over on Monday. Although this schedule seems like it would be difficult to adjust to, Ivy says it is easier with a 12-hour shift. Shifts used to be eight hours, which meant some shifts started in the middle of the night.

The Zion nuclear plant has two units. Each shift crew consists of two NROs for each unit, with one extra NRO. The crew also has one unit supervisor, a field foreman, and a shift engineer, who supervises the whole crew. There are five crews.

Ivy says the crew concept started in the 1980s and allows an NRO to work with the same people all the time. There is not a lot of movement in and out of the positions, so a crew will remain intact for a long time, she says.

It is difficult to describe a typical day, Ivy admits, because of the rotating shifts. Working at night is much different than working days, and the work on weekends varies significantly from the activities Monday through Friday. A lot of testing is done during the quiet times at night and on weekends.

During a weekday, the phone never stops ringing and people are in and out with requests for action in the field. Ivy describes the control room as command central, being the hub of the nuclear plant.

During each 24-hour period, NROs have to "take rounds" four times. This means that the NRO has to review his or her unit's control board and write down the parameters of the instruments. He or she records information on temperature, pressure, and flow rates. Each hour a computer generates a reading indicating the amount of power the unit is generating.

The most difficult part of her job, Ivy says, is keeping track and remembering all the pieces of information for which an NRO is responsible. "Lots of information comes in at once that has to be processed," she says, "and information on one system can affect other systems." An NRO has to remember how each of the systems are interconnected.

Lots of information comes in at once that has to be processed, and information on one system can affect other systems.

There are stretches of time, Ivy admits, that are "very, very boring, with nothing to do but look at the control boards." Other times are very hectic, especially during refueling outages, certain tests, and reactor trips. A reactor trip causes the nuclear chain reaction to shut down, although the unit itself is still at full power.

Being in the same environment for 12 hours at a time can be stressful, especially as the crew the NRO works with does not vary. Crew members are not supposed to leave the control room and often eat their lunches at their station. The Zion station does, however, have a cafeteria. If an NRO does leave the control room, he or she has to carry a beeper and must return immediately if beeped.

The NROs and supervisors work in a windowless control room that is kept very clean and well lit. Because NROs spend a majority of their time on the job in the control room, most employers have made great efforts to make it as comfortable as possible. Some control rooms have been painted in bright, stimulating colors, and some are kept a little cooler than is standard in

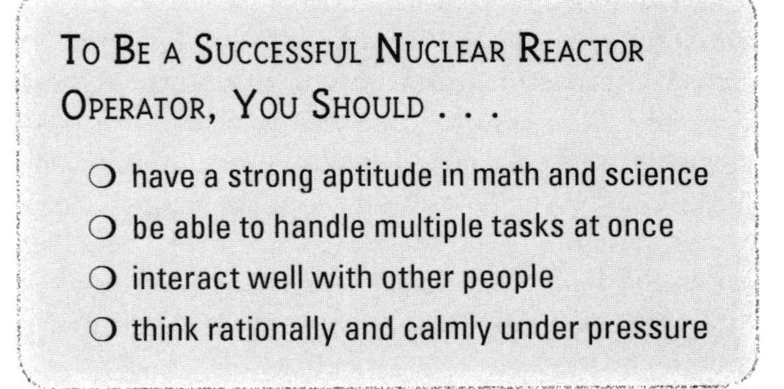

most offices. There are even some utility companies that have brought in exercise equipment for their NROs to use during quiet times.

Although NROs may continue to work at one station of control boards for a long time, they are not allowed to personalize their space. Ivy explains that each station in the control room is used by more than one person, as the shifts rotate in and out.

An added stress to the position is the tough scrutiny that NROs must submit to by the Nuclear Regulatory Commission (NRC). The NRC is the agency that establishes requirements for and grants licensing of the NROs. Plant management, the local community, and the national and local press are also on watch for compliance with regulatory and safety issues.

Ivy reports that during the more than seven years she has worked at the Zion nuclear plant, she has had no significant exposure to radiation, which is always a concern among plant personnel. Lead shielding, automatic alarm systems, and radiation detection devices are used to protect employees.

Do I Have What It Takes to Be a Nuclear Reactor Operator?

Ivy believes the most important quality to possess in becoming a licensed NRO is the ability to learn technology and to think in mathematical and scientific terms. During training, the NRO operator must learn and understand nuclear science theory, specifically nuclear radiology, radiation detection, and reactor design, operation, and control.

In addition, the NRO operator must become knowledgeable about nuclear power plant materials, processes, material balances, plant operating equipment, pipe systems, electrical systems, and process control. It is vital that the NRO understands how each activity within the unit affects other instruments or systems.

Prospective NROs must also possess a high degree of precision and accuracy. Because of the dangerous nature of nuclear energy, the NRO's performance is critical to the safety of other employees, the community, and the environment. The NRO must be able to shoulder this responsibility.

The NRO must be able to make quick decisions based on sound judgement and skill. The operator must be able to work under stress and remain calm, alert, and professional. There are numerous occasions when the NRO has to be able to perform multiple tasks at once.

During quiet times, however, the NRO must also be able to handle the monotony of routine readings and testings. The NRO must be alert at all times for changes in the controls.

Because the NRO must respond to requests from personnel in the field, he or she must also be able to deal effectively with and work well with other team members and plant personnel.

Nuclear reactor operators position a fuel rod manipulator over the reactor core at the Trojan nuclear power station, Rainier, Oregon. *(U.S. Department of Energy / Photo Researchers Inc.)*

How Do I Become a Nuclear Reactor Operator?

Some people in the industry believe that one of the most difficult aspects of becoming a nuclear reactor operator is getting hired. Because electric utilities must make an enormous investment in time and money training NROs, they are very selective when hiring.

Each applicant must go through intense screening, including identity checks, FBI fingerprint checks, drug and alcohol screening, psychological tests, and credit checks. After passing these initial screenings, the applicant must then take a range of math and science aptitude tests.

Potential nuclear reactor operators are recruited from three sources: local high schools and colleges, fossil fuel plants (utilities using nonnuclear sources for energy), and nuclear navy programs. Navy veterans from a nuclear program are considered excellent candidates because of their prior nuclear knowledge and the discipline and professionalism gained from the navy experience.

Ivy received her electrical engineering degree at the University of Wisconsin in Milwaukee. She says she "fell" into her work for CECO at the Zion plant. After graduation and some job market research, she decided that CECO would be a good company to work for, and the Zion plant was conveniently located near her home.

Ivy started at the Zion plant in one department and then moved into operations as an NRO. A good way into the field, says Ivy, is to come into the plant in one area and then move into operations after gaining nuclear experience. Work areas that Ivy mentions as possible entries include systems engineering, station labor, and the clerical union.

In some nuclear plants, new employees in operations are first placed in positions as auxiliary operators or equipment operators. These positions are not licensed and can be used to gain the necessary nuclear experience to become an NRO operator or trainee.

EDUCATION

High School

High school students interested in pursuing a career as an NRO should take a heavy concentration of classes in math and science. Courses should include

In-depth

Nuclear Energy: What Is It?

To better understand the job of a nuclear reactor operator, it may help to have a simple understanding of nuclear energy.

In a nonnuclear power plant, some sort of fuel, usually gas or coal, is used to heat water into steam in a steam boiler. The steam is released under high pressure through pipes into a turbine. The pressure causes the turbine to rotate, driving an electric generator that produces electricity.

A nuclear power plant uses a fuel in much the same way. The difference is that the fuel is uranium, which undergoes a fission reaction producing enormous quantities of heat. The fission takes place in a nuclear reactor.

In a fission reaction, the nucleus of an atom is split into energized particles, called neutrons. The neutrons are released at such great speed that they collide with other atomic nuclei and cause additional splitting to occur. This chain reaction would be uncontrollable if it were not contained within the reactor core.

The heat generated by the fission reaction creates steam from water circulating around the reactor core. The steam is carried away under very high pressure through pipes. The pressure rotates the turbine, which drives the electric generator that produces the electricity.

physics, chemistry, algebra, geometry, and calculus. In addition, courses in computer science and beginning electronics provide good preparation for the required training.

Although a college degree or experience is not required, many utilities use the completion of some postsecondary education as a screening tool. Ivy says that more and more NROs have at least two years of college experience, and about 25 percent have a four-year degree. Having a two-year or four-year degree gives employees more flexibility in the positions for which they may qualify.

Not having college experience, however, does not exclude an applicant from being hired. Selection of high school graduates is based on class curriculum and aptitude testing.

Postsecondary Training

Employers often hire graduates of a two-year science program at a local junior or community college. Many two-year programs are aimed specifically at the nuclear power industry. Graduates of these programs are considered excellent candidates for NRO training positions, called nuclear reactor operator technicians, because of their understanding of nuclear technology. Technical institutes also offer operator training programs, but they tend to emphasize theory less than junior or community colleges.

First-year courses for students enrolled in a two-year nuclear technology program will usually include an introduction to nuclear technology, radiation physics, applied mathematics, introduction to electricity and electronics, introduction to technical communications, basic industrial economics, radiation detection and measurement, introductory inorganic chemistry, radiation protection, advanced mathematics, basic mechanics, introduction to quality assurance and quality control, principles of process instrumentation, heat transfer and fluid flow, metallurgy, and metal properties.

Course selection for the second year includes technical writing and reporting, introduction to nuclear systems, blueprint reading, mechanical component characteristics and specifications, reactor physics, reactor safety, power plant systems, instrumentation and control of reactors and plant systems, power plant chemistry, reactor operations, reactor auxiliary systems, and industrial organizations and institutions.

The course content of and standards for all nuclear training programs are established by the NRC. Each nuclear power plant training program must also be accredited by the Institute of Nuclear Power Operations (INPO), which was founded in 1979 by industry leaders to promote excellence in nuclear generating plant operations.

A large portion of the course work in a two-year program is conducted in a laboratory or work-study situation. Although graduates of these programs have completed intensive classroom and laboratory training, they still have to undergo extensive on-the-job training once they are hired by a nuclear power plant.

The initial training for a new nuclear reactor operator technician at the nuclear station will continue for six months to two years, depending upon the employee's previous education and training. The primary goal of on-the-job training is for the trainee to learn in detail the workings of the plant.

Part of the training conducted at the nuclear station takes place in a control room simulator, which is an exact replica of the station's real control room. The controls in the simulator are connected to an interactive computer. Trainees experience mock events in the simulator, which teach them how to safely handle potential emergencies. Training also involves working under the supervision of a licensed NRO.

Throughout this training period, NRO technicians are subject to exams, both written and oral, sometimes as often as once a week. In some companies, trainees are let go for failing to pass any one training examination.

CERTIFICATION OR LICENSING

Once the technician has completed the required training at the plant, he or she is eligible to take the licensing exam administered by the NRC. Nuclear reactor operators must be licensed by the NRC.

The licensing exam consists of three parts: a written test, usually lasting one day; an oral exam lasting about half a day; and an actual demonstration. These exams are all designed to demonstrate that the technician has been properly trained and that he or she has demonstrated the ability to operate the controls safely and competently.

The NRO license is issued for a six-year period and may be renewed after passing a requalification exam. The license is valid for the specific power plant and a specific unit only. Approximately 90 percent of candidates taking the exam pass the first time, according to the NRC.

If an NRO fails when taking the relicensing exam, he or she is placed in remedial training to improve knowledge in weak areas. The test may then be retaken in six months. In addition to the license requalification exams, NROs must take an annual operating test given by the nuclear station and a written test every two years.

Because NROs are subject to continuous exams, training does not stop once the license has been obtained. As Ivy described, NROs must attend classes and participate in training in the simulator as part of their rotating work schedule. NROs train more than 70 hours each year in the simulator.

SCHOLARSHIPS AND GRANTS

There are a number of scholarships and grants available for students pursuing a career in nuclear energy. The financial assistance office at two-year and four-year colleges can provide a detailed list of the scholarships available. Additional scholarship information can be found by contacting the American Nuclear Society (ANS). The American Nuclear Society also has student chapters at many colleges and universities throughout the United States.

INTERNSHIPS AND VOLUNTEERSHIPS

Nuclear power plants usually do not offer internships in operations because of the intense training needed. It is possible, however, to work as an intern at some nonnuclear utilities to gain experience in the workings of a power plant. Check with the personnel offices of utility companies in your area to see about such opportunities.

LABOR UNIONS

Most nonmanagement operating personnel at most nuclear power stations are represented by a labor union. As an NRO at Zion, Ivy is a member of the labor union representing nuclear operation employees. All members of the operation team, except for management positions, are union members. Approximately 50 percent of utilities have labor unions representing employees.

Who Will Hire Me?

Almost all positions as a nuclear reactor operator are found at nuclear power plants or stations owned and operated by electric utilities. In 2000, there

FYI

Nuclear energy provides about 20 percent of the electricity needed in the United States, according to the Nuclear Energy Institute.

were 103 operating reactors in the United States. The Department of Energy hopes to build at least one additional nuclear plant in the United States by 2010.

Other possible, although limited, employment opportunities may be found at research reactors associated with major universities and scientific foundations.

Where Can I Go from Here?

Depending upon an NRO's experience, there are a number of advancement possibilities. Upon completing a required number of years as a licensed operator, he or she may take an exam to obtain a senior reactor operator license. To be certified as a senior reactor operator (SRO), the operator must demonstrate a broader and more detailed knowledge of the power plant, plant procedures, and company policies. In some locations, the SRO position may have supervisory responsibilities over other licensed operators.

SROs may have the opportunity to move into the positions of field foreman and then control room supervisor or unit supervisor. Because there are differences in the design of each nuclear station, there may be variations in the actual position titles. These are management positions responsible for an operating crew. Successful supervisors can also be promoted to shift engineer. It is even possible to eventually become the plant manager.

In addition to positions in operations, NROs and SROs can move into other fields in the nuclear industry. There may be positions at the nuclear station in training and education, safety, quality control, and other engineering functions.

Operators may also find jobs teaching at colleges or universities. Many operators have been successful moving into positions at nonnuclear power plants. Other job possibilities include working for a reactor manufacturer or in research and development consulting or other outside consulting. The NRC also offers a wide variety of job possibilities for reactor operators.

What Are the Salary Ranges?

Salaries of NRO technicians and licensed NROs vary, depending upon experience, training, employer, and location. Technicians who have little or no nuclear training can expect a beginning salary between $18,000 and $22,000 a year. Technicians who have graduated from a two-year nuclear technology program can be paid up to $30,000 a year. Nuclear power reactor operators earned median annual salaries of $63,300 in 2003, according to the U.S. Department of Labor. The lowest paid 10 percent earned $49,000, while the highest paid 10 percent earned $83,200 a year. Of course, as technicians gain experience and complete training, salaries will usually increase.

In addition to a regular salary, some NROs are paid a premium for working shifts and overtime. There also may be an hourly amount added for maintaining a license. Standard benefits for salaried NROs include medical and life insurance, paid holidays and vacations, and retirement benefits. Employers also pay for on-the-job and formal class training.

What Is the Job Outlook?

It is difficult to predict the future of the nuclear industry. There are those who believe there will be moderate growth and others who see only a decline in the presence of nuclear power. The U.S. Department of Labor predicts a decline in job growth through 2012.

However, with the launch in 2002 of the U.S. Department of Energy's (DOE) program *Nuclear Energy 2010*, which has the goal of creating a "public private partnership" for building a new nuclear plant in the United States by 2010, employment opportunities may improve. The Nuclear Energy Institute (NEI) reported that three energy companies applied for early site permits in 2003 and the NRC has certified several advanced design nuclear reactors. Among energy companies joining three different groups testing the construction and operating license process developed by the DOE are GE Energy, Hitachi America, and Bechtel Corp. Others are Florida Power & Light, Westinghouse Electric, and Toshiba.

Also potentially improving the employment outlook is a future industry-wide worker shortage predicted by the NEI. A 2004 survey by the NEI reports that about 29,000 workers will have to be recruited to fill vacancies in 13 job classifications over the next decade. Survey data indicates that about 55 percent of employees will be lost to other industries, and beginning in 2005 retirement is expected to add to the loss of staff.

To insiders, nuclear energy is a clean, reliable, relatively safe source of power. To those not in the industry, however, questions and concerns have been raised about safety, in great part because of the accidents at Three Mile Island and Chernobyl. There are also unresolved questions about environmental effects and waste disposal and reprocessing. In addition, construction and maintenance costs of nuclear plants have rapidly increased.

Until these issues are resolved, the future is uncertain. Most new job openings will be created by retirements or transfers to other positions. There may be new positions created, however, by increased regulations, plant license extension efforts, decommissioning, and waste disposal research.

There are growing opportunities for work in nuclear power plants located overseas. Currently, 31 foreign countries operate about 435 nuclear power plants; 38 new nuclear plants are under construction in 13 countries. Some U.S. companies are expanding outside the United States, and many foreign countries rely much more heavily on nuclear power than the United States.

Advancement Possibilities

Nuclear equipment sales engineers sell nuclear machinery and equipment and provide technical services to clients.

Technical advisers for nuclear plants monitor plant safety status, advise operations staff, and prepare technical reports for operation of thermal-nuclear reactors at electric-power generating stations.

Nuclear test reactor program coordinators evaluate, coordinate, and oversee testing of nuclear reactor equipment.

Radiation protection engineers supervise and coordinate activities of workers engaged in monitoring radiation levels and condition of equipment used to generate nuclear energy to ensure safe operation of plant facilities.

How Do I Learn More?

PROFESSIONAL ORGANIZATIONS

The following are organizations that provide information on nuclear reactor operator careers, accredited schools, and employers:

American Nuclear Society
555 North Kensington Avenue
La Grange Park, IL 60526
708-352-6611
http://www.ans.org

Nuclear Energy Institute
1776 I Street, NW, Suite 400
Washington, DC 20006-3708
202-739-8000
http://www.nei.org

Professional Reactor Operator Society
PO Box 484
Byron, IL 61010-0484
http://www.nucpros.com

BIBLIOGRAPHY

The following is a sampling of materials relating to the professional concerns and development of nuclear reactor operators:

Bodansky, David. *Nuclear Energy: Principles, Practices, and Prospects.* 2d ed. New York: Springer, 2004.

Lamarsh, John R., and Anthony J. Baratta. *Introduction to Nuclear Engineering.* 3d ed. Paramas, N.J.: Prentice Hall, 2001.

McPhee, John A. *The Curve of Binding Energy.* New York: Noonday Press, 1994.

Murray, Raymond L. *Nuclear Energy: An Introduction to the Concepts, Systems and Applications of Nuclear Processes.* 5th ed. Woburn, Mass.: Butterworth-Heinemann, 2001.

OCCUPATIONAL THERAPY ASSISTANTS

Definition

Occupational therapy assistants aid people with mental, physical, developmental, or emotional limitations using a variety of activities to improve basic motor functions and reasoning abilities. Under the supervision of registered occupational therapists, occupational therapy assistants help plan, carry out, and evaluate rehabilitation programs designed to help patients regain self-sufficiency and to restore their physical and mental functions.

High School Subjects

Biology
Health

Personal Skills

Helping/teaching
Leadership/management

Salary Range

$25,830 to $37,400 to $25,830

Minimum Educational Level

Associate's degree

Certification or Licensing

Required by all states

Outlook

Much faster than the average

DOT

076

GOE

14.06.01

NOC

6631

O*NET-SOC

31-2011.00, 31-2012.00

The aroma of grilled cheese sandwiches, toast, and scrambled eggs may linger in the air when Corrine Shields is at work. Dishes may sit in the sink waiting to be rinsed, but Corrine is not a cook or a dishwasher. She is a certified occupational therapy assistant, and she's in the kitchen in order to watch over rehabilitation patients.

Her goal is to teach them skills so that they can regain muscle tone, improve mental abilities, and become more self-sufficient. "By practicing basic living skills," Corrine says, "patients learn to care for themselves once again." Therapeutic activities such as working in the kitchen help rehabilitate patients. "Besides building up their bodies," Corrine says, "it's my job to watch out for their cognitive needs as well. For example, performing the 'simple' task of making toast can be difficult for stroke victims.

"As they move about the kitchen, I evaluate how well they handle safety concerns. I note how well they follow directions and how well they are able to sequence their actions in order to succeed."

When problems arise, Corrine works with her supervisor, a registered occupational therapist, to tailor adaptive strategies for each patient's needs. "It's challenging work," says Corrine. "No two patients are alike. It takes a very creative person to be a good occupational therapy assistant."

What Does an Occupational Therapy Assistant Do?

Before World War I, there were no occupational therapists or occupational therapy assistants. One consequence of modern warfare is a huge rise in the number of soldiers who survived combat but were disabled, both mentally and physically. These veterans needed special support and training in order to learn to live with the effects of their injuries. Occupational therapy developed in response to the need for services that helped soldiers regain self-sufficiency and mental health. Today, occupational therapy deals with a wide variety of patients.

Occupational therapy assistants work in hospitals, mental health facilities, hospices, substance abuse programs, schools, nursing homes, rehabilitation centers, clinics, and in private physicians' practices. They may work with children, developmentally disabled persons, or victims of accidents or illnesses. Many patients benefit from working with occupational therapy assistants, including people with arthritis, cancer, sports-related injuries, hand trauma, amputation, head or spinal cord injuries, strokes, burns, developmental disabilities, and mental illnesses.

Occupational therapy is not the same as physical therapy. Physical therapy helps people with disabilities or injuries regain movement and is mainly concerned with the well-being of patients' bodies. Occupational therapy also deals with physical rehabilitation, but it goes further and includes concern for the psychological and social effects of disabilities and injuries. The goal of occupational therapy is more than restoring physical mobility. Occupational therapy seeks to help patients develop skills that will allow them to re-enter the workplace and care for themselves at home.

Occupational therapy assistants work under the supervision of registered occupational therapists. In general, occupational therapists are responsible for developing programs while occupational therapy assistants are responsible for carrying out the programs.

Often occupational therapy assistants work more directly with individual patients than do occupational therapists. Occupational therapy assistants teach people with permanent functional disabilities how to use special equipment. For example, a person with a spinal cord injury needs to learn how to get around in a wheelchair. A stroke victim may have lost the use of one hand and has to learn how to put on shoes using a long-handled shoe horn. People with cerebral palsy or muscular dystrophy require special adaptive devices that allow them to feed themselves. Computers and computer-related equipment help speech-impaired patients to talk or amputees to walk. Learning to use such complicated equipment takes time, patience, and the support of occupational therapy assistants.

Occupational therapy assistants also work with people who have mental disorders. These disorders may be developmental or the result of emotional disturbances. They may also result from the effects of alcohol abuse, drug abuse, or eating disorders.

The goal of occupational therapy assistants working with this population is to provide strategies to cope with the tasks of daily life, reduce stress, and increase productivity. For instance, when substance abusers leave their rehabilitation programs, they need new skills in order to avoid unproductive behaviors that might lead to relapses. Recovering alcoholics, for example, benefit from practice with time management and budget preparation. Occupational therapy assistants help them develop these skills and avoid repeated substance abuse.

Working with developmentally disabled children or adults presents a different kind of challenge. Basic personal skills such as hygiene, dressing, or eating may require attention. Occupational therapy assistants observe the level at which developmentally disabled persons function and, after consultation with registered occupational therapists, implement strategies to increase self-sufficiency.

Occupational therapy assistants help developmentally disabled persons learn to ride the school bus or take public transportation to their workplace. They help disabled persons learn to do routine household chores such as cooking and cleaning.

Some occupational therapy assistants work in schools. Along with registered occupational therapists, they assess student needs and provide ways to increase active participation in the school day. For example, a child recovering from cancer therapy may need a desk modified to make sitting more comfortable. Another student needs a special splint in order to hold a pencil better. Other children benefit from game-type activities that improve balance and increase both gross and fine motor coordination.

A special branch of occupational therapy seeks to return injured workers to their jobs. Occupational therapy assistants help these people resume, as closely as possible, their original working roles. When necessary, occupational therapy assistants provide strategies, therapies, or adaptive equipment to modify individual work situations.

What Is It Like to Be an Occupational Therapy Assistant?

Corrine Shields works at St. Joseph's Hospital in Tucson, Arizona. Her primary work area is outpatient services, but she may also work in acute care, rehabilitation, or intensive care. A typical day begins with rehabilitation therapy for transitional care patients. Transitional care is a facility within the hospital for people with cerebral-vascular trauma, or stroke.

Corrine sees these patients once a day, Monday through Friday. She works with them using a variety of exercises. For instance, practice making lists is valuable for people with short-term memory loss. Other people need tasks to improve hand-eye coordination. Some patients need help with balance. To help one patient, Corrine has the patient stand beside an elevated table and play a game of cards with her. Another patient, recovering from a different type of injury but who also needs help restoring balance, stands on a foam mat and plays a more active ball exercise.

Lingo to Learn

Adaptive equipment Tools, aids, or devices that persons with reduced or limited mobility use to hold, reach, steady, or pick up objects.

ADL (Activities of daily living) Basic functions (showering, dressing, cooking, eating, going to the bathroom) that the average person performs every day, independently or with the aid of adaptive equipment, such as a sock-aid or a long-handled shoehorn.

Reacher Long-handled implement with a trigger mechanism that "pinches" or "scissors" together to allow the user to grab onto items, such as objects on a high shelf.

Sub-acute care Short-term care facility that patients visit prior to going home in order to learn strengthening and endurance exercises, as well as activities of daily living.

A big part of Corrine's morning is spent with patients who require assistance with the activities of daily living. She helps these people learn, or relearn, how to dress and feed themselves, use the telephone, and write messages. She may also teach them how to safely move from a reclining position on a bed to a sitting position in a chair.

In the afternoon Corrine works in the outpatient clinic with people who require a variety of therapeutic strategies. For example, patients who have had hip replacement surgery need exercises to improve their upper body strength. Pulmonary patients sometimes panic when they are unable to "catch their breath." High levels of anxiety can slow the healing process. Corrine helps pulmonary patients recognize approaching anxiety and finds ways to circumvent it when possible.

Some people with perceptual difficulties benefit from visual activities. Corrine sets up a peg board and asks them to complete a design following a pattern on a graph. By observing their progress, she can determine how well the patients are able to follow directions. She notes how they correct errors and evaluates their general problem-solving abilities.

Patients with cognitive disabilities are taken into the kitchen and asked to perform a basic task such as making scrambled eggs. Corrine watches how well they follow directions and how well they sequence the many steps needed to cook. If patients start to make mistakes, Corrine is there to correct them. She also reminds patients how to work safely within the kitchen.

The kitchen is also a great place to teach new skills to arthritis patients, people with hand injuries, or amputees who are learning to use artificial limbs. Occupational therapy assistants teach these people how to reduce their activity levels to basic movements, conserve their range of motion, and save energy.

In between patients, Corrine makes notes on medical charts, describing that day's activities. She consults with her supervisor, a registered occupational therapist, and discusses future patient care. Sometimes she meets with other hospital staff.

Nancy White works in a nursing home, and because she works exclusively with an older population, her job is slightly different than Corrine's. She observes residents and, when needed, devises adaptable equipment. For example, older people sometimes lose their full range of motion and cannot easily bend over to put on their shoes, so Nancy teaches them how to use long-handled shoehorns. "Reachers," a long handle with grippers that open and close, help mobility-impaired seniors pull on their clothing and dress themselves. Other people grow weaker as they grow older and find it difficult to feed themselves. The solution may be something as simple as creating a weighted eating utensil.

"Our goal as occupational therapy assistants," says Nancy, "is to keep nursing home residents as independent as possible, for as long as possible." Some of her work is similar to what goes on in the hospital. For instance, Nancy helps nursing home residents learn how to stay safe while using the bathroom. When necessary, she raises the level of the toilet seat by using special equipment. She checks to see that there is a grab bar in the shower and advises how to use it. She discusses transfer techniques for getting in and out of the bathtub safely.

Do I Have What It Takes to Be an Occupational Therapy Assistant?

"I'm a people person," says Corrine. "Being an occupational therapy assistant is a good profession for a people person. I get to work directly with patients and not worry about paperwork as much as an occupational therapist has to." A good occupational therapy assistant is a good observer. "You have to be able to pick up on things," says Corrine, "and watch for subtle emotional signs that telegraph how the patient is really feeling. You have to establish rapport with both the patient and the nursing staff. You need to be able to observe what's going on with patients' minds and bodies, seek out more information when necessary, and then, based on what you've discovered, provide the necessary service.

"You can't be squeamish about being close to people either or worry about dealing with all sorts of bodily functions," she adds. "Also, occupational therapy assistance is a physically demanding field. Sometimes you're supporting the weight of patients or helping transfer them from one place to another."

I'm a people person. Being an occupational therapy assistant is a good profession for a people person.

Barbara Rom, director of the Green River Community College program in Auburn, Washington, emphasizes that occupational therapy assistants should be good with their hands. "You can't be awkward," she says, "because you need to make or adapt all kinds of equipment, such as hand splints. It's a great help if you are nimble, creative, and like to make things with your hands." It's also important that you are able to write clearly, concisely, and legibly. Every activity an occupational therapy assistant does is noted on medical charts. Both written and oral communication skills are important. More and more, computer literacy is also needed.

Occupational therapy assistants always work under the supervision of registered occupational therapists. While you may work as a team in most circumstances, occupational therapy assistants are not the lead members. Above all, occupational therapy assistants must be flexible.

"The methods for delivering health care are changing," Corrine stresses. "Supervisors sometimes change, and patients and their needs change daily . . . if you're not flexible, this is not the profession for you."

How Do I Become an Occupational Therapy Assistant?

Corrine Shields has worked as an occupational therapy assistant for nine years. She received her associate's degree from Fox Valley Technical College in Appleton, Wisconsin.

Course work at accredited schools is intense and thorough. Students receive a broad education, including serving a supervised apprenticeship. "The goal," Corrine says, "is to produce graduates who can function immediately as staff members at whatever institution they join."

EDUCATION

High School

Classes in biology, chemistry, physics, social science, health, English, and computer use are helpful to students planning to pursue a career in occupational therapy.

Postsecondary Training

Occupational therapy assistants need more than a high school diploma. There are two ways to enter the profession. Most students attend a two-year program and receive an associate of applied science degree. A few students (those with many years of experience as health care workers or with several years of education past high school) may qualify instead for one-year certificate programs. Both one- and two-year programs include academic study as well as clinical fieldwork.

To Be a Successful Occupational Therapy Assistant, You Should . . .

- enjoy working with people
- be willing to work under supervision
- have good manual dexterity and be physically fit
- be flexible and creative

In-depth

History

Since about the 14th century, physicians have recognized the therapeutic value of providing activities and occupations for their patients. Observations that mental patients tended to recover more quickly from their illnesses led physicians to involve their patients in such activities as agriculture, weaving, working with animals, and sewing. Over time, this practice became quite common, and the conditions of many patients improved.

Occupational therapy as we know it today had its beginning after World War I. The need to help disabled veterans of that war, and years later the veterans of World War II, stimulated the growth of the field. Even though its inception was in the psychiatric field, occupational therapy has developed an equally important role in other medical fields, including rehabilitation of physically disabled patients.

Traditionally, occupational therapists taught creative arts such as weaving, clay modeling, leather work, jewelry making, and other crafts to promote their patients' functional skills. Today, occupational therapists focus more on providing activities that are designed to promote skills needed in daily living, including self-care; employment education and job skills, such as typing, the operation of computers and computer programs, or the use of power tools; and community and social skills.

It is important to note the difference between occupational therapists and physical therapists. Physical therapy is chiefly concerned with helping people with physical disabilities or injuries to regain functions, or adapt to or overcome their physical limitations. Occupational therapists work with physical factors, but also the psychological and social elements of their clients' disabilities, helping them become as independent as possible in the home, school, and workplace. Occupational therapists work not only with the physically challenged, but with people with mental and emotional disabilities as well.

College course work includes medical terminology, basic anatomy and physiology, gerontology and aging, construction of adaptive equipment, note taking and documentation, first aid and CPR, musculoskeletal system disorders, human development, basic health care skills, and therapeutic techniques.

CERTIFICATION OR LICENSING

Every state requires that occupational therapy assistants be certified. Twice a year the National Board for Certification in Occupational Therapy administers a national test to determine certification. The test is rigorous and comprehensive.

SCHOLARSHIPS AND GRANTS

Colleges may reserve scholarships for students pursuing health careers and make specific funds available for students wishing to become occupational therapy assistants. Certain employers, especially long-term care facilities such as nursing homes, may offer stipends to students. In exchange for agreeing to work for the facility after graduation (usually for at least one year), the facility pays a portion of the student's tuition. The American Occupational Therapy Foundation sponsors a number of state association scholarships for students at the associate's degree level and one national scholarship for students pursuing two-year degrees (see "How Do I Learn More?").

Who Will Hire Me?

Occupational therapy assistants work in a variety of institutions including hospitals, mental health facilities, hospices, substance abuse programs, schools, nursing homes, rehabilitation centers, clinics, and private physicians' practices. The majority work for hospitals or nursing homes. Since demand is great for occupational therapy assistants, employers often contact schools to inquire about recent graduates. The American Occupational Therapy Association (AOTA) reports that new occupational therapy assistants find their first jobs, on average, within two months.

Where Can I Go from Here?

Because occupational therapy assistants always work under the supervision of occupational therapists, there is not much room for advancement. Unless you are willing to return to school, obtain a four-year degree, and become an occupational therapist, the highest level that occupational therapy assistants can advance to is lead assistant. These people have more responsibility and may assist in making evaluations. They may schedule work for other occupational therapy assistants and help train students.

What Are the Salary Ranges?

According to the U.S. Department of Labor, the median annual salary for occupational therapy assistants was $37,400 in 2003. Those in the lowest 10 percent made less than $25,830, while those in the highest 10 percent made more than $50,290.

Those working in day care programs and within school systems receive slightly lower incomes while those working in skilled nursing facilities, rehabilitation centers, and hospitals receive higher incomes. Generally, full-time occupational therapy assistants receive standard worker benefits, including health insurance.

Occupational therapy assistants may work some nights and weekends, depending on the needs of the facilities where they work. Those assistants involved with schools work more regular hours than those who work in nursing homes, for example.

Advancement Possibilities

Lead occupational therapy assistants are responsible for making work schedules of other assistants and for the training of occupational therapy students.

Occupational therapists select and direct therapeutic activities designed to develop or restore maximum function to individuals with disabilities.

What Is the Job Outlook?

The U.S. Department of Labor predicts that employment of occupational therapy assistants will grow much faster than the average for all other occupations. Contributing to this growth is the aging population and the large numbers of elderly who need therapy. Also, medical advancements are allowing for people with major injuries to live longer and physically improve, requiring the aid of those in occupational therapy. In addition, insurance companies will be encouraging occupational therapists to assign more work to occupational

FYI

Occupational therapy assistants work with people with a variety of different injuries, disabilities, and illnesses, including:

- Alzheimer's
- arthritis
- depression
- learning disabilities
- multiple sclerosis
- spinal cord injury
- stroke

therapy assistants, thereby lowering costs of care. This trend will also encourage job growth for this profession.

How Do I Learn More?

PROFESSIONAL ORGANIZATIONS

For more information about this career, contact

American Occupational Therapy Association
4720 Montgomery Lane
PO Box 31220
Bethesda, MD 20824-1220
301-652-2682
educate@aota.org
http://www.aota.org

American Occupational Therapy Foundation
4720 Montgomery Lane
PO Box 31220
Bethesda, MD 20824-1220
301-652-2682
aotf@aotf.org
http://www.aotf.org

National Board for Certification in Occupational Therapy
800 South Frederick Avenue, Suite 200
Gaithersburg, MD 20877-4150
301-990-7979
http://www.nbcot.org

BIBLIOGRAPHY

The following is a sampling of materials relating to the professional concerns and development of occupational therapy assistants:

Anderson, Laura L. Swanson, and Christine Malaski. *Occupational Therapy as a Career: An Introduction to the Field and a Structured Method for Observation.* Philadelphia: F. A. Davis Company, 1998.

Quinlan, Kathyrn A. *Occupational Therapy Aide.* Mankato, Minn.: Capstone Press, 1998.

Sladyk, Karen. *Ryan's Occupational Therapy Assistant: Principles, Practice, Issues, and Techniques.* 3d ed. Florence, Ky.: Delmar Learning, 2000.

Weeks, Zona R. *Opportunities in Occupational Therapy Careers.* New York: McGraw-Hill, 2000.

OPHTHALMIC TECHNICIANS

Martha is sitting in the examining room with her eyes closed. "I see these shooting silver arrows going back and forth," she explains to Cathy Brown, the eye doctor's assistant. "It's like lightning bolts going on inside my brain or something. And it doesn't really stop when I open my eyes."

Cathy asks Martha more questions about how her eye problem is affecting her. Has it happened before? How long has it been going on this time? Does she experience headaches along with the "lightning bolts"?

"Okay, Martha. I'm going to look at your eyes more closely." Cathy uses a pen-size flashlight to check Martha's eyelids. "There's no infection or inflammation here, so we'll do a few more things." She shines the light into one eye and then the other, noticing that both eyes constrict equally and quickly to the light. Then she checks Martha's eye muscles by covering one eye and then the other as Martha reads the eye chart. Her muscles seem to be fine.

"Martha, I want you to move forward a little; rest your chin here and your forehead here. I'm going to look into your eyes using this machine. I'm looking now at your cornea, your iris, and your lens. Now I'm going to blow a bit of air into your eye, so try to keep it open as wide as you can. . . . Are you still doing a lot of reading in your work? I'm thinking that maybe these shooting arrows are just a sign that you should be resting your eyes more. Okay, here comes the shot of air. Good.

"The last thing I'm going to do is put some drops in your eyes to dilate your pupils. Dr. Berliner will come in to see you then, and he'll look into your eyes with a scope to see what's going on back there."

Definition

Ophthalmic technicians work with ophthalmologists (eye doctors) in examining patients' eye functions. They measure vision, perform routine tests on eyes, and help to diagnose and treat eye diseases and problems.

Alternative Job Titles

Ophthalmic allied health professionals
Ophthalmic assistants
Ophthalmic medical technologists

High School Subjects

Biology
Chemistry
Mathematics

Personal Skills

Helping/teaching
Technical/scientific

Salary Range

$17,840 to $24,170 to $34,200+

Minimum Educational Level

Some postsecondary training

Certification or Licensing

Recommended

Outlook

Much faster than the average

DOT

079

GOE

10.03.02

NOC

6631

O*NET-SOC

31-9092.00

What Does an Ophthalmic Technician Do?

Ophthalmic technicians can be considered eye nurses: They help eye doctors perform their work. If you have had eye checkups in either an optometrist's or an ophthalmologist's office, you have probably been taken care of by an ophthalmic technician. The difference between the two types of eye doctors is that the ophthalmologist works mainly with eye disease and injury and optometrists work mainly with healthy eyes that do not function properly.

Ophthalmic technicians take patient histories, perform lensometries (measure the lens of the eye), and operate various types of ocular equipment. They must be skilled in patient services such as putting on ocular dressings and shields, administering drops and ointments, and otherwise assisting patients. They must know how to work with all kinds of patients: the elderly, children, the physically disabled, and the visually disabled.

Technicians have knowledge of clinical optics, including retinoscopy, refractometry, spectacle principles, and basic ocular motility. Because contact

Lingo to Learn

Cataract A condition that exists when the eye lens is opaque, causing loss of vision.

Cornea The part of the eyeball that covers the iris and pupil.

Dilate To administer liquid drops to the eye to cause the pupil to enlarge briefly for examination.

Glaucoma An eye disease characterized by such things as loss of vision, hardening of the eye, and a damaged optic disk.

Keratometry Measurement of the cornea.

Ophthalmology The branch of medicine dealing with the structure, functions, and diseases of the eye.

Refraction The ability of the eye to bend light so that an image is focused on the retina; a procedure performed by ophthalmic technicians to determine the eye's refractive characteristics.

Retina The membrane in the eye that allows one to see; it is connected to the brain by the optic nerve.

Retinoscopy Observation of the retina.

Visual acuity The extent to which one can see clearly.

lenses are popular vision aids, technicians have to understand the basic principles of lenses, fitting procedures, patient instruction, and troubleshooting. In addition, they should have an understanding of general medical knowledge, including anatomy, physiology, and pathology (illness and disease), and they must know CPR (cardiopulmonary resuscitation) and other first aid procedures.

The ophthalmic technician must have the same skills that assistants have, as well as knowledge of more advanced procedures. First, in taking patient histories, they ask about the presenting complaint: why the patient has come to see the doctor. Taking the history is like interviewing the patient. What is the family history? Is there diabetes, glaucoma, or hypertension in the family? What medications is the patient taking: aspirin, steroids, birth control pills? Does the patient have allergies? And finally, if the patient wears glasses or contact lenses, how long have they worn them and how is their vision now?

Working directly with patients is the task with which the ophthalmic technician is involved the most. Many patients are elderly; they visit the ophthalmologist when they have symptoms related to eye problems, such as cataracts and glaucoma. These are the two most common eye conditions leading to loss of sight. (When you have cataracts, it's like trying to see through a steamed-up window; vision is very blurry and opaque.) The technician will help the ophthalmologist to monitor the patient's cataracts, which develop gradually as one gets older, and then will assist the doctor when it is time for the cataracts to be removed.

Certified ophthalmic medical personnel help to bring peace of mind to both patients and the doctors with whom they work. Because ophthalmic technicians work with other professionals, there is a sense of teamwork in the office setting.

What Is It Like to Be an Ophthalmic Technician?

Cathy Brown works with ophthalmologists at Maine Eye Center, an eye-care clinic in Portland, Maine. She greets patients, settles them into examining rooms, and performs initial tests on patients' eyes. Because of her training and certification, she is qualified to take medical histories, one of the first tasks that need to be done with new patients. She asks new patients about such things as why they need an eye exam, what their family history of disease is, what their vision is like, and what types of medications, if any, they take, all the while keeping up a friendly conversation to set them at ease.

Cathy's other basic skills include measuring and recording visual acuity (that is, how sharp one's vision is). Somewhere in the doctor's office you'll probably find a Snellen chart, which shows 11 lines of progressively smaller letters, starting with the big "E" at the top and ending with PEZOLCFTD at the bottom. Your visual acuity is determined by how much of the chart you can read without corrective lenses. Cathy also will use color plates to test eyes for color vision.

Many ophthalmologists work in the clinic where Cathy works. Each has a different specialty, such as pediatric ophthalmology (working with children), retinal or corneal ophthalmology, ophthalmic plastic surgery, and cataracts/glaucoma. At this point in her career, Cathy assists mainly with the plastics ophthalmologist, which means that she's involved with conditions like orbital reconstruction and tearing problems. Floating technicians, or technicians who move (or "float") to wherever needed, are required to fill in when any one of the doctors in the office needs help. Cathy says that this is the hardest part of the job, being skilled in just about every specialty so that you can handle any situation that comes up (be it cataracts, corneal problems, or even a simple vision test for a child).

Cathy performs routine exams as well: checking vision, pressure, and muscle reactions and motility; doing retinoscopies and refractometries; and dilating pupils. She does a lot of patient screening, taking histories and basically talking with the patients about their eye conditions. One of the most important things she does is to reassure patients about their particular complaints. Their needs and concerns require patience and understanding.

Although much of the work is routine, every now and then an emergency comes up. Perhaps a patient comes in complaining that her vision is dark or that she sees flashes of light. Cathy says that this should set off an alarm in the technician's mind: Is the retina attached? Is something wrong with the cornea? The patient will be screened by the ophthalmic assistant or technician, examined by the ophthalmologist, and then perhaps will go to the operating room or be sent to the hospital.

Cathy likes her work schedule. Her average workweek is about 36 to 40 hours, and she has Sundays and Mondays off. She is usually finished by about five in the afternoon, but she says that the ophthalmic photographers and those who work with angiograms sometimes have to stay later to wait for photos or X rays to develop.

Do I Have What It Takes to Be an Ophthalmic Technician?

"You definitely must have patience, especially because lots of the people you see are elderly," says Cathy. "You really get to learn a lot about people. It's actually really fun."

Advancement Possibilities

Ophthalmic medical technologists become certified after going through a two-year training program and passing certification exams. Their duties are similar to the technician's but more in-depth and advanced. Basically, technologists might use more specialized equipment, measure intraocular pressure, plot visual fields, and do other jobs that technicians are not certified to do.

Orthoptists are even more specialized than technologists. An orthoptist will assess the patient's eye alignment and measure how the eyes work together.

Ophthalmic surgical assistants work with ophthalmologists in preparing patients for eye surgery. They must be able to identify, select, and maintain ophthalmic surgical instruments; sterilize and set up instruments for surgical procedures; and otherwise assist the ophthalmic surgeon in either an office or a hospital operating room.

Cathy explains that on hectic days, when she might see 40 to 50 patients in one morning, "you need to be as pleasant as you can, but you have to move things along." In other words, you have to be very organized. "The doctors put a lot of trust in your hands. You have to be self-motivated, use your own judgment," Cathy says.

The doctors put a lot of trust in your hands. You have to be self-motivated, use your own judgment.

Communication skills are very important, as well as keeping abreast of new technology and knowledge in the field. You should expect to attend meetings, conventions, and a yearly educational program. You need to maintain your continuing education

In-depth

20/20

What does 20/20 vision really mean? To test your visual acuity (how well you see), the ophthalmic technician at your doctor's office will have you read the Snellen chart (the one with the big E at the top and the tiny letters at the bottom). This chart hangs at a distance of 20 feet from the examining chair. If you can read all the letters on the chart without glasses or contact lenses, that means you have 20/20 vision. It means that you can see at 20 feet what the "optically normal" eye can see at that distance.

If the technician tells you that you have 20/40 vision, It means that your eyes are less strong; you have to be only 20 feet away from something that the "optically normal" eye can see at 40 feet. The larger the bottom number is, the weaker your visual acuity. So if you can't see the PEZOLCFTD at the bottom of the chart, the ophthalmic technician will probably begin fitting you for glasses!

credits within three-year cycles, so you have to be comfortable with taking tests fairly often.

Every now and then there are volunteer opportunities for technicians. For example, Cathy and her colleagues once volunteered at a school for the deaf, where they examined the eyes of about 100 children.

How Do I Become an Ophthalmic Technician?

There are two general routes to becoming an ophthalmic technician: formal training and on-the-job training. In either case, you need to study for certification exams, take the exams (both written and performance), and continue to periodically update your certification. According to Dr. Melvin Freeman, "certification shows the dedication and professionalism of the employee and their dedication to the best care for patients under the ophthalmologist's guidance."

In Cathy's case, she was in a training program for ophthalmic surgical assisting when a job opened up at Maine Eye Center. She was hired as an on-the-job trainee with the obligation of going through a home-study course and 10 weeks of reviewing with the resident optometrists. She eventually took her exam and was certified as an assistant. Her next step is to take courses leading to certification as a technician.

Cathy says that many doctors hire people to work their way up in the office, as she is doing. At one point, the doctors at Maine Eye Center needed an ophthalmic photographer but realized it was difficult to find a trained worker. They put an ad in the paper and eventually hired someone who was a skilled photographer to be trained on the job.

EDUCATION

High School

Cathy recalls that it was helpful to have taken basic science and math courses in high school. She was able to take certain vocational classes in her junior and senior years, which gave her an awareness of the medical field. These classes included CPR and chemistry lab. Cathy knew that she wanted to work in a medical occupation, so she became involved in a nurses' assistant program. Going on field trips and taking tours of places like hospitals also opened doors for her, and she became further aware of job opportunities in ophthalmology.

As with many careers, it is wise to concentrate on basic subjects like English because in this job you'll find yourself doing various administrative tasks such as writing patient histories. You'll need to be able to communicate well, both on paper and in person. As Cathy mentioned, working for so many doctors involves teamwork and cooperation. Experience with team sports and with groups like the debate team and drama club gives you opportunities to learn how to work with others.

Postsecondary Training

University degrees are not required for this career. However, you must either successfully complete an accredited ophthalmic technician's program or be certified as an active ophthalmic assistant, have at least one year of full-time work experience as a certified ophthalmic assistant, and finish 18 hours of approved continuing education credits.

The courses involved can be taken while you are working as an ophthalmic assistant, or you can enroll in a one-year full-time training program. You can expect to be quite challenged in most of your courses for this career. At this stage, classes follow a pretty standard outline and curriculum, including basic anatomy and physiology, medical terminology, medical laws and ethics, psychology, ocular anatomy and physiology, optics, microbiology, and diseases of the eye. You also learn about patient services (such as preparing ocular shields, delivering drugs, and otherwise assisting the patient), ophthalmic skills and lensometry, and instrument operation and maintenance (you have to be familiar with such equipment as ophthalmoscopes, retinoscopes, and slit lamps).

Cathy recalls her training experience as somewhat overwhelming. But even though there was so much involved, she continued through her own motivation. She carefully watched others perform their jobs, gained the confidence to try the tasks herself, and eventually learned everything she needed for her own certification. "Everything that was presented in the courses was necessary," she says.

CERTIFICATION OR LICENSING

In brief, to be an ophthalmic technician you have to be certified by the Joint Commission on Allied Health Personnel in Ophthalmology (JCAHPO). The certification requirements are quite straightforward, consisting of five basic elements: (1) evidence of successful completion of education and training; (2) evidence of satisfactory work experience; (3) a current CPR certificate; (4) endorsement by a sponsoring ophthalmologist; and (5) successful completion of a skills evaluation and a written exam.

After becoming certified as a technician, you are required to maintain your credentials by renewing your certification periodically. It is your responsibility to apply for recertification every three years. This means that you must take a certain number of continuing education courses throughout your career. Accepted courses include those offered by JCAHPO at the Continuing Education Program held each year, regional courses, and self-study courses (for example, tapes, readings, and videos).

SCHOLARSHIPS AND GRANTS

JCAHPO selects certain students each year to receive scholarships. These students are usually enrolled in accredited education programs for ophthalmic medical personnel. For more information and application instructions, visit http://www.jcahpo.org/Foundation.htm.

Also, individual schools may have their own financial aid programs, so you should talk with a counselor at the financial aid office wherever you are applying.

Who Will Hire Me?

Ophthalmic technicians work wherever there are ophthalmologists: doctors' offices, eye clinics, and hospitals. They also work in university research and training centers. Some technicians work as teachers, technical writers, and consultants.

Where Can I Go from Here?

Becoming an ophthalmic medical technologist is definitely a step up the career ladder. According to one worker, "Being a COMT [certified ophthalmic medical technologist] is a very rewarding career. There's an abundance of opportunities throughout the country." Lisa Rovick is a COMT in a large multispecialty clinic in the Minneapolis/St. Paul area. She says that other options for advancement include going into the business side of ophthalmology, perhaps becoming a partner with the ophthalmologists at a busy office.

Other ophthalmic workers have become contractors, which means that they offer their services at various medical settings and work on a freelance basis. Education is another area of specialization. Some technicians perform in-service training and teach continuing education courses. Others work as sales representatives or researchers for manufacturers of ophthalmic equipment and pharmaceuticals.

Although it is not actually a higher-level position, ophthalmic surgical assisting is a specialty in which

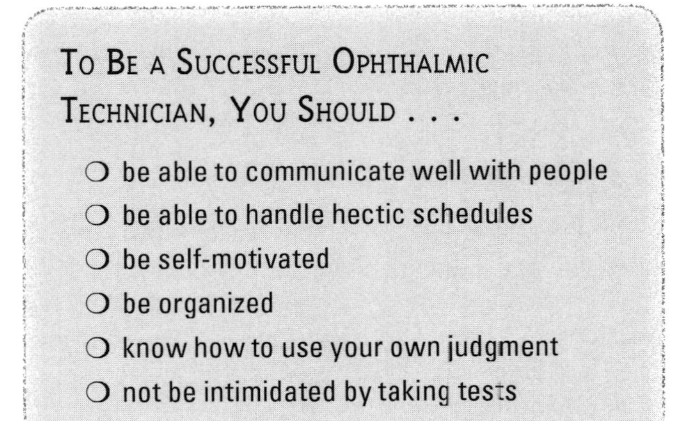

you may be examined and awarded a certificate. Cathy has been assisting with surgery and plans to become more involved in that aspect of the work. "I first assist in surgery," Cathy says, "meaning I assist the doctor, and also suture."

What Are the Salary Ranges?

According to JCAHPO, salaries for ophthalmic medical personnel vary from $20,000 to $50,000 a year. The *Occupational Outlook Handbook* reports that median annual earnings for medical assistants were $24,170 in 2003. Those in the lowest 10 percent earned less than $17,840, and those in the highest 10 percent earned more than $34,200. Full-time technicians are usually provided with health and life insurance, and receive vacation pay and sick leave.

What Is the Job Outlook?

The U.S. Department of Labor expects employment of medical assistants to grow much faster than the average for all other occupations. In fact, the medical assistants field is projected to be the fastest growing occupation through 2012. Part of the reason for this growth is the aging population and the number of medical assistants that will be needed to provide eye care to the elderly.

Some programs across the country, such as the Emory University School of Medicine in Atlanta, are beginning to offer higher degrees in ophthalmic technology. Emory awards a master's degree, which allows ophthalmic technologists to advance into management roles. Graduates of these programs also receive better starting salaries; the Emory program has had graduates receive offers of between $36,000 and $55,000 annually.

How Do I Learn More?

PROFESSIONAL ORGANIZATIONS

The following are organizations that provide information on ophthalmic technician careers, accredited schools and scholarships, and employers:

American Academy of Ophthalmology
PO Box 7424
San Francisco, CA 94120-7424
415-561-8500
http://www.aao.org

American Academy of Optometry
6110 Executive Boulevard, Suite 506
Rockville, MD 20852
301-984-1441
aaoptm@aol.com
http://www.aaopt.org

American Optometric Association
243 North Lindbergh Boulevard
St. Louis, MO 63141
314-991-4100
http://www.aoanet.org

Association of Technical Personnel in Ophthalmology
2025 Woodlane Drive
St. Paul, MN 55125-2998
800-482-4858
http://www.atpo.org

Joint Commission on Allied Health Personnel in Ophthalmology
2025 Woodlane Drive
St. Paul, MN 55125-2998
800-284-3937
jcahpo@jcahpo.org
http://www.jcahpo.org

BIBLIOGRAPHY

The following is a sampling of material relating to the professional concerns and development of ophthalmic technicians:

Anshel, Jeffrey. *Smart Medicine for Your Eyes*. New York: Avery Publishing, 1999.

Cassin, Barbara. *Fundamentals for Ophthalmic Technical Personnel*. Philadelphia: W.B. Saunders, 1995.

Ledford, Janice K. *Certified Ophthalmic Technician Exam Review Manual*. 2d ed. Thorofare, N.J.: Slack Inc., 2004.

Stein, Harold A., Bernard J. Slatt, and Raymond M. Stein. *The Ophthalmic Assistant: A Guide for Ophthalmic Medicine Personnel*. 7th ed. St. Louis: Mosby, 2000.

OPTICS TECHNICIANS

At 1:00 P.M. the lab at Lenscrafters bustles with activity. The store is packed with business people on their lunch hour, checking their watches, and waiting for their eyeglasses to be finished. Rich Crockett circles the optical lab, checking on the progress of six pairs of glasses that have to be ready within an hour.

One of the optics technicians Rich stops to observe is Ron Miranda. Although on the job for only three months, Ron has already mastered the operation of many high-tech instruments, compounds, and hand tools in the lab. As Rich watches Ron work on a lens, he's pleased with how quickly his newest employee has become proficient at the 20-step process.

As the most experienced member of the lab, Rich offers Ron a few tips on using the precision grinding instruments. Rich glances at the clock. It will be at least another hour before the flurry of business subsides.

Definition
Optics technicians produce lenses for prescription eyeglasses. They also assemble the lenses and frame into the finished eyeglass. Some optics technicians also produce lenses for cameras, telescopes, binoculars, and other optical instruments.

Alternative Job Titles
Optical technicians
Precision-lens technicians

High School Subjects
Biology
Mathematics
Technical/Shop

Personal Skills
Following instructions
Mechanical/manipulative

Salary Range
$15,720 to $22,194 to $34,810

Minimum Educational Level
High school diploma

Certification or Licensing
Required by certain states

Outlook
Little change or more slowly than the average

DOT
716

GOE
08.02.02

NOC
N/A

O*NET-SOC
51-9083.02

What Does an Optics Technician Do?

Lenses are part of countless aspects of daily, scientific, and professional life. Thus, there is a tremendous need for *optics technicians* to make, assemble, and maintain lenses. In addition, optics technicians are needed to help invent new types of lenses and new uses for lenses.

Though most people think of optics technicians as the men and women who grind and polish the lenses for eyeglasses, there are a number of areas in which optics technicians may work. These areas include lens fabrication, product manufacturing, maintenance and operations, and research and development.

Lens fabrication is the area most associated with producing eyeglasses. An optics technician working in lens fabrication might fill any of the following roles: lens molder, lens blocker, lens generator, lens grinder, lens polisher, lens centerer or edger, lens coater, or lens inspector. Depending on the size and organization of the laboratory, an optics technician can perform several or all of these tasks. A technician may also be responsible for supervising the work done by other technicians.

A *lens molder* works with partially melted glass, plastic, or polycarbonate to press and form a lens blank, which is a generic lens used to produce the prescribed finished lens.

A *lens blocker* places the lens blanks into blocks so that they are secured in place during the rest of the grinding and polishing.

A *lens generator* works with an instrument that grinds the lens into its rough curve and thickness.

A *lens grinder* finishes shaping the lens into its prescribed curve and thickness, using cup-shaped tools and fine grinding powders.

A *lens polisher* uses various compounds, pads, and machines to polish the lens so that there are no obstructions when checking the power of the lens and light refraction.

A *lens centerer* or *edger* uses a lensometer to check the degree and placement of the curves that determine the strength of the lens. Using handstones, the edger finishes shaping the lens to fit in the frame.

A *lens coater* performs all the finishing steps in the fabrication of the lens, including the application of tints or coatings and final polishing.

A *lens inspector* checks the lens for required hardness, inspects for scratches or other defects, and ensures that all government standards have been met.

The area of product manufacturing deals mostly with fabricating lenses for use in products other than eyeglasses. An optics technician working in this field assembles, aligns, calibrates, and tests optical instruments, which include microscopes, telescopes, binoculars, and cameras, as well as less common equipment used for land surveying, night surveillance, or medical research and diagnosis.

Optics technicians in maintenance and operations are responsible for keeping large-scale optical instruments working, such as technical and scientific cameras, large observatory telescopes, and spectrophometers. Most of the work is done at the site where the instrument is being used. These include places such as observatories, hospitals, and missile or satellite tracking stations.

Optics technicians working in research and development help develop new types of lenses and new uses for them. Working closely with engineers or scientists, they conduct tests, take measurements, and fabricate new optical instruments. These technicians may choose to specialize in surveillance equipment, security devices, precision measuring instruments, medical implements, or environmental tools.

Lingo to Learn

Aberration A condition that causes blurring, loss of clearness, or distortion of shape in the images formed by lenses or curved mirrors.

Diffraction The spreading out of waves as they pass around an obstacle or go through an opening. For example, light waves are diffracted when they pass through a small sheet of glass marked with thousands of parallel lines, producing a spectrum.

Index of refraction The ratio of the speed of light in a vacuum to its speed in the particular substance being measured.

Lens A curved, transparent body that bends (refracts) light rays.

Reflection The bending back of waves, such as light waves, from a surface.

Refraction The bending of waves, such as light waves, when they pass from one substance to another. Refraction occurs because waves travel at different speeds through different substances.

Spherical aberration Rays of light striking near the edges of the lens or mirror are brought to focus closer to the lens or mirror than are the central rays. The result is that the image of a point appears as a small disk.

What Is It Like to Be an Optics Technician?

The general, day-to-day responsibilities of an optics technician are similar throughout the entire field of optics technology. Whether you are making a pair of glasses for someone, a lens for a NASA telescope, or a crystal for a 16th-century museum piece, the tasks of grinding, polishing, and aligning are usually involved. Work environments, on the other hand, can vary greatly. While the majority of technicians work in laboratories that are clean, ventilated, and well lighted, *maintenance and operations technicians* will find themselves working at night or outdoors at places such as missile and satellite stations. It's not unusual for these technicians to work in cramped positions and on greasy or dirty equipment.

Rich Crockett manages the optics laboratory for a Lenscrafters store in Chicago. He's been an optics technician for more than 25 years. "The size of the lab varies from place to place, and the number of tasks each technician is responsible for may be lesser or greater, but they all look pretty much the same," says Rich.

Ron Miranda is newer to the job. He sees the lab as a very new type of work environment. "I worked as a florist before coming to the lab at Lenscrafters,"

ADVANCEMENT POSSIBILITIES

Precision-lens centerers and edgers, also known as **lead technicians**, set up, operate, and train workers on the grinder and collimator. The grinder edges and bevels precision ophthalmic optical lenses, and the collimator centers a beam of light through the lens.

Precision inspectors, also known as **optical elements inspectors** and **lens inspectors,** use precision measuring instruments to inspect optical and ophthalmic lenses at various stages of production and ensure that standards have been met.

Supervisors, also known as **inspecting supervisors and lens generating supervisors,** coordinate the activities of workers engaged in fabricating and inspecting optical lenses. The supervisor inspects lenses for defects and adherence to specifications using devices such as a polariscope, magnifying glass, protractor, or power determining instrument.

he says. "Here everything is so bright and clean and organized. At my other job it was completely the opposite."

Lenscrafters provides one-hour service, as do most retail lens fabricators these days. While Rich and Ron try to stick to an eight-hour schedule, the work occasionally extends into the evening. Rich says, "Sometimes I have to be here from before the store opens at 8:00 A.M. until after the store closes at 7:00 P.M. because we have a problem with one of the machines, or maybe someone came in just before we closed and needs their glasses when we open the next day. Usually on those days, though, I'm so busy I don't even realize how long I've been working."

"Yeah, but sometimes you really know you've been working a long day," adds Ron. "Still, when it's over you feel good." He explains that even after a tiring day, he feels proud of having accomplished something tangible. "When you're done, you know you've made a well-crafted product for two or three dozen people." He also notes that the more hours he works, the more money he makes and the closer he is to earning a promotion to lab manager himself.

Optics technicians usually work 40-hour weeks. Some retail eyeglass stores are open seven days a week. Research laboratories at private companies and in the government are generally open Monday through Friday.

An optics technician working in photo-optics maintenance might work at a rocket or missile test range or at a satellite tracking station. A typical day might involve assembling, adjusting, aligning, and operating telescopic cameras that track the missiles or satellites.

Technicians employed by private companies or government laboratories are usually specialized in production or in research and development. *Production technicians* sometimes assemble the entire product, right up to the final inspection, or they may focus on one production task. Other responsibilities include maintaining an inventory of parts and materials, performing precision assembly using microscopes, and working with the engineering staff on special projects. *Research and development technicians* work in laboratories with scientists and engineers. They are often charged with tracking and recording test results and building prototypes.

Regardless of the setting, safety and efficiency are mandatory for optics technicians. Certain chemicals that technicians use can be dangerous if mixed inappropriately, and the fumes they give off can be unhealthy in an unventilated room. Technicians are careful to protect their eyes, especially when they're using grinding instruments, because the particles of glass, plastic, and other materials can be hazardous.

"Everyone wears protective eye gear in the lab, whether they are working on a lens or not," Rich says. "We have emergency equipment all around the lab in case a chemical gets on someone, in their eyes, or explodes. The lab is safer than most people's workplaces. It only seems dangerous when everyone is busy and all the machines are making noise."

Do I Have What It Takes to Be an Optics Technician?

An optics technician working in retail has to be good with customers, as well as skilled at the manual aspects of the job. For Rich, the moment when someone puts on that first pair of eyeglasses and looks in the mirror is what makes his job great. "They look around the room and can't believe the detail they can see," says Rich. "Then they look in the mirror and say, 'Hey, I don't look bad at all. I look pretty darn good, in fact.'"

In retail, the production process can be almost nonstop. "It can be a very high-stress job during the times when the store is filled with customers," Rich says. Ron adds, "You have to pay very close attention to detail in every step of lens production." It's important that technicians not be easily flustered. They need to take the time to make sure they're using the right tool and following the specifications of the prescription.

You have to pay very close attention to detail in every step of lens production.

While new, high-tech equipment performs a lot of detail work automatically, most of the precision work still requires a certain feel or manual dexterity on the part of the optics technician. That feel only comes with experience and ability, like any craft work. "You get to believing that every pair of eyeglasses that comes out of this lab is your creation," says Rich. For example, the lens generator encloses the lens in a chamber while it grinds the lens to its prescription rough curve and thickness and then aligns the prism-axes. The technician works entirely by feel and knowledge of the requirements for each lens. Rich likens the work on the generator to peeling a potato blindfolded.

In other areas of optics technology, it's critical that technicians have an aptitude for math and science, as they will be working on complex projects. Good communication skills are also important because optics technicians need to report their findings in a clear manner, whether in a written report or a verbal briefing.

How Do I Become an Optics Technician?

The quickest way to become an optics technician is to apply for a position as a lab technician at a wholesale or retail lens fabricator. Most often these companies are looking for individuals whom they can train according to their own specific needs.

Rich Crockett hires optics technicians for the Lenscrafters labs he manages. "What I am most looking for is someone who gives it all they have in learning the skills. And I want someone who is interested in advancing in a career as an optics tech," he says. "I will train them so they will not only know every detail in making a pair of glasses for Lenscrafters, but also be thoroughly proficient in all phases of setup, grinding, generating, aligning, polishing, and finishing."

After a retail training program, which lasts anywhere from six to 18 months, optics technicians are knowledgeable in the materials that lenses are made out of, the chemicals used as adhesives, polishes, and tints, and also any innovations in optical goods. Some optics technicians are then able to move into other areas of optics. However, most advanced optics positions require some formal postsecondary training as well as on-the-job experience.

EDUCATION

High School

While not all retail lens fabrication laboratories insist on their optics technicians being high school graduates, most prefer hiring individuals with diplomas. If you have your eye on a job in production, maintenance and operations, or research and development, a high school diploma is a must, as you will need to pursue postsecondary training.

High school courses in mathematics, science, and shop are useful. Optics technicians will need some knowledge of algebra, geometry, physics, chemistry, technical reading and writing, mechanical drawing, glass working, and photography. Ideal courses are those that increase your manual dexterity and your ability to follow scientific procedures.

Postsecondary Training

A common way to become an optics technician is to train in an optics laboratory. These are usually on-the-job training programs and therefore provide the added benefit of income while learning. In some of the technical or industrial labs, training is in preparation for a job with the lab and therefore provides no income until training is successfully completed.

Another route is to attend a technical institute or community college that offers a two- or three-year program in engineering, optics, or physics. Useful courses are those that deal with geometrical optics, trigonometry, lens polishing, technical writing, optical instruments, analytical geometry, specification writing, physics, optical shop practices, manual preparation, mechanical drawing, and report preparation.

A handful of colleges and universities offer specific training and degrees for optics technicians. The University of Rochester, for instance, offers a two-year certification program for technicians. For advanced or highly technical positions as an optics technician, you may be required to have a bachelor's degree in optics, engineering, physics, or even astronomy.

CERTIFICATION OR LICENSING

Certification or licensing is usually not required for optics technicians, although some states have a license requirement for retail optics technicians. The licensing examinations in these states may be written, practical, or both. Inquire at an optics laboratory in the state you wish to practice to find out about licensing requirements.

Often, the laboratory will provide a certification upon completion of your training program. You may then be required by the lab to update this certification regularly by completing courses, seminars, conferences, written exams, practical exams, or any combination of them.

SCHOLARSHIPS AND GRANTS

Scholarships are available for students pursuing bachelor's degrees in optics engineering and physics at four-year universities, and to a lesser degree, for students in two-year technical programs. You should contact financial aid offices at the programs you're applying to in order to get information on eligibility, application requirements, and deadlines.

Who Will Hire Me?

Thirty-three percent of all optics technicians in the United States work in labs at retail eyeglass stores. One-hour eyeglass stores such as Pearle Vision and Lenscrafters have sprung up in almost every city, suburb, and town. Department stores often offer eyeglass services as well. With new stores opening up all the time and turnover in existing stores high, opportunities at the retail level are good.

Many other technicians are employed by government laboratories and by private manufacturers who make optical goods for medical, defense, and consumer markets. Several professional organizations offer employment listings and useful contact information. Other optics technicians are employed by optometrists or ophthalmologists in smaller labs.

Where Can I Go from Here?

Rich hopes to be promoted soon from lab manager to district manager of 17 stores. "The next step after I've supervised all the local stores is to move into the regional area." Rich can become a regional lab manager of all the labs in a section of a state, an entire state, or a group of states. This position is also called the RQC (regional quality control) because the individual must make sure that all the labs adhere to company and government standards. At this level, Rich would no longer be responsible for doing hands-on lens fabrication.

Ron sees himself becoming the lead technician in a lab eventually. Lead technicians supervise other optics technicians and handle the lab's administrative tasks.

Experienced technicians who work in production or research and development can aspire to some of the following positions. They can become photographic technicians who operate cameras in research or engineering projects. Advanced production technicians

To Be a Successful Optics Technician, You Should . . .

- have manual dexterity
- be attentive to detail
- have an aptitude for math and science
- have the desire to learn a craft
- be a good communicator
- work with energy and ambition

might help produce specialized optical goods such as reticles (the cross hairs in the focus of an optical instrument's eyepiece) or integrate electronic circuits that are used in calculators, computers, and other electronic systems. Instrument assemblers and testers perform the assembly of optical instruments, checking alignment, functioning, and appearance. Technicians can also advance to become optical model makers, who assemble prototypes of new optical devices.

What Are the Salary Ranges?

According to the U.S. Department of Labor, ophthalmic laboratory technicians had median hourly wages of $10.67 in 2003. For full-time workers, this comes to about $22,194 a year. Those in the lowest 10 percent made less than $7.56 an hour ($15,720 annually), while those in the highest 10 percent made more than $16.73 an hour ($34,810).

In a retail setting, technicians may have to complete a probationary employment period before receiving benefits such as health insurance and paid vacation and sick leave. Benefits packages at optics manufacturers and government laboratories are usually generous and include health insurance, paid vacation and sick leave, disability insurance, and some form of retirement plan.

What Is the Job Outlook?

Optics technicians will experience little or no job growth over the next 10 years. Although job growth in the realm of manufacturing lenses for eyeglasses should grow at an average rate, jobs in other areas of optics manufacturing will decrease because of increased use of automation. But even with government cutbacks in space and weapons technology, consumer demand for complex cameras, binoculars, telescopes, and medical tools will sustain employment levels for technicians in production, maintenance and operations, and research and development.

How Do I Learn More?

PROFESSIONAL ORGANIZATIONS

For information on optics technician careers, accredited schools, and employers, contact

American Optometric Association
243 North Lindbergh Boulevard
St. Louis, MO 63141
314-991-4100
http://www.aoanet.org

BIBLIOGRAPHY

The following is a sampling of materials relating to the professional concerns and development of optics technicians:

Belikoff, Kathleen M. *Opportunities in Eye Care Careers.* New York: McGraw-Hill, 2003.

Shannon, Robert F. *The Art and Science of Optical Design.* New York: Cambridge University Press, 1997.

Smith, Gregory Hallock. *Practical Computer-Aided Lens Design.* Richmond, Va.: Willmann Bell, 1998.

ORTHOTIC AND PROSTHETIC TECHNICIANS

The scene is controlled chaos in the Pueblo, Colorado, office of Mike Manship and Russ Miller, orthotic and prosthetic practitioners. From seeing patients who have come in with scheduled appointments and others who have walked in without an appointment, to answering phone calls, and dashing between examining rooms to the office's lab where they adjust patients' orthotic or prosthetic devices, there is never a dull day for the two men.

"If we're not working and talking with people," Russ says, "we are in the lab fabricating devices that will be fit on these people. The people that come into the office that already have the devices, we are oftentimes running from the exam rooms to the lab area to adjust their devices."

Definition
Orthotic and prosthetic technicians make, fit, repair, and maintain orthotic and prosthetic devices according to established specifications under the direction of orthotists and prothetists.

Alternative Job Titles
Arch-support technician
Orthotic and prosthetic practitioner

High School Subjects
Art
Biology
Technical/shop

Personal Skills
Helping/teaching
Mechanical/manipulative

Salary Range
$17,600 to $28,500 to $47,300+

Minimum Educational Requirements
Some postsecondary training

Certification or Licensing
Required by all states (licensing)
Voluntary (certification)

Outlook
Faster than the average

DOT
712

GOE
14.05.01

NOC
3219

O*NET-SOC
N/A

What Does an Orthotic and Prosthetic Technician Do?

Orthotic and prosthetic technicians read and follow specific instructions provided by orthotist and prothetists to choose the appropriate materials and tools necessary to make braces. These braces are used to support weak or ineffective joints and muscles, to correct physical defects, or to build artificial limbs for patients.

Mike and Russ are *orthotic and prosthetic practitioners*, a job which involves not only fabricating and fitting orthotic and prosthetic devices like a technician, but also for performing clinical evaluations of patients, for making recommendations regarding the best type of device to meet each patient's needs, and for the patient's post-rehabilitation care. We do "fabrication of these devices, fitting of the devices, and follow up to make sure that the patient is indeed seeing the benefits of orthosis and prosthesis," Russ says.

Similar to the work of orthotic and prosthetic technicians, *arch-support technicians* make steel arch-supports for a patient's foot, following the instructions of a podiatrist, orthotist, or prosthetist.

Like other skilled craftsmen, those working in the field of orthotics and prosthetics must read diagrams and follow written specifications to build medical appliances.

To make a plastic replacement for ears, noses, or hands, prosthetic technicians use wax or plastic to create an impression of the patient's amputated body area. A plaster cast is made from a mold of the impression. To ensure that the final replacement matches the patient's body part, the technician may have to carve, grind, or build up parts of the plaster model. When the basic device is ready, the technician will fit it with an outer cover using a sewing machine, riveting guns, and other hand tools. If necessary, the technician will mix pigments to match the patient's skin coloring and apply them to the outer covering of the prosthesis.

Orthotic devices are built by technicians who use a variety of tools such as hammers, anvils, welding equipment, and saws to cut and shape pieces of metal or plastic into the specified device's structural components. To be sure the finished device fits properly, the technician may shape the metal or plastic parts around a cast model of the patient's torso or limbs. When the technician completes the basic parts of the device, it is assembled with rivets, covered and padded with layers of rubber, felt, plastic, and leather.

Arch-support technicians work with plaster casts of a patient's foot to determine the proper size and shape of the support to be built. They must select stainless steel sheets of the correct thickness and cut the sheets to the correct size. Once the steel is formed to the specified shape the technician checks the support against the plaster model to be sure it fits accurately. The support is then polished with abrasive polishing wheels and leather is glued to it for additional patient comfort.

What Is It Like to Be an Orthotic and Prosthetic Technician?

"A typical work day is very chaotic," Russ says, ticking off a list of daily activities that include seeing scheduled and nonscheduled patients, in-house appointments, home visits, hospital calls, and time in the lab fabricating devices.

"In-house appointments, home visits, and hospital calls are often unscheduled so [the job] demands a flexible individual," Russ says.

Russ describes his office as "medical and technical," with examination rooms where he and Mike consult with patients, and a laboratory area where they fabricate orthotic and prosthetic devices for patients.

Not all of Russ's time is spent in the office, he says. "The job involves some travel to see patients that are home bound, or seeing patients in the hospital."

Lingo to Learn

AFO Ankle-foot orthosis. A brace used to support the ankle and foot.

KAFO Knee-ankle-foot orthosis. A brace used to support the knee, ankle, and foot.

Myoelectrics The technology of taking human nerve impulses or electrical impulses outside of the body and converting them to electric current, which is used to move the artificial parts in a prothesis.

Orthosis Orthotic device. An appliance that supports, aligns, corrects, or prevents deformities. Also used to improve the function of moveable body parts.

Prosthesis Prosthetic device. An artificial substitute for a missing body part such as an arm, leg, hand, or foot that is used for functional or cosmetic reasons or both.

Do I Have What It Takes to Be an Orthotic and Prosthetic Technician?

Technicians generally are not required to work overtime, evenings, or weekends. To be successful you should be comfortable working in workshops with power and hand tools, and with a variety of materials like plastic, metal, and leather. You also must be willing to adhere to strict safety procedures and be able to interpret written directions and follow precise instructions. You must also be committed to learning new technologies and advancements continually being developed in the field.

Russ says that good interpersonal communication skills are key to being successful in this profession. Also, "you need to be able to think on your feet and think outside of the box. In dealing with people there is no recipe, there is no one solution for one problem."

He continues, "This [profession] does require some kind of hand skills and mechanical skills and if you're truly going to advance in the field it would help to have some business experience, such as knowledge of accounting and marketing."

How Do I Become an Orthotic and Prosthetic Technician?

Having worked as a practitioner in orthotics and prosthetics for 20 years, Russ says he has found that working with people is "very rewarding. Being able to impact people's lives is something you will never forget."

FYI

- The ancient Greeks, Egyptians, and Romans were among the first societies that looked for different ways to use artificial methods to replace lost limbs and to support or correct the function of weak body parts.
- Modern orthotics and prosthetics are usually traced back to the 16th century French surgeon Ambroise Paré. Devices dating from that century include metal corsets, splints made of leather and other materials used for deformities of the hips and legs, special shoes, and solid metal hands.
- The Poor Relief Act of 1601, which established some government responsibility for the disabled, helped fuel the rapid development of orthotics in England at that time. Leather-covered wooden hands and single metal hooks to replace lost hands were among the devices developed.
- Improvements in the design and materials used for orthotic and prosthetic devices were prevalent following World Wars I and II, the Korean War, and the Vietnam War. An increase in sports-related injuries and those resulting from automobile accidents have also played a role in improvements to devices.

EDUCATION

High School

If you plan to pursue a career as an orthotic or prosthetic technician, you should take all the shop classes your school offers. Courses in metal, wood, and machine shop will provide a strong background for working with the tools and materials used in this profession. Algebra and geometry classes will teach you to work with numbers and measurements. To help develop eye-hand coordination, a sense of design and proportions, and to gain skills working with materials like leather, metals, and plastics you should take art classes. Courses in biology, health, and anatomy will provide an understanding of the human body. Because computer technology is used to design devices computer science courses are beneficial, and English will help improve your communication skills.

Postsecondary Training

There are two training options to become an orthotic or prosthetic technician. You may enroll in a two-year program of supervised clinical experience and training under the supervision of a certified orthotist or prosthetist. Upon successful completion of the program technician status is granted.

The second option is to enroll in a one- or two-year educational program that leads to a certificate or an associate's degree in orthotics-prosthetics technology. Educational programs typically include classes in anatomy, physiology, properties of materials, prosthetic and orthotic techniques, building devices, and supervised clinical experience.

To date, the National Commission on Orthotic and Prosthetic Education (NCOPE) accredits only five technician programs: Baker College of Flint, Flint, Michigan; Century College, White Bear Lake, Minnesota; Francis Tuttle, Oklahoma City; Meridian School of Allied Health Careers, Pittsburgh; and Spokane Falls Community College, Spokane, Washington. Each of these programs leads to an associate's degree and certification.

Russ says that to advance and become an orthotic or prosthetic practitioner requires a bachelor's degree in orthotics and prosthetics or in health sciences. "And there is no substitute for on-the-job training," he adds.

CERTIFICATION OR LICENSING

Although there are no licensing requirements at this time for orthotic and prosthetic technicians, the American Board for Certification in Orthotics and Prosthetics (ABC) offers a voluntary registration program. The minimum requirements for candidates seeking registration are a high school diploma and either completion of the two-year supervised on-the-job training program or a one- or two-year educational program at an NCOPE accredited school. Depending on the area of specialty, technicians who pass the ABC exam are designated as registered technician-orthotic, registered technician-prosthetic, or registered technician-orthotic/prosthetic. To maintain registration technicians must complete a required number of ABC-approved continuing education credits every five years.

SCHOLARSHIPS AND GRANTS

Qualified students may apply for scholarships through the O & P Educational and Development Fund. In 2004 one $500 scholarship and three $1,000 scholarships were awarded. Century College in Minnesota also offers scholarships, and the Orthotic and Prosthetic Assistance Fund (http://www.opfund.org) provides scholarships.

INTERNSHIPS AND VOLUNTEERSHIPS

Without training it is difficult to find internships or part-time or summer employment in this field, but volunteer opportunities may be available at local hospitals or rehabilitation centers. Since this profession is so specialized, Russ advises, "the best way [to get involved] is to express an interest in a local facility and get some exposure."

Who Will Hire Me?

According to a 2004 survey by the American Orthotic and Prosthetic Association (AOPA), 100 percent of O&P program graduates find employment. Orthotic and prosthetic technicians work for hospitals, rehabilitation centers, specialty clinics and home health settings, nursing homes, private brace and limb companies, and the Veterans Health Administration.

Graduates of one- or two-year educational programs generally get job placement assistance through the school they attended. Trade journals and professional organizations also provide job listings.

> **To Be a Successful Orthotic and Prosthetic Technician, You Should . . .**
>
> - enjoy working with your hands
> - have excellent eye-hand coordination
> - be patient and detail oriented
> - have strong interpersonal communication skills

Where Can I Go from Here?

Many technicians employed by large hospitals or rehabilitation facilities advance to orthotic or prosthetic assistants once they have acquired enough experience, and eventually they may move into supervisory positions. Advancement opportunities are also available to those who specialize in one area of the field.

Significant career advancement is usually only available, however, to technicians who further their educations. By earning a four-year degree in orthotics or prosthetics, or completing a one-year certificate program technicians may become certified orthotists or prothetists.

Russ says, "Advancement in this field is really based on your expertise and longevity in an office. Most offices are independently owned at this time, although 40 to 50 percent are corporately owned." He says advancement in a corporately owned company is usually based on experience and length of employment as well as a proven ability to provide good care and demonstrating good technical knowledge.

If you own your own company, success will be determined by "your ability to be flexible, think on your feet, and to wear as many hats as you can," Russ says.

What Are the Salary Ranges?

Salaries for orthotic and prosthetic technicians vary depending on the location of employment, the size and type of employer, years of experience, and certification. According to the U.S. Department of Labor, in 2003 the median annual earnings for medical appliance technicians were $28,500. The lowest paid 10 percent earned $17,600, and the highest paid 10 percent earned $47,300. According to the AOPA 2004 survey, the average annual salary

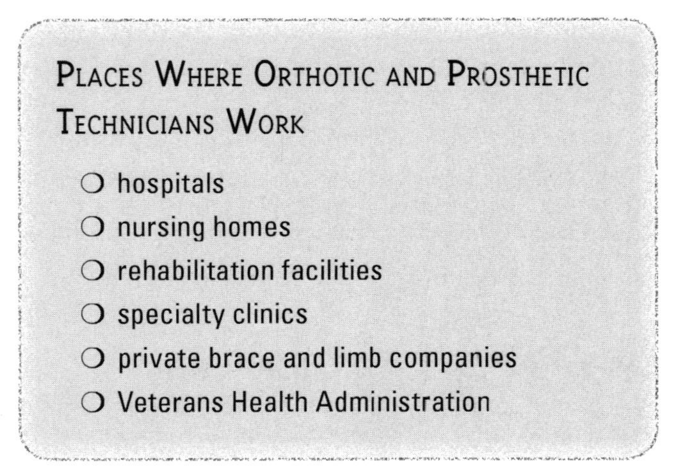

of ABC registered technicians was $40,454, and the average salary for fitters was $34,386. Noncertified licensed orthotists and prothetists with an average of seven years of experience earned $56,040 annually, and ABC-certified orthotists and prosthetists with 15 years of experience reported earning $91,452.

What Is the Job Outlook?

The U.S. Department of Labor projects employment opportunities for orthotic and prosthetic technicians will grow faster than the average through 2012. A study completed for the National Commission on Prosthetic Education reports that the aging baby boom population will increase the demand for orthotics and prosthetics by 2015, and by 2020 the number of people who have amputations and need prosthetic devices is expected to increase by 47 percent. In addition, there are more positions available than there are trained technicians to fill them, so employment opportunities should be good for technicians who graduate from accredited programs.

How Do I Learn More?

PROFESSIONAL ORGANIZATIONS

For information about the profession, accredited educational programs, scholarships, certification, and employment opportunities, contact the following organizations:

American Academy of Orthotists and Prosthetists
526 King Street, Suite 201
Alexandria, VA 22314
703-836-0788
http://www.oandp.org

American Board for Certification in Orthotics and Prosthetics
1521 Technology Drive
Chesapeake, VA 23320
757-548-5653
http://www/americanopcenter.com

American Orthotic and Prosthetic Association
330 John Carlyle Street, Suite 200
Alexandria, VA 22314
571-431-0876
info@aopanet.org
http://www.aopanet.org

National Commission on Orthotic and Prosthetic Education
330 John Carlyle Street, Suite 200
Alexandria, VA 22314
703-836-7114
info@ncope.org
http://www.ncope.org

O & P Educational Development Fund
c/o The Academy
526 King Street
Alexandria, VA 22314
703-836-0788
scholarships@oandp.org
http://www.opcareers.org/education/scholarships.html

BIBLIOGRAPHY

The following is a list of materials relevant to the professions of orthotics and prosthetics:

Edelstein, Joan. *Orthotics: A Comprehensive Clinical Approach*. Thorofare, N.J.: Slack, 2002.

Lusardi, Michelle M., and Caroline C. Nielson. *Orthotics and Prosthetics in Rehabilitation*, Boston: Butterworth-Heinemann, 2000.

Shurr, Donald G., and John W. Michael. *Prosthetics and Orthotics*. 2d ed. Paramus, N.J.: Prentice Hall, 2001.

Wilson, A. Bennet. *A Primer on Limb Prosthetics*. Springfield, Ill.: Charles C. Thomas, 1998.

PACKAGING MACHINERY TECHNICIANS

The large room Steve Polich enters is filled with rows of gleaming packaging machinery in various stages of assembly. Outside, even though it is only 7:00 A.M., it is already shaping up to be a hot, muggy day. Here, it is cool and comfortable. Steve crosses the assembly floor to his workstation, where an unassembled toothbrush-packaging machine awaits him. He hooks his thumbs in the pockets of his jeans and contemplates the machine he has been building for the last 10 weeks.

"Hey, Rick, got a second?" Steve asks the technician next to him, who is making a machine that will one day be wrapping bubble gum.

"Sure. What's up?"

"Take a look at this part I made the other day in the machine shop," Steve asks Rick.

"Didn't you do something similar last month when you were working on that carton for oil filters?"

Rick looks it over. "Looks like it might do the trick. Have you talked to engineering yet?"

Steve says, "More than once. If this doesn't work, looks like I'll be talking to them, again."

"Well, you always say you like a challenge," Rick says.

Steve smiles a bit ruefully. "I sure got my wish."

Definition
Packaging machinery technicians build and install automated packaging machines as well as maintain and repair them.

Alternative Job Titles
Assemblers
Automated packaging systems technicians
Fabricators
Field service technicians
Packaging machinery mechanics

High School Subjects
Computer science
English
Mathematics
Technical/shop

Personal Skills
Mechanical/manipulative
Technical/scientific

Salary Range
$20,000 to $33,900 to $53,650

Minimum Educational Requirements
High school diploma

Certification or Licensing
Voluntary

Outlook
Decline

DOT
638

GOE
08.03.01

NOC
7311

O*NET-SOC
51-9111.00

What Does a Packaging Machinery Technician Do?

Food, cosmetics, toiletries, pharmaceuticals, hardware, toys, nearly everything consumers buy is packaged by automated packaging machinery. *Packaging machinery technicians* work with the automated machinery that packages products into bottles, cans, bags, boxes, cartons, and other containers. The machines perform various operations, such as forming, filling, closing, labeling, and marking. The systems and technologies that packaging machinery technicians work with are diverse. Depending on the job, packaging machinery technicians may work with mechanical, hydraulic, or pneumatic systems, in addition to computerized controllers, fiber-optic transmitters, and robotic units.

Packaging machinery technicians do their jobs in the packaging plants of various industries or where the packaging machinery is manufactured. Their jobs entail building machines according to the engineer's blueprint, setting up equipment, training operators of the equipment, maintaining equipment, troubleshooting, and repairing machines.

Machinery builders, also called *assemblers,* assist engineers in the development and modification of new and existing designs. They build all kinds of packaging machinery, following engineering blueprints, wiring schematics, and pneumatic diagrams. Beginning with a mainframe that has

Lingo to Learn

Fiber optics Transmission of messages or information by light pulses along hair-thin glass fibers. Fiber optic sensors transmit to hard-to-reach places inside machinery.

Mainframe A bare metal frame that holds all the components of a packaging machine.

Packaging machinery industry Manufacturers who build, install, and service the machinery that packages products into boxes, cartons, bottles, cans, and other containers.

Product level The top level of a packaging machine where the product is wrapped, boxed, stacked, or somehow packaged.

Robotics Technology dealing with the design, construction, and operation of robots in automation.

been welded in another department, they assemble electrical circuitry, mechanical components, and fabricated items that may include parts they made themselves in the plant's machine shop. They may also need to bolt on any additional parts of the frame that are needed. After the machine is assembled, they test-run the machinery to make sure it is performing according to specifications.

Field service technicians, also called *field service representatives,* are employed by packaging machinery manufacturers and do most of their work at the plants where the packaging machinery is being used. In some companies, the assembler may serve as the field service technician; in others, the field service representative is a technician other than the assembler. In either case, they install new machinery at customer plants and train in-plant machine operators and maintenance personnel to use it.

The first thing field service technicians do is level the new machinery and anchor it to the floor. Then, following engineering drawings and wiring plans, they install the system's electrical and electromechanical components. They also regulate the controls and setup for the size, thickness, and type of material to be processed and ensure the correct sequence of processing stages. After installation, the technicians test-run the machinery and make any necessary adjustments, then teach machine operators the proper operating and maintenance procedures. The entire process takes about a week and is carefully documented. Field service representatives help the plant's in-house mechanics troubleshoot equipment already in operation. That includes making adjustments so the equipment runs as safely and efficiently as possible.

Automated packaging machine mechanics, also called *maintenance technicians,* perform scheduled preventive maintenance as well as diagnose machinery problems and make repairs. Preventive maintenance is done on a regular basis, following the manufacturer's guidelines in the service manual. During routine maintenance, technicians do such things as change filters in vacuum pumps, change oil in gearboxes, and replace worn bushings, chains, and belts. When machines do break down, maintenance technicians must work fast to fix them so production can resume as quickly as possible. In a small plant, a single mechanic may be responsible for all the duties required to keep a packaging line running; in a large plant, a team of mechanics may divide the duties. They might be responsible for all the machinery in the plant, one or more packaging lines, or a single machine.

What Is It Like to Be a Packaging Machinery Technician?

"I've always been into going fast," says Steve Polich, whose hobbies include racing cars and snowmobiles. "And basically, that's what packaging machinery is; the biggest reason that we're building automated machinery is to speed up the process."

Like the other assemblers at MGS Machinery Corp., Steve's day begins at 7:00 A.M. and often extends one or two hours beyond his scheduled quitting time of 4:30 P.M. The technicians are paid time-and-a-half for their overtime hours and some, like Steve, put in extra time beyond that requested by management. "I don't even really notice," he says of the extra hours. "The day goes by fast."

Steve works inside a large, climate-controlled assembly room with about 60 other assemblers, building machinery that is custom-made for a particular product. "You don't build a hundred of one kind of machine. Just about every machine we do has a specific job that's completely custom."

"Because the machinery is brand-new, assembly is cleaner work than maintenance," says Steve, who also has experience as a maintenance technician.

Before the actual building begins, Steve helps with the planning. "Generally speaking, it's run through engineering first. They come up with what they think is going to work. Then we all get together: the engineer, the shop foreman, the technician who's going to build it, and the salesperson with the sample product. Everybody voices whatever concerns they might have."

Steve spends anywhere from 10 to 16 weeks building, for example, a collator that packages an assortment of gift boxes into packs of six before feeding it to a wrapping machine. "You'll start out building from the mainframe. You generally start at the bottom and work your way to the top of the machine up to the product level. Where I'm at on the machine, that's where my day's work is."

Although Steve follows engineering blueprints to build the machine, he also has to be able to figure out how to make things work himself. "When you start getting into the top product level of the machine—where you're actually getting the product in there, getting the flaps closed or glued shut or taped shut or whatever—a lot of that is done on the fly, as we build it. I probably spend 30 percent of my week in the machine shop custom-making parts the way I feel will work best."

If Steve is having any trouble, he may ask an engineer for help. Or he may turn to a fellow technician. "If we have a problem, we grab the guy next to us to help us out. His machine may be doing something completely different from yours, but a lot of the problems are the same. Everybody kind of works together."

After the machine is built, Steve runs it for 60 to 80 hours with samples of the customer's product to make sure everything is working correctly. Then he does a customer checkout, in which the customer comes to the plant to see the machine in operation. After customer approval, Steve replaces any machined prototype parts with new ones. Then it's ready to be shipped.

In Steve's company, the assemblers also work as field service representatives, so his job is not over yet. "You do the training with the customer and their technicians. You go out in the field and do the installation and training of the operators in-house. When you return from that, they've got you posted to start another machine."

Do I Have What It Takes to Be a Packaging Machinery Technician?

"Packaging machinery technicians must be able to work under time pressure. Unless machinery is shut down intentionally for scheduled maintenance, it's supposed to be running 24 hours a day. Maintenance technicians are expected to make repairs as quickly as possible, because when you're working, that means they're not making production. Whereas the pressure in assembly is the deadline to get the machine done by its shipping date," says Steve.

Steve's job can be difficult, he says. "In custom machinery, there's no set way that it's going to be done. You don't know what's going to work. Some little task, and you can't get it—it's just not working. You can spend weeks just trying to get a machine to close a box, and that can get frustrating."

On the plus side, Steve likes getting to work on new and different machines all the time. He also likes the variety of his job; he may be on the assembly floor, in the machine shop, in a meeting with engineers, or at a customer's plant.

Steve enjoys the relative independence of his job. "We're pretty much on our own. We're given the project, given the day it's supposed to ship. We have a weekly meeting every Wednesday and we go in and give a project report on where we're at on our machine and how many days ahead or behind schedule we are. We're pretty much in control of ourselves."

"Being flexible, mechanically inclined, and self-motivated are all important qualities of a packaging machinery technician," Steve says.

How Do I Become a Packaging Machinery Technician?

Steve followed his father and brother into the packaging machinery field. After graduating from a two-year technical college, he spent six years as a maintenance technician for Anheuser-Busch before becoming an assembler at MGS. He recalls that he was always into mechanical things, including working on cars, boats, and snowmobiles. He remembers his high school math and machine shop

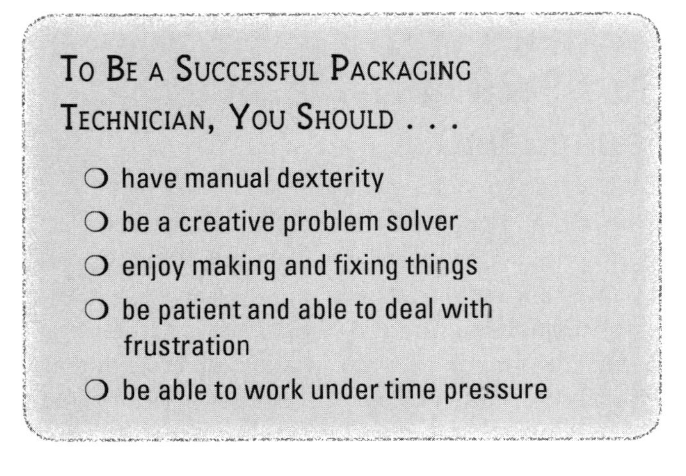

classes as being particularly useful in his future career choice.

EDUCATION

High School

Although it may be possible to get a job in the packaging machinery field without a high school diploma, the opportunities will be extremely limited, particularly those for advancement. And while a high school diploma may not be required by an employer, it is necessary for admission to any technical college or trade school offering packaging machinery courses.

Those interested in a career in packaging machinery should plan a course of study in high school that includes mathematics, geometry, electrical shop, machine shop, and mechanical drawing. Being able to communicate effectively with others, including engineers, plant management, and customers, is also important. So, in addition to developing your mechanical abilities, you should work on communication skills in English and writing courses.

FYI

The following industries employ packaging machinery technicians:

- food and beverages
- chemicals
- pharmaceuticals
- cosmetics and toiletries
- hardware
- household products
- apparel
- toys, sporting goods, and hobby items

Postsecondary Training

Although machinery training programs can be found across the country, either at community colleges or at any number of trade and technical schools, there are only a handful of technical colleges that specialize in packaging machinery and award a degree or certificate in automated packaging machinery systems. Programs generally last two years and involve extensive hands-on training as well as classroom study. Students practice with simple hand tools such as hacksaws and drill gauges and learn to run lathes, mills, and grinders. Other technical courses cover sheet metal and welding work; power transmission, electrical, and mechanical systems; maintenance operations; and industrial safety and the handling of hazardous materials.

Classes in packaging operations include bag making, loading, and closing; case loading; blister packaging; palletizing, conveying, and accumulating; and labeling and bar coding. There are also classes in form fill and seal wrap and carton machines as well as packaging quality control and package design and testing. In an industry where technology is increasingly sophisticated, highly desirable courses to take are PLC, or programmable computer logic, auto CAD (computer-aided design), and robotics.

Steve particularly enjoyed his electricity and PLC classes. One classroom project that stands out in his memory is building a do-nothing machine. "All it is is a bunch of shafts and gears and belts and pulleys and an electric motor. After you build this machine from a blueprint and hook it up to the motor, then all the shafts have to turn. It doesn't do anything, that's why they call it a do-nothing machine, but you do it to learn the skill of getting all the shafts turning the way they're supposed to and reading the blueprints."

SCHOLARSHIPS AND GRANTS

The National Institute of Packaging, Handling, and Logistic Engineers offers a scholarship program for university students majoring in Packaging, Handling, Logistics, or Related Fields. Write early for information on eligibility, application requirements, and deadlines.

Many schools offer scholarships that are funded through the Packaging Education Forum. To be eligible you must be enrolled at the school. Follow that school's procedures regarding eligibility, application requirements, and deadlines. For further information, contact the school you're interested in attending.

LABOR UNIONS

Union membership may be a requirement for some jobs, depending on whether or not a union is active at a particular company. Unions are more likely to be found in large-scale national and international corporations. Field service technicians are usually not unionized. Maintenance technicians and assemblers may be organized by the International Brotherhood of Teamsters, Chauffeurs, Warehousemen, and Helpers of America, or the International Association of Machinists and Aerospace Workers. Some technicians may be represented by the International Longshoremen and Warehousemen's Union.

In a union shop, union membership is required after a period of time that varies according to the management-labor contract. There is usually a probationary period of three to six months. Unionized technicians pay weekly or monthly dues to the union and work under a contract that determines their pay, benefits, and work rules.

Who Will Hire Me?

Packaging machinery technicians are in high demand both by companies who manufacture packaging machinery and by those who use the machinery. Glenn Davis, director of technical education for the Packaging Machinery Manufacturers Institute and author of several industry textbooks, estimates there are 60,000 openings per year and less than 200 qualified applicants. "Most of the jobs are unadvertised," he says, explaining, "There are so few qualified applicants that employers rely on industry sources to find employees."

With packaging one of the largest industries in the United States, jobs can be found across the country, in small towns and large cities, in small companies or multi-plant international corporations. Opportunities for packaging can be found in almost any company that produces a product. Food, chemicals, cosmetics, electronic components, pharmaceuticals, automotive parts, hardware, plastics, and almost any product you can think of use packaging machinery. The jobs are not restricted to any one industry or geographic location; wherever there is industry, there is some kind of packaging going on.

To break into the business, newly trained technicians should visit packaging plants and companies and ask for tours, making their wish for employment known. Contacts made while in school or during on-the-job training could also be approached.

And, *Packaging Digest* magazine (http://www.packagingdigest.com) advertises job openings and includes company profiles in each issue.

ADVANCEMENT POSSIBILITIES

Assembly supervisors oversee and coordinate activities of workers engaged in assembling parts and applying knowledge of the assembly process and production methods.

Field service managers supervise and coordinate activities of field service technicians engaged in installing packaging machinery at customer plants and training operators and maintenance personnel in its operation.

Where Can I Go from Here?

In five years, Steve can see himself supervising an assembly floor or a packaging department "where I would call the shots on the type of machinery I needed in there." He sees being a field service manager as another advancement possibility.

Many successful technicians later move into sales. Some, like Steve's brother, travel the world purchasing packaging machinery for companies with international plants.

Advancement possibilities for a high school graduate without a two-year technical school diploma will be drastically lower, while those with the degree may need additional training depending on their ultimate career goal. One possible career or education path for a technician with a two-year degree is to continue on to get a four-year engineering degree and become a research engineer in a company's research and development department. A technician with additional training might also move into administrative or executive positions.

Paul Desens, an instructor at Hennepin Technical College, where Steve graduated, notes, "A two-year degree gives you ground-floor entry into the packaging industry, one of the largest industries in the country. You can use that to launch your career in many ways."

What Are the Salary Ranges?

Earnings vary with geographic area, the skill level of the employee, and his or her duties. The type of industry the technician is working in, such as the food and beverage industry or the chemical industry, for example, also helps determine salary. So does the size of the company. In addition, technicians who work at companies with unions usually earn larger salaries.

According to the U.S. Department of Labor, median salaries paid by general purpose machinery manufacturers for assemblers in 2003 were $33,900 for entry-level positions to more than $53,650 for experienced workers. Learn to Earn (http://www.12evt.org) reports salaries for packaging machinery technicians range between $20,000 and $40,000.

An inexperienced technician's salary typically starts around $20,000 and with experience can increase to $35,000. At larger companies, some seasoned workers with two-year degrees may earn between $50,000 and $70,000 a year, particularly those in field service jobs. Salary.com lists earnings between $21,030 and $30,943 for manufactuing technicians in 2005.

What Is the Job Outlook?

Acccording to the U.S. Department of Labor, due to an increase in automation and technology job opportunities for machine assemblers and fabricators is expected to decline through 2012. Adding to the decline will be the trend of companies sending more jobs offshore to countries with lower labor costs.

The Packaging Machinery Manufacturers Institute 10th annual packaging machinery shipments and outlook study also forecasts only a 3.9 percent increase in demand for packaging machinery shipments through 2006. Select machinery categories and growth rates include: cartoning and multipacking machinery, 3.2 percent increase; labeling machinery, 6.9 percent increase; shrink film and heat sealing machinery, 4 percent increase; and pallet unitizing machinery, 2.8 percent increase.

The introduction of computers, robotics, and fiber optics into the industry has added new skill requirements and job opportunities for packaging machinery mechanics and technicians. There is already widespread application of computer-aided design and computer-aided manufacture (CAD/CAM). The use of computers in packaging machinery will continue to increase, with computer-to-computer communication regarding the status of operations and diagnostic maintenance information. The role of robotics, fiber optics, and electronics will also expand. To be prepared for the jobs of the future, you need to seek training in the newest technologies.

How Do I Learn More?

PROFESSIONAL ORGANIZATIONS

The following organizations provide information on packaging machinery technician careers, accredited schools, and possible employers:

Institute of Packaging Professionals
1601 North Bond Street, Suite 101
Naperville, IL 60563
630-544-5050
info@iopp.org
http://www.iopp.org

National Institute for Certification in Engineering Technologies
1420 King Street
Alexandria, VA 22314-2794
888-476-4238
http://www.nicet.org

National Institute of Packaging, Handling, and Logistic Engineers
6902 Lyle Street

Lanham, MD 20706-3454
301-459-9105
niphle@erols.com
http://www.niphle.org

Packaging Machinery Manufacturers Institute
Packaging Education Forum
4350 N. Fairfax Drive, Suite 600
Arlington, VA 22203
888-275-7664
http://www.pmmi.org

Technical Association of the Pulp & Paper Industry
15 Technology Parkway
Norcross, GA 30092
800-332-8686
http://www.tappi.org

BIBLIOGRAPHY

The following is a sampling of materials relating to the professional concerns and development of packaging machinery technicians:

Camenson, Blythe. *Real People Working in Mechanics, Installation, and Repair.* Lincolnwood, Ill.: VGM Career Horizons, 1999.

Carter, David E. *Power Packaging.* New York: Hearst Book International, 1999.

Cliff, Stafford. *50 Trade Secrets of Great Design: Packaging.* 2d ed. Gloucester, Mass.: Rockport Publishers, 2002.

Roth, Lazlo, and George L. Wybenga. *The Packaging Designer's Book of Patterns.* 2d ed. New York: John Wiley and Sons, 2000.

PARALEGALS

Definition
Paralegals research laws, investigate facts, prepare documents, and do background work for lawyers, who review their work and assume legal responsibility for the projects.

Alternative Job Title
Legal assistants

High School Subjects
Computer science
English
Government
Sociology
Speech

Personal Skills
Communication/ideas
Following instructions

Salary Range
$25,000 to $38,400 to $61,900+

Minimum Educational Requirements
Some postsecondary training

Certification or Licensing
Recommended

Outlook
Faster than the average

DOT
119

GOE
04.02.02

NOC
4211

O*NET-SOC
23-2011.00

In hindsight, Kathey Mehle realizes that going to the house was a dangerous thing to do. She was working for an attorney, trying to locate some people to provide information for a legal case, but the people did not want to be found.

When the attorney asked Kathey to go to the people's home, she did it without hesitation. She walked to the door and knocked, but no one answered. Kathey surveyed the yard and noticed a trash can. She opened the lid, looked at some of the items on top, and discovered a few envelopes with a different address. That is where the missing people were found. Kathey's employer was impressed.

"He was just amazed that I would go to that length, to actually open up a lid of a garbage can like that," she recalls with a chuckle. "Attorneys really appreciate it when they give somebody an assignment and the person just doesn't stop.

"I've always felt that, as a paralegal, your job is to make the attorneys' lives easier and help them any way you can. For the most part, the attorneys I've worked for have been really good guys. You see the services that they do for the clients, and you feel that you should be just as dedicated."

What Does a Paralegal Do?

Paralegals, also known as *legal assistants,* do background work for attorneys. They research laws, investigate facts, prepare documents, and help lawyers prepare for trials. Most paralegals have some legal training, but they are not lawyers and cannot give legal advice, set fees, accept cases, or represent clients in court. They perform their work under the oversight of lawyers, who assume responsibility for it. Paralegals work for corporations, government agencies, community legal services, individual attorneys, and law firms that include many attorneys.

In conducting research, a paralegal typically goes to a law library and reads constitutions, treaties, statutes, court cases, legal articles, or legal codes. The paralegal uses this information to prepare documents for the use of attorneys: everything from contracts and wills to deeds, legal briefs, and stock certificates. Sometimes research turns up information the attorney can use in a case. The paralegal often writes a report that helps the lawyer decide how to proceed with the case. Paralegals also prepare affidavits, maintain files of documents, and file pleadings with court clerks. In some states, anyone who is at least 18 years old can serve subpoenas, which might be part of a paralegal's duties.

In government jobs paralegals also analyze policies and regulations pertaining to an agency, then compile reports for the public and the people who work in the agency. They might collect evidence for hearings or talk to employers to learn why health and safety standards are not being met. In community service jobs legal assistants help provide legal aid to the poor by filing forms, conducting research, and preparing documents. In corporate jobs paralegals deal with financial reports, shareholder agreements, contracts, employee benefit plans, minutes of meetings, corporate resolutions, and government regulations.

As a paralegal, you might work on many types of legal cases or focus on certain areas of the law, depending on the types of projects your supervising attorney accepts. Paralegals usually have the widest variety of duties if they work for small law firms that accept many types of cases.

Conversely, you might work for a larger firm that specializes in one aspect of the law, such as bankruptcy, corporate law, criminal law, labor law, patents and copyrights, real estate, or medical malpractice. In that type of setting, the paralegal's duties might be highly specialized. For example, you might work only on cases that deal with employee benefits. In general, a firm is considered small if it employs 15 or fewer lawyers, medium if it employs 15 to 50, and large if it employs more than 50.

Some paralegals coordinate the work of other employees, such as *legal secretaries*. In large law firms or corporations, *paralegal administrators* direct other paralegals. In contrast, *legal administrators* are the business managers in law offices.

Lingo to Learn

Affidavit A document listing statements that a person provided voluntarily and confirmed with an oath.

Appeal The request that a higher court reverse or correct the decision of a lower court on the grounds that an injustice was done or error was committed.

Brief A condensed version of a large document, series of papers, facts, or propositions.

Deposition The testimony of a witness, taken during an investigation and written down to be used later in court.

Discovery The disclosure of facts that were previously hidden; lawyers commonly disclose the facts of their cases to each other before court trials begin.

Litigation A lawsuit.

Subpoena Legal papers that command a witness to appear in court and testify.

What Is It Like to Be a Paralegal?

Kathey Mehle works in the law offices of Ian L. Mattoch in Honolulu, Hawaii. She usually arrives at 6:30 in the morning and leaves by 4:00 in the afternoon. There is always a stack of mail to review, letters and legal documents to write, and various tasks to finish. "I'm on the phone a lot. There can be days when clients are calling me all day long," she says. She spends most of her time at her desk, but previous jobs frequently took her away from the office, conducting research and doing other projects.

"The good thing about being a paralegal is you have a lot of diversity in your job," she says. "I have a lot of freedom."

Kathey has worked in various types of law offices during her more than 20 years in the profession, and she likes almost everything about her career, but she notes, "There just seem to be a lot of crazy people in the world. I found family law the most discouraging, but I have a friend who does family law, and she loves it. Criminal law is the same way. You see these people ruining their lives."

As a paralegal, Kathey has witnessed families falling apart and people going to prison. In most offices paralegals must sometimes deal with difficult clients, but some positions with corporations, for instance, would not involve much public contact. Although there are difficult moments, Kathey generally enjoys interacting with the public.

"Clients appreciate the paralegal, because the attorneys have a tendency to speak above them," she explains. "Many times, they call back, and they want to speak to the paralegal for clarification."

Clients can feel free to talk to Kathey or any other employee of the firm, because there is a strict rule against discussing clients outside the office. "The privacy issue is really important in a law firm. Everything is strictly confidential," Kathey says.

Kathey works with seven attorneys, four other paralegals, two paralegal assistants, three legal secretaries, and a word processing specialist. She is supervised by an attorney who is responsible for her work, and she makes sure to keep him informed at all times. "You have to be really careful and let him know what you're doing," she says.

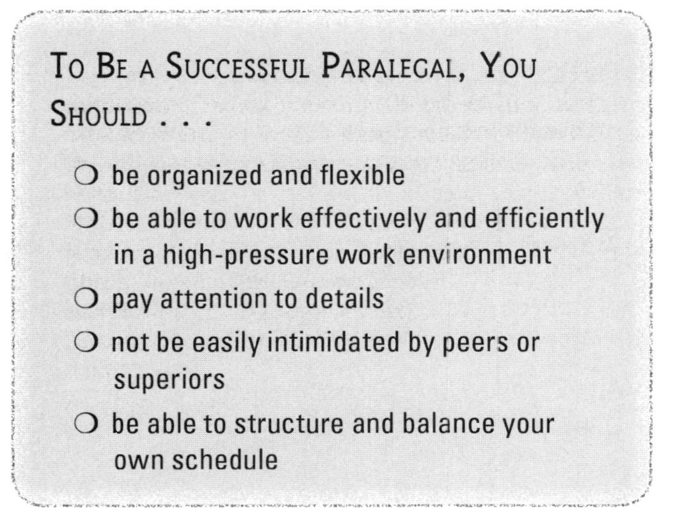

To Be a Successful Paralegal, You Should . . .

- be organized and flexible
- be able to work effectively and efficiently in a high-pressure work environment
- pay attention to details
- not be easily intimidated by peers or superiors
- be able to structure and balance your own schedule

Another paralegal, Donna Smith, is in and out of her office all day. She works for a small law firm that specializes in environmental litigation, such as recovering the cost of cleaning up pollution at sites that violate standards set by the Environmental Protection Agency. Paralegals spend many hours helping prepare each case before it goes to court. For example, Donna might find documents that disprove claims by the opposing attorneys, and she would type data from those documents into tables to be used by her supervising attorney.

Currently, Donna and several temporary paralegals are reviewing all the documents from a three-year-old case to separate those that the opposing lawyers should not be allowed to examine. They have six days to finish summarizing the contents of these "privileged" documents on computer, and the stack of documents still to be summarized is two feet tall. One of the temporary paralegals is taking some documents home to work on them over the weekend.

Donna's job involves a great deal of paperwork that must be sorted and filed. Boxes of documents are stacked beneath her desk, labeled "discovery," "depositions," and "settlement negotiations." Piles of documents from at least six cases cover her desk, all in various stages of processing. She makes copies of papers and sometimes travels to other law offices to review documents there or to deliver documents to them. Like Kathey, she spends a great deal of time making telephone calls. She usually eats her lunch on the run, but she considers it a tradeoff for not having to be tied to a desk all day. Her job might appear overwhelming, but she says it is all about "managing and prioritizing time. If you can't be organized, you won't be able to do the job well."

Do I Have What It Takes to Be a Paralegal?

Paralegals need to be good at writing and speaking, since they prepare a large number of documents and discuss projects with attorneys and many other people. They need analytical and organizational skills to help attorneys prepare for trials, to make sense of large amounts of information, and to manage their own busy schedules. "You review a lot of documents, and the attorney is looking at you to find these facts for him," Kathey says. She once worked for an attorney who used to say that his paralegal was his "keeper of all the facts."

Investigative skills are important for a job that often revolves around research. "Now, with the Internet, there is so much out there that you can find," Kathey comments. She also conducts research in locations such as the Secretary of State's office or the Department of Consumer Affairs, typically when she is helping investigate a corporation. Kathey sometimes tries to locate people who are trying to elude attorneys, but her job does not require her to deliver subpoenas.

A paralegal should be prepared to handle responsibility. On a real estate deal, for example, a paralegal must prepare, copy, notarize, and file documents in time to meet specific deadlines. Millions of dollars, a person's civil rights, or the reputation of the law firm or corporation could be at stake.

Paralegals sometimes work under pressure. Attorneys can be impatient, last-minute changes can require that the staff work late, and rush deliveries might have to be made to city officials. The paralegal must think and act quickly but remain calm enough to avoid careless errors. It is also helpful to be assertive and not easily intimidated, whether you're dealing with cantankerous senior partners or slow-moving county clerks.

How Do I Become a Paralegal?

Kathey Mehle became interested in the legal professions at the age of 17, when she was issued a traffic ticket and saw how confusing the court system could be. Initially, she envisioned herself becoming an attorney, but as she learned more about her options, she decided to enter a paralegal training program after high school. "I was lucky to have found something that fit me," she says.

Some paralegals begin as clerical workers and are given more training on the job, but most enter the profession by completing training courses. In Hawaii, Kathey says, it is common for document clerks, legal secretaries, and others employed in law offices to work during the day and take paralegal classes in the evenings. Because requirements vary, it is important to inquire at local offices of paralegal associations to learn the specifics for your area.

EDUCATION

High School

The most important skill for any paralegal is the ability to read and analyze complex information. Skills in researching, investigating, and summarizing information are also necessary. Therefore, any language courses (English, Spanish, and other foreign languages), literature, writing, speech, and logic will help you prepare for a career in this field. Donna Smith remembers that she enjoyed English and writing classes in high school. "To understand sentence structure is so important to what I do that I still diagram sentences to help me really know what the words actually say," she comments.

Kathey agrees that speaking and writing are essential skills for her profession, and she notes that many high school students have inadequate writing skills. She also recommends classes in typing, computer applications, and social sciences. "Civics is probably the most important, because it gives you an introduction to what courts are about," she says.

You can also sometimes attend paralegal presentations during Career Days. Drama club, speech teams, and debate teams will help sharpen your ability to research a topic, communicate your findings, and defend them with logical arguments.

Postsecondary Training

Most paralegals have completed some type of training program, and a large percentage hold a two- or four-year college degree. Training typically runs from one to three years and is available through colleges and universities, law schools, business schools, proprietary schools, and paralegal associations. Some programs admit only students who hold a bachelor's degree. Distance learning (taking college classes via the Internet or by correspondence) is an acceptable and fairly common way of obtaining a paralegal education. Some schools are considering offering a master's degree in the field, but that is not yet available. Of about 600 programs nationwide available through colleges, universities, and law schools, about 250 have been approved by the American Bar Association.

Kathey completed a two-year program, which was about all that was available during the 1970s when she attended school. She says the two-year program is still the most common, but it seems that many firms are recruiting employees with four-year degrees, not necessarily in paralegal studies. "Law firms are looking for some specialization and experience," she explains. For example, a degree in health science would be useful at a law firm that handles personal injury or medical malpractice cases. A science major might focus on patents and copyrights.

Kathey's training included general studies and classes in real estate, research, and litigation. "The primary focus was legal courses," she says. "They made you learn the courthouse, where to find things." She was taught how local and national courts are organized, how to do legal research, and how to write briefs about specific cases. She also studied topics such as corporate structure, shareholders, and stocks. "There were some classes I just hated. For me, the legal research was kind of hard," she recalls.

FYI

The paralegal profession began to develop during the 1960s, when the number of lawsuits in the United States started increasing significantly. Attorneys hired assistants to help them handle a larger number of cases and to reduce costs.

At first, many paralegals were legal secretaries who assumed a steadily increasing number of responsibilities. Today, paralegals are usually graduates of formal training programs, and they perform many routine duties that used to be done by lawyers.

In-depth

Not Just for Lawyers

Paralegals can be found all over corporate America, but they often aren't called paralegals. Although these professionals deal with laws and regulations, they do not work under lawyers and attorneys; in fact, some paralegals work for themselves. Check out this short list of just a few of the different jobs you can set your sights on as a paralegal:

- *Health care paralegals* use medical experience or knowledge to compile information to be used in medical malpractice hearings.
- *Real estate paralegals* work with leases and negotiate their terms.
- *Housing law paralegals* help protect the housing rights of the poor.
- *Freelance paralegals* can work from home for various lawyers or corporations; they hire their services out on contract.
- *Compliance paralegals* work to ensure that their company is following the guidelines and regulations established by their area of business.

Other programs often include classes in public speaking, criminology, psychology, and sociology.

Donna Smith studied criminology while earning her bachelor of arts degree in sociology. Later she enrolled in a lawyer's assistant program that consisted of eight months of three-hour classes, three evenings a week. "I found the work harder than college, because it was specific, substantive, and focused, whereas college courses are designed to be theoretical. Paralegal studies are more like, 'This is the law, and this is how it applies,'" she remarks.

CERTIFICATION OR LICENSING

Paralegals are not required to be licensed or certified, but credentials are available through the National Association of Legal Assistants Certifying Board. Paralegals who have passed the board's examination are called Certified Legal Assistants (CLA). Those who hold a bachelor's degree, have at least two years of experience, and have passed the Paralegal Advanced Competency Exam are called Registered Paralegals (RP). Requirements vary widely, depending on the state and the attorney who employs you. Kathey says she expects certification to be more widely required in the future.

SCHOLARSHIPS AND GRANTS

The National Federation of Paralegal Associations administers many scholarships and other awards. Schools that offer paralegal programs also provide information about various types of financial aid.

INTERNSHIPS AND VOLUNTEERSHIPS

On-the-job experience can help you decide whether this is the career for you. It improves your job skills and shows potential employers what sort of worker you are. Applying for internships will also give you experience in writing a resume and being interviewed.

Kathey suggests investigating the possibilities at state legal aid offices, even if you're still in high school. You might be able to work there during the summer, for example. "They're always looking for free help," she says. "They get free help, and you get great skills." During paralegal school, Kathy volunteered for a state Department of Welfare, where she interviewed people to determine whether they qualified for Aid to Families with Dependent Children. "Interviewing skills are very important for a paralegal, depending on the area of law where you're working," she notes.

Another paralegal who completed an unpaid internship, Karen Greene, accepted the position to learn more about her area of specialization, civil litigation. During her internship with the Equal Opportunity Employment Commission, Karen interviewed candidates for participation in class-action lawsuits, developed a questionnaire, chose a database to organize the information, and conducted research.

Kathey found the Department of Welfare position through her school, which kept a list of volunteer opportunities. Local offices of the American Bar Association and legal secretaries associations can frequently provide information about internships. By dropping off resumes at law offices, you have a good chance of finding an internship or even a temporary, paying job, possibly as a secretary or in the mail room.

Who Will Hire Me?

Kathey Mehle's second internship during school led to her first job in the field; the same company offered her permanent employment. "The relationship just developed," she says.

Donna Smith found her first permanent job through the placement center at the school where she studied to become a paralegal. Like many legal assistants, she had previously worked temporary jobs in the field. Temporary jobs are a good way to try different types of work environments before you decide what type of position you prefer.

Most paralegals are employed by law firms. Others work for corporations, government agencies, or community law services. Jobs are available with insurance companies, real estate and title insurance firms, prepaid legal insurance services, banks and trusts, social agencies, offices of public defenders and attorneys general, the judicial system, hospital and school administration, and legal publishing houses. Some paralegals are self-employed freelancers.

"You can go in so many different areas," Kathey says. "Knowing what your interest is, that's where you try to find a job." For example, paralegals can choose jobs that allow them to work with defendants, plaintiffs, corporate law, or environmental law. You could even be a civilian paralegal for the military.

To find job leads, start with the career placement office of the school where you received your paralegal education. Schools often help their students prepare resumes, learn interview skills, arrange internships, and find permanent employment. Mail resumes to attorneys' offices and other organizations. Many openings for paralegals are listed in the classified advertisements of newspapers, particularly in legal newspapers.

Check the job banks maintained by paralegal associations, sometimes on the Internet and sometimes in the organizations' newsletters; many employers advertise there first. Call or visit local divisions of paralegal associations. Some associations offer student memberships. Attend association meetings and seminars to meet paralegals and others in the profession who might refer you to prospective employers.

Register with agencies that specialize in placing paralegals in temporary employment. Temporary jobs often lead to permanent positions. Experienced paralegals often find employment through executive search firms.

Where Can I Go from Here?

Donna Smith would eventually like to become a paralegal administrator who supervises other paralegals. To do that, she would need to work for an organization that employed at least five or six legal assistants.

In most organizations there are few opportunities to advance through a hierarchy of paralegal positions. Paralegals with more experience are given more responsibility, however, and you can specialize in a field to prepare for a move to a larger firm. With an aptitude for management and training in business, a paralegal can advance to legal administrator, overseeing the expenses and other daily business of law firms. Many legal assistants return to school to become attorneys. Some experienced paralegals operate as freelancers or consultants, working independently for various attorneys; such a venture requires planning, some understanding of business practices, office space, and financing.

The paralegal profession is a young one that is still developing, and new positions will develop with it. One area that shows promise is prepaid legal services, which are often offered in corporate benefits packages. These services allow the corporation's employees to obtain the aid of attorneys to settle legal matters, including divorces, wills and estate planning, consumer debt, and real estate issues.

No matter what type of job you find, you will probably need to continue your education to keep up with changing laws and other developments in the field. Kathey Mehle, who frequently attends in-house training seminars, says that despite more than 20 years in the profession, she still learns something every day.

Advancement Possibilities

Paralegal administrators supervise other paralegals, helping them with assignments when necessary and ensuring that caseloads are distributed evenly. A paralegal administrator might also function as both the liaison between the paralegals and attorneys and the spokesperson for the paralegals whenever a concern arises that requires discussion.

Legal administrators manage the business aspects of a law firm. A board of attorneys monitors and runs the law firm, but a legal administrator might sit on this board and provide an accounting of office expenses.

Attorneys perform a variety of legal services for clients, such as conducting legal research, filing deeds and other documents, drawing up wills and prenuptial agreements, writing briefs, and presenting arguments in civil and criminal courts of law.

Donna also occasionally attends training seminars and workshops. She belongs to the Illinois Paralegal Association, and she makes a habit of reading *Legal Assistant Today* (http://www.legalassistanttoday.com), which she says features "cutting edge and up-to-the-minute coverage of practical issues in case management and ethics."

What Are the Salary Ranges?

Earnings vary with geographic location, employer, and the employee's education and experience. Jobs with large firms in urban areas usually pay the most. According to Salary.com, in 2005 the median annual earnings for entry-level paralegals were $39,442 with the lowest paid earning $34,678 and the highest paid earning $45,100. Those with experience had salaries ranging from $48,070 to $60,386 with a median of $53,588 annually.

The U.S. Department of Labor reports that paralegals earned median annual salaries of $38,400 in 2003. The highest paid 10 percent earned $61,900, while the lowest paid 10 percent earned $25,000. Paralegals employed by the federal government averaged about $53,770 in 2002. Most also received paid vacations, paid sick leave, a pension plan, health insurance, and life insurance and their employers paid the paralegals' professional dues.

What Is the Job Outlook?

The paralegal profession is expected to be among the fastest-growing occupatios through 2012, because employers have begun to realize that legal assistants can perform many services at lower salaries than lawyers. Attorneys are also hiring paralegals to cut their own expenses, improve their efficiency, and make legal services more available to clients. There will probably be competition for paralegal jobs, however, as more people graduate from training programs.

New jobs will be created as the field rapidly expands. Private law firms will continue to offer

FYI

Various federal agencies employ paralegal specialists, particularly the Department of Justice, the Treasury Department, and the Department of Health and Human Services. Workers in federal positions are frequently involved in hearings, appeals, litigation, and advisory services.

To obtain an entry-level position, applicants must pass the Administrative Careers with America Examination for Benefits Review, Tax and Legal Occupations. For details, including when the test is offered and what job openings exist, contact an Office of Personnel Management, Federal Job Information Center/Testing Office near where you want to work. Those offices are listed in telephone books under "U.S. Government."

the largest number of openings, in part because of increasing demand for legal services to settle issues regarding intellectual property, health care, international law, matters pertaining to the elderly, sexual harassment, and the environment.

Corporate legal departments, banks, real estate and title insurance firms, insurance companies, and many other organizations will also hire legal assistants. In addition, the increasing number of prepaid legal plans will create jobs.

Community legal services, which operate on limited budgets, will hire paralegals to reduce expenses; these organizations provide legal assistance to the poor, the elderly, minorities, and middle-income families. There will also be an increasing number of positions in various levels of government, the courts, and consumer organizations.

There might be some slowing of growth in the field if the nation experiences a recession, since the economy affects the public's tendency to pay for optional legal services, such as drafting wills, planning estates, and handling real estate transactions. During economic slumps, when sales and profits drop, corporations initiate fewer lawsuits. Other legal problems, such as bankruptcies, foreclosures, and divorces, are more apt to arise during a recession, however. Because paralegals provide legal services at a lower cost than attorneys, they might weather a recession better than would lawyers.

How Do I Learn More?

PROFESSIONAL ORGANIZATIONS

The following organizations provide information on paralegal careers, accredited schools, and possible employers:

American Association for Paralegal Education
2965 Flowers Road South, Suite 105
Atlanta, GA 30341
770-452-9877
info@aafpe.org
http://www.aafpe.org

American Bar Association
740 15th Street, NW
Washington, DC 20005-1019
202-662-1000
http://www.abanet.org

Association of Legal Administrators
75 Tri-State International, Suite 222
Lincolnshire, IL 60069-4435
847-267-1252
http://www.alanet.org

National Association of Legal Assistants
1516 South Boston Avenue, Suite 200
Tulsa, OK 74119
918-587-6828
http://www.nala.org

National Federation of Paralegal Associations
2517 Eastlake Avenue East, Suite 200
Seattle, WA 98102
206-652-4120
info@paralegals.org
http://www.paralegals.org

National Paralegal Association
PO Box 406
Solebury, PA 18963
215-297-8333
admin@nationalparalegal.org
http://www.nationalparalegal.org

BIBLIOGRAPHY

The following is a sampling of materials relating to the professional concerns and development of paralegals:

Brittain, Vicki, and Terry L. Hull. *The Paralegal Handbook*. Clifton Park, N.Y.: Thomson Delmar Learning, 2002.

Fins, Alice, and Marguerite Duffy. *Opportunities in Paralegal Careers*. Lincolnwood, Ill.: VGM Career Horizons, 1999.

Post, Ruth-Ellen. *Paralegal Internships: Finding, Managing and Transitioning Your Career*. Albany, N.Y.: Delmar Publishers, 1998.

Southard, Jo. *Paralegal Career Starter*. 2d ed. New York: Learning Express, 2002.

Wagner, Andrea. *How to Land Your First Paralegal Job*. 3d ed. Upper Saddle River, N.J.: Prentice Hall, 2000.

PERFUSIONISTS

Carol Zografas shuts the door behind her and glances around the sterile cardiac operating room. It is only 7:00 A.M. and she has already read her patient's chart and knows what to expect. It is the first procedure of the day, a neonatal case involving two-month-old Kristen. Carol will be working with Maxine, the anesthesiologist, and Dr. Cardwell, the heart surgeon, as well as with the other operating room staff, to repair complex defects in Kristen's heart.

Carol turns on the heart-lung machine and goes through her preoperative checklist. Is the tubing the right size for the infant? Are all the parts of the machine working properly? She checks off one item after another on her list. Once the operation begins, Kristen's life could depend on Carol's skills and the heart-lung machine.

Finally, she puts the list down, satisfied that she is as prepared as she can be to begin the operation. She looks across the room at Maxine. "I'm all set, Max. Are you ready?" she asks.

Definition
Perfusionists operate and monitor extracorporeal circulation equipment, such as heart-lung machines and artificial hearts, during any medical situation where it is necessary to support or temporarily replace the patient's cardiopulmonary-circulatory function.

Alternative Job Titles
Cardiovascular perfusionists
Extracorporeal technologists
Perfusion technicians

High School Subjects
Biology
Chemistry
Mathematics
Physics

Personal Skills
Helping/teaching
Technical/scientific

Salary Range
$50,000 to $97,424 to $165,000

Minimum Educational Requirements
Bachelor's degree

Certification or Licensing
Recommended

Outlook
About as fast as the average

DOT
078

GOE
14.02.01

NOC
3214

O*NET-SOC
29-2031.00

What Does a Perfusionist Do?

The heart is the main tool of the circulatory system, beating about 70 times a minute to circulate the oxygen and nutrients that provide energy for human action and thought. This tool, basically a pump at the heart of our lives, must move 2,000 gallons of blood through 60,000 miles of arteries and veins every minute of every day.

When one's heart is not functioning correctly, or when one has a heart disease, surgery is often performed to repair the damage or to control the illness. During an operation such as open-heart surgery, coronary bypass, or any other procedure that involves the heart and lungs, the *perfusionist* is indispensable. Before the cardiologist can begin to operate on the heart, it is necessary to interrupt or replace the functioning of the heart by circulating the blood through machines outside of the patient's body. This process of circulating the blood outside the patient's body is called extracorporeal circulation.

Perfusionists are experts in extracorporeal circulation. They perform complex, delicate procedures to transfer the functions of the heart to special machines while the cardiologist operates on the patient. These machines are called heart-lung machines; they take over the job of the heart and lungs. When the surgery is over, perfusionists also may help to start the heart pumping again if it doesn't start up by itself.

During heart surgery, the doctor will pierce the patient's breastbone and the membrane surrounding the heart (called the pericardial sac). Then the perfusionist will activate the heart-lung machine by inserting two tubes into the heart; one tube circulates blood from the heart to the machine, and the other tube circulates blood from the machine back into the heart. Using the heart-lung machine, the perfusionist maintains the functions of the patient's circulatory system and the appropriate levels of the patient's heart, including oxygen, carbon dioxide, and other nutrient levels.

Operating the heart-lung machine is the foundation of the perfusionist's job. During the medical procedure, perfusionists may also administer prescriptive drugs, anaesthetic agents, or blood products through the blood. They may also induce hypothermia, which means that the patient's body temperature is lowered to about 70 degrees (the human body's average temperature is about 98 degrees) so that the metabolism and stress levels are slowed down, allowing for less risk to the patient's bodily functions. Perfusionists use probes in other parts of the body to monitor the blood pressure and kidney activity during the surgical procedures. They also perform blood gas analysis and check for normal brain activity.

Perfusionists perform a technique called blood salvaging, which means that they try to save as much of the patient's blood as possible so they don't have to depend on donated blood. Blood salvaging is especially important these days because of the high rate of AIDS cases; the HIV virus, which causes AIDS, is transmitted through blood (as well as through other body fluids). Some patients donate their own blood supply prior to their surgery. Perfusionists also sometimes work with cell savers, which are machines that separate plasma, damaged platelets, and saline from blood that should not be returned to the patient's body.

During an operation, a patient must have a precise and consistent amount of blood flowing through the body and to the brain. The perfusionist must make sure that the heart-lung machine is delivering the proper amount of blood back into the patient's body to prevent damage to the brain and other major organs. Before the patient is taken off the heart-lung machine, the perfusionist makes sure that the patient's temperature is back to normal; he or she also does a blood test (called a hemocrit) on the patient to ensure that the red blood cell count is normal.

After surgery, the perfusionist slows down the blood flow to the patient and shuts off one of the lines to the heart-lung machine. When the patient's body takes over on its own, the machinery is shut off. If the patient's heart does not start on its own, the perfusionist may have to provide temporary cardiac support (with either the heart-lung machine or an artificial heart) until the patient's heart is ready to beat on its own.

Lingo to Learn

Blood salvaging Using as much of the patient's blood as possible so as not to depend on donated blood. Some patients donate their own blood supply prior to their surgery.

Cardiac Relating to the heart.

Cardiologist Heart surgeon.

Cardiopulmonary Relating to the heart and lungs.

Cell savers Machines that separate plasma, damaged platelets, and saline from blood that should not be returned to the patient's body.

Extracorporeal circulation Circulation of the patient's blood outside the body.

Heart-lung machine A machine used to take over the function of the patient's heart and lungs during surgery or respiratory failure. The machine draws blood from the patient's body, reoxygenates it, and pumps it back into the patient's body.

Induced hypothermia A condition that the perfusionist may inflict on the patient to reduce body temperature to 70 degrees or below; this slows the patient's metabolism and reduces stress on the heart.

Pulmonary circulation Blood flow to and from the lungs.

Perfusionists are responsible for assembling, setting up, monitoring, and operating all the equipment that assists the circulation of blood during a medical procedure. They may also be responsible for ensuring that the equipment is maintained in accurate working order.

Specialized perfusionists assist at-risk patients such as premature babies and heart patients who have just had surgery (postoperative, or post-op patients). In these cases, the workers perform extracorporeal membrane oxygenation, using a machine that draws blood from the patient's body, reoxygenates it, and pumps it back into the patient through the arteries. For newborns and very young infants, this

In-depth

History of Heart Surgery

Considering the age of humankind and the evolution of the medical sciences, heart surgery is still in its infancy. The first bypass operation was performed in 1944 by Dr. John Blalok, whose patient was a newborn infant with oxygen-poor blood. The baby was born with a bluish tint because blood was not circulating correctly. Dr. Blalock operated on the baby, bypassing a blocked blood vessel.

The most significant breakthrough in open heart surgery occurred 10 years later, when Dr. John Gibbon used a machine to pump blood and supply oxygen to an 18-year-old patient, giving the surgeon needed time for delicate heart surgery. The machine was the heart-lung machine, which is now a standard fixture in cardiac operating rooms.

buys crucial time until the infant's respiratory and circulatory systems can work on their own; for heart patients, it may buy time until the heart is able to pump on its own or until a donor heart is found.

Perfusionists have also recently become important in the treatment of trauma. In such cases, they are called upon to rapidly infuse or replace lost blood or to lower the blood volume. Perfusion is now being used in the treatment of patients undergoing cancer surgery, organ transplants, and orthopedic surgery. As medical technology evolves, new uses for perfusion will most likely be developed.

What Is It Like to Be a Perfusionist?

Carol Zografas is the chief cardiovascular perfusionist at Maine Medical Center in Portland. It is 6:30 in the morning when she arrives at the hospital. She checks the schedule to find out what procedure she will be doing today and finds that she will be assisting the surgical team to repair extensive defects in the heart of a newborn baby.

Carol reads the patient's chart and looks for anything out of the ordinary that she may have to consult with the surgeon about. Does the baby have diabetes? Is the kidney function normal? It will be Carol's job to monitor and adjust the infant's kidney function, blood sugar, brain activity, and other bodily functions while the infant is in surgery.

After she is sure she knows all she needs to know, Carol gathers her equipment together and assembles it in the cardiac operating room. She goes through her page-long preoperative checklist to be sure that all the equipment is running properly. She checks the contents of the prepackaged parts for sterility and integrity. Are the tubes for the artificial heart placed in the right areas to make sure the circuits are complete? Have the proper drugs been administered in the prime fluid? Are all the parts of the heart-lung machine working properly? Are all the alarms operational?

When Carol is satisfied that her checklist is complete, she is ready to begin her work with the rest of the surgical team. She will be in the operating room anywhere from four to six hours for a typical surgical procedure. Her machinery is next to the operating table, and she works closely with the surgeon, the anesthesiologist, and other operating room staff.

Carol and her staff perform approximately 150 procedures each year. As chief of her department, Carol usually performs perfusions two days a week. The remaining hours in her workweek are filled with administrative and managerial tasks and teaching. Maine Medical Center has one of the three largest heart programs in New England and is a clinical teaching site for Northeastern University in Boston.

Carol supervises seven full-time and one half-time staff members. For quality control reasons, she tries not to schedule her staff for more than one procedure a day; she fills in herself when someone gets sick. The rest of her time is spent monitoring quality standards, performing preventive maintenance on equipment, solving staffing problems, chairing department meetings, attending meetings with other departments, counseling staff, and keeping up with the accreditation requirements for the hospital.

Although Carol's day begins promptly at 6:30 in the morning, she is never sure when it will end. "All the perfusionists in my department average about five hours of overtime per week. Overtime has its peaks and valleys," she says. "We always have two staff members on call in case of an emergency, and we work every day of the week."

Do I Have What It Takes to Be a Perfusionist?

Perfusionists perform some of the most delicate and vital services for patients during heart and lung surgery, yet most patients have never heard of perfusionists and aren't aware of the services they perform. Although their profession is not well known, perfusionists can take pride in the knowledge that the procedures they perform are crucial to their patients' lives.

Perfusionists make decisions that could affect the well-being of the patient for years to come. "It is so technical," Carol says. "There is always the possibility of us doing some permanent damage. This is why we have so many checklists and check things so often. We build our systems to be as safe as possible."

Carol tries not to schedule her staff for more than one procedure a day, because each procedure takes hours of total focused concentration. "This is not a job you should take because you want to make money," Carol says. "You have to be able to commit yourself to each and every patient, and that takes a lot of compassion. You have to be able to react quickly in emergency situations, keep a cool head. Suppose you've got a patient who comes in to the emergency room, and his heart isn't working. You've got to keep your head and get that patient on bypass as soon as possible." She concludes, "This job is a major commitment on your life, and your family, not unlike that of a surgeon. It can have a major impact on your lifestyle."

You have to be able to commit yourself to each and every patient, and that takes a lot of compassion.

Occasionally, medical situations occur in which all the combined effort and talent of the surgical team are unable to help the patient. Perfusionists must have strength of character to accept the limitations of modern medicine, as well as its successes. "You need to know how to deal with death," Carol says, "and sometimes that only comes with age. It's really hard when you have children you're working with and you lose a patient. You have to learn some way to deal with it."

What Carol likes best about her job is the peace of mind she gets from knowing she's helped another human being. She especially likes working in the neonatal department. It gives her a sense of satisfaction to see a listless newborn with pale, clammy skin transformed through the surgery into a healthy, rosy-skinned infant. Carol's satisfaction comes from knowing that the contributions she makes during any successful surgical procedure help the patient to live a normal life.

Carol likes working in a field where new developments and new technologies are always coming along. She never has time to be bored. She also enjoys teaching. Because Maine Medical Center is a clinical supervision site for Boston's Northeastern University, Carol is able to share her skills with students.

Carol says that it helps to have a great staff. "The surgeons here are wonderful," she says. However, she doesn't really enjoy the administrative work as much as working in the operating room. She also doesn't like what's happening in the health care industry itself. "It's so cost-driven these days," she says. "All you hear is cost, cost, cost; streamline your team. I'm concerned that there isn't much nonprocedural time left for my staff to keep educated about new developments. I'm also concerned that cutting the costs of medical services will adversely affect patient care, although this hospital has assured us over the years that would never happen here." Carol regularly reads various professional journals to keep up with new developments in her field.

How Do I Become a Perfusionist?

Carol was an operating room nurse at Maine Medical Center in 1967 when she entered an on-the-job training program for perfusionists. She characterizes her training as rigorous "baptism by fire." She became board-certified when that became standard, which was in 1972. She says that today you cannot learn perfusionism on the job alone. There is too much technical knowledge required, and too many technological developments have occurred for that to work.

When Carol began her studies, her nursing background was helpful to her, but she had to take a

To Be a Successful Perfusionist, You Should . . .

- have good communication skills
- have a strong sense of responsibility
- work well as part of a team
- think independently
- act quickly and calmly in emergencies
- cope well under extreme stress
- know how to deal with occasional failure

lot of extra classes and study a lot on her own to be successful.

EDUCATION

High School

In preparation for any perfusion technology program, it is very important to take natural science classes such as biology and chemistry. Also essential are courses in higher mathematics and physics. You must have a high school diploma before you can be accepted by an accredited educational program.

Postsecondary Training

On-the-job training and apprenticeships are no longer available for positions in the perfusion field. To prepare for a career in perfusion, you must attend one of the 23 nationally accredited schools in the United States. Some of these schools require you to have a bachelor of science (B.S.) degree before you enter their program; others include course work toward the B.S. as part of their training. Program length varies from one to four years, depending on the schooling required for acceptance.

Occasionally, an accrediting institution will accept applicants who have trained at nursing schools or other technical schools and who have had experience as nurses or health technicians.

The accredited school carefully examines the student's personal character, academic achievement record, and personal temperament before accepting new students. There is intense competition for admission to these programs. Only 10 to 20 percent of the applicants are accepted.

It takes a unique type of person to work successfully under the kind of stress and challenge required. Intense course work is good preparation for such a challenging job. Courses include physiology, cardiology, respiratory therapy, general surgical procedure, and pharmacology. Also covered are courses in heart-lung bypass for adult, young children, and infant patients undergoing heart surgery; extracorporeal circulation; monitoring of the patient; and special applications.

You'll also receive clinical training for one and a half to two years. Most of the accredited perfusion programs try to begin their students' clinical training as soon as possible. The practice of perfusion requires extensive actual operating room experience. It is in the operating room that you observe and learn about extracorporeal circulation, respiratory therapy, general surgical procedures, and anesthesia. In clinical practice, you begin to perform perfusion procedures and perfect their skills.

CERTIFICATION OR LICENSING

Certification currently is not an absolute requirement for perfusionists, but it is rapidly becoming a practical requirement as more than 70 percent of perfusionists nationally are now certified. Certification is administered by the American Board of Cardiovascular Perfusion. Applicants must be graduates of an accredited training program, have performed a minimum of 75 instructor-supervised

FYI

What is extracorporeal membrane oxygenation?

Used for premature babies suffering respiratory distress and for postoperative heart patients, a machine draws blood from the patient's body, reoxygenates it, and pumps it back into the patient through the arteries. For premature babies, this buys crucial time until the infant's respiratory system can work on its own. For heart patients, it may buy time until the heart is able to pump on its own or until a donor heart is found.

clinical perfusions during the educational program, and pass a certification examination, which consists of two separate parts: the Clinical Applications in Perfusion Examination and the Perfusion Basic Science Examination. Applicants who successfully complete these requirements may use the designation certified clinical perfusionist.

Perfusionists must renew their certification every year. To be eligible for recertification, perfusionists must have performed at least 40 clinical perfusions per year and complete continuing education programs (45 continuing education units every three years). At present, perfusionists do not need separate state licenses to practice their profession.

SCHOLARSHIPS AND GRANTS

Scholarships for perfusion programs are available from the American Society of Extra-Corporeal Technology (AmSECT). Be sure to write well in advance of your planned study for application requirements and procedures (see "How Do I Learn More?"). In addition, financial aid in the form of scholarships and grants is often available through the financial aid office where the student is applying to go to school.

Who Will Hire Me?

Carol's first job experience was at Maine Medical Center, the hospital where she continues to work today. Typically, the perfusionist works in the cardiac operating room in a hospital as part of the surgery team. The perfusionist might be employed by the hospital itself, by a medical services group, or even by an individual cardiologist.

Many perfusionists are self-employed, meaning that they are independent contractors who offer their services to one or more hospitals. Those who are self-employed must take care of their own business affairs, including purchasing medical insurance, scheduling vacation time, and buying uniforms and other necessary materials.

A clinical perfusionist may find employment in any of the hospitals with open-heart surgery facilities in the United States. Some perfusionists find work as clinical consultants for companies that develop and sell perfusion equipment to hospitals. Perfusionists with graduate school education may conduct research and write about their findings.

ADVANCEMENT POSSIBILITIES

Chief cardiovascular perfusionists are in charge of the perfusionists on staff at a hospital. The chief perfusionist supervises others' work, performs administrative tasks, counsels staff, and maintains and monitors quality standards. If the hospital where you work is part of a university or other educational setting, as chief perfusionist you would instruct students

AmSECT, the professional society for perfusion technologists, recommends that students who have entered a program investigate the field first with professors and teachers and then join the AmSECT student membership division. This group holds meetings and conferences where you can get information on job openings in the field.

Where Can I Go from Here?

Perfusionism is a highly specialized field. As chief perfusionist in her department at Maine Medical Center, Carol has advanced as far as she can. Her position requires her to be responsible for managing a large staff as well as maintaining quality control. She is also responsible for supervising the purchase of supplies and equipment and for educating her staff about new techniques.

The typical career path involves learning more complex and specific procedures. Carol says that the foreseeable future in perfusionism will be increasingly technical and specialized. Neonatal perfusionism, one of Carol's most rewarding job responsibilities, is a good example of one specialization.

Perfusionists with graduate education and experience may conduct research and write about their work. Others choose to teach in colleges and accredited schools.

What Are the Salary Ranges?

Salaries for perfusionists compare favorably with those of other health technicians. According to a survey by

FYI

What is a coronary bypass?
A surgical procedure performed on patients with diseased or obstructed coronary arteries or veins.

During surgery, a nonessential vein from another part of the patient's body is grafted onto the obstructed coronary artery, thus bypassing it and allowing essential blood flow to and from the heart.

Perfusion.com, the average salary for perfusionists employed by hospitals was $97,424 in 2003, with earnings ranging from $50,000 to $165,000. Those employed by private perfusionist groups earned an average of $88,102, with a range of $32,000 to $275,000. Self-employed perfusionists earned an average of $115,258, with salaries ranging from $50,000 to $260,000. The average national income for all perfusionists was $87,439. Perfusionists usually receive a standard benefits package that includes paid vacation and holidays, insurance, and 401(k) plan options.

Perfusionists employed by hospitals and medical services groups get benefits such as sick leave, vacation, and medical insurance. Self-employed and physician-employed perfusionists usually pay for their own insurance, as well as for such items as uniforms and other minor equipment needed on the job.

What Is the Job Outlook?

This highly specialized field employs only about 3,700 individuals nationwide. However, the job outlook for perfusionists is good. Employment is expected to grow at a rate that is about as fast as the average for all other occupations. The number of Americans age 65 and over continues to rise. This demographic group is at a higher risk for developing cardiovascular disease, therefore requiring the professional expertise of perfusionists.

A number of factors may limit growth in this field. Open-heart surgery is very complex and many hospitals are not capable of performing such procedures; they are usually performed only in medical centers with 300 or more beds. Secondly, many hospitals have tried to cut costs by reducing the number of new perfusionist hires and asking perfusionists to take on more procedures without additional compensation. Finally, the development of new medical techniques, specifically ones that do not require the use of a heart-lung machine during surgery, may limit the need for these workers. It is still too early to tell, though, whether these new techniques will replace existing treatment options.

How Do I Learn More?

PROFESSIONAL ORGANIZATIONS

The following are organizations that provide information on perfusionist careers, certification, accredited schools and scholarships, and employers:

American Board of Cardiovascular Perfusion
207 North 25th Avenue
Hattiesburg, MS 39401
601-582-2227
http://www.abcp.org

American Medical Association
515 North State Street
Chicago, IL 60610
800-621-8335
http://www.ama-assn.org

American Society of Extra-Corporeal Technology
503 Carlisle Drive, Suite 125
Herndon, VA 20170
703-435-8556
http://www.amsect.org

The following Web site provides information on all aspects of perfusion:

The Perfusion Home Page
http://www.perfusion.com

BIBLIOGRAPHY

The following is a sampling of materials relating to the professional concerns and development of perfusionists:

Levitzky, Michael G. *Pulmonary Physiology*. 6th ed. New York: McGraw-Hill, 2002.

Wischnitzer, Saul, and Edith Wischnitzer. *Health-Care Careers for the 21st Century*. Indianapolis, Ind.: JIST Works, 2000.

PETROLEUM TECHNICIANS

In her cubicle in the engineering department, Lisa Whiting sits down at her computer. She has just returned from the "log library," where the company logs are stored. These logs contain the graphic representation of physical information collected from inside an oil well. They examine the electrical and radioactive properties of the rocks and give information about rock type and how much fluid, oil, gas, or water it contains. Lisa needs production information about the well, too, before she can go to work. She signs onto the online service where she can access the scout tickets that have the data she wants.

Carefully, she updates the reserves database, knowing the report she provides to the engineers will be the basis for future decisions made on the well, such as whether or not there is enough oil to keep drilling or how to maximize production on wells the company already owns. The responsibility is a big one, but Lisa enjoys it.

Definition
Petroleum technicians assist in the exploration of petroleum fields and in the production of oil and gas. They test potential sources, drill test wells, improve drilling technology, collect petroleum from producing wells, and deliver oil to pipelines.

Alternative Job Titles
Chemical technicians
Engineering technicians
Laboratory technicians
Maintenance technicians

High School Subjects
Chemistry
Computer science
Mathematics

Personal Skills
Helping/teaching
Technical/scientific

Salary Range
$22,000 to $40,800 to $67,700

Minimum Educational Requirements
Some postsecondary training

Certification or Licensing
None available

Outlook
Little or no growth

DOT
010

GOE
02.05.01, 06.03.01

NOC
2212

O*NET-SOC
19-4041.00, 47-5011.00, 47-5012.00, 47-5013.00, 47-5021.00

What Does a Petroleum Technician Do?

By the close of the 1960s, the Middle Eastern countries had come to dominate the oil business, and in the next two decades America's oil giants witnessed wildly fluctuating oil prices. They also saw increasing instability due to international conflicts and realized that depending on oil from this region was risky.

In the mid-1980s, the price of oil dropped, and America's oil producers came to understand what it would take to stay competitive with the foreign petroleum market: They needed to find more economic ways to run their oil operations. In this quest, scientists soon discovered in many abandoned oil wells almost as much petroleum as had been produced from older methods. Extracting the leftover oil required new technologies that would result in a profit.

The *petroleum technician* occupation was created to meet these challenges. Technological changes in the oil business called for highly scientific and technological workers to be crew members out in the field, drilling for oil and managing other aspects of the business. Petroleum technicians give the needed support to oil and gas exploration and production. They usually work as part of a team, assisting scientists, engineers, and managers in the business of finding and marketing petroleum. Sometimes called *geological* or *mineral technicians,* petroleum technicians assist in drilling test wells, help to measure the flow rates of oil, and assist in the testing of geological formations that promise oil. They prepare notes, sketches, maps, and survey data of certain areas and wells and analyze well logs or other geophysical data. Technicians operate and maintain the equipment that keeps records of the kinds of stone, clay, or mineral layers

FYI

In August 1859 Edwin Drake drilled the first oil well at Titusville, Pennsylvania. Petroleum was discovered 69 feet below the surface of the earth at Oil Creek.

a drill passes through and collect petroleum samples from producing wells.

The oil business is made up of companies who do one, some, or all of the following: explore for new oil fields, drill and retrieve oil, transport oil from refineries to distribution centers via tankers, barges, and pipelines, and refine crude oil into the stuff we all use every day. There is also some marketing and distribution going on to get the finished product to gas stations, airlines, factories, and people's houses. Petroleum technicians work in all these areas and carry many different titles.

Before anyone drills for oil, they have to know where to find it. And to know where to find it, they have to know how to look and what to look for. Petroleum technicians, working with geologists, geophysicists, and petroleum engineers, assist in the exploration of petroleum fields.

Laboratory technicians help in various kinds of studies, including exploration and production research, drilling research, and process and product research. They collect and examine geological data or test samples to determine the oil and mineral content. Some petroleum technicians, called scouts, collect information about oil and gas wells already in existence and land or lease contracts. Once exploration teams have determined a possible oil reservoir, drilling crews take over.

Drilling for oil is tricky business. In the long run, it is the drill bit that proves if the oil is there, and it takes several kinds of technicians to keep an oil rig operation running smoothly and successfully. *Drillers, derrick operators, engine operators*, and *tool pushers* can all be found out on the rig, each performing their own part in the action.

The most common type of drilling involves a drill bit suspended on a drilling string of 30-foot pipes joined together. As the bit goes deeper, the string is added. As drilling progresses, the bit gets more and more worn, till eventually it has to be replaced. In order for the bit to be replaced, the whole string has to be lugged up to the surface and taken apart section by section. Once done, the string can be put back together and the bit lowered to the well once again. This operation, called a round trip, takes most drilling crews 12 hours to complete. Recently, mechanized drill rigs handle the pipe automatically, making life much safer for drill crews.

Drillers supervise the drilling crew and make sure the machinery is running properly. They also keep a record of how deep they drill and through what, each day. Derrick operators work high atop the derrick, or framework, that sits over the well and help with the replacement of the drilling string. They work to keep the drill bit cool and control the flow of oil. Engine operators run and oversee the maintenance of the engines used to operate the drill, and tool pushers select what drill bits to use and make sure the drilling machinery is working the way it is supposed to. They also make sure the drilling rig is well supplied with just about anything it needs for smooth operations.

A *mud logger,* also called a *mud test technician,* takes the cuttings as they are pumped out of the well and analyzes them under a microscope in a portable laboratory at the well site to determine the presence of gas or oil. As drilling progresses the mud logger, who usually has training in geology, also uses a variety of computer-operated instruments to analyze well fluids at varying depths.

Next, technicians called *well loggers* lower logging tools to the bottom of the well on cable called wireline. Using logs, the well loggers measure the rock layers for such things as formation density and radioactivity. Electronic messages are sent back up the cable to instruments on board a logging truck. Many types of logs, all resembling an electrocardiogram, are generated for further study and interpretation by experienced geologists and engineers to determine the presence of oil or gas.

If mud and well logging indicate the well is a source for commercial oil, *well-servicing technicians* put the well in production. How they do it depends on what the reservoir is like: Shape, depth, and rock formation all play a part. Production facilities are then operated, monitored and maintained by the *pumpers,* while *gaugers* make sure the company's oil measurement and sale policy is followed.

Production engineering technicians regulate gas production, read charts at wells, gather fluid data on liquid-producing wells, and work with the production engineer to get the most out of the well.

Reservoir engineering technicians provide technical assistance to reservoir engineers for special projects involving computerized analyses of well production, budgets, and other data.

What Is It Like to Be a Petroleum Technician?

As a petroleum technician, you could work on land or sea, in an office or a laboratory, at a drilling site in the desert, or at a big-city refinery. The workplace varies as much as the many jobs petroleum techs do. If you work on a drilling crew or a production well, you will work outdoors, in all kinds of weather. Drillers work around the clock in three shifts, sometimes in isolated remote areas, living in quarters furnished by the company. They often move from place to place since work in a particular field may be completed in a few weeks or months. On the other hand, technicians who work on production wells usually remain in the same location for long periods.

If you work on offshore drilling rigs and platforms, be prepared to experience strong ocean currents, tides, and storms. You will generally work seven days a week, 12 hours a day, living on the drilling platform in small but comfortable quarters. After seven days on, you will get seven days off, returning to shore by helicopter or crewboat. Those who work on shore in oil production operations may work all over the world, in swamps, plains, deserts, or mountains ranges.

As an engineering technician, Lisa Whiting does all her work indoors, unlike some engineering technicians who spend part of the time in the field. Lisa says for her, working a regular 40-hour week is the norm and overtime is seldom required. "I definitely stay busy and always have work to do."

Lisa assists six engineers in the engineering and acquisitions department of Parker & Parsley Petroleum Company. She uses a computer to set up spreadsheets needed for analyses by engineers who make economic evaluations and forecasts of the wells. Working with the operations department, she researches and organizes well histories, including production revenue, on both company-owned and outside-operated properties.

Other jobs done by engineering technicians include plotting production curves on graphs and maintaining various databases, including the status

A petroleum engineer at a petrochemical plant inspects equipment in her area. *(Peter Bowater / Photo Researchers Inc.)*

of reserves, drilling programs, and daily oil and gas production per well. Lisa and the other engineering techs also perform clerical tasks such as typing letters, memos, and other correspondence.

"I really love my job and enjoy the many people I get to work with, the different libraries I get to go to, and getting out of the office at times. I'm always

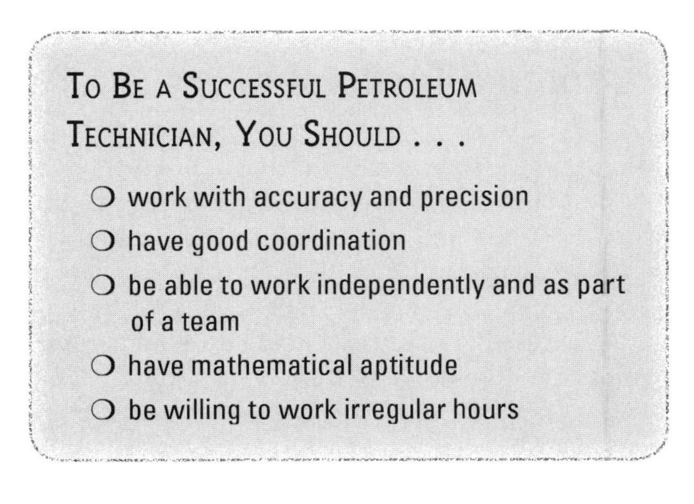

To Be a Successful Petroleum Technician, You Should . . .

- work with accuracy and precision
- have good coordination
- be able to work independently and as part of a team
- have mathematical aptitude
- be willing to work irregular hours

Lingo to Learn

Formation evaluation Methods of obtaining and analyzing data on oil- and gas-producing formations.

Gas lift Gas injected into the well to lighten and raise the fluid by expansion of the gas in order to help raise the fluid to the surface and obtain the maximum recovery of oil for maximum profit to the producer.

Sucker rod pumps Commonly known as rod pumping, this surface equipment imparts a motion to bring the fluid up to the surface and obtain the maximum recovery of oil for maximum profit to the producer.

Well completion The operations necessary to put the well in production.

Well log The product of a survey operation. Provides a permanent record of one or more physical measurements. Used to identify underground rocks and to determine the mineralogy and physical properties of potential reservoir rocks and the nature of the fluids they contain.

Well stimulation To employ methods to break up the formation and increase the flow of oil and gas. Explosives (perforating), special acid (acidizing), or sand solutions (fracturing) may be injected through the casing pipe.

doing different types of work and not the same thing all the time. It is not a boring job," Lisa says.

Do I Have What It Takes to Be a Petroleum Technician?

Much of the work in the petroleum industry involves physical labor and is potentially dangerous. You must be strong and healthy, enjoy the outdoors in all weather, and not mind getting dirty on the job. Flexibility is also an important quality to have. If you adapt well to changing working conditions, long hours, and a home away from home, you could do well working on an oil rig. Exploration or drilling crews may be away from their home base for several days at a time, while technicians on offshore rigs must be able to deal with a restricted environment for extended periods. Petroleum technicians must like working with machinery and scientific equipment and instruments.

Tana Priest, a senior engineering assistant at Lisa's company, says being quick to grasp and follow instructions, taking action without being reminded, and having organizational skills are qualities engineering technicians need. Lisa adds that being a quick learner and enjoying learning new programs on the computer is important for engineering technicians. "You have to be the type who enjoys a fast pace and doesn't want repetitious work."

How Do I Become a Petroleum Technician?

Lisa Whiting became an engineering technician over five years ago after starting out as a geological technician. "I was fortunate enough to get into this line of work by having the employer train me," she says. In fact, technicians usually begin working somewhere as a trainee, under the direct supervision of a scientist or a more experienced technician. If you have hands-on job experience, or an educational background with some work in a research or computer lab, you are more likely to land a tech job or to require a shorter period of on-the-job training. As you gain more experience, you will require only minimal supervision and could someday become a manager. Usually a technician is an engineer just starting out, says Tana Priest, or an engineering/production secretary who has advanced to the position of technician after two to five years of on-the-job experience. Tana's first job was as a production manager's secretary, where

FYI

According to the American Petroleum Institute, the U.S. oil industry employs about 1.4 million people. Oil provides about 40 percent of the energy we consume and 97 percent of our transportation fuels.

In-depth

Oil in the Family

From the Beverly Hillbillies to Dallas, striking it rich with oil is as much a part of American folklore as King Cotton and the Gold Rush. For those with dollar signs in their eyes, mineral oils are the important ones. Mineral oils include petroleum and its products, coal tar and its products, and shale oil. Mineral oils are often called hydrocarbon oils because they are composed chiefly of hydrocarbons, chemical compounds containing only hydrogen and carbon.

Petroleum, the most important mineral oil, is a major source of energy throughout most of the world. A liquid mixture of more than 100 complex mineral compounds, petroleum is usually obtained by drilling wells in the earth. Ordinarily black in color, petroleum can also be yellow or almost any other color. Products of petroleum include gasoline, kerosene, fuel oil, and lubricating oil.

Coal tar is a black, sticky substance derived from coal. Pitch, naphthalene, and phenol are among its products.

Shale oil, a substance that closely resembles petroleum, is obtained by heating certain types of shales known as oil shales. Shale oil is more expensive to produce than petroleum and, because of this, the world's vast reserves of shale oil remain intact.

The crude, petroleum, and natural gas industry is made up of establishments operating oil and gas fields. The activities of the industry include exploration for crude petroleum and natural gas; drilling, completing, and equipping wells; operating separators and emulsion breakers, and all other activities involved in making oil and gas marketable, up to the point of shipment from the producing property.

Major industry players include such large integrated oil and gas companies as BP, Atlantic Richfield, ExxonMobil, ChevronTexaco, Royal Dutch/Shell, Phillips Petroleum, and USX, as well as independent producers Oryx Petroleum and Mitchell Energy and Development Corporation.

she gained experience in taking drilling reports and typing correspondence for engineers.

"I don't think it is difficult to get a job as an engineering tech. From what I've seen, good techs are hard to find," Lisa says.

EDUCATION

High School

Math was Lisa's favorite course in high school and proved helpful in her future career, as did her algebra and calculus classes. Typing and English courses also helped prepare her for her job. Geometry and trigonometry are other math classes students considering a career as a petroleum technician should take. In addition, chemistry and physics classes provide you with a working knowledge of geology. Any classes that provide you with background information on the processing of crude oil into petroleum products and the use of the scientific principles in the operation of various types of equipment would be helpful. For mechanical jobs, shop courses and blueprint reading are useful; for laboratory, research, and engineering technician jobs, computer skills are important.

Postsecondary Training

Most employers prefer you to have at least two years of specialized training or education. Because the overall trend toward hiring technicians is slowing, any additional schooling is a huge plus. Laboratory and radio technicians generally need at least one year of training, while a mud test technician will need a minimum of a bachelor's degree in geology. Postsecondary training is not usually required for drilling and production jobs, but many petroleum technician positions require familiarity with specified basic processes that can be gained through special education in technical or community colleges.

Petroleum technology programs, found primarily in the West and Southwest, are helpful both for newcomers to the field and for those already working who want to upgrade their job skills. An associate's degree in applied science can be earned with technical courses plus general education studies. Certificates in a specified area of study are awarded for completion of technical courses only.

Petroleum technology programs provide training in drilling operations, fluids, and equipment; production methods such as sucker rod pumping and gas lift; formation evaluation, including well logging methods along with the basics of core analysis; well completion methods such as open hole completion, perforating, acidizing, and fracturing; and petroleum property evaluation, including evaluation of production history data and basic theories and techniques of economic analysis.

Other training includes specialized programs designed for oil company employees. These programs are often offered by the suppliers of the special materials, equipment, or services.

LABOR UNIONS

Most petroleum technician jobs are not unionized. Only about 25 percent of all firms employing oil field operation workers, and less than 5 percent of firms employing contract drilling workers, are covered by union contracts. Union representation is largely restricted to workers in the refining and transportation areas of the petroleum industry. Workers in establishments with collective bargaining agreements are represented by the Associated Petroleum Employees Union or by the Oil, Chemical and Atomic Workers International Union.

Who Will Hire Me?

The U.S. Department of Labor reports that in 2002 geological and petroleum technicians held 11,000 jobs and of those one-fifth were with oil and gas extraction companies.

Although drilling for oil and gas is done in a large number of states, about 60 percent of all workers are employed in four states: Texas, Louisiana, Oklahoma, and California. Employers in the crude petroleum and natural gas industry include major oil companies and independent producers. The oil and gas field services industry, which includes drilling contractors, logging companies, and well servicing contractors, is the other major source of employment. Most jobs are full-time, permanent positions, while some are temporary.

Check with the local office of your state employment service for job leads or check directly with oil companies and oil services companies. Names and addresses can be found in the *U.S.A. Oil Industry Directory* (http://www.osti.gov/energycitations/product.biblio.jsp?osti_id=5867385).

Employment sources for qualified petroleum technicians include a placement service offered by the Society of Petroleum Engineers for their members. Those interested in engineering or engineering technician opportunities can find job listings in the Journal of Petroleum Technology, published by the Society of Petroleum Engineers.

Where Can I Go from Here?

"I have room to grow to be a senior engineering tech then an engineering assistant, and on to a senior engineering assistant," says Lisa. With additional schooling and a degree, an engineering technician could also go on to be an engineer.

The advancement opportunities for other kinds of petroleum technicians vary greatly. In drilling, a rotary driller can advance to head driller to tool pusher to oil production manager. With enough capital, technicians can become independent owners and operators of drilling rigs. Pumpers and gaugers can go on to become oil company production or operations foremen on up to operations management, overseeing an entire district.

In many areas advancement requires further education. Well loggers who want to analyze logs need a minimum of a bachelor's degree in geology or petroleum engineering. For advanced level engineering, a master's is the minimum requirement and a doctorate is the standard level of education. Upper-level researchers also need a doctorate.

During periods of rapid growth in the oil industry, advancement opportunities are plentiful for capable workers. However, downsizing in recent years has made advancement more difficult, and in many cases technicians, geologists, engineers, and others have accepted lesser positions for which they are overqualified.

What Are the Salary Ranges?

Because of their many work situations and conditions, petroleum technicians' salaries vary widely. Salaries also vary according to geographic location, experience, and education. According to the U.S. Department of Labor Occupational Information Network, media annual earnings for geological and petroleum technicians were $40,800. Those in the middle 50 percent earned between $29,900 and $53,600 annually. The lowest paid 10 percent earned $22,000, while the highest paid 10 percent earned $67,700. In general, technicians working in remote areas and under severe weather conditions usually receive higher rates of pay, as do technicians who work at major oil companies and companies with unions.

What Is the Job Outlook?

Employment is expected to decline as a result of reduced exploration and falling production in the domestic oil industry. In recent years there has been a worldwide surplus of oil. The Occupational Information Network predicts only about a 1 percent increase in jobs opportunities from 11,000 in 2002 to 11,300 in 2012. The U.S. Department of Labor expects employment to show little or no growth for geological and petroleum technicians through 2012.

Major oil finds around the world and increased production by key foreign oil producers, such as the Middle Eastern and North Sea nations, have increased the supply of oil. At the same time, domestic conservation of oil by industries and the public has reduced the demand for oil. The surplus has resulted in low oil prices and a reduced incentive for exploration and drilling. In an effort to cut costs, oil companies have streamlined operations and maintained their production levels with fewer workers.

Environmental measures being imposed in industrialized countries and the concentration on conserving energy through greater efficiency are expected to lead to lower energy-consumption growth rates. According to the Energy Information Administration, crude oil production is expected to continue to decline in the United States. Consumption and production of U.S. natural gas, however, is expected to increase.

Oil still maintains a powerful role in the world's economy and employment. While the industry has seen tough times in the last decades of the 20th century, the pattern could easily reverse itself. Drilling for oil in the Gulf of Mexico has picked up, legislation passed at the end of 1995 called for an end to the 22-year export ban of Alaskan oil to Japan, South Korea, and other Asian countries, and in 2005 the U.S. Senate approved legislation that opens a portion of the Arctic National Wildlife Refuge to oil exploration. Though there will still be new jobs for petroleum technicians, most of the jobs will be filled by current technicians. The more skilled and specialized you are, the better chance you will have of getting a job in the industry.

Advancement Possibilities

Petroleum engineers analyze the technical and cost factors to plan methods for recovering the maximum amount of oil and gas in oil-field operations.

Petroleum geologists explore and chart the arrangement of strata and structure of the earth to locate gas and oil deposits. They also study well logs, analyze cores and cuttings from well drillings, and interpret data obtained by electrical or radioactive well logging.

Well-logging captains supervise and coordinate activities of workers engaged in analysis of mud and oil well cuttings during drilling operations to detect presence of oil or gas and identify productive areas.

How Do I Learn More?

PROFESSIONAL ORGANIZATIONS

The following organizations provide information on petroleum technicians careers, correspondence courses, accredited schools, scholarships, and employers:

American Association of Petroleum Geologists
PO Box 979
Tulsa, OK 74101-0979
918-584-2555
http://www.aapg.org

American Petroleum Institute
1220 L Street, NW
Washington, DC 20005-4070
202-682-8000
http://www.api.org

Junior Engineering Technical Society Inc.
1420 King Street, Suite 405
Alexandria, VA 22314-2715
703-548-5387
info@jets.org
http://www.jets.org

Society of Petroleum Engineers
PO Box 833836
Richardson, TX 75080
800-456-6863
spedal@spe.org
http://www.spe.org

The University of Texas at Austin
Petroleum Extension Service
One University Station, R8100
Austin, TX 78712-1100
800-687-4132
http://www.utexas.edu/cee/petex

BIBLIOGRAPHY

The following is a sampling of materials relating to the professional concerns and development of petroleum technicians:

Hyne, Norman J. *Nontechnical Guide to Petroleum Geology, Exploration, Drilling and Production*. 2d ed. Tulsa, Okla.: Pennwell Books, 2001.

Krueger, Gretchen Dewailly. *Opportunities in Petroleum Careers*. Lincolnwood, Ill.: VGM Career Horizons, 1998.

Leffler, William L. *Petroleum Refining in Nontechnical Language*. Tulsa, Okla.: Pennwell Books, 2000.

Yergin, Daniel, and Joseph Stanislaw (contributor). *The Prize: The Epic Quest for Oil, Money, and Power*. New York: Free Press, 1993.

PHARMACY TECHNICIANS

Definition

Pharmacy technicians work with pharmacists in preparing medication and keeping patient records. They fill and label bottles with prescribed tablets and capsules, prepare IV packs, take inventory, clean equipment, and enter data into a computer.

Alternative Job Titles

Pharmacy assistants
Pharmacy clerks
Pharmacy medication technicians
Pharmacy technologists

High School Subjects

Chemistry
Health
Mathematics

Personal Skills

Helping/teaching
Technical/scientific

Salary Range

$18,740 to $22,755 to $33,780

Minimum Educational Level

Some postsecondary training

Certification or Licensing

Recommended

Outlook

Faster than the average

DOT

074

GOE

14.02.01

NOC

3414

O*NET-SOC

29-2052.00

The medical center pharmacy is brightly lit. The fluorescent light bounces off the clean white shelves and counters, off the glass bottles and beakers. Like scientists in a laboratory, the pharmacy technicians in their white coats hover over vials and weights and measures. One technician prepares an intravenous solution (IV), while another, wearing a special hood, carefully prepares an investigational drug.

A beeper pierces the quiet of the room. It's a Code 5000, the call for the hospital emergency team, and one of the pharmacy technicians moves into action. Critical situations occur every day in the hospital, and he has become very familiar with emergency procedure.

He takes the cart stocked with medications, equipment, and a monitor defibrillator and quickly makes his way through the hospital. At the end of the corridor, nurses, physicians, and an anesthesiologist stream into the patient's room. They all work hurriedly, yet smoothly and precisely. When the pharmacy tech arrives with the cart, it becomes his responsibility to write down everything that happens in order to maintain a legal record of the emergency scene. He listens and watches carefully and also performs his other duties, such as preparing an IV or resuscitation equipment.

What Does a Pharmacy Technician Do?

You've probably stood many times at a pharmacist's counter, waiting for a prescription to be filled. You've watched the pharmacist count out pills or prepare capsules. You've been advised on how to use each medication safely and effectively. And you've probably noticed how much the pharmacist relies on his or her assistants. These assistants are known as *pharmacy technicians,* and they have become a recognized force in the health care industry.

Whether in a drug store, hospital, clinic, or nursing care facility, pharmacy technicians perform a number of duties, many of which require precision and attention to detail. In a retail pharmacy, technicians work under the direction of a pharmacist. Their responsibilities include filling prescriptions and preparing prescription labels, as well as stocking and taking inventory of prescriptions and over-the-counter medications. They also have a number of clerical duties, such as maintaining a database of patient medication records, preparing insurance claim forms, and managing the cash register. The pharmacy technician also cleans and sterilizes glassware and equipment.

In a hospital, pharmacy technicians perform many of the same duties as in a retail setting, along

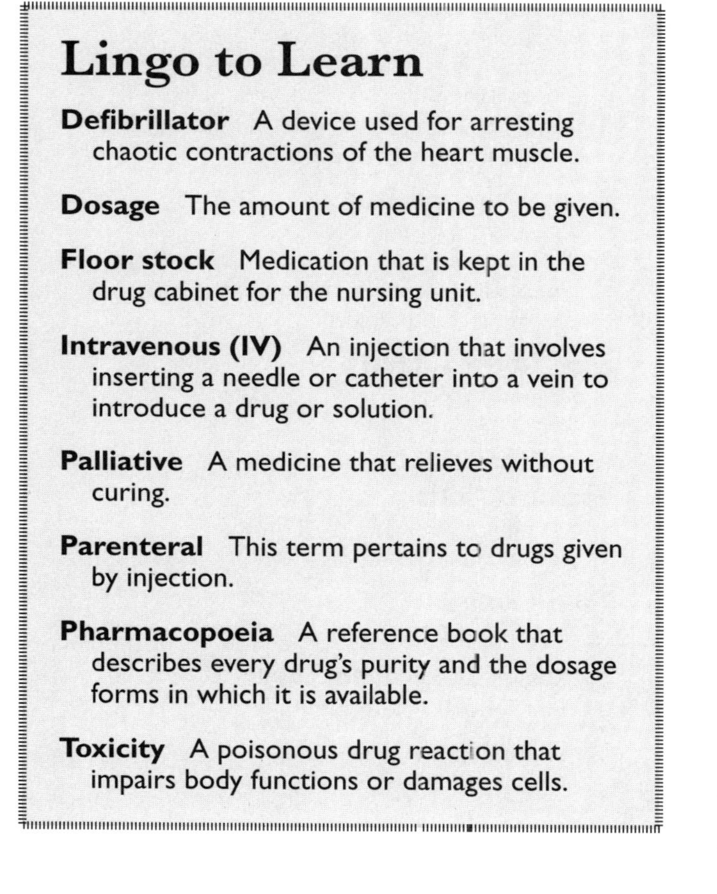

Lingo to Learn

Defibrillator A device used for arresting chaotic contractions of the heart muscle.

Dosage The amount of medicine to be given.

Floor stock Medication that is kept in the drug cabinet for the nursing unit.

Intravenous (IV) An injection that involves inserting a needle or catheter into a vein to introduce a drug or solution.

Palliative A medicine that relieves without curing.

Parenteral This term pertains to drugs given by injection.

Pharmacopoeia A reference book that describes every drug's purity and the dosage forms in which it is available.

Toxicity A poisonous drug reaction that impairs body functions or damages cells.

with some added responsibilities. For instance, *hospital pharmacy technicians* often assemble 24-hour supplies of medication for patients, prepare commercially unavailable medications, prepare sterile intravenous medications, and deliver medications to patient rooms. They also maintain medications at nursing stations and in operation rooms. Sometimes, a pharmacy technician distributes medications to smaller, outpatient clinics. In large hospitals where computerized or robotic dispensing equipment is used, technicians are usually in charge of operating and maintaining the equipment.

In some hospitals, pharmacy technicians are also important members of the emergency team. They prepare resuscitation equipment and keep a special cart stocked with medications and a monitor defibrillator, which they bring with them when summoned to an emergency in the hospital.

Preparing medication, whether it be for a customer or a hospital patient, often requires more than counting pills and filling bottles. Pharmacy technicians work with a variety of substances and tools, such as a mortar and pestle (typically made of glass or porcelain), which is used to grind crystalline or granular substances. Conical and cylindrical graduates are glasses used for measuring liquids. Technicians use spatulas to prepare ointments or to remove substances from the mortar and pestle. An experienced technician in a hospital or research facility works with investigational drugs: new drugs approved for human use but with unknown side effects; some patients agree to try these new drugs when all other prescribed drugs and treatments have failed. Preparing the investigational drugs requires special gloves and hoods. These experienced technicians also work with chemotherapy agents and live bacteria.

Pharmacy technicians are responsible for the handling and safe delivery of controlled substances, drugs or substances with a high potential for abuse, which, when abused, may lead to severe dependence. Amphetamines, methamphetamines, codeine, and morphine are among these substances. In 1970, Congress passed the Controlled Substances Act to improve the regulation of manufacturing, distributing, and dispensing of these drugs.

What Is It Like to Be a Pharmacy Technician?

Mark McCrory, CPhT, is the senior technician in a hospital pharmacy. His duties include preparing the daily dosing for all the inpatients. "I'm also IV trained," he says, "so I make the IV fluids. I also do a lot of compounding of drugs that are not standard doses. We usually get drugs that are packaged per pill, per unit dose, and sometimes the drugs aren't available as unit doses, or the dosing for the patient requires only half a tab. Our hospital policy is that anytime there's a half a tab, or not a full tab, they're repackaged before they go to the floors." The techs also repackage when drugs have been bought in bulk to save expenses.

To prepare the drugs, the techs work in the manufacturing area of the pharmacy. "Sometimes drugs are not commercially available in suspension [particles of a drug mixed with fluid]. Patients who are in a comatose state are given drugs intravenously, or more often than not, through a gastrointestinal tube. It goes right into their stomachs and is broken down through the body."

The pharmacy also includes a unit dose area, where the unit doses are prepared for the next day. "That's basically counting pills," Mark says. "We have a sheet of patients generated by units, and each shift has the responsibility for filling certain units. The unit dose techs are also responsible for answering the phones and triaging the questions from nurses. There are certain things that techs can answer. Any kind of dosing or compatibility questions, medication-type questions. We can answer those if we're directed from the pharmacist."

Mark typically works in the IV room, where his first task of the shift is to put labels in order. "The labels are generated by the computer for scheduled doses," he says. "Sometimes they're PRN, as the patient needs them. Those labels come up on a different schedule and printer. Some drugs have short expiration times, and once they're mixed up, they're only good for four or six hours. We do those just before they're due. Other drugs have longer expirations of 24, 48, or 72 hours. We can get those out first thing." Mark also works in a biological safety hood to prepare chemotherapeutic drugs. "We do work with some caustic materials. We work with a lot of acids. Particularly with the chemotherapeutics, there are certain protocols with chemo gloves, chemo gowns. Some of the techs wear full plastic aprons. I wear the paper-type sleeves with heavy-duty rubber gloves."

Mark is also the Pixis coordinator. "The Pixis is the automatic drug dispensing machine," he explains. "Most in-house pharmacies are going with automation. It's robotics. A nurse will ask for a certain drug, a drawer with the drug will pop open, the patient is charged, the drug is dispensed, all through the computer system. I'm sometimes on call, and when there's a problem with the machine, I have to repair it. Usually if there's a problem, it's that the machine has accidentally charged a patient for a drug they don't need." Maintaining the Pixis involves changing drawers, refilling medications, and even replacing a motherboard when necessary.

Cathy Guay works in another area of technician work; she is a pharmacy technician at Palmer's Drugs, an independently owned drug store in Missoula, Montana. As the senior technician at Palmer's, she works the coveted day shift from 9:00 A.M. to 4:00 P.M. The first thing she does in the morning is check on the orders that were placed and filled the evening before, to see if there are prescriptions waiting to be filled. If so, she types the prescription and patient data into the computer, prints out a label, gets the medication from the shelf, and counts or measures the appropriate amount. She places the filled order in a designated area where the pharmacist can review it before putting it in a bag for the customer.

In the morning, Cathy also reviews the order that the night technician faxed to their wholesale drug supplier so she'll know what to expect in that day's shipment. She spends most of her day helping walk-in customers and answering phone calls from doctors' offices, customers, and health insurance providers. "I try to answer every call by the second ring," she says. She notes that independent retail pharmacies, as opposed to chain pharmacies, have to compete by offering better customer service. For instance, when customers have a question about their insurance coverage, Cathy finds out the answer. She also delivers prescriptions to customers who are unable to pick them up in person.

Cathy says there's much personal interaction with customers in a retail setting. "You've got that customer on the phone or in front of you," she describes. "You want to take the time to find out how their day is going."

FYI

- Rx, a symbol meaning prescription, was originally a symbol of the gods in early medical writings. The symbol was used as a prayer for healing.
- A 5,000-year-old clay tablet, discovered in the Middle East, records drug remedies used by the Sumerians. Listed on the table are prescriptions for vegetable extracts, ointments, and solutions.
- In ancient Mesopotamia, doctors tested drugs and poisons on slaves and prisoners.

Do I Have What It Takes to Be a Pharmacy Technician?

It's crucial that pharmacy technicians be neat, conscientious, and highly reliable. In this field, mistakes can have serious consequences. If you're the

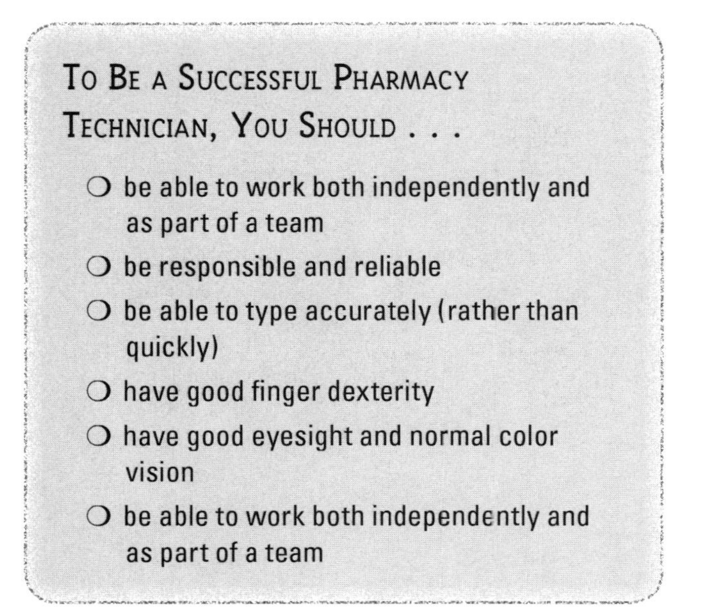

To Be a Successful Pharmacy Technician, You Should . . .

- be able to work both independently and as part of a team
- be responsible and reliable
- be able to type accurately (rather than quickly)
- have good finger dexterity
- have good eyesight and normal color vision
- be able to work both independently and as part of a team

kind of person who pays scrupulous attention to detail and can't stand to leave a room messy, this line of work is probably right for you. "The stress level is very high," Mark says, "because of the demand. You've got somebody's life in your hands. One error could kill a patient. The nurses who call down are under a lot of stress, with doctors breathing down their necks."

You're working under the pharmacist's license. They have to be able to trust you.

During the course of a workday, pharmacy technicians may handle addictive and expensive drugs, so they need to be ethical. "You're working with controlled substances," Mark says. "You're working under the pharmacist's license. They have to be able to trust you." It's also important for pharmacy technicians to not divulge personal information about patients or customers. Good communication skills are also essential because pharmacy technicians are expected to provide customers or patients with instructions on taking the drugs they've been prescribed. Moreover, pharmacy technicians must relate well to a variety of people, including customers, patients, and medical professionals.

Cathy Guay says that retail pharmacy technicians must have especially good interpersonal skills because they're working closely with customers who often have important questions or concerns.

Typing is another essential, if underrated, skill. While pharmacy technicians don't need to be rocket-fast typists, they do need to be accurate. Again, a mistyped prescription label could have a dire effect on a patient's health. Because pharmacy technicians must handle needles and syringes while they're preparing drugs, good hand-eye coordination and finger dexterity are essential. In addition, technicians need good eyesight in order to identify the various pills and medications. Correct color vision is a must since some drugs are color-coded.

How Do I Become a Pharmacy Technician?

Mark went through a pharmacy technology program at a local community college. "It involves a lot of memorization of drugs, body parts, physiology," he says. Mark also believes that certification is important. "You're given more respect. It's not required to work here, but it helps. Also, we pay 50 cents more an hour to certified techs." For retail pharmacy technicians, informal, on-the-job training is still the most common way to enter the profession. However, many employers can no longer afford to train technicians and prefer to hire formally educated technicians.

Cathy Guay entered the field by working as an errand runner for a nursing home pharmacy in Seattle. When her employer offered to pay for a nine-month technician training program, Cathy jumped at the chance. Training is offered at community colleges, vocational/technical schools, and hospital community pharmacies throughout the United States. The programs usually last from six months to two years, leading to a certificate or an associate's degree.

EDUCATION

High School

To become a pharmacy technician, you need a high school diploma or its equivalent. You should take courses that develop your basic math skills, since a pharmacy technician's job demands accuracy in numerical calculations and record keeping. To test your aptitude for the scientific nature of a pharmacy tech's job, take some courses in biology and chemistry. By working on projects in your high school's chemistry lab, you learn how important it is to follow instructions to the letter. Health courses can familiarize you with medical and pharmaceutical terminology. Finally, taking English and speech courses will polish your communication skills for the job.

Postsecondary Training

Formalized pharmacy technician training was first offered by the armed forces and is now offered by many hospitals, vocational and technical schools, and community colleges. Some courses offered in these training programs include introduction to pharmacy and health care systems, pharmacy laws and ethics, medical terminology, anatomy, therapeutic agents, biology, and higher math. In addition, courses in microcomputers, writing, IV preparation, and interview and intercommunication skills are also part of some programs. In addition to the class work, you may be required to perform an internship or clerkship in a pharmacy. Since 1983, the American Society of Health-System Pharmacists (ASHP) has accredited pharmacy technician programs in order to ensure certain standards of training. To find out what programs are offered near you, contact the Pharmacy Technician Educators Council (http://www.rxptec.org).

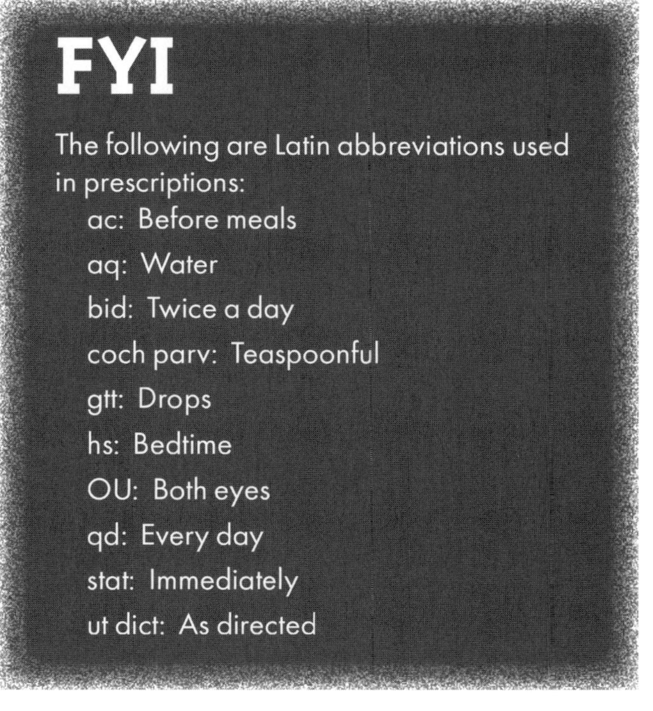

CERTIFICATION OR LICENSING

While certification is not required, it is highly recommended. In the past, certification was handled on a state-by-state basis. However, in 1995 the Pharmacy Technician Certification Board (PTCB) was established to create a single, national voluntary certification program for pharmacy technicians. Since that time, more than 195,000 pharmacy technicians in the United States have taken the National Pharmacy Technician Certification Examination and received the designation certified pharmacy technicians (CPhT). Certification shows an employer that you have received the training and gained the knowledge needed to perform the duties of a pharmacy technician. On-the-job experience or a hospital training program is usually adequate preparation for taking the exam. Some national drugstore chains have developed incentives for their pharmacy technicians to become certified. Walgreens, for instance, has created its own training program and materials, and the company offers a pay raise to technicians who become certified.

After passing the exam, pharmacy technicians must take 20 hours of continuing education every two years in order to maintain their certification. Certification must be renewed every two years.

Who Will Hire Me?

Mark got his job as a tech immediately following his community college program. "My program required an internship," he says, "where I had to work in an inpatient and outpatient setting. I was offered my job before I was even finished with my internship, which is often the case. We hire a lot of our techs from internship programs."

Most pharmacy technicians begin their job search on the local level. Newspaper ads, employment agencies, and hospital job listings are all good starting points. Graduates of training programs sometimes move into technician positions with the hospital or retail pharmacy where they served as interns.

The majority of pharmacy technicians will find work in hospital pharmacies, retail drugstores,

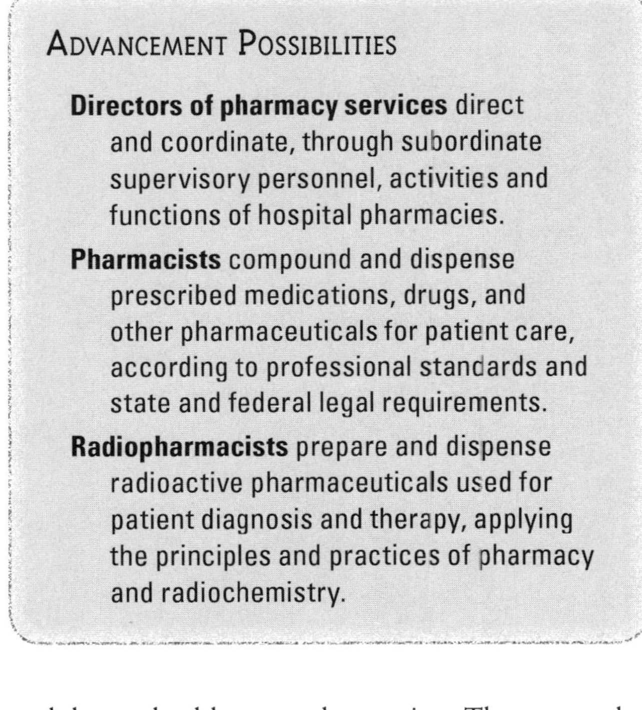

Advancement Possibilities

Directors of pharmacy services direct and coordinate, through subordinate supervisory personnel, activities and functions of hospital pharmacies.

Pharmacists compound and dispense prescribed medications, drugs, and other pharmaceuticals for patient care, according to professional standards and state and federal legal requirements.

Radiopharmacists prepare and dispense radioactive pharmaceuticals used for patient diagnosis and therapy, applying the principles and practices of pharmacy and radiochemistry.

and home health care pharmacies. There are also positions available in nursing home pharmacies, clinic pharmacies, and mail-order prescription pharmacies. In addition, experienced technicians are sometimes hired by nontraditional employers, such as medical insurance companies, medical computer software companies, drug manufacturers, food processing companies, and as instructors in pharmacy technician training programs.

More job opportunities are available in those areas with an older population, because more medical services are generally required by the elderly. These areas typically include New York, Florida, California, Arizona, and New Mexico.

Where Can I Go from Here?

The advancement prospects for pharmacy technicians are somewhat determined by the size of the pharmacies where they work. Mark describes the line of advancement at his workplace: "You start off as a tech trainee. You do tests and skill evaluations to move up the ladder. We have Tech 1, Tech 2, then Senior Tech. Many of our techs tend to go into pharmacy school. A number of the pharmacists we work with started at the hospital as pharmacy techs." This is the path Mark wants to take, with plans of getting his Pharm.D.

Experienced pharmacy technicians may also choose to specialize in a particular area of pharmacy work, such as in narcotics control or chemotherapy preparation. Others may choose to work primarily in the emergency room or operating room of a hospital or clinic. In a smaller retail pharmacy, advancement is not always possible.

What Are the Salary Ranges?

According to the *Occupational Outlook Handbook*, the median hourly wage for pharmacy technicians was $10.94 in 2003, or $22,755 annually for full-time employees. The middle 50 percent earned between $9.01 and $13.50 an hour, while those in the highest 10 percent earned more than $16.24 an hour.

Graduates of accredited training programs, along with technicians who are certified, are usually paid in the higher ranges. In addition, salaries are higher on the East and West coasts and in large cities. Benefits for pharmacy technicians often include medical and dental insurance, retirement savings plans, and paid sick, personal, and vacation days.

What Is the Job Outlook?

According to the *Occupational Outlook Handbook*, employment for pharmacy technicians will grow faster than the average for all other occupations. This demand can be attributed to the changing role of pharmacists, the increasing pharmacy workload due to the growing elderly population, and the need to control health care costs. In particular, as pharmacists spend more time in consultation with customers, skilled pharmacy technicians will be needed to handle the assembly and dispensing of medications. While the use of computerized and robotic dispensing equipment eliminates some traditional duties, there will always be a need for a skilled technician to maintain these devices, as well as to handle the other technical and clerical responsibilities.

Pharmacists are getting jobs with many different kinds of health care providers, which means more opportunities for pharmacy technicians as well. As technicians continue to gain recognition for their skilled and specialized work, more career, training, and scholarship opportunities will arise. Those interested in pursing a career as a pharmacy technician should keep an eye on health care trends and government health care reform. Also watch for the changing role of hospitals, as hybrids between hospitals and nursing homes develop.

How Do I Learn More?

PROFESSIONAL ORGANIZATIONS

To learn about continuing education, contact

American Association of Pharmacy Technicians
PO Box 1447
Greensboro, NC 27402
aapt@pharmacytechnician.com
http://www.pharmacytechnician.com

To learn about an online certification course, contact

National Pharmacy Technician Association
PO Box 683148
Houston, TX 77268
888-247-8700
http://www.pharmacytechnician.org

To learn about certification, contact

Pharmacy Technician Certification Board
2215 Constitution Avenue, NW
Washington, DC 20037-2985
800-363-8012
http://www.ptcb.org

BIBLIOGRAPHY

The following is a sampling of materials relating to the professional concerns and development of pharmacy technicians:

Generali, Joyce A. *The Pharmacy Technician's Pocket Drug Reference*. 2d ed. Washington, D.C.: APhA Publications, 2003.

Reddy, Indra K., and Mansoor A. Kahn. *Essential Math and Calculations for Pharmacy Technicians*. Boca Raton, Fla.: CRC Press, 2003.

Reifman, Noah. *Certification Review for Pharmacy Technicians*. Washington, D.C.: PTCB Books, 2004.

Weetfeet. *Careers in Biotech and Pharmaceuticals: The WetFeet Insider Guide*. Reissue ed. San Francisco: WetFeet, 2004.

PHLEBOTOMY TECHNICIANS

"It's my job to draw blood from donors," says Sherry Southerland, who works as a phlebotomy technician at a branch office of the Bonfils Blood Center, a blood bank that supplies most of the hospitals in Colorado. "I go over the donors' medical histories, ask them additional questions, scrub the skin, find the vein, collect, and label the blood. Like any job, after a while, things can get pretty routine." She sighs and adds, "But when my dad got sick and I saw him being transfused, I realized that phlebotomy technicians are not just some cog in a machine. I could see the other end of the process and it made a real difference."

Sherry stresses the vital role phlebotomy technicians serve in the collection of the nation's blood supply. "We've got to have this resource," she says, "and it must be screened well. When my dad was sick, I hoped that the phlebotomy technicians who had drawn the blood that he was receiving had done a good job screening donors. Did they ask enough questions, I wondered. Did they take time to explain why those questions were necessary? The importance of what I was doing as a phlebotomy technician suddenly came through."

Definition
Phlebotomy technicians draw blood from patients or donors in hospitals, blood banks, clinics, physicians' offices, or other facilities. They assemble equipment, verify patient identification numbers, and withdraw blood either through a finger puncture or with a needle syringe.

Alternative Job Titles
Blood technicians
Phlebotomists

High School Subjects
Biology
English
Health

Personal Skills
Helping/teaching
Technical/scientific

Salary Range
$18,720 to $21,944 to $33,488

Minimum Educational Level
Some postsecondary training

Certification or Licensing
Required by certain states

Outlook
About as fast as the average

DOT
079

GOE
14.05.01

NOC
3212

O*NET-SOC
N/A

What Does a Phlebotomy Technician Do?

Ancient people did not understand the role of blood, but they knew it was vital. Some believed that it might even be the home of the soul. Early Egyptians bathed in blood, hoping this act would cure illness or reverse the aging process. Some Romans drank the blood of dying gladiators in order to acquire the athletes' strength and bravery.

Over time, scientists began to understand how blood functioned and they searched for ways to collect it or transfer it from one person to another. Quills or silver needles were attached to silver tubing and the tubings were attached to animal bladders in order to construct blood-collection devices. Arteries were punctured and blood gushed out. Sometimes the donor died, as well as the patient. Little care was taken with the cleanliness of instruments. No one understood why blood sometimes failed to coagulate or coagulated too quickly. No one could explain why blood could not always be transferred successfully from one person to another.

Modern techniques of blood collection, typing, and transfusion developed in the 20th century. Blood is now drawn by professionals called *phlebotomy technicians* or *phlebotomists*. They work in clean, well-lighted laboratories, hospitals, and clinics.

Blood is used for a variety of medical tests or is stored in blood banks for future use. There are three main methods by which blood can be drawn: venipuncture, arterial puncture, and capillary collection. Collecting through veins is the most common method, followed by artery collection, then capillary collection, which involves punctures of the fingers or heels.

The first steps in drawing blood are to take the patient's medical history and match the physician's testing order with the amount of blood to be drawn. Then the patient's temperature and pulse are taken. Next, the site of the withdrawal is located. Typically, the large vein that is visible on the underside of the arm near the elbow is used.

Finding a suitable vein, however, is not always easy because there is a great deal of anatomical difference among people. Once a suitable site is located, a tourniquet is wrapped high on the patient's upper arm, as far from the elbow as is convenient. The phlebotomy technician checks the site for lesions, other needle marks, and any skin disorders that might interfere with the collection process. Then the site is cleansed by swabbing with a sterile solution. The phlebotomy technician grasps the patient's forearm and retracts the arm downward in order to immobilize the soft tissue and steady the vein. Sometimes the patient is asked to open and close his or her hand a few times to make the vein more prominent. Making a proper puncture takes practice. After the sterile needle is uncovered, it must be grasped tightly but passed through the skin gently. The needle is inserted almost horizontal with the vein and as parallel to the skin as possible. Then the hub of the needle is raised and the angle toward the skin increased so that the needle can pierce the wall of the vein. After the needle is advanced slightly into the vein itself, blood may be withdrawn. Generally this is done by releasing a clamp attached to the blood collection device or to the tubing. When the required amount of blood is collected, the needle is removed and sealed, the site covered, and the tourniquet removed.

After collection, the phlebotomy technician labels the blood, coordinates its number with the worksheet order, and transports the blood to a storage facility or to another laboratory worker. The phlebotomy technician also checks to make sure that the patient is all right, notes any adverse reactions, and administers first aid or other medical assistance when necessary.

Specialists in blood-bank technology are professionals who perform a variety of tasks associated with blood banking. They test blood for compatibility, type and match it, and store it until needed. Phlebotomy technicians who are employed by blood banks may be supervised by specialists in blood-bank technology. Phlebotomy technicians who work in hospitals or clinics are supervised by other laboratory personnel.

What Is It Like to Be a Phlebotomy Technician?

"When I come to work," says Sherry Southerland, "I never know whether the lobby of the blood bank will be full or whether no one will show up for an hour or two. The day after a disaster occurs anywhere in the U.S., however, we're always mobbed by donors. Regardless, 80 percent of the people we see are repeats, folks who come here every 56 days because they know how great the need is for blood.

Lingo to Learn

Autologous donation A blood donation that is stored and reserved for return to the original donor during surgery.

Blood bank A facility responsible for collecting blood from donors, separating blood into its components, typing, and matching blood in order to ensure safe transfusions.

Blood components The red cells, white cells, platelets, and plasma that constitute blood.

Hematology The science of blood and blood diseases.

Plasma The liquid portion of blood, including protein, but excluding cellular components.

Platelets The cells in blood that are involved with clotting.

Transfusion A medical procedure to transfer blood from one body into another.

Typing A procedure to determine the blood group (A, B, AB, or O) within a particular sample.

Venipuncture The puncture of a vein with a hypodermic needle, commonly known as a needle stick.

They know that blood banks like ours are on the front lines and that together, we're the ones fighting this war to keep people healthy."

Sherry's job as a phlebotomy technician begins by greeting donors when they arrive at the Bonfils Blood Center branch office in Lakewood, Colorado. If they are first-time donors, she enters their names and medical information into the computer and if they are repeats, she pulls up their medical history cards. To give blood, donors must weigh more than 110 pounds, not have infections such as colds or the flu, not be taking certain medications, and not be engaging in a variety of at-risk behaviors. At-risk behaviors include illegal intravenous drug use and certain types of sexual activity.

Sherry asks each donor several questions, some of which are repeats of medical history information. "People skills are very important in this job," she says. "I'm not trying to be nosy when I ask these questions. We're trying to retain donors and yet we need to weed out the high-risk volunteers too. You have to be dedicated to the donors and to putting out a safe product."

Updating medical histories and asking questions help screen out people with illnesses or behaviors that might jeopardize the safety of the blood supply. In particular, phlebotomy technicians try to screen donors who might have active cases of or have been exposed to tuberculosis, malaria, hepatitis, syphilis, and HIV.

If the donors' medical histories are satisfactory, Sherry checks their temperatures and then, using a small centrifuge, does a quick blood test to verify iron levels. A low iron level indicates that the donor's body is in a weakened condition and there isn't enough hemoglobin present. (Hemoglobin is the iron-containing protein within red blood cells that carries oxygen.) If a patient should receive such hemoglobin-poor blood, there wouldn't be enough red blood cells to perform vital functions within the body. If, however, iron levels are sufficient, Sherry directs the donors to a reclining bed where she takes their pulse and blood pressure and swabs the skin with antiseptic.

Next comes the needle stick. "I can't look when it's my turn to give blood," she says. "And the first time I had to make a needle stick on someone else, I was so nervous. It's still a bit scary. You don't want to hurt people. Practice, that's the only way to learn." It takes about five minutes to collect a pint of blood. When the required amount is collected, Sherry uses a hematron, a device that heat-seals the tubing that extends from the needle in the donor's arm to the collection bag. Then the needle is removed and disposed of, and the blood is transported to the laboratory where it is typed by other workers. Next, she makes sure that the donor drinks some juice, eats cookies or crackers, and rests for 10 to 15 minutes before leaving the blood center. "Everybody reacts a bit differently to giving blood," she says. "Here, it's not like in a doctor's office where phlebotomy technicians draw only a small vial of blood." Taking a pint of blood makes some people turn white, others break out in cold sweats, and some people pass out completely. Still, only 1 percent of donors have any adverse reactions, at all.

Phlebotomy technicians are trained to watch for a range of responses from mild light-headedness to loss of consciousness. Each year Sherry renews her first aid and CPR training. She also has emergency medical training and a certificate that enables her to set up IVs, intravenous drips used to replace body fluids. Other portions of her day are spent performing quality checks on equipment, taking inventory of supplies, and attending meetings.

Specialists in blood-bank technology (persons who have advanced degrees) process the blood collected, type it, make cross matches with patients, check the blood for communicable diseases and infections, and store it for future use.

Do I Have What It Takes to Be a Phlebotomy Technician?

"Being a phlebotomy technician is challenging work," says Sherry. "You're constantly working with people. Good communication skills are essential because you have to stick the patient or donor with a needle in order to draw blood. Yes, you're following orders and doing routine work, but a sense of humor helps too."

Mary Anderson, program director at the Wichita Area Vocational Technical School in Wichita, Kansas, adds, "The patients have to feel like they are the most important thing in your world at that moment. Even when you have to work at a quick pace, you should not make the patients feel like they're on an assembly line. That's not always easy," she says, "particularly for phlebotomy technicians who work in hospitals. They have to deal with a variety of people under difficult circumstances. Often you're called to the bedside of a patient to draw blood, and not only are you dealing with a sick person who doesn't want to have another needle stuck in them, the doctors, the nurses, and sometimes the families are after you to hurry up and finish your work."

According to the American Society of Phlebotomy Technicians, phlebotomy technicians are "often the only part of the lab staff that a patient sees. . . . Yet, phlebotomists work difficult hours, the pay is low, the turnover rate high, and they often find themselves faced with cantankerous patients. . . . Although phlebotomists serve as valuable liaisons between the patient and the clinical laboratory, many times they suffer low professional esteem."

"No matter what the working situation," says Mary, "phlebotomy technicians have to be patient and not get upset. This is essential because the blood test won't be any better than the samples they collect."

No matter what the working situation, phlebotomy technicians have to be patient and not get upset. This is essential because the blood test won't be any better than the samples they collect.

Phlebotomy technicians need to have excellent interpersonal communication skills. They should be good listeners and able to speak precisely and clearly. They should be able to reassure patients as well as be able to explain medical procedures. Some shift work may be required. Those working in hospitals, in particular, can expect to work some weekends and holidays as well. People in this profession work with precise, often small, medical supplies. Good manual dexterity is essential.

Persons who are squeamish at the sight of blood or have difficulty working with needles would find it hard to succeed as a phlebotomy technician. There is a small risk of exposure to contaminated blood and other illness in this profession, but phlebotomy technicians always wear gloves and, when necessary, additional protective clothing. This, along with common sense and attention to procedure, minimizes risk.

To Be a Successful Phlebotomy Technician, You Should . . .

- enjoy working with people
- be patient
- be able to work under pressure
- be attentive to detail
- be an effective communicator and a good listener
- have good manual dexterity

How Do I Become a Phlebotomy Technician?

Sherry had been a home health care aide and a hospice volunteer before she started working for Bonfils Blood Center. "I was trained on the job. That was a common practice then," she says. Now, in order to achieve certification and to move ahead professionally, formal training programs are highly recommended.

EDUCATION

High School

Biology, health, and other science courses are helpful for students wishing to become phlebotomy technicians after graduation. Computer science, English, and speech classes are also important. In addition, if you plan on entering a formal phlebotomy training program, you should be sure to fulfill the entrance requirements for the program you plan to attend.

Postsecondary Training

Until recently, on-the-job training was the norm for phlebotomy technicians. Now formal programs are offered through independent training schools, community colleges, or hospitals. Most programs last

In-depth

Blood: Its Function and Purpose

Blood is a distinctive and recognizable type of tissue, but this does not mean it is a stable, uniform substance with a fixed proportion of ingredients. Quite the opposite is true; its composition is always changing in response to the demands of other body systems. Other organs are constantly pouring sources into the blood, or removing things from it. Blood in one part of the body at any given moment may be vastly different in chemical makeup from blood in another part of the body.

Blood does have certain basic components. A sample of blood left to stand for an hour or so separates into a clear, watery fluid with a yellowish tinge and a darker, more solid clump. The clear, yellow liquid is plasma and it accounts for approximately 55 percent of the volume of normal blood. The darker clump is composed mainly of the red cells that give blood its characteristic color.

Plasma enables our blood to carry out most of the transportation tasks our bodies assign it. Being more than 90 percent water, plasma, like water, can carry substances within it in two ways: in solution and in suspension. A substance in a water solution, such as salt in salt water, must be removed from the water by chemical or physical action, such as boiling. On the other hand, a substance in suspension, such as red blood cells in whole blood, separates more easily, particularly when its watery carrier has been contained and its flow stilled.

Red blood cells number in the trillions and are carried in suspension by the plasma. In turn, the red blood cells carry the single most important substance needed by the body's cells: oxygen. A complex iron-protein substance called hemoglobin is responsible for the oxygen-carrying capacity of red blood cells. Although water and plasma can also carry oxygen, hemoglobin is special because it increases by more than 50 times the oxygen-carrying capacity of our blood.

White blood cells are larger than red blood cells, but there are far fewer of them in our blood. We need every last one of them, however, as the white blood cells are the ones that attack foreign bodies that invade our tissues. Autoimmune diseases, such as multiple sclerosis, result when the white blood cells mistakenly attack healthy areas of our bodies.

Platelets, while not equipped with nuclei and therefore not fitting the definition of a cell, are nonetheless crucial. More like bits of cell substance, platelets initiate some of the first steps in the complex biochemical process that leads to the clotting of blood. Without them, we could easily bleed to death from the smallest of injuries.

from 10 weeks to one year and should be approved by the National Accrediting Agency for Clinical Laboratory Sciences or the American Society of Phlebotomy Technicians. They include both in-class study and supervised, clinical practice. Course work includes anatomy, physiology, introduction to laboratory practices, communication, medical terminology, phlebotomy techniques, emergency situations, and CPR training. Most of these programs are structured to prepare students for certification exams.

CERTIFICATION OR LICENSING

Certification and licensing for phlebotomy technicians varies according to state and employer. Several agencies grant certification. To be eligible to take the qualifying examination from the American Society of Phlebotomy Technicians or from the Board of Registry of the American Society of Clinical Pathologists (ASCP), applicants must have worked as a full-time phlebotomist for six months or as a part-time phlebotomist for one year, or have completed an accredited phlebotomy training program.

SCHOLARSHIPS AND GRANTS

Many community colleges offer general scholarships and financial aid, as do some hospitals and training programs. In addition, institutions with specific phlebotomy programs are sources of information on work-study and student internships.

Who Will Hire Me?

Phlebotomy technicians work in a variety of health care settings. The majority of them work in hospitals or in outpatient settings such as clinics, physicians' offices, reference laboratories, or blood banks. A few are hired by private industry or by insurance companies. The greatest need for phlebotomy technicians is in small hospitals (that is, those with fewer than 100 beds). Many of the publications serving health care professionals list job advertisements, as do daily newspapers. In addition, some employers actively recruit graduating students through visits to accredited programs.

Where Can I Go from Here?

Sherry worked in the Bonfils Blood Center's mobile units for several years. Her next move was to become a supervisor at the Lakewood branch office. After a few years as supervisor, however, she stepped out of administration and moved back to working directly with donors. "Ten minutes after the 1995 explosion at the Federal Center in Oklahoma City, we were flooded with donors," she says. "People know the need for donated blood is always there. Working with generous, concerned people is what I like best about my job and I wanted to continue doing just that."

One of the most common career paths for phlebotomy technicians is to work for a few years in a hospital or laboratory and then return to school to study medical laboratory technology or some other branch of clinical laboratory medicine.

ADVANCEMENT POSSIBILITIES

Blood bank technologists are responsible for all the activities within blood banks, including the collection, testing, storage, and transportation of blood.

Phlebotomy supervisors oversee the work of other phlebotomy technicians, coordinating schedules and making certain the strict safety guidelines of the field are followed.

Training instructors work in technical schools, community colleges, and hospital educational programs to train phlebotomists in their duties. They might also supervise the clinical practice portion of the training in a hospital.

If you are interested in advancing within blood-bank centers, one option is to return to school, obtain a bachelor's degree, attend a specialized fifth-year program, and become a certified specialist in blood-bank technology. Specialists in blood-bank technology are responsible for all the activities and staff within blood banks. They coordinate educational programs, oversee blood collection, direct testing, and arrange for storage and transportation of blood and blood products.

What Are the Salary Ranges?

Experience, level of education, employer, and work performed determine the salary ranges for phlebotomy technicians. According to a survey by the American Society of Clinical Pathologists' Board of Registry, the median annual salary for phlebotomy technicians was $21,944 in 2002. Salaries ranged from $18,720 to $25,168. Phlebotomist supervisors had median annual salaries of $33,488 in 2002.

A specialist in blood bank technology with a bachelor's degree and advanced training can usually expect a starting salary of approximately $40,000 a year.

Benefits such as vacation time, sick leave, insurance, and other fringe benefits vary by employer, but are usually consistent with other full-time health care workers.

What Is the Job Outlook?

According to the *Occupational Outlook Handbook*, employment of clinical laboratory workers is expected to grow about as fast as the average for all other occupations over the next 10 years. Across the United States, demand for phlebotomy technicians is highest in small hospitals. Demand for all kinds of health care professionals, including phlebotomy technicians, will grow as the percentage of Americans aged 65 and older continues to rise. There is a particular demand for workers who are qualified to draw blood at patients' bedsides. The number of patients with certain diseases, such as HIV and AIDS, also increases the need for phlebotomy technicians.

How Do I Learn More?

PROFESSIONAL ORGANIZATIONS

For information on careers and answers to questions about the field, contact

American Association of Blood Banks
8101 Glenbrook Road
Bethesda, MD 20814-2749
301-907-6977
aabb@aabb.org
http://www.aabb.org

For a career brochure, contact

American Society for Clinical Pathology
2100 West Harrison Street
Chicago, IL 60612
312-738-1336
http://www.ascp.org

To learn about phlebotomy programs, contact the following organizations:

American Society of Phlebotomy Technicians
PO Box 1831
Hickory, NC 28603
828-294-0078
http://www.aspt.org

National Accrediting Agency for Clinical Laboratory Sciences
8410 West Bryn Mawr Avenue, Suite 670
Chicago, IL 60631
773-714-8880
info@naacls.org
http://www.naacls.org

BIBLIOGRAPHY

The following is a sampling of materials relating to the professional concerns and development of phlebotomy technicians:

Garza, Diana, and Kathleen Becan-McBride. *Phlebotomy Handbook: Blood Collection Essentials*. 6th ed. Upper Saddle River, N.J.: Prentice Hall, 2002.

McCall, Ruth E., and Cathee M. Tankersley. *Phlebotomy Essentials*. 3d ed. Philadelphia: Lippincott Williams & Wilkins, 2002.

Pendergraph, Garland E., and Cynthia Barfield Pendergraph. *Handbook of Phlebotomy and Patient Service Techniques*. 4th ed. Philadelphia: Lippincott Williams & Wilkins, 1998.

PHOTOGRAPHIC EQUIPMENT TECHNICIANS

A brilliant red hue illuminates the horizon. The ocean is calm and reflects innumerable beams of the setting sunlight. "A gorgeous photograph," reflects James Valentin, a professional wildlife photographer, as he patiently waits for the dolphins he has been following to leap from the water. Suddenly they appear, splashing sprays of water into the air as they break the surface. Then the impossible happens. The camera does not release its shutter. He misses the shot. For the professional photographer, there is no experience more frustrating: equipment failure.

Stories like this are not new to photographic equipment technician and repair shop owner Larry Grabowski. "Ninety percent of the problems I see are the result of customer misuse," Larry comments. "Water, sand, deflecting bullets; pros put their equipment through a lot of rigorous work," he says, with the complacent grin of experience. On one shelf in his shop sit a dozen different cameras of all formats and brands. From each camera dangles a repair tag with specific instructions written neatly in black pen.

Larry arrives early every morning before any of his techs in order to inspect and prioritize the day's work, as well as to finish up on some work from the day before. From a clutter of hand tools on his workbench, he instinctively grabs the right screwdriver and inserts the final screws in a Hasselblad camera. He closes the back, winds the crank, and releases the shutter. "Perfect," he says beneath his breath. "Perfect."

Definition
Photographic equipment technicians repair, maintain, and test still and motion picture cameras. They disassemble cameras using a variety of hand tools and inspect for camera defects using specialized equipment. Repairs and adjustments are made using hand tools and computers.

Alternative Job Title
Camera repairers

High School Subjects
Chemistry
Mathematics
Technical/shop

Personal Skills
Mechanical/manipulative
Technical/scientific

Salary Range
$16,800 to $30,800 to $51,200

Minimum Educational Requirements
High school diploma

Certification or Licensing
None available

Outlook
Decline

DOT
714

GOE
05.03.03

NOC
9498

O*NET-SOC
49-9061.00

What Does a Photographic Equipment Technician Do?

A good camera is not like a toaster or a blow-dryer; when it malfunctions you do not just throw it out and buy a new one. Many of today's professional cameras cost anywhere from $700 to $6,000. These cameras are designed to endure, yet, as with any intricate machinery, a breakdown at some point in time is bound to happen. *Photographic equipment technicians* are trained to pinpoint a camera's problem, disassemble the camera, and make the necessary repairs and adjustments. Like any other repair person, they must speak clearly to their customers about what repairs or adjustments they have completed. The photographer will want to know precisely what the problem was so that he or she can take precautions against a repeated occurrence. Technicians also must be experienced in repairing the more commercial and inexpensive point-and-shoot cameras.

With the many different brands and formats of cameras available to photographers, it would be very difficult for the technician to become familiar with them all. However, there are certain standard features of a camera that make diagnosing specific problems

Lingo to Learn

Aperture An opening of variable size located in a camera lens that controls the amount of light that reaches the film.

Focal length For a simple lens focused on an infinitely distant subject, the distance between the center of the lens and the point on the axis of sharpest focus.

Light meter A device in photography, either hand held or built into the camera, that measures ambient or reflective light or both.

Oscilloscope An apparatus used to make visible any irregularities in the motion of rapidly oscillating machinery. Used to test the accuracy of the shutter.

Shutter A device in a camera consisting of curtains or overlapping blades designed to protect the film from exposure until the release is pressed.

Shutter release A button, lever, or plunger that is depressed to open the shutter.

SLR (single lens reflex) A camera design in which the image from the lens is deflected to a ground glass mirror that swings out of the way when the shutter is released.

Standard light Also called a light meter tester; a diffused light source of which the EV (exposure value) is known. Used to test the accuracy of camera exposure.

with all cameras very similar. The camera's shutter speed, for example, can be tested with a specialized electronic apparatus called an oscilloscope, to confirm the shutter's accuracy of up to one-eight thousandth of a second. Most modern cameras have built-in light meters, which should yield the same reading on any camera. Here again, the technician can test for accuracy using precision light metering instruments called exposure testers.

In order to study further possible problems, and to fix problems already diagnosed, the technician will need to disassemble the camera, and he or she must be very familiar with that specific camera's blueprint provided by the manufacturer. Technicians use simple hand tools (screwdrivers, pliers, ring wrenches) to disassemble the camera, as well as to make some adjustments and repairs. They must be proficient with small tools in order to make the necessary precision adjustments inside a camera's body. They need good eyesight (a jeweler's loupe can help with this) to work with very small parts.

The technician uses optical measuring equipment to test the focus of the camera's lens. Camera lenses have various aperture sizes called f-stops that determine the amount of light that falls on the film and controls the depth of field of each photograph. With computerized measuring equipment, technicians determine that the precise diameter of each f-stop on the lens conforms with manufacturer's specifications.

Essential to maintaining photographic equipment in error-free, top working order is keeping the camera clean and well lubricated. Technicians use vacuums and air pressure devices to remove harmful dust and dirt from the camera's mirrors, lens, and shutter. They use a syringe or fine cotton swab to apply special lubricants to many of the camera's gears. Some parts must be removed completely and soaked in a solvent to remove hardened dirt and excessive lubricant.

As the latest generation of cameras takes over the market, parts for older models become increasingly rare. In this case, when a part is no longer available from the manufacturer, technicians must fabricate the part using a drill press, bench grinder, lathe, and other tools.

Some new technologies have brought significant changes to photography in recent years, which in turn have required more skills of the photographic equipment technician. One of the major changes, now becoming standard on most cameras, is automatic focus. When this malfunctions, technicians must repair tiny motors housed inside the lens. Tests and adjustments to these motors are frequently made by computers called autocollimators and ZTS testers.

With today's cameras becoming increasingly more computerized, technicians will need a solid understanding of electronics. Many of the traditional analog knob controls on cameras have been replaced by simplified and more modern digital forms. Today's camera has taken on myriad new, high-tech features in an effort to make the photographic process a more precise and user-friendly experience, all of which has made the camera a more electronics-oriented machine than it was in the past. Whereas before technicians used a screwdriver for many adjustments, today they use a computer.

What Is It Like to Be a Photographic Equipment Technician?

As a repair shop owner, Larry Grabowski arrives at his shop early and leaves late, after his regular techs have already gone home. "There's always so much to be taken care of," he says, as he takes a camera from the shelf and looks at it inquisitively. His technicians work a normal eight-hour day, though a tech will usually stay later in order to finish a camera. "A good tech gets so absorbed in the repair," Larry says, "that he loses all sense of time. It's just you and this problem with the camera."

Depending on the problem and the type of camera, a repair job can take anywhere from an hour to an entire day. Technicians sit in well-lit shops at a bench for most of their day. The tools, machines, and test equipment that they will use for a repair are all close at hand. Technicians usually work alone on a camera but they often assist each other with difficulties. In a shop there are repair techs who specialize in various brands and formats of cameras. For example, one tech may know the 35mm Nikons and Canons very well but not the large format cameras such as Hasselblads and Rolleiflexes. "In my shop we all overlap with our specialties," Larry says. "That's very important, in case somebody is sick or quits."

When a camera is brought in for repair at Larry's shop, the technician asks the photographer for as much detailed information as possible about the problem. Often amateurs, as well as professionals, have no idea what is wrong with their camera when they bring it in for repair. Photographer James Valentin confesses, "I really don't know how these new, high-tech cameras work. When one of my babies breaks down, I usually haven't a clue as to the problem. I simply tell my repair guy, 'it's not working right.'"

It is then up to the technician to run a series of tests on the camera to pinpoint the possible problem. The technician tests for the correct exposure readings, if the shutter and aperture settings are at manufacturer's specifications, if the motor drive advances, if the automatic focus is operational and accurate, and if the light meter communicates correctly with the rest of the camera's features. The list of possibilities, especially with more advanced cameras, is lengthy. Some tests can be eliminated if the technician can find out more information from the photographer. Does the camera release its shutter? Are all of the pictures turning out overexposed? Did the photographer drop the camera in the ocean? Answers to these and other questions can help the photographic equipment technician pinpoint the exact problem.

To Be a Successful Photographic Equipment Technician, You Should . . .

- have manual dexterity and mechanical aptitude
- have patience
- be detail oriented
- work well with hand tools
- have good verbal skills
- have good eyesight

"Ninety percent of the cameras that come into my shop are torn down completely," Larry says, meaning that they are entirely disassembled. One malfunction in a camera could be the result of, or result in, another, less obvious malfunction, so a complete "tear down" is necessary in order to inspect for all possible part failures. "It's my business," he explains. "If I give a professional photographer a camera and he goes out on an assignment and that camera breaks down again, he misses the shot, and I'm in for big trouble. I'll be going out of business."

To "take or tear a camera down," as it is often called in the business, requires excellent mechanical skills. Photographic equipment technicians use a variety of hand tools when disassembling a camera. There are many small and sensitive parts in the camera's body that must be carefully handled or avoided. "You can have the smartest tech who knows everything about cameras and how they work, but if that tech doesn't have the ability to handle tools properly, then he's of no use to me," Larry says, as he clears a workbench of pliers, tweezers, and screwdrivers.

Larry's shop often receives older cameras for repair. Many models that are still used by professionals no longer have parts supplied by the manufacturer. "Occasionally I have to fabricate gears and other parts," he says. "My customers really appreciate this sort of service. Rather than waiting to have someone else make the parts and then ship them to me, I can make one immediately and get the camera back in the photographer's hands."

Do I Have What It Takes to Be a Photographic Equipment Technician?

"Patience," Larry says, is the key to being a good photographic equipment technician. "Especially with today's newer cameras, where you have a million and one things that can malfunction." Generally, technicians have a discerning knack for problem solving and love puzzles. Troubleshooting a camera (finding out what is wrong) is often the most challenging part of the job. When the seemingly logical answer to a problem is not the answer, the technician must have the patience to accurately deduce other likely causes and then go on with the repair.

Technicians need to be very detail oriented. A camera is composed of numerous tiny, interrelated parts that can easily be missed or misplaced. Paying close attention to these small details is essential to completing the repair successfully. Larry recalls a time when one of his newer techs spent an afternoon diagnosing and repairing a particularly difficult camera and after reassembling it, realized that he had forgotten to put in a spring. He had to disassemble the camera again. "I don't have time for those kinds of foul-ups," he says. "Those unnecessary mistakes can be costly."

As with any technical field, photographic equipment technicians should have good manual dexterity and must be mechanically proficient. Technicians should be familiar with and comfortable using a variety of hand tools. One of the most important prerequisites today in the business is having a good working knowledge of electronics. "You simply cannot survive in this field without an electronics background," Larry asserts.

You simply cannot survive in this field without an electronics background.

Though photographic equipment technicians spend most of their day at a bench hunkered over a camera, they often have direct contact with the public. Techs should be polite and genial with their customers in order to learn as much as possible about the camera's problem. When the repair job is completed, they will also need to speak clearly in nontechnical terms about what repairs were done. Technicians at repair shops that deal directly with customers can be put under stress to work quickly, while, of course, being thorough and accurate. Often customers are very demanding.

"The camera is the photographer's livelihood," Larry explains. "He needs it in top working order as fast as possible. It's often very difficult for me or one of my techs to explain to the photographer that I can't have the repair done in an hour. There are other photographer's cameras here in need of speedy repair."

How Do I Become a Photographic Equipment Technician?

Unlike doctors, astronauts, and movie stars, very few grow up aspiring to be a photographic equipment technician. It is more the sort of career that someone suddenly realizes, "Hey, that would be really interesting," and then pursues proper training. "I was always good at fixing things, and taking things apart as a kid," Larry remembers. And generally, this is indicative of people in the field; technicians are inquisitive, they are tinkerers, they enjoy figuring out how and why things work. They enjoy puzzles and are enthused by a challenge. Many technicians, before they entered the field, were amateur photographers or even professionals.

EDUCATION

High School

Few people who do not finish high school go on to become photographic equipment technicians. This is a highly technical field that requires keen and resourceful people. High school is where the skills required to become a technician can first be studied and tested. While it may not be a requirement for some shops that employees possess a high school diploma (a technician is hired mainly on his or her ability to efficiently diagnose a camera's problem and repair it), it is, however, necessary in order to enroll in certain training seminars and related classes at the postsecondary level.

High school classes in the applied technologies, such as mechanics, electronics, auto maintenance, shop, and home maintenance and repair, are essential in building a student's familiarity with tools and other technical machinery. A strong background in mathematics will be useful when working with camera exposure equipment as well as other precision computers. In addition, students will find a basic understanding of physics beneficial when working with the numerous, interrelated parts of a camera.

Of course, it would be to your advantage to take classes in photography. A photographic equipment technician will need to know the fundamental principles of photography: how good photographs are taken, the relationship of aperture, shutter speed, and focal plane, how a camera is expected to handle under specific conditions, and much more.

Postsecondary Training

The two most common ways of becoming a photographic equipment technician are either taking repair courses at technical institutions (which, at some places, may not always be specifically geared toward camera repair), or, and more common in the industry today, enrolling in home study training programs, which often offer the option of residency training. Enrollment in either requires a high school diploma or GED.

The advantage to home study training programs (besides being at home) is that you are free to work at your own pace, with, of course, some restrictions. Programs usually take a year to complete. Through video aids and manuals, students learn basic camera design and operating systems, how to use test equipment, the actual business of camera repair, and many other topics necessary to be competitive and successful in the field. Students are provided with camera subassemblies (the exact part of the camera being studied) or whole cameras to practice what they have learned. Upon completion of a home study training program, students receive a diploma; this will certainly be an advantage in finding a job at a repair shop or manufacturer.

Students can find other opportunities to learn camera repair at training seminars or conventions offered by the Society of Photo-Technologists (SPT) and the National Association of Photo Equipment Technicians (NAPET), a division of Photo Marketing Associations International (PMA). Such opportunities, however, are usually limited to their members. Both associations publish newsletters that cover an array of topics in the field. SPT publishes a bimonthly repair journal that focuses on the repair of specific makes of cameras. The annual PMA convention is a great place to make contacts and learn some of the latest information in the camera repair business.

Who Will Hire Me?

As a young man, Larry answered a newspaper ad asking for an apprentice at a camera repair shop. He had always been mechanically proficient, and through his hobby of photography he already knew the workings of a camera. He got the job, and there, from the ground floor, he discovered the intricacies of camera repair. He learned the trade from experienced professionals while on the job. This scenario is still possible today but certainly not as common. In fact, Larry says, "I won't hire inexperienced techs. I simply don't have the time to train them." Yet, when asked where a technician gets this experience, he replies with a smile, "At other shops."

When Larry hires a technician he looks for one thing: Can he or she repair a camera? "I ask a job applicant what kind of cameras he knows like the back of his hand, and then I pull one off my shelf and give it to him to repair. I can tell you in 10 minutes if he's going to make the grade."

There are several different possibilities for entering the job market as a photographic equipment technician. The first, and most obvious, is at a repair shop that specializes exclusively in repairing and maintaining equipment. You can locate such shops through the phone book or a trade magazine such as *Photo District News* (http://www.pdn-pix.com), which publishes a list of repair shops.

Manufacturers also hire technicians. The plus side to working for a manufacturer is that if you already know their cameras very well, you will have increased your chance of getting a job (if one is open). Also, you will not have to deal with the uncertainty and frustration of figuring out another brand's camera. Everything will be familiar ground. On the downside, you are limiting yourself and your

Advancement Possibilities

Motion picture equipment supervisors coordinate activities of workers engaged in assembling, repairing, remodeling, and maintaining photographic, sound, and motion picture equipment.

Photographic engineers design and construct special-purpose photographic equipment and materials for use in scientific or industrial applications.

Photojournalists photograph newsworthy events, locations, people, or other illustrative or educational material for use in publications or telecasts, using still cameras.

marketability. If you ever decide to look for a job elsewhere, at an independent shop, for example, you will most likely be forced to learn all the other cameras you never had to repair. Some shops make it a rule not to hire techs that come from manufacturers precisely because their knowledge is too limited. "All of my techs know several different brands, and that's a requirement at my shop," Larry explains.

Universities with large photography departments also hire photographic equipment technicians. Their cameras get a lot of wear and tear, and rather than always sending the equipment out for costly repairs, they have a technician in house to service them. Universities generally hire the more experienced, already established technician who will also be able to teach a course on repair. Some of the larger retail camera stores may employ a technician for maintenance services and minor repair jobs. Another option is to start your own business and put your experience and efforts to work for yourself. You may start off part time at home, and then, when business and earnings increase, expand to larger markets.

Because this is such a highly specialized field, most repair shops and manufactures do not advertise in newspaper want ads. The majority of job placement is done within the industry. Many individual repair shops and manufacturers will also post any available positions at technical and repair schools. If you graduated from a home study program, the school will often put you in contact with likely employers. Word of mouth, as well, is often used when hiring and should definitely not be overlooked as a viable job source. This is why it is very important to keep friendly contacts with people in the industry.

Where Can I Go from Here?

Advancement in photographic equipment repair is synonymous with gaining experience. The more you learn, the further you advance. As for Larry, he began as an apprentice, with very little knowledge or experience in the field, and now he owns and operates his own successful repair shop, as well as being a top-notch repair tech in his own right. "It's a long road building a reputation," he says. "You have to do consistently good and reliable work for a long time."

If you work at an independent repair shop or for a manufacturer, your advancement in the field will be essentially the same. There is no formal ladder with clearly definable levels other than trainee to experienced technician to supervisory position to, for the business-inclined, shop owner. Prestige in the business comes from what you know and how resourceful you are. If you work at a shop, your authority increases as you master more brands and formats of cameras, though, as Larry explains, "No one can know everything. Especially with the complexity of these new cameras." You advance at a manufacturer as you become more proficient and inventive in your repairs.

Teaching and other instructional opportunities are possible for the experienced repair technician who has an exceptional reputation in the business. In addition to teaching at a college or technical school, such people can lead discussion groups at training seminars or write manuals detailing their proven, and original, methods of repair.

What Are the Salary Ranges?

What you earn as a repair technician depends on how skilled you are and whether or not you are working at an independent shop, a manufacturer, or are in business for yourself. One factor that most employers consider when hiring new techs is whether or not the applicant holds a diploma from a reputable repair school. The U.S. Department of Labor reports median annual earnings for photographic equipment technicians were $30,800 in 2003. The top paid 10 percent earned $51,200 or more, while the lowest paid 10 percent earned $16,800.

A Salary.com 2005 review of earnings nationwide for camera and photographic equipment repairers found salaries ranged between $29,163 and $43,950 with median annual earnings of $35,906.

If you are in business for yourself, there is no limit to your income, depending, of course, on your productivity and business skills. One-person shops can save considerable overhead by setting up business at home. A shop owner in the right location with a good staff and state-of-the-art equipment can expect earnings in the $70,000 to $80,000 range.

For many, the right benefits package is important when choosing a job. Though repair shops normally provide some benefits, the larger manufacturers may offer a more comprehensive benefits package including health insurance, paid holidays, and vacation and sick leave.

What Is the Job Outlook?

The *Occupational Outlook Handbook* predicts a decline in employment growth for this occupation through 2012 primarily because of the popularity of inexpensive cameras, which are cheaper to replace than repair. In addition, rapid technological progress in digital cameras often means that when a digital camera breaks, not only is replacing it as inexpensive as repairing it, but the new models are also more advanced.

Generally, it takes a repair technician one to three months to find a job. There are camera repair shops in all 50 states, though some areas, particularly the West Coast, East Coast, and Florida, have the greatest shop density. The technician with experience in repairing a wide variety of brands and formats will have the highest success in obtaining a job.

Job security for photographic equipment technicians rests largely on the success of photography as a business and art form. With the growing popularity of digital still cameras (28 percent of U.S. households owned digital cameras in 2003, acccording to the Photo Marketing Association International), an increasing number of people will take on photography as a hobby. As more amateur photographers produce high quality images, the chances that they will begin to break into the professional markets are good, all of which will provide a healthy, competitive environment in the field. As a result, more cameras will be in demand.

The Photo Marketing Association reported that in the United States in 2004, about 8.2 million analog cameras were owned, compared to 16.9 million digital cameras. This figure, when compared to the 15.6 million analog cameras owned in 1997 and 700,000 digital cameras owned, reveals that there has been a steady increase in sales of digital cameras.

Even the most well-built analog camera and top-of-the-line digital cameras will require maintenance from time to time. Aside from regular maintenance, repair shops will continue to see the "ailing" camera. "A lot of the cameras that come into my shop are here because of unintentional customer abuse," Larry explains

An additional concern for potential camera repair shop owners concerns the need to purchase more precision testing equipment to repair today's more sophisticated digital cameras. Although this is of little matter to major manufacturers and large repair shops, the high cost of this equipment is forcing the independent camera repairer out of business.

How Do I Learn More?

PROFESSIONAL ORGANIZATIONS

The following organizations provide information on photographic equipment technician careers, accredited schools, and employers:

National Association of Photo Equipment Technicians
3000 Picture Place
Jackson, MI 49201
517-788-8100
http://www.pmai.org/sections/napet.htm

Society of Photo-Technologists
11112 Spotted Road
Cheney, WA 99004
888-662-7678
http://www.s-p-t.org

BIBLIOGRAPHY

The following is a sampling of materials relating to the professional concerns and development of photographic equipment technicians:

Borowsky, Irvin J. *Opportunities in Photography Careers*. New York: McGraw-Hill, 2004.

Careers in Focus: Arts and Entertainment. Chicago: Ferguson Publishing Company, 1998.

Gilbert, George. *Career Opportunities in Photography*. Chicago: Ferguson Publishing Company, 2005.

Johnson, Bervin M. et al. *Opportunities in Photography Careers*. Lincolnwood, Ill.: VGM Career Horizons, 1998.

PHOTOGRAPHIC LABORATORY TECHNICIANS

The darkroom glows a soft yellow and boxes of photographic paper reach halfway to the ceiling. Photographs cover the walls, some of them marked in pen, others simply tacked there, the models of a perfect black-and-white photograph. Tom stands before an enlarger and focuses the image of a grinning man. With the image sharply in focus he turns off the enlarger's light and pulls a box from the stack. "Double," he mutters to himself, "one eight-by-ten, double-weight, glossy." He pulls out a sheet of the photo paper and inserts it in a holder below the enlarger's lens. He hits a button and the image is projected onto the paper.

Tom checks the wall clock and waits for the second hand to reach 12, then he slides the paper into the first bath. He lifts the corner of the tray slightly while the image slowly emerges. At first, it is ghostlike and then, magically, the life in the man's eyes appears. Tom checks the clock, then the paper, then the clock again. After exactly three minutes he removes the paper and submerges it into the next bath. In 30 seconds he pulls out the paper and studies it intensely. "Ten more seconds," he says. "Ten and a number three filter."

Definition
Photographic laboratory technicians develop films and slides in chemical baths, print photographs from the developed negatives, and duplicate, retouch, sort, and package photographs for customers.

Alternative Job Titles
Darkroom technicians
Photofinishing processors
Photographic process workers
Photoimaging technicians

High School Subjects
Art
Chemistry

Personal Skills
Artistic
Mechanical/manipulative

Salary Range
$14,100 to $20,500 to $36,000

Minimum Educational Level
High school diploma

Certification or Licensing
None available

Outlook
More slowly than the average

DOT
714

GOE
05.03.03

NOC
9498

ONET-SOC
49-9061.00

What Does a Photographic Laboratory Technician Do?

After you snap a picture with an analog camera, two major procedures happen before you get your photograph. First, the film is developed producing a negative, and second, from this negative, a print is made. How a *photographic laboratory technician* performs these jobs depends largely on where he or she is employed: at a professional or commercial laboratory, where much of the work is done by hand, or at a wholesaler or one-hour minilab, where most of the work is done by machines. Professional and commercial labs require highly skilled workers who perform a variety of specialized tasks. Though wholesalers and minilabs require a less technically skilled staff, their workers must be mechanically proficient to operate the sensitive computerized machines.

Photo labs are divided into four separate departments: processing, where all film is developed according to manufacturers' specifications; color printing, where color negatives are read and printed to customer specifications; black-and-white printing, where negatives are printed to customer specifications; and duping film, where transparency reproductions are made from other slides, film, or flat artwork.

At a minilab, where exclusively color film is processed, only two machines do the processing: the developing machine and the printing machine.

Processing workers are responsible for developing color, black-and-white, and slide films in a series of chemical baths. The procedure they use is commonly called dip and dunk processing. In complete darkness

Lingo to Learn

Burn To increase the exposure of a particular area of a photographic print by allowing more light to fall on that spot for a set amount of time.

C-41 process The industry standard, established by Kodak, for processing color negative films for prints.

Contact print Positive images of the actual negatives.

Contrast In photographic printing, the various shades of dark and light tones in a print.

Developer A chemical solution that converts latent film and paper images to visible images.

Dodge To decrease the exposure of a particular area of a photographic print by blocking the light during exposure for a set amount of time.

E-6 process The industry standard, established by Kodak, for developing positive color transparency films.

Enlarger A darkroom device used for projecting the negative's image to a sheet of photographic paper. It consists of a column with a movable head containing a light source, a negative carrier, and a lens.

Exposure The total amount and time of light a film or photographic paper receives.

Fixer A chemical that removes undeveloped and unexposed silver salts from film or paper, rendering it no longer light-sensitive.

Primary colors Red, blue, and green, in the additive color system, which if combined in equal intensity produce white light.

Safelight A darkroom light that provides illumination of the correct color for working with light-sensitive photographic paper.

the technician removes the film from its canister and fastens it to two clips, one at the top of the film, the other at the bottom. He or she then attaches the film to a dip and dunk machine, where it is led (or dipped) through a series of chemicals for a specific amount of time. Each type of film requires a different series of chemicals. Black-and-white films are completely processed in four baths: developer, stop, fixer, and wash. Color films are completely processed in six baths: developer, bleach, wash, fixer, a second wash, and stabilizer. Color slides undergo a process similar to color films.

Color printing technicians make prints from developed negatives. First the technician reads the negative for its color values in a negative reading analyzer. This tells the technician how much cyan (greenish blue), magenta (purplish red), or yellow to add or subtract from the negative when printing. The technician then inserts the negative into a color enlarger and makes the appropriate settings. Certain parts of the negative may require longer or shorter exposure than the negative as a whole. In this case, the technician dodges (blocking some light from exposing a specific portion of the print) or burns (allowing more light to fall on a specific area of the print) during the exposure process using simple tools. After the photographic paper is exposed to the enlarger's light, the technician transfers the paper in complete darkness to a series of chemical baths to bring out the positive image.

Black-and-white printing technicians read the developed negative for its density to determine the amount of light each area requires for correct exposures. This is often a guessing process that comes with experience. With the negative in the enlarger and the image projected onto a flat surface, the technician checks the focus of the image with a focusing magnifier and adjusts the enlarger accordingly. At this point, the technician crops the image to customer specifications. After the sensitized paper is exposed to a specific amount and duration of light, the technician transfers the print to three chemical baths: developer, stop, and fixer. A final water bath washes away the residual chemicals.

Film duplicating technicians use film transparency reproduction machines that copy the original image onto another film with minimal loss of picture quality. Technicians mount the transparencies in cardboard or plastic mounts with specialized machines.

Photographic laboratory technicians at professional and commercial labs doing custom work often must spot prints. Using very fine-tipped paint brushes, the technician adds dye to scratch or dust marks on a print to match its surrounding tone and color. A similar task, airbrushing, is used to alter prints by adding either transparent dyes or opaque paints to the prints. Other tasks include checking for any errors in the work and preparing and receiving customer orders.

What Is It Like to Be a Photographic Laboratory Technician?

Technicians in photo labs generally do only their job, depending on which branch they specialize in. They are either in processing, color printing, black-and-white printing, or film duplication. As manager of a busy professional lab, Tom Banks knows how to work in all areas. "When things get backed up I have to help out sometimes, especially if one of my techs is sick. The work has to get done," he explains as he prepares a customer order for development.

Customer service at a photo lab is often what distinguishes a good lab from a bad lab. Depending on the lab, some technicians may receive orders for a part of the day, especially new techs. "It's important for a newcomer to understand what goes on in all aspects of a lab," Tom says. When a customer drops off film or negatives, the technician must note on the purchase order precisely what the customer wants. "Do they want just a proof sheet, or do they want prints, and what size prints, and do they want a glossy or matte finish or something else? And if they bring negatives, do they want them custom cropped, and if so, how?" Tom explains. "If you don't give the customer exactly what he wants then he won't be coming back."

After a roll of film is received for processing, a technician brings it to the color or black-and-white processor for development. For black-and-white film the processing technician notes the ASA (film speed) and brand of film. This will determine how long the film should be submerged in each chemical bath. The technician brings the film into a darkroom where absolutely no light may enter (once the film is out of its canister any exposure to light would ruin it). The technician then attaches the film to the developing machines, again in complete darkness, and leaves the darkroom through a specially designed revolving door. "After awhile you get used to doing things in complete darkness," Tom says. "You simply learn where everything is by touch."

Periodically the processing technicians must test the freshness of the chemicals. They run a control strip of film through the chemicals and read the results with a machine called a densitometer. If certain color patterns do not appear, the chemicals are ready to be changed. "Color chemicals are especially sensitive," Tom says. "The temperature must be accurate within one half of one degree. If the main developer is old and you develop a roll of film in it, the film's not going to turn out as well as it should. The same is true with any of the other chemicals." The technician makes a fresh batch of chemicals from either a powder or concentrate and temperature-controlled water.

The processing technician then places the negatives in a dust-free drying cabinet. From here, the printers take over. The negatives are attached to their original order slip where the printer reads what to do next. Often the first print made from a fresh roll of developed film is a contact, or proof, sheet (a sheet of positive images the same size as the negative). From the contact sheet the customer can choose which images he or she would like to enlarge. "Most people who bring in a roll of film want contact sheets first," Tom says, cutting a strip of 35-millimeter negatives into strips of five to prepare them for the contact printing machine. "If they want immediate pictures of lesser quality they go to minilabs."

The main difference between color and black-and-white printing is that color must be developed in complete darkness, often in developing tubes. "With black-and-white, you can work with a safe light, and your prints are processed in trays," Tom explains. Black-and-white printers are mainly concerned with gray tones and contrast levels. "In a good print you want some true whites, some true, rich blacks, and as many grays in between as you can get." Technicians use colored filters inserted in the enlarger below the light source to help them bring out the contrast of a print. When custom cropping an image, printers can lower or raise the enlarger's lens housing unit to manipulate the size of the image; the higher the lens, the larger the image. The technician then makes test strips of the image to find its correct exposure value. With each print the technician determines the exposure that will yield the best contrast and distribution of gray tones. This is done by setting both the aperture of the lens (which controls the amount of light) and the number of seconds the paper will be exposed to that light.

Once the printing technician has found the best exposure value, the print is ready to be developed. If the exposure was correct, the technician only has to watch the image emerge from the developer bath and remove it promptly with tongs when it appears fully developed. Development is stopped in the stop bath, and then made insensitive to light in the fixer bath. The technician washes away the residual chemicals and then inserts the print in a drying machine.

Do I Have What It Takes to Be a Photographic Laboratory Technician?

Only half of the artistic process is completed when the photographer composes and snaps the picture; the other half happens in the lab. "You really need to be creative to succeed at the job," says Tom. "You need to see things as an artist to be a good technician, otherwise everything is just another picture." On the other hand, at wholesalers and minilabs, where the customers are largely amateurs, machine printers are mostly concerned with quality control: making sure each image is free of defects. "There's little art in a thousand different children in front of a thousand different Christmas trees," Joe Cimino, manager of a busy one-hour minilab, says. "Our customers aren't trying to make art. They're concerned with making memories."

You need to see things as an artist to be a good technician, otherwise everything is just another picture.

An understanding of photography is a must for any photographic laboratory technician. "Everyone in my lab is a photographer," Tom says. "Either amateur or part-time pro, they know photography. If they didn't, it would be like a car mechanic who didn't know how to drive." Technicians can also gain valuable experience when working from their own negatives.

Color printing technicians need to determine from a mere glance if a print has correct color balance. "Color techs absolutely must have a precise sense of color," says Tom. "Good color techs can look at a negative and set the correct color balance for a print in less than 30 seconds." When checking color prints, technicians observe the hue (specific color), value (color luminance), and saturation (color purity) of the image. If any of these color factors are not at their optimal value for the quality of the negative, the technician must make the necessary adjustments and reprint. "This is one of the biggest challenges for beginners," Tom explains. "To look at a flawed print and then refer back to the negative to determine if that's a mistake the photographer made, or me, the printer."

Photographic laboratory technicians need strong organizational skills. At many professional labs, service is completed within 24 hours. Lab workers must not only prioritize customer orders, but also plan their work so the most orders can be done in the least amount of time. "For example, we work with all different sizes of negatives," Tom explains. "You need to plan your time working with one size of negative and then going to the next. Otherwise, you'll be adjusting your enlarger all day." Processors spend much of their time checking and preparing chemicals. "Every detail counts when dealing with the chemicals," Tom says. "There's no turning back if a mistake is made in the process. My chemistry man is the most important person on my staff. If he makes errors then we're all in for a late night."

Minilab operators must speak clearly and comfortably with their customers when receiving and returning orders. Joe says his most difficult job is finding out what the customer wants. "Most amateurs simply don't speak the language," he says. "I'll get customers who'll give me negatives they've had stuffed in their wallet for a year and expect good prints from them. I've got to tell them that that's now pretty impossible. Eighty percent of my work is customer service; the machines do the rest."

How Do I Become a Photographic Laboratory Technician?

In high school Tom took a class in photography and continued the hobby throughout college, where he was a member of a photo club. He graduated from college with a bachelor's degree in art history. After receiving his degree, he enrolled in a photography program at a community college to enhance his darkroom skills, where after three years of night classes he received a certificate. Two months after he completed the

To Be a Successful Photographic Laboratory Technician, You Should . . .

- understand and be proficient with a camera
- understand and appreciate the arts, especially photography
- have a good sense of color
- be detail oriented
- have good verbal skills when talking with customers
- be familiar with computers

program he found a job in a lab developing black-and-white prints. "Ever since then I've had jobs in photo labs, doing really everything, but my specialty is still black-and-white printing. A lot of my training came from on-the-job experience." Classes Tom took at his community college prepared him for his first job. "That's where I learned the magic of the darkroom," he says. "I took classes in photo theory. Though most of the students found it pretty boring, it's absolutely essential for building good experience in the lab." In photo theory classes students learn the highly technical aspects of photography, and Tom maintains he won't hire a tech unless he can demonstrate proficiency.

EDUCATION

High School

While in high school, take as many photography classes as your school offers. Work as a photographer for your school newspaper or yearbook. Yearbook or newspaper experience will also give you an opportunity to learn about desktop publishing, or electronic prepress, an aspect of processing that many photo labs are branching into.

Because of the chemicals you deal with in the lab, chemistry is an important subject, especially if you want to specialize in photo processing. Mathematics will prove useful if you go on to study photo theory at a more advanced level. You should also take as many classes as possible in art history and read books on this subject.

It would be next to impossible to find a job as a photographic lab technician without a high school diploma, and the higher-paying jobs require advanced training at technical schools and colleges as well.

Postsecondary Training

After high school you can pursue a one-, two-, or four-year photoimaging education. What you choose depends on the kind of job you want. If you are interested in a career as a minilab operator, the one-year program works well. Your courses include photographic science, minilab systems, and lab management. In a two-year program, you learn the basics of the photographic process, including basic photography, portrait photography, color and black-and-white film processing, and creative darkroom techniques. Four-year programs teach electronic imaging, the future of photo imaging, and business management. Many two-year digital imaging programs are developing across the country; these programs prepare students for work as photographic laboratory technicians, as well as for work in publishing and graphic design.

In-depth

Digital Photography

Digital cameras have advantages over traditional 35-millimeter film cameras. They can store images on floppy disks and memory cards, which can easily be transferred onto your computer hard drive and save you the expense of film and processing. You can choose which images are worth saving and printing, and can even view them on the camera's LCD screen as you take the pictures. With film, you may pay for the whole roll of film to be processed only to discover that you had your eyes closed and spinach between your teeth in every single shot. With software programs, you can edit that nasty spinach out of your teeth and give yourself glamorous pearly whites.

> **Advancement Possibilities**
>
> **Photographic laboratory supervisors** coordinate the activities of workers who develop prints from negatives, copy and enlarge prints, and airbrush and retouch prints.
>
> **Film processing supervisors** oversee the activities of workers engaged in photofinishing operations, such as repairing photographic negatives, and in developing, sorting, and checking prints.

Other opportunities for gaining experience in the field can be found through photography clubs and workshops offered at high schools, community centers, and continuing adult education classes. Clubs and workshops are the best informal methods for learning the basics in camera and darkroom procedures. They are great places to really find out if photoimaging is for you before you invest in a formal education.

You should be aware that photography is an expensive field to study and pursue. Cameras, film, photo paper, filters, and many other tools of the trade are quite costly. A student can easily spend over $300 on supplies, not including the camera. Once you become proficient, the endless extras available can quickly shrink your wallet.

SCHOLARSHIPS AND GRANTS

Some four-year photoimaging programs offer scholarships to students who have demonstrated both their skill in the field and a commitment to learn more. To be considered, you should keep a portfolio of your work.

INTERNSHIPS AND VOLUNTEERSHIPS

Most four-year photoimaging programs offer internship possibilities for students seeking firsthand, on-the-job experience at a real professional photo lab.

Who Will Hire Me?

"Twenty years ago I walked into a black-and-white photo studio in New York with my portfolio in hand," Tom recalls. "They just happened to be looking for a part-time printer, and they were impressed enough with my portfolio to give me the job. After four months I was full time." Today the field is more competitive and usually people are not hired on a walk-in basis. To land a good job with either a minilab chain or a photo lab you should have proven experience. For those just starting in the field, most employers view a diploma or certificate from a photo school as a sign of practical experience and a willingness to learn more.

Minilabs offer a large market for employment. As technological advances in 35-millimeter cameras make photo taking easier and bring camera costs down, more and more people are becoming amateur photo enthusiasts who want quick results. As a result, "there's been a minilab boom," says Joe.

For graduates with more technical skills, professional labs, commercial labs, and some wholesale labs are the best places to look for employment. Laboratories require highly skilled people who must be able to begin their new job with very minimal training. "It takes a lot of time to train someone to be a processor or printer. I really don't have that kind of time," Tom says. Employers at any of the three types of labs look for people who specialize in one branch of photoimaging but also like to see applicants who have a working understanding of the other branches. Labs often post job descriptions at photo schools rather than advertise in newspapers.

Professional labs offer the widest variety of services and require the most technically proficient staff. They work with professional photographers and serious amateurs. Commercial labs deal mainly with ad agencies and professional photographers rather than the general public. They work chiefly with quality custom color and black-and-white printing, and now more frequently with electronic imaging. Wholesale labs do high-volume, machine-operated printing, as well as custom printing. Many of their clients are photography stores and pharmacies where film is received for processing.

Where Can I Go from Here?

Photographic laboratory technicians generally advance in the field by stepping up to supervisory and managerial positions. Advancement is also measured by way of salary increases. As less technically skilled workers gain experience at a lab, they advance by taking on more responsibilities, such as being put in charge of a particular account. Color print machine operators at minilabs can advance to managing the store. Managerial responsibilities include new-hire training, inventory control, customer relations, equipment maintenance, and market forecasting.

"There is one downside to advancement," Tom confesses. "If you take on managerial positions you don't really get the opportunity to do the job you love. I was a custom black-and-white printer for 20 years, and I loved it. Now, as manager, I sort of miss it. But my salary is significantly higher than before." Tom spends much of his time in customer relations and departmental forecasting. "This is a rapidly changing field," he says. "Once you think you know it all, the rules change all over again. That's why we have departmental forecasting." With new technologies continually redefining the business, Tom has to keep up with new trends to stay competitive and provide quality service.

More experienced technicians can increase their earnings by teaching photography workshops. High schools, colleges, and universities hire technicians to teach classes in photography and darkroom techniques; however, some training in education is required for these positions. For the business inclined, opening your own studio can provide great satisfaction and unlimited earnings.

What Are the Salary Ranges?

According to the *Occupational Outlook Handbook*, photographic process workers and processing machine operators had a median annual salary of $20,500 in 2003. Those in the middle 50 percent earned between $16,400 and $27,400 a year, while those in the highest paid 10 percent earned $36,000. The lowest paid 10 percent earned $14,100 annually. A 2005 review by Salary.com of earning nationwide for film laboratory technicians reported average annual earnings between $18,495 and $28,000. Managers can expect to earn more, and employees working for established labs generally receive health and life insurance and retirement plans in their benefits packages.

What Is the Job Outlook?

Most new openings for machine operators and precision process workers will tend to be replacement positions, not new positions, and for this reason the U.S. Department of Labor expects employment to grow more slowly than the averge through 2012.

Electronic imaging (EI) photography, which incorporates digital printing, and graphic and Web page design, is expected to change the profession in the future. Beth Castaldi of Burrell Colour Incorporated in Crown Point, Indiana, does not believe EI will decrease the number of workers in the field, but that it will only change the nature of needed skills. "There will be a need for more upfront type skills," says Beth, "such as computer entry. A typical printer operator may do different kinds of things than he or she did in the past, but we'll still need them. I think the prognosis for employment in the field is good." Schools are adapting to the new changes by offering curriculum in EI, and many labs are jumping on the bandwagon with EI services for customers.

The price of digital cameras is steadily dropping and the quality of photos they produce is improving while the popularity of the cameras is increasing. According to the Photo Marketing Association International (PMAI), by the end of 2003 28 percent of U.S. households owned digital cameras and the demand for related services is growing. In 2004, while the majority of digital photo prints were made at home, 32 percent of photographic prints from digital cameras were made in retail outlets, and PMAI projects that the number will increase to 39 percent in 2005. The number of photo prints ordered online is expected to reach 9.6 percent in 2005, so those working in photo labs will also have to have some understanding of the Internet and be able to advise customers on how to get the most from their digital images.

Many consumers still use film rather than digital, however traditional film processing declined 8.4 percent in 2004, reflecting a gradual shift from film to digital technology. The minilab may stay competitive in the wave of new technology by providing portraits and wedding photography.

How Do I Learn More?

PROFESSIONAL ORGANIZATIONS

For information about the photo industry, training and educational programs, and employment opportunities, contact the following organizations:

Association of Professional Color Imagers
APCI Headquarters
3000 Picture Place
Jackson, MI 49201
517-788-8146
http://apci.pmai.org

Digital Imaging Marketing Association
3000 Picture Place
Jackson, MI 49201
517-788-8146
http://dima.pmai.org

Photo Imaging Education Association
3000 Picture Place
Jackson, MI 49201
517-788-8146
http://www.pieapma.org

Photo Marketing Association International
3000 Picture Place
Jackson, MI 49201
517-788-8100
http://www.pmai.org

BIBLIOGRAPHY

The following is a sampling of materials relating to the professional concerns and development of photographic laboratory technicians:

Blacklow, Laura. *New Dimensions in Photo Processes: A Step by Step Manual*. 3d ed. Woburn, Mass.: Focal Press, 2000.

Busselle, Julien. *Processing and Printing (B & W Photo-Lab Series)*. Rochester, N.Y.: Silver Pixel Press, 2000.

Careers in Focus: Arts and Entertainment. Chicago: Ferguson Publishing Company, 1998.

James, Christopher. *The Book of Alternative Photographic Processes*. Albany, N.Y.: Thomson Delmar Learning, 2001.

PHYSICAL THERAPY ASSISTANTS

Definition
Physical therapy assistants work under the supervision of physical therapists to help patients improve mobility, relieve pain, and prevent or lessen long-term physical disability.

Alternative Job Titles
Physical therapist assistants
Physical therapy technicians

High School Subjects
Health
Physical education
Psychology

Personal Skills
Following instructions
Helping/teaching

Salary Range
$24,230 to $36,610 to $49,650

Minimum Educational Level
Associate's degree

Certification or Licensing
Required by certain states

Outlook
Much faster than the average

DOT
076

GOE
14.06.01

NOC
6631

O*NET-SOC
31-2021.00

Tracey Anderson believes that the most demanding aspects of her work as a physical therapy assistant (PTA) are also the most rewarding. "We're working with people who are hurting, angry, and some of their families don't understand," she says of the patients who visit the private clinic for which she works. "We have one patient who is very young and has had multiple surgeries. Her body is covered with scars. One time she told me, 'No one's going to love me like this.' These people are stressed out and they tell you so many things."

This level of closeness isn't surprising to Tracey. "You do develop relationships with these people. You're very close to them physically, working with their bodies, helping them with exercises. They're in pain, they're crying." Though Tracey finds it difficult to separate herself from her patients' suffering, she's happy to have the opportunity to make her patients feel better. "I've had people who come in and who are cantankerous and mean, and I've seen them lose that anger. You make a lot of friends. It's amazing."

What Does a Physical Therapy Assistant Do?

Disease and injury can profoundly impair the performance and mobility of the human body. For centuries, forms of exercise, massage, and the use of heat and other techniques have been used to treat disabling conditions. Modern physical therapy has evolved, becoming more sophisticated and broader in scope. In addition to restoring mobility and alleviating pain and suffering, physical therapy now aims at preventing and mitigating permanent disability. Under the supervision and direction of a physical therapist, the *physical therapy assistant* works with patients to instruct and assist them in achieving the maximum functional performance of their bodies.

Injuries to the back, a common source of pain and immobility, often respond well to physical therapy. For some conditions, such as stroke, therapy may involve relearning such basic tasks as standing, eating, bathing, and walking. Other patients may be required to adapt to the permanent use of a wheelchair or an artificial limb. Patients with such severe impairments are often emotionally overwhelmed by these limitations of their bodies. A physical therapy assistant must also work with them to improve their state of mind. Ultimately, the goal of a physical therapy assistant is to help patients regain a maximum degree of independence.

As part of a team including the patient's physician, nurses, physical therapist, and, often, a psychologist and social worker, the physical therapy assistant participates in the evaluation of a patient's condition. An evaluation can include measuring the patient's strength, range of motion, and functional ability; that is, how well the patient performs certain physical

Lingo to Learn

Disassociation Passive exercises performed on the patient by the physical therapist or PTA that involve stretching parts of the body in order to loosen rigid or locked joints.

Iontophoresis Using electrical impulses to introduce anti-inflammatory medication through the skin into an inflamed area.

Quality of life In medicine, quality of life refers to the overall nature of a patient's physical and psychological well-being.

Traction A therapy that uses mechanical equipment to stretch, pull, or hold a part of the patient's body into position. It is used for fractures, muscle spasms, or other injuries to aid proper healing and to relieve pain caused by physical pressure.

Ultrasound Ultrasound is commonly used in physical therapy to relieve pain and swelling of joints and improve muscle condition.

Vestibular stimulation The vestibular nerve in the ear affects a person's balance; some patients require therapy to restore their sense of balance.

tasks. Once the physical therapist has developed a treatment plan, it is the responsibility of the physical therapy assistant to carry out the therapy, to take notes on the patient's progress, and to report observations, particularly if he or she perceives that a patient is having severe difficulties or experiencing problems with the prescribed therapy. During complicated therapeutic procedures, the physical therapy assistant works side-by-side with the physical therapist; more routine procedures are usually carried out by the physical therapy assistant alone.

An important role of the physical therapy assistant is teaching patients the use of canes, walkers, crutches, or wheelchairs, and how to apply, remove, care for, and live with devices such as braces, or artificial limbs and joints. Many patients, especially geriatric (elderly) patients, need to learn how to climb stairs, or to transport themselves from bed or from a wheelchair to the shower or toilet.

The emotional and psychological condition of a patient is often a key factor in their response to therapy. A physical therapy assistant plays a part in helping their patients overcome the feelings of hopelessness, loss, and fear that often accompany illness and disability.

Physical therapy assistants work with a variety of patients, ranging from the elderly to the very young. In an acute care hospital, patients may include those with back problems, severe burns, cancer, and those recovering from motorcycle or car accidents. In a rehabilitation facility, physical therapy assistants work closely with newly disabled patients to help restore them as fully as possible to an independent lifestyle. These intensive therapy sessions—lasting three hours or more—often involve helping the patient relearn the basic tasks of life. They sometimes incorporate occupational and speech therapy as well (see the article Occupational Therapy Assistants).

Home health therapy allows still more individual contact with the patient. The physical therapy assistant visits a patient in his or her home, which allows the assistant to assess the patient's abilities for performing everyday tasks like sweeping, washing dishes, or making a bed. The assistant teaches the patient how to accomplish these tasks safely. Many home health patients are elderly and confined to their homes, and the physical therapy assistant provides a welcome link to the outside world.

Other physical therapy assistants work with disabled children at schools and children's hospitals. By doing "play" therapy, a physical therapy assistant can work on a child's motor control, vestibular stimulation, balance, and coordination. The physical therapy assistant helps children learn to crawl, sit, stand, or walk, and over the years, helps them achieve the most possible independence.

In all of these job settings, a physical therapy assistant may also perform clerical duties, such as filling out reports, devising schedules, maintaining patient records, and coordinating inventory and supplies. A physical therapy assistant may also be responsible for coordinating the patient's treatment with the patient's insurance plans.

What Is It Like to Be a Physical Therapy Assistant?

"A patient usually requires a procedure prior to the therapist seeing them," says Tracey Anderson, a physical therapy assistant in a private clinic, "such as hot pack, electrical stimulation, or ultrasound. That takes about 20 minutes, then you prepare them for the therapist to see them."

When Tracey first gets to work, she prepares the procedure room. "I make sure everything's ready, turning on equipment, making sure we have hot packs and cold packs. There are some procedures that require an injection that freezes the area to be worked on. So I get everything set up, then go through the schedule to see which patients are coming in, then I pull their records." Tracey is also required to keep her work area clean, which includes making the bed and doing some laundry. Though Tracey doesn't have to deal with progress reports or the maintaining of files, she mentions that PTAs in some offices must transcribe notes, keep records, schedule, and perform other administrative duties.

"Our office has a casual atmosphere," she says. "We've found that really does make people much more comfortable. We don't wear lab coats. Our waiting room has a dining room table, and we give the patients coffee or tea. If a patient has to wait a little while, we sit with them and talk. Once they're comfortable, it's easier to work with them."

A patient may require 15 or 20 minutes of therapeutic exercises. The therapist gives me the exercises, and then I teach the patient how to do them.

Many physical therapy facilities focus on sports medicine, but Tracey's clinic primarily provides wound care. She often works with people who have scar tissue from multiple surgeries. When a patient arrives, Tracey leads them to the back where the patient can change clothes and get into the bed. "I then apply electrical stimulation to whichever part of the body we're working—the lower back or shoulder, for example. Usually we cover patients with hot packs and they stay that way for about 20 minutes. If an ultrasound is required in that area, then I'll do that. Then the therapist takes over." Patients at the clinic are scheduled for every half hour, so Tracey sees about 16 patients a day.

Tracey learned how to use the electrical stimulation machine while on the job. "We attach electrodes to the area of the body being worked on. The electricity sort of grabs the muscles and works them. The idea is that it will tire the muscles so that they will relax. That makes it much easier for the therapist to work on the patient. You have to be very careful, though; it's easy to apply too much electricity."

The clinic also features a gym area. "A patient may require 15 or 20 minutes of therapeutic exercises. The therapist gives me the exercises, and then I teach the patient how to do them."

Tracey also provides emotional support, as well. "I can't tell you how many stories I've heard," she says. "Many patients need to talk about their circumstances, and how their families are reacting to their injuries. You really have to be able to talk to them and listen."

Do I Have What It Takes to Be a Physical Therapy Assistant?

Some of the most important qualities for a physical therapy assistant to have are physical stamina, patience, and good communication skills. If you are thinking of entering this field, you must also genuinely enjoy working with people, including those under the stress of illness, aging, or injury. When a condition will not permit patients to regain full use of their bodies, the physical therapy assistant helps them to adjust to this, and to discover ways to become as self-sufficient as possible. "You're dealing with people who are in pain," Tracey says. "Usually by the time they get to the physical therapist, they've been through doctors, insurance companies, and paperwork, and they're not always the nicest people. You just have to love what you're doing and really get along well with people."

Physical therapy assistants are often responsible for many patients in a day, so they need to be organized, efficient, and realistic about what can be accomplished. Mastery of the many therapy techniques is obviously essential. A physical therapy assistant must also have good observational skills in order to recognize what is and is not working for a patient. These observations must then be communicated to the patient's physical therapist and physician.

A physical therapy assistant is constantly challenged in his or her work. Not only does this

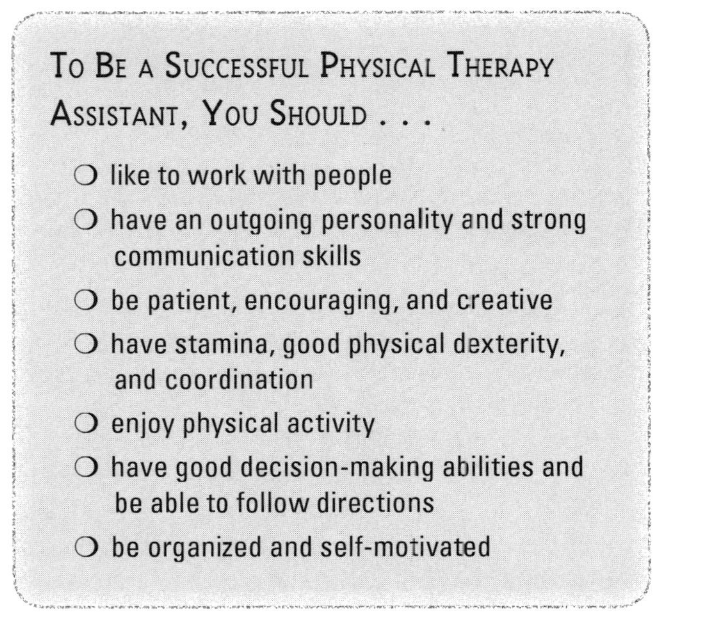

To Be a Successful Physical Therapy Assistant, You Should . . .

- like to work with people
- have an outgoing personality and strong communication skills
- be patient, encouraging, and creative
- have stamina, good physical dexterity, and coordination
- enjoy physical activity
- have good decision-making abilities and be able to follow directions
- be organized and self-motivated

career require a great deal of stamina and physical strength, but, because of the often slow healing process and the repetitive nature of many therapy techniques, the therapy assistant must have patience as well. The ability to communicate enthusiasm and encouragement is a great asset. "You have to have a great personality," Tracey says. "I find a sense of humor to be very important. You have to make people very comfortable. People need to trust you."

How Do I Become a Physical Therapy Assistant?

EDUCATION

High School

While you are in high school, you should take courses in biology, health, math, psychology, speech, and English to prepare for a career as a physical therapy assistant. Classes that enable you to become comfortable on computers are also useful.

Some high schools offer work-study programs in health, which combine classes in health and medical subjects with practical work experience. Volunteering at a local hospital is also an excellent way to explore the hospital environment and to become familiar with aspects of this career. Working with children, the physically disabled, or the elderly is another way to gain practical experience.

Postsecondary Training

Students must attend an accredited physical therapy assistant program, offered at many community and junior colleges, vocational schools, and universities. The American Physical Therapy Association (APTA) sets the standards for accreditation and educational requirements for these programs. There are about 245 accredited physical therapy assistant programs in the United States, according to APTA.

Physical therapy assistant programs are designed to last two years and result in an associate's degree. The programs are divided into academic course work and hands-on clinical field experience. The course work includes anatomy, physiology, biology, the history and philosophy of rehabilitation, human growth and development, chemistry, and psychology. In addition, students take some courses in mathematics and applied physical sciences in order to gain an understanding of the apparatus and the principles behind the therapeutic procedures they will use. Students also receive training in the variety of physical therapy techniques, including massage, therapeutic exercise, and heat and cold therapy. Before students can begin their clinical work, many programs require that they gain certifications in CPR and first aid. During the clinical rotation period, students apply the education, techniques, and skills they have learned in various health facility settings, under the supervision of senior physical therapy assistants and physical therapists.

CERTIFICATION OR LICENSING

Upon graduation from an accredited program, most states require that a candidate pass a written examination administered by the state in order to become a licensed physical therapy assistant. The process for renewing the physical therapy assistant license also varies by state. In addition, physical therapy assistants must be certified in CPR and first aid.

SCHOLARSHIPS AND GRANTS

The APTA offers a minority scholarship to students enrolled in physical therapy assistant programs accredited by the APTA. This award is given to outstanding minority students on a competitive basis. Visit the APTA Web site, http://www.apta.org, for more information.

INTERNSHIPS AND VOLUNTEERSHIPS

If you are interested in becoming a physical therapy assistant, look for a summer or part-time position working or volunteering in the physical therapy department of a hospital or clinic. Many public and private schools also enlist volunteers to work with their disabled students. Jobs at summer camps for disabled children are also excellent experience for prospective physical therapy assistants. Nursing homes and other elderly facilities are another source of work experience and volunteerships. Any of these volunteer positions will help you determine whether you have the personal qualities needed for this career.

Another way to gain more knowledge about this field is to speak with physical therapists and physical therapy assistants.

Who Will Hire Me?

Tracey first started working for the clinic in a clerical position. "I started talking to some of the therapists," she says, "and they decided to start training me for working with patients."

There are about 50,000 physical therapy assistants in the United States, about three-quarters of whom work in hospitals or the offices of health care practitioners. Physical therapy assistants also find employment in rehabilitation centers, home health therapy, extended-care facilities, schools for disabled children, nursing homes, physicians' offices, and private physical therapy offices. The clinical rotation you do during your training program will give you a good feel for which environment is right for you.

Your training program's placement office offers an excellent route to finding your first job. (In fact, one way to evaluate a prospective school is to ask how many of its graduates find work as physical therapy assistants.) Once you've graduated, your placement office should provide listings of available jobs in the area, along with advice on putting together your resume.

Other ways to find a job include looking at classified ads, visiting employment agencies, and browsing hospital and job sites on the Internet. Many newspapers have a section in their classified ads specifically for health care positions. Employment agencies sometimes handle all hiring for local hospitals; call around to see if that's the case in your area. You should also check the Web sites for your local hospitals, as they may post job openings online. There are also a number of free Internet sites dedicated to helping people in certain health professions locate work nationwide.

In-depth

Physical Therapy (PT) vs. Occupational Therapy (OT)

Assessment In physical therapy, the therapist assesses the patient's body structure and physiology.

In occupational therapy, the therapist conducts activity analysis, in which a person's ability to do an activity is compared to the demands of that activity.

Treatment Goals and Methods Physical therapy treatment seeks to moderate pain and enhance healing through applications of heat and cold, ultrasound, and electrical stimulation; improve normal function and movement through joint mobilization, stretching, and exercise; and improve overall conditioning to allow for an improved level of physical activity. Occupational therapy treatment seeks to enable a person to perform activities that are necessary or desirable by improving the patient's technique, adapting the environment, or modifying the task itself.

Where Can I Go from Here?

A physical therapy assistant's responsibilities may increase as his or her level of experience increases. At a larger facility, a physical therapy assistant may receive promotions to a supervisory position; in a smaller facility, an assistant may gradually receive more and more responsibility for the coordination of the physical therapy office. As physical therapy assistants develop greater experience and responsibilities, they can expect to earn higher salaries.

Physical therapy assistants may also choose to advance by changing facilities, such as moving from a hospital setting to a home health setting, or from the acute care facility to the outpatient unit of a physical therapy department. Each area of physical therapy brings its own challenges and rewards.

Some physical therapy assistants return to school in order to become fully qualified physical therapists. Many universities and colleges offer bachelor's-to-master's degree programs in physical therapy. (The master's degree is now the minimum requirement for employment as a physical therapist.) Competition for placement in a physical therapy program is expected to remain keen; a physical therapy assistant with a degree from an accredited program, good grades, and strong work experience may find acceptance into a physical therapy program easier than those with no prior experience in this field. There are APTA-accredited programs in California, Ohio, and Pennsylvania that allow physical therapy assistants to keep working during the week while they pursue a master's degree in physical therapy on the weekends.

Some physical therapists and physical therapy assistants may find opportunities for conducting research into the effectiveness of physical therapy techniques or participating in the development of new therapies. Still others may develop a desire to move into other health and medical careers.

What Are the Salary Ranges?

Physical therapy assistant salaries vary according to facility type, geographical location, employer, and the physical therapy assistant's experience level. The U.S. Department of Labor reports that median annual salaries for physical therapy assistants were $36,610 in 2003. Salaries ranged from less than $24,230 a year to more than $49,650. Benefits for physical therapy assistants vary but usually include paid holidays and vacations, health insurance, and pension plans.

What Is the Job Outlook?

"For a long time," says Tracey, "physical therapy wasn't seen as a medical profession. Many people didn't take it seriously, and insurance companies didn't want to pay [for it]. But I've seen that change a lot over the last 10 years. People are recognizing physical therapy as a very viable procedure, not just a glorified massage."

According to the *Occupational Outlook Handbook,* employment of physical therapy assistants is expected to grow much faster than the average for all other occupations over the next 10 years. As medical technology advances, more patients will be saved and will be in need of physical therapy. New abilities to treat disabling conditions will also prompt more demand for physical therapy assistants to work with these patients. Also, as the population grows older and as more and more people survive into advanced age, the number of elderly people with chronic and debilitating conditions will also increase as will their need for physical therapy. Also, the technologies that permit more infants and young children to survive severe birth defects are also a factor in the forecast for strong growth in jobs in the field.

An additional factor in the growth of the number of jobs for physical therapy assistants is the need for containing the rise of medical costs: Many hospitals will look for physical therapy assistants to fill out their physical therapy staff, rather than increasing the number of higher-paid physical therapists.

How Do I Learn More?

PROFESSIONAL ORGANIZATIONS

The following are organizations that provide information on physical therapy assistant careers, accredited schools, and employers:

Advancement Possibilities

Physical therapists plan and administer medically prescribed physical therapy treatment for patients suffering from injuries, or muscle, nerve, joint, and bone diseases, to restore function, relieve pain, and prevent disability.

Physiatrists are medical doctors who specialize in clinical and diagnostic use of physical agents and exercises to provide physiotherapy for physical, mental, and occupational rehabilitation of patients.

American Physical Therapy Association
1111 North Fairfax Street
Alexandria, VA 22314-1488
http://www.apta.org

American Congress of Rehabilitation Medicine
5987 East 71st Street, Suite 111
Indianapolis, IN 46220-4049
acrm@acrm.org
http://www.acrm.org

BIBLIOGRAPHY

The following is a sampling of materials relating to the professional concerns and development of physical therapy assistants:

Curtis, Kathleen A. *Physical Therapy Professional Foundations: Keys to Success in School and Career.* Delmar Learning, 2002.

Krumhansl, Bernice, and Kathy Siebel. *Opportunities in Physical Therapy Careers.* New York: McGraw-Hill, 1999.

Moffat, Marilyn, and Steve Vickery. *The American Physical Therapy Association Book of Body Maintenance and Repair.* New York: Henry Holt, 1999.

Quinlan, Kathryn A. *Physical Therapist Assistant.* Careers Without College. Mankato, Minn.: Capstone Press, 1998.

PLASTICS TECHNICIANS

Definition
: Plastics technicians are skilled workers who help develop, manufacture, and market plastic products.

Alternative Job Titles
Composite workers
Plastics fabricators
Plastics repairers

High School Subjects
Mathematics
Technical/shop

Personal Skills
Following instructions
Mechanical/manipulative

Salary Range
$16,100 to $30,400 to $38,300

Minimum Educational Level
High school diploma

Certification or Licensing
Voluntary

Outlook
More slowly than the average

DOT
754

GOE
08.02.01

NOC
2233

O*NET-SOC
51-4072.00

Production at a major candy manufacturer has ground to a halt. Broken bearings and gears prevent the 60-year-old machinery from operating, costing the company more money with each passing shift. The company has two choices. It can replace the costly machinery, or it can have new parts made to replace the broken ones. The company opts for replacement, but with a twist. The new parts will not be made of metal but of a specially molded, high-performance plastic.

Standing over the aluminum injection mold, the plastics technician is extremely focused as he completes the setup of his machinery. He checks the material feed, temperature, and pressure of the machine, making sure that the mold is set to create a part exactly six inches wide by 10 inches long; miscalculation in any part of the process will create an unusable part, costing the company even more time and money.

The technician closes the mold and presses a button that sends molten plastic pouring through a hole at the top into the mold. He waits the appropriate time for the part to cool, checking the hardening rate as the minutes pass. When the part has cooled and solidified, he opens the mold and releases the part, which is perfectly dimensioned and ready for shipment to the candy company.

What Does a Plastics Technician Do?

Plastics manufacturing is a major industry whose products play a role in almost every aspect of our lives. The electronics industry uses plastics to make computers, radar equipment, video games, televisions, and telephones. In the aerospace industry, plastics can be found in rocket nozzles, re-entry heat shields, and astronauts' clothing. Modern packaging uses billions of pounds of plastics annually, and a variety of consumer goods are made from plastic—appliances, toys, dinnerware, luggage, and furniture, for example.

Plastics technicians are often considered the middle men of plastics: Their job falls somewhere between that of the scientist, who actually combines the materials that make up different plastics; the engineer, who designs the finished plastics into products; and the worker, who carries out the production of the finished plastics products. Technicians help design engineers, scientists, research groups, and manufacturers develop, manufacture, and market plastics products. They may work in research and development, mold and tool making, manufacturing, sales and service, or other related areas.

Research and development technicians work on prototypes, assist in the design and manufacture of specialized tools and machinery, and monitor the manufacturing process. These technicians often work in a laboratory, monitoring chemical reactions, testing materials, evaluating the test results, keeping records, and submitting reports.

Mold and tool designers, also known as *drawing detailers,* may be involved in overall product design, as well as mold and tool design. Molding requires the technician to install molds in production machines, like the one at the candy manufacturer, establish correct molding cycles, monitor the molding process, maintain production schedules, test incoming raw materials, inspect goods in production, and ensure that the final product meets specifications. Projects may be as simple as making the handle of a cooking pot or as complex as creating a small, intricate part for a computer, which could take hours of calculations and numerous attempts to make it perfect.

Plastics manufacturing technicians work in either molding, laminating, or fabrication. Technicians in laminating superimpose materials in a predetermined pattern. This process is used to make aircraft, aerospace, and mass-transit vehicles; boats; surfboards; and furniture. Laminating entails benchwork for small parts and teamwork for large parts. A reinforced plastics item the size of a shoebox can be built by one person, but a large motorized vehicle requires the work of several technicians.

Technicians employed as *fabricators* work with plastic sheets, rods, and tubes, using equipment similar to that used in woodworking. Aircraft windshields, solariums, and computer housings are some of the products made by fabricators, who use basic machine shop methods combined with heat-forming, polishing, and bonding to complete their work.

Sales representatives for materials suppliers help customers select the right grade of plastic. They serve as a liaison between the customer and the company, assist in product and mold design, and help solve problems that may arise in manufacturing. They might, for example, call on the U.S. Air Force or Coast Guard, especially if they work for a laminating company. Representatives who work for machinery manufacturers help customers select the proper equipment. A background in science helps them understand the machines they sell and their customers' manufacturing processes.

What Is It Like to Be a Plastics Technician?

A typical day for a plastics technician includes setting up molds in production machines, checking

Lingo to Learn

Additives Chemicals added during plastics processing to modify the behavior of plastics.

Celluloid A strong, durable thermoplastic, which is used for shoe heal covers and fabric coatings.

Compounding Using additives in plastics processing; important in the processing of recycled materials.

Epoxy A plastics material used as an adhesive because of its strong resistance to chemicals and weathering.

Extrusion A plastics processing technique of melting and heating resins.

Feedstock The raw material used to produce plastics.

Injection molding A process of injecting melted resin into a mold.

Polymers What plastics are made of; chains of many molecules linked to form one large molecule. Polymers have their origin in nature but are man-made materials.

Pyrolysis The decomposition of organic material by heat.

Recycling The process of using materials recovered from waste to create new products.

Resins The basic building blocks for all plastic products, which are made up of polymers. Before being made into plastic products, resins may be stored in the form of liquids, pellets, or film.

Silicones Plastic material noted for its high heat resistance. Silicones are also water repellent and weather resistant. Some silicone products include insulation for motors, some toys, molds, and models.

Stabilizers Additives used to increase the strength of plastics, making them more resistant to heat.

Thermoplastics Materials that may be melted and reshaped many times under heat. These materials harden as they cool.

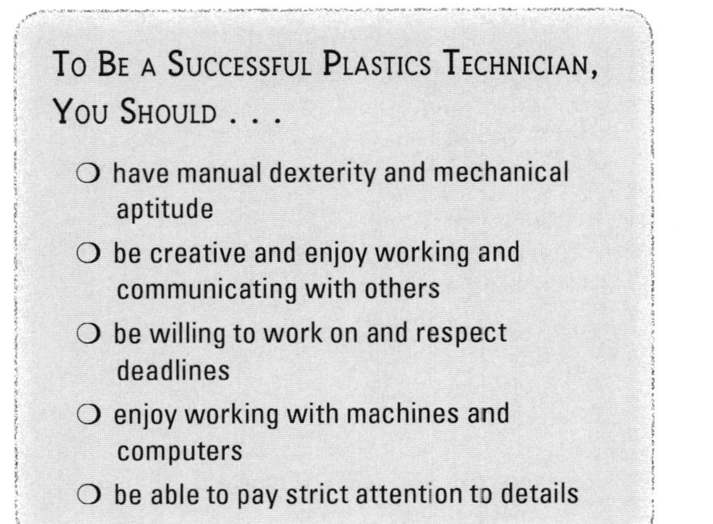

molding cycles by computer, and testing raw materials, such as resin, plastic fiber, and adhesives that form the plastic end-products. Technicians also load material into the machines, make minor adjustments, and monitor the molding process. When each process is complete, technicians unload and inspect the finished product. They may also remove clogged material from the molds. Each technician must follow safety procedures to protect the workers, while giving attention to the care and upkeep of the machinery, which includes expensive molds and dies.

Scott Jones works in injection molding as a process technician. "When we do a die set on the injection molding machines, change the mold on the press to a different part, my responsibility is to set all the parameters on the machine and get it so it's running quality parts," Scott says. "I make any needed adjustments. It's pretty much like a computer controller, a computer screen on the press. You go into that and manually enter in any changes to the parameters on the press."

The work does not require that Scott keep many tools. "Every now and again a part gets stuck in a mold," he says, "and I have brass or aluminum tools that I use to get in there and remove any parts that are stuck without damaging them."

Scott sees this job as one that is always changing. "The computers that control the presses are being upgraded constantly. The design for the molds we use has improved a lot, which makes my job easier." To keep up on changes, Scott reads magazines about injection molding technology.

"You don't have to do a lot of hard physical work," Scott says. "It gives you a chance to use your head a little bit. You're not just on an assembly line doing the same thing over and over." There is some stress that goes along with the job, however. "It's your responsibility to keep these presses running. There are times when you're fighting things that are out of your control. I'm also responsible for the shift, so if any of the presses go down and I can't get them running, then I'm the one who has to answer for it."

> You don't have to do a lot of hard physical work. It gives you a chance to use your head a little bit. You're not just on an assembly line doing the same thing over and over.

Matt Mckeown also works as a process technician, for a manufacturing company that produces outdoor furniture, health care products, toilet seats, and other plastics. The company also contracts to do molding for other companies. "I set up the machines and do the die changes," he says. "I think we're different from a lot of injection molding companies because we do it all, from machine maintenance to processing, troubleshooting." When Matt first arrives for work, he meets with the previous shift. "We talk about what went on, what's not running well, what's down. We have a priority list set by the schedulers." Matt works on injection molding machines and auxiliary equipment. "All of our presses are run by robots," he says, "so we have programming to do. We change a tool, we change the robot program."

Do I Have What It Takes to Be a Plastics Technician?

Plastics technicians should have good manual dexterity, good hand-eye coordination, and be free from color blindness. They need to demonstrate flexibility when working with others, including fellow technicians, engineers, chemists, and managers. Technicians also need to be flexible and open-minded in absorbing and mastering the different skills that are part of the field, such as molding, laminating, and fabricating. They must be aware that they will constantly need to update and expand their skills so as to compete in the ever-changing field of plastics technology.

Communication skills are also paramount to being a successful plastics technician. One must be able to speak clearly and concisely with customers in order to address and solve problems, and also with other technicians in order to create a product using precise specifications and demands. Technicians need to be inquisitive to be able to learn to work with evolving machinery, new compounds, and techniques.

"Companies sometimes look to hire people with mechanical aptitude," Scott says, "people who are good with tools, but that's not necessarily the quality you need for the job. You need to be good at analyzing problems and troubleshooting."

Some mechanical experience can be helpful, however, in certain aspects of the work. "The best background you can have for the job," says Matt, "is a degree in electro-mechanicals. That will teach you pretty much everything you need to know, from hydraulics to electronics."

How Do I Become a Plastics Technician?

Those seeking a career in plastics have two educational choices. One option is to go directly from high school to an apprenticeship program at a plastics factory, which lasts from six months to several years. The other option is to enroll in a college program offering a degree in plastics technology.

Matt's training was mostly in-house, with some outside courses in programming. He also attends annual seminars on processing.

EDUCATION

High School

A high school diploma is the minimum educational requirement for a career as a plastics technician, but this will only qualify you for the most basic positions. While in high school, you should take subjects designated as college preparatory. These subjects will provide a solid foundation for the specialized knowledge required of a plastics technician. Courses should include mathematics, including one year each of algebra, geometry, and trigonometry, and courses in the laboratory sciences, preferably organic chemistry and physics. English and speech classes will also help you hone your communications skills. Mechanical drawing and shop will also be useful.

FYI

The SPI reports that plastics is the United States's fourth largest manufacturing industry, employing over 1.4 million people in 2002 and shipping products valued at $310 billion.

Postsecondary Training

While still in high school, you should investigate programs offered by community colleges, technical institutes, and vocational-technical schools. Some schools include plastics courses as part of mechanical or chemical technicians programs. Also, an increasing number of colleges offer bachelor's degrees in plastics technology.

A typical two-year curriculum for plastics technicians at a community college includes course work, laboratory, and, sometimes, work experience. In the first year, courses typically include introduction to plastics, applied mathematics, compression molding procedures, fabrication of plastics, properties of thermoplastics, injection molding, and extrusion molding.

Second-year courses typically include reinforced plastics procedures, applied chemistry of plastic materials, dies and molds, thermo-forming, synthetic elastomers, foamed plastics procedures, test procedures, and basic employment information.

Another training option is to participate in apprenticeship programs or in-plant training programs while earning a degree. Many companies operate on a three-shift basis; hours can be arranged around your class schedules. As part of the learning experience, it is possible to participate in cooperative education or work-study programs. This is a joint venture between the school and the industry where students can work a limited number of hours per month and often receive college credit.

A plastics technician tests the power of an adhesive made from raw sugar. *(Scott Bauer / U.S. Department of Agriculture)*

If you plan to enter the military, investigate branches of service that offer training in plastics. The U.S. Air Force, Navy, Coast Guard, and Army publish procurement specifications, operate repair facilities, and carry on their own research and development.

In the plastics industry, each process requires a specific knowledge. For example, injection molding skills are completely different from those required for laminating. The technician who specializes in compression molding has skills not common to other processes. Certain bodies of knowledge, however, are common to all areas of the plastics industry.

CERTIFICATION OR LICENSING

The Society of the Plastics Industry (SPI) offers National Certification in Plastics (NCP). With a minimum of two years' experience and some formal training in plastics processing, technicians can take a test to become NCP Certified Operators.

SCHOLARSHIPS AND GRANTS

The Plastics Pioneers Association Scholarships are offered through the Plastics Institute of America to students in two- and four-year degree and certificate programs leading to careers in the plastics industry. Several awards of $1,500 are granted each year. The SPI also offers scholarships for those pursuing a career in the plastics industry.

Who Will Hire Me?

Primary plastic producers are the main employers of plastic technicians. A smaller number of technicians are employed by other manufacturers who have in-house plastic departments. Major employers of plastics technicians include such well-known

In-depth

The Birth of Plastics

The plastics industry traces its beginnings to 1869, when a billiard ball manufacturer in New York offered a prize of $10,000 to anyone who could create an alternative material to ivory for the production of billiard balls. Balls had been made from the ivory taken from elephant tusks, which had grown increasingly rare and expensive to obtain.

A printer named John Wesley Hyatt experimented with a mixture of cellulose nitrate and camphor, creating what he called celluloid. Although he did not win the prize, his invention, patented in 1872, brought about a revolution in production and manufacturing. By 1892, more than 2,500 articles were being produced from celluloid, including, incidentally, piano keys, the first plastic false teeth, the first movie film, frames for eyeglasses, and, of course, billiard balls.

companies as DuPont, General Motors, and Dow Chemical.

A good way to find a job in this field is to enter an apprenticeship or in-house training program. You can apply for these programs through local employment agencies or through the personnel offices of employers. If you graduate with a four-year degree in plastics technology, you may want to join the local student chapter of the Society of Plastics Engineers. These student chapters maintain close ties with the parent organization and offer numerous opportunities for networking and establishing contacts that are invaluable when seeking employment.

Apprenticeships and in-plant training programs also exist for prospective technicians. Direct application through employment agencies and personnel officers of plastic employers will also prove successful. A student chapter of the Society of Plastic Engineers exists to offer assistance in finding jobs, and employment opportunities and job listings are available from the SPI as well.

Advancement Possibilities

Plant managers formulate and execute plant policies and direct production activities to meet sales objectives.

Plastics inspectors test and inspect finished products for size, strength, and uniformity.

Product designers create designs for plastic products and determine the practicability of designs in relation to cost, industry specifications, and the limitations of plant equipment.

Plastics engineers engage in the manufacture, fabrication, and end use of existing materials, as well as with the development of new materials, processes, and equipment.

Where Can I Go from Here?

Well-trained and experienced technicians have a variety of advancement opportunities open to them. Some manufacturers conduct in-house training sessions; others offer incentives to those who further their education and expertise at accredited institutions. "Most of the people who do this work start out in plastics as a machine operator," Scott says, "then become a material handler, and die-setter, then a process technician."

Those with advanced education will progress to supervisory and management positions. Others may become involved in sales and marketing or even ownership of a plastics manufacturing enterprise. Some machine operators may go on to become tool and die makers.

Plastics technicians with a background in design may advance to the position of *product designer.* These plastics workers create designs for products to be produced from plastic materials. They research the practicality of designs in relation to the limitations of plant equipment, cost, probable selling price, and industry specifications.

Plastics engineers engage in the manufacture, fabrication, and use of existing materials, as well as the creation of new materials, processes, and equipment.

Quality control supervisors interpret and enforce quality standards. They direct and instruct the *quality control inspectors* assigned to the processing and finishing departments.

Production managers direct the work of various production departments, either directly or through subordinate supervisors. They provide information on new production methods and equipment, problems, and the need for maintenance of all plant machinery and equipment. They also work closely with union representatives.

Purchasing agents are responsible for overall direction and coordination of buyers who secure raw materials, components, packaging material, office equipment, supplies, machinery, and services for a production plant.

What Are the Salary Ranges?

The *Occupational Outlook Handbook* lists median annual earnings for plastic molding machine setters and operators at $30,400 in 2003. Those in the lowest paid 10 percent earned $16,100 annually, and the highest paid 10 percent earned $38,300. Tool and die makers working in the plastics products manufacturing industry earned $42,600 annually.

Benefits often include paid vacations, health and dental insurance, pension plans, production bonuses, and industry-sponsored education. These benefits will vary with the size and nature of the company.

What Is the Job Outlook?

Although the plastics industry plays a role in so many essential aspects of daily life, competition from foreign companies, reduced consumer demand, and technological advancements have resulted in declining employment opportunities. The U.S. Department of Labor predicts slower than average job growth in this industry through 2012.

In a 2003 report the SPI noted a significant downturn in the domestic plastics industry that began in 2000. The organization reported a decrease of 8.4 percent in the number of employees between 2000 and 2002. It also reported a 5.4 percent decrease in the compound annual growth of shipments during that time period. The largest decline in product demand was for urethane and other foam products (down 13.9 percent); nonpackaging film (down 11.5 percent); and laminated plate, sheet, and film (down 11.7 percent).

How Do I Learn More?

PROFESSIONAL ORGANIZATIONS

The following organizations can provide information about the plastics industry, educational programs and scholarships, certification, careers, and employment opportunities:

American Plastics Council
1300 Wilson Boulevard
Arlington VA 22209
800-243-5790
http://www.plastics.org

Junior Engineering Technical Society Inc.
1420 King Street, Suite 405
Alexandria, VA 22314-2794
703-548-5387
info@jets.org
http://www.jets.org

Plastics Institute of America
333 Aiken Street
Lowell, MA 01854
978-934-3130
info@plasticinstitute.org
http://www.plasticinstitute.org

Society of Plastics Engineers
14 Fairfield Drive
Brookfield, CT 06804-3911
203-775-0471
http://www.4spe.org

Society of the Plastics Industry
1667 K Street, NW, Suite 1000
Washington, DC 20006
202-296-7005
http://www.socplas.org

BIBLIOGRAPHY

The following is a sampling of materials relating to the professional concerns and development of plastics technicians:

Bone, Jan. *Opportunities in Plastics Careers*. Lincolnwood, Ill.: VGM Career Horizons, 1991.

Careers in Focus: Technicians. Chicago: Ferguson Publishing Company, 2001.

Harper, Charles A., ed. *Handbook of Plastics, Elastomers, and Composites*, 4th ed. New York: McGraw-Hill, 2002.

Harper, Charles A. *Modern Plastics Handbook*. New York: McGraw-Hill, 2000.

Strong, Brent A. *Plastics: Materials and Processing*. Paramus, N.J.: Prentice Hall, 1999.

POLLUTION CONTROL TECHNICIANS

Definition
Pollution control technicians conduct tests and field investigations to obtain data for use by environmental, engineering, and scientific personnel in determining sources and methods of controlling pollutants in air, water, and soil.

Alternative Job Title
Environmental technicians

High School Subjects
Biology
Earth science
Health

Personal Skills
Mechanical/manipulative
Technical/scientific

Salary Range
$21,500 to $35,800 to $56,500+

Minimum Educational Level
Some postsecondary training

Certification or Licensing
Required by certain states

Outlook
Much faster than the average

DOT
029

GOE
02.05.02

NOC
2231

O*NET-SOC
19-4091.00

As people become more concerned about the air they breathe both indoors and out, environmental companies are sending air quality control technicians like Dean Spencer to residential and commercial properties. While some environmental technicians test outdoor air for pollutants, Dean is actively involved in cleaning and sanitizing indoor systems, sometimes even crawling into the ductwork with a vacuum.

"In an office building," Dean says, "I'll either have to crawl through or send a viper [a high pressure air hose] through and blow out the trash that's inside—the accumulated mold or dust or whatever's in the bottom of the metal air ducts—and it blows back to the heavy duty vacuum we use." Good ventilation helps prevent illnesses and allergic reactions and carries indoor air pollutants out of the home. "People are just starting to realize that this is something important," Dean says.

What Does a Pollution Control Technician Do?

The two most identifiable specializations in pollution control are air pollution control and water pollution control (sometimes called water and wastewater technology). Other types of specializations focus on noise, light pollution, or soil quality. The goal of all these technologies is to make public resources suitable and safe for reuse. Each area of specialization, however, is distinguished by the vast assortment of conditions that technicians work under. The generically termed *pollution control technician (PCT)* works in a vast number of places, for a diverse group of employers, with a myriad of duties and responsibilities. These technicians may be involved in testing and monitoring, or they may install or repair systems, such as ventilation.

Air quality technicians focus on both industrial pollution and the monitoring of the quality of open air. In terms of industry, these technicians may test and monitor specific pollutants, such as exhaust from smokestacks and chimneys of manufacturing plants or a specific reaction such as an internal combustion engine. They gauge smoke density using samples culled from a specific site, or they may re-create the same condition of contamination in the laboratory. Their laboratory work may involve use of gas chromatographs, atomic absorption spectrophotometers, and flame photometers.

When checking the quality of open air, technicians gather data from rooftop sampling devices or stationary trailers equipped with constant monitoring machinery. These trailers are like mobile laboratories, capable of analyzing outside air 24 hours a day for solid particles and specific gases. Information gathered in these trailers may be stored on 30-day printouts or cross-referenced and combined with preexisting data stored in a computer.

Noise technicians use rooftop devices and mobile units in pollution areas in the same manner as air technicians. They take readings and collect data from factories, highways, airports, and other outdoor locations, gauging noise exposure levels for workers and the general public. They sometimes test potentially hazardous manufactured goods such as construction equipment, chain saws, snow blowers, and lawn mowers. In teams of two, the technicians gather data, one member "listening" with electronic instrumentation as his or her partner records the results. Such information is used in research, in determining compliance with noise regulations, and in writing environmental impact assessments.

Noise technicians must take into account the effects of sound-absorbing and sound-reflecting material at the observation site and must also be aware of the distance the sound source is from their observation area. Government noise technicians may act as mediators and arbiters in nuisance disputes and may issue summons to violators as part of their responsibilities.

Water pollution control technicians work to pinpoint the source of water pollution and attempt to reduce its effects by collecting samples from natural bodies of water, industrial sites, and other water sources. They sometimes perform physical and chemical tests with a field kit to determine the origin of the pollution. Some water pollution control technicians set up monitoring devices that compile readings of turbidity (muddiness), water flow, temperature, and pressure.

Water pollution control technicians spend considerable time outdoors, regardless of weather, aboard boats, possibly amid unpleasant smells, in close proximity to hazardous substances such as oil, PCBs, and cyanide. Field sites are sometimes spread far apart or in inaccessible areas, making travel difficult and sometimes keeping technicians away from home for long periods of time.

Water pollution control technicians must be able to analyze incoming data from advanced, automated equipment and be able to combine that data with their own experience and preexisting data already in a computer. They must be able to prepare reports, oral and written, as well as charts, graphs, and tables to communicate data to others who have a role in the analytical process.

Estuarine resource technology is a specialty related to water pollution control, particularly suitable for those with training and interest in biology. Estuaries are coastal regions where salt and fresh water come together. A wide variety of ecologically fragile plant and animal species coexist in these bays, salt marshes, inlets, and tidal pools. They are extremely vulnerable to pollution from nearby towns, cities, and industry. *Estuarine resource technicians* study the environmental impact of these external factors. Their work may take them from the laboratory to boats, even into the water clad in diving gear.

Estuarine resource technicians must be familiar with the upkeep and functions of their specific technology. They must be able to collect and analyze samples, record data, and tolerate any climactic conditions that arise as they go about their job.

Hazardous waste technicians focus on the safe disposal of toxic waste. This waste is usually created in the form of a by-product when chemicals and other industrial products are manufactured.

In the cleanup process, technicians are required to remove hazardous material to an intermediary processing center or a new disposal site. They may gather water and soil samples at the pollution site and

Lingo to Learn

Air quality standards The level of pollutants released into outside air that is not allowed to be exceeded by industry.

Carcinogenic A substance capable of causing cancer.

Centrifuge A mechanical device consisting of a container that spins very rapidly, exerting great centrifugal force on its contents, causing rapid separation of substances.

Emission The release of gases or particulates into the environment.

Exposure levels The permissible quantity of an allowable pollutant according to rule or regulation.

Microscope One of several types of instruments used to obtain an enlarged visual or photographic image of minute objects or minute details of objects.

pH meter A device that gives a numerical value that indicates the relative acidity or alkalinity of a substance on a scale of one to 14, with seven being neutral.

perform laboratory tests to determine the identity of a pollutant and how much of it is present. Onsite, technicians use pumps, drilling equipment, and chemical-sensing devices.

Hazardous waste technicians must also be trained to assess and eliminate the remains of compromised underground gasoline storage tanks and even the presence of improperly disposed household chemicals.

What Is It Like to Be a Pollution Control Technician?

Ryan Windall works in "fossil operations," which primarily involves testing smokestacks. "I go to coal-fired plants and perform opacity audits on the stack meters," Ryan says. "Opacity is the measure of dirt going up and out of the stack. We have combustion turbines that are fired with fuel oil or natural gas, plus all the power plants with the coal."

Checking the opacity involves the use of neutral density filters. Different shades of glass on the filters simulate the amount of dirt in the air. Clear glass simulates little dirt, while smoke-colored glass simulates more dirt in the air. "Some days I'm 350 feet up in the air on a catwalk outside the stack," he says. "I ride an elevator up the outside of the stack. In some places, I go up 200 feet inside a stack. I may be only feet from the peregrine falcons we have on boxes mounted to the stacks. We use them to control pigeons and other birds that home in on our structures."

Ryan may also be involved in a variety of other tests, including testing for mercury in the coal so that turbines are not burning heavy metals. He also takes well samples from ash landfill sites.

Back in the office, Ryan writes reports for completed audits. Usually the power plants test out fine, requiring no changes. "I'll also draw up models or designs for testing," he says. "Once, I designed a stack extension for testing one of our turbines. I worked with engineers and contractors in modeling the piece and building it."

While Ryan focuses on pollutants released into outside air, Dean Spencer works as an indoor air quality technician, cleaning and sanitizing ventilation systems in homes and offices. His day begins with preparing his truck. "I make sure I have all my tools," he says. "We need a coil cleaner, deodorizing and sanitizing liquid we spray into the system, cleaner for the air registers because we take them down and there's normally dust and mold on them. We also use this material that's basically like a plaster for sealing up holes we make in the ductwork. We seal it up with metal tape, then we smooth on the plaster over it."

Dean typically works on a two or three person crew, with each residential job taking about three hours. "A job may take longer if we come across something difficult," Dean says, "like if we have to get up in the attic and cut into old metal stovepipe-type systems. Flex duct is more prevalent now, because it's easier to store as far as construction. It basically looks like a slinky covered with insulation and plastic."

For a typical residential job, Dean will set up tarps beneath registers to prevent anything falling onto the floor and making a mess. "Then we'll take down registers and place them outside so we can clean them. Then I'll go to work on the air handler, which is usually in the garage, or it may be inside a closet in the house, or in the attic. I take the air handler apart, take the panel off and take the blower out and place it outside where I can blow out the fan and get off all the dust that's clinging to that. I then vacuum out the air handler because there's usually mold and dust clinging to the insulation side. I'll clean with high pressure air and a cleaning solution. I'll clean the coils also, because the air filter can let really fine dust inside the coils, which transfers the heat or coldness to the inside air, and the dust will cling to the moisture. During the summer, it sweats because it's cold from the air-conditioning, and the moisture condenses on the coils. It forms like a mud that clings to the inside and impedes the air flow."

When finished with the air handler, Dean and a crew member will go inside the house to send a high pressure air hose through the air duct system. "At the same time, we hook up a heavy duty vacuum to the air handler, and it sucks all the air backwards, sucking the air in through the ducts instead of blowing it out." Dean then puts the air handler back together and returns the registers to the walls.

Eye goggles and a mask are sometimes required for the work, but Dean mostly makes use of ear muffs. "When you're working with high pressure air," he says, "like when you're outside cleaning the air blower, you're working with a lot of high-decibel noise."

Do I Have What It Takes to Be a Pollution Control Technician?

PCTs must enjoy working with their hands and be at ease with a variety of instruments and equipment.

A technician collects data from a laboratory test simulation of the damage to fir trees by air pollution. *(Maximilian Stock Ltd. / Photo Researchers Inc.)*

Basic manual skills are necessary, along with good overall physical conditioning. Air technicians must climb ladders and stretch in uncomfortable, unnatural positions. Water technicians must be able to move boats in and out of bodies of water. "You can't be allergic to hard work," Dean says.

Dean says he is expected to work as part of a team. "You have to either take directions efficiently or be good at directing people."

An often overlooked quality for being a successful PCT is skill in communication, both oral and written. Technicians may be required to convey field findings in a concise manner to experts, environmental engineers, and fellow technicians who may not have been to the site. PCTs may also be called on to speak authoritatively to professional meetings, science clubs, and the public.

"You need interpersonal skills," Ryan says. "You should appreciate diversity, because you're working with people with a range of ages and personalities. And sometimes when you go to other plants, people are territorial."

Depending on the area of work, pollution control technicians need to be precision-minded, detail-oriented people. They must be good at reading maps, charts, blueprints, and diagrams.

Furthermore, those students interested in pursuing a career in pollution control technology must be able to tolerate long hours and a floating schedule. Some jobs require the PCT to spend several days at one site. Pollution control is a job driven by the situations that arise; flexibility and the ability to adapt to a variety of situations are crucial. PCTs must also have patience and endurance to travel considerable distances between sites.

How Do I Become a Pollution Control Technician?

Ryan majored in chemistry in college but took his first job before completing his degree. He has worked for his current employer in various capacities as a chemical technician and a metrologist for over 20 years.

EDUCATION

High School

High school students who intend to pursue a career in pollution control technology should take courses in the sciences, namely biology, chemistry, and physics, especially those that offer lab-intensive training. Mathematics and computer science should also be a focus. Additionally, you should put specific emphasis on speech, English, and technical writing classes that are offered to strengthen your communication skills. If you want to work with the repair and maintenance

To Be a Successful Pollution Control Technician, You Should . . .

- be precision minded and detail oriented
- have manual skills, physical dexterity, and good overall physical conditioning
- be extroverted and able to speak and write authoritatively and intelligently
- have a flexible personality in order to tolerate repetitious procedures, long hours, and sometimes long-distance travel

of systems, you should enroll in shop classes to gain experience working with tools and hone your mechanical aptitude.

Postsecondary Training

For a limited number of jobs, only a high school education will be required. For most entry-level jobs in pollution control technology, however, two years of post-high school education is the average basic requirement. Because the field is rapidly expanding, requirements may vary. Both associate's and bachelor's degree programs are offered in environmental technology, as well as in specific areas such as wastewater treatment technology. Many programs incorporate an internship with a local employer into their curriculum.

CERTIFICATION OR LICENSING

Because of the vast diversity of specialization in the field, certification is not uniformly mandatory. Certification for PCTs depends on the level of employment, experience required, and the degree of hazard or threat to the worker or public. Government employers usually require certification of their technicians, especially for jobs that deal with public health, such as sanitation, public water supply, or when sewage treatment is dissolved.

The National Environmental Health Association (NEHA) offers seven related credentials such as registered environmental technician (RET), certified environmental health technician (CEHT), and certified food safety professional (CFSP). The Institute of Professional Environmental Practice also offers certification to environmental professionals with four-year degrees.

SCHOLARSHIPS AND GRANTS

Information regarding scholarships and grants may be accessed through technical and four-year schools with degree programs in the environmental sciences. NEHA also offers scholarships to encourage students to pursue careers in environmental health.

INTERNSHIPS AND VOLUNTEERSHIPS

Internships are usually offered as part of a PCT degree program. A volunteership in a laboratory, forest service summer program, or not-for-profit environmental organization, such as Greenpeace, may provide practical experience and contacts to advance in the field. The Environmental Career Center provides info about summer jobs and paid internships. The Environmental Careers Organization promotes hundreds of paid environmental internships, typically for those with bachelor's degrees.

In-depth

What Causes Indoor Air Pollution?

Do you find yourself having headaches, throat irritation, nausea? You may be working or living in a space that has "tight building syndrome," meaning that it has reduced outside air exchange. Because of this inadequate ventilation, pollutants remain in the air. One of the most dangerous of these pollutants is asbestos, which can come from damaged insulation and can cause lung disease and cancer. Formaldehyde from plywood and tobacco smoke can cause coughing, fatigue, allergic reactions, and cancer. The mercury found in some latex paints can cause kidney and brain damage. Biological pollutants from bacteria, animal dander, and pollen can cause shortness of breath; eye, nose, and throat irritation; and digestive problems.

Who Will Hire Me?

There are two areas of employment for PCTs—the private sector and the government. The private sector, namely manufacturing companies producing steel and oil, seeks technicians who can work in environmental divisions to ensure safety and maintain pollution standards. Construction firms need technicians to survey sites, document existing conditions, draw blueprints, and foresee environmental problems that might hinder completion of a project.

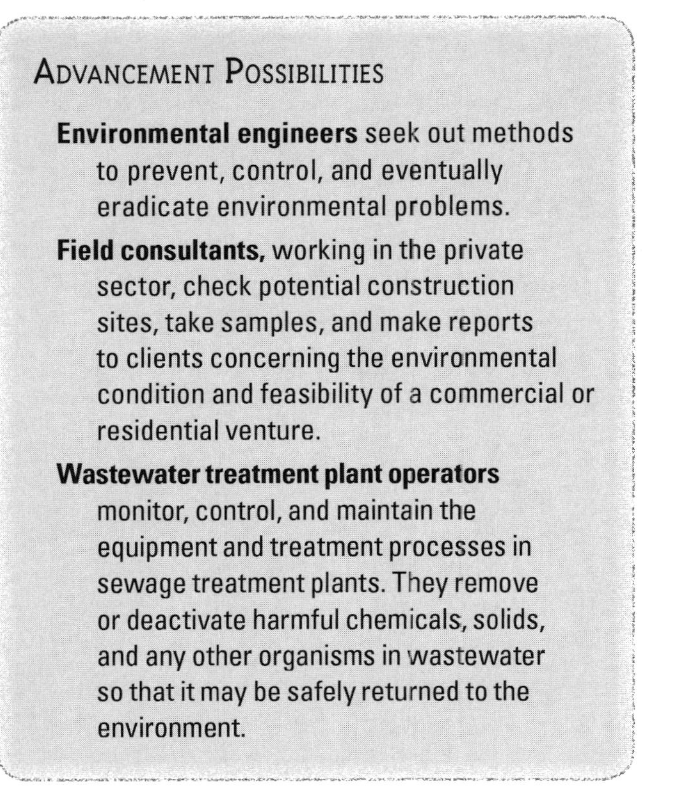

Advancement Possibilities

Environmental engineers seek out methods to prevent, control, and eventually eradicate environmental problems.

Field consultants, working in the private sector, check potential construction sites, take samples, and make reports to clients concerning the environmental condition and feasibility of a commercial or residential venture.

Wastewater treatment plant operators monitor, control, and maintain the equipment and treatment processes in sewage treatment plants. They remove or deactivate harmful chemicals, solids, and any other organisms in wastewater so that it may be safely returned to the environment.

Government agencies at the federal, state, and local levels need technicians to respond to citizen complaints, monitor industry through constant testing and sampling, and clean up pollution areas. The Environmental Protection Agency and the Occupational Safety and Health Administration are key employers of PCTs.

Where Can I Go from Here?

As pollution control technicians gain experience, they may earn more pay and acquire greater responsibility. In private industry, experienced technicians may train new hires, act as supervisors, or oversee quality control operations. A technician with considerable mechanical experience may become an expert in his or her specific subspecialty. Others may become inspectors, technical representatives, or executives in management, sales, or public relations. With further education, pollution control technicians can become environmental engineers.

Bill Pickett, a former pollution control technician now involved in management, sales, and public relations, says, "Most employers like a grounding in the actual nuts and bolts of the field—actual experience that may help your knowledge when working in other areas." Experience as a PCT may provide the raw material and skills to advance to another area of pollution control.

Most employers like a grounding in the actual nuts and bolts of the field—actual experience that may help your knowledge when working in other areas.

Despite these possibilities, and as with many fields, technicians may run into dead-ends, discovering that advancement is only possible with the continuance of formal education.

What Are the Salary Ranges?

Because of the varied nature of the work, the salaries range widely. According to the *Occupational Outlook Handbook,* the median annual earnings of environmental science and protection technicians were $35,800. Those in the lowest paid 10 percent earned $21,500, while those in the highest paid 10 percent earned $56,500.

In 2004, *Environmental Protection* magazine (http://www.eponline.com) published the results of its salary survey of the environmental industry: regulatory compliance specialists with bachelor's degrees earned $54,518 annually, while those with master's degrees made $60,024. A plant level manager had median earnings of $68,922 with an average annual bonus of $3,489. The average bonus for regulatory compliance specialists was $3,453.

It is important to note that pay scales and compensation for PCTs vary based on the level of education attained, experience, and the location of the employer; urban employers tend to pay more than suburban employers in relation to the cost of living and demand.

What Is the Job Outlook?

The U.S. Department of Labor projects faster than average job growth in the environmental science and protection industry through 2012. Employment growth can be judged, as in any other field, by the overall expansion of the population and economy, although, in terms of pollution control, this must be weighed against the ever-present need for pure resources. New treatment plants will have to be constructed to satisfy the demands of the residential and industrial sectors of the country. More qualified people will be needed to supervise and test in these facilities and in other areas of the environmental field. In addition, existing treatment plants will be forced to upgrade and expand to satisfy new government regulations and the widening needs of their surrounding communities.

Other factors that will influence growth include continuing public concern for the environment, continued lobbying of government and industry regarding pollution standards, the availability of government funding, and the degree of government enforcement.

Clearly, education will provide the best tool for advancement in pollution control. According to the *Environmental Protection* magazine survey, fewer than five of the approximately 450 respondents reported having no post-secondary training or only a high school diploma. The most desirable future jobs will go to those who have kept up with changing technology and pollution conditions. Those who continue their education through technical and university settings, government seminars, and conferences, will do well. Continuing education will allow technicians to become more diversified and thus more qualified in a wide variety of related fields.

It is also important to consider that pollution control jobs, while necessary throughout the country, are not evenly distributed. Job applicants who have flexibility in terms of location may have greater success in obtaining a job. Finally, it is significant to mention that a recent trend toward privatization has emerged in the pollution control field. PCTs who work in the private sector for companies that offer these pollution-related services stand to do the best in future job markets.

How Do I Learn More?

PROFESSIONAL ORGANIZATIONS

For information about career opportunities, educational programs, scholarships, internships, certification, and water conservation and quality management, contact the following organizations:

Air and Waste Management Association
One Gateway Center, Third Floor
Pittsburgh, PA 15222-1435
412-232-3444
info@awma.org
http://www.awma.org

American Water Works Association
6666 West Quincy Avenue
Denver, CO 80235
800-926-7337
http://www.awwa.org

Environmental Career Center
Two Eaton Street, Suite 711
Hampton, VA 23669
757-727-7895
http://www.environmentalcareers.info

Environmental Careers Organization
30 Winter Street
Boston, MA 02180
617-426-4375
http://www.eco.org

Institute of Professional Environmental Practice
600 Forbes Avenue
333 Fisher Hall
Pittsburgh, PA 15282
412-396-1703
http://www.ipep.org

National Environmental Health Association
720 South Colorado Boulevard, Suite 970-S
Denver, CO 80246-1925
303-756-9090
http://www.neha.org

BIBLIOGRAPHY

The following is a sampling of materials relating to the professional concerns and development of pollution control technicians:

Careers in Focus: Environment. Chicago: Ferguson Publishing Company, 1999.

Doyle, Kevin et al. *The Complete Guide to Environmental Careers in the 21st Century*. Washington, D.C.: Island Press, 1998.

Fanning, Odom. *Opportunities in Environmental Careers*. Revised ed. New York: VGM Career Books, 2002.

Hocking, Martin B. *Handbook of Chemical Technology and Pollution Control*. San Diego: Academic Press, 1999.

PSYCHIATRIC TECHNICIANS

A young boy charges through the adolescent psych ward, raging, his words choked in screams and tears. Full of fury, he pounds the walls with his fists. The boy has just been told he is being discharged from the hospital that day. Sue Jones, a psychiatric technician, stands nearby with a junior technician.

"Should I take him down?" the junior technician asks Sue.

"No," Sue answers, "Let him work it out."

It is a calculated risk.

Sue has worked with the boy. She knows that he comes from the streets, out of control, neglected by a mother who sold her body for drugs right in front of him. After four months in the ward, he's made little progress. But this is only his first time in treatment. Given time . . .

The boy stands there, screaming. The staff moves between him and the other patients, ready to restrain him if he turns violent.

But it is better to do it this way, Sue thinks. Let him feel his anger. For the first time in his life he's found a structured environment, and now they are sending him away. And in this anger, there is hope, a chance to heal.

Definition
Psychiatric technicians provide skilled nursing care and assist in treatment programs for patients with mental illnesses and emotional disturbances and patients with developmental disabilities.

Alternative Job Titles
Human services technicians
Mental health technicians
Psychiatric nursing specialists
Psychiatric technologists

High School Subjects
Health
Psychology

Personal Skills
Communication/ideas
Helping/teaching

Salary Range
$17,390 to $25,667 to $43,805

Minimum Educational Requirements
Associate's degree or some postsecondary training

Certification or Licensing
Voluntary (certification)
Required in some states (licensing)

Outlook
More slowly than the average

DOT
079

GOE
14.07.01

NOC
3413

O*NET-SOC
29-2053.00, 31-1013.00

What Does a Psychiatric Technician Do?

People with mental illnesses and emotional disturbances, and those with developmental disabilities, require special care to prevent them from becoming a danger to themselves or others and treatment toward the possibility of functioning to the fullest extent possible in mainstream life. Whether in a psychiatric hospital or clinic, a residential halfway house, or a school for the developmentally disabled, the health professional with whom these patients most often interact is the *psychiatric technician*.

Psychiatric technicians work intensively with patients and perform a variety of tasks, including participating in prescribed treatment programs, such as group therapy; administering oral and hypodermic medications; and taking basic health measurements, such as blood pressure and temperature readings. Psychiatric technicians are also responsible for maintaining patient hygiene and assisting in other routine activities, including feeding and bathing patients and keeping their clothing and living areas clean; when possible, the psychiatric technician encourages and trains patients to perform these activities for themselves.

One of the most important roles of the psychiatric technician is to observe patients and to provide written and oral reports on their observations to the patients' medical and psychiatric physicians. A psychiatric technician spends a great deal of time with patients, speaking with them, playing cards, chess, and other games, and escorting patients to medical appointments, church services, movies, museums, sports events, and other places. The psychiatric technician also facilitates patient-to-patient interaction, encouraging patients to participate in social and recreational activities as a means of promoting the rehabilitative process. By developing a relationship with patients, psychiatric technicians provide regularity and trust in a structured environment, which may be beneficial and necessary to the patient's progress.

Under the supervision of psychiatrists, psychologists, and other mental health professionals, the psychiatric technician participates in the planning of treatment strategies and is chiefly responsible for their implementation. Activities may include physical and mental rehabilitation exercises in recreational and occupational settings designed to build social and mental skills, modify behavior, and encourage a sense of personal responsibility and confidence often lacking in psychiatric patients.

Because of their direct association with patients, psychiatric technicians are an important component of the psychiatric team. Their observations provide insight into the effectiveness of treatment strategies so that each patient will receive the most appropriate care possible. Close contact with a patient also allows the psychiatric technician an important awareness into the patient's behavior and state of mind, which enables the psychiatric staff to recognize times of stress and possible harmful behavior. Timely intervention may prevent the patient from becoming a danger to him- or herself or others.

Psychiatric technicians may also be responsible for maintaining contact with the patient's family, arranging family meetings, and conducting initial admission interviews and psychological testing. In a hospital setting, the psychiatric technician becomes involved in every part of their patients' lives. In other settings, such as clinics, halfway houses, and day centers, the psychiatric technician sees many patients who have left the hospital and are making the transition to everyday life. These patients require special attention from the psychiatric technician who, while working with families, government services, and other mental health agencies, will help to coordinate the patient's housing, finances, and employment. The psychiatric technician will also establish continuing psychiatric and medical treatment.

Community mental health is another area that employs psychiatric technicians. In this particular setting, patients generally do not require hospitalization, but nonetheless need help in dealing with such problems as drug and alcohol abuse. Sometimes called *human services technicians,* the patients of these psychiatric technicians may also include the elderly, victims of spousal and sexual abuse, and clients of social welfare programs, child care centers, vocational rehabilitation workshops, and schools for people with developmental disabilities.

What Is It Like to Be a Psychiatric Technician?

Sue Jones has been a psychiatric technician for almost 10 years. She is a senior member of a nursing staff, working with adolescent inpatients at a private psychiatric hospital in New Hampshire. "The unit I work on is very violent at times. But not all are like that. It's quieter to work with adults, because many of them have been in the system a long time, and they're often depressed," Sue says. "I prefer to work with adolescents because you seem to have more of a chance to help them. There's still a chance to get them out of the system and back into normal life."

Typically, there are 30 patients in Sue's unit, ranging in age from 12 to 17, with varying degrees of emotional and mental disabilities, and with varying levels of functional ability. Assigned to this unit are 10 or more staff, including nurses, psychiatric aides, and psychiatric technicians. The high ratio of staff to patients allows intensive supervision, observation, and interaction, which are key elements to psychiatric treatment.

"We keep patients on a highly structured schedule, from the moment they wake up to the time they go to sleep," Sue explains. "Their day begins at 8:00 A.M., when they're expected to have prepared their rooms, made their beds, cleaned, showered, and dressed. We call this 'milieu' therapy, which is an important part of their treatment. By holding them responsible for their own behavior, we encourage them to function at the highest level possible for them."

Patients are divided into two groups according to their functional level. Throughout the day, Sue and the other psychiatric staff lead patients through a variety of group and individual activities, each designed to coordinate therapeutic and rehabilitative skills that may allow the patient to leave the hospital setting and return to the community. The typical day for these patients includes group therapy and individual counseling sessions, schooling, group and individual activities, and therapies such as art therapy. Sue also leads "life school" classes in which patients are exposed to and taught skills they will need in the community, such as how to handle money and shop for groceries. Relieving the stressfulness of these activities may be an important factor in a patient's successful return to the community.

As a senior member of the staff, and because she is continuing her studies, Sue is considered a psychology intern. As such, she leads group counseling sessions under the supervision of a staff psychologist. "By talking about their problems, patients can help each other feel better. In group, they can talk through their problems and maybe learn to avoid the behavior that brought them here in the first place."

Sue is also responsible, along with the other members of the staff, for maintaining a safe environment in her unit. "Things can get physical two or three times a shift," Sue says. "Often, I eat lunch on the fly. If there's a crisis, for example, if one of the patients begins to attack someone on the staff, or themselves, or one of the other patients, I have to be ready to help intervene. But a big part of my job is observing my patients, recognizing when things are going badly for them, figuring out where they are in an emotional cycle and at what point to intervene. I try to get to them before they turn violent, to talk it through, and help them resolve an emotional crisis themselves.

"It's part of what we call MAP, or Managing Aggressive Patients. By first recognizing anxiety and working with patients to create an alliance, we assist them in verbalizing their conflict instead of acting it out," Sue explains.

Despite the stressfulness of her work, Sue finds being a psychiatric technician very rewarding. "For me, it's exciting watching these kids grow, seeing the things that happen in the course of the day that make them feel better or worse about themselves. Although I've had many traumatic experiences here, I do have the reward of seeing a few people heal."

Do I Have What It Takes to Be a Psychiatric Technician?

Psychiatric technicians work with people who, because of their illnesses, may exhibit extreme forms of behavior. Often they may be unpleasant or disagreeable to work with, or even abusive to themselves and others. The job of psychiatric technicians requires them to work closely with these patients; compassion, sensitivity, and a strong motivation to help others are necessities. Sue Jones agrees. "I really care for my patients, and I love the work I do. It's very hard work, and I had to grow a lot to do it."

It's very hard work, and I had to grow a lot to do it.

Patience is often required on the job, especially with patients whose disabilities allow for only slow, often insubstantial, improvement. What may outwardly appear to be a minor event may, for these patients, be a major moment of progress. Through encouragement, empathy, and an awareness of the patient's condition, the psychiatric technician is instrumental in motivating patients to reach these accomplishments and encouraging them to continue. A keen sense of observation allows the psychiatric technician to recognize not only times of stress in the patient but also the activities, events, and situations that help the patient's condition. Being able to relate to their patients and to present their observations to the patients' psychiatric and medical doctors allows the psychiatric technician to function as an important bridge in the therapeutic process.

This field also requires physical prowess, if not strength. Restraining individuals who become violent can be a traumatic experience. "I've had to rescue one boy who tried to hang himself. Another girl tied her neck off with a strip of cloth she tore off her shirt. I've also had to interfere with a kid who reduced a room full of furniture to nails and boards," Sue says. "We diffuse situations like that as a team. We also process and debrief traumatic events as a team, and we'll discuss them informally with each other, too. Some of us have also had individual sessions to overcome traumatic events." But, at 5'6" and 125 pounds, Sue says that she is stronger than she looks. "I'm very active physically, anyway, and I've developed physically as a result of the job. And I know what I'm doing—I know when to ask for help. I would say that my strength is as much in my honesty and consistency as in my physical preparedness. I don't hesitate. And I don't bargain."

Sue finds the work very challenging. But there are frustrations too, Sue says. "Before we dispose—that is, transfer a patient to another facility—sometimes, the best we're able to achieve is to function as a sort of bandage. We have to work within the patient's insurance requirements," she explains, "which often means we can only provide the lowest level of care. Their insurance won't pay for anything more."

Sue's work as a psychiatric technician is never boring. "There's never a dull moment. I go in each morning knowing that I have to deal with what happens or has happened in the shift before, and that I will deal with it no matter what. I've amazed myself by doing this. I do what has to be done. It's the ultimate internship, and I have very little fear about the work I do."

How Do I Become a Psychiatric Technician?

The educational requirements for becoming a psychiatric technician can vary widely from state to state and from facility to facility. In some cases, no specialized schooling is required and training is given on the job. Elsewhere, a psychiatric technician may be required to have a two-year associate's degree or even a four-year bachelor's degree from a psychiatric technician program. These schools also feature clinical fieldwork in which a student participates in on-the-job training at a variety of facilities requiring psychiatric technicians. Sue Jones, for example, has continued her studies while working and expects to receive her bachelor's degree shortly. "It's because I'm still studying that I've received more and more responsibilities, and now I'm considered one of the senior staff in my unit," Sue says.

EDUCATION

High School

Students considering this field should plan to continue their education in either a two-year or four-year academic program. This will allow them greater growth in the field, increasing their responsibilities as they gain experience with corresponding increases in pay. While in high school, students should take on courses in psychology, biology and other natural sciences, and mathematics. Developing good communication skills is important, too, so taking English and other courses that will build strong written and verbal skills is highly recommended. Because a psychiatric technician becomes intimately involved in the lives of his or her patients, subjects that prepare you for human interaction, such as social sciences courses, peer counseling, and tutoring programs, will also be an asset as you begin your career.

"Looking back," Sue reflects, sighing, "I wish I had concentrated more on biology, because that is the basis of much of psychiatric work. But one course I had in high school really helped—government. We're part of a system here, and it's helped me to understand why certain things like the insurance system are the way they are. And I deal with a lot of governmental agencies on behalf of my patients. I think it's important to understand the structure of our society."

Postsecondary Training

For those students pursuing postsecondary education as a psychiatric technician, two-year programs

Lingo to Learn

Neurosis A mental and emotional disorder that affects only part of the personality. A neurosis does not disturb the use of language and is accompanied by various physical, physiological, and mental disturbances, the most usual being anxieties or phobias.

Obsessive-compulsive A neurosis that results in the patient's compulsion to carry out certain acts, no matter how odd or illogical or repetitive they are. This sort of neurosis is evident once the obsession or compulsive act interferes with normal life. For example, a person obsessed with cleanliness might take a dozen or more showers a day.

Paranoid schizophrenic The most common and destructive of the psychotic disorders, characterized by departure from reality, inability to think clearly, difficulty feeling and expressing emotions, and a retreat into a fantasy life.

Phobias An irrational or overblown fear that prevent a person from living a normal life.

Psychosis A more complete disintegration of personality and a loss of contact with the outside world than with neuroses.

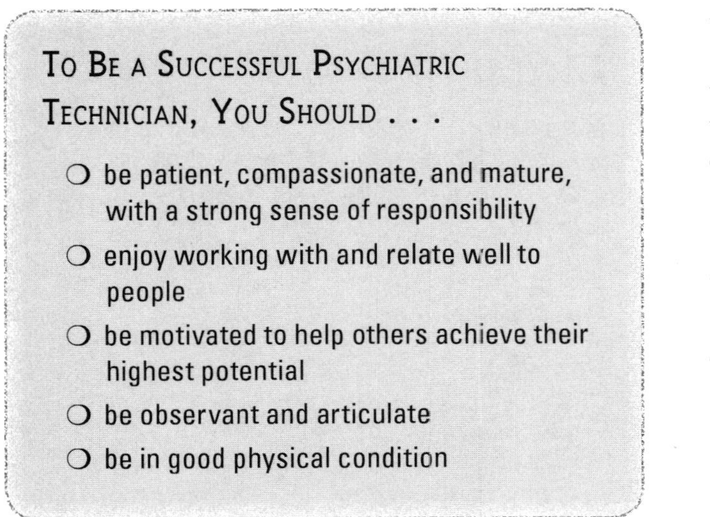

To Be a Successful Psychiatric Technician, You Should . . .

- be patient, compassionate, and mature, with a strong sense of responsibility
- enjoy working with and relate well to people
- be motivated to help others achieve their highest potential
- be observant and articulate
- be in good physical condition

leading to an associate's degree and four-year programs leading to a bachelor's degree will usually include courses in human development, personality structure, and the nature of mental illness; anatomy, physiology, and basic medical science; and training in nursing techniques. Social science courses give the prospective psychiatric technician understanding of family and community relationships, and programs will also offer an overview of the mental health and medical system.

An important element of all programs is the practical and clinical phase of study in which students receive training and experience in the actual work of psychiatric technicians. A student's field experience may comprise as much as one-third of his or her study program.

Other postsecondary courses a psychiatric technician can expect to take include English, psychology, sociology, and mental health-related courses, including early childhood development, general and abnormal psychology, classes in family and social welfare institutions, psychopathology, general nursing, community mental health, and techniques of therapy.

Apart from field experience, many programs offer training in interviewing and observation skills. Students may be trained in recognizing meanings behind certain tones of voice, in what people say and do, and ways of speaking and behaving. Because psychiatric technicians often administer psychological tests, students may also be trained in the proper administration of such tests, which are often in the form of questionnaires and have been designed to give health professionals insight into a patient's state of mind. Psychiatric technician students also receive training in crisis intervention, group counseling, behavior modification, child guidance, and family therapy, as well as training in consulting and working with the variety of agencies, both public and private, concerned with mental health and the public welfare.

Finally, prospective psychiatric technicians may also enter the field through military service. Military personnel may request, as part of their military service, secondary schooling as a hospital corpsman and choose to specialize as a psychiatric technician. The Navy, for example, offers a 15-week general course at a hospital corpsman school, followed by two six-week training periods in psychiatric technology. The first of these periods features course work; the second period is the clinical phase.

CERTIFICATION OR LICENSING

The American Association of Psychiatric Technicians (AAPT) offers four levels of national certification. According to the AAPT, first level certification is achieved by passing a comprehensive test, but requires no postsecondary training or practical experience. Level II requires 30 hours of college course work and one year of practical experience; Level III requires 60 college course credits, or an associate's degree, and two years of field experience. Level IV certification is available to psychiatric technicians with at least three years of experience and a bachelor's degree in psychiatric technology or a related psychology major. AAPT certification is voluntary, but it will probably be helpful when you seek your first job in the field. In addition, certification may make you eligible for increases in salary and responsibilities as you progress in your career (see "How Do I Learn More?").

Currently only four states—Arkansas, California, Colorado, and Kansas—require psychiatric technicians to be licensed. These four states also have various agreements regarding reciprocity. Licensing requirements may include completing specific amounts of classroom instruction and hands-on experience and passing a written test. Continuing education courses are usually required for license renewals.

INTERNSHIPS AND VOLUNTEERSHIPS

It is possible to find work in the field during high school, either part time or during the summer. Students may apply for positions as psychiatric aides, trainees, or orderlies or find work in housekeeping, maintenance, or administrative positions. These positions generally do not require formal education or training and are excellent opportunities for gaining experience and insight into the field.

Prospective psychiatric technicians may also gain practical experience by applying for jobs as a nurse's aide at a local hospital or clinic or participating in volunteer programs related to this field. Many schools also offer peer counseling experience, and schools with developmentally delayed students may have need of student volunteers or tutors. This kind of work will help you decide if the field is right for you.

In addition, volunteering in local mental health and community service organizations or working at playgrounds, swimming pools, and summer camps will help you gain both experience and insight into the field and the nature of the work involved.

Students interested in these opportunities should talk to their school guidance counselor or contact local hospitals and mental health clinics.

Who Will Hire Me?

Apart from state mental institutions and private psychiatric hospitals and clinics, there are a great many facilities that need skilled psychiatric technicians. For example, nursing homes, family service centers, public housing programs, public schools, prisons, and courts of law are all places that employ psychiatric technicians.

A growing number of psychiatric technicians are finding employment in the community, rather than in the hospital setting. The trend is toward treating psychiatric patients in the home or school, allowing them to continue to be a part of the community. A psychiatric technician may work in a school or participate in half-day programs where patients can receive therapy and specialized attention without disrupting their daily life. Psychiatric technicians specializing in patients with developmental disabilities may find employment in training centers devoted to teaching these patients job and life skills.

In addition, a growing number of psychiatric technicians are working as part of privately funded family stabilization teams. Much like social workers, these psychiatric technicians are assigned to specific patients and the family and are available to intervene in periods of difficulty or crisis, working with the entire family to resolve personal relationship issues, coordinate their access to community support services, such as welfare, medical treatment, and housing, and resolve financial and legal issues. This work involves visiting patients in their own homes and communities, where living and social conditions may vary widely. Many members of family stabilization teams are required to carry beepers and to be on call 24 hours a day. Their intervention can often make a great difference in resolving a situation before it reaches a crisis point.

Where Can I Go from Here?

For Sue Jones, her work is part of a career path that will eventually result in her receiving a Ph.D. in clinical psychology. "Although, looking back on it," she says, "if I had started early enough, I would have gone to medical school to become a psychiatrist."

Apart from gaining practical experience that will help in future studies, many aspiring psychologists and senior nursing staff find that their work as a psychiatric technician combines well with continued educational efforts, allowing them an opportunity to study, as well as to see in practice, many of the theoretical concepts included in their class work.

For psychiatric technicians, the increase in experience will lead to increased responsibilities and increased pay. With the proper experience, a psychiatric technician can also achieve positions with supervisory duties.

In general, continuing educational growth will greatly expand a psychiatric technician's advancement opportunities. A psychiatric technician may choose to enter other specialties in the psychiatric field, which may require more specialized training. With experience and education or additional training, psychiatric technicians may also choose to become instructors for other psychiatric technicians.

What Are the Salary Ranges?

Salary depends on a variety of factors, including geographical location, the type of facility, and the level of education and experience. The U.S. Department of Labor reports that psychiatric technicians earned a median hourly wage of $12.34 in 2003, which translates into about $25,667 a year, based on a 40-hour workweek. The lowest paid 10 percent earned less than $8.36 an hour ($17,390 a year), and the highest paid 10 percent earned more than $21.06 an hour ($43,805 a year). Technicians employed in

ADVANCEMENT POSSIBILITIES

Senior psychiatric technicians supervise and instruct junior psychiatric technicians, help coordinate schedules, and serve as the liaison between management and the technicians.

Psychiatric technician instructors work in hospitals and at technical schools to train psychiatric technicians. They may also teach certification courses.

Psychiatrists are physicians who treat patients with mental, emotional, and behavioral symptoms. They have completed all of the training required to become licensed medical doctors (M.D.'s) and then have taken additional training to specialize in psychiatry.

Psychologists teach, counsel, and work in research and administration to help understand people, their capacities, traits, and behavior and to explain their needs. They normally hold doctorates in psychology, but they are not medical doctors and cannot prescribe medication.

physicians' offices generally receive higher pay than those in institutional settings.

Most psychiatric technicians work a 40-hour week, which may include at least one weekend shift. Many psychiatric facilities require trained staff 24 hours a day, and psychiatric technicians may have their choice of day, evening, night, or weekend shifts. Fringe benefits often include health insurance, paid sick days, and paid vacations. Some state institutions and agencies may also grant financial assistance for continuing study.

What Is the Job Outlook?

The U.S. Department of Labor projects employment for psychiatric technicians to grow more slowly than the average through 2012. Demand for technicians, though, is expected to continue in large part because of a well-established trend of returning hospitalized patients to their communities after shorter and shorter periods of hospitalization. This trend has encouraged development of comprehensive community mental health centers and has led to a strong demand for psychiatric technicians to staff these facilities.

Concerns over rising health care costs should increase employment levels for technicians, because they and other paraprofessionals can take over some functions of higher paid professionals. This kind of substitution has been demonstrated to be an effective way of reducing costs without reducing quality of care.

How Do I Learn More?

PROFESSIONAL ORGANIZATIONS

The following are organizations that provide information on psychiatric technician careers, accredited schools and scholarships, and employers:

American Association of Psychiatric Technicians
2000 O Street, Suite 250
Sacramento, CA 95814
800-391-7589
aapt@psych-health.com
http://www.psychtechs.org

American Psychiatric Association
1000 Wilson Boulevard, Suite 1825
Arlington, VA 22209
703-907-7300
apa@psych.org
http://www.psych.org

Child Welfare League of America
Child Mental Health Program
440 First Street, NW, Third Floor
Washington, D.C. 20001-2085
202-638-2952
http://www.cwla.org/programs/bhd/mhdefault.htm

BIBLIOGRAPHY

The following is a sampling of materials relating to the professional concerns and development of psychiatric technicians:

Careers in Focus: Medical Technicians. 3d ed. New York: Facts On File, 2004.

McClelland, Lucille Hudlin. *Textbook for Psychiatric Technicians*. 2d ed. St Louis, Mo.: Mosby, 1971.

Sternberg, Robert J. *Career Paths in Psychology: Where Your Degree Can Take You*. Washington, D.C.: American Psychological Association, 1997.

QUALITY ASSURANCE TECHNICIANS

Definition
Quality assurance technicians evaluate a wide range of new or modified products to verify that they perform in accordance with company and legal specifications.

Alternative Job Titles
Quality assurance analysts
Quality assurance specialists
Quality control technicians or analysts

High School Subjects
Computer science
English
Speech

Personal Skills
Mechanical/manipulative
Technical/scientific

Salary Range
$38,800 to $55,011 to $79,755+

Minimum Educational Requirements
Associate's or bachelor's degree

Certification or Licensing
Voluntary

Outlook
Much faster than the average

DOT
033

GOE
08.02.03

NOC
2233

O*NET-SOC
51-9061.00

Stu played the same downhill ski computer game for several hours. He had become quite skilled at it, not "falling" at all. He was so good, in fact, he was getting bored. But he could not quit because he was actually at work in the quality assurance laboratory of a software company in Novato, California. Just then, a man walked into the lab and asked Stu what he thought about the game he was testing.

"I don't know why a company like ours would waste its time on such a boring game. This game first came out five years ago; who's going to buy it now? Look—the skier just goes from the left to the right, up and down, over and over again."

The man looked at Stu a moment and left, thanking him for the comments. When he was gone, a colleague leaned over and asked Stu, "Do you know who that was? That was the president of the company," he continued, "and probably the person who decided to sell that game you dislike so much."

Stu was initially embarrassed, but later, when he found out his company had discontinued work on the game, he remembered the unique privilege quality assurance technicians have in software companies. They are there, in part, to play, talk, and act like consumers.

What Does a Quality Assurance Technician Do?

Every product that comes out on the market has passed through either a quality assurance or quality control department or laboratory. Some products, such as clothes, may only need to be visually inspected for imperfections in sewing or sizing, while products that include a lot of different pieces, like games, might be counted or weighed. But products that are highly technical in nature, such as engines, computers, and software, usually require equally technical quality assurance tests. For example, engines are tested with diagnostic computers for which technicians must be specially trained.

Before being released in consumer markets, most products, especially computer products, are put through a series of quality assurance tests designed to anticipate and help solve problems that the user might encounter. *Quality assurance technicians* evaluate and test new or modified software programs to determine whether or not they perform according to designer specifications and user requirements. They also "test the tests," that is, they evaluate automated procedures used to verify that software programs function properly.

Some quality assurance technicians, like Stu, spend most of their time actually using the software applications, attempting to simulate the way in which the average consumer would use it. If it is a computer game, they play it over and over and over for hours, trying to make it crash. When the program

Lingo to Learn

Alpha testing The first formal testing of new hardware or software. Alpha testing is typically done by and within the company that is developing the product.

Application A software program that allows users to perform certain tasks, such as word processing, database record keeping, or spreadsheets.

Beta testing Hardware or software testing performed by a limited number of users under normal conditions. Beta testing occurs after in-house (alpha) testing.

Glitch A bug or problem with a computer program, hardware design, or software application.

Hardware The physical equipment inside a computer that makes it operate.

Software Programs or the logical sequence of commands making up a computer program.

Software development tools Special programs used to develop, analyze, debug, and perfect software.

crashes, or stops working, they fill out special forms explaining the combination of moves or commands that apparently made the program crash.

Each program or product arrives in the lab with a request for testing during a specified number of hours. After the quality assurance technicians have logged in those hours and have completed detailed performance reports and documentation, the program or software product is sent back to the programmer for revisions and corrections. Some technicians have direct contact with the programmers in order to describe the problems more accurately and advise about the ways in which they might go about solving the glitches. They might also make suggestions about how to make the program more user-friendly, efficient, exciting, or fun.

The trend in the computer industry is toward the development of automated quality assurance tests. Often times, even the automated tests require a "live" technician to administer and supervise them, as well as to interpret results and write reports explaining conclusions. Technicians in this area tell the computer which tests to run and verify that tests run properly by watching the computer monitor for interruption codes and breakdown signals. They run the results through special testing programs that verify their accuracy and reliability.

Some quality assurance technicians work with consumers who are experiencing specific problems with already-purchased software. They usually listen to the customer's complaint and try to identify exactly what sequence of commands led to the problem. Then they attempt to duplicate the problem in the lab in order to perform more in-depth tests on the program and eventually contact the programmers about correcting it.

Quality assurance technicians with solid work experience in the industry and some formal education in computer programming may work as *quality assurance analysts*. Analysts write and revise the quality standards or specifications for each software program. They also create the quality assurance tests that technicians use to verify that the program operates well, a task which involves computer programming. They evaluate proposals for future software developments, deciding whether or not the proposed project is capable of doing what it aims to do. As individuals most familiar with the performance of certain programs, they might become involved in training software users.

What Is It Like to Be a Quality Assurance Technician?

Stu Smeglane works for Broderbund Software, a company that sells a wide variety of computer software, from graphic printing packages to word processors to specialty games. As a high school student, he worked there full time during the summers, earning $11 an hour as an independent contractor. "Independent contractor translates as very good hourly wage, no benefits," says Stu. But, he explains, working a couple months as a "QA" person gives an individual a good taste of what it is like. "My mom always yelled at me when I was young for playing too many video games. Then, there I was, still in high school, making more money than anyone else in my family for doing just that!"

Some entry-level quality assurance work can be boring, according to Stu. Just before the holidays one year, for example, his company wanted to release a graphic software package that printed out holiday decorations like wreaths and candy canes. "For eight hours a day, I would stare at these things, trying to find even just the slightest imperfections."

The important thing to keep in mind, however, is that despite the boring tasks that a quality assurance technician may have to endure, this position is generally a gateway to bigger and better computer-related jobs. And this is especially helpful for individuals with little or no experience or formal education in computers. "Unless you have an ingenious idea that will make you a million dollars, you break into the industry any way you can," says Stu.

Stu's desk is one of several in a large, well-lit computer laboratory. Working with a computer screen eight hours a day may have detrimental effects on an individual's vision, though Stu has not yet personally experienced this. When he arrives in the morning, he checks in with his supervisor to see what program he is assigned for the day. Then, he takes it to his desk and starts playing. "We look for glitches," says Stu, "and pretty soon you get good at finding them." He tries all kinds of things, like typing very fast or clicking the mouse on the border of an icon instead of square on it. "It can be really fun to see how quickly you can make a program crash."

When Stu is successful in making a program crash, he reboots the system to see if he can reenact the crisis. "The idea is to isolate those moves or commands that were too much for the program to handle. I have to be able to write down in my report exactly what went wrong so that the programmer can locate the problem quickly and accurately." The bug sheets—forms technicians fill out when they find problems—must be clear, concise, neat, and detailed.

I have to be able to write down in my report exactly what went wrong so that the programmer can locate the problem quickly and accurately.

Sometimes, instead of testing programs that will definitely be sold by the company, the technicians test a whole group of games the company is considering buying for resale on the mass market. "I love playing games and imagining ways to make them better. Some games people come up with are downright stupid." This aspect of his job is very satisfying to Stu because his opinions and ideas have a lot to do with determining which products his company sells.

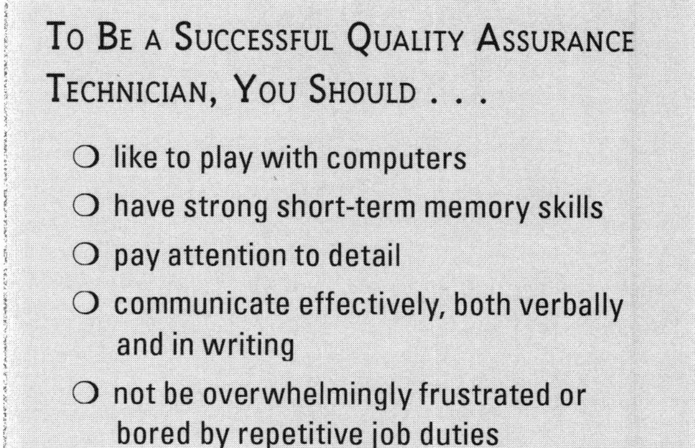
To Be a Successful Quality Assurance Technician, You Should . . .

- like to play with computers
- have strong short-term memory skills
- pay attention to detail
- communicate effectively, both verbally and in writing
- not be overwhelmingly frustrated or bored by repetitive job duties

Like most areas of business and industry, quality assurance is relying more and more on technological advancements. It is becoming a science and branch of engineering in its own right. Individuals with experience in it as well as formal education in computer science will have many opportunities in the years to come.

Do I Have What It Takes to Be a Quality Assurance Technician?

In the computer industry, most quality assurance tasks involve playing around on the computer, so individuals who dislike computers should stay away from this field. Although most labs set up quality assurance tests so that a technician need not have prior computer experience, it is helpful to have a basic understanding of how computers work. This foundational knowledge enables a technician to move swiftly through computer setups and program procedures. It also helps the technician identify more accurately the potential source of a particular problem as well as more clearly explain the problem in the report to the programmer.

Quality assurance technicians should also have strong short-term memory skills. "You can be playing along and then all of a sudden crash the game, and you have to be able to remember what you just did,

In-depth

Crash, Break, and Debug: Nice Work, If You Can Find It

At 16, Marcus Duerod went to work as a quality assurance play tester for Broderbund Software. His job? "To play all of the games Broderbund created, even break them, if necessary," Marcus says with a grin. "I had to test everything, try to find the bugs." He quickly advanced from play tester to regular tester. "The jobs were pretty much the same," he explains. "Except that instead of testing games, I tested productivity products, like Printshop."

Now, four years later, Marcus has already been promoted to the position of quality assurance technician and has worked on two wildly popular computer programs—the action-packed animated computer game, Prince of Persia, and KidPix Studio, a paint program that lets kids create movies and slide shows.

"In QA, we're like kids," Marcus says. "We get to break everything and complain about it all not working, but somebody else has to fix it. That's not our headache."

With his promotion, of course, came greater responsibilities. "As a technician, you're completely in charge of a product. When they assigned me the KidPix CD-ROM project, I had done a couple of updates to programs that had already been released," Marcus explains. "But, this was different. This was a new product with six different programs inside of it, including a slide show program and a digital puppets program. The older version didn't have as many features and was released on floppy. So, I was nervous."

Marcus describes the process involved in testing and evaluating a product like KidPix Studio. "The product manager—who's the liaison between the programmer and the QA tech—gives me the specs for the program, what it's supposed to do, along with a rough draft of the product's user manual, and an alpha version, or demonstration, of the product. This gives me the chance to see and use the product. Then, I review it and create a test plan. I write down any problems I find and what I'll need to test to make sure it works. Every game, every program is different," he stresses. "You have to cover anything that a normal, or not-so-normal, user would encounter. I submit the test plan to the product manager, who passes it along to programming. A week or two later, I get the program disks back from the programmer and then I supervise the testers who have been assigned to that product, using my test plan. Every week or so the product manager brings corrected disks back from programming and I make sure the bugs are really gone.

"The Kidpix project was really complicated, with a lot of content, like digitized sound and pictures. The biggest hassle was that it had to run on so many different computers. There were so many configurations and it had to work on all of them."

Marcus loves computers and has played with them since he was a kid. "We had a Commodore 64 when I was 12 or 13," Marcus says. "I used to mess around on it all the time with my brother." So, it comes as no surprise that he likes what he does, even considers himself lucky. "I love my job," Marcus says. "We're on the cutting edge of technology here.

"We always have the best computers and software. They're paying me to play with the newest, coolest stuff!"

And will the guy who is the first to play with all of the games begin creating them? "Actually, I'd like to move away from software into building and designing electronic devices," Marcus says. "I'm good with electronics." And, probably, a little tired of playing games.

even if you were in 'auto-pilot,'" explains Stu. The ability to pay close attention to detail is important for the same reason. Computer programming is a very precise science; a technician must be just as precise and detailed in his or her explanations of problems. "You can't say to a programmer, 'it kind of messes up when I do something like this.' You have to explain exactly what happens and what precipitates it, down to the last keystroke."

Since technicians have a lot of indirect and direct contact with programmers and marketing representatives, they should be able to communicate effectively, both verbally and in writing. And, given the amount of repetitive work, quality assurance technicians should not allow themselves to become overwhelmed, stressed, or frustrated by a certain degree of monotony in their job duties. "Even video games can get boring," cautions Stu.

In addition, good technicians are generally not the kind of people who get upset when things break. "After all that's our job—to make these things break down!" says Stu. Individuals who succeed in this field generally have their eye on professional advancement, keeping up with technological advances and pursuing formal education in a computer-related discipline.

How Do I Become a Quality Assurance Technician?

Stu found out about the opening at Broderbund through a friend. "A lot of jobs in the computer industry are made known by word of mouth," says Stu. Initially hired as an independent contractor, Stu maintained contact with his supervisor even during periods in which he did not work. He was called back for several summers and various special projects throughout the year and was offered a full-time job upon graduation.

EDUCATION

High School

For most temporary or independent contracting jobs as quality assurance technicians, a high school diploma is not required. In fact, some technicians, like Stu, are still in high school when they obtain their first job in this field.

However, a high school diploma is required for most full-time positions in the computer industry as a whole. There are always exceptions, of course, for those computer geniuses who come up with a software idea on their own and make millions on it (one of Stu's high school classmates did this at age 17, while still a senior), but most individuals interested in a career in a computer-related field should at least finish high school.

Any high school course on computers, whether programming, operating, or fundamentals, provides a solid background in computer basics that is valuable for quality assurance technicians. An academic background in computers is not necessary for all quality assurance technician jobs, however. This is because a company may want to hire people with computer skills comparable to those held by their customers, who may have no prior experience at all.

Math and science classes, especially those that incorporate the use of flowcharts, are also good preparation. English and speech courses give students multiple opportunities to improve both written and verbal communication skills.

Postsecondary Training

Entry-level jobs in quality assurance require no formal education beyond high school. Many companies have in-house training programs for new employees and, depending upon the nature of the testing to be done, some allow trainees to learn through hands-on experience.

Since most quality assurance technicians envision eventual promotion, however, postsecondary education is a good idea for anyone interested in this field. Many technical and vocational schools offer a wide range of courses in computer-related technologies leading to a two-year associate's degree in computer engineering technology, for example. The curricula often include courses in hardware construction and design, software programming basics, network administration, single and multi-board microcomputing, and other basics in computer science. Since the thrust of the industry is toward the automation of quality assurance tests, individuals interested in this field should pursue at least an associate's degree in order to distinguish themselves from colleagues in case staffing cuts are made due to automation. As technicians learn the processes by which programs are written, tested, and revised, they tend quite naturally to become interested in increasing their involvement with projects. Some formal education is a helpful stepping-stone in this pursuit.

FYI

If you are good with words and computer programs, you may be able to combine these skills in a career as a freelance writer. Computer magazines such as *PC Computing* regularly feature articles on software development and columns on fixing bugs.

Another option for a quality assurance technician is to complete a bachelor's or advanced degree in computer science or computer-related discipline. The field of quality assurance engineering is an up-and-coming field. Who better to work on test design and product development than those technicians most familiar with how quality assurance tests perform in the lab? College classes in computer science can be rigorous and competitive, but they definitely pay off in the professional long run. As competition in the industry continues to grow, a university education becomes more and more important during job hunting.

CERTIFICATION OR LICENSING

As the information technology industry becomes more competitive, the necessity for management to be able to distinguish professional and skilled individuals in the field becomes mandatory, according to the Quality Assurance Institute. Certification demonstrates a level of understanding in carrying out relevant principles and practices, as well as providing a common ground for communication among professionals in the field of software quality. The organization offers certification programs in certified quality analyst, certified software test engineer, and certified SPICE assessor.

SCHOLARSHIPS AND GRANTS

Since no formal education or training is required of quality assurance technicians, there are currently no scholarships or grants reserved exclusively for individuals seeking careers in this area.

Technical school or university students should work closely with their school's financial aid office in order to obtain information about possible sources of financial awards. These offices usually maintain a complete list of available scholarships and grants and a profile of the requirements of each. They should be contacted directly.

In addition, if an individual is currently employed and wants to pursue a degree in a computer-related field that may benefit the employer directly, he or she may be eligible for any tuition reimbursement programs the company offers. Interested employees should contact their company's personnel or benefits office.

INTERNSHIPS AND VOLUNTEERSHIPS

Since it is an entry-level position, and since many people are hired on an independent contractor basis, there are very few internships in this area. An independent contractor is an individual who is hired for a specific amount of time or to complete a specific job or set of tasks within a time limit agreed to by the employer and the contractor. Independent contractors are usually paid relatively well, but they do not receive any benefits and are responsible for paying their own taxes since no taxes are withheld from their earnings. Many computer companies offer summer jobs to students or other individuals as independent contractors. School placement offices usually maintain information about these kinds of opportunities. Local newspapers, computer trade magazines, and computer professionals are also good job hunting sources.

Who Will Hire Me?

Many quality assurance technicians work for hardware or software development companies that have numerous permanent, full-time positions in quality assurance.

Computer companies tend to be clustered in the same geographical area, like the Silicon Valley between San Francisco and San Jose in Northern California, for example. There, computer companies open and close seemingly overnight; it is not at all uncommon for a company to be created in order to develop just one product. If the product fails on the market or even before it gets to market, the company folds. For the period of time the "start-ups" stay open, however, they may hire quality assurance technicians to evaluate and test their products on an independent contracting basis.

Some of these jobs are advertised in computer trade magazines, such as *Computerworld, PC Computing, PC World,* and *Macworld*. But they might also be publicized by word of mouth. A friend told Stu about the job in quality assurance at Broderbund that he eventually obtained. Professional networking in the computer industry is very important; an interested individual should stay in contact with as many computer professionals as he or she can. Otherwise, close attention must be paid to newspaper and magazine advertisements.

As quality assurance grows in stature, service companies designed only to provide quality assurance evaluation to product manufacturers and developers are also increasing in number. Currently, these firms are mostly found in those areas where computer companies are clustered. Interested individuals should consult a local telephone directory to determine if such companies exist in their area.

General consulting companies, particularly those specializing in computer system integration or analysis, might also hire quality assurance technicians. Many large corporations like insurance companies and banks are beginning to investigate ways to automate forms and other kinds of paperwork. Much of this development work is being subcontracted to outside computer programmers, but some is being performed in-house. People interested in quality assurance should check with any major employers in the area to see if they are hiring quality assurance technicians. The further away an individual goes from a full-fledged computer company, however, the harder it will be for him or her to move up the ranks of the computer industry's hierarchy.

Where Can I Go from Here?

Stu is currently pursuing a bachelor's degree in computer engineering. He hopes eventually to go into software design and programming, but is also thinking about computer management. "There are basically two roads to take—the technical one or the management one. And they both require more school."

If a quality assurance technician wants to stay deeply involved in the technical side of operations, he or she will eventually have to decide what area of computer technology is the most appealing—quality assurance, software or hardware engineering, networks, systems—the list could go on and on.

After some experience and maybe even some formal education, a technician is a good candidate for promotion to a supervisory position. Such a position would involve a few administrative duties, such as schedule writing and assignment distribution. But supervisory positions also involve more complex and interesting technical duties. "The supervisor always saves the best jobs for himself or herself. The last supervisor I had played a very popular video game for three weeks straight," says Stu, shaking his head. Supervisors also have greater responsibility than technicians in terms of report and technical writing and meetings with the programmers.

Positions above those in quality assurance supervision require more education (probably at least a bachelor's degree), more experience, and more definite goals. In the technical track, supervisors can be promoted to quality assurance or software engineering positions. They may also be promoted to programming positions.

Those who wish to focus mainly on the managerial side of operations might go into product sales. Technicians are particularly well suited for sales since they are extremely familiar with the products they have tested. They might also go into marketing or low-level and middle management. Many of these positions require formal education after a certain point. Education requirements vary with the company and with the potential, expertise, and experience of the individual.

What Are the Salary Ranges?

A quality assurance technician working as an independent contractor typically earns between $9 and $15 an hour. The exact hourly range is generally dependent on the individual's work history, the proposed length of employment, and the level of technical difficulty incorporated into the specific tests to be run.

A review by Salary.com of earnings nationwide found that in 2005 full-time, entry-level quality assurance specialists earned between $38,800 and $49,379 with a median of $43,502 annually. Those with bachelor's degrees who have worked in the industry for less than 10 years reported earnings between $46,369

ADVANCEMENT POSSIBILITIES

Quality assurance supervisors assign testing projects to the quality assurance technicians. They also do quality assurance testing themselves but may tend to work with more complicated procedures or interesting products. They have more report-writing responsibilities and work more closely with computer programmers, who try to correct product glitches by revising the programs.

Quality assurance engineers are members of a growing field. Currently, the computer industry is pushing for automated quality assurance tests that would not necessarily require a technician to run them. Quality assurance engineers are working in part on such large-scale projects. These engineers work on quality assurance test design, methods of interpreting test results and correcting diagnosed problems, and on writing specification manuals and technical sheets.

Software engineers analyze industrial, business, and scientific problems and conceive software programs that can provide solutions to them. They meet with clients to determine the specific nature of the problem, give presentations of software proposals and demonstrations of finished products, and consult with other engineers in the regular course of their work.

and $57,581 per year. Salaryexpert.com reports annual earnings nationwide for quality assurance coordinators ranged from $44,097 to $79,755 with median earnings of $55,011. Testers also generally receive a full benefits package as well, including health insurance, paid vacation, and sick leave.

Technicians promoted to supervisory positions can expect to make several thousand dollars more annually. *Computerworld*'s salary survey reported that quality assurance managers could expect annual earnings between $64,750 and $86,750 in 2005. Salaries also increase dramatically as a technician completes higher levels of education. Those with an associate's degree in a computer-related discipline and who are promoted from a technician position make more than their nondegreed counterparts.

What Is the Job Outlook?

The U.S. Department of Labor projects that the number of positions in quality assurance is expected to grow at a rate much faster than the average through 2012. According to the 2005 *Computerworld* survey, quality assurance professionals are in great demand and job opportunities are among the fastest growing in the information technology industry. One reason for this is somewhat complicated but important to understand. Many computer products on the market are basically replicas of one another; they perform the same function but under a different brand name. Thus, there are many word processors available, all of which work reasonably well. Where before a computer company could distinguish itself by introducing a one-of-a-kind product, like spreadsheet software, it no longer can.

Many computer companies are taking a different approach in order to distinguish their products from the competition. Simply put, they aim to offer higher performance levels and better technical support, including user training, than anyone else. This market trend translates into a boom for quality assurance. It is now crucial that products be near perfect before they are put on the market and quality assurance is responsible for just that.

This situation also helps explain why quality assurance is being treated more and more as a science. Companies want the most accurate, most efficient, and most financially feasible ways to test their products. This means, of course, increased automation; so quality assurance technicians should prepare themselves for the future by becoming educated and experienced in software design and programming. In this way, they can be the ones creating the tests that, as technicians, they only run.

Like any industry, the availability of jobs depends on current sales. Quality assurance jobs in insurance companies and financial institutions are good bets since those industries are overhauling their systems for managing and processing forms.

As for computer companies, the more money they earmark for research and development of new or modified products, the more jobs there will be in quality assurance. But in the computer industry, economic indicators of this type are always relative; start-up companies, each hoping to be the pioneer in an unexplored market niche, continue to be established every day.

How Do I Learn More?

PROFESSIONAL ORGANIZATIONS

The following are organizations that provide information on quality assurance careers, accredited schools, certification, and employers:

IEEE Computer Society
1730 Massachusetts Avenue, NW
Washington DC 20036-1992
202-371-0101
http://www.ieee.org

National Committee for Quality Assurance
2000 L Street, NW, Suite 500
Washington, DC 20036
202-955-3500
http://www.ncqa.org

Quality Assurance Institute
Windsor at Metro Center
2102 Park Center Drive, Suite 200
Orlando, FL 32835-7614
407-363-1111
http://www.qaiusa.com

BIBLIOGRAPHY

The following is a sampling of materials relating to the professional concerns and development of quality assurance technicians:

Benbaw, Donald W. et al. *The Certified Quality Technician Handbook*. Milwaukee: ASQ Quality Press, 2003.

Careers in Focus: Manufacturing. 2d ed. Chicago: Ferguson Publishing Company, 2002.

Evans, James R., and William M. Lindsay. *Management and the Control of Quality*, 5th ed. Cincinnati: South-Western College Publishing, 2001.

Griffith, Gary K. *The Quality Technician's Handbook*. 5th ed. Upper Saddle River, N.J.: Prentice Hall, 2002.

QUALITY CONTROL TECHNICIANS

Definition
: Quality control technicians inspect products and processes, conduct tests, and collect data to ensure that products and processes conform to quality standards.

Alternative Job Titles
Quality control inspectors
Quality engineering technicians
Quality inspectors
Quality technicians

High School Subjects
Chemistry
Mathematics
Physics

Personal Skills
Mechanical/manipulative
Technical/scientific

Salary Range
$17,200 to $28,200 to $50,500+

Minimum Educational Requirements
Some postsecondary training recommended

Certification or Licensing
Voluntary

Outlook
More slowly than the average

DOT
012

GOE
N/A

NOC
2261

O*NET-SOC
N/A

Wearing goggles, rubber gloves, and a protective apron, Donna Batsch looks ready to enter a biohazard zone, but instead she is mixing a bleach solution to test some sweater yarns for fiber content. She cuts a small piece of yarn and weighs it on a scale to determine the number of grams. Donna then places the yarn on a watch plate and puts it in the incubator for 30 minutes to dry. When she takes the yarn out, she weighs it again and makes a note of the dry weight. She drops the yarn into the bleach solution, removes it, and places it back into the incubator. Donna rinses the yarn, dries it again, and weighs it. The yarn is supposed to be 100 percent wool, and the bleach solution should have dissolved all the wool, but a percentage remains, which means the yarn is not 100 percent wool. The supplier of the yarn had made an error. Without quality control and technicians like Donna, thousands of mislabeled sweaters could have been produced and sold, potentially costing the company money and its reputation.

What Does a Quality Control Technician Do?

Quality control technicians test and inspect products and processes to make sure they meet clearly defined standards. They use various tools, including computers, gauges, analytical devices, and testing instruments, to monitor and perform the tests and record the outcomes. Quality control technicians determine whether the test results conform to requirements and produce reports with the findings and recommendations. They work primarily in manufacturing industries but can work in any industry or department where quality must be measured and recorded. For instance, quality control technicians may have played a role in making sure the pants you are wearing are of durable, high-quality fabric. They may also have conducted tests on the components in your home computer to ensure they will function up to the manufacturer's standards. Quality control technicians probably analyzed and tested the ingredients in the juice you drank for breakfast to guarantee adherence to regulations and approved standards.

Quality control technicians can be involved at each stage of the manufacturing or production process. They may test individual components or materials from suppliers or inspect finished products to determine whether they meet standards. Checking for quality can take the form of a quick visual inspection or a detailed analysis that might involve elaborate processes and highly technical equipment. Technicians may also be responsible for setting up test equipment or calibrating instruments to make sure they measure and record accurately.

The work of quality control technicians can range from inspection and testing to supervision and training of inspectors; their work may also involve statistical analysis and reporting of test and experiment results or meeting with clients. Although test standards and procedures are well defined, quality control technicians are often called upon to use their judgment and expertise in evaluating, analyzing, and interpreting results.

In the manufacturing industry, quality control is closely related to quality assurance. While quality control focuses on the operational techniques and regulatory processes used to measure actual quality and compare this with the standards, quality assurance deals more with the overall processes of quality systems. Quality assurance involves the planned order of events that extends throughout the life cycle of a product. These events are designed to demonstrate whether quality requirements will be fulfilled. For example, in a food processing company, quality control might be responsible for inspecting and testing the vegetable shortening that will be used to make crackers. Technicians will analyze the content of the shortening to make sure it conforms to the standards: Does it have the correct percentage of soybean oil and the prescribed amount of canola oil? Is the quality acceptable? Quality assurance, on the other hand, is concerned with the entire process of producing the crackers, from the acquisition of ingredients to the production line to the packaging. Is each step efficient, or is there room for improvement? Are all of the quality requirements fulfilled?

The job of a quality control technician is similar to that of an *inspector*. Although the terms may sometimes be used interchangeably, quality control technicians usually handle more complex procedures. They may make decisions regarding the types of tests to conduct, write inspection and test procedures, and analyze processes. Inspectors, on the other hand, may be involved primarily with monitoring the quality standards of individual components or products. Their tasks may not include interpretation or analysis of test results.

Quality control technicians work in a variety of environments and conditions. They may be employed in laboratories and wear lab coats, or they may work in factories and wear hard hats. Technicians might work outdoors and travel from location to location, or they may remain indoors at one workstation for an entire day.

What Is It Like to Be a Quality Control Technician?

Donna Batsch is a senior lab technician for Jantzen Incorporated, a sportswear manufacturer in Portland, Oregon. Donna is responsible for performing a variety of tests on fabrics to make sure they conform to the standards set by Jantzen. She may test for color fastness, fabric strength or stretch, shrinkage, flammability, or fiber content, just to name a few. All of the test methods are from ASTM International (formerly the American Society for Testing and Materials) and the American Association of Textile Colorists and Chemists (AATCC).

Donna gets to work as early as 6 A.M. She and the other lab technicians work in a controlled laboratory environment where the temperature is always 70 degrees Fahrenheit and 65 percent humidity. After putting on a vest to protect her clothes, she unloads fabrics from machines that have been running overnight then gets ready to make up batches of testing solutions. Jantzen works with four main solutions: seawater, chlorinated pool water, acid perspiration solution, and clear, or deionized, water.

Lingo to Learn

Control A device or object used as a standard of comparison in judging the results of a test or experiment.

Mean, mode, median Different ways to calculate averages.

Metrology The science of weights and measures.

Process capability The degree to which the output of a process meets specification requirements.

Sampling The process or technique of selecting a representative part from a larger group.

Standard deviation The measure of variation from the norm.

Statistical process control The use of statistical methods to efficiently manage processes.

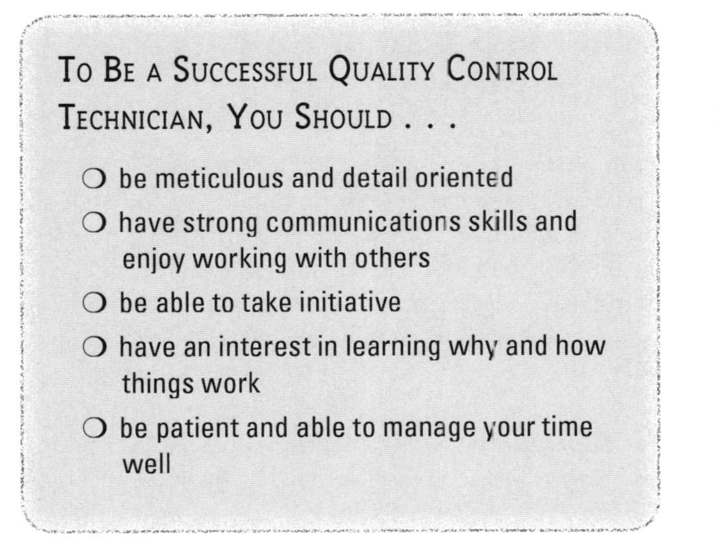

To Be a Successful Quality Control Technician, You Should . . .

- be meticulous and detail oriented
- have strong communications skills and enjoy working with others
- be able to take initiative
- have an interest in learning why and how things work
- be patient and able to manage your time well

Occasionally, Donna will have special testing requests to carry out. Today, she performs seam slippage and tensile strength tests on fabric that will be used to make backpacks. Tensile strength refers to the most longitudinal stress that can be placed on the fabric before it tears. After sewing up seams on samples of fabric, Donna uses a special machine equipped with pneumatic grips that hold the fabric then pull it apart. "First of all you tear the seam until it breaks," she explains, "and then you turn it around and pull the fabric until it breaks, and then the computer measures if there is a gap of a quarter inch. That might indicate that there might be a slippage problem." With backpack fabric, slippage is not an issue, but Donna is still required to perform the testing and keep detailed records of each test she runs along with the results.

Jantzen is probably most well known for its swimwear, and Donna often tests swimwear fabric to make sure the colors do not fade in chlorine or sunlight, the fabric will not droop when you get the swimsuit wet, and the seams will not tear when you are diving from the high board. The pool water test is used to determine how color will hold up to the chlorine. "It doesn't show how the fabric will hold up to the chlorine. It just shows how the color will hold up," Donna says. "And all the bright, pretty neon colors don't always hold up as well." Donna mixes up a solution using clear water (for consistency), a bit of chlorine, and pool acid, a blend of acidic acid and hardness concentrate used to standardize the test. After testing the solution for the correct pH and chlorine content, Donna pours some of the solution into a specialized dry-cleaning machine, which is basically a stainless steel can, along with a five-gram load of test fabric. Donna also includes a control piece. "All of our loads contain a control piece so that when everything is said and done, and the control is dry, we can compare it to our standards and know if the solution was done correctly."

After the swimwear fabric tumbles in the solution for 45 minutes, Donna runs the fabric through a wringer, rinses it in clear water, wrings it again, then dries the fabric on paper towels. Donna must complete a report on each fabric. Each report lists all the test methods and results, such as the shrinkage results and the ratings for color fastness. All of the information is then entered into a computer network database so that managers, designers, production personnel, and others needing access to the information will have it readily available.

Do I Have What It Takes to Be a Quality Control Technician?

If you are interested in becoming a quality control technician, you must be attentive, conscientious, and extremely detail oriented. Quality control is all about accuracy; if one element of the test is off, all the results might have to be discarded. You must, therefore, be able to follow directions and carry them out with precision. You should also have good communication skills and work well with others—you may work in a small laboratory with other technicians, you might have to report to management, or you may be the one to break the news to a supplier or department when something does not meet standards.

Donna adds, "You need to be able to organize your time, and you need to be able to see what needs to be done and just do it." Initiative is important, and so is patience. And although quality control may involve repetitive tasks, Donna does not consider this a drawback. "Even though we're doing the same things over and over, it's still different because we're seeing so many different fabrics," she says. "There's always something different." Donna also enjoys the technical aspect of being a quality control technician, though she stresses that she does not believe technical skills are mandatory for the job.

At Jantzen, quality control technicians work a 40-hour workweek. There might be an occasional rush job, but Donna rarely has to work late. Aside from sewing and cleaning up when something ignites

A quality control technician inspects the lasting power of fluorescent light bulbs. *(Volker Steger / Siemens / Photo Researchers Inc.)*

during a flammability test, there is not much Donna does not like about her job.

Donna has a need for things to be right, and she believes this helps her in her job. "I've been told that I'm a little tough on some of my ratings," Donna notes, "but the way I feel is, I'd rather be a little tough than not tough enough and have a problem down the line."

How Do I Become a Quality Control Technician?

Donna had been working in the sewing factory at Jantzen when she learned about the opening in quality control. "I really didn't want to sew anymore," she recalls. "It was piecework, and I was more interested in making sure I had good quality, so I could never make any money. I had good quality, and that's why they tolerated my slowness!"

EDUCATION

High School

If you are interested in quality control work, mathematics will come in handy. There are many calculations, percentages, and statistics involved in quality control, so you need to be comfortable with mathematical operations. Algebra and geometry are both good choices.

Sciences are also helpful, and although the particular discipline you should study may depend

In-depth

Quality Assurance versus Quality Control

Although quality assurance is a term used throughout every industry, most people relate the term to the computer software business or high-tech industries. Quality assurance technicians and quality control technicians may have similar titles, but their job responsibilities differ. In general, quality control technicians spend time testing products to make sure they meet specified standards.

If they don't pass the slew of tests, the products are returned. Quality control technicians can work in any industry, but they are predominantly employed in the realm of manufacturing.

Quality assurance technicians test computer software applications to determine whether or not they perform at the desired level. Like the quality control technician, quality assurance technicians test products to make sure they are of high quality and meet standards. Unlike quality control technicians, however, quality assurance technicians try to break or crash computer programs to find every possible bug or error in the application. They must test the same program repeatedly, searching for problems so that it will run perfectly by the time it reaches the consumer.

on the industry you enter, both physics and chemistry will benefit you. The lab work involved with science classes is especially helpful—you will learn how to follow instructions, complete individual steps, and record data and report your findings, which are all things quality control technicians do on a daily basis. Donna deals with acids and hazardous substances at times, and chemistry is involved with the mixing of solutions. She enjoys working with chemicals, especially for fiber analysis. One chemical will dissolve one type of fiber, while another chemical may eliminate another type of fiber. "To me that's very fascinating," Donna says. "It makes me regret that I never took chemistry."

If you have an idea of the industry you are interested in, it would be a good idea to take some relevant classes. For example, if you are interested in entering the textile industry, you may wish to take some home economics classes to gain an understanding of fabrics and clothing construction. If you think you may enter the aviation field, you need some knowledge about flying and aviation equipment and instruments, so joining an aviation club or taking some flying lessons might help. If agriculture is your niche, you should take some agriculture classes and join the Future Farmers of America or similar organizations.

Postsecondary Training

Donna received all of her training on the job and does not have a college degree. Her fellow technicians also received in-house training. College requirements generally vary from employer to employer and may depend on the industry. For instance, if you plan to work in quality control at a biomedical engineering firm, you may be required to have completed college courses in biology or microbiology. Unless you select a highly specialized field, however, a college degree is ordinarily not mandatory.

It never hurts to undergo some formal training, and a college degree may provide you with an advantage when you are looking for a job. A two-year program at a community college or technical school can give you a solid background and knowledge that you can apply to quality control. Some schools may offer certificate programs or associate's degrees in quality control. If a quality control program is not available, however, classes in statistics or mathematics should be helpful. You may also want to seek out classes such as metrology and calibration, data analysis, quality costs, probability theory, and sampling techniques.

CERTIFICATION OR LICENSING

Certification is not mandatory to be a quality control technician, but some employers may list certification as a job requirement. The American

Society for Quality (ASQ) offers a certification program for Certified Quality Technicians. A combination of work experience and education is necessary before the candidate is allowed to sit for the written examination. Knowledge of quality control concepts and techniques, fundamentals of practical statistical methods, sampling principles, quality data analysis, and problem solving are a few of the topics covered.

ASQ frequently offers preparatory courses for those interested in becoming certified. Some community colleges and technical schools may offer classes or programs to prepare students for certification as well. For instance, Clackamas Community College in Oregon City, Oregon, has a quality control technician program designed to help students working full time in the quality field prepare for the ASQ certification exam. Students who earn 45 credits in the program will also earn a certificate. With three years of full-time work experience and the certificate, students are qualified to take the certification examination.

SCHOLARSHIPS AND GRANTS

For scholarship opportunities, contact the financial aid office of your school for information. Because quality control is a specialized field and there are few programs dedicated solely to quality control, your best bet may be to find general scholarship opportunities. Professional organizations such as ASQ may be able to provide you with lists of scholarships and financial awards, although the scholarships may be geared more toward students seeking a bachelor's degree in engineering or management.

INTERNSHIPS AND VOLUNTEERSHIPS

Large manufacturers often offer internship opportunities. These may not specifically be in the quality control department, but that does not mean you should discount them. Some internships may take place in several departments, and if you voice your interest in quality control and show promise and initiative, chances are the quality control department will be eager to bring you on board. Jantzen frequently employs interns, and although the lab has not had any interns in the past, Donna has expressed a desire for an intern to join the quality control team.

Who Will Hire Me?

Donna applied for a technician position in the laboratory at Jantzen more than nine years ago. "When I started, I was in the sewing factory," she recalls. "The job in the lab opened up, and it was a part-time position. I had just had a baby and decided that I only wanted to work part time. So I applied for it, thinking they would never hire me because I'm just a sewing machine operator, and lo and behold, they did." Donna went to full time after a year and a half, and she has been there ever since.

Opportunities for quality control technicians exist in all areas of business and industry. You should be able to find positions in the health care industry, the food production field, the textile industry, computer manufacturing, the automotive industry, and more.

Conventional methods for locating job opportunities should work when you are seeking employment as a quality control technician. Newspaper classified ads, employment agencies, and trade publications are all excellent sources for finding open positions. Searching on the Internet is also a good resource for finding jobs and for researching specific industries or companies you are interested in. Many companies post current job listings with online employment databases and also on company Web sites. Professional organizations such as ASQ generally offer employment assistance and job listing services to members.

Word of mouth is always an excellent method for learning about job opportunities. Stay active in local business organizations or clubs to establish connections and to learn about hiring trends. If you are a student, your school's placement office may be of assistance. The office may host job fairs or provide you with lists of open positions.

If you have a good idea of the industry in which you would like to work, you may wish to write directly to employers in that industry to find out about job possibilities. You can also try to contact the quality control department directly and request an informational interview, which is designed for you to find out more about the company and the duties of the quality control department. This may provide you with some insight as to whether you would be a good fit with the company, and it also gives the quality control department a chance to get an impression of your qualifications and your level of interest. If an opportunity happens to arise at a

Advancement Possibilities

Quality managers or quality supervisors oversee the operation of quality control departments and supervise quality control technicians. They plan, coordinate, and direct quality control programs, working with other departments and management.

Quality engineers design, apply, and maintain quality systems and standards for industrial processes, materials, and products.

later point, the company may contact you if you left a positive impression.

Where Can I Go from Here?

Donna does not foresee any big changes in her future. "Actually," she says, "I'm very comfortable where I am. The people I work with, we all get along very well. It's like a little family." She enjoys her work and has no desire to change. Donna supposes that the natural progression within the company would be to an administrative position, such as manager of quality control, which is the position her boss holds, but she prefers to stay in the lab. "It's not a position I'm interested in," she explains matter-of-factly, "because his level of stress is a lot higher than mine." The manager of quality control supervises the department and acts as the liaison between the technicians and other departments and clients.

As quality control technicians gain more experience, they may become responsible for more complicated or more technical tasks. They may also specialize. For instance, Donna generally assumes the tasks of rating color shades, though she attributes this to the need for consistency rather than her years of experience. Donna is also the only technician who is certified to work with hazardous chemicals and wear a respirator.

With a bachelor's degree, quality control technicians can also become quality engineers. Quality engineers are involved with designing quality systems and processes. They plan and direct activities concerned with the development, application, and maintenance of quality standards. Statistical experiments and evaluations may be part of a quality engineer's duties.

What Are the Salary Ranges?

Salaries of quality control technicians depend on many variables, including the industry, level of experience, and education. In higher-paying industries such as the high-tech industry, quality control technicians can expect to earn more.

According to the U.S. Department of Labor Occupational Information Network, the median annual earnings of inspectors, testers, and graders were $28,200 in 2003. The job of a quality control technician is generally considered to be a more advanced position, but job duties are sometimes interchangeable. The lowest paid 10 percent of inspectors, testers, and graders earned $17,200, while the highest paid 10 percent made $50,500.

A 2005 survey by Salary.com of earnings nationwide for entry-level quality control inspectors found salaries ranged from $25,636 to $32,919. Senior-level inspectors with at least five years of experience earned between $37,777 and $46,795.

Most companies offer benefits that include paid vacations, paid holidays, and health insurance. Actual benefits depend upon the company, but may also include pension plans, profit sharing, 401(k) plans, and tuition assistance programs.

What Is the Job Outlook?

The U.S. Department of Labor predicts slower than average growth in employment through 2012 for this field. But the job outlook for quality control technicians depends in large part on the industry in which the technician is employed. While some manufacturing sectors may experience slow growth, others, such as high-tech industries, will continue to grow rapidly. As the emphasis on total quality management and quality control grows and becomes more integrated into the production processes of manufacturing companies, a need for experienced quality control technicians should increase.

Donna feels confident that the job outlook is positive. "My feeling is that it looks pretty good," she notes. "I think people are foolish not to have quality control because there are so many problems that can arise, and you really have no way of knowing that unless you have done some testing." The lab at Jantzen has grown from a one-person operation to a staff of more than three, which indicates that there is plenty of work to keep the lab busy. Donna knows that some of the fabric vendors have started building small in-house labs to test fabrics before they are sent to Jantzen. This saves the vendor from having fabric returned if it does not meet specifications. Qualified technicians will be needed to fill openings in these small labs.

The *Occupational Outlook Handbook* notes that an emphasis on quality will continue to grow. Companies will become more automated and implement systematic approaches to quality inspection. While this may eliminate some positions for inspectors, technicians will be needed to maintain the equipment and oversee the processes. Also, companies will integrate quality control systems into production processes, and technicians will be in demand to monitor and implement procedures. The best employment opportunities will be for those with experience and advanced skills.

How Do I Learn More?

PROFESSIONAL ORGANIZATIONS

The following organizations provide information on quality control technician careers, certification, employers, and schools:

American Society for Quality
PO Box 3005
600 North Planakinton Avenue
Milwaukee, WI 53203-3005
800-248-1946
http://www.asq.org

Association for Quality and Participation
PO Box 2055
Milwaukee, WI 532201-2055
800-733-3310
aqp@aqp.org
http://www.asq.org

ASTM International
100 Barr Harbor Drive
PO Box C700
West Conshohocken, PA 19428-2959
610-832-9585
http://www.astm.org

BIBLIOGRAPHY

The following is a sampling of materials relating to the professional concerns and development of quality control technicians:

Benbow, Donald W. et al. *The Certified Quality Techncian Handbook*. Milwaukee: ASQ Quality Press, 2003.

Careers in Focus: Manufacturing. 2d ed. Chicago: Ferguson Publishing Company, 2002.

Evans, James R., and William M. Lindsay. *Management and the Control of Quality*, 5th ed. Cincinnati: South-Western College Publishing, 2001.

Griffith, Gary K. *The Quality Technician's Handbook*. 5th ed. Upper Saddle River, N.J.: Prentice Hall, 2002.

RADIATION PROTECTION TECHNICIANS

It is called "the canyon," a concrete section of a building at a federal nuclear reservation in Washington State. Bonnie Judy brings her radiation monitoring equipment and spends the morning there, overseeing a crew of hazardous materials handlers, riggers, and other workers who are wrapping hazardous waste and carefully lowering it into a railroad tunnel for disposal. Bonnie checks the area for dangerous levels of radiation and watches the workers, making sure they observe safety regulations designed to protect them.

In the afternoon she accompanies another team of workers who are planning to pull tumbleweeds that have sprung up among the buildings and surrounding areas. In the past the soil and groundwater at the facility have been contaminated with radioactive particles. The surface dirt might not be particularly dangerous now, but a tumbleweed's long tap root can reach deep into the earth and draw contaminants up into the weed. Bonnie is responsible for ensuring that the workers pulling the weeds are not being exposed to dangerous levels of radiation. It is also her job to survey the weeds and identify those that are contaminated; they must be treated as hazardous waste and cannot be burned or thrown away like ordinary weeds. The project takes hours. Bonnie scans one tumbleweed after another, working with patience and thoroughness. Her job is important, the danger from radiation is real, and she takes it seriously.

Definition
Radiation protection technicians monitor radiation levels, protect workers, and decontaminate radioactive areas, often in a nuclear power plant.

Alternative Job Titles
Health physics technicians
Radiation analysts
Radiation chemistry technicians
Radiation control technicians
Radiation monitoring technicians

High School Subjects
Mathematics
Physics

Personal Skills
Mechanical/manipulative
Technical/scientific

Salary Range
$40,890 to $42,137 to $47,615+

Minimum Educational Requirements
Associate's degree

Certification or Licensing
Required for certain specialties

Outlook
Little or no growth

DOT
199

GOE
N/A

NOC
2263

O*NET-SOC
N/A

What Does a Radiation Protection Technician Do?

Some elements, such as uranium and radium, are said to be "radioactive," because they give off rays of energy that cannot be seen. Radiation has always existed in elements that occur naturally on Earth and in cosmic rays that come from outer space. Some radiation always bombards every part of the planet. These natural amounts of radiation pose small threat to human health or the environment, but in larger doses, radiation can cause great damage.

During the 20th century and the early years of the 21st century, technological advances have given humans the ability to generate unnatural amounts of radiation for many purposes, including the production of nuclear power and the curing of cancer through the use of radiation therapy. It is the job of *radiation protection technicians* to ensure that workers, the public, and the environment are not harmed by unacceptable levels of radiation.

Radiation protection technicians use ion counters and Geiger counters to measure radiation in work areas and the environment. Sometimes they collect and analyze samples of air, water, soil, plants, and other materials to determine their level of radioactivity. They use special instruments, such as dosimeters, to reveal how much radiation the workers in nuclear facilities have experienced. Most often, a dosimeter is a badge that the employee wears; it uses photographic film to reveal exposure to radioactivity.

In determining how long a worker can safely remain in a contaminated area, the technician considers time, distance from the source, and shielding. Time is a factor because, after becoming radioactive, some materials break down into harmless, stable elements within minutes or days, but others remain radioactive for thousands of years. For example, used nuclear fuel is highly radioactive, and workers must always handle it with extreme caution. Next, the technician bases calculations on the fact that workers close to a source of radiation will experience higher exposures than those who are farther away. Also, workers shielded by materials such as lead and concrete will experience lower exposures to radiation.

Technicians take measurements, record them, and inform their supervisors of any unacceptable levels of exposure. They also compile numerous reports for the Nuclear Regulatory Commission (NRC) and other supervisory and regulatory agencies. The job requires a thorough understanding of federal regulations and the ability to make sure that workers follow strict procedures.

Some radiation protection technicians help teach a facility's various employees how to work around radiation and how to use monitoring equipment. Technicians also help workers set up equipment that indicates whether processes at the facility are operating within standard limits. The radiation protection technician is responsible for calibrating and maintaining these instruments and must be knowledgeable about machines throughout the plant.

In addition to routine measuring and control, radiation protection technicians must be prepared to deal with abnormal situations and emergencies. They commonly wear safety glasses, safety shoes with rubber soles, cotton booties, gloves and glove liners, coveralls, and other protective gear on the job.

Radiation protection technicians are supervised by power plant managers, nuclear scientists, and engineers. When they adjust equipment, they typically work with operators in the control room. When they repair equipment, they work with instrumentation technicians. When they help ship radioactive waste, they work with nuclear material handlers and hazardous waste management technicians. They also interact with dozens of other employees who constitute the work community at a nuclear site.

Lingo to Learn

Dosimeter A device that measures the amount of radioactivity absorbed.

Geiger counter An instrument used to detect, measure, and record nuclear emanations, cosmic rays, and artificially produced subatomic particles.

Ion An atom, group of atoms, or molecule that has acquired a net electric charge by gaining or losing electrons.

Nuclear reaction A chain reaction in which the energized subatomic particles of split atomic nuclei collide with and split other atomic nuclei.

Radiation The emission and propagation of waves or particles, such as light, sound, radiant heat, or particles emitted by radioactivity.

Radioactivity The spontaneous emission of radiation either directly from unstable atomic nuclei or as a consequence of a nuclear reaction.

Reactor A device in which a nuclear chain reaction is initiated and controlled.

What Is It Like to Be a Radiation Protection Technician?

Bonnie Judy is a lead radiological control technician for Fluor Daniel Hanford, a private contracting company that performs maintenance, operations, decommissioning, and decontamination at the Hanford Nuclear Reservation near Richland, Washington. Hanford used to produce plutonium for nuclear weapons and is now the largest environmental cleanup project in the world. The facility is one of the few national disposal sites for low-level radioactive waste. It is also the site of Washington's only commercial nuclear power plant.

Bonnie is currently working at an old building that is scheduled to be closed. "Our job is to put it in safe condition," she says. Her team of radiation protection technicians oversees other workers who are cleaning up hazardous waste, removing combustibles in the

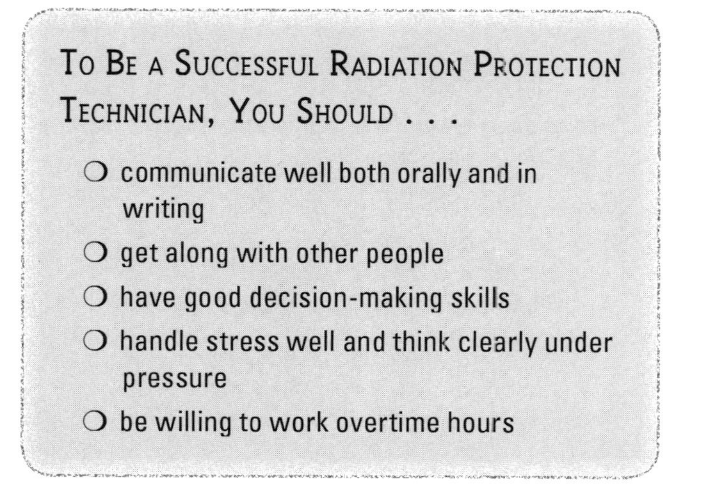

To Be a Successful Radiation Protection Technician, You Should . . .

- communicate well both orally and in writing
- get along with other people
- have good decision-making skills
- handle stress well and think clearly under pressure
- be willing to work overtime hours

building, and generally stabilizing the structure. Bonnie and her crew work on various projects at this nuclear reservation that covers hundreds of acres.

She and the other radiation protection technicians have two primary duties. First, they set dose rates for people who work at the site. This involves using instruments to take measurements in areas that contain radiation. "A radiation dose is the only thing that can actually penetrate your body and do some harm," she explains. Her job is to make calculations to determine how long the workers can remain in a radiation area without being harmed.

Second, Bonnie conducts surveys to detect contamination. To do that, she uses sensitive instruments to scan the surface of a tool, a piece of equipment, or a person's entire body.

Another aspect of Bonnie's job is educating and overseeing workers to make sure they comply with safety regulations and take seriously their danger of exposure to radiation. "We help them and keep them safe," she says. Radiation protection technicians have medical training and carry medic cards. "That's also handy off the job," Bonnie notes; in any emergency, her medical training could prove useful.

On the job Bonnie interacts with workers in many professions, from millwrights and riggers to instrumentation technicians and engineers. "It's a fun job," she says. "I've met a lot of smart, neat people. We go out on a different job almost every day."

Before workers begin a project, Bonnie fills out radiological work permits that spell out details such as the conditions the crews will encounter and what clothing they will need to wear. In deciding what to put in the permit, she considers surveillance maps and reports compiled by her team of radiation protection technicians. Because Bonnie is a supervisor, she spends a large part of the day at her desk. Other technicians do more hands-on work around the site, although they also sometimes work at computers.

"It's a physically active job but not a physically demanding job," Bonnie remarks. "Women can do it just as well as the men."

Bonnie is enthused about most aspects of her career, but she admits, "The thing I don't like the most is I commute for two hours a day." She has to drive more than 40 miles to work, since a radiation protection technician cannot live on a nuclear site. The town nearest the Hanford reservation is about 30 miles away.

Some radiation protection technicians spend a great deal of time on the road, because they work temporary jobs at various sites instead of being employed steadily at one. The reactor unit at a nuclear power plant must be shut down periodically so its fuel can be exchanged for new fuel. During these "fuel outages," additional technicians are hired to help oversee repairs and testing done by workers from other departments. The plant's regular employees usually work much longer hours during outages, often putting in 10 hours a day for six days a week. At other times they typically work five days a week with occasional overtime.

Do I Have What It Takes to Be a Radiation Protection Technician?

Radiation protection technicians must be able to work with precision, perform well under stress, communicate clearly, cooperate as part of a team, and maintain a pleasant but firm manner when directing other employees. They must make sure that workers take the danger of their jobs seriously instead of becoming complacent and ignoring safety procedures.

"I really feel the people who do this job should be very responsible," Bonnie says. "You need a strong personality. You're in charge of making sure those people are the same when they come out as when they came in. You have to assert yourself."

This is probably not a good job for someone who is shy or not confident. "You will be questioned," Bonnie warns; workers will ask, "'Who said you were God today?'"

Technicians constantly interact with workers in many professions. They need to be able to communicate and get along with other people.

It is also vital that the technician be able to make quick decisions and think clearly under pressure. The job can be stressful because of the radiological conditions and the decisions that must be made. People rely on radiation protection technicians to make decisions that could affect the entire plant.

The job involves long hours, including frequent overtime, and the technician must be able to keep working without making mistakes. Attention to detail is essential, since technicians are responsible for documentation and making mathematical calculations. Bonnie says an aptitude for science is not the most important quality for this job, because most people can learn the scientific knowledge they would need. It is an occupation that deals with science, however, and it would be helpful to have an interest in subjects such as atomic energy, biology, and environmental issues.

How Do I Become a Radiation Protection Technician?

Before she became a radiation protection technician, Bonnie stayed home to raise her two children until they were old enough to attend school. Then she found a job as an operator at the Hanford nuclear site, making fuels to load into the reactor. When her job in the fuel fabrication group was discontinued, the company sent her to its own school, the Hanford Technical Training Center, to study radiation protection for about six months. Next, she completed on-the-job training for a week or two at each of 10 or 12 facilities. Then she was given a permanent job assignment. Bonnie was in the first class ever offered at the training center and she still works for the same company.

It is common to learn this profession through on-the-job training, especially when workers are laid off, as Bonnie was, from other positions within the company. Other technicians who work at Hanford have completed training at vocational or technical schools.

FYI

Hazardous materials must be packaged securely when they are shipped. Spent nuclear fuel and other high-level wastes are transported in containers designed to remain intact through fires, immersion in water, high-impact collisions, and other accidents. Highly radioactive materials are usually transported as solids, not liquids, and they would probably not contaminate a wide area even if the container broke open.

EDUCATION

High School

A high school diploma is the minimum requirement for entry into the radiation protection field. To begin preparing in high school, take at least one year of science and two years of mathematics, including physics, chemistry, biology, algebra, cal-culus, and geometry. Four years of English are also recommended, since radiation protection technicians need to communicate well with other employees. Computer programming and applications, vocational machine shop operations, and blueprint reading are also helpful.

"Take plenty of algebra classes and calculus. Don't be afraid of the math," Bonnie advises.

Postsecondary Training

Although the job does not require a college degree, some college education is becoming more common. Many technical schools and community colleges offer programs that lead to a certificate or associate's degree in radiation protection or in related areas, such as health physics, nuclear materials handling, and nuclear technology. The U.S. Navy also offers excellent technical training programs for nuclear specialties.

Classes in radiation protection typically include radiological safety; radiological emergencies; radiation detection, measurement, shielding, and monitoring; disposal of radioactive wastes; and radiation physics. In addition, students learn about electricity, electronics, computers, chemistry, nuclear technology, blueprint reading, plant communications, and power

In-depth

The Storage of Nuclear Waste

Different types of nuclear waste are stored in different ways. High-level waste emits a great deal of radiation and must be stored in containers made of materials that will prevent radiation from reaching people nearby. One kind of shielded container, designed to last for hundreds of years, is a stainless steel bin inside a concrete vault.

Fuel that has been used in a nuclear reactor is highly radioactive. Spent nuclear fuel, which comes from sources such as nuclear power plants and nuclear submarines, can be stored in various ways. Usually it is placed in water pools, which cool the fuel and shield workers from radiation. Some older fuels that have cooled and are no longer as radioactive can be "dry stored" in casks made of lead or concrete or in buildings with thick concrete walls. Spent nuclear fuel can be processed to recover the uranium it contains, but currently this is not being done, because the country has a surplus of uranium.

Clothes, gloves, tools, and other items contaminated with small amounts of plutonium are called transuranic waste. They are not very radioactive and can usually be stored in unshielded metal drums. The drums are placed on concrete in a metal building. Air is continually pulled into the building to ensure that if a drum were damaged any radioactive particles that escaped would be contained within the building instead of moving outside.

In the past some types of nuclear waste were released directly into aquifers, the layers of water that occur naturally in the ground. This practice has been halted, and the radionuclides that were placed in the aquifers are decaying naturally. Because they have been diluted and dispersed by the movement of the groundwater, the amounts of contaminants in specific areas of the aquifers have become somewhat less concentrated.

plant quality control. The curriculum usually features a year or two of chemistry, physics, laboratory procedures, and technical writing.

Electric utilities and other nuclear facilities frequently recruit students from these technical programs immediately after they graduate. Technicians then complete further in-depth training on the job.

CERTIFICATION OR LICENSING

No law requires radiation protection technicians to be licensed or certified, but Bonnie says that companies are now hiring only certified workers. Various certifications are available, often through colleges, technical schools, and company training programs. Whatever the certification, it is usually accepted by employers when the technician moves to another job, but each company typically requires all new employees to pass a competency test.

Technicians who travel to projects at various sites are usually registered by passing a certification examination administered by the National Registry of Radiation Protection Technicians (NRRPT). "It's nationally recognized as saying you know your stuff," Bonnie explains. As of now, the NRRPT certification never expires, but the rules might soon be changed to require periodic recertification.

Bonnie earned her certification from the Hanford Technical Training Center when she completed her training there. All technicians at Hanford are certified and must complete continuing education every two years. If they lose their certification, they have a brief time to regain it or lose their jobs. They independently learn the material in study guides, and they participate in training sessions that take about two and a half days every four months. After every six modules, they take a composite test. In that way they are recertified on every facet of the job every two years.

The second part of the recertification process is an oral test. A board of supervisors proposes a hypothetical situation in which something goes wrong at the plant, and the technician states aloud how the problem should be handled. Then the technician must respond to the board's incisive questions. "Those oral boards are agony, even for us extroverts. It's basically to see how well you think on your feet, because a lot of times that's what we have to do," Bonnie explains.

LABOR UNIONS

Like Bonnie, most radiation protection technicians are represented by the International Brotherhood of Electrical Workers (IBEW). Bonnie's union membership ensures that she will not be fired but will be transferred to new contracting companies as they take over operations at the nuclear site. Technicians may belong to other labor unions, depending on the plant and the location. Supervisory and management personnel do not belong to unions.

Who Will Hire Me?

During her more than 16 years at the Hanford nuclear reservation, Bonnie has worked for a series of contracting companies that help maintain and operate the facility. First, she was an operator in a fuel fabrication group for the Westinghouse Corporation. Then the company sent her to radiation protection school. She worked as a trainee and received promotions about every six months, and within about three years she had progressed to a senior-level technician. She has worked for the Fluor Daniel Hanford Corporation since it took over, about a year and a half ago. The Bechtel Hanford Corporation and the Pacific Northwest National Laboratory also hire radiation protection technicians at this nuclear site.

Radiation protection technicians usually work at nuclear facilities or for companies that have radioactive elements or machinery that produces radiation. Most work for electric utilities that operate nuclear reactors. Other employers include regulatory agencies, nondestructive testing firms, radiopharmaceutical industries, and companies that handle and process nuclear materials or handle nuclear waste. Jobs are also available with regulatory agencies and federal and state agencies. University research departments and national research facilities also hire radiation protection technicians.

Jobs for radiation protection technicians are listed in technical magazines and on the Internet. You can also send resumes to nuclear reservations. Many companies recruit new employees from schools that offer training in the field, and students in the best programs often receive several job offers before they have graduated.

To work in a job that involves national security, you will need federal security clearance, such as clearance from the Nuclear Regulatory Commission or military clearance. Your employer would most likely help you make the necessary arrangements. Many jobs in this field are at federal nuclear sites, often overseen by the U.S. Department of Energy.

FYI

Research on how radiation affects a human body is ongoing. We do know some of the more common short-term and long-term effects. Immediate symptoms include nausea, hemorrhage, and fatigue. Conditions that show up after a longer period of time include cancer, lower fertility, and possible birth defects.

Throughout the world there are documented cases of severe birth defects directly attributed to prolonged exposure to radiation. Because of these facts and all that is still unknown about exposure, it is apparent that the radiation protection technician's job is vital to the safety of everyone.

Where Can I Go from Here?

A technician can advance to various positions within the field. Instrumentation specialists work within the radiation protection department, distinctive from the

Advancement Possibilities

Research technicians invent new ideas and techniques for handling nuclear and radioactive materials.

Health physics technicians teach new radiation monitors, study existing procedures, and test experimental designs and safety procedures.

Soils evaluation technicians assess soil density, radioactivity, and moisture content to determine sources of unusually high levels of radioactivity.

Radioactive waste analysts prepare waste for disposal, develop methods for disposing of it, and keep inventories of stored wastes.

X-ray calibration technicians check the calibration, reliability, and safety of X-ray equipment; and they evaluate the performance of filters.

plant's general instrumentation protection technicians. ALARA ("As Low as Reasonably Achievable") specialists ensure that radiation exposures are kept as low as possible.

Experts in the field may be offered attractive positions with laboratories or as consultants. They may work as nuclear engineering or nuclear industry consultants, or they may be self-employed.

What Are the Salary Ranges?

"Without overtime, which is practically unheard of, once you get to be a full-fledged radiation-contamination technician, you can expect to make $45,000 to $48,000 a year. A lot of them make more than that, because of the overtime," Bonnie says. She adds that technicians who travel to work temporarily during outages at various facilities can make $80,000 to $90,000 in eight months or so.

The U.S. Department of Labor reports that in 2003 nuclear monitoring technicians had annual median salaries of $60,300, with those in the middle 50 percent earning between $48,300 and $72,700. The lowest paid 10 percent earned $30,600, and the highest paid 10 percent earned $87,500 annually.

A review by Salary.com of earnings nationwide found that in 2005 radiation technicians had annual salaries between $40,890 and $47,615 with a median of $42,137.

Benefits typically include health insurance, paid vacations and holidays, and retirement plans. Since the field changes rapidly, some companies offer tuition reimbursement for employees to continue their education by attending seminars and workshops.

What Is the Job Outlook?

"You used to be able to make a really good living if you went on the road, moving from one outage to another," Bonnie comments. "A lot of that has begun to disappear, so we're getting a lot of technicians who used to work on the road and are now looking for a steady job."

She adds that radiation protection technicians will probably not enjoy steady work in their profession indefinitely. "In my opinion, I would not recommend it for a person looking for a lifelong vocation, because I've got to hope we won't have this kind of work to do forever. The new plants and new facilities are being built so there are fewer times when a person would have to make an entry [into a contaminated area]," she says.

According to the U.S. Department of Labor Occupational Information Network, nuclear monitoring technicians held 5,700 jobs in 2002. The number of new jobs is projected to increase by only 1 percent to 5,800 positions in 2012.

In addition, the number of nuclear power plants operating in the United States declined to 103 in 2005 from 110 in the late 1990s, and the future of nuclear energy is in question because of concerns over safety and environmental issues. Still, even if the industry grows slowly or declines, there should be demand for radiation protection technicians. Jobs will become available as technicians retire, are promoted, or seek other employment. Regulatory and other government agencies might create new jobs as they increasingly enforce safety standards.

In related fields a number of jobs will probably become available. For example, the use of radiation in science, medicine, and industry is expected to increase. Radiation protection technicians could find employment with manufacturing companies or research and development laboratories. Jobs will be available in laboratories that process radioisotopes and in plants that make equipment that detects, measures, and controls radiation. Also, more industries will be using X-ray technology. Employment opportunities are expected to be best for technicians with degrees in applied science technologies.

How Do I Learn More?

PROFESSIONAL ORGANIZATIONS

The following organizations provide information on radiation protection careers, accredited schools and scholarships, registration, and employment opportunities:

American Nuclear Society
555 North Kensington Avenue
La Grange Park, IL 60526
708-352-6611
http://www.ans.org

American Society for Nondestructive Testing
PO Box 28518
Columbus, OH 43228-0518
800-222-2768
http://www.asnt.org

National Council on Radiation Protection and Measurements
7910 Woodmont Avenue, Suite 400
Bethesda, MD 20814-3095
301-657-2652
http://www.ncrp.com

National Registry of Radiation Protection Technicians
PO Box 6974
Kennewick, WA 99336
509-736-5400
nrrpt@nrrpt.org
http://www/nrrpt.org

Nuclear Energy Institute
1776 I Street, NW, Suite 400
Washington, DC 20006-3708
202-739-8000
http://www.nei.org

BIBLIOGRAPHY

The following is a sampling of materials relating to the professional concerns and development of radiation protection technicians:

Shapiro, Jacob. *Radiation Protection: A Guide for Scientists, Regulators, and Physicians.* 4th ed. Cambridge, Mass.: Harvard University Press, 2002.

Walker, J. Samuel. *Permissible Dose: A History of Radiation Protection in the Twentieth Century.* Berkeley: University of California Press, 2000.

RADIOLOGIC TECHNOLOGISTS

Definition
Radiologic technologists operate equipment that creates an image of the human body for the purpose of medical diagnosis. They are responsible for accurately positioning the patient and ensuring that the minimum amount of radiation is used to produce a quality diagnostic image.

Alternative Job Titles
Radiographers
X-ray technologists

High School Subjects
Health
Mathematics
Physics

Personal Skills
Helping/teaching
Technical/scientific

Salary Range
$29,340 to $41,850 to $58,300

Minimum Educational Level
Associate's degree

Certification or Licensing
Required by all states

Outlook
Faster than the average

DOT
078

GOE
14.05.01

NOC
3215

O*NET-SOC
29-2034.01

A boy, frightened and still wearing his baseball cap and uniform, is wheeled into radiology. The radiologic technologist, who has significant experience in dealing with worried young children, instinctively knows that the best way to calm the boy and accomplish her job is to divert his attention from his throbbing leg.

With a smile and a few quick questions, she learns the boy's name—Billy; the position he plays—pitcher and sometimes second base; and his team's record—not that great.

The boy grows more relaxed as she explains the X-ray procedure. As she talks, she positions the boy beneath the X-ray camera for the optimum filming angle. She sets the controls of the X-ray machine so as to be able to produce a picture of the correct density, contrast, and detail. She then adjusts a columnator, which is a knob that reduces the size of the X-ray area, therefore ensuring that the boy's leg will be exposed to the least amount of radiation for the shortest duration of time.

The radiologic technologist is acutely aware of the potential harmful effects of the radiation on both herself and the boy, and as a result, she wears protective clothing and a radiation badge as a matter of rule. Most importantly, she properly and professionally covers the boy with lead shielding before beginning the procedure. She makes the exposure, removes the film so that it can be developed, and then tells the boy the procedure is complete.

Billy is wheeled away and she reloads the "bucky" with X-ray film and prepares for her next assignment. Before the day is over, she will have completed 20 to 25 X-ray procedures; among those are scans that reveal broken bones, chest examinations, lung cancer, and pneumonia, as well as scans to determine problems in the spinal column, kidneys, and upper and lower gastrointestinal tract.

As a result of his fracture, the boy will be lost to his team for the rest of the season, but his leg will heal perfectly as the result of the technologist's competent imaging, which provided the physician with the precise view he needed to accurately set the broken bone and begin the healing process.

What Does a Radiologic Technologist Do?

Radiologic technologists, sometimes called *radiographers* or *X-ray technologists,* operate equipment that creates images of the human body for the purpose of medical diagnosis. Since all work is done at the request and under the supervision of a supervisor, radiologist, or attending physician, radiologic technologists do not complete any procedures on their own.

To do their job, radiologic technologists, or RTs, must help prepare the patient by explaining the procedure and answering any questions the patient might have. In some instances, an RT may administer, under the supervision of a radiologist, a substance called a contrast medium, which is usually barium sulfate given orally or rectally, so as to make specific body parts, such as the kidney or abdomen, better able to be viewed. They must also make sure that the patient is free of jewelry or any other metal that would obstruct the X-ray process. RTs position the person sitting, standing, or lying so that the correct view of the body can be radiographed. Technologists are also responsible for protecting the test subject from radiation, covering adjacent areas with lead shielding. Special attention and protection is given to the very young and women in their childbearing years, since they are the most susceptible to the effects of radiation. Radiologic technologists are keenly aware of the welfare of the patient in relation to radiation, ascribing to the term "ALARA," which means, "as low as reasonably allowable."

The technologist is responsible for the positioning of the X-ray equipment at the proper angle and distance from the part to be radiographed, and determining exposure time based on the location of the bone or organ and the thickness of the body in that area. Universal formulas that relate to body weight, degree of illness, and density of tissue and bone exist to help the RT determine the appropriate settings. The RT must set the controls of the X-ray machine to produce pictures of the correct contrast, detail, and density. The RT then places the photographic film on the far side of the patient's body to make the necessary exposures. The film is then developed for the radiologist or other physician to interpret.

Secondary duties for RTs may include the performance of routine administrative tasks such as maintaining patient files and keeping detailed records of equipment maintenance and usage. RTs may also be responsible for managing a radiation quality assurance program and, with considerable experience, manage other technologists in regard to work schedules and assignment of duties.

Lingo to Learn

Bucky The tray in which X-ray film is loaded.

Columnator A dial on the X-ray machinery that controls and adjusts the area of radiation exposure.

Contrast medium A solution of barium sulfate that is administered orally or rectally to highlight organs such as the abdomen, which normally can't be distinguished. This medium is used for upper and lower gastrointestinal examinations(GIs).

Diagnostic imaging Preliminary testing of the body tissues and skeletal structures through the use of X rays, sound waves, tomographic scans, and magnetic scans.

Fluoroscopy A procedure that examines the upper or lower gastrointestinal areas.

Pigastat A device used for children that immobilizes them during an examination, lifting arms and holding them in place.

Radiographs X-ray films.

What Is It Like to Be a Radiologic Technologist?

Diane Libertini has been a radiologic technologist for 25 years and has worked in hospitals and in private practice. Currently, she works at an imaging center, where she works as a billing manager and quality control manager and also performs mammograms. "Before you see the first patient," Diane says, "you must perform quality control tests on the CT [computerized tomography] machine, mammo machine, and processors. We have one CT room, one tomographic/radiographic room, one flouroscopy/radiographic room, one sonogram room, one mammogram room, one DEXA [dual energy X-ray absorptiometry, which measures bone mass], and a nuclear medicine department." The technologists must rotate through the different rooms each day. "We begin seeing patients at 8:30. We start with the patients who must be without food and water and do the exams that require prep first. The CT room begins by feeding the patients who need an oral contrast and then waiting one hour to scan the patient."

While waiting, scans not requiring prep can be performed. A CT scan takes from 15 minutes to over an hour. "Each CT is set up on a computer," Diane explains. "A machine scans the patient, making 360 degrees around the patient. We usually perform five to seven CTs per day."

Technologists also perform IVPs (intravenous pyelograms), diagnostic X rays of the kidneys, ureters, and bladder. "The tomographic/radiographic room is used for IVPs," Diane says. "You inject a contrast material and then take timed pictures of the urinary tract. These tests are done first thing in the morning and usually take one hour. In this room, the X-ray tube moves in a linear fashion."

The fluoroscopy/radiographic room is reserved for prepped tests such as upper GIs, (gastrointestinal), which are X-ray examinations of the esophagus and stomach. "The fluoroscopy unit allows the radiologist to watch as the test is being done. The tests require a contrast material called barium to be administered. The oral cholecystogram requires pills to be taken ahead of time to show up the gallbladder. Each of these takes about 30 minutes, and we schedule four or so a day."

The imaging center schedules many mammograms (X rays of the breast) throughout the day, one every 15 minutes. "The screening mammogram consists of four images. Each patient leaves with a preliminary report. The radiologist must check and speak to every patient."

Common tests performed in the sonogram room are pelvic, obstetrical, and breast sonograms. This exam uses sound waves instead of X ray. "We also do vascular sonograms that measure flow and velocity of the blood. Each patient receives their results before they leave and they talk to the radiologist." In the DEXA room, 20-minute tests are performed that involve a small amount of X ray to take a picture of the hip and lumbar spine.

The nuclear medicine department requires a specially licensed technologist. "Each patient is injected with a small amount of radioactive isotope and the images are obtained with a gamma camera."

Diane says each technologist is also expected to take on front desk duties. Her schedule is 6:30 A.M. to 3:30 P.M. Monday through Friday, with every other Friday off.

Do I Have What It Takes to Be a Radiologic Technologist?

Radiologic technologists should be skilled at technical work and have a mastery of medical technology. They must enjoy helping and working with the sick, who are sometimes worried or frightened. Clearly, a personal touch is mandatory for success in the field. "It's a 'people' business," Diane says, "where the people are often being sick, scared, and not wanting to be at the doctor's office. You must be very patient, very detail oriented, and willing to work late if an emergency comes up."

FYI

A beam of tiny particles from the nuclei of atoms might help cure some cancers. In boron neutron capture therapy, the patient is injected with a boron compound. The compound accumulates in cancerous tumors only. A nuclear reactor or particle accelerator is used to generate a beam of neutrons, which is focused on the cancerous area. The beam stimulates the boron compound, which kills the cancer cells but does no harm to healthy tissue.

It's a "people" business, where the people are often being sick, scared, and not wanting to be at the doctor's office.

Communication skills, as previously mentioned, play a significant role in an RT's daily duties. The RT must be able to relay information to radiologists and other technologists, and help patients into the proper position so a procedure can be completed.

Prospective RTs should be aware of the repetitiveness of the job and that RTs spend long hours on their feet and are subject to frequent overtime. The physical stress of lifting and moving patients and the emotional stress, especially in a hospital setting, of knowing a patient, sometimes a child, has a life-threatening illness can be difficult.

"You are exposed to radiation," Diane points out, "so there is an element of hazardous duty. Also, some techs have developed chemical allergies to the darkroom chemicals." RTs wear lead aprons when performing fluoroscopies and other procedures. They also wear radiation badges that are checked once a month for exposure levels. In terms of disease exposure, RTs prescribe to universal standards when dealing with diseases such as AIDS, hepatitis, and tuberculosis, wearing rubber gloves, gowns, and masks to maintain health and safety standards. Although radiation and disease pose a risk, RTs can be diligent and aware so as to avoid exposure in the fulfillment of their duties.

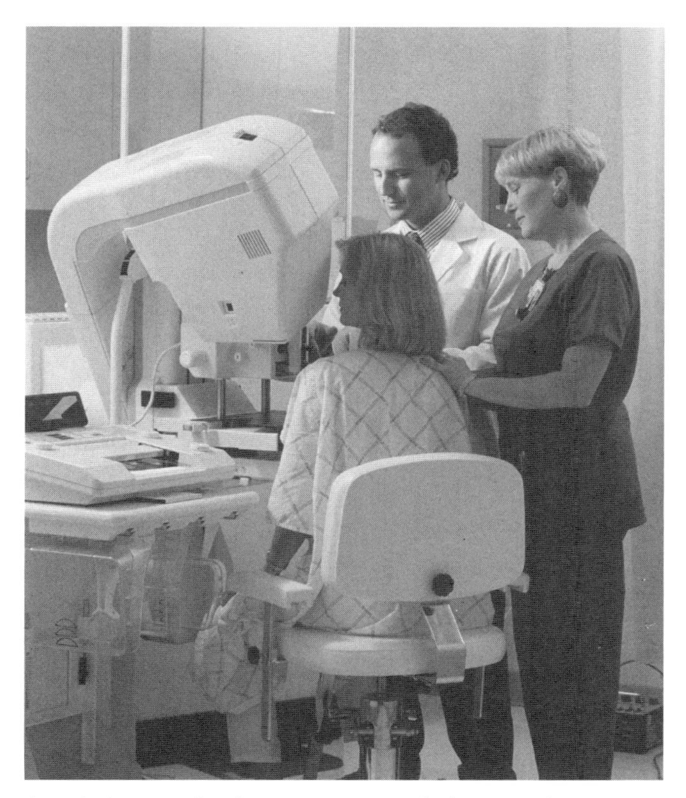

A radiologic technologist assists a radiologist and a patient during a mammogram. *(Photo Disc)*

How Do I Become a Radiologic Technologist?

After graduating from high school, Diane stepped right into an approved two-year school of radiologic technology in a hospital-based program. "At the end of the program," she says, "you take the exam from the American Registry of Radiologic Technologists to receive your license, which enables you to perform X rays. You then may sit for the advanced certification exams in mammography, computed technology, magnetic resonance imaging, quality management, radiation therapy, nuclear medicine, and sonography. New exams are coming down the road."

EDUCATION

High School

Students who intend to pursue a career as a radiologic technologist should take courses in the sciences—namely, biology, anatomy, physics, and chemistry. You should also take courses in mathematics and take advantage of writing and speech classes, which will allow you to hone your communication skills. Unlike a few other technical careers, a high school degree is required for entry into radiologic technology training programs.

Postsecondary Training

Instruction in the radiologic sciences is offered at universities and colleges in the form of four-year baccalaureate programs and two-year associate degree programs, in hospitals in the form of a two-year hospital certificate program, and also in the armed forces.

A two-year associate's program consists of a mixture of theory and practical hours. Due to the intense nature of the education, many students take an additional year to complete the educational requirements.

The curriculum that aspiring RTs will experience includes instruction in anatomy and physiology, radiation physics and biology, pathology, medical technology instruction and procedures, principles and techniques of diagnostic imaging, patient care and medical ethics, and radiation safety and protection.

To Be a Successful Radiologic Technologist, You Should . . .

- have compassion and a personal touch
- have patience and a flexible personality
- be extroverted and able to communicate in a clear and concise manner
- have an understanding of medical terminology and procedures

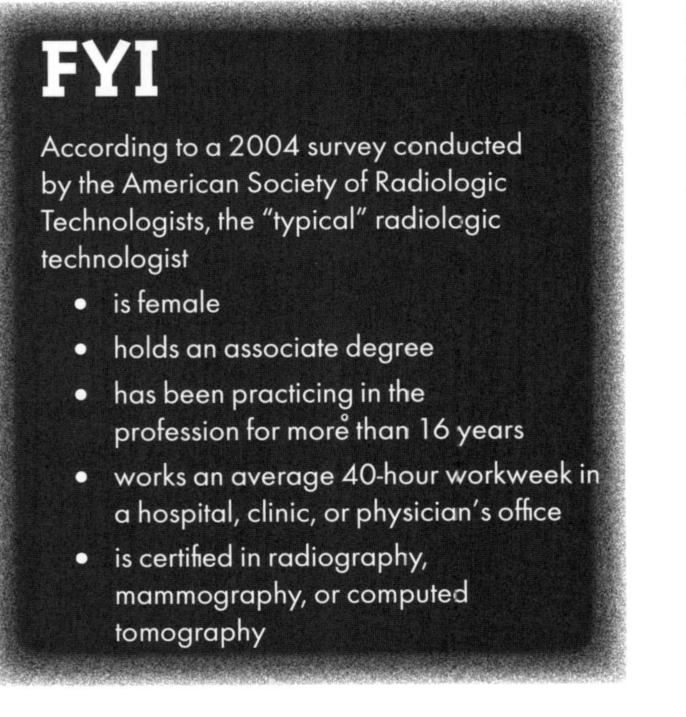

FYI

According to a 2004 survey conducted by the American Society of Radiologic Technologists, the "typical" radiologic technologist

- is female
- holds an associate degree
- has been practicing in the profession for more than 16 years
- works an average 40-hour workweek in a hospital, clinic, or physician's office
- is certified in radiography, mammography, or computed tomography

Programs should be accredited by the Joint Review Committee on Education in Radiologic Technology (JRCERT). See http://www.jrcert.org for more details.

CERTIFICATION OR LICENSING

Most medical employers require certification by the American Registry of Radiologic Technologists (ARRT). Radiologic students, upon completion of their education, are expected to take and pass the National Registry Boards to allow employment. All students must be registry-eligible, which means registered with the ARRT to take the test the next time it is offered. The Registry Boards are offered four times a year.

In addition to standard certification, a significant amount of continuing education exists in the radiologic field. In order to maintain proper certification, RTs must take 24 hours of continuing education in the course of two years. These courses are offered by technical-type programs and also the Institute for Professional Growth (IFPG), which offers X-ray seminars at area hotels.

Currently, 38 states require that radiologic technologists be registered.

INTERNSHIPS AND VOLUNTEERSHIPS

Radiologic technologists gain valuable internship experience in the course of the practical hours that are required to gain a degree. Those in a hospital certificate program will gain experience on-site throughout their education. "I was lucky," Diane says. "I was in a work-study program in high school. I worked in the radiology department of a hospital for school credit, so I knew what I was getting into, and I had a head start when I actually got into X-ray school."

A guidance counselor may be able to set up a meeting with a professional radiologic technologist at his or her place of work. This way, you could observe the duties, facilities, and equipment used, as well as ask questions of the technologist. Another way to gain more information and make a good contact in the field is to speak with a teacher of radiology at an educational program.

Who Will Hire Me?

While most RTs work in hospitals, others may work in physicians' offices, HMOs (health maintenance organizations), mobile imaging clinics, nursing homes, or extended health care facilities. "My first job was at the hospital where I trained," Diane says. "I worked part time during training and was offered a job at graduation."

Hospitals provide radiologic technologists with the best opportunity for employment. Half of RTs work in hospitals. Application through employment services or through the personnel officers of potential health care employers is a good way to locate job openings.

While rural areas and small towns offer more opportunity for employment than cities, pay and benefits are usually better with an urban employer.

Where Can I Go from Here?

Those interested in moving beyond a career in radiologic technology should be aware that advanced jobs can only be acquired through further education. This education may be provided in-house, at a teaching hospital, or in a technical school or college setting. Those obtaining a bachelor's degree will have the best chance for advancement. Further education will allow RTs to become certified in CT, ultrasound, MRI (magnetic resonance imaging), nuclear medicine, and other fields, thereby gaining experience and flexibility to prosper in the workplace.

"I first worked on the third shift," Diane says, "pulling 40 hours from Monday to Friday. I then went to nuclear medicine and CT working days, weekends, and on call. We worked all the time."

With considerable experience, radiologic technologists can move into teaching positions or train new technologists in-house or at other locations. Other RTs may use their experience to work in sales and marketing, demonstrating new equipment for medically oriented businesses.

Radiologic technologists employed in hospitals have the opportunity to advance to administrative and supervisory positions. Those who gain their bachelor's degree and then a master's degree in health administration may choose to seek a position as a hospital administrator or manage a business for radiologists.

What Are the Salary Ranges?

According to the *Occupational Outlook Handbook*, radiologic technologists had median annual earnings of $41,850 in 2003. Those in the lowest 10 percent earned less than $29,340, while those in the highest earned more than $58,300 annually. On average, RTs working for medical and diagnostic laboratories earned the highest salaries in this field.

Compensation and pay scales will vary based on the location of the employer—with urban areas more lucrative than rural areas and small towns—and on the level of education attained, the experience, and the responsibilities of the technologist.

What Is the Job Outlook?

The field of radiologic technology is expected to faster than the average for all other occupations. This is due to the vast clinical potential of diagnostic imaging. New uses for radiologic technology will continue to be discovered, therefore increasing demand. Opportunities in small towns and rural areas exist for those flexible about location and compensation.

Another factor that will influence growth is the aging of the American population. As the median age rises, more attention will be focused on diseases that are prominent in older people. Many of these diseases require the use of imaging equipment and technologists. The Southeast and Southwest regions of the United States offer significant employment opportunity due to their large populations of retirement-age Americans. The aging workforce will also create more positions in the radiology field, since may radiologic technologists will reach retirement age. The ARRT and ASRT have found that the majority of RTs are 40 years or older, part of the reason the organizations are predicting a severe shortage of RTs by 2010.

Another reason for this shortage is that fewer people are entering the field than ever before. The career may be unattractive to some because of the long hours and wages that don't properly compensate. In an effort to bring some standardization to the field, ARRT is considering requiring technologists to have a bachelor's degree in order to become certified. Currently, RT students are putting in nearly four years of training anyway, because of the practical requirements of associate's degrees.

While a shortage in the workforce may exist, prospective RTs should be aware that there is stiff competition for good jobs. One must be prepared to

Advancement Possibilities

Computed tomography (CT) technologists, working closely with physicians, are responsible for taking detailed cross-sectional pictures of the internal structures of the human body.

Magnetic resonance imaging (MRI) technologists use computers, radio waves, and powerful magnets to create images of specific parts of the body.

Diagnostic medical sonographers use high-frequency sound waves, not radiation, to create images of internal body structures.

Chief technologists and technical administrators are radiologic technologists who have, through experience and further education, risen to supervisory positions in hospitals and other health care settings.

Radiologic instructors teach in university settings, teaching hospitals, and in two-year technical programs.

be flexible in order to prosper in the field. Education will provide the best tool for competition and advancement. Those technologists with advanced training in mammography, CT imaging, MRI, ultrasound, and other technologies stand to prosper in the years ahead.

How Do I Learn More?

PROFESSIONAL ORGANIZATIONS

To learn about certification, contact

American Registry of Radiologic Technologists
1255 Northland Drive
St. Paul, MN 55120-1155
651-687-0048
http://www.arrt.org

For extensive information about careers in radiologic technology, visit the ASRT Web site.

American Society of Radiologic Technologists (ASRT)
15000 Central Avenue, SE
Albuquerque, NM 87123-3917
505-298-4500
http://www.asrt.org

To learn about accredited educational programs, contact

Joint Review Committee on Education in Radiologic Technology
20 North Wacker Drive, Suite 2850
Chicago, IL 60606-3182
312-704-5300
mail@jrcert.org
http://www.jrcert.org

BIBLIOGRAPHY

Following is a sampling of materials relating to the professional concerns and development of radiologic technologists.

Anderson, Anthony, ed. *The Radiology Technologist's Handbook to Surgical Procedures*. Boca Raton, Fla.: CRC Press, 1999.

Bushing, Stewart C. *Radiologic Science for Technologists: Physics, Biology, and Protection*. 8th ed. St. Louis, Mo.: Mosby, 2004.

Statkiewicz Sherer, Mary Alice, Paul J. Visconti, and Russell E. Ritenour. *Radiation Protection in Medical Radiography*. 4th ed. St. Louis, Mo.: Mosby, 2002.

Stedman's Radiolology Words. 4th ed. Philadelphia: Lippincott Williams & Wilkins, 2003.

RESPIRATORY CARE WORKERS

Tom Garcia reports to work at 7:00 P.M. at Northwestern Memorial Hospital, one of Chicago's major teaching hospitals. He greets coworkers as he gets a cup of coffee and collects the reports of the day shift. When he sits down to read them over, he looks for important messages, patients who have undergone surgery that morning, and new admissions requiring evaluation. He makes notes of changes in therapy or medication. When Tom finishes scanning the last report, he realizes that one chart is missing. He dials the nurse's station on the pediatric floor.

"Hi, Joanie, it's Tom Garcia. Where's Jessica Brandon's chart?" Tom has been giving Jessica chest physiotherapy since she was admitted a month ago with complications of cystic fibrosis. There is a pause on the other end, then a sigh.

"Tom," Joanie says finally, "Jessica died this afternoon."

Tom covers his eyes with his hand and sits quietly for a moment. This is the part of the job Tom hates. He sees Jessica's smile as he left her room just last night. "You be sweet now," he told her, "and I'll see you tomorrow." Sometimes all the knowledge and skilled care in the world are not enough. The feelings of failure—however irrational—and having to witness the grief of survivors can be excruciating.

But right now Tom can't indulge his feelings. It's going to be a tough night. Two other respiratory care workers are out with the flu bug that's going around. He'll have to work twice as hard, yet give each patient the same focused attention as he would on a slow day.

Definition
Respiratory care workers administer general respiratory care to persons with heart and lung problems.

Alternative Job Titles
Inhalation therapists
Respiratory care practitioners

High School Subjects
Biology
Chemistry
Health

Personal Skills
Helping/teaching
Technical/scientific

Salary Range
$31,420 to $42,050 to $56,480

Minimum Educational Level
Associate's degree

Certification or Licensing
Required by certain states

Outlook
Faster than the average

DOT
079

GOE
14.06.01

NOC
3214

O*NET-SOC
29-1126.00, 29-2054.00

What Does a Respiratory Care Worker Do?

In extraordinary circumstances, it is possible to go without food for a few weeks or without water for a few days. But without air, brain damage occurs within minutes; death follows after about nine minutes.

Respiratory care workers include *therapists, technicians,* and *assistants* (or *aides*). Assistants clean, sterilize, store, and maintain inventory and care for equipment. They are usually beginners on their way to certification and registration and have little patient contact. The duties of *registered respiratory therapists* (RRTs) and *certified respiratory therapists* (CRTs) are similar. They both treat patients with cardiorespiratory problems.

RRTs have more clinical experience, however. They apply scientific knowledge and theory to the practical problems of respiratory care under the supervision of doctors. They may be required to exercise independent clinical judgement. Sometimes they even advise doctors on appropriate therapy. Licensed RRTs can also order medication with a physician's approval. In addition, their responsibilities often entail training, teaching, and supervising other workers, such as CRTs.

Respiratory care workers review clinical data, patient histories, and respiratory therapy orders.

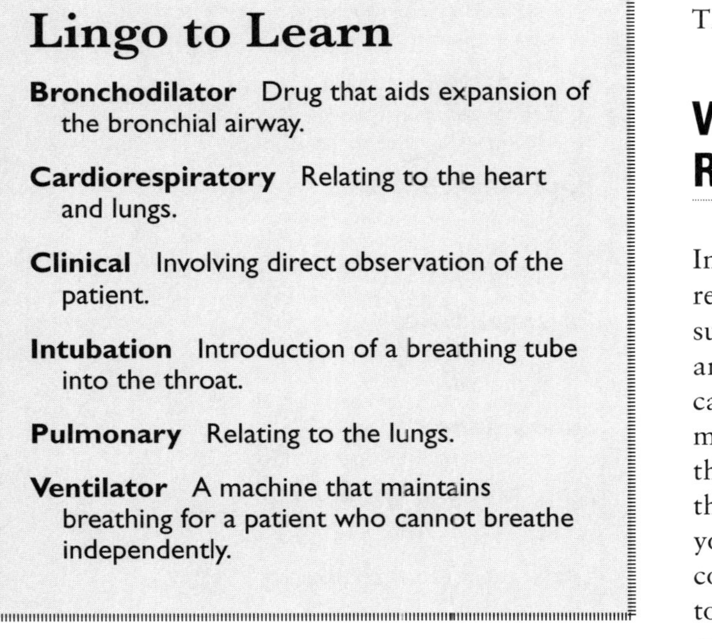

Lingo to Learn

Bronchodilator Drug that aids expansion of the bronchial airway.

Cardiorespiratory Relating to the heart and lungs.

Clinical Involving direct observation of the patient.

Intubation Introduction of a breathing tube into the throat.

Pulmonary Relating to the lungs.

Ventilator A machine that maintains breathing for a patient who cannot breathe independently.

They interview and examine patients and perform or recommend X rays and laboratory tests. They evaluate patient information in order to determine the appropriateness of specific therapies. They perform and modify prescribed therapeutic procedures, such as the administration of aerosol inhalants that confine medication to the lungs. They are also responsible for assembling, maintaining, and monitoring equipment and for ensuring cleanliness and sterility. Equipment includes ventilators (respirators), positive-pressure breathing machines, or environmental control systems. The patients of respiratory care workers may be recovering from surgery and need respiratory care to restore full breathing capacity and to prevent respiratory illnesses. Other patients suffer from chronic conditions like asthma or emphysema. Victims of heart failure, stroke, drowning, or other trauma need life support. Respiratory care workers observe patients' physiological responses to therapy and consult with physicians if there are adverse reactions. They are often called to emergency rooms and intensive care units where their skill and devotion can mean the difference between life and death. Now that home care is becoming more widespread, respiratory care workers sometimes instruct patients and their families in the use of respiratory equipment at home.

An important aspect of the job is record keeping. Respiratory care workers record critical information on patients' charts, make reports, and keep track of the cost of materials and charges to the patients. There is always a lot of paperwork.

What Is It Like to Be a Respiratory Care Worker?

In the intensive care unit, Tom Garcia, a registered respiratory therapist, inspects ventilators for recent surgery patients. Since these people are intubated and cannot speak, Tom asks yes or no questions that can be answered with hand squeezes. He takes a few moments to reassure these critical patients and let them know he's there for them. As he finishes up, the pager summons him to operating room seven. A young woman, the victim of a drunk driver, has just come out of emergency surgery. Tom connects her to a ventilator and confirms that the equipment is operating properly.

The surgeon asks Tom questions about an oddity in the patient's blood gas analysis. It's something Tom has seen before. He explains it to the surgeon and makes a recommendation. Tom smiles to himself as he leaves the intensive care unit, reflecting that only a few years ago, doctors didn't ask the advice of lower-level professionals. But that's changing with specialization, the increasing sophistication of equipment, and new options in therapeutic technique.

It's nearly midnight when Tom sits down to eat a quick lunch. After leaving the ICU, Tom administered bronchodilator aerosols to two pulmonary disease patients. He coached them on how to cough in order to clear their lungs. He also performed chest physiotherapy on a man recovering from pneumonia. This technique involves placing the patient in a posture to promote drainage and thumping and vibrating the rib cage. Tom expands the sketchy notes he made on his rounds. Finally, he writes out a to-do list for the remainder of his shift. He has to check on the car accident victim again and call the equipment manufacturer about a recurring problem with one of the ventilators. Since one of the aides has the flu, he'll check to see that there are enough supplies for the next shift.

"This is not a job for someone who wants a nice, predictable nine-to-five existence," Tom says. "And you'll never get rich. On the other hand, you'll never be bored either. The rewards of a career in respiratory therapy are the constant challenge and knowing that you help people. You see results. What you do makes a difference."

The rewards of a career in respiratory therapy are the constant challenge and knowing that you help people. You see results.

Advancement Possibilities

Pediatric neonatal specialists work with premature newborns and newborns with respiratory problems. The needs of these infants are unique; since many more premature infants now survive, this is a rapidly growing field.

Pulmonary function technologists use advanced techniques to diagnose pulmonary diseases.

Do I Have What It Takes to Be a Respiratory Care Worker?

Because people can die so quickly if they stop breathing, respiratory care workers play a critical role in medical institutions. In cases of cardiac arrest, drowning, electric shock, and other kinds of trauma, they may literally hold people's lives in their hands. For this reason, respiratory care workers need to develop maturity, the capacity to accept grave responsibilities, and a genuine desire to care for others.

"You can't be squeamish," says Tom. "Especially in a big city hospital, you see lots of bad injuries. You've got to keep your cool because the patient and the trauma team depend on you. And since you work with ventilators and other sophisticated machinery, it helps if you're good with your hands or have mechanical aptitude."

Pat Adney is director of respiratory care and rehabilitation services at Chicago's Weiss Memorial Hospital. In addition to the qualities already described, Pat says having a natural curiosity and interest in the field is a plus. "A really good respiratory care worker possesses intellectual curiosity. Most of your education comes from the job; you constantly have to figure things out and learn on your own initiative because there's always something new." Pat also stresses emotional equilibrium. "You must strike a balance so you neither burn out nor become heartless and unfeeling."

Since respiratory care workers have to process a lot of paperwork, writing skills are a must. "You work with doctors and other highly educated people," says Tom. "In order to have credibility, you must be articulate and well read in your field. There's always so much to read because there are new things happening all the time."

Another factor to keep in mind is the necessity for shift work. Medical facilities operate 24 hours a day, so there are three shifts. Most respiratory care workers are expected to be flexible about shift changes, overtime, and holidays. Remember, too, that they are on their feet for most of the 40-hour week. They must also be able to take orders from superiors—even when they come from people who are not always pleasant. "You have to deal with professional egos," Tom comments, "and sometimes you're pulled in different directions because of great needs and a too small staff."

Finally, one important factor to consider is safety. The pressurized gases used in respiratory therapy are potentially hazardous; and every respiratory care worker runs the risk of contracting an infectious disease from a patient. Following safety precautions, regular maintenance, and equipment testing reduce the possibility of injury from pressurized gases, while strict adherence to proper procedure minimizes the risk of exposure to infectious disease.

How Do I Become a Respiratory Care Worker?

Tom's career grew out of two major boyhood interests. "I always liked fooling around with mechanical things, and I was interested in science. Applying mechanics to the human body is fascinating." Tom recalls his training period as being a tough two years. "There was a lot of memorization. Everything was very concentrated. In the second year you get thrown into patient care—you have to be an adult right away."

EDUCATION

High School

Respiratory care requires a lot of fundamental mathematical problem solving. For instance, in their daily work, respiratory care workers must compute medication dosages and calculate gas concentrations. Tom advises that high school students take courses in algebra, physics, chemistry, biology, English composition, and reading comprehension. Classes in health, computer skills, general mathematics, and bookkeeping are also helpful.

A summer job in a hospital is a good way to see what the field is like. Although the job assignment may not relate to respiratory therapy, there will be chances to observe and perhaps get acquainted with respiratory care workers. If no part-time or temporary work is available, you might consider volunteer service.

Postsecondary Training

To work as an aide, you may only need a high school degree and on-the-job training. Formal training in respiratory care is provided in one-year certificate programs, which certify an individual for entry-level respiratory therapy work, or two-year associate degree or four-year bachelor degree programs that prepare you for the registry examination and advanced work. There are 59 entry-level and 319 advanced respiratory therapy programs in the United States and Puerto Rico. A high school diploma or equivalent is required for all. Training is available through hospitals, medical schools, colleges and universities, trade schools, vocation-technical institutes, and the armed forces. It is imperative that the training institution be accredited by the Committee on Allied Health Education and Accreditation (CAHEA) of the American Medical Association (AMA) or the Committee on Accreditation for Respiratory Care (CoARC). A list of accredited programs is available from the American Association for Respiratory Care (AARC) (see "How Do I Learn More?").

Two-year schools should include enough credit hours of clinical training (treating patients under supervision) to qualify the student to take both the certification and registry examinations. (Certification is required in order to sit for the registry examination.)

Course work consists of anatomy, physiology, medical terminology, chemistry, mathematics, microbiology, physics, therapeutic procedures, clinical medicine, and clinical expressions. Students learn to do procedures such as venous punctures, arterial blood draws, intubation, stress testing, and electrocardiograms. Social science classes in communication skills, psychology, and medical ethics support the basic science studies.

In respiratory care, as well as all other areas of medicine, education is ongoing. Constant improvements in equipment, medication, and therapeutic technique make continuing education a must. In addition to registry, a respiratory care worker may pursue specialties in pulmonary function technology, pulmonary function therapy, pediatric neonatology, and many other areas. Supervising RRTs or equipment manufacturers often present in-service training seminars. Good hospitals support additional training.

CERTIFICATION OR LICENSING

Typically, a hospital hires uncertified new graduates providing that they pass the certification exam in six months to a year. Tom took the registry exam two years after certification. As an RRT, Tom is now a supervisor. "I enjoy teaching," he says. "I like to pass on knowledge, to help shape the careers of new people."

Certification and registry examinations are offered by the National Board for Respiratory Care (see "How Do I Learn More?"), usually through a state licensure agency. Forty-two states license respiratory care personnel. The certified respiratory therapists (CRT) designation is the standard for licensure in most states. As of 2006, candidates for the CRT must hold an associate's degree from an accredited respiratory therapy education program. To sit for the registered respiratory therapist (RRT) exam, applicants must hold the CRT designation and an associate's degree from an accredited program.

SCHOLARSHIPS AND GRANTS

The American Respiratory Care Foundation (the philanthropic organization of the AARC)

To Be a Successful Respiratory Care Worker, You Should . . .

- have compassion, courtesy, and flexibility
- be able to articulate your thoughts, ideas, and opinions
- have a cool head under stress
- be willing to follow instructions and be a team player
- pay attention to details
- have mechanical aptitude and good manual dexterity

offers scholarships specifically for respiratory care education (see "How Do I Learn More?"). Some hospitals may sponsor students on an as-needed basis. Individual states sponsor general scholarships.

Who Will Hire Me?

AARC reports that there are more than 110,000 respiratory therapists in the United States. According to the *Occupational Outlook Handbook,* 90 percent of respiratory care workers had jobs in hospitals in departments of respiratory care, anesthesiology, and pulmonary medicine. The remaining jobs were in home health care services, medical equipment rental companies, and nursing homes. Nevertheless, more and more respiratory care workers are now finding employment in skilled nursing and rehabilitation facilities, doctors' offices, companies that provide emergency oxygen services, and municipal services such as fire departments.

Many CAHEA-accredited schools have placement services to help graduates find jobs. The American Association for Respiratory Care publishes a monthly magazine, *The AARC Times,* which features classified job ads (see "How Do I Learn More?"). Networking with people already employed in the profession is also a source of job referrals.

Many new graduates apply directly to potential employers. They do research by talking to respiratory care workers already working there. They ask about the quality of training and the general quality of health care available through the employing institution. It's a good idea to find out whether there will be support for additional training. Will the employer reimburse tuition expenses? Will it allow a flexible schedule to accommodate class time? Teaching hospitals are especially good places to begin a career. Equipment, technology, and training are likely to be first rate, with opportunities for varied duties and working with a range of patient needs.

Employers look for applicants who have made good grades and who have excellent attendance records. They evaluate personal qualities too, like courtesy, communication skills, enthusiasm, maturity, and a responsible, cooperative attitude.

Where Can I Go from Here?

Tom Garcia started out as respiratory therapy technician and later took the registry exam. "It's common to go into nursing or medical school or several ancillary fields once you acquire some technical skills," Tom says. "Many decide to stay in respiratory care, but usually a CRT will want to become an RRT so that he or she can get into supervisory or administrative levels."

Pat Adney, who started her medical career as a physical therapist, says, "Many respiratory care workers go into home care after a few years. At first, you're on call on a rotating basis. You may have to go out on weekends or holidays, but eventually you get some options that allow more flexibility."

What Are the Salary Ranges?

An AARC study found nearly half of the respiratory therapists in the United States made more than $48,000 a year in 2002, which was an increase of $10,000 from the previous year. According to the *Occupational Outlook Handbook,* respiratory therapists earned a median salary of $42,050 in 2002. Those in the lowest 10 percent earned less than $31,420 annually, while those in the highest 10 percent earned more than $56,480.

Hospital workers usually enjoy excellent fringe benefits including health insurance, paid vacation and sick leave, and pension plans. Additional benefits may include free parking, cafeteria discounts, uniform allowances, tuition reimbursement for job-related studies, and on-site day care.

What Is the Job Outlook?

Employment in respiratory care is expanding rapidly. The U.S. Department of Labor expects employment to increase faster than the average for all occupations over the next decade.

Even though efforts to control rising health care costs have slowed down job opportunities in hospitals in recent years, this slow-growth trend is not expected to last. On the contrary, respiratory care professionals with credentials in neonatal care and pulmonary disease will be particularly in demand.

Several factors are involved, including the rapid increase in the middle-aged and elderly populations. The elderly are the most likely to suffer heart and lung ailments such as pneumonia, chronic bronchitis, emphysema, and heart disease. As the Baby Boomers move from middle age into old age, the need for respiratory care workers will increase.

Advances in the treatment of heart attack, traumatic injury, and premature birth also bode well for the respiratory care field, since all these groups require respiratory care for some part of their treatment. The AIDS epidemic also continues to spread, and these patients often have secondary lung ailments. This and other disease populations will boost the demand for respiratory therapy professionals.

The home health care field is also expanding. This expansion has been fostered to some extent by the insurance industry's demand for less expensive alternatives to hospital care. Equipment manufacturers and rental firms, as well as companies that provide respiratory care on a contract basis, will also employ more respiratory care professionals.

How Do I Learn More?

PROFESSIONAL ORGANIZATIONS

For career and accredited programs information, contact

American Association for Respiratory Care
9425 North MacArthur Boulevard, Suite 100
Irving, TX 75063
(972) 243-2272
info@aarc.org
http://www.aarc.org

For accreditation information, contact

Committee on Accreditation for Respiratory Care
1248 Harwood Road
Bedford, TX 76021-4244
817-283-2835
http://www.coarc.com

For a list of accredited respiratory care programs, contact

National Board for Respiratory Care
8310 Nieman Road
Lenexa, KS 66214-1579
http://www.nbrc.org

BIBLIOGRAPHY

The following is a sampling of materials relating to the professional concerns and development of respiratory care workers:

Egan, Donald F., Craig L. Scanlan, Robert L. Wilkins, and James K. Stoller, eds. *Egan's Fundamentals of Respiratory Care.* 7th ed. St. Louis, MO: Mosby Year-Book, 1999.

Persing, Gary. *Respiratory Care Exam Review: Review for the Entry Level and Advanced Exams.* Kent, U.K.: W. B. Saunders, 2004.

Wilkins, Robert L., Thomas J. Butler, and James R. Dexter. *A Pocket Guide to Respiratory Disease.* Philadelphia: F. A. Davis, 2001.

ROBOTICS TECHNICIANS

Clanking noises on the plant testing floor aren't exactly irritating to Jim Ryers. He's a pretty seasoned robotics technician and is accustomed to working around noisy machines.

Today, though, Jim has a lot on his mind—even more than usual—and the squeaking noise coming from the arm of this prototype robot is making it hard for him to concentrate. He has an appointment with one of the head engineers in less than 20 minutes, and in an hour he's due to leave for the General Motors plant where his expertise in arc-welding robots is needed to straighten out a misbehaving robot on the assembly line.

"It's not welding doors anymore, Jim," the foreman at General Motors yelled over the phone. "It's burning holes in them!"

"Watch it!" yells another technician, who is teamed up with Jim to teach this prototype robot how to move its welding arm as the specification sheet says it should.

"Huh?" mumbles Jim, turning absentmindedly toward his colleague.

Wham! The robot's arm swings around and lands Jim a painful, but ultimately harmless, blow to the head. Jim's colleague makes certain Jim is okay and then they both share a laugh.

They know what it's like to have a thousand things on their minds. And they both know how dangerous it is.

Definition

Robotics technicians install, program, and repair robots and related equipment by applying knowledge of electronics, electrical circuits, mechanics, pneumatics, hydraulics, and programming.

Alternative Job Titles

Field service technicians
Manufacturing installation engineers

High School Subjects

Mathematics
Physics
Technical/shop

Personal Skills

Mechanical/manipulative
Technical/scientific

Salary Range

$28,380 to $45,930 to $66,810+

Work Environment

Primarily indoors
Primarily one location

Minimum Educational Level

Associate's degree

Certification or Licensing

Recommended

Outlook

About as fast as the average

DOT

638

GOE

N/A

NOC

2232

O*NET-SOC

N/A

What Does a Robotics Technician Do?

Robots are increasingly complex machines, and it takes increasingly well-trained and multiskilled people to build and service them. That's why *robotics technicians* can be considered the jacks-of-all-trades of robotics engineering. They not only install, repair, and maintain finished robots, but they help design and develop new kinds of robotics equipment.

Many robotics technicians work for robotics manufacturing companies that specialize in designing and building machines for a wide variety of customers. Whether robots are needed to weld or paint automobile bodies, perform precision medical procedures, help clean up toxic wastes, or perform any other task in the place of a traditional human worker, several robotics technicians will always be in the background to repair, fine-tune, or replace them. Thus, while robots may replace human workers in many ways, each robot's existence depends on the skill and care of robotics technicians and other specialists.

While all robotics technicians perform many tasks, most specialize in a particular field. *Robotics*

Lingo to Learn

Field robot or service robot A robot that does jobs in nonmanufacturing environments that are hazardous, dreary, or inaccessible to humans. Examples include machines that manipulate radioactive material, "astrobots," that are stationed in orbit around Earth, and rodent-sized robots, also known as "pipe mice," that look for corrosion in pipelines.

Industrial robot A machine or device designed to both manipulate and transport parts, tools, implements, and other objects through a programmed manufacturing task.

Prototype robot A first full-scale and usually functional form of a new type or design of robot. A tested and successful prototype usually serves as the model from which several robots are assembled to fill a customer's order.

Robot The general name for a unit or machine that is able to perform human-type actions and functions, without necessarily having a human appearance.

Sensor A device for the detection or measurement of a physical property to which a robot may respond. The machine derives input signals relative to tracking, altitude, distance, grip, or any other coordinates that may help it perform a specific task along a determined course.

design technicians, for example, focus their energies near the drawing boards, where they team up with engineers and other technicians to design and develop new robotics devices. The engineers are responsible for analyzing the tasks that the robots will have to perform and the settings in which they will perform those tasks. Customers for whom the robots are being designed are often very particular about the specifications—including the cost—of the robots they've ordered. The engineers must meet those specifications as closely as possible, while designing the best robot for the job.

Once the engineers have come up with the initial design for a robotics system, it's time for the robotics technicians to get involved. They first familiarize themselves with the specifications and any diagrams, blueprints, or sketches. Referring to that information, they then run a series of tests on the various systems and materials that will be used to build the robotics device. They keep careful records of all their test procedures and results and may be asked to clearly present those test results with tables, diagrams, and written reports. If a particular system, subsystem, or material does not meet test requirements, the robotics technician is often responsible for suggesting alternative materials or more effective ways of configuring a system for the best possible results.

After completing the testing process, robotics design technicians often oversee the building of a robot prototype (the first full-scale and functional model of the robot). The technicians often apply their skills in sketching and mechanical drawing so that machine shop workers can actually make all the necessary parts. Once those parts are assembled and the robot prototype passes further testing, the robotics design technicians help produce the formal documentation, including blueprints and manufacturing specifications sheets. Those specifications, in turn, are used by other technicians and workers to produce the actual robots that a customer ordered. *Materials handling technicians,* for example, locate and deliver components and materials for robot assembly. *Robot assemblers* are then responsible for actually putting those parts together. Those assemblers who specialize in the moving parts, hardware, and robot components are often referred to as *mechanical assembly technicians.* In addition, *electrical assembly technicians* put together electrical components, including circuit boards and automatic switching devices, the "gray matter" of robotics brains.

Once robots are designed and assembled, their lives have only just begun. They must be put to work for the customers who ordered them. Special robotics technicians serve as the bridge between the company that made the robots and the customer who ordered them. Such technicians install, repair, and maintain robots in their specific work environments. After reviewing the work order and instructional information, they must make sure that the site is suitable for the robots. The proper electrical wires, switches, circuit breakers, and other parts must be in place before a robot can be positioned and secured, often with the help of cranes or other heavy equipment. Robots, after all, often move sheets of steel large enough to make car frames or ship bows, so they may themselves be quite large. In addition, various fixtures—hoses, cables, and connectors for hydraulic systems or welding arms, for example—must be installed. And once the robot is operational, the technicians must use its programming language, or operating system, to program the robot for specific tasks. A palette-stacking robot in a warehouse, for example, must be programmed to stack a certain number of boxes from left to right and from bottom to top, over and over again without fail.

Most robotics technicians perform a number of specialized jobs, and many of their jobs overlap. A design technician may visit a customer's manufacturing floor to help update a robotics system. It is not surprising, therefore, that most robotics technicians boast broad skills in electronics, electrical circuitry, mechanics, pneumatics, hydraulics, computer programming, and mechanical drawing, in addition to excellent communication and teamwork skills.

What Is It Like to Be a Robotics Technician?

Jim Byers is a robotics technician with FANUC Robotics Inc., a leader in U.S. industrial robot production. When faced with the difficult task of describing what he and FANUC Robotics are all about, Jim often resorts to a simple, real-life example. "If you've seen the Saturn car commercials, and you've seen the yellow robots building the cars, that's us." Indeed, FANUC Robotics specializes in robotics systems used to build automobiles and, not surprisingly, does a lot of business with the "Big Three" U.S. automakers: General Motors, Ford, and Daimler-Chrysler.

On a day-to-day basis, Jim contributes to the design, testing, assembly, and maintenance of such robots. His surroundings change accordingly, depending on the project with which he is involved. One day, for example, Jim may be at his desk, drafting plans for parts that will help turn a prototype robot into the actual machine that FANUC will deliver to a given customer. Another day, he may be on the machine floor, surrounded by mechanical instruments and computer controllers, trying to program a robot arm to clutch a certain object and rotate it a specific number of degrees.

"Once a project has come through engineering and has actually hit the manufacturing floor," Jim explains, "I do the buildup on the robots." At such times, Jim assembles the entire system with test parts to make sure it functions properly. If all goes well, the robot system is then dismantled and shipped to the customer.

Jim's responsibilities are by no means over when a robot he's worked on is sent out to a customer. "There are times when I go on the road—actually go to the customer's plant—to help install a robot, get it running," he explains. Such jobs really put Jim's skills to the test, as he can be confronted with any number of new situations, must work with customers he may not know well, and must be able to think on his feet. "You head out there, and you basically have to be a mechanical engineer, an electrical engineer, plus you've got to be familiar with what robot is out there, the software that's in it, what type of controller it has, how the application works," he explains. Often, Jim is alone on such jobs. "When you head out to a job, that's it," he says. "You're the only representative; you have to know everything."

There are times when I go on the road—actually go to the customer's plant—to help install a robot, get it running

Obviously, no robotics technician can know everything. Still, the technician will usually know a lot more about robotics systems than customers who depend on those systems. As an additional service to those customers, the technicians often teach them the necessary skills to rectify common problems. That way, time and money can be saved when a robot doesn't function properly or, in Jim's words, "when it gets hung up on something."

Not all robotics technicians perform as broad a range of duties as Jim. Many technicians stick to specific fields of concentration with less varied work environments. Robotics technicians primarily involved in development and testing, for example, spend most of their days at a desk, worktable, or test laboratory. Those who specialize in robot installation, operation, or maintenance, however, tend to move considerably, often carrying assorted objects and tools around bustling, often noisy factory floors. Different robotics technicians also work different hours. While Jim tends to work a standard 9-to-5 schedule, maintenance technicians and robot operators may work less regular hours, depending on the demands of a particular customer. Many auto manufacturers, for example, break the workday into three eight-hour shifts; if a robot needs service at three in the morning, a robot maintenance technician may have to go on call (and go without much sleep).

Some technicians may work in potentially dangerous environments. Robots, after all, are often used for tasks that may be hazardous to human workers, such as handling laser beams, arc-welding equipment, radioactive substances, or toxic chemicals, detecting and detonating bombs, or exploring the depths of oceans or outer space. Technicians who work with these so-called field or service robots may face occupational hazards unknown to their colleagues who work around more conventional factory robots.

While field robots continue to grow in popularity, most robotics technicians face few risks if they follow strict safety regulations and remain attentive on the job. For Jim, the most common danger is being hit by a robot when programming it for a path of motion—hardly a life-threatening event in most cases.

"If you're in there teaching a path, teaching the robot how to go through the motions, you think it's going to one point, and it'll go to a different point," Jim says. "And if you happen to be standing in the way of that point—unless you get the robot stopped—it will hit you."

Do I Have What It Takes to Be a Robotics Technician?

Robotics makes use of the latest cutting-edge technology in areas as diverse as computers, artificial intelligence, and materials design. A successful robotics technician is, therefore, not only someone who can work well with his or her hands and with mechanical devices, but someone who is willing to work very hard to keep up with the rapid pace of technological change. Jim compares robotics to the computer industry, where specialists master the intricacies of one system (like the 486 microcomputer chip) only to discover that its successor (the Pentium chip, for example) has been developed and must now be learned as well. In much the same way, robots are made up of systems and subsystems that continuously change at lightning speed. They incorporate microprocessors, computer languages (commonly called operating systems by robotics technicians), computer controllers and feedback systems, new materials, and so forth. Trying to keep up with rapid changes in all these areas can be a daunting task. "It seems like every time you get a different robot, they've changed the version of the software. Different parameters are moved," says Jim. "We've got some people who know how to run four different generations of robots," he says, noting that this is an accomplishment worthy of much respect.

While keeping up with technology can be tough, even frustrating, Jim also points out that it is extremely interesting and rewarding. "What's more," he says, "no robotics technician is expected to know it all. The challenge is to learn broad enough skills to get by and to prioritize those areas of knowledge that will be most useful. You have to work in a lot of different areas to do robotics. You really don't master any of them. You just have to be familiar with all of them," Jim explains.

The ideal robotics technician should also be able to strike a delicate balance between working well alone and acting as a team player. A technician must often confront complex situations without any assistance; in such cases, self-sufficiency is a real asset. On the other hand, a good part of any technician's time is spent on crowded manufacturing floors, with groups of customers who use a robotics system, or among other robotics workers. "If you're out on a customer site, you can't be rude or pushy with them," says Jim. "When you're working on the floor here, there's a lot you have to know . . . so many types of robots, so many systems we build. If you need a question answered, you need to be able to get along

To Be a Successful Robotics Technician, You Should . . .

- have excellent mechanical aptitude and coordination
- be neat, precise, and patient
- think methodically and communicate effectively
- be able to work independently and as part of a team
- enjoy learning new skills and programs

with employees. You always need a helping hand—whether something's heavy, or you need something lifted—it's always good to have contacts within the plant."

How Do I Become a Robotics Technician?

Anyone with a strong mechanical background and a willingness to learn can become a fine robotics technician. Jim points out that it's a field that's hard to train for and that the best way to start moving up the ladder is to get a foot in the door, even if it's at the bottom rung. "When I was younger, I did a lot of model building, and when I turned 16, I started working on cars," Jim recalls. "Basically, I knew robotics was an up-and-coming field that looked exciting . . . something I wanted to try." When he finally did try his hand in robotics, the combination of spatial and mechanical dexterity from his hobbies served him exceptionally well.

EDUCATION

High School

A high school diploma is the minimum educational requirement for a robotics technician, and additional work experience is also helpful. Interested high school students should take courses that provide a solid background in mathematics, physics, machine shop skills, drafting, and electronics. For Jim, the most useful classes in high school were physics, calculus, and three years of drafting, including computer-aided drafting (CAD).

Postsecondary Training

While some entry-level positions in robotics are open to technicians with only a high school diploma, most successful robotics technicians have received formal training in a related technical field, usually in a two-year postsecondary school associate's degree program. In an effort to best educate their existing workforces, some companies pay for the educational costs of employees who work toward certification or associate's degree in robotics or related fields. Jim, for example, has almost completed an associate's degree in robotics technology, for which FANUC fully reimburses his tuition. Jim says that working a full-time job while attending school is a lot of work, but the feeling of satisfaction and hope for future payoff make it all worthwhile. Jim also lists two reasons why his associate's degree is taking him considerably longer than two years to complete. First, it is hard to take a full course load and also work full time, so he balances the two by taking a little longer; second, such a degree requires more credits than many others.

"I probably have an additional 18 credit hours," he explains. "There are so many different classes you have to take. Eight core robotics classes and support classes, two electrical, a microprocessor course, two hydraulics, two pneumatics classes, drafting, and CAD." Some programs also require courses in technical writing, communications, social sciences, and the humanities.

In addition to training toward a formal degree, robotics technicians may register for on-the-job technical training, for which their companies may issue certificates of completion. Jim has benefited from several classes offered by FANUC Robotics. He took an introductory course in Carol (the company's proprietary operating software for robotics controllers), a one-week training class on Arc Tool (the operating system for robots used for automatic welding operations), a buildup class for the Arc Mate Robot (a system primarily used in FANUC's weld systems), various electrical training classes, and a controller debugging class.

CERTIFICATION OR LICENSING

To date, there is no national licensing bureau for robotics technicians. However, while most robotics technicians do not need to obtain a license or certificate in order to get a job, in some industrial settings a company might hire someone with the provision that he or she successfully passes courses or training in a particular program. Learning new technology is the key to success in the robotics field and the ideal technician welcomes the challenge of keeping up-to-date.

INTERNSHIPS AND VOLUNTEERSHIPS

The student trying to get a first job as a robotics technician faces a catch-22. It's very difficult to find that first job in robotics, even a part-time or summer position. Still, the only way to find your first job is to get a foot in the door. Thus, while first attempts to land a job in robotics might be initially frustrating, perseverance and resourcefulness usually lead to openings.

One way to increase your odds of being hired for a first job in robotics is to look into related jobs in other engineering fields such as electronics or mechanics. Such jobs offer experience and skills that can be transferred to robotics if and when an opportunity in that field opens up.

Other activities that will foster knowledge and skills relevant to a career in robotics include membership in high school science clubs, participation in science fairs, and pursuing hobbies that involve electronics, mechanical equipment, model building, or reading books and articles about technical topics.

Who Will Hire Me?

Students who graduate from a two-year college or technical institute can usually receive job-placement assistance from the school's placement office. Corporate recruiters from robotics manufacturers and other automated equipment industries may also visit schools to interview and hire students who meet their needs.

There are numerous other ways of locating prospective employers in the robotics industry. State or private employment agencies may be able to help. Want ads in newspapers and professional journals are another source of information. In addition, students should not hesitate to directly contact companies by email, phone, or letter to describe their education, interests, and experience. One fruitful way to learn more about a specific company or job title is to set up an informational interview—over the phone or in person—in which you merely try to gather information and ask general questions rather than asking for or about a specific job.

The Internet can also assist in the job search; *Robotics Online* (http://www.roboticsonline.com), sponsored by the Robotics Industries Association (RIA), features job listings along with news and information about changes in the industry.

Jim's first job in the field was a combination of lucky timing and extremely hard work. After graduating from high school, a family friend and employee of FANUC Robotics Inc. saw promise in Jim's mechanical inclinations with cars and models and helped him land an entry-level position at the firm. Jim started out as a job runner.

"Basically, I came in, I had a clipboard, and I just drove a company car and picked up parts for the systems." After nearly two months of running, Jim told his boss that he knew how to drive a car; now he wanted some work experience he could use.

Jim was assigned a basic job on the robot assembly floor and given the opportunity to prove himself in order to advance. "When they see you can do a job, they keep moving you up," he explains. After five different advancements in four different areas, Jim ended up working primarily with arc-welding robots used in automobile manufacturing. As FANUC often gets orders for as many as 500 to 1,000 robots for a spot welding plant, Jim is able to make substantial contributions to the company's bottom line.

Where Can I Go from Here?

After several years on the job, robotics technicians who have proven their ability to handle more responsibility may be assigned some supervisory work or may train new technicians. Experienced technicians may teach courses at their workplace or at local schools or community colleges.

Other routes for advancement include becoming a sales representative for a robotics company or working as an independent contractor for companies that use or manufacture robots. Jim points out that many seasoned robotics technicians subcontract their time out to customers for a lot of money, basing their worth on the skills and experience they've developed over the years. "Those guys can work when they want to and make about $100 an hour."

With additional training and education, especially a bachelor's degree, technicians can become eligible for positions such as robotics technologists or robotics engineers. Jim would like to earn his bachelor's degree in robotics engineering so that he can get into design work and build entire systems. Then he will be in a position to apply expertise and creativity to robotics-related problems. "When a customer asks for a process to build a certain part or perform a certain task," Jim explains, "I will figure out what type of robots and tooling to use and design them, the fixturing to hold the needed parts—the whole works."

Jim also points out that his experience as a robotics technician—and all of his work that led up to that job—will give him an edge as an engineer. "If you're building a system, you can tell the difference between a seasoned engineer and someone who's just come out of school," he says, stressing that many engineers just out of school are still exceptionally good at what they do. Nevertheless, there's no schooling like the job itself.

What Are the Salary Ranges?

Earnings and benefits for robotics technicians vary widely in different parts of the country and among jobs with different training requirements and responsibilities. The Fluid Power Educational Foundation reports that trained technicians in the fluid power industry (which includes robotics technicians) had average starting salaries of $38,500 annually. According to the *Occupational Outlook Handbook,* electrical and electronics engineering technicians had median annual earnings of $45,930 in 2003. The lowest paid 10 percent earned less than $28,380 annually, while the highest paid 10 percent earned more than $66,810. Full-time positions in robotics often include health, life, and disability insurance, as well as 401(k) plans.

What Is the Job Outlook?

Technological breakthroughs in computer feedback systems and microcomputers, as well as advanced material design, bode well for robots and the technicians who keep them running. The U.S. Department of Labor expects employment of engineering technicians in general to increase about as fast as the average through 2012. Automation of manufacturing work will ensure a healthy employment outlook for robotics technicians. According to the RIA, in 2004 North American companies purchased almost $1 billion of robots, which represented a 20 percent increase over 2003 purchases. Although auto manufacturers still purchase the greatest number of robots, industries such as pharmaceuticals, food, life sciences, aerospace, and electronics are also realizing the value of robots in manufacturing. In addition to industrial robots, so-called field robots are expected to enjoy wide popularity as their uses explode in areas such as nuclear waste management, bomb detection and detonation, and pollution control. In order for companies to compete globally, they are relying on robotics to help them improve manufacturing processes. According to RIA, material handling, spot welding, arc welding, dispensing/coating, and assembly are the leading applications for new robot orders.

This proliferation of industrial and field robots means that more technicians will be needed to service the growing number of robots in use. Whether they choose to design, build, install, maintain, repair, or operate the machines, robotics technicians have a promising future.

Advancement Possibilities

Automated equipment engineers confer with a customer's engineering staff to determine layout of equipment, to resolve problems of machine design, and to avoid construction problems in the plant. They also instruct equipment operators and engineering and maintenance personnel regarding the setup, operation, and maintenance of equipment.

Maintenance mechanics repair and maintain machinery and mechanical equipment and may initiate purchase orders for parts and machines.

How Do I Learn More?

PROFESSIONAL ORGANIZATIONS

The following are organizations that provide information on robotics technician careers, accredited schools and scholarships, and possible employment:

Robotics and Automation Society
Institute of Electrical and Electronic Engineers
Education Information
3 Park Avenue, 17th Floor
New York, NY 10016-5997
212-419-7900
http://www.ncsu.edu/IEEE-RAS

Robotics Industries Association
PO Box 3724
900 Victors Way, Suite 140

Ann Arbor, MI 48106
734-994-6088
http://www.roboticsonline.com

Society of Manufacturing Engineers
One SME Drive
Dearborn, MI 48121
800-733-4763
http://www.sme.org

BIBLIOGRAPHY

The following is some recommended reading for robotics technicians:

Cook, David. *Robotics Experiments for Beginners.* Technology in Action Series. Berkeley, Calif.: APress, 2002.

Craig, John J. *Introduction to Robotics: Mechanics and Control.* Pearson Education, 2004.

Kuo, Benjamin C., and Farid Golnaraghi. *Automatic Control Systems.* 8th ed. New York: John Wiley & Sons, 2002.

Masterson, James W., Robert L. Towers, and Stephen W. Fardo. *Robotics Technology.* Chicago: Goodheart-Willcox, 1997.

SEMICONDUCTOR TECHNICIANS

Definition
Semiconductor technicians work in the development and processing of semiconductor materials and devices.

Alternative Job Titles
Microelectronics technicians
Semiconductor development technicians
Semiconductor processing technicians

High School Subjects
Computer science
English
Mathematics

Personal Skills
Mechanical/manipulative
Technical/scientific

Salary Range
$19,427 to $27,477 to $40,768+

Work Environment
Primarily indoors
Primarily one location

Minimum Educational Level
Associate's degree

Certification or Licensing
Voluntary

Outlook
Decline

DOT
003

GOE
08.03.02

NOC
9483

O*NET-SOC
51-9141.00

The etch rates, used to indicate the conducting properties of the semiconductor wafers, are mysteriously high. Michael McCollum, the technician responsible for the area, goes over the operator's calculations. "Seem fine," he says. "We'll run another set of wafers, and then we'll check the equipment. By the way, anyone know if the day shift changed the chemical bath? Could that be it?"

The next set of wafers, slices of cylinder rods made of silicon, read the same—the etch rate is still too high. Mike checks the etching bath's hardware. The lamps might have malfunctioned, heating the bath to too high of a temperature. Mike tests that. "Normal," Mike says. "It's got to be the chemical. Let me dig around the database, see what the day shift did."

A check in the production database shows him that a chemical change was made just before the day shift left, which isn't enough to cause the problem. So Mike digs deeper. Scanning the computer files, he notices that the new batch number is different from the last few chemical changes.

"There it is," Mike says, returning to the wet-etch area. "I'll bet if we sample it, we'll find a higher percentage of hydrofluoric acid in the new batch. Once we adjust the temp offset, we'll be on our merry way."

What Does a Semiconductor Technician Do?

Semiconductors and devices utilizing them are found in nearly every electronic product made today, from complicated weapons systems and space technology, to personal computers, DVD players, cell phones, and programmable coffee makers. The making of semiconductors and microelectronics devices requires the efforts of a variety of people, from the engineers who design them, to the technicians who process, construct, and test them.

Although the word *semiconductor* is often used to refer to microchips or integrated circuits, a semiconductor is actually the basic material of these devices. Semiconductor materials are so titled because they can be treated to act with properties between that of an insulator, which does not conduct electrical current, and that of a true conductor of electrical current, such as metal.

Silicon is the most common material used as a semiconductor. Other semiconductor materials may be gallium arsenide, germanium, selenium, silicon carbide, and cuprous oxide. Doping, or treating, these materials with substances such as aluminum, arsenic, boron, and phosphorous gives them conducting properties. By applying these substances according to a specifically designed layout, engineers and technicians construct the tiny electronic devices—

Lingo to Learn

Bit A unit of information, used when referring to the information storage capacity available on a microchip. 1,000 bits is equal to 1K of information.

Capacitor Element in electrical circuit used to store charge temporarily.

Clean room Specially designed, dust-free, air-filtered room where the semiconductor wafers are processed and where the circuit layout is imprinted on the wafer. Must be kept extremely clean due to the sensitivity of semiconductor processing. A clean room is often 100 times cleaner than a hospital room.

Conductor Substance that conducts an electrical charge.

Doping Refers to the adding of chemicals and other substances to semiconductor material.

Etching The process of preparing wafers, usually by treating (doping) the semiconductor with various substances that will give it the desired conducting properties.

Insulator Material that does not conduct electricity.

Integrated circuit Tiny chip of material imprinted or etched with many interconnected electronic components.

transistors, capacitors, and resistors—of an integrated circuit. A microchip no larger than a fingernail may contain many thousands of these devices.

There are many steps that occur in processing semiconductors into integrated circuits. The technicians involved in these processes are called *semiconductor development technicians* and *semiconductor processing technicians*. They may be involved in several or many of the steps of semiconductor manufacturing, depending on where they work. Often, semiconductor technicians function as a link between the engineering staff and the production staff in the large-scale manufacturing of semiconductor products.

The making of semiconductors begins with silicon. To be used, the silicon must be extremely pure. The silicon used for semiconductors is heated in a furnace and formed into cylinder rods between one and six inches in diameter, and three or more feet in length. These rods are smoothed and polished until they are perfectly round, and then sliced into wafers of between one-quarter and one-half millimeter in thickness. Then the wafers are processed, by etching, polishing, heat treating, and lapping, to produce the desired dimensions and surface finish. After the wafers are tested, measured, and inspected for any defects, they are coated with a photo-sensitive substance called a photoresist.

The engineering staff and the technicians assigned to assist them prepare designs for the layout of the microchip. This work is generally done using a computer-aided design (CAD) system. The large, completed design is then miniaturized as a photomask when it is applied to the wafer. The photomask is placed over the wafer and the photoresist is developed, much like film in a camera, with ultraviolet light, so that the layout of the microchip is reproduced many times on the same wafer. This work takes place in a specially equipped clean room (a laboratory kept completely free of dust and other impurities). During the miniaturization process, the tiniest speck of dust will ruin the reproduction of the layout on the wafer.

Next, the wafer is doped with chemical substances that will give it the necessary conducting properties. Technicians follow the layout, like a road map, when adding these substances. The proper combinations of materials create the various components of the integrated circuit. When this process is complete, computerized equipment tests the wafer's many thousands of components in a matter of seconds. Many of the integrated circuits on the wafer will not function properly, and these are marked and discarded. After testing, the wafer is cut up into its individual chips.

The chips are then packaged in a casing usually made of plastic or ceramic, which also contains metal leads for connecting the microchip into the electronic circuitry of the device for which it will be used. It is this package that people usually refer to as a chip or semiconductor.

Semiconductor process technicians are generally responsible for the fabrication and processing of the semiconductor wafer. Semiconductor-development technicians usually assist with the basic design and development of rough sketches of a prototype chip; they may be involved in transferring the layout to the wafer and in assembling and testing the semiconductor. Both types of technicians gather and evaluate data on the semiconductor, wafer, or chip. They are responsible for making certain that each step of the process precisely meets test specifications, and also for identifying flaws and problems in the material and design. Technicians may also assist in designing and building new test equipment and in communicating test data and production instructions for large-scale manufacture. Technicians may also be responsible for maintaining the equipment and in training operators on their use.

What Is It Like to Be a Semiconductor Technician?

Michael McCollum is a process technician for Atmel Corporation in Colorado Springs, Colorado. He began at Atmel as an operator and was promoted to his current position in the main wafer fab (clean room) after one year. "My particular area of responsibility is the wet-etch area, which is the area of etching that uses hydrofluoric acid baths," Mike says.

Atmel runs 24 hours a day on a compressed week schedule, which means that Mike works from Wednesday to Saturday, beginning his 12-hour shift at 7:30 P.M. "I start a little early to read my email," he says.

Michael's shift begins with a "passdown," or briefing by the technicians and engineering staff of the previous shift, who will inform him of the events of the day and the status of production that will affect his work for the evening. Equipment that has failed during the day will be brought to his attention, and he is also given the production schedule for the night's shift.

"Most nights are very self-structured until something major comes up," Michael says. "Usually after the passdown I go into the fab—what we call the clean room—and take care of the pressing problems there, which can include lots on hold, down machines, things like that. If that clears up, I then work on my own assigned projects or experiments. During quiet times, I can also clear up my paperwork."

Part of Mike's job is to perform tests and experiments on new semiconductor devices. "Or I'll investigate problem lots that may have been scrapped. For that I'll use a microscope and other equipment or dig around in the online lot histories for any clues to what has happened to them." Mike's training for the job involved becoming what is called a visual inspection expert. "When I was first starting, one of the senior techs told me to look at a lot of wafers, because you can spot some unusual defects that way. I look at basically every problem wafer under the scope first, before doing anything else. The microscope is probably the most used tool in a fab."

Another tool that Mike uses is a tox tool, which measures the oxide thickness on a wafer after the etching process. "We have to be certain we've met

In-depth

The Downsizing of Computer Technology

The earliest computers filled entire rooms because of the large size of the semiconductors available before the development of microelectronics technology. Since then, efforts have been focused on fitting more and more components on a single chip. The more components, the faster (because the electrical current does not have to travel as far) and more capable of complex operations the chip will be.

Today, microchips are generally classified in three sizes, depending on how many transistors are fitted, or integrated, on a chip. Small-scale integration (SSI) chips contain approximately 4,000 transistors (referred to as 4K). LSI, or large-scale integration, chips can contain between 16K and 64K transistors. Finally, VLSI, or very large-scale integration, chips contain 64,000 or more transistors on a single chip, containing as much as four million bits of information. All of this is on a chip often not much larger than the size of a fingernail (and some chips can be as small as 1.3 millimeters). VLSI chips have made possible the personal computer, which is even more powerful than the former room-sized computers of a few decades ago.

the etch target," Mike says. "Most areas of a fab rely on inspection and measurement tools. There are also fully automated systems that use pattern recognition software for alignments and measurements. In fact, one of my current projects is setting up the pattern recognition on a new tool. That's been very interesting, but frustrating too."

One of Michael's responsibilities is to work with newly hired operators. "I train them on the equipment, and I also certify them, giving them quizzes on their job skills. When operators or their supervisors have questions, I answer them, or I'll find out the answers for them."

Throughout his shift, Michael must be available to troubleshoot any problems that may arise. "Work is always being interrupted," Michael says. "I'll get paged to solve a quick problem on the production line, or asked to look at an unusual lot, or answer someone's question. If I have a problem or question I can't solve, I'll email the other techs or the engineers about it. And if there's a serious problem, I may be the unlucky one to wake an engineer up at 2:00 or 3:00 in the morning!"

Michael's shift officially ends at 8:00 A.M. "That's when we get to present the formal morning passdown to a full meeting of all the etch process engineers, equipment engineers, and incoming technicians. Then I wrap up with any final meetings I need to attend or email I have to send. I usually get to go home—and to bed!—by about nine in the morning."

Do I Have What It Takes to Be a Semiconductor Technician?

"I've learned a lot about working in a high-volume production environment," Mike says, "I really enjoy it. I get the chance to work on many different facets of the manufacturing process, from the physical processes of creating the integrated circuits, to the more human aspects of teaching operators and keeping everyone and everything on track."

An important component in most manufacturing processes is the speed with which products are produced. Technicians and other employees may find themselves under a great deal of pressure to maintain a certain level of production volume. The ability to work under a sometimes stressful environment while retaining composure is an important aspect for any prospective semiconductor technician. "Atmel is very high volume," Mike says, "and often there can be conflicts between engineering and production, especially when there's a problem and machines or processes are down. Conflicts and arguments can be pretty common here, and being diplomatic about that can be really difficult at times."

The technicians kind of fill the role of liaison between manufacturing and engineering . . .

Unlike the operators, the people who run a specific piece of equipment on the production line, the semiconductor technician is given a variety of responsibilities and duties. Prioritizing one's work, while still responding to the needs and demands of the engineering staff and other aspects of the production process, is an essential ability for the successful semiconductor technician. "But for me," Mike says, "the best part of the job is the unpredictability of it. If something suddenly goes wrong, you have to drop everything and get on top of the problem, often while being pulled a dozen different ways from production, engineering, and management. The frustrating part is that the job is often feast or famine. Everything often goes wrong at once, and it gets difficult to stay on top of it all."

Mike sees communication skills and problem-solving skills as the two most important aspects of his job. "Most of my job actually involves communication. Being able to write coherently and speak effectively are very important." Mike's position requires him to work with a variety of people, and his communication skills are constantly called into play. Not only do his duties require him to prepare reports, he must also speak with the engineers, production supervisors, other technicians and operators, and personnel from management throughout his shift.

"The technicians kind of fill the role of liaison between manufacturing and engineering," Mike says, "which is never a comfortable place to be since manufacturing always wants to damn the torpedoes and run full steam ahead, while the engineers always want 500 pages of data before committing anything to process."

A thorough understanding of semiconductors, electronics, and the production process is also necessary. Investigative and research skills, and a basic knowledge of computers and computer programs are also important skills for the prospective semiconductor technician.

"The other big aspect of the job is problem-solving, trying to find out what's wrong or what happened to cause a particular event or situation," Mike says. "Someone will find something unusual or have a problem and call us in to evaluate the problem and try to resolve it, or decide who to call in next. And the computer system itself is an important tool, since there is a lot of good information in there, if you can dig it up. When there's a problem, you have to be able to sift through and analyze a lot of different information in order to solve it."

The work of semiconductor technicians is not physically strenuous and is usually done in an extremely clean environment. Technicians may work with hazardous chemicals, however, and proper safety precautions must be strictly followed. Because of the large demand for semiconductors and related devices, many facilities, like Atmel, will operate on a 24-hour schedule, meaning that a technician may be assigned to the night or weekend shift or work a rotating schedule.

To Be a Successful Semiconductor Technician, You Should . . .

- have a strong science and math background
- have well-developed communication skills, especially written and verbal skills
- be detail-oriented, analytical, and flexible
- be self-motivated and self-disciplined
- be able to work independently or as part of a team
- have good problem-solving abilities

How Do I Become a Semiconductor Technician?

The nature of the microelectronics industry, where technological advances are continuous and rapid, means that some form of higher education, whether in a two-year or four-year program, is a must. An early interest in and excitement for electronics and computers is encouraged for anyone considering entering this field. Math and science skills also play an important part in every aspect of this career.

Mike holds an associate's degree in electronic technology. "Although I actually kind of fell into semiconductors," he says. "I was working at a hamburger joint while going to school, when I decided to get into something more exciting."

EDUCATION

High School

Math and science courses, as well as classes in computer science, are obvious requirements for students wishing to enter the semiconductor and microelectronics field. Physics and chemistry will be helpful for understanding many of the processes involved in developing and fabricating semiconductors and semiconductor components. Mike also emphasizes the need for strong communication skills. "It's most of my job," he says. "So, while math and science are important, English and being able to speak effectively and to write coherently are also very important."

You can develop your own interests in computers and microelectronics while in school. Because of the rapid advances in electronics technology, most schools will be unable to keep up, and you are encouraged to read and explore on your own. Joining extracurricular clubs in computers or electronics will give you an opportunity for hands-on learning experiences.

Finally, you should begin to seek out the higher education appropriate for your future career interests. The high school guidance office can be helpful in locating the right program for the future semiconductor technician's needs.

Postsecondary Training

Technician jobs in microelectronics and semiconductor technology require at least an associate's degree in electronic or electrical engineering or technology. Two-year programs are available at community colleges or vocational/training schools. If you are interested in a career at the engineering level, consider studying for a bachelor's degree. The trend

FYI

Silicon is the second most common element on Earth, after oxygen. When combined with oxygen and other elements, silicon forms sand, quartz, agate, and other rocks. In order for silicon to be used as a semiconductor, it must be 99.9999 percent pure.

toward greater specialization within the industry may eventually make a bachelor's degree more desirable than an associate's degree.

An electronics engineering program will include courses in electronics theory, as well as math, science, and English courses. You can expect to study such subjects as the principles and models of semiconductor devices; physics for solid state electronics; solid state theory; introduction to VLSI (very large scale integration) systems; and basic courses in computer organization, electromagnetic fundamentals, digital and analog laboratories, and the design of circuits and active networks.

"I found the most important classes to be tech writing, physics, mathematics, and electronic theory," Mike says. "And statistics knowledge is important for using quality control methods. Also, here at Atmel all our correspondence is done with email, and all the processing and data gathering is done on a real-time network, so basic computer knowledge is a must." Companies will also provide additional training on the specific equipment and software they use. Many companies also offer training programs and educational opportunities to employees to increase their skills and their responsibilities.

Courses are available at many community and junior colleges, which may be more flexible in their curriculum and better able to keep up with technological advances than vocational training schools. The latter, however, will often have programs geared specifically to the needs of the employers in their area and may have job placement programs and relationships with different companies as well. Do some research to determine whether the training offered is thorough, and that the school has a good placement record. Training institutes should also be accredited by the National Association of Trade and Technical Schools.

Military service will also provide a strong background in electronics. In addition, the tuition credits available to military personnel will be helpful when continuing your education.

CERTIFICATION OR LICENSING

Certification is not mandatory, but voluntary certification may prove useful in locating work, and in increasing your pay and responsibilities. The International Society of Certified Electronics Technicians (ISCET) offers certification testing at various levels and in various fields of electronics. The ISCET also offers a variety of study and training material to help prepare for the certification tests (see "Sources of Additional Information").

Who Will Hire Me?

Semiconductor technician positions can be located through the job placement office of a community college or vocational training school. Job listings in the newspaper, or at local employment agencies, are also good places for locating job opportunities. You can also find lower-skilled positions in the semiconductor industry and work hard for promotion to a technician position.

"That's how it worked for me," Mike says. "I applied for and got a job at Atmel as an operator while I was still in school. And after a year, I was promoted to process technician."

The huge market for semiconductors and the devices related to them means that many job opportunities are available to qualified people. The largest names in semiconductors are companies such as Intel, Motorola, Texas Instruments, National Semiconductor, and Western Digital. In addition, there are certain areas of the country where the semiconductor industry is most active, including California, Texas, and Massachusetts. Other states where semiconductor manufacturers can be found are Illinois, Idaho, Pennsylvania, Arizona, New York, Colorado, Connecticut, and Nebraska.

Where Can I Go from Here?

As in any manufacturing industry, the advancement possibilities available to semiconductor technicians will depend on their levels of skill, education, and experience. Technicians may advance to more senior technician roles and may find themselves in supervisory or management positions. Technicians with two-year associate's degrees may elect to continue their education. Often, their course work will be transferable to a four-year engineering program. They may ultimately choose to enter the engineering and design phases of semiconductor development. Also, a background in semiconductor processing and development may lead to a career in sales or purchasing of semiconductor components, materials, and equipment.

What Are the Salary Ranges?

According to the *Occupational Outlook Handbook,* the median hourly earnings of electronic semiconductor processors were $13.21 in 2003 (or approximately $27,477 annually for full-time employees). Those in the lowest 10 percent earned less than $9.34 an hour ($19,427 a year), and those in the highest 10 percent earned more than $19.60 an hour ($40,768 a year). Wages and benefits will vary according to employer, location, and the level of experience, education, and actual title and responsibilities. Overtime and holiday pay is generally available, as well as pay differentials for night and weekend shift work.

What Is the Job Outlook?

The U.S. Department of Labor expects that employment of electronic semiconductor processors in the United States will decline over the next 10 years. The main reasons for this are a rising number of imports from non-U.S. companies and increased productivity in semiconductor manufacturing methods.

Many semiconductor manufacturers are upgrading their fabs with newer equipment that makes 12-inch wafers. These larger wafers produce twice as many chips as the older, 8-inch wafers. The increased use and efficiency of automated manufacturing techniques has enabled manufacturers are able to increase their output with the same number of technicians or fewer. In addition, some manufacturers are building plants overseas, where manufacturing and labor costs are cheaper, thereby limiting opportunities in this field in the United States.

Advancement Possibilities

Senior technicians are supervisory or management positions.

Semiconductor sales representatives work in sales of semiconductor components, materials, and equipment.

Semiconductor purchasing representatives/agents work in the evaluation and purchasing of semiconductor components, materials, and equipment.

Despite this general decline in employment in this field, the demand for semiconductors will remain very high. The existing use of semiconductors in computers, appliances, cell phones, and vehicles will only increase, and new applications are under constant development. This factor, combined with the need to replace workers who retire or otherwise leave the field, will ensure that jobs will be available for qualified applicants. Technicians with postsecondary education in electronics and semiconductor technology will have a distinct advantage in this job market.

How Do I Learn More?

PROFESSIONAL ORGANIZATIONS

The following are organizations that provide information on semiconductor technician careers, certification, accredited schools and scholarships, and possible employment:

Electronics Technicians Association International
5 Depot Street
Greencastle, IN 46135
800-288-3824
eta@eta-i.org
http://www.eta-i.org

International Society of Certified Electronics Technicians
2708 West Berry Street
Fort Worth, TX 76109-2356
817-921-9101
http://www.iscet.org

Semiconductor Equipment and Materials International
3081 Zanker Road
San Jose, CA 95134

408-943-6900
semihq@semi.org
http://www.semi.org

Semiconductor Industry Association
181 Metro Drive, Suite 450
San Jose, CA 95110
408-436-6600
mailbox@sia-online.org
http://www.sia-online.org

BIBLIOGRAPHY

The following is a sampling of materials relating to the professional concerns and development of semiconductor technicians:

May, Gary S., and Simon M. Sze. *Fundamentals of Semiconductor Fabrication*. New York: John Wiley and Sons, 2003.

Quirk, Michael, and Julian Serda. *Semiconductor Manufacturing Technology*. Upper Saddle River, N.J.: Prentice Hall, 2000.

Sze, Simon M. *Semiconductor Technology: Physics and Technology*. 2d ed. New York: John Wiley and Sons, 2001.

Turley, Jim. *The Essential Guide to Semiconductors*. Upper Saddle River, N.J.: Prentice Hall, 2002.

SOIL CONSERVATION TECHNICIANS

Soil conservation technician DeAnn Denton scoots down the gully, carrying her 25-foot survey stick with her. The steep embankment drops down into a stream that runs alongside a railroad track. Over the years the bank has been a big erosion problem, washing away back into a farmer's field. Last week the farmer called DeAnn's office at the Natural Resources Conservation Service, a federal agency that assists land users with their conservation problems. "What can I do?" he asked DeAnn. "I'm losing my field."

When DeAnn and a few others go out to survey the area, the survey stick proves way too short for the job. "When I'm at the bottom," DeAnn says, "the rod's supposed to be at the top." DeAnn decides to solve the problem by measuring from top to bottom and bottom to top until the two meet in the middle. "It was an interesting technique," she says, "and it worked.

"We learned the embankment's 12 percent grade and 80-foot drop were causing a tremendous amount of water to fall along this waterway. We don't like our water to fall more than 1/2 percent in 100 feet. Water here falls four times that amount, and the force of water running is what causes erosion."

DeAnn presents a few different plans to the farmer, who picks the one he likes and can best afford. Two weeks later, 80 feet of pipe are buried in his hillside. The pipes redirect the water into a rock-filled settling basin lined with antierosion fabric. "The flow of water is slowed down considerably," says DeAnn, "and the tubes don't disrupt the stream."

Definition
Soil conservation technicians develop conservation plans for landowners, such as farmers and ranchers, that help preserve the earth's natural resources: soil, water, wildlife, and forests.

Alternative Job Titles
Cartographic technicians
Engineering technician aides
Physical science technicians
Range conservationists
Range technicians
Surveying technicians

High School Subjects
Agriculture
Earth science

Personal Skills
Following instructions
Technical/scientific

Salary Range
$23,442 to $57,084 to $100,000+

Work Environment
Primarily outdoors
Primarily multiple locations

Minimum Educational Requirements
High school diploma

Certification or Licensing
None available

Outlook
More slowly than the average

DOT
040

GOE
02.03.03

NOC
2115

O*NET-SOC
19-1031.00, 19-4093.00, 45-4011.00

What Does a Soil Conservation Technician Do?

Soil conservation technicians work with landowners to help preserve and protect the earth's natural resources. They devise plans to control land and water erosion, reforest lands, and improve and preserve wildlife habitat that adhere to government conservation regulations. "We look at the problem and give suggestions," says DeAnn. Soil conservation technicians assist landowners in conserving woodlands, pastures, and range land. They typically work with farmers and ranchers, but recreational landowners often request help, as do home owners. With their knowledge of conservation practices and engineering and agricultural science, soil technicians know best how to minimize the damage that we humans may cause to the land.

Most soil conservation technicians work for the federal government, and several programs are

Lingo to Learn

Cartography The science and practice of mapmaking.

Cover crop A temporary crop grown to reduce or prevent erosion to farmland. It builds up the soil's organic content to make it more fertile.

Geotextile An anti-erosion fabric used to line settling basins, or large holes filled with rocks, dug to displace water flowage.

Loam Soil that contains a variable mixture of sand, silt, and clay.

Rangeland The vast area of land, primarily in the western United States, where livestock roam and feed.

Sheep's foot A piece of equipment used to tightly pack soil. A five-by-eight-foot roller with blunt prongs sits on the front of a machine, packing dirt as it burrows through the ground.

Topsoil The surface soil that includes the layer where most plants have their roots.

available to assist land users with specific problems. "We have a program to close abandoned wells, and an exclusion program to keep livestock out of streams. We do stream inventories throughout the state, to make sure farmers' streams aren't contaminated with livestock waste. We work a lot with manure control on farms," says DeAnn, "and with people who want to attract wildlife to their backyard." By using survey and field information, soil conservationists are able to put together plans according to the landowner's needs, finances, and maintenance requirements. In their work, technicians use basic engineering surveys. They design and implement conservation practices like terraces and grassed waterways. They lay out contours, tile drainage, and irrigation systems; plant grasses and trees; collect soil samples and gather information from field notes; improve woodlands; assist in farm pond design; build manure storage units; make maps; and inspect areas to determine conservation needs.

Some soil conservation technicians work for the Bureau of Land Management, which oversees millions of acres in the public domain. They help survey publicly owned lands and help find features that determine the best way to use the land. They may be called upon to supervise a survey team. Technicians in the Bureau of Reclamation assist civil, construction, and general engineers with dam construction and irrigation planning. Soil conservation technicians can also assist scientists, engineers, and other professionals to obtain the data they need to develop water and soil conservation plans.

When starting their careers, soil conservation technicians may begin in a variety of aide-level positions that enable them to develop their skills. *Cartographic survey technician aides* assist mapmakers in surveying public lands and pinpointing certain land features. *Engineering technician aides* conduct field studies and oversee some phases of construction or irrigation projects. They also manage water resources and define drainage areas on maps. *Physical science technician aides* study the physical characteristics of soil and produce aerial survey maps used by soil conservationists.

In addition to aide positions, soil conservation technicians can also hold a variety of entry-level technician positions. *Range technicians* work closely with range conservationists to manage rangeland, mostly in the western part of the United States. They determine the value of the rangeland, the number of livestock it can support, and the potential for damage caused by animals and erosion. *Cartographic technicians* perform technical work in mapping or charting the earth. *Geodetic survey technicians,* who are concerned with measuring the size and shape of the earth, do nonprofessional work in analyzing and evaluating geodetic survey information. *Physical science technicians* assist professional scientists to set up and operate measuring instruments and testing equipment, and make routine chemical analysis. Finally, *survey technicians* conduct field measurements for mapmaking, construction, and dredging operations. They also gather measurements for highways and dams.

What Is It Like to Be a Soil Conservation Technician?

At 7:00 A.M., DeAnn rides out to a dairy farm about five miles from her office to see how things are going. "Right now, I'm in the middle of constructing a waste storage unit," says DeAnn, "and I want to make sure there aren't any problems. I typically begin my day by checking out any job sites that are in progress.

"This project is just two days along. Yesterday, they started removing the topsoil, and today they dig the actual hole. It'll take two weeks to do the whole thing," says DeAnn. An excavation company is doing the work, and they have a complete set of plans to go by that DeAnn drew up herself. Waste management projects are something DeAnn does a lot of in her home state of Michigan, where cattle are often kept in confined spaces. "The waste must be stored properly," DeAnn explains, "so it doesn't seep into groundwater."

When DeAnn first started the project, she did a soil boring to determine the soil's makeup. To build a manure pond, a hole is dug to hold the waste. "If the soil has enough clay, it'll keep the waste contained and we can just dig the hole. If the soil has sand and water present, it's too porous and the waste will seep right through. Then, we need to line the pond with cement." This farmer's soil had enough clay, so DeAnn drew up a plan to create a manure pond far away from streambeds. The hole would be dug by a sheep's foot, a piece of equipment that packs the clay soil tight as it tunnels through it. In Michigan, the Natural Resources Conservation Service does farm inventory to determine if certain guidelines are being followed. "If farmers receive federal payment, they have to follow our guidelines," says DeAnn.

The various tasks of a soil technician usually depend on the state where she or he works. Each state has their own annual plan, and every state's needs are different. "In Michigan," says DeAnn, "because we're surrounded by the Great Lakes, people realized we had to clean up our waters. A lot of our conservation programs grew out of that." DeAnn works on a task force made up of farmers, private companies, concerned citizens, and government workers. It meets quarterly to oversee the Environmental Quality Incentive Program, which is present in all seven of Michigan's watersheds. "The state is divided into watersheds," says DeAnn, "and each watershed gets federal funding. The task force decides the best use of the funds, and anyone who wants to be on it can."

After DeAnn checks out the waste storage construction site, she heads back to her office to plan her day. In the afternoon, she has appointments with five different farmers who are interested in various programs. "They called for some literature so I sent it out," says DeAnn. "After reading it they called back. They're interested in some of what we have to offer." DeAnn will probably go visit the farmers with the department's resource conservationist (RC), who is her supervisor and coworker. The two work closely together as a team, and DeAnn often shows her preliminary conservation plans to him for approval. "The RC does the final plan," says DeAnn, "based on what I've come up with."

Periodically through the day, DeAnn continues to check on the waste manure project to make sure it's progressing smoothly. If she has time, she visits nearby sites of projects already completed. "On the way back to the office, I swung by the 80-foot gully that we worked on a few months back. It's already green with new vegetation. After I've seen an eroded gully made all nice and smooth and green again, I know it's what I'm here for."

Do I Have What It Takes to Be a Soil Conservation Technician?

Like DeAnn, most soil conservation technicians have a love for the environment. They care about the planet's fragile natural resources and feel deeply committed to seeing those resources protected so future generations can enjoy their use.

But love for the outdoors isn't all it takes to be a soil conservation technician. You must have a working knowledge of land and water characteristics and be able to apply that knowledge to practical solutions. You must understand how humans, livestock, and weather affect natural resources, both in the long and short terms. Soil technicians are analytical and can assess complex data, use surveys and other equipment, and read and interpret maps.

Because your main job is to provide assistance, you must be willing to work with communities to solve problems. Clear communication, both oral and written, is important. Technicians write clear, concise plans; explain the results of tests and assessments; and make recommendations. Often they do this with people who are either skeptical or resistant to their suggestions, so an agreeable manner, patience, and a willingness to listen to others are imperative. "You deal with people all day long, and many aren't open to your way of thinking," says DeAnn. "You must be a good listener and accepting of people's decisions, even if you don't agree with them."

DeAnn feels being a people person is the most valuable quality a soil conservation technician can have. "You must be outgoing and willing to go talk with folks," DeAnn says. The hardest part of her job is telling people no. "If we don't have any money for them because they don't qualify, or we can't do what they want to do because it's against regulations, we have to say no. You better have good people skills for that," says DeAnn. DeAnn also believes good soil conservation technicians are self-starters. "You can't stand around and wait for someone to tell you what to do." There's a lot of independence and one-on-one contact with people. To be a soil technician, you have to like working with those conditions.

You also have to like the outdoors and be prepared for the weather. Soil technicians work outside most of the time. "The best part about my job is walking through the fields on a sunny day," says DeAnn. And the worst? "When it pours rain, of course," DeAnn laughs.

The best part about my job is walking through the fields on a sunny day. And the worst? When it pours rain, of course.

A soil conservation technician studies the effects of wind erosion while a local farmer observes. *(Jack Dykinga / U.S. Department of Agriculture)*

How Do I Become a Soil Conservation Technician?

DeAnn grew up on a 600-acre farm in Michigan and was around conservation all her life. She and her four sisters worked the farm as they grew up, and DeAnn still lives on the family farm and helps with its crops. "We started with dairy heifers and went to beef cows and cash crops of soybeans, corn, and wheat. My father was doing conservation before anyone heard of it. He was the first farmer in the area to do no-till farming," says DeAnn. She contributes her love for her job to being on the farm. "It's where I learned about soil, water, and conservation practices. I had a great background going into this profession because of the farm."

EDUCATION

High School

While in high school, would-be soil conservation technicians should concentrate on mathematics, especially algebra. Figuring out conservation plans involves working extensively with numbers, measurements, and ratios. "You have to be able to figure out how fast water is running down a gorge," says DeAnn, "or how big to dig a hole. This takes math skills most of all." Both oral and written communication is needed for report writing and discussing complex issues with land users. You also want to take biology, for a background in plants, and vocational agriculture if it's available, to help understand the complex problems and issues facing today's farmers and rangers. DeAnn took four years of architectural drawing in high school, which helped her tremendously with the surveys and mapmaking she's required to do. She also thinks mechanical drawing and drafting classes are a good idea.

DeAnn strongly recommends joining 4-H if you can, or spending time on a farm during summers if you get the chance. "I was a 4-H member for eight years,"

DeAnn says. "It taught me to be outgoing, and soil conservation technicians have to have this." Joining Future Farmers of America (FFA) is another good way to explore what this career is all about. Science clubs that focus on problem solving, such as Science Olympiad, would also provide valuable experience.

Postsecondary Training

Very few colleges or universities offer programs or degrees in soil conservation. Although it's still possible to become a soil conservation technician with just a high school diploma, many soil technicians have degrees in environmental studies, agronomy, general agriculture, or crop soil science. A few have degrees in related fields such as wildlife biology, forestry, and range management.

Soil technicians must have some practical knowledge in soil conservation before they enter the field, and a lot of this is obtained through on-the-job training and experience like DeAnn had on her family farm. Employment by government agencies requires prospective employees to pass a competitive civil service exam. "You can study for it," says DeAnn. "It tests your knowledge of conservation and the job we do."

Once you begin working in most government agencies, you receive both on-the-job training and formal instruction. The Natural Resources Conservation Service (NRCS) provides a weeklong course in conservation training, which is required for anyone who wants to move up the rank and become a resource conservationist. There is also training held on engineering, water control structures, strip cropping, field boundary borders for wind erosion, and other conservation measures. These are usually statewide trainings. Government employees receive promotions according to years of experience and additional training.

CERTIFICATION OR LICENSING

No certification or license is required of soil conservation technicians; however, becoming certified could improve your skills and professional standing. The American Society of Agronomy offers certification in soil science.

SCHOLARSHIPS AND GRANTS

Once you begin working for the government, opportunities are available to take training courses and college classes that are paid for by the agency. The Employee Development Program provides scholarship money to NRCS workers for up to two university classes a year.

To obtain information about the availability of scholarships or grants in a field of study related to soil conservation, contact the financial aid office of the school you plan to attend.

INTERNSHIPS AND VOLUNTEERSHIPS

The Bureau of Land Management (BLM) and the U.S. Forest Service participate in summer programs for high school students that offer opportunities to learn and experience conservation practices and techniques in the wild. The U.S. Forest Service offers volunteer opportunities across the country. In addition, the Forest Service sponsors the Youth Conservation Corps Program, a summer employment program in which a limited number of high school students work on completing conservation projects on public lands. For programs in your area, contact the BLM and U.S. Forest Service offices nearest you. Also, check out the BLM Environmental Education Web site at http://www.blm.gov/education and the U.S. Forest Service programs site at http://www.fs.fed.us/aboutus/national.shtml.

Who Will Hire Me?

DeAnn was working in a Michigan soil conservation district as an office manager when a position opened up at NRCS. "Our district shared the same office with NRCS and our work was intertwined. I did data entry for them, and we were offered a lot of the same training as federal employees. Just working with the resource conservationists gave me experience," says DeAnn, "and of course the farm gave me practical experience. I applied for a job as a soil technician when one came available and I got it."

Most soil conservation technicians find work at county, state, or federal agencies. The federal government is the largest employer of soil conservation technicians. In most states, soil conservation technicians are assigned to a county district office where they provide their services to the area's land users. At present, there are more than 3,000 field locations located across the United States, so entry-level candidates are likely to find openings available if they're willing to go where the jobs are.

ADVANCEMENT POSSIBILITIES

Soil scientists study soil characteristics, map soil types, and investigate responses of soils to known management practices to determine how soil can be used and the effects of alternative practices on soil productivity.

Agronomists conduct experiments or investigations in field-crop problems and develop new methods of growing crops to secure more efficient production, higher yield, and improved quality.

Soil conservationists plan and develop coordinated practices for soil erosion control, moisture conservation, and sound land use.

To become employed by the Natural Resources Conservation Service, an entry-level candidate must have at least six months of general experience that provides a basic knowledge of agriculture operations, machinery, and terminology. Some of this basic experience may be substituted with educational course work in range management, conservation, agriculture, forestry, or some other combination of natural and physical science. In DeAnn's case, she got it working in a soil conservation district and on the farm.

If you're in school, you can gain experience by working a summer job in your field of interest. Contacts made on summer jobs often lead to permanent employment, and your school career placement office should be able to help you find work. In the spring, government representatives usually come to schools to talk with graduating students about opportunities in their agencies, and these recruitment sessions could lead to a job. In order to be considered for a position, you can expect to take the civil service examination and fill out the required government application. Many students begin this application procedure during their final semester before graduation.

Some soil conservation technicians are hired by public utility companies, banks and loan agencies, and mining or steel companies. Employment in the private sector can also include working as surveyors or drafters with surveying or architectural firms. The number of soil technicians employed in the private sector, however, is small compared to those working for government agencies.

Where Can I Go from Here?

DeAnn would eventually like to become a *resource conservationist.* "I'll have to go through the steps to get there," she says, "and take some required classes." Soil conservation technicians can move up to soil conservationist, resource conservationist, then into specialized management and supervisory positions. With more education, they can also advance to jobs as *soil scientists* and *agronomists.* "But I like being in the field," says DeAnn, "and plan on staying in a position that keeps me out there."

The Natural Resources Conservation Service classifies different ranks, or grades, of soil conservation technician, and what separates one rank from another is usually the number of years of experience you have and the specialized skills you've acquired through field work and training courses. Many soil conservation technicians choose to go to higher ranks, and with each advancement comes an increase in salary as well as additional duties and responsibilities. As these duties increase, the amount of time spent in the field tends to decrease while the amount of time spent behind a desk increases. For some soil technicians, like DeAnn, working outdoors and being with people and solving their problems are the parts of the job she loves.

The NRCS offers weeklong conservation training for those who want to move into soil or resource conservation. The course requires you to work intensively with a farmer developing a comprehensive conservation plan that meets his or her needs. Once you've completed it and become a certified conservationist, you wait for a position to open up so you can transfer into it. Government agencies offer promotions from within, so your chances of advancing are good, especially if you're willing to relocate. "Where the jobs are depends on a state's individual plan and whether they want field workers or administrative staff," says DeAnn.

Soil conservation technicians also have the option of becoming *conservationists* with private companies. Research and testing firms have increased their hiring of conservationists in response to the demand for environmental impact statements and erosion control plans. These firms help private companies monitor water near logging sites and advise on tree harvesting practices.

According to federal regulation, when workers retire from government service they're prohibited from accepting work in the private sector for one year. "It's so people in the private sector can stay competitive," says DeAnn. "We're so well-trained, we're the leaders in conservation."

What Are the Salary Ranges?

The salaries of soil conservation technicians working for federal government agencies are set by the government according to experience and training. In 2003, the average salary for soil conservationists working for the federal government was $57,084 a year. Soil conservation technicians with bachelor's degrees entering into employment with the federal government in 2003 earned between $23,442 and $29,037 a year, depending on academic achievement. Technicians with master's degrees made starting salaries between $35,519 and $42,976. Those with doctorates made $51,500. Pay raises occur in annual steps depending on years on the job. Soil and resource conservationists with high levels of management responsibilities can make as much as $100,000 a year.

DeAnn enjoys a full health insurance and benefits package. She can choose from a variety of health plans and receives vacation and sick leave that increases yearly. She's also on a pension plan. Soil conservation technicians who work for large private firms and local, state, and federal government agencies usually receive generous benefit packages.

What Is the Job Outlook?

Because most soil conservation technicians are employed by the federal government, employment opportunities are largely tied to government spending. Fewer opportunities in the federal government will exist for foresters and soil scientists, however, due partly to budget constraints, and partly to a growing trend in government to hire contract workers from private industry to take on conservation work. The U.S. Forest Service is de-emphasizing their timber program and focusing more on wildlife habitat, recreation, and sustaining ecosystems. As DeAnn pointed out, the Natural Resources Conservation Service works with all aspects of conservation and land use, including wildlife habitat, reforestation, and recreation. As more soil technicians and conservationists are needed to provide technical assistance to land users, more jobs in the NRCS should open up. Overall, however, the U.S. Department of Labor predicts slower than average job growth for the field of conservation science, which includes soil conservation technicians.

Because government regulations require private companies to comply with standards and procedures to assure environmental protection, there should be an increase in jobs for soil technicians and conservationists in the private sector. Most of these jobs will be in research and testing firms who do environmental impact statements and ground and water testing.

Right now, there is a strong emphasis on protecting our natural resources, preventing further damage to our environment, and cleaning up our soil and water. As long as this trend continues, we can expect there to be jobs for technicians who know how to do this work.

How Do I Learn More?

PROFESSIONAL ORGANIZATIONS

The following are organizations and associations that provide information on schools, soil conservation careers, and employment opportunities:

American Society of Agronomy
Career Development and Placement Service
677 South Segoe Road
Madison, WI 53711
608-273-8080
http://www.agronomy.org

Bureau of Land Management
1849 C Street, Room 406-LS
Washington, DC 20240
202-452-5125
http://www.blm.gov

Natural Resources Conservation Service
U.S. Department of Agriculture
Attn: Conservation Communications Staff
14th and Independence Avenues
Washington, DC 20250
http://www.nrcs.usda.gov

Soil and Water Conservation Society
945 SW Ankeny Road
Ankeny, IA 50021-9764
512-289-2331
http://www.swcs.org

Soil Science Society of America
677 South Segoe Road
Madison, WI 53711
608-273-8095
headquarters@Soils.org
http://www.soils.org

USDA Forest Service
1400 Independence Avenue, SW
Washington, DC 20250-0003
202-205-8333
http://www.fs.fed.us

BIBLIOGRAPHY

The following is a sampling of materials relating to the professional concerns and development of soil conservation technicians:

Kohnke, Helmut, and D. P. Franzmeier. *Soil Science Simplified*. 4th ed. Long Grive, Ill.: Waveland Press, 1995.

Morgan, Roy. *Soil Erosion and Conservation*. 3d ed. Malden, Mass.: Blackwell, 2005.

Sumner, Malcolm E., ed. *Handbook of Soil Science*. Boca Raton, Fla.: CRC Press, 1999.

White, William C., Donald N. Collins. *Opportunities in Farming and Agriculture Careers*. Lincolnwood, Ill.: NTC/Contemporary Publishing Group, 1995.

SPECIAL EFFECTS TECHNICIANS

As a special effects technician for the film industry, Tom Chesney is sometimes involved with the design of an effect. "Sometimes it's somebody else's design, and you're doing the hands-on fabrication work," he says. Though his work may vary from project to project, he is generally only involved with mechanical effects. "Special effects is an awfully broad category these days," he says. "When I did low-budget films, we did makeup effects and everything. Now there's a job for makeup effects, for model makers, for prop makers." As the jobs have become more specialized, Tom has focused on certain aspects of mechanical work, such as welding and electrical. He also works with pyrotechnics. "We design it, we build it, we wreck it," he says.

Definition
Special effects technicians are crafts persons who use technical skills to create effects, illusions, and computer generated images for motion pictures, theatre productions, television broadcasts and video games.

Alternative Job Titles
Computer animation specialists
Makeup effects specialists
Mechanical effects specialists
Pyrotechnic effects specialists

High School Subjects
Computer science
Theater/dance

Personal Skills
Artistic
Communication/ideas

Salary Range
$45,000 to $60,000 to $100,000+

Work Environment
Indoors and outdoors
Primarily multiple locations

Minimum educational level
Some postsecondary training

Certification or Licensing
None available

Outlook
About as fact as the average

DOT
962

GOE
N/A

NOC
5226

O*NET-SOC
N/A

What Does a Special Effects Technician Do?

Special effects technicians make what we see when we watch a movie, television broadcast, or theater production look and seem real. If a scene in a script calls for actors to walk down a 1920s Paris street, a Tyrannosaurus Rex to cause havoc in modern times, or a 25th-century spacecraft to go to warp speed in a blinding flash of light, it is the job of the special effects technician to make the viewer believe that it is really happening on-screen.

Special effects technicians are crafts persons who build, install, and operate equipment used to produce the effects called for in scripts for motion picture, television, and theatrical productions. They read the script before filming to determine the type and number of special effects required. Depending on the effects needed for a production, they will mix chemicals, build large and elaborate sets or models, and fabricate costumes and other required backdrops from materials such as wood, metal, plaster, and clay.

What's known generally as special effects is actually a number of specialized trades. There are companies—known in the industry as special effects shops or houses—that offer specialized services in such diverse areas as computer animation, make-up, and mechanical effects. A special effects shop might provide just one or a combination of these services, and the crafts persons who work at the shops are often skilled in more than one area.

Computer animation specialists use high-tech computer programs to create effects that are otherwise impossible or too costly to build by traditional means. They typically work in an office, separate from the actual filming location. Because much of the technology they use is on the cutting edge of the industry, computer animation specialists are highly skilled in working with and developing unique computer applications and software programs.

Lingo to Learn

Computer-generated image (CGI) A special effect for a motion picture that was developed using complex computer software.

Latex A malleable plastic used in the construction of masks and costumes for actors in film and theatrical productions.

Matte Background paintings, of mountains or a futuristic city for example, which are used in movies in place of elaborate or costly sets.

On-location A site, usually outdoors, where the filming of a motion picture takes place. Filming may also take place on a set.

Producer The individual, or group of individuals or a company, who arranges the financing for the filming of a motion picture, oversees the hiring and activities of all employees involved in a production, and determines the schedule for bringing the production to completion.

Pyrotechnics The art of making and using of fireworks and explosives.

Shop A company that provides special effects for motion pictures, theatrical productions, and television broadcasts.

Special effects coordinator The individual who leads a team of special effects technicians in providing effects for a motion picture.

Storyboard A scene-by-scene script of a motion picture that indicates when and where special effects are required.

Tricks The term used for "special effects" by those who work in the motion picture industry.

Makepup effects specialists create elaborate costumes and masks for actors to wear in a film or theatrical production. They also build prosthetic devices to simulate human—or nonhuman—limbs, hands, and heads. They work with a variety of materials, from latex plastic to create a monster's mask, to human hair they weave into wigs, to plain cotton cloth for a costume. They are skilled at sewing, weaving, applying makeup, and mixing colored dyes.

Mechanical effects specialists build moving sets and backdrops for motion pictures and theatrical productions. They might also create moving or mechanized props, such as a futuristic automobile for a science fiction film. Because of a production's budget constraints, they are often required to construct miniature working models of such things as airplanes or submarines that, on film, will appear to be life-sized or larger. Mechanical effects specialists are usually skilled in a number of trades, including plumbing, welding, carpentry, costume design, electricity, and robotics.

Pyrotechnic effects specialists are experts with munitions and firearms. They create carefully planned explosions for dramatic scenes in motion pictures and television broadcasts. They build charges and mix chemicals used for explosions according to strict legal standards.

Most professionals working in the field of special effects offer their services as freelance special effects technicians. Some also work for special effects shops. The shops are contracted by motion picture or television broadcast producers and theatrical productions to provide the effects for a specific production. After reviewing the script and the type and number of the special effects required, the shop will send a special effects team to work on the production, or hire freelance technicians to assist on the job. Depending upon their level of expertise, many freelance technicians work for several shops.

Often, nonunion team members are required to help out with tasks that fall outside an area of expertise during the production. This may involve setting up and tearing down sets, moving heavy equipment, or pitching in on last-minute design changes. Union technicians are contracted to provide a specific service and rarely perform work outside an area of expertise.

What Is It Like to Be a Special Effects Technician?

Tom Chesney has been a special effects technician in the film industry for 20 years and has worked on such films as *Men in Black, Inspector Gadget, Waterworld,* and *Raising Arizona*. He also worked on the film *Swordfish* starring John Travolta, for which Tom handled some of the mechanical effects.

One scene involves a woman strapped with explosives and tubes of ball bearings. "The SWAT team pulls her out of the bank," Tom explains, "and she blows up. There's a lot of explosives and a lot of ball bearings, but of course it's not real. So we have all these police cars and buildings that are to look like they're riddled with ball bearings—sort of like machine gun fire, except it's all at once. We had to cut the metal of the cars, making holes that go into the car on one side, and out the opposite side. We made the dents the way they were supposed to be, and then put a charge in each hole. You Bondo [apply auto-body filler paste] over it, so that when the explosive goes off, it reveals the hole dented in the way you prepped it. If it's got to blow out, then you have to put a big enough charge that actually blows the metal toward the outside."

For the scene, the cars were also to be jerked out of the frame. This was accomplished with cables attached to the cars. Later, computer effects technicians will "erase" the cables from the scene. "When we used to fly somebody," Tom says, "we used to try to get pretty small wires on them and have it lit so that you can barely see the wires. Now we use fairly heavy cable painted orange, and they just erase it."

Not every project that Tom has worked on has required lavish, big-budget effects; in some cases, the effects are small, but necessary. "There are always effects in a movie," he says. "Even a fire in a fireplace or in a campfire is an effect, because it's usually fueled by propane. Throughout the filming of a scene, you want to keep the fire at the same size, so you're not going to just burn regular logs." Tom frequently works with the filmmakers Joel and Ethan Coen, which sometimes involves rigging more subtle effects. For the film *O Brother, Where Art Thou?* the effects technicians had to build an old-fashioned railroad handcart. "It was electric," he says. "Nobody really had to pump it. Those old ones were hard to work." They also had to build a burning cross for one scene, which was made of steel and plumbed with propane.

Tom describes a Coen brothers film as being very tightly managed, beginning with a complete script with no anticipated changes. "Many of the changes in scripts are due to the cost of a scene," Tom says. "It may cost too much to film. But the Coens pretty much know when they write a scene what it's going to cost them." A typical Coen film requires about nine weeks of work, with about three weeks preproduction to prepare the effects. Some films, however, can last months longer. "For *Waterworld,* some guys were there for over a year."

When a film is in production, Tom is usually on the set, working as an *on-set lead.* He works with the director and assistant director (AD) to make sure the effects are ready to go when needed. He works project to project, on a freelance basis. "The special effects coordinator gets hired for a show," Tom explains, "then he hires a crew to work on that show. Then when the show's over, you're unemployed." And during a project, an effects technician is expected to work many hours. "A 10-hour day is very short for us. Twelve hours is normal. You also get some 15-hour days."

Do I Have What It Takes to Be a Special Effects Technician?

Special effects work is physically and mentally challenging. "You have to be calm," Tom says. "Much of what we do is life threatening to other people. You have to know what your limits are. You don't get fired for not knowing how to do something. You get fired for saying you know how and then doing it wrong."

Because networking is such an important aspect of the work, Tom emphasizes that you should be good with people and also remain persistent in the face of rejection. "As with anything in the movie industry," Tom says, "you just keep going and don't accept 'No.' You're going to hear 'No' over and over. It has nothing to do with your talents—either they're hiring or not. Most of the time you're recommended for a job by somebody who's already working with the boss."

Depending on the production, mechanical effects specialists may find themselves knee-deep in mud in subzero temperatures, or working in a studio where they may have to wait hours inside a small cramped space for their cue to perform an effect. Makeup effects specialists most often spend their days working in a trailer at a filming location or at a shop where they can construct the masks and prostheses needed for an actor's costume. Computer animation specialists have to spend long hours sitting at computers, often performing painfully repetitive work.

Because the majority of special effects technicians work as freelance or independent contractors, they must often provide their own tools and equipment when hired for a job. That requires them to have large

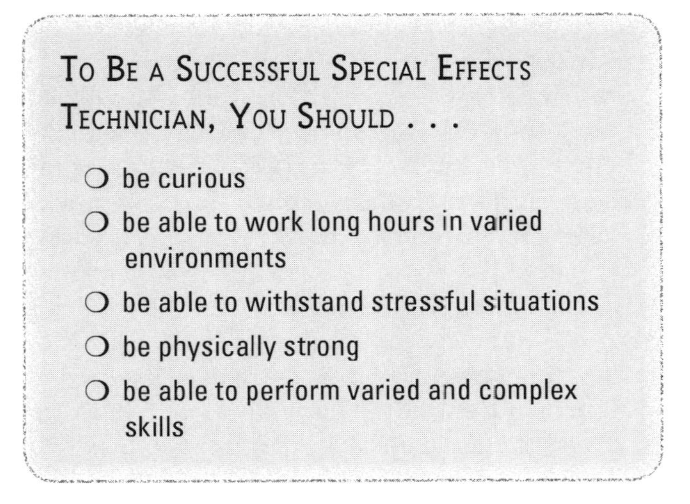

To Be a Successful Special Effects Technician, You Should . . .

- be curious
- be able to work long hours in varied environments
- be able to withstand stressful situations
- be physically strong
- be able to perform varied and complex skills

cash reserves to purchase or rent equipment they'll need to perform an effect. Cash reserves are also important because getting work is largely dependent upon the needs of filmmakers and theatrical producers. Special effects technicians have to be able to budget the money they do make to weather the lean periods between jobs.

How Do I Become a Special Effects Technician?

Tom got into special effects by working with his brother who had already established himself in the film industry. Tom was mechanically inclined and was a math major in college, all of which have helped him in the job. "A good effects person is just a good mechanic," Tom says. "We are the jacks of all trades. I weld, do carpentry, electrical work, plumbing work." The skills are more important than the college education. "I've hired people right out of high school. They were gofers until they learned different skills and started working in the movies." A movie set can be a great learning experience, especially on a lower-budget project where there's more of a mix of the experienced and inexperienced. "People in the business are really good about teaching others the ropes."

EDUCATION

High School

While companies that hire technicians in special effects are more concerned with applicants' past experience than whether or not they have a high school diploma, high school is one of the best places to learn many of the skills required to become successful as a technician in special effects.

High school courses in chemistry, mathematics, science, physics, computers, art, shop, and electronics are important to learn the basic skills that technicians in special effects use every day. Working on high school drama productions can also be helpful for learning lighting, set, and prop design.

"Physics are involved," Tom says, "and there's some math to figure in terms of building things out of steel. You use geometry to get angles and to get lengths of certain pieces."

Postsecondary Training

Some universities have film and theater schools that offer courses in special effects. Some special effects technicians major in theater, art history, photography, and related subjects. The bachelor's and master's of fine arts degrees offered at colleges across the country are studio programs in which you'll be able to gain hands-on experience in theater production and filmmaking with a faculty composed of practicing artists.

Many of the skills required to work in mechanical effects can be gained by learning a trade such as carpentry, welding, plumbing, or hydraulics and applying those skills by building sets or props for community theater productions. "Knowing electronics can be an easy in," Tom says. "Out of a crew of 25, there's a good chance no one's good at electronics. If they need somebody to build something like an electronic motor controller specific to a scene, there are people who can do that, but not many."

Some of the CGI (computer generated imagery) technicians working today have not had any special schooling or training, having mastered graphics programs on their own. Many young technicians invest in software programs in order to learn their way around computer effects. Those who can demonstrate a great deal of talent and originality in addition to computer skills will have the most success.

CERTIFICATION AND LICENSING

A mechanical special effects technician who works with fire and explosives generally needs a pyrotechnics operator's license issued by the state. A federal pyrotechnics license is also available.

INTERNSHIPS AND VOLUNTEERSHIPS

Since many of the skills needed to become a special effects technician are learned on the job, it is important for those interested in working in the field to get as much hands-on training as possible. And since employment is so competitive, working as a volunteer may be the best way to learn some of those skills.

Many small community theaters are so underfunded and understaffed that they must rely on volunteers to assist in prop construction and design, makeup, and simple mechanical effects. Student filmmakers often need volunteers to assist in their productions, and local haunted houses and amusement parks may have need for technicians. For further information on volunteer positions and internships in theatrical productions, contact your local community theater.

LABOR UNIONS

Some special effects technicians choose to join a union during their careers. One of the benefits of union membership is that some film studios, for example, will only hire union members to work on a production. This means that there is greater opportunity for union special effects technicians to work on a big-budget production early in their careers. The principal union organizing special effects technicians working in motion pictures and theatrical productions is the International Association of Theater and Stage Employees (IATSE). To work as a union special effects technician requires the completion of a six-year training program that includes serving as an apprentice in a prop-making shop, and passing an examination administered by the union. Unionized special effects technicians pay membership dues and work under a contract that determines their pay, benefits, and work rules.

Who Will Hire Me?

Networking is an important aspect of finding work in the film industry. "Every show I've worked on, other than on my brother's projects," Tom says, "has been because somebody else got on the show and I called them. It has never been because I looked in *Variety* and saw that there was a show going on. You have

In-depth

A Quick History of Special Effects in Motion Pictures

- At the turn of the century, a French filmmaker named Georges Méliès began using "special effects," including mechanical models, painted backdrops, and multiple film exposures. In order to simulate a spaceship's flight in his film *A Trip to the Moon* (1902), Méliès shot a model from a cannon and filmed its brief moment aloft.
- By the 1920s, nearly every major studio in Hollywood had a special effects department.
- In the 1939 film *The Wizard of Oz,* for example, a 90-pound costume transformed actor Bert Lahr into the Cowardly Lion; the tornado that swept away Dorothy's house was created with 30 feet of muslin hung from a gantry that moved.
- By the 1950s, the American viewing public were demanding films and television shows that were more realistic, and many studios closed their special effects departments.
- While special effects were still present in film and television commercials for the next few decades, it wasn't until the mid-1970s that the field experienced a rebirth. In 1975, George Lucas began filming *Star Wars,* and the crew of special effects technicians who assisted in the filming of the movie were the core of a special effects company he'd later form, Industrial Light & Magic (ILM). ILM is responsible for the effects in over 100 feature films, including six of the top 10 box office hits in movie history.

to know someone." Tom advises the mechanically inclined to simply promote themselves as special effects technicians, and to try to make contacts with those in the business. Check Web pages and AOL profiles of special effects technicians, and send email. The Internet Movie Database (http://www.imdb.com) is an extensive listing of professionals in many aspects of the industry. Another good resource is the LA 411 guide, a yellow pages of special effects coordinators, directors, production houses, and other industry insiders. (The guide can be accessed online at http://www.la411.com.) "Go around and look for jobs," Tom advises. "If they hire you, then you can say, 'Well, I don't know how to weld, but I can cut steel,' or, 'I can use some tools, but I can't use them all.' They'll find a place for you, and they'll teach you."

Most technicians in special effects are freelance or independent technicians who have started their own companies, or shops. Typically, a film or theater producer will hire a technician to provide the effects for a production. Depending upon the complexity of the required effects, the technician might then hire additional freelance technicians to assist on the job. The technician who was hired by the producer is considered the special effects coordinator of the special effects crew he or she assembles. It is not unusual for the coordinator on one job to be hired later as a crew member by the coordinator on another project.

As long as California remains the motion picture capital of the world, the majority of employment opportunities for technicians in special effects will be found in that state. Orange County, California, and the San Francisco area are two of the largest centers for special effects shops in the state. The number of theaters in and around New York City and Chicago makes them natural centers of employment for someone interested in working in theater effects.

Where Can I Go from Here?

Most special effects technicians have worked for several years to develop a reputation that will enable them to find sufficient work to support themselves, so leaving the field usually isn't in their immediate career plans. Instead, trying to work on bigger, more elaborate, and technically challenging productions is their primary goal.

After gaining experience working for several special effects shops and perfecting their skills working on different types of projects, technicians often start their own shops. Some shops have departments or subsidiary companies that build and sell equipment used for creating special effects.

What Are the Salary Ranges?

Some technicians have steady, salaried employment, while others work freelance for an hourly rate and may have periods with no work. The average daily rate for beginning technicians is $100 to $200 per day, while more experienced technicians can earn $300 per day or more. A member salary survey conducted by IATSE shows that employment in digital effects can pay very well, even in assistant positions. When adjusted to show annual figures, the survey found that character animators, CGI effects animators, and art directors had median yearly earnings of around $100,000. On the low end of the scale, these professionals earned around $55,000, and on the high end, $350,000. Effects assistants had beginning wages of around $45,000, and median wages of $60,000.

Those working freelance will not have the benefits of full-time work, having to provide their own health insurance. Those working for special effects houses have the usual benefit packages including health insurance, bonuses, and retirement.

What Is the Job Outlook?

According to the *Occupational Outlook Handbook*, employment of directors, producers, and others in the motion picture industry is expected to grow about as fast as the average through 2012. There is heavy competition for broadcast and motion picture technicians, and in general the plum jobs go to the best trained. While some technicians provide special effects for theater, few find the work steady or well paying enough to work in theater exclusively. Most supplement their incomes by providing effects for motion pictures and television commercials and industrial productions as well.

The competition for jobs in film special effects houses is fierce. For more than 20 years now, films of all genres have incorporated computer graphics and high-tech effects, inspiring a whole generation of young people with computers and imaginations. Many of today's top effects professionals credit their

Advancement Possibilities

Technical directors coordinate activities of radio or television studio and control-room personnel to ensure technical quality of picture and sound for programs originating in the studio or from remote pickup points.

Owners of special effects shops operate their own business specializing in the fabrication, installation, and activation of equipment to produce special effects for television, motion picture, and theatrical productions.

love for *Star Wars* with directing them toward careers in the industry. As the cost of powerful computers continues to decrease, even more people will be able to experiment with computer graphics and develop their skills and talents.

Though some special effects companies are very profitable, others are struggling to make enough money to meet their expenses. Production companies are attempting to tighten their budgets, and to turn out movies quickly. The cost of the effects, including salaries for top technicians, is increasing, while film producers decrease their special effects budgets. This will either be corrected by effects companies demanding more money, or only a few of the very top companies will be able to thrive.

How Do I Learn More?

PROFESSIONAL ORGANIZATIONS

The following organizations provide information on special effects technician careers and other careers in motion pictures, accredited schools, and possible employers:

American Film Institute
2021 North Western Avenue
Los Angeles, CA 90027
323-856-7600
http://www.afi.com

Animation World Network
6525 Sunset Boulevard, Garden Suite 10
Hollywood, CA 90028
323-606-4200
http://www.awn.com

Society of Motion Picture and Television Engineers
595 West Hartsdale Avenue
White Plains, NY 10607
smpte@smpte.org
914-761-1100
http://www.smpte.org

United State Institute of Theater Technology
6443 Ridings Road
Syracuse, NY 13206
800-938-7488
http://www.usitt.org

The Visual Effects Society
4121 Redwood Avenue, Suite 101
Los Angeles, CA 90066
310-822-9181
http://www.visualeffectssociety.com

BIBLIOGRAPHY

The following is a sampling of materials relating to the professional concerns and development of special effects technicians:

Rickitt, Rick. *Special Effects: The History and Technique*. New York: Watson-Guptill Publishing, 2000.

Rogers, Pauline B. *The Art of Visual Effects: Interviews on the Tools of the Trade*. Woburn, Mass.: Focal Press, 1999.

Yager, Fred, and Jan Yager. *Career Opportunities in the Film Industry*. New York: Facts On File, 2003.

SPECIAL PROCEDURES TECHNOLOGISTS

Something was wrong. Maybe David Brown felt it before he thought it. Maybe his years of training and experience as a cardiac catheterization technologist made him sense that Mrs. Smith was in trouble. She lay calmly, still under the anesthesia but disconnected from the EKG monitor now, as he transferred her from the table.

The other members of the cardiology team were in the second swing room, prepping for the next patient. The procedure had gone well—they'd found and removed significant blockage from Mrs. Smith's artery; she was stable . . . but something was wrong.

David lifted her eyelids. Only the whites showed. He called out: "She's crashed!" He lifted her back onto the table and hooked her up again to the monitor, as the rest of the team rushed to his side. To the cardiologist he said, "Seizures. She's fibrillating."

The team's response was immediate. With the third shock from the defibrillator, her heart beat again. The cardiologist snaked the catheter through the artery to her heart. Studying the image on the fluoroscope, he said, "Vessel wall collapsed. Good catch, David. You just saved her life. Now, let's get a stent in there."

Definition
Special procedures technologists operate medical diagnostic imaging equipment, such as computer tomography (CT) scanners and magnetic resonance imaging (MRI) scanners. They also may assist in procedures involving imaging, such as angiography and cardiac catheterization (CC).

Alternative Job Titles
Angiographers
Cardiac catheterization technologists
Computer tomography technologists
Special vascular imaging technologists

High School Subjects
Biology
Health

Personal Skills
Technical/scientific
Helping/teaching

Salary Range
$29,340 to $44,460 to $58,300+

Minimum Educational Level
Associate's degree

Certification or Licensing
Recommended (certification)
Required by certain states (licensing)

Outlook
Faster than the average

DOT
078

GOE
14.05.01

NOC
3215

O*NET-SOC
29-2031.00, 29-2034.00

What Does a Special Procedures Technologist Do?

Although X rays are a valuable diagnostic tool, advances in technology have allowed medical staff to capture even more precise images of the human body. Tools such as computer tomography (CT) scanners and magnetic resonance imagers (MRI), and techniques such as angiography and cardiac catheterization, allow physicians and specially trained technologists to pinpoint areas of medical concern. In some cases, intervention procedures may be performed right away, saving valuable time and allowing patients to avoid riskier surgical procedures.

Cardiac catheterization, computer tomography, angiography, and magnetic resonance imaging are four special procedures that are often grouped together, because each technique involves the making or using of visual images to assist physicians in treating their patients. Many of those who do this work began as radiologic technologists and then went on to receive advanced training in their specialized area. These professionals with advanced training are known as *special procedures technologists*. They are generally responsible for positioning the patient for examination, immobilizing them, preparing the equipment to be used, and monitoring the equipment and the patient's progress during the procedure.

Special diagnostic procedures may be grouped into two areas: invasive and noninvasive. CT scans and MRI scans are considered noninvasive because the equipment does not enter the body. Angiography and cardiac catheterization are considered invasive techniques because the imaging work is done from within the body. Sometimes patients will undergo more than one of these procedures so that their physicians will have a better understanding of their health conditions.

ANGIOGRAPHY

Blood vessels do not normally show up on X-ray photographs. Yet physicians need to be able to see the vessels of the circulatory system in order to detect and locate such life-threatening conditions as aneurysms, narrowing or blockage of the vessel, or the presence of clots in the vessel. Angiography accomplishes this by coating the vessels of the affected areas with a contrast medium, a substance that allows blood vessels to be seen because the contrast makes the vessels opaque to the X rays. In patients with tumors or injuries to their organs, an angiogram can show any changes that have occurred to the pattern of the vessels. Studying the flow of the contrast medium through the vessels also gives the physician important information about the way the patient's blood flows. With this information, the physician can assess the extent of damage or the progression of disease and determine the necessary treatment.

In order to perform an angiography, a small tube, called a catheter, is first inserted into the patient and moved through an artery to the area the physician wishes to examine. The special procedures technologist, called an *angiographer* in this case, assists the placement of the catheter by operating and monitoring an X-ray fluoroscope. The angiographer next prepares the contrast medium to be injected and is responsible for controlling the amount and rate of flow of the contrast medium into the patient's body. Using a video display, the angiographer will adjust the density and contrast of the image in order to make certain that the highest possible quality X rays will be taken. The angiographer then initiates the filming sequence, taking a rapid series of X rays that will function as a movie of the vessel. This will allow the physician to study the blood flow within the vessel.

An angiography procedure can last a few minutes or up to three hours. Once the X rays have been taken, the angiographer takes them to the hospital's darkroom to be developed. The angiographer then reviews the finished X rays for their quality and to be certain that they properly record the area under examination.

Lingo to Learn

Aneurysm A saclike bulging of a blood vessel, usually an artery; an extremely dangerous health condition.

Artery A vessel that carries blood away from the heart to the rest of the body.

Catheter A small, flexible, strong tube made of plastic, rubber, or metal, inserted into the body to inject medicines, drain fluids, and perform diagnostic procedures.

Catheterization The introduction of a catheter into the body.

Coronary stent A device inserted into a blood vessel in order to support a weakened or collapsed area of the vessel.

Diagnosis The determination, after examination, of the nature of the patient's health condition and extent of disease.

Electrocardiogram (EKG or ECG) A record of the electric current produced by the contractions of the heart. The EKG machine and monitor provide a graphic, real-time representation of this electric current.

Fluoroscope X-ray apparatus that uses a fluorescent screen of calcium tungstate to produce images of the varying densities of the body.

Imaging The creation of images of the parts of the body.

Intravenous Refers to the injection of medicines, contrast mediums, and other drugs directly into a vein.

Stroke A condition, often accompanied by seizures, brought on by the collapse or rupture of a blood vessel in the brain.

Vascular Pertaining to or containing vessels.

Vein A vessel that carries blood from other parts of the body back to the heart.

X ray A type of radiation beam used to record on film shadow images of the portions of the body.

Recent advances in technology allow angiographers to inject far less contrast medium into patients. Computers, in what is called digital subtraction angiography, enable the technologist to delete parts of the X rays that reduce the quality and visibility of the vessels. In some cases, this means that the contrast medium can be injected intravenously, eliminating the riskier catheterization procedure. Advances in intervention procedures, such as expanding a blocked artery or injecting medications directly into a tumor, mean that these can be performed while the catheter is still in place. In this way, surgery can often be avoided.

CARDIAC CATHETERIZATION

Like angiography, the cardiac catheterization (CC) procedure is invasive, in that it involves the introduction of a catheter into the patient's body in order to examine and treat heart conditions. As part of a team assisting the cardiologist, the *cardiac catheterization technologist* performs one or more of several functions, including positioning the patients and explaining to them the procedure they will undergo; monitoring such vital signs as the patient's blood pressure and respiration rates; documenting the procedure by inserting patient data into a computer system used to control the amount, quality, and sequence for filming the X rays of the patient's heart; and assisting the cardiology team in preprocedure sterilization by retrieving supplies and equipment necessary to the procedure.

During a cardiac catheterization procedure, a catheter is introduced through a small incision into a vein or artery and guided into the patient's heart. When the catheter is in position, it can be used for various diagnostic and intervention procedures, such as directly reading the heart's blood pressure, withdrawing blood to determine the amount of oxygen reaching the heart, injecting contrast medium for filming X rays, or introducing tools and medications to repair damaged vessels. When these procedures are called for, the cardiac catheterization technologist will assist in preparing whatever tools and medications are needed.

When X rays are required, the CC technologist will enter data on the amount, quality, and filming sequence of the radiation beam, initiate the introduction of the contrast medium into the heart, and activate the fluoroscope that will film the heart. CC technologists are also responsible for positioning the X-ray device and the table, raising and lowering them according to the cardiologist's request.

Finally, an important function of the cardiac catheterization technologist is to remain alert to changes in the patient's response throughout the procedure. Because patients undergoing this procedure generally suffer from life-threatening conditions, and because there remains a measure of risk to the procedure, the cardiologist and the other members of the cardiac catheterization team must be kept continually informed of the patient's progress.

CT (COMPUTER TOMOGRAPHY) SCAN

CT scanning (also known as CAT scanning, which stands for computer axial tomography) represents an important breakthrough in diagnostic imaging. While invasive techniques such as angiography entail not only a degree of risk to the patient, but are also limited in their usefulness in highly complex organs like the brain, CT scanning combines X rays with computer technology to create clear cross-section images. These cross sections, or slices, provide more detailed information than standard X-rays, while the technique minimizes the patient's exposure to the X-ray radiation. First developed in the early 1970s for studying the brain, CT scanning has proven a useful technique for examination of much of the body.

A CT scanner is a large device consisting of a rotating scanner and a table that may be placed in a variety of positions as it enters the scanner. The *CT technologist* is responsible for positioning the patient on the table, making certain that the head and body are immobilized. The placement of the patient must be precise and according to the radiologist's instructions in order to achieve the necessary images of the area under examination. Contrast media are also used in CT scanning. The medium is sometimes taken orally, at other times given intravenously. The CT technologist enters data into the scanner's computer control, including the type of scan to be performed, the time required, and the thickness of the slice to be made.

As the CT scan begins, large numbers of low dosage X rays are passed through the patient from a great many angles. These angles enable the computer to construct three-dimensional images of the parts of the patient's body. Different tissues in the body absorb X rays in different amounts; sensors allow the computer to gather this information and build the images. During the procedure, the CT technologist observes the patient through a window in the control room and speaks to the patient over an intercom system. Because the CT scan can be an uncomfortable procedure, the CT technologist is able to provide reassurance to the patient.

MAGNETIC RESONANCE IMAGING (MRI)

MRI is the latest advance in imaging technology. Unlike the other procedures, it does not involve X rays and, therefore, presents no risk to the patient. MRI scans also produce the most detailed and flexible images among the various imaging techniques. Because it is relatively new, however, it remains an extremely costly procedure.

As its name implies, MRI uses a strong magnetic field to affect the positioning of hydrogen protons (the nuclei of hydrogen) in the body. Normally, hydrogen protons are randomly positioned; when subjected to the magnetic field of the MRI, however, these protons will line up parallel to each other. A pulse of radio waves is then used to knock the protons out of this alignment. As the protons return to their magnetic alignment, they produce radio signals, and the MRI scanner reads these radio signals in order to construct its images. Because the different tissues of the body contain different levels of hydrogen, each tissue will produce a radio signal of a different strength. The MRI computer interprets the strength of the signals as it builds the images of the section of the body under examination.

The *MRI technologist* first speaks to the patient, explaining the MRI procedure, and makes certain that the patient is not carrying any metal objects. These can be hazardous to the patient and can damage the equipment once the magnetic field is activated. The MRI technologist is responsible for positioning the patient on the table that will be introduced into the MRI scanner. Special coils, or receivers, are positioned on the patient over the area the radiologist wishes to examine. A microphone inside the scanner allows the patient and technologist to communicate throughout the procedure, which generally requires half an hour, and the MRI technologist will explain the microphone's operation to the patient.

In the computer control room attached to the MRI scanning room, the MRI technologist enters the necessary data, such as the patient's history, the position for entry into the scanner, the part of the body to be scanned, and the orientation of the scan, into the computer. The MRI technologist initiates the scan and observes the patient through a window in the control room and on a closed-circuit video display, while maintaining voice contact. In this way, the MRI technologist can offer comfort and reassurance to the patient while remaining alert to the patient's safety.

MRI scans are particularly useful for examining the brain, spinal cord, and the eyes and ears and for determining the precise extent of tumors that may be present in the patient's body. MRI scans can provide detailed images of the heart, the circulatory system, as well as joints and soft tissues and organs such as the intestines. Continual refinements to MRI techniques are making possible the imaging of areas of the body that have previously resisted detailed examination.

What Is It Like to Be a Special Procedures Technologist?

Before the introduction of these special imaging procedures, physicians were dependent on X rays to give them an understanding of the conditions affecting their patients. X rays, however, are not usually precise enough to supply detailed images of many vital areas of the body. For some health conditions, exploratory surgery was the only way a physician could locate the source of a health problem. Yet even minor surgery can expose a patient to risk. Special imaging procedures have greatly enhanced the physician's diagnostic abilities; in some cases, these procedures allow the patient to avoid surgery altogether.

Special procedures have created a need for personnel trained to operate the equipment and assist the medical and nursing staff. The quality and precision of the images determine their usefulness in treating the patient. Technologists are the people responsible for this quality and precision.

David Brown is a cardiac catheterization technologist at the Texas Heart Center in St. Luke's Episcopal Hospital in Houston. "We're one of the premier cardiac centers in the world," David says. "We're a large facility, with 11 cath labs, which may be more than most places. But we're involved in research too. A lot of the procedures we perform are still experimental."

Typically David works in a team of four, including two nurses and two technologists, who assist the cardiologist. Teams are assigned to one of several different rooms, with each room set up according to the needs of its diagnostic specialty. Assignments to these rooms are rotated according to a daily schedule. In addition to these rooms, "swing labs," which are really two rooms joined together, allow the cardiac team to perform more than one procedure. "That way, when we finish one procedure, one of us will manipulate the patient from the table while the others are already preparing for the next procedure.

"The nature of the room's specialty determines its schedule. A room set up for peripheral vascular work, for example, may only see one or two patients in the day," David explains. "In a swing lab, we'll work on eight to 11 patients a day. Compare that to an X-ray lab, where it's more like an assembly line—they'll do 200 to 300 patients in one day. Because what we do may be very intensive, our schedule operates according to a specific structure."

When David arrives at the hospital at 7:00 A.M., he first meets with the other members of the cardiac staff to coordinate the day's schedule and receive his assignment. "There's a specific amount of time allotted for each procedure, based on how long they usually take. So I know at the beginning of the day what my schedule will be like." As part of the team, David is assigned to one of the four areas of the cardiac catheterization procedure described above.

"Each one is important, and I've been trained for all of the different fields of the procedure. Sometimes I drive the table, that is, position the patient, manipulate the X-ray camera. Other times, I do the procedural documentation, or I do what we call human dynamic monitoring, which means watching the EKG monitoring, reading the patient's blood pressure and other vital signs. Or I'll be the 'go-fer,' running supplies, sterilizing the equipment, and scrubbing up the other members of the team."

David's days are busy, and sometimes procedures can take longer than expected. "The nature of cardiac catheterization means that the procedure must always come first. So sometimes we're lucky when we can break for lunch, if there's another team available to fill in for us," David says. "And I'd say we run late almost every day."

The daily schedules of other special procedures technologists vary according to the size of the hospital, their patient load, and the type of imaging technique they perform. An angiographer's day may be similar to David Brown's, as they too assist in an invasive procedure. MRI technologists and CT technologists may find their schedules to be much different. "Also," David says, "the other special procedures are generally assigned to the radiology department, while we're a part of the cardiology department."

Do I Have What It Takes to Be a Special Procedures Technologist?

Special procedures technologists, as with all personnel involved in health care, work with people undergoing extremely stressful periods of their lives. "That can be a down side," says Kelly Yu, an MRI technologist at a New Haven, Connecticut, hospital. "Our job can be very stressful and full of hard situations. But the fact that I feel I am helping mankind helps balance the equation."

David Brown agrees. "We work with sick and dying people, and they are often pretty scared. I like it that I can interact with the patients, and I do my best to make them more comfortable. You really get to know your patients, and there's an extra satisfaction when the intervention is successful. But when things don't go well, it can be pretty rough."

You really get to know your patients, and there's an extra satisfaction when the intervention is successful.

Good communication skills are important not only for interacting with the patients, but also for working with other members of the medical staff. As a member of a cardiology team, David's contact with physicians, nurses, and other technologists is more intensive than Kelly's work in MRI. "But I like it that I'm allowed to interact with professionals on an equal level," says David, who is currently completing his premedical studies and expects to become a general surgeon. "I think being a cardiac tech allows me to prove myself to the others. There's more respect here than in other areas of radiology. They see me working; I'm part of the team, and really, the only thing that counts here is how well you perform your job. I think there's an attitude toward other radiology technologists that you're just a tech. I don't find that in cardiology."

For Kelly, the recent initiation of board certification for MRI technologists brings an added respect to her work. "Certification is a big step toward acknowledgment," she says. But Kelly finds a lot of satisfaction in the work itself. "I chose radiology and MRI because it's an up-and-coming career that's always taking steps toward being at the forefront of medicine in the years to come. Each year we get better upgrades, and we're able to do things that were never even imagined before, like magnetic resonance angiography, breast imaging, and imaging of heart, abdomen, and prostate. I like the fact that this career is always moving on, challenging me to become a better and more competent tech."

No matter where they work, though, technologists must have the desire to keep learning and stay current with new developments in the field. One of the exciting parts of David's work is the sometimes experimental nature of the procedures with which he assists. "A lot of the work we do is as part of major research studies into techniques and types of medication. For example, we pioneered the use of coronary stents. I like being involved in new technologies. And I get to see procedures that never make it to being approved too."

David, who began his radiology career as a radiologic technologist in the army, finds his work in cardiology to be an important step in his future career. "I've dreamed of becoming a surgeon since I was young. And the work I do here is a lot like surgery. It's giving me a real exposure to what I hope to do in the future. I get to put into practice a lot of the things I'm studying in school too. For that reason, I recommend this work to anyone considering a medical career."

Technologists must be able to concentrate on several tasks at once. Cardiology patients are often confronted with life-threatening conditions, and David must always be alert to signs that they are in trouble during the procedure. "I'm working with critical patients. I have to be able to see what can go wrong and be prepared for it. If a patient crashes suddenly, or if they can't tolerate the procedure, I have to know to call the anesthesiologist or to call for respiratory support. That can be stressful, knowing that a person's life depends on what you do."

Patients undergoing these procedures may require extra sensitivity from the technologists and other personnel involved in their care. "You have to be able to inspire confidence in them," Kelly says. "That's a big factor in a patient's health and whether they'll get better." Technologists, therefore, should enjoy working with people and be able to give reassurance.

Hospitals are, of course, sterile, well-lit work environments. However, working conditions may vary. A busy hospital, a critical care ward, or an emergency room may present a much more stressful environment than a health care clinic, a health maintenance organization (HMO), or a diagnostic imaging center. Hours may also vary widely. David Brown, for example, generally works eight hours a day, five days a week. "Although," David says, "they're considering adding a second shift, because of the increasing volume of patients we see." Other special procedures technologists may be assigned to work night or weekend shifts, or they may be on call, meaning they must be available to work 24 hours a day.

Advancement Possibilities

Radiologic equipment specialists test, repair, calibrate, and assist in the installation of radiological and related equipment used in medical diagnosis or therapy, applying technical knowledge of electronic, radiological, and mechanical systems, as well as user knowledge of computers, manuals, test equipment, measuring instruments, hand tools, and power tools.

Chief radiologic technologists direct and coordinate activities of radiology or diagnostic imaging departments in hospitals or other medical facilities.

Radiologists diagnose and treat diseases of the human body using X rays and radioactive substances.

Radiology administrators plan, direct, and coordinate administrative activities of radiology departments in hospital medical centers.

How Do I Become a Special Procedures Technologist?

Most special procedures technologists begin their careers in radiology as radiologic technologists.

Generally, they are required to hold an associate's degree in radiology, and then they receive additional training and education in their special procedure. In addition, many states and Puerto Rico require that radiologic technologists be licensed.

EDUCATION

High School

"In tenth grade," David says, "I sort of fell into an advanced course—human anatomy and physiology—where we had to dissect a cat. Ever since I've dreamed of becoming a surgeon." Biology, chemistry, and algebra were also important classes for David. "Having good math skills makes everything go easier," he adds. "And I'd say that my English and social science classes were really helpful, especially when I'm relating to patients and the other members of the cardiology team."

Advanced courses were also a feature of Kelly Yu's high school curriculum. "I found taking advanced courses in anatomy, physiology, math, and physics to be very useful," she says. Classes in communication, such as speech, and classes that reinforce written and verbal skills will help you throughout your career. Because most imaging specialties depend heavily on computer technology, you should gain a good understanding of the use of computers. Depending on where you will work, you will probably find yourself confronted with people from a great variety of cultural backgrounds and experiences. Therefore, you will do well to take a variety of social studies classes and gain an awareness of, and respect and understanding for, issues confronting other cultures.

Postsecondary Training

A high school diploma or equivalent is a requirement for anyone interested in entering this field. After high school, most students will find it necessary to attend a two-year program and earn an associate's degree in radiology before finding employment. These programs can be found at community colleges, vocational and technical training schools, or in the military.

David, for example, began his career in the army. "Actually, I applied for the physical therapy program, but that was filled. So I went into radiography. It was a pretty extensive course, with 20 weeks in the classroom and 23 weeks doing clinical practice. I was sent to a lot of different hospitals around the country for that part."

After he left the army, David applied for his job in the cardiology department. "I was taught everything I needed to know about cardiac catheterization, as well as EKG monitoring, here at the hospital. The training program here usually lasts from three to six months, depending on how quickly you pick it up and how much experience you've already had."

Kelly Yu received her associate's degree in radiology. "Then I was lucky enough to get into the Yale School of Medicine for a year to specialize in MRI."

Most radiologic technologists receive training through a program accredited by the Joint Review Committee on Education in Radiologic Technology (JRCERT). These programs include classroom work, laboratory training, and clinical experience. You can expect to study such subjects as human physiology; medical terminology; radiation physics and protection; diagnostic imaging techniques, principles, procedures, evaluation, and pathology; computer science; quality assurance; medical ethics and law; and patient care.

In all cases, special procedures technologists must complete additional training in their specialty area, which is usually offered through a hospital, medical center, college, or vocational or technical training school.

CERTIFICATION OR LICENSING

Graduates of accredited programs are eligible to take the certification examination offered by the American Registry of Radiologic Technologists (ARRT). Most states and Puerto Rico also require licensing for radiologic technologists. This requirement is usually satisfied by successfully receiving ARRT certification, but you will need to check with your state's licensing board for specific information. Certification requirements and opportunities vary by state for the individual special procedures. However, where certification is available, technologists are strongly advised to complete those requirements. This will enhance your chances of finding employment (see "How Do I Learn More?").

INTERNSHIPS AND VOLUNTEERSHIPS

If you are interested in entering the health care field, you can begin your involvement while still in high school. Most hospitals have volunteer programs that will allow you to explore the hospital environment and gain valuable insight into medicine and patient care. Many nursing homes, mental health centers, and other treatment facilities need dedicated volunteers to assist with patients. You may also be able to find part-time work in one of the lower-skilled medical fields; for example, as a nurse's aide or as an orderly. A job in administration, such as clerking at a hospital, health clinic, or health care center, will also give you valuable experience and exposure to the field. Because careers in health care can be as stressful as they are rewarding, you should consider if your personality is right for the field, and if the field is right for you. You can locate volunteer and employment opportunities by consulting with your high school guidance counselor, contacting local hospitals and health care facilities, or by searching job ads and contacting other employment services.

Who Will Hire Me?

As noted, special procedures technologists are employed in a variety of health care settings. Hospitals are the most likely source for employment, especially for techniques such as CT and MRI scanning, which require extremely costly equipment. Health maintenance organizations and other health care clinics and centers also need personnel trained to carry out the variety of testing procedures needed for medical care. There are also a great number of diagnostic imaging centers, often associated with hospitals, that are specifically dedicated to performing the battery of special imaging procedures. Also, the U.S. government employs radiologic and other imaging personnel, usually through the Department of Veterans Affairs or as members of the armed forces.

Where Can I Go from Here?

Advancement in special procedures fields is generally limited, as these specialties already represent advanced areas of radiology. With experience, however, a special procedures technologist may advance to greater responsibilities and to supervisory positions. Chief radiologic technologists, for example, oversee a radiology or imaging department at a hospital or other medial facility. Radiology administrators direct and coordinate the administration of hospital radiology departments. After working as a technologist you may also choose to continue your education in order to reach advanced positions. Radiologists, for example, have medical degrees and use X rays to diagnose and treat illnesses. David sees his special imaging procedures work as a valuable bridge to becoming a doctor. David, in fact, credits his decision to pursue a medical career to his work as a cardiac catheterization technologist.

Special procedures technologists will find demand for their skills throughout the country. Travel to other countries is also a possibility, as some countries, including Great Britain, South Africa, and Canada, recognize U.S. certification.

What Are the Salary Ranges?

According to the *Occupational Outlook Handbook*, radiologic technologists had median annual earnings of $41,850 in 2003. Those in the lowest 10 percent earned less than $29,340, while those in the highest 10 percent earned more than $58,300 annually. Medical and clinical laboratory technologists had median annual earnings of $44,460 in 2003. The lowest paid 10 percent earned less than $31,410, and the highest paid 10 percent made more than $60,790.

Compensation and pay scales will vary based on the location of the employer—with urban areas more lucrative than rural areas and small towns—and on the level of education attained, the experience, and the responsibilities of the technologist. Benefits vary widely from state to state and from employer to employer. Most packages, however, include paid vacation and holidays, as well as sick leave, medical and dental insurance, and some form of retirement plan. Some employers may offer additional benefits such as on-site day care and tuition reimbursement.

What Is the Job Outlook?

The job outlook for special procedures technologists is quite favorable. The U.S. Department of Labor expects employment of radiologic technologists to increase at a faster than average rate over the next 10 years. For certified special procedures technologists the outlook should be even better. Heart disease and cancer continue to be among the primary health concerns in the U.S. population, and there will be a high demand for skilled technologists to assist in the diagnosis and treatment of these and other conditions.

Because these procedures can reduce or even eliminate the need for riskier and costlier surgical interventions, their use can be expected to become more and more common in the health care industry. The ability to diagnose ailments precisely and accurately, and even before they become life-threatening, is an important factor in the increasingly cost-conscious health care arena. In addition, health insurance companies, especially malpractice insurance underwriters, will also require more and more testing in order to limit physician and hospital liability. While these procedures themselves may be expensive, they can reduce both hospital and physician liability costs and litigation and also reduce the need for the much more expensive treatment of advanced diseases and conditions.

Another factor that will influence growth is the aging of the American population. As the median age rises, more attention will be focused on diseases that are prominent in older people. Many of these diseases require the use of imaging equipment and technologists. The Southeast and Southwest regions of the United States offer significant employment opportunity due to their large populations of retirement-age Americans. The aging of the work force will also mean more retirement within the field and more positions to fill. ARRT has found that the majority of radiologic technologists are 40 years or older, part of the reason the organizations are predicting a severe shortage of technologists by 2010.

Another reason for this shortage is that fewer people are entering the field than ever before. The career may be unattractive to some because of the long hours and wages that don't properly compensate. In an effort to bring some standardization to the field, ARRT is considering requiring technologists to have bachelor's degrees in order to become certified. Currently, radiologic technology students are putting in nearly four years of training anyway, because of the practical requirements of associate's degrees.

How Do I Learn More?

PROFESSIONAL ORGANIZATIONS

The following are organizations that provide information on special procedures technologist careers, accredited schools and scholarships, and possible employers:

American Registry of Radiologic Technologists
1255 Northland Drive
St. Paul, MN 55120-1155
651-687-0048
http://www.arrt.org

American Society of Nuclear Cardiology
9111 Old Georgetown Road
Bethesda, MD 20814-1699
301-493-2360
admin@asnc.org
http://www.asnc.org

American Society of Radiologic Technologists
15000 Central Avenue, SE
Albuquerque, NM 87123-3917
800-444-2778
http://www.asrt.org

Joint Review Committee on Education in Radiologic Technology
20 North Wacker Drive, Suite 900
Chicago, IL 60606-2901
312-704-5300
mail@jrcert.org
http://www.jrcert.org

To learn more about credentialing in cardiovascular technology:

Cardiovascular Credentialing International
4456 Corporation Lane, Suite 120
Virginia Beach, VA 23462
804-497-3380
http://www.cci-online.org

BIBLIOGRAPHY

The following is a sampling of materials relating to the professional concerns and development of special procedures technologists:

Brant, William E., and Clyde A. Helms, eds. *Fundamentals of Diagnostic Radiology*. 2d ed. Baltimore: Lippincott Williams & Wilkins, 1999.

Careers in Focus: Medical Technicians. 4th ed. New York: Facts On File, 2004.

Juhl, John H., and Andrew B. Crummy, eds. *Paul and Juhl's Essentials of Radiologic Imaging*. 7th ed. Philadelphia, PA: J. B. Lippincott, 1998.

Mettler, Fred A., Jr., and Milton J. Guiberteau. *Essentials of Nuclear Medicine Imaging*. 4th ed. Philadelphia: W. B. Saunders, 1998.

STAGE TECHNICIANS

"Every show is memorable," says Molly P. Rosen, a stage technician in California. "I can remember every show that I've done." One show that Molly recalls as particularly challenging was a community theater production of *Sweeney Todd,* for which she served as a dresser. "It's a very fast show," she says. "We had a lot of quick changes. I would be in an area backstage where I'd have five guys all quickly changing out of costumes into tuxedos, out of tuxedos into other costumes. We had a matter of seconds to get them all dressed."

But such demands are part of why she finds the work so satisfying. She discovered very early on that stage technician work was in her blood. "When I was a junior," Molly says, "we were doing *Little Shop of Horrors* as a fund-raiser for our choral department. The school rented all the equipment we used, and one day one of the lights didn't work, so I helped to repair it. I didn't know what I was doing, but I looked at the light, and I looked at the person repairing it, and I said, 'This is what I want to do for the rest of my life.'"

Definition
Stage technicians install and operate lights, scenery, and sound equipment for plays, concerts, lectures, and other stage productions. Stage technicians also work in radio, television, video, and film.

Alternative Job Titles
Electrical technicians
Electricians
Light technicians
Sound technicians
Stage production workers

High School Subjects
Technical/shop
Theater/dance

Personal Skills
Artistic
Mechanical/manipulative

Salary Range
$32,726 to $39,918 to $48,299+

Work Environment
Primarily indoors
Primarily multiple locations

Minimum Educational Level
High school diploma
Apprenticeship/internship

Certification or Licensing
None available

Outlook
About as fast as the average

DOT
962

GOE
N/A

NOC
5226, 5227

O*NET-SOC
N/A

What Does a Stage Technician Do?

Whenever you go to a play or a concert, you witness more than the talent of the actors and musicians. You also witness the talent of the *stage technicians.* The hanging and the focusing of the lights, the adjustment of the sound, the construction of the sets, all these elements require the expertise of a knowledgeable technician. The technicians are quietly working backstage during the performance, making sure all goes smoothly, but they've also spent many hours before the show putting the stage together. For any production to work, for the audience to be drawn into the show, to see what they are supposed to see and hear what they are meant to hear, a theater must have a dedicated staff of stage technicians.

Because of the limited resources and funds of most theaters, play directors rely on their stage technicians and designers to pull off some real stunts. To make everything appear real, and for the effects of lighting and sound and set design to be convincing, requires both imagination and hard work. Stage technicians spend a lot of time crawling around in the small spaces beneath the stage, climbing up to the grid work high above the stage, knowing their way around a sound board. In other words, the success of any show can rely as much upon the people backstage as it does upon those on stage.

Usually, a designer or stage director will create blueprints and other diagrams and specifications for

Lingo to Learn

Dimmers An electrical device that dims the lights.

Flat A piece of stage scenery consisting of a wooden frame, usually rectangular, covered with lightweight board or fabric.

Flies Areas above the stage where scenery, lighting, and other equipment are kept.

Floods Lights that give a general fixed spread of illumination.

Focusing Fixing the lights on stage to light specific areas.

Gel A color medium introduced before light to alter the color of the beam.

Gobo A cut-out shape that is projected.

Hanging Attaching scenery, lights, or other equipment to bars.

Leko A lamp which gives a sharply defined image in outline of any object placed within its focal range.

Pyrotechnics Chemical effects used to create lighting or special effects.

the look of the show. A technician then works with these designs, installing lights, sound equipment, and building scenery. Sometimes these technicians are even required to build a whole stage for productions, such as a theater in a park or outside music concert.

These technicians gather props, sometimes making do with very limited resources. The smaller the theater or event, the less the technician is probably going to have to work with. This can require a great deal of imagination and ingenuity, as well as a clear technical understanding of how things work. Stage technicians must also understand the play or performance—with knowledge of the key scenes, a technician can better provide the required effects.

To create these effects, technicians use hammers, saws, and other hand tools or power tools. They climb ladders and work on scaffoldings. They situate the stage lights and set up cables for the raising and lowering curtains, scenery, and other equipment. They work with electronics and electrical wiring, and they position microphones, speakers, and amplifiers. A technician may also need computer skills, as some theaters have advanced equipment that is operated and controlled by computer.

Once the production begins, the stage technician is required to keep all these systems working. Technicians operate the lighting and sound equipment during a performance, as well as raise and lower equipment.

What Is It Like to Be a Stage Technician?

Molly P. Rosen works as a freelance stage technician in addition to her full-time job as a production manager for a university. Theaters across Orange County, California, call Molly when they need additional technical work, and her responsibilities vary. "If I'm called into the La Mirada Theater for the Performing Arts," she says, "I'm usually called in as an electrician. I'll come in to hang a show, focus the show, sometimes to help load in a show as an overhire carpenter."

Working as a carpenter involves building the sets. "Not so much actually getting out a hammer and nails and building," she says, "but building in a sense that it's in pieces and we need to put it together for a show. If it's a brand new show, the set is coming in from the shop where it was built, and we've got elements to put together. Or the theater will rent a set from a local rental company. A lot of things get screwed together, or they get hinge-pinned together."

Though every show is different, the work itself is fairly routine. "When I go into these theaters as an electrician, it's easy for me. Once you've hung a light, you know how to do it for the rest of your life." But each show can provide particular challenges. "Sometimes you're hanging out over a ledge hanging a light, or you're on a ladder." Molly works from a light plot that has been prepared by a lighting designer or the house master electrician. She has experience working as a designer herself. "I do design work for a local high school," she says. "I don't plot it out, because I'm also hanging my own design. I talk to the director and I see what he wants, and I see how the scenery looks. I work with what equipment the school has, and sometimes I bring in extra."

Molly sometimes works as part of a strike crew, as well. "The strike crew is the crew that comes in and makes it all go away," Molly explains. "We come in and strike the show after final curtain. We tear down the set, pack up the props, pack up the costumes, restore the lighting."

Molly has also worked with touring companies. "I spent three years touring: two with a small company and one with *Sesame Street Live*. I've been to almost all 50 states now. I love the touring aspects of theater. I was meeting new people every week. The first company I worked with, we were in a different city every day. A lot of the places where we performed were high schools, where we would have high school crews. So I got a chance to actually teach these students while they were helping us put on a show."

The technology is frequently changing. In her 10 years working in theater, she has watched as "moving lights" have become integral in theater work. "That's computer-controlled lighting," Molly explains. "You program in a computer how you want the lighting to look on stage, and the computer runs the lighting. With computerized moving lights, you can have a very small circle of white light in one scene, and in the next scene a big circle of red light with a star pattern." Molly learns about the latest technology on the job, and by talking to the people she knows in the industry. "I have friends who specialize in sound, in costumes, in scenery."

David Darland works full time as lighting and sound designer and technician for the Gaslight Theater in Arizona. This sometimes means more than just 40 hours a week. Each show at the Gaslight Theater runs 11 weeks, and preparing for the first week of a new production can mean working day and night, sometimes up to 120 hours a week. David must build and paint all the sets, and hang and focus the lights. He prepares the sound effects, the sampling machine, and programs the computer board. And he tends to just about every other technical detail, from changing light bulbs around the complex to locking the theater up at night. In the Gaslight Theater, David has a long list of job titles: light and sound designer/technician, guitarist, caddy, heating and air-conditioning specialist, light bulb maintenance man, pyrotechnics worker, tour guide, lumber materials distribution specialist, hydraulics engineer, and security officer.

Preparing for a show also means using his imagination and the limited resources of the theater to create interesting effects. He's often called upon to make something artificial seem real. "When there's the need for me to create a sunset on stage," David explains, "without having the sun or the clouds or diffraction of the atmosphere, I have to create all that using colored gels and different instruments."

But the job of stage technician appealed to more than his creative side. When working in high school on the stage and lighting crew, most of his fellow students wanted to be producers. "I was one of the few people who wanted to be a technician. I wanted to get dirty," David says. "I wanted to hang the lighting instrument 30 feet on the grid on a rickety old ladder."

To Be a Successful Stage Technician, You Should . . .

- have knowledge of the theater and how it operates
- have carpentry and electrical knowledge
- be in shape for climbing, balancing, and lifting
- work well with others
- be committed to making contacts

Do I Have What It Takes to Be a Stage Technician?

If working freelance, Molly says, you need to be prepared for a varied schedule and varied wages. "Sometimes you don't get the call until the day before," she says. "The last call I got from La Mirada, they were in a pinch and called me at 11:00 at night needing me at 8:00 the next morning." Though she was part of the union when she worked on *Sesame Street Live* and was guaranteed a certain wage each week, she's currently not with the union, and pay can be low. "Those are some of the disadvantages of the work," she says, "but I wouldn't trade it for anything in the world."

David also enjoys going to work. "I feel lucky," he says. "I'm able to imagine anything I want and somebody gives me the time and money to do that on stage." He feels that it's very rewarding to sit back and watch the results of his efforts, and to see the audience appreciating the effects he created. "Even newspaper criticism of a show's lighting and sound can lead to growth and learning." And despite

FYI

Tricks of the Trade

- Early theatrical machinery included the *eccyclema* (introduced in the 5th century B.C.), a platform that could wheel an actor or interior scene out onto the stage. A hoisting device called the *mechane* could lift actors up and down (to simulate mortals rising to heaven, or gods lowering themselves to earth).
- A revolving stage was invented in Osaka, Japan, by the Kado-za doll theater. The trapdoor is a 19th-century invention used on stage floors to lower lights or to raise and lower actors.
- In the later 19th century, theater audiences demanded spectacles. To meet this demand, theater owners built elaborate sets; a Victorian theater staged the chariot race in *Ben Hur* using actual chariots and horses supported by cradles and moved forward on a railway; the New Aquatic Theatre in Paris, 1895, featured a large pool for water acts.

his many years of experience, David thinks there remains a lot more for him to learn. "I'm constantly in training," he says.

> I'm able to imagine anything I want and somebody gives me the time and money to do that on stage.

A technician often has to rely on the imagination. Sometimes a technician has to stage a show with very limited tools and props. And no matter how limited a theater's resources, a director may have elaborate demands requiring the technician's creativity and knowledge of equipment.

Because of these sometimes elaborate demands, a stage technician must be patient and able to work well with people. Technicians must also make the commitment to the long hours. The entertainment industry revolves around weekends and holidays, as well as late nights.

But a commitment to the job, long hours and all, is essential to a stage technician's success. Someone pursuing stage technician work should be committed to making contacts, to getting to know the theater community and how a theater operates. "Study a manual," David says. "Find a summer or weekend job at a theater. Get into the box office, costume, carpentry, acting, music, dance, stage management. Starting out, you should be prepared to volunteer a lot of your time, and to remain open to any lighting or sound job that comes along."

How Do I Become a Stage Technician?

Though Molly took drama courses in high school, her teacher's background was in directing and acting. "We were lucky in that the school brought in professionals to do our sets and lights, so I could talk to them about the work." But most of Molly's knowledge of stage technology came from college. "I lucked out in that I had a graduate student who pulled me aside one day and said, 'If you have a question, ask. I'm going to teach you what you need to know.'"

EDUCATION

High School

As a student, you can get involved with your high school theater, or media group, or with the local community theater. Any aspect of theater work, whether as an actor, stagehand, or ticket-taker, can bring you valuable experience and expose you to theater operations. Courses such as wood shop and those that offer you hands-on experience with electronics or electrical wiring will provide you with technical knowledge you'll need. Some experience with computers can also help, as an increasing number of contemporary theaters use computers in their stage management.

Composition or technical writing courses can give you the writing skills you'll need to communicate ideas to other technicians. Should you choose to further your education, these writing skills will help you with grant proposals and scholarship applications. Literature courses that help you to become familiar with the history and analysis of plays can provide you with a knowledge that might impress theater managers. Understanding the theme, message, or sentiments in a play can also help you with decisions about lighting and sound effects.

Postsecondary Training

Some community and junior colleges offer stage technician programs, or programs in theater arts, or radio and TV. Or you may choose to pursue a degree in theater or theater production. In many university drama departments, you can receive a bachelor of arts, a bachelor of fine arts, or a master of fine arts, with concentrations in acting/directing, design/technical production, or dramatic theory. A good program will offer you a well-rounded education, combining courses in theoretical study with hands-on, practical experience to familiarize you with the tools of stage work. Above all, it is the hands-on experience that will make you most attractive to an employer. It is also through this experience that you will come to know the theater community and the people who can offer you job opportunities. School can open a lot of doors for you, but it doesn't guarantee work. Some people gain experience as technicians before they get a degree. They then have the practical experience and the education to move on to designing or directing jobs.

SCHOLARSHIPS AND GRANTS

If you are going on to a degree-granting program, you can pursue grants and scholarships on the local level, through your school. The National Academy of Television Arts and Sciences also offers some scholarships to those interested in stage lighting and sound. Many graduate programs offer teaching or research assistantships, which offer a stipend or fee-waiver. The Theater Communications Group (TCG) has available career development programs for directors and designers. The grants are available to scenic, costume, sound, and/or lighting designers who have designed three fully staged theatrical productions. (See "Professional Organizations" at the end of this article for contact information.)

> **Technical Jobs in TV and Film**
>
> **Gaffers** Set up and adjust lights according to the plan of the director of photography.
>
> **Special effects technicians** Design, build, and install equipment, and mix chemicals for special effects. (See the article "Special Effects Technicians.")
>
> **Grips** Move and store lights, props, scenery, scaffolds, and other equipment.
>
> **Camera operators** Film according to the plans of the director of photography.
>
> **Sound cutters** Edit and synchronize music, dialogue, and sound effects.

INTERNSHIPS AND VOLUNTEERSHIPS

Many community theaters need volunteers for the stage management of summer productions. National internships are listed in a directory from TCG. TCG also publishes a monthly journal called *ArtSEARCH*, which has information on summer theater positions.

LABOR UNIONS

The International Alliance of Theatrical Stage Employees, Moving Picture Technicians, Artists and Allied Crafts of the United States, Its Territories, and Canada (IATSE) is the labor union for theater workers. Most technicians and designers don't belong to the union. In the smaller, regional theaters across the United States, union membership is generally not required. But those technicians working in larger cities, or those working in television and film, may need to belong to a union to get the better jobs and better pay.

Who Will Hire Me?

To learn about jobs, Molly subscribes to *ArtSEARCH*. "Not every job out there is listed," she says, "but a lot of them are. There's also *Playbill* Online, which

ADVANCEMENT POSSIBILITIES

Technical directors coordinate activities of radio or television studios to ensure the technical quality of picture and sound for programs originating in the studio or from remote pickup points.

Sight-effects specialists provide special stage lighting and sight effects for theatrical performances and direct electrical crews in installing and arranging lighting and wiring equipment.

has a section for employment listings. Sometimes I'll look at *Backstage West*. Also, networking is a big thing." Molly mentions that she recently was called in to stage manage a brand new production. "They had just gotten my name from someone else who I'd never met, who had heard I was a good stage manager." Because of the tight-knit community in theater, technicians must be certain to make a good impression. Molly once worked for a summer stock theater where the prop person failed to fulfill his responsibilities. "This person was basically blackballed in the theater community in Orange County," she says. "Since that summer, I've heard his name a couple of times, but no one has hired him."

In addition to the directory of internships, TCG also publishes an annual theater directory that lists nonprofit professional theaters across the United States. Twice a year, they publish a theater profile book, which lists the individual shows being performed by these theaters.

Many technicians work as freelancers for theaters for only the run of a show. Because of the inconsistency of work, these technicians supplement their income with lighting or sound work outside of the theater. Technicians can find work in TV, film, and video production. They can also find work in other areas of entertainment, such as nightclubs and theme parks. Any organization that requires special lighting, such as museums, sports centers and arenas, or the government (for the lighting of monuments, public gardens, parks, and bridges) calls upon technicians.

Major cities offer technicians the best opportunities. The theaters and concert halls are larger, employ more people, and pay a better salary. Talented technicians and designers find the best work on Broadway, in Chicago, or in Hollywood, where they can command a high salary and work alongside the most ambitious people in the business. However, even in a city, there are smaller theaters that pay significantly less than the larger theaters.

Where Can I Go from Here?

Molly is currently pursuing work as a stage manager and is extremely devoted to the theater. "I had an opportunity to go into film when I was in college," she says, but doing so would have meant not finishing her degree. "That would have been good money. But when I'm on the run crew for a show, or stage managing, I can hear the audience's reaction to what's going on. That's really what has kept me in theater. You can hear the appreciation. With theater, you get more of a chance to affect someone's life, more so than with film."

Once stage technicians have gained enough experience and know their way around the lighting and sound equipment, they may choose to pursue work in a larger city. Or they can pursue permanent staff work with a theater, as a stage manager or production manager. Or they may choose to go back to school, so that they can get instruction in lighting design, or in direction. Others work as teachers in college drama programs.

Film and television also provide opportunities for experienced stage technicians. The best place for this work is in New York, Los Angeles, and Chicago. Local network affiliates or cable channels may produce their own programming and require technicians. Most technicians in the film industry need to belong to a union.

What Are the Salary Ranges?

Because so many stage technicians work on a freelance basis, their salaries can vary from year to year. One year, there may be many theatrical or musical productions in your area, and the next year there may be significantly fewer, requiring you to supplement your income in other areas. Beginning freelancers may make only $30 to $70 a day on a production, but experienced technicians can earn up to $300 a day.

Earnings vary widely according to the worker's experience, job responsibilities, the geographic location of the theater, and the budget of the performance. In addition, the International Alliance of Theatrical Stage Employees reports that different local chapters have different pay scales, although its members, who are mostly employed at the largest commercial houses and on Broadway, generally earn more than nonmembers.

According to the Web site Salary.com, the average salary for stage designers in 2005 was $39,918, with most designers making between $32,726 and $48,299 a year. Most full-time workers receive health insurance and other benefits, as established by the local union contract. Because workers are hired for a particular time period, vacations are rarely provided.

Freelance technicians generally don't receive benefits, but full-time employment will include vacation pay, and insurance benefits. Union membership may include health insurance opportunities.

What Is the Job Outlook?

According to Theatre Communications Group, overall theater attendance has been up over the past several years, but most theaters are still operating a deficit. Thus, there are few new or small theaters that can pay living wages for stage production workers and technicians. Thus, many people working in theater production—especially at small or nonprofit theaters—supplement their incomes with other sources of work.

Today, theaters tend to be concentrated in large metropolitan areas, so the number of job possibilities is greatest there, but so too is the competition for those jobs. Many stage workers start out instead with small theatrical groups. After they develop skills and a local reputation, they may be able to move to bigger, better-paying markets. They may have to work part time, do volunteer work in amateur theater, or support themselves in unrelated fields for extended periods while waiting for better theater jobs.

However, theater remains a popular form of entertainment and an important cultural resource. Thus, those who are skilled in a variety of production areas and are persistent and creative in their job searches stand the best chance of employment. For example, someone who knows about both lighting and sound systems, or both set design and props, is more likely to get a desirable position in theater.

How Do I Learn More?

PROFESSIONAL ORGANIZATIONS

For information about job openings and community theaters across the country, contact

American Association of Community Theater
8402 Briarwood Circle
Lago Vista, TX 78645
866-687-2228
info@aact.org
http://www.aact.org

This labor union represents technicians, artisans and craftspersons in the entertainment industry, including live theater, film, and television production. It negotiates salaries and offers pension, insurance, and educational programs.

International Alliance of Theatrical Stage Employees, Moving Picture Technicians, Artists and Allied Crafts Workers of the United States, Its Territories, and Canada
1430 Broadway, 20th Floor
New York, NY 10018
212-730-1770
http://www.iatse-intl.org

To learn about ArtSEARCH and career development programs:

Theater Communications Group
520 Eighth Avenue, 24th Floor
New York, NY 10018
212-609-5900
tcg@tcg.org
http://www.tcg.org

For information on student chapters, contact

United States Institute for Theatre Technology
6443 Ridings Road
Syracuse, NY 13206
800-938-7488
info@office.usitt.org
http://www.usitt.org

BIBLIOGRAPHY

The following is a sampling of materials relating to the professional concerns and development of stage technicians:

Field, Shelly. *Career Opportunities in Theater and the Performing Arts.* 3d ed. New York: Facts On File, 2006.

Fitt, Brian. *A–Z of Lighting Terms*. Woburn, Mass.: Focal Press, 1999.

Ionazzi, Daniel A. *The Stagecraft Handbook*. Crozet, Va.: Betterway Books, 1996.

Parker, W. Oren B., R. Craig Wolf, and Dick Block. *Scenic Design and Stage Lighting*. 8th ed. Belmont, Calif.: Thomson/Wadsworth, 2003.

Pilbrow, Richard. *Stage Lighting Design: The Art, the Craft, the Life*. Design Press, 2000.

SURGICAL TECHNOLOGISTS

Definition
Surgical technologists are integral members of the surgical team. They work closely with surgeons, nurses, anesthesiologists, and other personnel to ensure the success of operations and assume appropriate responsibilities before, during, and after surgery.

Alternative Job Title
Operating room technicians

High School Subjects
Biology
Chemistry

Personal Skills
Following instructions
Helping/teaching

Salary Range
$23,290 to $33,150 to $45,000+

Minimum Educational Level
Some postsecondary training

Certification or Licensing
Recommended

Outlook
Faster than the average

DOT
079

GOE
14.02.01

NOC
3219

O*NET-SOC
29-2055.00

The operating lounge is empty, except for two people sitting at one of the round tables, quietly joking around and drinking their coffee while they draw up the following week's schedule. A high-pitched series of beeps jars their banter and the surgical technologist reaches down for his pager. Through a background of static, he hears: "Stab wound. OR. Stat." John Houck is on his feet and headed toward the operating room before the message clears from his pager.

In emergencies like this, there is no time to set up for surgery. John has nearly finished scrubbing when the patient, a woman in her mid-30s, is wheeled into the operating room. Within minutes, a nurse, anesthesiologist, and surgeon arrive. John has to be doubly efficient in emergencies, not having had the time to organize the instruments, sutures, or sponges. He helps the other members of the surgical team to scrub, and the operation begins.

John hands instruments to the surgeon as needed and counts the sponges. He will help with suturing at the close of the surgery. Once the initial frenzy is over, surgery becomes a familiar rhythm, everyone working together to ensure the survival of the patient.

"I think we've got her," the doctor says finally, as he finishes stitching up the woman. "She's going to hurt a little, but she'll make it."

An orderly wheels the woman to the recovery room. The members of the surgical team pull off their gloves and masks. John collects the instruments that need sterilizing, throws the garbage away, and begins cleaning the operating room in preparation for the next operation.

What Does a Surgical Technologist Do?

Surgical technologists are an integral part of the surgery team, providing assistance and assurance that, from start to finish, operations run as smoothly as possible.

During World War II, there was a shortage of doctors and nurses to perform operations. From this need came the idea of specially training someone to assist in the surgical process. Today, there are thousands of certified surgical technologists, without whom successful operations would be difficult.

The role of a surgical technologist begins before the patient arrives in surgery and continues after surgery is completed. The operating room must be set up for whatever kind of surgery will be performed, from organizing drapes and equipment to preparing the sterile field, which means placing the necessary sterilized instruments on a special sterilized tray and making sure nothing unsterilized touches them. The technologist scrubs and puts on a gown, cap, mask, shoe covers, and gloves, and then helps the surgeons and nurses get gloved and gowned after scrubbing. The surgical technologist's most important role is maintaining the sterile field. "It could be so easy for

Lingo to Learn

Drape Sterile cloth used to surround and isolate the actual site or location of the operation on the patient's body.

-ectomy Surgery that involves the partial or complete removal of an organ, as in appendectomy (removal of the appendix).

Forceps Instrument that is very similar in appearance to cooking tongs. Used by surgeons to hold back skin or other soft tissue.

On call Surgical assistants remain available via pager to come to work on a moment's notice in case of an emergency.

-otomy Surgery that involves the perforation or incision of organs or tissue, as in radial kerototomy (laser surgery performed on the eye).

-plasty Surgery to restore, reconstruct, or refigure body parts, as in rhinoplasty (surgery to reshape the nose).

Scalpel A thin-bladed knife that is used as a surgical tool.

Scrub The process of thoroughly washing the hands and forearms before surgery to ensure sterility.

Scrubbing Literally, the physical cleaning of the hands, wrists, and forearms of the surgeon and each member of the surgical staff. Scrubbing is performed prior to all surgeries in order to kill germs and harmful bacteria.

Sterile field The part of the operating room where the instruments, equipment, and surfaces are entirely free of germs.

Sterilize A procedure in which living microorganisms are removed from an area or instrument.

Sutures The stitches used to close a wound or surgical incision.

a patient to get infected if someone's not monitoring the room," John Houck says.

Once the surgery is underway, the technologist pays attention to the needs of the surgeon, handing instruments, sutures, and sponges, perhaps holding back flaps of skin with forceps if need be. "You are the surgeon's right-hand person," John says. "You have to be almost a mind-reader. You definitely have to know your procedures."

> You are the surgeon's right-hand person.

Technologists count the sponges, sutures, and needles frequently to make sure nothing is left inside a patient. If there are specimens to be taken to the lab to be analyzed, it is the technologist who helps prepare, care for, and dispose of these specimens. They help apply dressings to the patient and may be asked to operate sterilizers, lights, or suction machines.

After the operation, the technologist makes sure the patient is transported to the recovery room by an orderly. If an orderly is not available, then the technologist transports the patient. They are responsible for cleaning up after the surgery, including disposing of soiled drapes and disposable instruments and equipment, sterilizing instruments, and restocking the operating room for the next operation.

What Is It Like to Be a Surgical Technologist?

John Houck has worked as a surgical technologist since 1982. He works the 3:00 P.M. to 11:00 P.M. shift at Illinois Masonic Hospital. He likes to arrive early for his shift so that he can relax for a few minutes, hear about the morning from his coworkers, and organize his schedule for the evening. Surgical technologists who work the morning shifts handle scheduled surgeries. At hospitals, surgeries are scheduled in the mornings or early afternoons, so it's rare that there are a lot of scheduled surgeries for John's shift. A morning technologist may have back-to-back surgeries through his or her entire shift. John's shift involves simply finishing with the scheduled surgeries and then waiting for emergencies to come in. "The day-shift people don't get much emergency action," John says. "This shift, we see a lot of trauma cases—stabbings, shootings, accidents. We get at least three unscheduled cases a night, even during the slowest times."

In emergency situations, John says, a technologist has to move fast. "You'll get a call, 'gunshot coming up in five,' and you've got five minutes to get everything ready—to prepare the sterile field, to prepare the room. Sometimes you don't even get five minutes." He laughs. "One thing you get good at around here is fast set-up."

In any situation, John makes sure that the operating room is ready for the surgery that is about to take place. He helps the surgeons with their gowns and gloves and stands by during surgery ready to pass whatever instruments are needed and keeping careful count of everything: sponges, needles, sutures.

At the end of an operation, an orderly comes to wheel the patient to the recovery room and John cleans up. He throws away used surgical drapes and throws away, washes, or sterilizes equipment and instruments.

"You don't have a lot of awake contact with the patient," he says, "so it's not like you get to know them, but it's rewarding work. It's a good feeling when you hear that someone who was near death made it and is doing well."

Do I Have What It Takes to Be a Surgical Technologist?

"I used to get adrenaline rushes," John says. "And I'll admit, it gets crazy. But now I'm used to the pace. Now it's just part of my job." There is no doubt that surgical technologists work under great pressure and tension. Not only do they need to be able to react quickly and efficiently to high-stress emergency situations, but they also need to realize that flaring tempers are a part of the work. They have to learn not to take anger personally. "This is a place where you need to stand up for yourself," says John. "You need to be confident and good at your job. No one has time for someone who doesn't know what they're doing. If you're meek and timid in this business, you get yelled at and walked all over."

Technologists must be good at organizing, pay attention to details, and be very attentive to the surgeon during surgery. "There is a lot of responsibility here," John says. "But I like that there's a lot of variety to the work."

Technologists often stand for long periods of time. They should have manual dexterity as they are often required to quickly handle instruments. They should be interested in helping people and sensitive to the needs of the patient, even though most often the patient is not conscious. They should be able to withstand strong odors and unpleasant sights.

The operating room environment, whether in a hospital or private setting, is a clean, brightly lit, fairly quiet, and cool environment. Technologists must be able to focus on the task at hand, even when it may be long and tedious. They must be able to adapt to emergency situations. While most technologists work 40-hour weeks, schedules are not always fixed, and technologists may be expected to work different shifts as a part of that work week. Most technologists are expected to be available to work on call from time to time.

How Do I Become a Surgical Technologist?

As a member of the military, John decided that work as a surgical technologist would be interesting to him, and he was sent to the training program on the Texas base where he was stationed. He became certified and worked in the hospital on his army base for some time. John was a fairly good student in high school, where his favorite subject was science.

EDUCATION

High School

Surgical technologists are required to have their high school diplomas to enter a training program. Students who haven't finished high school are encouraged to complete their GED, which enables them admission to surgical technology programs at hospitals and community colleges. High school courses in basic sciences are important, as well as anatomy and physiology if possible.

Postsecondary Training

Surgical technologists receive their training in programs offered by community colleges, technical schools, hospitals, and the military. There are 150 accredited programs for surgical technology throughout the country.

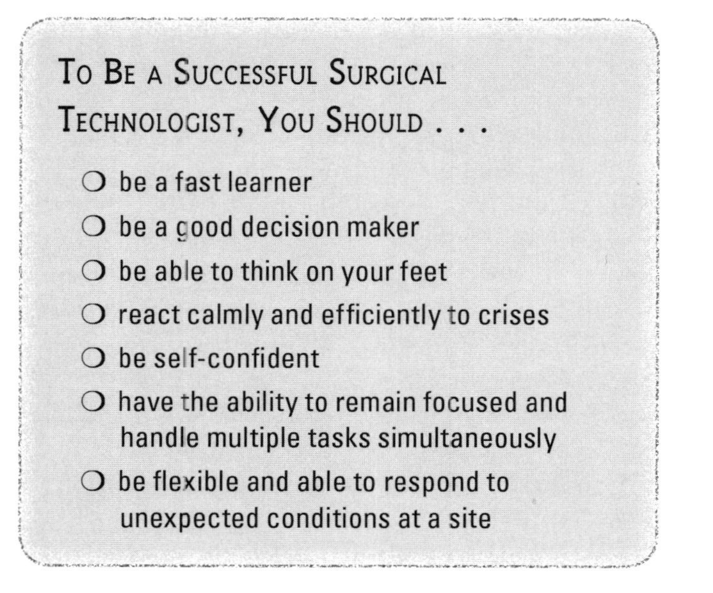

Training programs last anywhere from nine to 24 months and lead to a certificate, diploma, or associate's degree. In 2002 there were 361 surgical technology training programs accredited by the Commission on Accreditation of Allied Health Education Programs (CAAHEP). Required courses include anatomy, physiology, pharmacology, microbiology, and medical terminology. Students learn about the safety and care of patients during surgery, surgical procedures, and aseptic techniques. They learn to sterilize instruments, to prevent infection, and to handle drugs and equipment. Graduates of surgical technology programs know how to apply their knowledge appropriately, are prepared to assume the full range of responsibilities encompassed by their profession, and have received extensive clinical experience in circulating and scrubbing. They are comfortable handling equipment and maintaining a sterile field, monitoring fluids, and organizing the operating room.

CERTIFICATION OR LICENSING

Certification is recommended but not required; however, to advance in the profession, becoming certified is a good idea. "Being certified is not the only way to work as a technologist," John says, "but it's smart. Employers look on it as a sign of commitment. You put time in to get certified. They think: This person is serious about this type of work. Employers like that."

National certification is provided by the Liaison Counsel on Certification for the Surgical Technologist. Applicants must either be currently certified or must be graduates of surgical technology programs accredited by CAAHEP. Recertification is required every six years, either in the form of an exam or by keeping up a required number of points by attending conferences offered throughout the year. "Last month I went to a conference where we took gallbladders out of live pigs," John says. "It was really interesting. Going to conferences gives you points toward recertification and the conferences are a tax deduction." He laughs. "And it doesn't hurt that they're held in great places. Great warm places in the winter."

SCHOLARSHIPS AND GRANTS

Scholarships are available through the Foundation for Surgical Technology through the Association of Surgical Technologists (AST). Applicants must be students of programs accredited by CAAHEP. Selection is based on academic performance and financial need. Contact AST for more information (see "How Do I Learn More?").

Who Will Hire Me?

John received his training through the military in Texas. "That's how a lot of us were trained," he says. After completing his training, he was certified and worked as a surgical technologist in the military for a few years. Upon returning to Chicago, John had no trouble finding employment. "There are always openings for qualified surgical techs," he says.

About three quarters of surgical technologists work in hospitals, and students who go through hospital training programs are often hired by those hospitals after graduation. Community colleges that offer programs have placement centers and work with hospitals in the area, which like to hire technologists trained locally.

Within hospitals, surgical technologists may work in operating rooms, ambulatory areas, and central supply departments. Surgical technologists also work in the offices of physicians and dentists who perform outpatient surgical procedures. Others, known as private scrubs, are employed by surgeons who have special surgical teams that perform complex procedures such as liver transplants.

Where Can I Go from Here?

Advancement begins in the form of salary raises, but once a surgical technologist has acquired some experience, he or she can be employed in a number of diverse areas. "The training we get is really broad," John says. "It's a good thing, because you're able to adapt to different jobs from the start. And once you know what you're doing, there are a lot of possibilities." Experienced surgical technologists work as central service managers, surgery schedulers, and managers of materials such as instruments, equipment, and surgical supplies. Assistant operating room administrators order supplies and arrange work schedules. Assistant operating room supervisors direct the surgical technologists in the operating room.

For those who would like to get out of the operating room atmosphere, there are positions available in sales and management with companies that sell operating room equipment or supplies to hospitals. Some technologists find that they want to impart their knowledge and experience to others and become instructors in surgical technology training programs.

Advancement Possibilities

Assistant operating room administrators are responsible for ordering all of the medical supplies necessary for any surgery that might take place and making certain that they are available to the operating team during surgery. They are also responsible for creating shift schedules, as well as for supervising and monitoring the other surgical technologists.

Assistant operating room supervisors direct and monitor the work of the surgical technologists working as part of the surgical team. Should any problem arise during a surgery, it is up to the operating room supervisor to make certain the problem—whether it is a missing instrument or a personality conflict—does not affect the surgery being performed.

Medical supplies salespeople work for sterile equipment companies or operating room equipment companies and sell medical supplies and/or equipment to hospitals, clinics, and private practices.

What Are the Salary Ranges?

The *Occupational Outlook Handbook* reports that surgical technologists had annual median earnings of $33,150 in 2003. Those in the lowest 10 percent made less than $23,290, while those in the highest 10 percent made more than $45,000.

Full-time employees are generally provided with a benefits package that includes health and life insurance.

What Is the Job Outlook?

According to the U.S. Department of Labor, job opportunities for surgical technologists are expected to grow faster than the average for all occupations. Competent surgical technologists are in great demand. Population growth, longevity, and more advanced medical procedures have contributed to a growing demand for surgical services and therefore surgical technologists. While general economic conditions could affect the growth of this field, it is probable that the trend will continue for years to come.

Due to the rising cost of health care, more surgery is being done on an out-patient basis. If this continues, there will be a great need for surgical technologists. But if more surgeries are performed in non-hospital settings, demand will drop because fewer technologists are hired in those settings.

Some hospitals are discussing the employment of staff members who will handle a wider range of tasks than surgical technologists are qualified to do. While this will limit the need for technologists, there is presently the issue of staff shortages involving nurses, and this works in the favor of surgical technologists, making it desirable to assign them more tasks. Technologists will also need to adapt to new developments in surgery, such as increased use of fiber optics and laser technology.

To be competitive for the best positions as surgical technologists, students should pursue advanced training in anatomy and physiology and aim for certification upon completion of training programs.

How Do I Learn More?

PROFESSIONAL ORGANIZATIONS

For career information and information about education and scholarships contact

Association of Surgical Technologists
7108-C South Alton Way
Englewood, CO 80112
800-637-7433
http://www.ast.org

For certification information contact

Liaison Council on Certification for the Surgical Technologist
128 South Tejon Street, Suite 301
Colorado Springs, CO 80903
719-328-0800
mail@lcc-st.org
http://www.lcc-st.org

BIBLIOGRAPHY

The following is a sampling of material relating to the professional concerns and development of surgical technologists:

Hinton, Debbie, and Tammy Allhoff. *Surgical Mayo Set-Ups*. Albany, N.Y.: Delmar Learning, 2002.

Price, Paul, and Teri Junge, eds. *Surgical Technology for the Surgical Technologist: A Positive Care Approach*. Albany, N.Y.: Delmar Learning, 2000.

Snyder, Katherine, and Chris Keegan. *Pharmacology for the Surgical Technologist*. Philadelphia: W. B. Saunders, 1999.

Wells, Maryann P., and Mary Bradley. *Pocket Guide to Surgical Instruments*. 2d ed. Philadelphia: W. B. Saunders, 1998.

SURVEYING AND MAPPING TECHNICIANS

Robert Benjamin rubs his eyes and stands up from his computer. He needs to pace himself so he doesn't strain his eyes—good vision is important to a mapping technician. The computer has become his main work tool, though he can remember the days when he drew everything with pencil and triangle and worked with prism instruments and plotters.

After a short break, he returns to the photographs for another hour of detailed work. He looks at the projection of the aerial photographs and works with the computer to produce a three-dimensional model. Engineers will work from his map, relying on its accuracy to plan for the city or state.

Definition
Surveying and mapping technicians help determine and record geographic areas or features.

Alternative Job Titles
Cartographic aides
Surveyor assistants
Survey helpers

High School Subjects
Art
Earth science
Geography

Personal Skills
Artistic
Technical/scientific

Salary Range
$18,782 to $29,972 to $50,336+

Work Environment
Indoors and outdoors
Primarily multiple locations

Minimum Educational Level
Some postsecondary training

Certification or Licensing
Voluntary

Outlook
Faster than the average

DOT
018

GOE
02.08.01

NOC
2254

O*NET-SOC
17-3031.00, 17-3031.01, 17-3031.02

What Does a Surveying and Mapping Technician Do?

Surveying and mapping technicians have mapped more than city and state boundaries and highways; they've been involved in the recovery of space vehicles, the navigation of the moon and of the ocean floor, the mapping of wildlife ecology, and the charting of tornado paths. They assist with the building and design of airports, housing developments, bridges, and buildings. A variety of professionals, such as civil engineers, cartographers, photogrammetrists, and surveyors, rely on technicians to measure and map geographic areas and features.

Some of the earliest civilizations required maps to define boundaries and to record routes for transportation and commerce. In ancient Egypt and Rome, surveyors used chains and wheel rotations to measure fields, canals, and irrigation ditches. Today's surveying technician works with decidedly more sophisticated tools, such as computers, satellite imagery, and remote-sensing devices.

Surveying technicians can find work in the areas of land, construction, mining, geodetic, and marine surveying. Most land surveying technicians are employed by engineering and architectural firms. To gather the information that's used to establish township or property lines, a survey party—made up of a party chief and several survey technicians—goes on location. The *party chief,* who is either a senior surveying technician or a land surveyor, organizes and leads the daily activities. Technicians operate surveying instruments and electronic distance-measuring equipment, compile notes, make sketches, and enter data into computers.

Construction operations employ a large number of surveying technicians. These technicians are usually the first to be involved in the development of highways, railways, buildings, and bridges. They

Lingo to Learn

Cadastral Mapping that records legal property boundaries.

Geodesy The science concerned with determining the exact size and shape of the earth.

GIS (Geographical Information System) Computerized databases of spatial and cartographic information.

GPS (Global Positioning System) A system that precisely locates points on the earth using radio signals transmitted by satellite.

Imagery Infrared or radar equipment used to record characteristics of the landscape for mapping.

Level The instrument most commonly used for determining elevations in the field.

Oceanographic charting Charting for the exploration and development of ocean resources.

Thematic Maps that depict details of the environment, such as soil and vegetation.

Topographic A map representing important features of the landscape, such as elevation contours, transportation lines, and bodies of water.

locate construction points on the job site as specified on the architectural plans. For example, they locate corners of buildings, foundation detail points, center points for columns and walls, the height of floors or ceilings, and other points that require precision location.

Mining surveying technicians work on the geological staffs of mining or exploration companies. At existing mines, they map underground geology, calculate tonnage of ore and broken rock, take samples, locate diamond drill holes, and compile geological data derived from boreholes. In searching for new mining sites, technicians operate instruments that measure variations in the earth's magnetic field, its conductivity, or gravity. This data is used to define boundaries for future in-depth explorations.

Geodetic surveying technicians take measurements of large masses of land, sea, or space. These measurements help set major points of reference for smaller land surveys, determine national boundaries, and prepare maps. Because of the precision that's required, geodetic surveying technicians must take the size and shape of the earth into account in their measurements.

Marine surveying technicians survey harbors, rivers, and other bodies of water to determine shorelines, topography of the bottom, and water depth. Their surveys aid in the exploration of mineral resources, oceanographic mapping, nautical charting, and shoreline and water circulatory research.

Mapping technicians help scientists measure, map, and chart the earth's surface. One type of mapping technician is a cartographic technician, who takes the information provided by surveys, aerial photography, other maps, and cultural and geographical research and produces a map or chart of the area. *Cartographic technicians* are involved in the production of a variety of maps: maps for use in navigation by sailors and pilots; topographic maps for representing landscape features such as elevation, boundaries, and bodies of water; and maps detailing a region's soil, vegetation, and climate. A cartographic technician probably helped create the maps you've used to travel on highways, to find the location of a distant country, or to navigate your way around an unfamiliar city.

Photogrammetric technicians are mapping technicians who use aerial photographs to study and measure details of the environment. With information obtained by air, satellite, or radar, photogrammetric technicians can prepare maps and drawings of areas that are usually inaccessible or difficult to survey by other means. Photogrammetry is used, for example, to measure farmland planted with certain crops and to confirm crop allotments under government production quotas.

What Is It Like to Be a Surveying and Mapping Technician?

Robert Benjamin does photogrammetry work. As a stereo compiler for Aerial Mapping in Phoenix, Arizona, he produces maps from aerial photographs. The small company he works for subcontracts work from engineering companies who do projects for the government. He works from projections of two photographs, taken from different positions for stereoscopic viewing. Using the computer as a plotting instrument, Robert produces accurate preliminary maps drawn from photographs into a three-dimensional (3-D) model.

Robert took his first stereo compiler job in Texas in 1964 and has since worked in Colorado, Missouri, and Arizona. Over the years and from place to place, Robert has seen many changes. The emergence of computers as mapping tools is one of the most fundamental changes. Robert began using computers to draw images more than a decade years ago. Prior to that, he worked with mechanical instruments that required adjustments, such as multiplexes and plotters. "Technology has made the work easier," he says.

On a typical day, Robert works in his office on two or three assignments, though some jobs can require up to three weeks. To prevent strain on his eyes from the level of detail, Robert generally takes a short break every hour. "The job can be very hard on the eyes," says Robert. "You must walk away from it from time to time."

Robert enjoys the fact that he sets his own schedule. "I work about any hours I want," he says. He notes that when his company's overall workload increases, so do his hours. "Over the years, I've worked a lot of overtime," he says. Long days of work can be draining for Robert because he must maintain the same level of meticulous detail.

Unlike mapping technicians, you won't find most surveying technicians behind a desk. That's certainly true for Russ Kluesner, a senior surveying technician for Druyvestein, Johnson & Anderson, an engineering and surveying firm in Missoula, Montana. Russ arrives at the office by 7:00 A.M. to pick up equipment and to discuss the day's project with his supervisor. The rest of his day is spent out on location with a surveying crew. The workday typically ends at 5:00 P.M., but it's not unusual for crews to work until twilight.

Being a surveying technician can require a good deal of travel. Last year, Russ spent 10 months on the road as crew chief for a survey team. His assignments have recently taken him to an island in Alaska, duck ponds in North Dakota, and to the base of the Grand Canyon. As Russ puts it, "There are only so many maps you can make in your own backyard."

In Alaska, he and his crew took a boat each morning to an island where they used satellite tracking equipment to mark the center line for a proposed road. In order to cut through the heavy brush, they used axes, machetes, and even chainsaws. After dark, the crew caught the boat back to the mainland. "You've got to love the outdoors," Russ says. "There are nice, easygoing days, and then there are rough days."

You've got to love the outdoors.

One of the things he especially enjoys about his work is being able to come up with innovative solutions on location. For instance, his firm was hired to map duck ponds for an environmental organization. Surveying on foot in the marshlands proved nearly impossible, so Russ and his crew mounted the global positioning system (GPS) equipment on four-wheelers.

The equipment that he most often uses is the geodetic-grade GPS, which measures accurately within two to three millimeters and the total station. A total station is essentially a telescope and keyboard set up on a tripod, used to provide accurate angles and distances. Russ notes that today's high-tech gear is no substitute for understanding the basic theories behind surveying. "If you're going to do this, you've got to know how to do math longhand," he says, "and how to hold a plumb bob."

Do I Have What It Takes to Be a Surveying and Mapping Technician?

To be a good surveying or mapping technician you'll need to have a knack for computers and mathematics. Most mapping and surveying that's done today relies on a technician's skilled use of computers and other computerized technology. Having an aptitude for math as well as computers can help a technician learn and adapt to rapidly changing technologies.

Mapping technicians need good visual perception in order to see things three-dimensionally so that they can interpret photographs, maps, and drawings. Robert notes that someone working with maps should also be prepared for the amount of detail work and have the patience to perform meticulous work over long periods of time. Having an artistic sensibility can also help technicians to interpret and

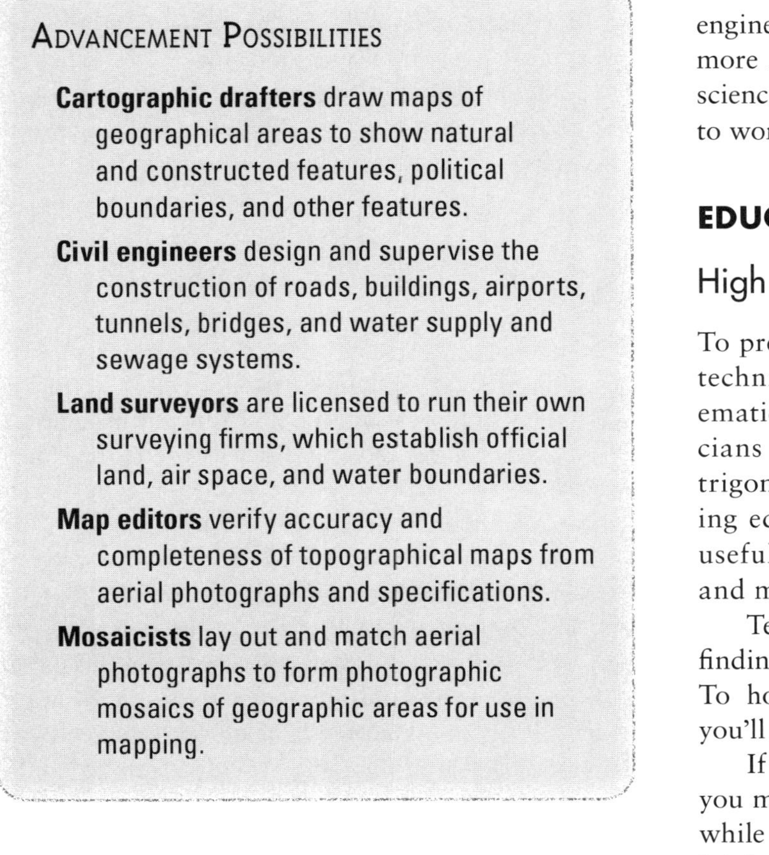

ADVANCEMENT POSSIBILITIES

Cartographic drafters draw maps of geographical areas to show natural and constructed features, political boundaries, and other features.

Civil engineers design and supervise the construction of roads, buildings, airports, tunnels, bridges, and water supply and sewage systems.

Land surveyors are licensed to run their own surveying firms, which establish official land, air space, and water boundaries.

Map editors verify accuracy and completeness of topographical maps from aerial photographs and specifications.

Mosaicists lay out and match aerial photographs to form photographic mosaics of geographic areas for use in mapping.

clarify all the research that goes into producing a comprehensive map.

A strong interest in geography and the environment is important for mapping technicians and essential for surveying technicians, who spend the bulk of their time in diverse, outdoor locations. Russ considers the hours that he spends outdoors each day as a perk of the job.

As members of a survey party in the field, technicians are usually required to be in good physical condition and able to cross all types of terrain. Surveying technicians are on their feet much of the time, and often they must carry the surveying instruments and equipment.

How Do I Become a Surveying and Mapping Technician?

Russ started working on a land surveying crew right out of high school, but he feels that it's best to have some postsecondary training in science, mathematics, and computers first. "In this day and age," he says, "it's tough to advance without some education."

Robert notes that his two years of college engineering helped him learn how to do mapping more readily. He agrees that a solid background in science and math is important for anyone who wants to work in this field.

EDUCATION

High School

To prepare for a career as a surveying or mapping technician, you should study geography, mathematics, and computers. Russ notes that technicians who have a basic grasp of geometry and trigonometry are able to catch on to using surveying equipment much faster. Shop classes are also useful as an introduction to working with tools and machines.

Technicians are often expected to turn in their findings in either a written report or a verbal briefing. To hone your communication and writing skills, you'll want to take English and speech classes.

If you want to work as a surveying technician, you may want to take environmental studies classes while in high school. You should also look into joining hiking or orienteering clubs at your school or in your community.

Mechanical drawing or art classes can help you develop the coordination and spatial relations you need for drawing maps.

Postsecondary Training

It's possible for surveying and mapping technicians to begin their careers as assistants or "gofers" at the surveying site. Russ, for example, was hired by a civil engineering firm when he finished high school in 1981. In addition to providing on the job training, the firm paid for him to study geodesy and engineering at night school.

However, graduates of accredited postsecondary training programs in surveying, photogrammetry, or mapping are in a stronger position to be hired as beginning technicians. These two-year programs are offered at junior colleges and technical institutes. The first year of courses typically includes English, composition, drafting, applied mathematics, surveying and measurements, construction materials and methods, applied physics, statistics, and computer applications. The second year introduces you to technical physics, advanced surveying, photogrammetry and mapping, soils and foundations, technical reporting, legal practices and problems, industrial organizations and institutions, and transportation and environmental engineering. Often, students are expected to do a summer internship in the field between their first and second years of course work.

To get a list of accredited surveying and cartography programs, contact the American Congress on Surveying and Mapping (ACSM).

CERTIFICATION OR LICENSING

The National Society of Professional Surveyors (NSPS) of the ACSM has a voluntary certification program for survey technicians. The program has four levels of certification and two tracks (field and office). The advanced field track certifies technicians to work as boundary party chiefs and/or construction party chiefs, while the advanced office track certifies technicians as chief computer operators or chief drafters. For details on the program, including sample problems and a bibliography for self-study, contact ACSM (http://www.acsm.net).

Licensing is required in all 50 states for land surveyors but not for technicians. Technicians who wish to advance to land surveyor, however, will need to have a four-year degree, 10 to 12 years of experience, and a passing score on two written exams, depending on the requirements of the state.

SCHOLARSHIPS AND GRANTS

The ACSM Map Design Competition Awards are given to a student from an academic program and a student from a technical program. The ACSM also offers the Berntsen Scholarship in Surveying for students in two-year programs.

You should also contact the financial aid office at your school. They can provide you with information on academic, leadership, and minority scholarships, as well as need-based grants.

If you begin working for a firm right out of high school, ask about their policy on tuition reimbursement. Many companies encourage employees to pursue higher education and will pay a portion of the costs. Most firms will also cover the costs of continuing education seminars, workshops, and books.

To Be a Successful Surveying and Mapping Technician, You Should . . .

- be good at math, computers, and mechanics
- have patience for detailed work
- have good eyesight, hearing, and coordination
- be in good physical shape in order to carry surveying equipment
- be able to discriminate among the shapes and sizes of objects
- enjoy traveling and the outdoors

INTERNSHIPS AND VOLUNTEERSHIPS

Many engineering and surveying firms hire students to help with the increased workload during the summer season. For instance, the company that Russ works for in Montana typically hires work-study students to do basic chores, such as cutting brush and carrying equipment. Doing outdoor work like this will give you a sense of what it's like to be a surveying technician. To find out about internships near you, contact local surveying and engineering firms.

Students interested in an internship in mapmaking should contact government agencies and mapmaking companies. Some mapmaking companies offer apprenticeships with senior cartographers. You can contact the American Society for Photogrammetry and Remote Sensing to get the names of major employers (http://www.asprs.org).

Who Will Hire Me?

Most mapping and surveying technicians work in the private sector for engineering, construction, and architectural firms. You can look in your phone book under "Surveyors" and "Engineering–Civil" to see what kind of opportunities there are locally.

You could also work as a technician for the federal, state, or local government. Major federal employers include the U.S. Geological Survey, the Forest Service, the Bureau of Land Management, the Army Corps of Engineers, the National Imagery

In-depth

Surveying History

Surveying probably began in ancient Egypt, where it was used for reestablishing land boundaries after the annual flooding of the Nile. About 130 B.C. the Greeks used an instrument called the dioptra to level and lay off right angles. The Romans built roads and aqueducts with the aid of an aligning instrument known as the *groma*.

A simple type of transit, an instrument used to measure angles, was first used in Europe during the 16th century. Transits with telescopic sights came into use in the 18th century. By the end of the 18th century, many of the present instruments of surveying were in use, although in crude form. Electronic surveying instruments were introduced in the 1950s.

In the United States, the Coast Survey was established in 1807 by Congress to survey and chart the coastal waters and offshore islands of the United States. (The Coast Survey later became the Coast and Geodetic Survey and finally the National Ocean Service.) The need for information regarding natural resources, international and state boundaries, railroad routes, flood control, soil conservation, and national defense eventually led to the establishment of other agencies, such as the Bureau of Land Management, the Geological Survey, the Soil Conservation Service, and the Corps of Engineers of the U.S. Army.

and Mapping Agency, the National Ocean Survey, the Department of Commerce in the Bureau of the Census, the National Weather Service, the Department of Agriculture, and the National Environmental Satellite Service. State and local governments often hire surveying technicians to work for highway departments and urban planning agencies.

Some oil companies also keep a staff of surveying technicians. Mapping technicians can find work with photogrammetric firms and commercial map and atlas publishers.

Where Can I Go from Here?

Robert hopes to eventually move from his job as stereo compiler into a management position or a sales job. "Most good map salesmen have been compilers," he says. "They know what needs to be done."

Some mapping technicians work toward a professional degree in cartography or photogrammetry. Others work toward becoming *field map editors*. Editors identify features on aerial photographs and verify information used in mapmaking. They travel over the land that the map is supposed to cover and record features needed in the completed map. They also obtain information from county records about boundary lines and other official information.

Russ is currently working on obtaining his Montana surveyor's license so that he can open his own business and do a bit less traveling himself. In the majority of states, becoming a licensed land surveyor requires additional education and a number of years experience. Some of the professional organizations are working to increase the requirements needed to become a licensed land surveyor. One requirement being considered is a bachelor's degree in engineering.

What Are the Salary Ranges?

According to the U.S. Department of Labor, the median hourly wage for surveying and mapping technicians in 2003 was $14.41 an hour. Based on a 40-hour workweek, this amounts to an annual salary of $29,972. The lowest-paid 10 percent made less than $9.03 an hour ($18,782 a year), and the highest-paid 10 percent made more than $24.20 an hour ($50,336 a year). Full-time employment often includes a benefit package of health and life insurance, retirement, and mileage reimbursement.

What Is the Job Outlook?

Jobs for surveying and mapping technicians are expected to grow faster than the average through 2012, according to the U.S. Department of Labor. The uses of advanced technologies, such as GPS, Geographic Information Systems (GIS), and remote sensing, have increased the accuracy and productivity of surveying and mapping technicians. The increased demand for people to perform basic GIS-related data entry work, and the current lack of formal licensing or testing for technicians should contribute to the growth of jobs in this field.

Most of the opportunities will continue to come from engineering, architectural, and surveying services firms. Surveying technicians will be needed to lay out new streets, homes, shopping centers, and schools. They will also be needed to locate gas and water property boundary lines. An increasing number of urban redevelopment programs will also mean more jobs for surveying technicians.

New equipment and technology introduced into surveying and cartography also translates into a steady demand for mapping technicians. As maps are being used to represent new features of the environment and new phenomena, technicians are needed to produce the maps.

How Do I Learn More?

PROFESSIONAL ORGANIZATIONS

The following are organizations that provide information on surveying and mapping technician careers, schools, and employers:

American Congress on Surveying and Mapping
6 Montgomery Village Avenue, Suite 403
Gaithersburg, MD 20879
240-632-9716
http://www.acsm.net

American Society for Photogrammetry and Remote Sensing
5410 Grosvenor Lane, Suite 210
Bethesda, MD 20814
301-493-0290
asprs@asprs.org
http://www.asprs.org

BIBLIOGRAPHY

The following is a sampling of materials relating to the professional concerns and development of surveying and mapping technicians:

Harbin, Andrew L. *Land Surveyor Reference Manual*. 3d ed. Belmont, Calif.: Professional Publications, 2001.

Kavanagh, Barry F. *Surveying with Construction Applications*, 5th ed. Upper Saddle River, N.J.: Prentice Hall, 2003.

Van Sickle, Jan. *1001 Solved Surveying Fundamentals Problems*. 2d ed. Belmont, Calif.: Professional Publications, 1998.

———. *GPS for Land Surveyors*. 2d ed. Boca Raton. Fla. CRC press, 2002.

Whyte, W., and R. Paul. *Basic Surveying*. 4th ed. Woburn, Mass.: Butterworth-Heinemann, 1999.

TEACHER AIDES

The resource room (RR) at Custer County School in rural Colorado looks like a typical elementary school classroom. It is full of bright colors and has activity centers for reading, math, and computers; "cubbies" where students stash their belongings; individual student desks; and large worktables. But the room also has some furnishings not usually found in a classroom: a comfortable sofa for curling up on, and a small kitchen area with a refrigerator, microwave oven, and toaster.

Teacher aide Loretta Remington explains that "resource room" is the name given to the classroom where kindergarten through fifth grade students with disabilities or special needs spend part or all of their school day. Like teacher aides in all types of classrooms classrooms, Loretta is in the resource room each day to help students and to support the teaching staff.

Definition
Teacher aides help teachers run classrooms by performing a variety of duties, including preparing instructional materials; completing administrative tasks like grading papers and keeping records; helping students with classroom work; and supervising students in the library, on the playground, and in the lunchroom.

Alternative Job Titles
Education paraprofessional
Instructional aide
Paraeducator
Teacher assistant

High School Subjects
Art
English
History
Personal Skills
Helping/teaching
Leadership/management

Salary Range
$12,890 to $19,080 to $28,830+

Educational Requirements
High school diploma
Some college (varies by state and school district)

Certification or Licensing
Required in some states

Outlook
Somewhat faster than the average

DOT
099

GOE
12.03.03

NOC
6472

O*NET-SOC
25-9041.00

What Does a Teacher Aide Do?

The need for classroom support for teachers was first noticed early in the 20th century. Teachers' job responsibilities became more difficult to manage due to increasing class sizes and bureaucratic demands that detailed records of student achievements and classroom activities be maintained. Technological advances, the variety of educational materials available, and other changes added to the time teachers were required to spend preparing instructional materials and took away from the time they spent doing what they were trained to do: teaching.

Today *teacher aides* work in schools and educational settings across the country to provide instructional and clerical support to teachers. Clerical duties may include photocopying, typing or word processing, filing, grading students' homework assignments and tests, keeping class attendance records, and helping prepare instructional materials. Teacher aides also may be responsible for stocking classroom supplies, maintaining classroom equipment, and operating audiovisual equipment.

Instructional duties, which are usually performed under the guidance of a teacher, vary widely depending on the school and the students' needs. In elementary schools, teacher aides may provide instructional support to children, such as working with individual students or small groups of students who need extra help with reading, writing assignments, or math and science problems. They may assist students in gathering information for reports or other projects. Teacher aides working in secondary schools may specialize in certain subjects such as math, science, or English.

Some aides work in computer labs, helping students use computers and educational software;

others work in libraries, where in addition to basic clerical duties, they check books in and out, shelve returned books, and help students doing research use materials available in the library.

Besides classroom responsibilities, teacher aides often supervise students in the cafeteria, on the school grounds, in the hallways, and on field trips. Aides also help design bulletin boards and other classroom displays, arrange student workstations, and may participate in parent-teacher conferences to discuss students' progress.

Many teacher aides choose to work exclusively with special education students, such as Loretta does, or in bilingual classrooms. Aides working in special education classrooms attend to disabled students' needs, which may include feeding them, teaching them good grooming habits, or helping them on and off the school bus.

Teacher aides working in bilingual classrooms may help students who speak English as a second language understand and work on assignments. They also may help assess each student's progress by observing his or her performance on assignments and in class then keeping records of related information.

Lingo to Learn

Bilingual classroom These are classes in English-language school systems where students who are not fluent in English are taught in both their native language and in English.

IEP Individualized education plan. A federal document used by schools with special needs students that defines an individual child's educational plan. It is created by an IEP team that includes the student, the student's parents, classroom teachers, special education teachers, social workers, and others. Each student's IEP is reviewed annually and is reviewed every three years by a psychologist.

Inclusive classroom Situations in which students with disabilities or special needs are integrated into general education classrooms.

Paraprofessional Someone specially trained to assist a professional person such as a teacher.

Title I schools Schools located in communities that have a high proportion of students from low-income homes.

Tutor A person who provides individual instruction or guidance to another person.

What Is It Like to Be a Teacher Aide?

At Custer County School Loretta works with students in kindergarten through fifth grade with a wide range of disabilities. "Our situation here is unusual because we have a resource room for elementary students and another one for middle and high school students. Also, because we are a small school [about 450 students in grades kindergarten through 12] we don't have a separate classroom for emotionally disturbed children like they do in larger districts. So they are in regular classrooms unless they are having difficulties—then they spend time in the RR."

She says her work in the classroom is challenging. "What makes this job challenging is the differentiation that is necessary within the curriculum. Students that come into the RR require assistance in all content areas and at all grade levels."

The RR Loretta helps staff has four students full time and about 16 others who are in and out during the day for help in various subjects. "Some come in for math, some come in for reading, some come in for both," Loretta says "and some come in for affective." She explains that affective is for students that need help dealing with emotional problems. The small kitchen is used to teach students basic cooking skills, "like making toast."

Regardless of why each student spends time in the resource room every day, the process is usually the same. "When they come in they get their rubric and then get to work on the activities listed," Loretta says, adding that the rubric is a document she and the student create together to clearly establish learning goals and objectives for that child and how he or she can successfully accomplish them.

"Because kids aren't intrinsically motivated, we have a reward system for doing their best. We use play money and a till. Each task has a monetary value for completing it well. If they do a good job they get money; if they don't do a good job they put money into the till. It teaches them how to count and the value of money and how to use it," Loretta says. Once a month students are treated to a party. The play money students have earned by successfully achieving their goals becomes a part of the activity. "We had a pizza and movie party and the kids used their play money to buy slices of pizza and drinks," she says.

Although she worked in a corporate job for many years, Loretta has a background in education and was a licensed elementary school teacher in Rhode Island before moving to Colorado. So she says there were no surprises when she began working as a teacher aide. "My expectations were fairly realistic. I knew what the workday was like."

Do I Have What It Takes to Be a Teacher Aide?

A career as a teacher aide is for someone who likes children and enjoys watching them experience the pleasure of learning new things. However, the work may be emotionally tiring and physically demanding, especially in work with special education students, which may require strenuous tasks such as lifting.

> If you enjoy working with children and adults and can display patience, flexibility, and perseverance, then this would be an enjoyable career for you.

The job also may require you to work outdoors, supervising playground activities. Teacher aides often spend a lot of time each day standing, walking, and kneeling as part of their activities with the children. You should be comfortable communicating and working with teachers, administrators, and parents as well as with children.

To be a successful teacher aide you should enjoy working with children from diverse cultural backgrounds and from a variety of family/home environments. You should also be able to handle different classroom situations with fairness and patience, be flexible and willing to follow teachers' instructions, and have the initiative to complete assigned projects.

Loretta advises anyone planning to pursue a career as a teacher aide to "Search within. If you enjoy working with children and adults and can display patience, flexibility, and perseverance, then this would be an enjoyable career for you."

How Do I Become a Teacher Aide?

Loretta says the best way to find work as a teacher aide is to network within your community. After deciding to go back to her roots as an educator, Loretta used networking and learned about an opening for a special education aide at the school where she now works. Loretta says another way to learn about job openings is to sign on as a volunteer at the school where you would like to work, and to check the classified advertisements in the local paper. Many school districts and state departments of education also maintain a list of available jobs.

EDUCATION

High School

While in high school you should take courses such as English, history, social studies, math, science, art, drama, speech, and physical education, all of which will provide you with a broad knowledge base. Taking a foreign language will be helpful if you plan to work in a district with a large bilingual population. Courses in computers, child care and development, home economics, and psychology are beneficial as well.

Postsecondary Training

Requirements for advanced training vary by state and school districts. If your job responsibilities are limited to clerical duties a high school diploma may be the minimum requirement, while those assisting in classroom instruction may be required to have completed some postsecondary education. Loretta says the school where she works requires that teacher aides have an associate's degree or two years of college.

According to the federal 2001 No Child Left Behind Act, teacher aides working in Title 1 schools are now required to meet one of three requirements: have at least two years of college, hold a two-year associate's degree or higher, or pass specific state and local assessments. In addition, teacher aides working in special education classrooms are required to meet specific state standards.

Numerous community colleges offer certificate and two-year associate degree programs that will prepare you to work as a teacher aide, but most aides receive training on the job. Schools often provide orientation sessions, workshops, and other training to familiarize new teacher aides with the school's organization, policies, operation, and philosophy.

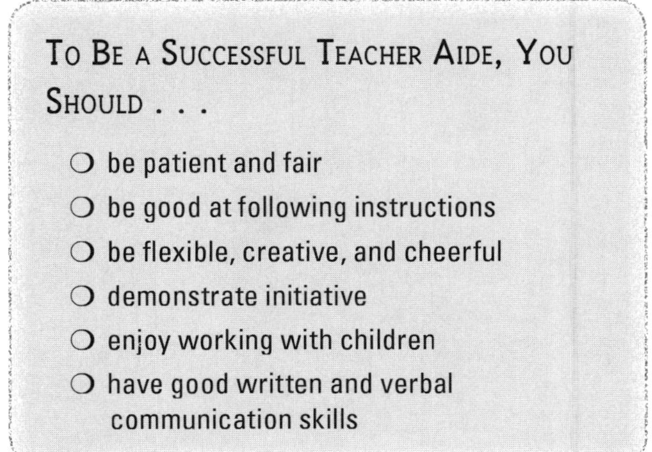

To Be a Successful Teacher Aide, You Should . . .

- be patient and fair
- be good at following instructions
- be flexible, creative, and cheerful
- demonstrate initiative
- enjoy working with children
- have good written and verbal communication skills

CERTIFICATION OR LICENSING

Based on the federally mandated requirements for education paraprofessionals established by the No Child Left Behind Act, the American Federation of Teachers (AFT) has been actively advocating a state-level certification system. However, currently 16 states have no certification or licensing requirements. All other states require some form of certification or licensing. For example, Georgia requires that teacher aides have two years of college or 50 hours advanced education for a state license, which is renewable every two years. For specific licensing and certification requirements, contact the school district in the state where you plan to seek employment. Many schools now also require that teacher aides have previous experience working with children, a valid driver's license, and some require applicants to pass a background check.

SCHOLARSHIPS AND GRANTS

Professional organizations, such as the AFT, now offer scholarships and grants to graduating high school seniors pursuing advanced education. Check with your school guidance counselor or with the specific organization for information. Some school districts also may help pay for the cost of attending required in-service training, seminars, and conferences related to the job.

INTERNSHIPS AND VOLUNTEERSHIPS

To help prepare for a career as a teacher aide you may want to volunteer with a Boy Scout or Girl Scout troop in your community, offer to coach a children's athletic team, or work with children in after-school programs at community centers. Volunteering to help with religious education classes at your church will provide classroom experience. Babysitting or working as a counselor at a summer camp is another way to gain experience.

Who Will Hire Me?

According to the AFT, there are about 980,000 education paraprofessionals working under various job titles, including teacher aide, instructional aide, special education assistant, bilingual assistant, library assistant, and early childhood assistant. Most are employed by preschools and day care centers, public or private elementary and secondary schools, vocational education centers, community colleges, and adult education centers.

Where Can I Go from Here?

Advancement for teacher aides usually is only through salary increases based on increased job responsibilities and experience. Some teacher aides use their positions as a starting point to pursue bachelor's and master's degrees to become licensed teachers.

Loretta said she enjoyed her work as a special education aide so much that she decided to pursue a master's degree in special education so she can move into a teaching position. In addition to special education, she is getting a dual endorsement in English as a Second Language, which prepares her to work with bilingual students.

FYI

- Across the country, "para-to-teacher" programs are helping members of minority groups become teachers. The Latino and Language Minority Teacher Project in Los Angeles is one such program. Teacher aides pursuing teacher certification can receive stipends and mentorships through these programs.
- Each year the National Education Association honors the Education Support Professional of the Year with a $10,000 prize. The recognition is the highest honor for professionals in the field of educational support. The 2004 recipient was a teacher aide from Cedar Rapids, Iowa.
- In 2005, education support professionals, which include teacher aides, school nurses, school bus drivers, custodians, office staff, and cafeteria workers, were more than 40 percent of the entire kindergarten through 12th grade workforce.

What Are the Salary Ranges?

The American Federation of Teachers reports that education paraprofessionals typically are paid an hourly rate that can range from as low as minimum wage ($5.15 per hour in 2005) to as much as $20 per hour. Salaries vary by school district, region of the country, and duties performed. Many teacher aides work part time and most work only during the nine to ten month school year.

The *Occupational Outlook Handbook* reports that the median earnings in 2003 for teacher aides were $19,080. The middle 50 percent earned between $15,170 and $24,000. Those in the lowest paid 10 percent earned less than $12,890 annually, while the highest paid 10 percent earned more than $28,830.

Teacher aides working part time normally do not receive benefits, but full-time paraprofessionals usually receive health insurance and other benefits.

What Is the Job Outlook?

According to the U.S. Department of Labor, employment of teacher aides is expected to grow somewhat faster than the average for all occupations through 2012. Despite a projected slowdown in general school-age enrollments over the next decade, the student populations for which teacher aides are most needed—special education students and those with English as a second language—are expected to increase. School districts meeting the requirements of educational reforms such as the No Child Left Behind Act will also likely increase the demand for teacher aides.

Employment opportunities will be greatest for persons with at least two years of formal education after high school. Those who speak a foreign language should be in particular demand in school districts where a large number of students do not speak English in their homes.

How Do I Learn More?

PROFESSIONAL ORGANIZATIONS

The following organizations can provide information about paraprofessionals working in education, including research, publications and journals, training programs, and employment opportunities:

American Federation of Teachers
555 New Jersey Avenue, NW

Places Where Teacher Aides Work

- charter schools
- daycare centers
- parochial schools
- private and public schools
- preschools
- religious organizations

Washington, DC 20001
202-879-4400
http://www.aft.org

Association for Childhood Education International
17904 Georgia Avenue, Suite 215
Olney, MD
800-423-3563
aceihq@aol.com
http://www.acei.org

National Education Association
Educational Support Personnel Division
1201 16th Street, NW
Washington, DC 20036
http://www.nea.org

National Resource Center for Paraprofessionals
Utah State University
6526 Old Main Hill
Logan, UT 84322-6526
435-797-7272
twallace@nrcpara.org
http://www.nrcpara.org

BIBLIOGRAPHY

Doyle, Mary Beth. *The Paraprofessional's Guide to the Inclusive Classroom: Working as a Team.* 2d ed. Baltimore: Paul H. Brookes Publishing Co., 2002.

Hammeken, Peggy A. *Inclusion: An Essential Guide for the Paraprofessional.* 2d ed. Minnetonka, Minn.: Peytral Publications, 2003.

———. *450 Strategies for Success: A Practical Guide for All Educators Who Teach Students with Disabilities.* Minnetonka, Minn.: Peytral Publications, 2000.

Naftali, Lee and Joel E. Naftali. *You're Certifiable: The Alternative Career Guide to More Than 700 Certificate Programs, Trade Schools, and Job Opportunities.* New York: Fireside, 1999.

Skelton, Kathryn Jane. *Paraprofessionals in Education.* Albany, N.Y.: Delmar Learning, 1997.

Twachtman-Cullen, Diane and David DeLorenzo. *How to Be a Para Pro: A Comprehensive Training Manual for Paraprofessionals.* Higganum, Conn.: Starfish Specialty Press, 2000.

TECHNICAL SUPPORT SPECIALISTS

Some technical support specialists work for software and hardware companies advising users through a phone help-line, while others work within individual companies just down the hall from the computer users. Scott Kruize keeps the computers of a gift import company up and running, instructing coworkers on the use of software, hardware, and peripherals such as printers. "In the modern world, you're likely to have a job where you wear many hats," Scott explains, while he works on two units before him, repairing keyboard and battery connections that have gotten loose. "Few people end up in a Dilbert-esque cubicle doing just one thing. So I'm also the systems administrator, which means I do things like change the backup tapes, monitor the system for performance and for locked out users, and things like that."

Definition
Technical support specialists investigate and resolve problems with the hardware, software, and peripherals of computer systems. They also answer phone calls from users experiencing problems and walk them through appropriate procedures.

Alternative Job Titles
End user consultants
Help desk representatives
Information center specialists
Microcomputer support specialists
User support analysts

High School Subjects
Computer science
English
Mathematics

Personal Skills
Helping/teaching
Technical/scientific

Salary Range
$23,690 to $39,900 to $68,000+

Work Environment
Primarily indoors
Primarily one location

Minimum Educational Level
Associate's degree

Certification or Licensing
Voluntary

Outlook
Faster than the average

DOT
033

GOE
02.06.01

NOC
6221

O*NET-SOC
15-1041.00

What Does a Technical Support Specialist Do?

Businesses and individuals rely on computers for everything from basic word processing to complex databases. People who use computers on a daily basis recognize how lost they would be without them. But just like all technological products, computer systems break down—and they break down relatively often. *Technical support specialists* investigate and resolve problems in computer functioning. When computer users, consumers, and business colleagues run into problems, they contact a technical support specialist for help.

The professional area known as technical support can officially be broken down into several categories: user support, technical support, and microcomputer support, among others. Positions in the computer industry differ among companies; the duties of a technical support specialist in one company might be the responsibility of the user support specialist in another. Job titles and descriptions vary depending on the nature, size, and needs of the company. However, almost all technical support specialists perform some combination of the tasks described below.

Technical support specialists fall into several categories, according to what they fix and who they assist. *User support specialists* direct much of their efforts at the users themselves, training them in proper procedures and explaining how to resolve recurrent problems. They answer phone calls, taking notes on the precise nature of the user's problem and the commands he or she entered that led to that problem. In some companies, they might enter a description of the problem into a special computer program that tells them how to help the user.

Their goal is to locate the source of the problem. If it is the user, specialists explain procedures related to the program in question, maybe a statistical, graphics, database, printing, word processing, or email program. If the source of the problem is located in the program or hardware, the user support specialists consult with technical support specialists, programmers, and other computer professionals to work out a solution.

Technical support specialists employed by computer companies are mainly involved with solving problems caused by the computer system's operating system, other software, or hardware. They consult manuals, meet with programmers, and inspect peripheral equipment in order to isolate the problem. Then, they try to solve the problems through a variety of methods, including program modifications and the replacement of certain hardware or software.

Technical support specialists employed by the information processing departments of large corporations do this kind of troubleshooting as well, but they also oversee the daily performance of their office's computer systems. They compare their department's projected work load on a computer system with its specified capacity in order to determine whether a given system is sufficient or if it should be upgraded and how. They might also test and modify commercial programs to customize them to their particular needs.

Microcomputer support specialists specialize in preparing a computer for delivery to a client, including loading the appropriate operating system and other software, installing the unit at the client's location, answering the client's immediate questions, and fielding later questions over the telephone. They also diagnose problems, repairing minor ones themselves and referring major ones to other support specialists.

All technical support specialists evaluate software programs in some capacity. They write technical reports of their findings and offer suggestions to designers and programmers about how to improve the program. They may be involved with the writing of training manuals and with the training of users. Most specialists read trade magazines and current books in order to keep up with changes in the field.

Lingo to Learn

Application A software program that helps you do word processing, build databases, or create spreadsheets.

Backup Copies of computer files on tape or diskette stored in a place other than the main work site, to be used in case of an emergency.

Crash When a computer freezes up and must be rebooted in order to operate; a "hard drive crash" means the computer can't be repaired.

Data dictionary Information about data, including name, description, source of data item, and key words for categorizing and searching for data items.

Glitch A "bug" or error in programming that causes interruptions or problems in computer operations.

Hardware The physical equipment inside a computer that makes it work.

Peripheral Any machine connected to a computer, such as a printer or an external modem or CD-ROM.

Software Programs that can be added to a computer so it can perform additional functions.

Technical support Maintenance and repair performed by a computer technician on computers, peripherals, or software applications.

User A person who uses a computer.

User support Online or live telephone assistance offered by a computer technician to a system user.

What Is It Like to Be a Technical Support Specialist?

"I'm the point of contact for all the users here," Scott Kruize says of his role at the import company, "if something goes wrong with their computer program, or if they have a question, or their printer doesn't work. I cope with about 100 people here in the home office, and we've got about a dozen showrooms, and also reps out in the field. I talk to them all."

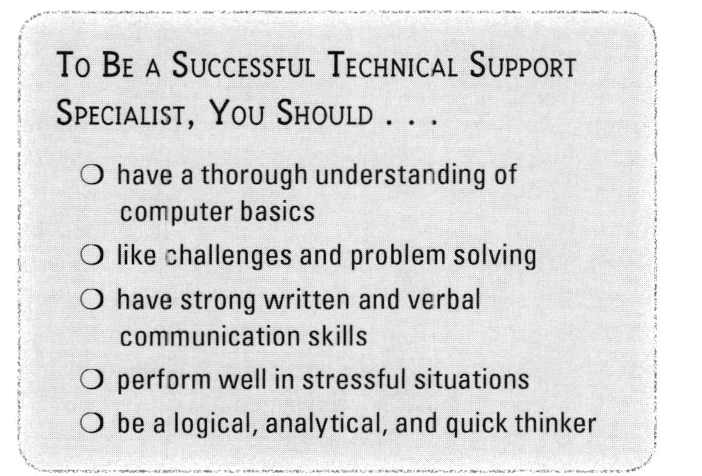

To Be a Successful Technical Support Specialist, You Should . . .

- have a thorough understanding of computer basics
- like challenges and problem solving
- have strong written and verbal communication skills
- perform well in stressful situations
- be a logical, analytical, and quick thinker

Though Scott's day usually begins and ends the same—assuring that the main system is running okay—the rest of his day doesn't follow a set routine. "The phone rings from users around the building who need help with something," he says. "If I can't help them on the phone, I walk there and free up the printer jam, or unlog them from the database that's not answering their query, or whatever it might be." Often, users will have questions about the word processing program, such as how to change the case of a particular font. "Also, from time to time, I take screwdriver in hand and adjust loose connections. If anything truly is broken, then I call the manufacturer and arrange to have it professionally fixed by the factory."

For repairing hardware, Scott has a miscellaneous collection of tools that he's gathered over his 12 years of working with computers. "I have one of those zipper cases with a set of computer tools, and I just augment it with regular tools like pliers and screw drivers. I don't have an electronics bench or anything like that. Computer tech support people don't get into the circuit-level stuff."

Scott also tests new equipment when it arrives from the manufacturer. "We just got in new laptop computers which the boss insists we check out and make sure are working before he puts them to use in the field." Scott also must keep records of his work. "As I move pieces of equipment from place to place, I have to key the new location into a database."

When working on computers, Scott relies on as many resources as possible. "My colleagues will sometimes know more on a given topic than I do, and vice versa, so we share knowledge. You need to stay on good terms with a wide variety of people. I do read manuals, and get information from the Web. And I'll get on the phone with tech support at companies that make the software and hardware we're running here. There is no source of information that I don't use." To keep up on the constantly changing industry, Scott reads technical publications. "Some of them are connected specifically with network administration that you can't buy on the newsstand. This is a job for a person who doesn't mind being a student every day."

Scott works a regular Monday through Friday workweek, usually putting in some overtime. "In this particular business, there are times of the year when we have rushes and a lot of users on the system." Scott likes working with people and helping them with their computer problems. "This is not a burden to me," he says. "It's something I enjoy."

Do I Have What It Takes to Be a Technical Support Specialist?

"Good interpersonal skills are important," Scott says, "because you're going to have to get along with users and management." Good stress management techniques can help specialists keep a clear mind. Strong logical and analytical thinking skills enable them to understand on the spot how a user complaint is linked to software programming.

"You have to be resourceful and flexible," he says. "You can't be too rigid in your thinking—don't look in your manuals and say, 'Well, the answer's not here, so I don't know what to do.' You have to have some ability to think for yourself, and to think on your feet, and to use alternative sources of information if necessary."

You have to have some ability to think for yourself, and to think on your feet, and to use alternative sources of information if necessary.

Quick analysis of this kind also requires thorough knowledge of computer basics. Specialists are not expected to know everything about a particular program before they begin work, of course, but rather they should have a broad understanding of computer principles that allows them to learn specifics relatively easily.

Technical support specialists like challenges and finding creative ways to deal with them.

Solid written and verbal communications skills are a must for a prospective technical support specialist. To write technical materials, it's especially important to be clear and concise.

How Do I Become a Technical Support Specialist?

Scott hasn't had a great deal of formal training. He learned most of what he knows about computers from hands-on experience. "You should spend some time with your hands on the computer," he advises students, "and I don't mean playing video games. You should fire up your word processor, or a simple CAD program, or an elementary database." Scott also suggests actually opening a computer and exploring. "Pull video cards, or install a replacement floppy disk drive. They're not mechanically complicated. That hands-on experience goes a long way."

EDUCATION

High School

You need at least a high school diploma to become a technical support specialist. Courses in mathematics, such as algebra and geometry, can give you the opportunity to develop strong logical and analytical thinking skills. Science classes are equally important, as they teach you to analyze and investigate the world around you. In physics and chemistry, for instance, you will use analytical methods similar to those used by technical support specialists when they are solving a problem.

English and speech classes are important because they teach you the basic communication skills vital to being a good technical support specialist. Computer classes, such as basic principles, business applications, programming, or computer science, can give you excellent background information about computers. Business classes like accounting or statistics might help you down the line when you're involved in administrative decision making. Drafting and mechanical drawing classes let you practice skills that carry over to the proper use of flow charts.

Postsecondary Training

In deciding whether to pursue formal postsecondary training, you need to think about which area of technical support interests you the most. If you would like to work in the computer information service department of a large corporation, an associate's degree in PC support and administration can be a strong asset. These companies often hire technical support specialists who can double as system administrators, and they take the educational background of an applicant into consideration. Technical schools offer many majors in business-related computer technologies, such as computer communications or PC support and administration. A two-year associate's degree in PC support and administration, for instance, emphasizes hardware and software support, PC DOS data communications, and networking, along with general business classes. In addition to the associate's degree, some companies prefer applicants with training or vendor-certification in a specific area like networking.

However, an associate's degree is by no means a requisite for employment as a technical support specialist. Most major computer companies who hire people to field user calls and do other minor technical or microcomputer support look for someone with general computer proficiency and demonstrated potential to learn their systems quickly through in-house training programs. One good way to prepare yourself for this field—and to get promoted from within a company—is through self-study.

Once you're hired by a company, you can also participate in vendor-sponsored in-house workshops to expand your knowledge. At these workshops, the manufacturer of a program sends its best employees to train new users on the product.

While vast computer experience and talent may be enough for success in the field, many computer professionals eventually feel the need to earn a bachelor's degree in order to stay competitive in the job market. Not only could a four-year degree give you an edge when looking for a job, but it could lead to better pay. Universities offer a wide spectrum of majors in computer science, from computer software engineering to computer-generated graphic design. Fortunately, many technology companies like to promote from within and will pay the cost of an employee's educational expenses in return for a work commitment of a specified number of years.

Advancement Possibilities

Technical support supervisors are generally responsible for solving the more complicated problems and for implementing the more complex solutions and programming changes. They have some administrative duties as well.

Computer network engineers are commercially certified. They design, install, maintain, modify, and repair computer networks for business applications.

Software engineers analyze industrial, business, and scientific problems and conceive software programs that can provide solutions to them.

CERTIFICATION OR LICENSING

There is no standard certification for technical support specialists. Certain hardware and software vendors or employers might offer training certificates when their workshops or in-house training classes are completed successfully, but these carry relatively little weight with new employers. "The requirements for the certificates change rapidly," Scott says, "and your ability to be employed doing the kind of work I do is not dependent on holding a certificate like that." Scott does think that certification may help you get that first job if you have little experience in the field, "but it won't sustain you through your whole career."

Nationally recognized certification programs offered by commercial associations and companies are springing up in other computer fields, such as network administration. Similar programs may develop in the technical support field, so interested individuals should watch for advertised announcements of such programs in computer magazines, industry newsletters, and Internet sites.

SCHOLARSHIPS AND GRANTS

There are currently no scholarships or grants specifically designated for individuals wishing to pursue education in computer technical support. However, certain employers may offer tuition reimbursement and scheduled time-off as a benefit to employees. These programs are generally more readily available in medium- and large-sized companies. In those that do not have educational funds, employees should be sure to discuss academic plans with supervisors and managers in the event that such on-staff expertise is desired. In some cases, employers may be willing to pay educational costs in order to improve company operations.

Individuals seeking formal education should work closely with their school's financial aid department, which disburses scholarships, grants, and federally subsidized student loans.

INTERNSHIPS AND VOLUNTEERSHIPS

Internships in technical support are not abundant. There may be some summer opportunities in computer companies, especially in geographical areas where computer companies are clustered. Technical support positions require so much in-house training that it is usually considered a bad investment to employ people only in the short-term. However, in areas like the Silicon Valley in northern California, job turnaround may be great, causing a steady demand for specialists and perhaps the willingness on the part of the employer to accept interns.

Technical school or university students might be required to complete part of their curricula by working in school-organized internships or co-op programs, which vary greatly by school. If your school doesn't organize such programs, you can work with your placement offices to find summer or off-quarter employment.

Any opportunity you have to practice technical support skills should be taken. One way to test technical support prowess is to offer to help friends and relatives when they run into problems on their computers. You might also offer user support and training to a church or nonprofit organization.

Who Will Hire Me?

Scott says his position was created at the import company out of necessity. "The system grew," he says, "more users, more equipment, more activity. They needed somebody to help out. The job was created; it hadn't existed before."

Technical support specialists work in any medium- to large-sized business or corporation that maintains an in-house computer information service or technical support department. Commercial databases and online services, retail stores, catalog companies, insurance companies, banks, financial institutions, hospitals, governmental agencies, universities, public and private school systems, and any other big service industry firm are some of the organizations that hire technical support specialists.

Another big employer of technical support specialists is computer companies, including those specializing in the research, development, or manufacture of hardware, software, and peripherals. As mentioned above, many computer companies tend to be established in the same geographical areas. Research Triangle in North Carolina and the Silicon Valley in northern California are two of the major ones. Potential employers can be identified simply by taking note of brand names on a walk through a computer store or perusal of a computer magazine.

Internet service providers (ISPs) are also good prospective employers of technical support specialists. Most local ISPs also have a technical support staff. Companies that produce CD-ROMs and computer games employ a support staff as well.

You can consult the classified listings in your local newspapers, as well as in computer trade magazines. The newest way to find a job is to check out the many Web sites for computer-industry jobseekers. You might also browse online job postings for individual companies.

In the geographical clusters of computer companies, many job openings are made known by word-of-mouth. Network with employed computer professionals and try to get "in the information loop." Talk to instructors and counselors in your school's placement office.

Where Can I Go from Here?

Scott is happy with the work he does, and he supplements it by teaching classes at a community college and by consulting privately. "But this isn't a good position for people who are on the fast-track to success," he says. "You don't go from computer tech support to manager of a company. It's much more a technical job than an executive one. But I don't really wish to manage departments full of people. I'd rather help everybody, have my hands on computer hardware and software."

After working in an entry-level technical support position, you have a good chance of being promoted to *support supervisor*. This position entails more complicated technical work as well as performing some managerial duties, like scheduling appointments with clients and vendors, and ordering supplies. Supervisors usually do more technical writing than specialists, preparing performance reports for programmers and design analysts. They may also train new employees or participate as teachers in training workshops offered to customers.

Technical support specialists might use their positions to springboard to an area requiring more specialization and a higher level of training. Some may become *certified network engineers* (CNEs). CNEs determine and analyze client networking needs, select appropriate hardware and software, make any necessary changes, supervise installation and initial operations of the system, and sometimes provide training to network users. Many technical support specialists develop the basic knowledge needed to succeed in the additional education and certification programs required of these positions.

Software engineering is another field that technical support specialists might consider. *Software engineers and engineering specialists* use computers to solve problems, increase productivity, and allow for business efficiency. They meet with clients to determine the specific nature of the problem, give presentations of software proposals and demonstrations of finished products, and consult with other engineers in the regular course of their work. A bachelor's degree or equivalent work experience is usually required for these positions.

What Are the Salary Ranges?

Technical support specialists made median annual salaries of $39,900 a year in 2003, according to the U.S. Department of Labor. Salaries ranged from a low of $23,690 at the entry level to more than $68,000 a year for senior specialists with management responsibilities.

Most specialists work for companies that provide a complete benefits package, which may include health care coverage, a pension plan, paid sick leave and vacation days, and educational expense reimbursement.

What Is the Job Outlook?

Computer support specialists should experience faster than average job growth over the next 10 years, according to the U.S. Department of Labor. As long as new technological inventions enter the market, there will be the need for technical support specialists to solve problems. Many companies cite the shortage of information technology (IT) professionals as one of the most significant obstacles to business success. As a result, those with solid computer skills have many options when entering the workplace. Though some of the more talented workers are stepping into jobs right out of high school, most industry experts say this is rare, and that some basis of college education is required for promotion and higher salaries.

The number of technical support specialists hired varies according to a number of factors. When the computer industry experiences higher sales or when a new product hits the market, companies will need additional technical support specialists, since increased sales automatically means increased calls to technical support. But even when sales at one company are down, job opportunities are still strong for technically flexible applicants. The key is to keep up-to-date on the newest technologies by surfing the Internet and talking with other computer professionals.

As large service industries continue to invest in computer systems as an automated alternative to record keeping and forms management, technical support positions there will increase in number as well. Computer companies are beginning to offer longer warranties and full-coverage service contracts to new customers as a strategy to distinguish their product from the competitors'. In order to fulfill these contractual obligations, computer companies will hire more technical support staff or subcontract the work out to computer service companies described above.

How Do I Learn More?

PROFESSIONAL ORGANIZATIONS

The following organizations provide information on technical support specialist careers, schools, and employers:

Association for Computing Machinery
1515 Broadway
New York, NY 10036
800-342-6626
http://www.acm.org

Association of Support Professionals
122 Barnard Avenue
Watertown, MA 02472
617-924-3944
http://www.asponline.com

IEEE Computer Society
1730 Massachusetts Avenue, NW
Washington, DC 20036
202-371-0101
http://www.computer.org

BIBLIOGRAPHY

The following is a sampling of materials relating to the professional concerns and development of technical support specialists:

Eberts, Marjorie, Margaret Gisler, and Maria Olson. *Careers for Computer Buffs & Other Technological Types*. New York: McGraw-Hill, 1999.

Gookin, Dan. *Troubleshooting Your PC For Dummies*. 2d ed. Hoboken, N.J.: Wiley, 2005.

Henderson, Harry. *Career Opportunities in Computers and Cyberspace*. 2d ed. New York: Facts On File, 2004.

Pogue, David, ed. *Tales from the Tech Line: Hilarious Strange-But-True Stories from the Computer Industry's Technical-Support Hotlines*. New York: Berkley Publishing Group, 1998.

TEXTILE TECHNICIANS

When you get dressed in the morning, you probably don't know the thread of your shirt, and when you sweep the floor, it's unlikely that you care what the broom's bristles are made of. But for Mark Burris, shirt threads and broom bristles are not only interesting but exciting at times. "There's always something new to learn, something new to experience, or something to relearn," he says as he does a quality check on a run of microdenier fabric. As a process technician at Cookson Fibers in Charlotte, North Carolina, for the last seven years, Mark has gleaned a great deal of knowledge about different fabrics and fibers and the equipment that's used to create and process them.

Mark's responsibilities often take him from the fabric manufacturing floor, to the computer room, to the testing labs. This variety is one of the things he enjoys most about his workday. He raises his voice to compete with the noise of the machinery in the background. "Earlier," he says, "I was in the mill's laboratory doing physical testing on a brand new synthetic fabric to verify that it performs the way the customer expects."

Definition
Textile technicians research, design, and produce fibers and textiles. They develop improved manufacturing methods, conduct quality control tests, and are involved in sales and customer service.

Alternative Job Titles
Fiber technologists
Process technicians
Research associates

High School Subjects
Chemistry
Computer science
Family and consumer sScience

Personal Skills
Mechanical/manipulative
Technical/scientific

Salary Range
$27,000 to $39,921 to $60,000+

Work Environment
Primarily indoors
Primarily one location

Minimum Educational Requirements
Associate's degree

Certification or Licensing
None available

Outlook
Decline

DOT
040

GOE
N/A

NOC
2233

O*NET-SOC
N/A

What Does a Textile Technician Do?

The textile industry is one of the oldest and largest industries in the United States. The development of synthetic fibers more than 75 years ago revolutionized the industry, making fabrics more versatile and functional. Besides making fabrics for clothing, the textile industry manufactures household goods, such as towels, sheets, and tablecloths. It also creates durable carpets, draperies, and upholstery. Numerous textiles are also used by automakers for safety belts and shoulder harnesses and to reinforce tires, belts, and hoses.

During the past decade, the U.S. textile industry has reacted to intense foreign competition by improving its technology and processing methods. For example, a new technique called open-end spinning has increased yarn production by four times the rate of the old method. Another example is the computerized knitting machine, which produces sweaters in a fraction of the time it used to take.

As the textile industry continues to evolve, there's a need for skilled and educated textile technicians who can manage the more complex processes. *Textile technicians* have a hand in all aspects of textile production, from research and development, to quality testing, to sales of finished products. *Research and development* technicians are involved

A textile technician inspects several silk moth (Bombyx mori) cocoons in water that are having their silk threads harvested. *(Pascal Goetgheluck / Photo Researchers Inc.)*

in polymer science, fiber chemistry, yarn production, fabrication efficiency and flexibility, dyeing and finishing, development or modification of production machinery, and application of new technology to solve problems. Some research technicians develop new textiles to be used for a specific purpose, while others design new uses for existing textiles.

Product development technicians work with the research and development staff to develop prototypes of products. They test sample products for tensile strength, abrasion resistance, washability, flammability, elasticity, and comfort, using specialized testing equipment. Depending on test results, technicians may then modify the product.

Quality control technicians make sure products meet or exceed standards and specifications—such as weight and count characteristics, colorfastness, or stability—in a safe and cost-effective manner. They also find solutions to problems in purchasing, product specifications, or production.

Production technicians work with raw materials; oversee the production of fiber, yarn, and fabric; do dyeing and finishing of fabrics; and manufacture textile products.Some production technicians work on the electronic controls of a knitting machine or a loom; others develop dyes and finishes. They develop improved methods for converting fibers into textiles and textile products. These methods may include combing and carding, spinning, weaving, knitting, or extruding or casting film solutions.

Other textile technicians work in *customer service and sales*. These technicians need to have a thorough knowledge of production and quality control, along with good communication skills. They find out what customers want and need and convey these ideas to the research and development staff.

Textile technicians also work for the U.S. government, one of the world's largest consumers of textile products. *Purchasing officers* locate producers and suppliers of specific textile products and make sure they meet government requirements. *Textile testing engineers* test and evaluate a product or prototype, using Federal Test Methods and Standards to verify that its performance meets the government's requirements. *Customs inspectors* examine all imported goods for correct quotas and labeling requirements and to make sure they are free of insects and disease organisms. Government research facilities also hire technicians to develop textile products such as uniforms for adverse weather conditions, space suits, interiors for space vehicles and submarines, and suits to protect against biological and chemical warfare.

What Is It Like to Be a Textile Technician?

When Mark Burris began his career at Cookson as an entry-level textile technician, he was responsible for checking certain stages in the production process at regular intervals. To produce the microdenier fabric that Cookson is known for, technicians begin with raw resin chips made of plastic. The chips are placed in a nitrogen atmosphere, which pulls moisture out. In the next stage of production, moisture is added back in at a specified level. The chips are then moved out of the nitrogen dryers and spun into various denier and filament combinations. Mark says that the production process varies according to the fabric they are making. "We try to customize our process to meet the customer's specifications," he says. "For instance, do they want high-strength yarn? Do they want something with high bow? Do they want something that dyes a particular shade?"

Handling the production checkpoints gave Mark a good introduction to the textile mill and its equipment. As he gained experience, he started doing other tasks around the mill. His manager took note and expanded his job; Mark now oversees all production. He credits his career growth to a can-do attitude. "Now there's nothing in this plant that I cannot do or am not willing to try," he says. The most demanding aspect of his job involves thinking quickly to solve glitches in the production process. "I spend a lot of time putting out 'brush fires,'" he says. When he notices a problem, he analyzes the production process to determine what adjustments or changes are needed, then he implements those changes.

Lingo to Learn

Abrasion resistance The ability of a fiber to withstand rubbing or abrasion.

Absorbency or moisture regain The percentage of moisture a dry fiber will absorb from the air under standard conditions of temperature and moisture.

Bow A type of off-grain fabric in which the filling yarn sags between the selvages.

Chemical reactivity The type of chemical reaction to which individual fibers are susceptible.

Cohesiveness The ability of fibers to cling together, especially important in yarn spinning.

Count Yarns per inch in warp and filling direction in woven fabrics.

Denier Yarn or fiber size, defined as weight in grams for 9,000 meters of fiber or yarn.

Elastic recovery The ability of fibers to recover from strain.

Elongation The ability of a fiber to be stretched, extended, or lengthened.

Fire retardance A material's resistance to combustion when tested under specific conditions.

Heat sensitivity The ability of a material to soften, melt, or shrink when subjected to heat.

Resiliency The ability to return to original shape after bending, twisting, or compressing.

Tenacity The strength of a fiber; usually referred to as breaking tenacity, which describes the force at which the fiber ruptures or breaks.

While Mark spends most of his time right on the plant floor, he occasionally works from his desk, tracking processes and keeping records. In addition, he sometimes meets with customers. After five years of working a swing shift, he now enjoys working the weekday shift from 8:00 A.M. to 5:00 P.M. Like most

To Be a Successful Textile Technician, You Should . . .

- be detail-oriented
- have good communication skills
- have good eyesight
- have problem-solving skills
- have an aptitude for science

textile mills, his plant keeps its machines running seven days a week, 52 weeks a year.

Mark is also responsible for maintaining machinery to meet safety standards. While somewhat noisy, all new machinery is designed with noise shields to cut the risk of hearing loss. Production technicians are required to wear protective face masks, earplugs, and protective clothing when appropriate.

Problem solving is a big part of Terry Olano's job, too. She manages quality control for the piece goods area of the Lilli Group in New Jersey, an apparel manufacturer. After earning a bachelor's degree in textile engineering, Terry first worked in a laboratory, testing garments and fabrics for quality, color, and durability. In her current position, she conducts fabric inspections. "We do a 10 to 20 percent inspection of every dye lot to verify quality," she explains. "I give advice to the cutting room about how to spread and cut the fabric. I also help make claims valid when we have to send fabric back to the manufacturer."

Bennett Baird is a supervisor for the research and development staff of a major chemical firm that manufactures fibers and textiles. His staff includes technicians with varying educational backgrounds, from a high school diploma to a master's degree. Bennett says, "Most technicians work under a senior researcher or technical person who plans project priority, objectives, and strategies. The degree of independence depends on the technician's experience and capability." In Bennett's laboratory, technicians run physical, chemical, and flammability tests, as well as microscopy and advanced photo lab tests. As in most laboratories, testing is carried out under carefully controlled conditions. Atmospheric moisture, in particular, affects the performance of fibers and textiles, so temperatures are maintained at 70°F and relative humidity at 65 percent. Samples are first measured to determine dimensions, weight, thickness, and count, or number of warp and filling threads. Experiments are repeated several times to verify results for strength, elongation, and recovery from stretching, shrinkage, abrasion resistance and pilling, colorfastness, and flammability.

Do I Have What It Takes to Be a Textile Technician?

To be a textile technician, you'll need to have strong interest in science and new technologies. Technicians who work in research and development, in particular, need to be able to communicate with the scientists they work with. They must be meticulous and resourceful. Those in product development must be creative and able to sell their ideas.

Interpersonal skills are also important, especially for technicians who move into sales and customer service. Terry notes, "You have to be able to communicate with workers and customers from different cultures and educational backgrounds. It takes patience, and you can't be afraid to ask questions."

You have to be able to communicate with workers and customers from different cultures and educational backgrounds. It takes patience, and you can't be afraid to ask questions.

Mark suggests technicians be detail-oriented and diplomatic, "because when it comes down to it, you are the one that's going to be held responsible. It's my job to spot problems, and since most problems are human error, you have to be diplomatic in how you handle them."

How Do I Become a Textile Technician?

In the past, technicians could begin their careers as machine operators and work their way up. However, most companies today are looking for graduates of a two-year college or technical school with degrees in textile technology. Some even require a four-year degree.

Bennett Baird confirms this trend. "It's desirable to have some technical training, including math, chemistry, physics, statistics, and engineering." His company now requires employees to have at least a two-year degree. Terry Olano adds, "You can learn on the job, but you need education to understand results. You need the theoretical knowledge and at least a two-year degree."

While Mark got his training on the job, he agrees that the industry has changed. "You've got to have that education. You're going to get left behind if you don't have it, because things are modernizing so quickly to compete with [textile mills] overseas." To further his career, Mark plans to take night classes in computer programming.

EDUCATION

High School

If you're interested in becoming a textile technician, you should take as many science classes as possible. Having a background in chemistry, physics, and biology will provide a solid foundation for the more advanced science courses in a postsecondary training program. The lab work involved in science classes is especially helpful. You learn how to follow instructions, complete individual steps, and report your findings, which are all aspects of a textile technician's job.

Courses in mathematics and computer science are also recommended. Once you're working as a textile technician, you'll need to be able to understand calculations, percentages, and statistics. Knowledge of computer programming is useful since most of the machinery that textile technicians operate is computerized.

Most high schools offer classes in home economics, fashion design, or sewing, all of which will help familiarize you with various fabrics and sewing methods.

If you're drawn to the notion of working for a textile mill in another country, it wouldn't hurt to take a foreign language. Spanish or Chinese, in particular, would be an asset.

Postsecondary Training

To enter the field of textile technology, you'll need to have an associate's degree. Some technicians choose to attend two-year programs in chemistry, physics, or another science, which gives them the general training necessary for a textile career. There are also technical schools and community colleges that offer more specialized two-year programs in textile technology.

An increasing number of textile companies are requiring technicians to have a bachelor's degree, especially for supervisory positions. A bachelor's degree in chemistry or science technologies will give you the appropriate skills and knowledge. You could also choose to get a four-year degree in textile technology, textile engineering, textile management, textile design, textile chemistry, and textile marketing. Terry Olano, who earned a bachelor's degree in textile engineering, feels the training was invaluable. "I wanted to be a fashion designer when I graduated from high school," she says. "My father made me get a degree in engineering. Now I have a much better understanding of textiles, and I am able to judge whether a garment can be produced from a particular fabric."

A bachelor's degree in textile technology includes courses in chemistry, geometry, calculus, yarn production systems, physics, textile form and structure, fiber science, knitting systems, technology of dyeing and finishing, weaving systems, textile yarn production and properties, textile measurement and quality control, physical properties of textile fibers, fiberweb and nonwoven production, and technical fabric design.

Most textile engineering degree programs offer concentrations in polymer chemistry, dyeing and finishing science, dyeing and finishing operations, or dyeing and finishing management.

Major centers for textile education include North Carolina State University in Raleigh, North

FYI

Natural fibers include wool, mohair, cashmere, camel's hair, alpaca, bristles, feathers, and plant fibers, such as cotton, linen, and jute.

Manufactured fibers include rayon and acetate.

Synthetic fibers include nylon, polyester, olefin, and acrylic.

Carolina; Center for Applied Textile Technology in Belmont, Georgia; Institute of Technology in Atlanta; Clemson University in South Carolina; and Philadelphia University.

Additional on-the-job training helps technicians learn specific skills for a particular company or piece of equipment. Bennett Baird says, "Technicians are expected to stay aware of developments in the textile area. They read trade journals and use resources like vendor and supplier magazines so they know who's supplying what to their areas. They also attend training seminars and association events."

SCHOLARSHIPS AND GRANTS

For scholarship opportunities, contact the financial aid office of your school for information. Many schools with textile programs offer academic, leadership, and minority scholarships and grants. In addition, professional organizations like the National Council of Textile Organizations and the American Fiber Manufacturers Association may be able to provide you with a list of scholarships and financial awards (see the end of this article for more information).

INTERNSHIPS AND VOLUNTEERSHIPS

Many textile, fiber, and chemical companies offer internship and co-op opportunities. These firms sometimes work with local colleges and trade schools to develop programs where students work part time while attending school. DuPont, for example, offers a co-operative education program in which college students alternate full-time classroom study with periods of full-time employment in their discipline. Because of the time commitment involved with the employment periods, students usually need to extend their graduation date by one year. However, the on-the-job experience they get is an invaluable asset. Dupont also offers internships to college students. These normally take place during the summer between the junior and senior year. Check with your college placement office for information on other companies that offer such programs.

Who Will Hire Me?

Textile manufacturing jobs are concentrated in California, New York, North Carolina, Pennsylvania, Tennessee, and Georgia. The remaining jobs in the United States are found almost exclusively in the South and Northeast, particularly Pennsylvania, Tennessee, and New York. Textile technicians are employed by research institutions, textile manufacturers, raw materials manufacturers, testing facilities, apparel companies, or manufacturers of home furnishings. Companies need not necessarily be textile based, however, to have opportunities for textile technicians. There are also many jobs in industrial settings, such as automotive industries; chemical companies that make binders for textiles; and biomedical companies that make textiles for a variety of uses in the health care field.

If you are willing to live in another country, there are many opportunities for textile technicians abroad. Anderson & Associates, an executive search firm for the apparel, textile, and home furnishing industry, is placing an increasing number of technicians in manufacturing plants in countries with emerging textile industries, such as Honduras, Mexico, and El Salvador. Fluency in Spanish is a must for these jobs.

Where Can I Go from Here?

Mark advanced quickly in his company because he worked hard and was willing to take on more responsibilities. However, further advancement for him will require that he obtain an associate's or bachelor's degree. Opportunities for advancement are generally good for textile technicians with postsecondary degrees. They can become section supervisors, production superintendents, or plant managers. There are also advanced positions in industrial engineering, quality control, and production control.

Technicians who have gained an expert knowledge of textile manufacturing and machinery can become *fabric development specialists* for a textile fiber producer or textile weaving firm. This job involves translating a designer's ideas into an actual fabric. Another advanced position is *textile converter,* who decides how textile materials are to be dyed or printed.

Technicians might choose a career in merchandising; for example, buying fiber for spinning companies. They work in retail settings, representing companies that produce textile products. Other technicians become *sourcing agents* who find suppliers of components, evaluate their products, and determine costs and the ability of the suppliers to meet delivery deadlines.

Those technicians who take an active interest in on-the-job safety might choose to become *plant training specialists* or *plant safety experts*.

What Are the Salary Ranges?

Graduates of two-year postsecondary textile manufacturing technician programs who have little or no previous textile experience start off making about $27,000 a year, according to the North Carolina Center for Applied Textile Technology. After four to six years of experience, textile manufacturing technicians usually advance to annual salaries in the mid-30s.

College graduates of four-year textile programs can start out as management trainees and typically earn more than those with two-year degrees. According to the North Carolina State University College of Textiles, the average student graduating with a degree in textile management or textile technology from the class of 2002 earns about $39,921.

After 10 to 20 years of advancement to top-level positions, persons who started as technicians can earn annual salaries up to and above $60,000.

Government positions generally pay less than those with private companies, and research and development technicians usually earn more than production technicians.

Textile technicians usually receive the benefits of salaried staff such as paid holidays, vacations, group insurance benefits, and employee retirement plans. In addition, they often have the benefit of company support for all or a part of educational programs. This is an important benefit because these technicians must continually study to keep up to date with technological changes in this rapidly developing field.

Advancement Possibilities

Chemical technicians work with chemists to develop chemicals and related products. For instance, they might test packaging for environmental acceptability or develop new production techniques.

Fabric development specialists help translate a designer's concepts into a new fabric.

Textile converters determine how to dye or print on textile materials.

Textile engineers manage or supervise other textile workers in research, product development, and production.

What Is the Job Outlook?

Automation has changed textiles from a labor-intensive industry to a technology-intensive one. As a result, fewer people are needed in production, and the educational requirements for other jobs are becoming more rigorous.

Although the demand for textiles is likely to increase, job opportunities in the U.S. textile industry are expected to decline as a result of the increased use of automation and competition from foreign manufacturers.

Nick Simpson, a technical marketing official at Cortaulds, Inc., in Axis, Alabama, says, "Textiles have taken a bit of a beating in the last couple of decades in all the developed countries. I would say the job numbers are going to decrease in the future rather than increase." He indicates, however, that the job placement of textile graduates over the last few years has been pretty good. "I think there are fewer jobs, but they're more high tech," he explains.

Mark maintains a positive outlook, saying, "As more modernization takes place, it's going to take highly skilled, educated people. You can have a computer that will run things all day long for you, but someone has to oversee that computer."

How Do I Learn More?

PROFESSIONAL ORGANIZATIONS

The following organizations provide information on textile technician careers, accredited schools, and employers:

American Apparel and Footwear Association
1601 North Kent Street, Suite 1200
Arlington, VA 22209
800-520-2262
http://www.apparelandfootwear.org

American Fiber Manufacturers Association
1530 Wilson Boulevard, Suite 690

Arlington, VA 22209
703-875-0432
afma@afma.org
http://www.afma.com

Institute of Textile Technology
2551 Ivy Road
Charlottesville, VA 22903
804-296-5511
http://www.itt.edu

National Council of Textile Organizations
1776 I Street, Suite 900
Washington, DC 20006
202-756-4878
info@ncto.org
http://www.ncto.org

BIBLIOGRAPHY

The following is a sampling of materials relating to the professional concerns and development of textile technicians:

Collier, Billie, and Phyllis Tortora. *Understanding Textiles*. 6th ed. Paramus, N.J.: Prentice Hall, 2000.

Conway, George L. *Garment and Textile Dictionary*. Albany, N.Y.: Delmar Publishing, 1996.

Harris, Jennifer, ed. *5,000 Years of Textiles: An International History and Illustrated Survey*. Washington, D.C.: Smithsonian Books, 2004.

Johnson, Maurice J., and Evelyn C. Moore. *So You Want to Work in the Fashion Business? A Practical Look at Apparel Product Development and Global Manufacturing*. Paramus, N.J.: Prentice Hall, 1998.

TIRE TECHNICIANS

Roaring engines drown out the noise of 400,000 fans as 33 cars speed around curves at more than 100 miles an hour, just barely missing one another as they fight for position in the greatest spectacle in racing.

It's the 10th lap of the Indy 500. The drivers are concentrating on the task at hand—keeping the tires on the road around the curves and picking up speed on the straightaway. With their hearts pumping quickly, every muscle tensed, their minds focused in intense concentration on every move of their cars, the last thing these drivers need to worry about is the safety of the tires carrying them around the track. And they don't. These tires, just like the tires on the family sedan, have been tested and tested and tested again by tire technicians before they ever hit the road.

Definition
Tire technicians are employed by tire manufacturers to test prototype tires, determine their strength and durability, and find any defects in their design and construction.

Alternative Job Title
Tire test equipment technician

High School Subjects
Chemistry
Mathematics
Technical/shop

Personal Skills
Technical/scientific
Mechanical/manipulative

Salary Range
$17,160 to $28,200 to $50,000+

Work Environment
Primarily indoors
Primarily one location

Minimum Educational Level
Some postsecondary training

Certification or Licensing
None available

Outlook
More slowly than the average

DOT
750

GOE
08.02.03

NOC
9423

O*NET-SOC
51-9061.01, 51-9197.00

What Does a Tire Technician Do?

Every time a race car takes a turn around a track, a truck makes a long haul across country, a bus carries kids to and from school, or a car takes someone to the grocery store, the very safety of not only the occupants but of everyone on the road depends in part on the tires they're riding on. *Tire technicians,* or *tire test equipment technicians,* like Bob Dornhecker, ensure tire safety.

The tires that carry all our automotive conveyances are tested over and over again in several stages before they ever hit the streets. Prototypes may never even leave the research stage because tire technicians discover flaws in either the design or materials of the tires.

Bob is employed by Goodyear, a large tire manufacturer. He works closely with engineers and other technicians in determining what types of testing to perform and how long each product should remain in the testing facility. It's Bob's job to carry out testing procedures and make sure Goodyear tires live up to both government and company standards. Bob says safety is first and foremost. "It's always on my mind that the customer is going to be riding on this. It's up to me to provide the highest quality product."

Most tire technicians work with experimental models or production samples as they come out of the factory. Bob works mostly with developmental models, often in the areas of race car or aircraft tires. To do the testing, technicians mount the tires on testing machines, or fly wheels, that simulate the road experience. These recreate the stresses of actual road conditions, such as traveling at high speeds, traversing bumpy roads, making quick stops, or carrying heavy loads.

The testing machines used by technicians are operated through computers, allowing Bob and other technicians to adjust them as needed. The technicians can change the weight of the load or the type of simulated road surface the tire is traveling on. Readouts provide the data the tire technician uses to determine if there are any flaws in the tire.

There are mainly two different types of testing that technicians perform—dedicated and free flow, or general, testing. Dedicated testing is a high-tech, electronically run procedure that measures rolling resistance. This is the resistance at which a tire meets force and momentum. It measures the forces acting against the tire. Dedicated testing requires the technician to be there at all times during the procedure, watching the machines, programming variables, and collecting the data.

Free flowing or general testing is a durability type testing. It may last for days or even weeks and cover many different operations that test the tire's durability. A technician might have 45 tires being tested at once under different procedures.

A tire technician uses several types of tools to measure the strength, reliability, and durability of the tire. Computers, gauges, meters, and micrometers all play a large role in the course of their work. Bob uses gauges to detect whether parts of the tire are damaged and to evaluate uniformity and quality.

During the course of testing, a flaw may be found. The technician would then record the data collected and report it to the supervisor or engineer in charge. The safety of all vehicles riding on tires is dependent on the tire technician and the role he or she plays in the tire manufacturing process.

What Is It Like to Be a Tire Technician?

Tire technicians work in shifts. At Goodyear, tire testing is a 24-hour process. Younger technicians, or those just starting out, often have to work the off-shifts, meaning nights and weekends. Bob has been there for six years and works the second shift, in the afternoons.

When he arrives for work, Bob first finds out what location he'll be working at that day. There are various test sites, and sometimes a tire technician will be sent on assignment to another location that is different from the regular testing facilities.

When Bob arrives at his location, he consults with the technician who worked the shift before him, getting all the pertinent information about his assignment, either through written records or personally discussing the situation. He'll then check the area of work and look over the data, making sure it's correct and everything is on schedule.

After he locates the test tire, Bob interprets the testing specifications as laid out by the engineer. When all the preliminary work is in order, he loads the tire onto the testing machine, and "then we finally get rolling," says Bob.

"The job of the technician is to make sure everything's on schedule. There's always a lot to do," Bob says. He sometimes runs simultaneous tests or has to switch quickly from one project to another. Schedule changes are common, and a technician has to be flexible and able to change focus as priorities change. "Flexibility is key," he says. "You have to be able to switch gears quickly from something that was hot to something else completely."

Sometimes the work can be frustrating, according to Bob. "Say a hot project comes up, tires for Boeing's new aircraft. We're working fast and furious to get the tires out. I get to the last 30 seconds of a cycle and have a failure. I have to start the entire procedure all over again."

When Bob actually finds a flaw in a tire, he removes it from the testing device and determines the failure type. Is the fault in the tire tread, the compound, or in the materials inside the tire? Does it have to do with traveling speed or road surface conditions? Going over all the data, he locates the apparent problem.

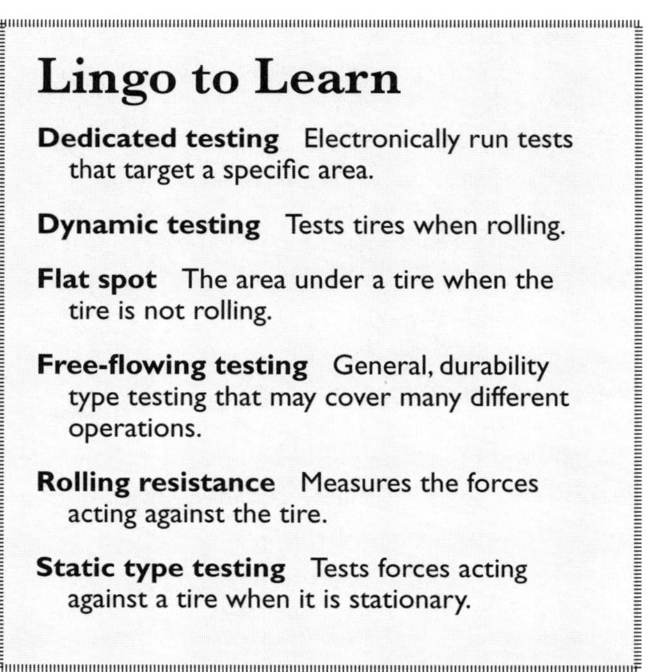

Lingo to Learn

Dedicated testing Electronically run tests that target a specific area.

Dynamic testing Tests tires when rolling.

Flat spot The area under a tire when the tire is not rolling.

Free-flowing testing General, durability type testing that may cover many different operations.

Rolling resistance Measures the forces acting against the tire.

Static type testing Tests forces acting against a tire when it is stationary.

"A big percentage of what we do is actually interpreting data," says Bob. Going over the accumulated data allows the tire technician to find errors, which he reports to the supervisor of engineering. Bob also spends a lot of time documenting his work. Tire technicians are responsible for filling out reports, making charts and graphs, and relaying important information, both verbally and in writing.

Occasionally, Bob has trouble with one of the machines he uses for testing. Not only does he have to locate problems in tires but sometimes in the testing equipment itself. "We do a lot of troubleshooting, checking for machine failure."

Do I Have What It Takes to Be a Tire Technician?

Tire technicians have a lot of responsibility. They are part of a team of people directly responsible for the safety of anyone who comes in contact with a motorized vehicle on wheels. Even if you don't drive or fly in an airplane, tires are present in the lives of anyone living in the modern world. Tire technicians need to be detail oriented and organized. They also must be able to work under pressure. "It can be a little stressful," says Bob. "I'm always making sure that all the data is of the highest quality. It's always on my mind."

Dealing with schedule changes and being flexible and cooperative are important characteristics for a tire technician. Tire testing is a never-ending job. There are always projects going on and new products being developed. A tire technician needs to have good reasoning ability and be able to think clearly even when juggling several different tasks.

Good communication skills are very important. Tire technicians spend a lot of time interacting with other technicians, engineers, managers, and supervisors. Bob actually took a class offered through his workplace on this topic. "It taught me how to interface with my supervisors. How to determine their expectations and how I can meet them."

Bob must be able to communicate his results to a number of people not only verbally but also in writing. He spends a lot of time writing reports and recording findings. For this he needs to be able to write clearly and concisely and to accurately interpret data on charts and graphs. "Our whole job relies on effective communication," stresses Bob. "Our product is data. If we can't communicate that data, information gets lost in the process."

Flexibility is key. You have to be able to switch gears quickly from something that was hot to something else completely.

Computers play a big role in the job duties of tire technicians. Technicians need to be comfortable operating computers and to be familiar with basic programs. According to Bob, "Much of the testing equipment is PC-based. It all runs through computers."

Being in good shape physically is another important characteristic of a tire technician. "Technicians must have a certain level of physical ability. We use lifts for the really heavy stuff, but your endurance level needs to be high. You're always on your feet," says Bob.

Unusual work hours are often a necessity, especially if a technician is new to the job. "The newer technicians work off-shifts and weekends," Bob says. "That's kind of a drawback. But working Sunday pays double time."

For Bob, the best part of his job is, "knowing I have a direct impact on the business. They rely on our data to make a multimillion-dollar decision."

How Do I Become a Tire Technician?

Tire technicians need to have at least a high school diploma. Employers increasingly prefer their technicians to have some post-high school training in an area related to electronics.

EDUCATION

High School

Students interested in becoming a tire technician should take classes in mathematics and science while

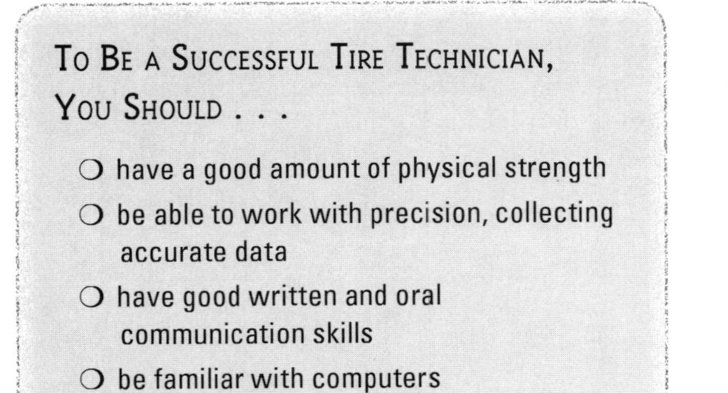

in high school. Algebra and geometry are important in developing reasoning skills. "It's the ability to do problem solving that's important," says Bob.

English, writing, and communications classes are important because technicians write reports and give oral presentations about their work.

Shop classes, such as electronics, and laboratory science courses, such as chemistry, are helpful in becoming familiar with measuring devices, electrical machinery, and electronic testing equipment.

"Take any computer classes you can," advises Bob. "They have more advanced computer equipment in high schools now. Become familiar with everything you can. Testing equipment is PC-based."

Postsecondary Training

It was once possible to become a tire technician with just a high school diploma and a background in technical work. But today, most employers are looking for people with some amount of postsecondary training. Goodyear reports it now requires a two-year technical certificate or an associate's degree in electronics. An equivalent, such as military training in electronics, is also acceptable.

Bob went to a community college and earned a two-year degree in electronic engineering technology. Before going to college, he had experience as a woodworker and a background in electronic repair. "I saw it as an opportunity to apply some of my knowledge and learn a lot more," he says.

Once he was employed by Goodyear, Bob went through an extensive on-the-job training program, spending months learning the testing procedures and following other, more experienced technicians. Later, he went back to school and received his bachelor's degree in industrial technology. Bob participated in an employee reimbursement program, and his tuition was paid by Goodyear.

Prospective tire technicians should take classes in mathematics and science, especially the applied sciences. "You need to know how to read a micrometer, how to interpret a scale in millimeters and convert metric," Bob advises.

According to Bob, psychology classes are important in learning to work with others, develop reasoning skills, and deal with stress. "It's important to handle situations without becoming too stressed," he says. You should also take communications and writing classes. "Good writing skills are the most important part of the career path, especially technical writing. We interface with both people and machines," says Bob.

Finally, computer classes are crucial. You should be familiar with personal computers and be able to use Windows and spreadsheets.

In addition, Bob participates in continuing education programs sponsored by his employer. Courses on giving effective presentations, how to use a media chart, and making charts and graphs are some that he has found helpful.

Who Will Hire Me?

Tire technicians are employed by tire manufacturers. The large manufacturing companies all employ technicians to conduct testing on new tires.

How did Bob get his first job as a tire technician? "I went right to the employment office at Goodyear, left my resume, and kept on bugging them," he says. "I called them once a week."

Eventually, his diligence paid off. He got the job and has been working there for the last six years. The large tire manufacturers have employment offices where interested technicians can apply.

Employment placement services at technical institutes and vocational schools are also good sources of information. Often employers looking for qualified technicians will contact a local school when there are job openings.

Where Can I Go from Here?

Tire technicians usually follow a typical career path. Technicians just starting out and without some form of postsecondary education will likely begin their careers as a *lab operator, junior.* They may then progress to *lab operator, senior; lab technician;* and then to *tire test equipment technician.*

Bob's official title is tire test equipment technician. This is the starting level for a technician with a college degree. The next levels are *master technician* and finally *chief technician.*

"To make the move to master and then chief technician would be nice," says Bob. He points out that advancement is based on individual skills and abilities. Bob is motivated and constantly continuing his education and looking to the future.

"I would like to stay in testing. I think it's an exciting area," says Bob. "I could go into test engineering with my current degree and the right level of knowledge gained here."

There are also opportunities in engineering and support personnel. If a tire technician pursues an education in engineering, job options expand. "If you have the skills and ability, it will get you considered for a tire test engineer or information processor," says Bob. Good communication skills can lead to jobs outside of a traditional technician's role. Inspectors may be responsible for quality control and maintaining product standards.

After a certain amount of years with a company and proven organizational, communication, and people skills, a tire technician can move into the ranks of management. Becoming a supervisor in the tire testing area and other sections of a facility is possible.

What Are the Salary Ranges?

Tire technicians fall into the category of inspectors, testers, and graders. According to the *Occupational Outlook Handbook,* in 2003 inspectors, testers, and graders had median hourly wages of approximately $13.56, which would translate into a yearly income of approximately $28,200. The lowest paid 10 percent had hourly wages of approximately $8.25 ($17,160 per year), while the highest paid 10 percent earned approximately $24 per hour (about $50,000 per year).

Employees of large manufacturing facilities generally receive benefits such as paid vacations and holidays, sick days, and insurance benefits. Many facilities operate around the clock, and opportunities to work off-shifts, Sundays, and holidays bring time and a half and double-time pay.

Advancement Possibilities

Tire inspectors inspect cured tires to ensure conformance to standards.

Tire test engineers or information processors are involved in the design and testing procedures of tires.

Supervisors coordinate and supervise activities of workers engaged in manufacturing rubber tires and tubes. They inspect products in process to ensure adherence to specifications.

Quality control inspectors inspect completed products and those in process for conformance to specifications. They tag substandard products and discuss defects with department supervisors to correct them.

What Is the Job Outlook?

The U.S. Department of Labor expects employment for testers, inspectors, and graders to grow more slowly than the average through 2012. This slow growth can be attributed both to increased automation of some testing processes, in addition to a growing trend towards shifting testing duties from inspectors to production workers, thereby streamlining staff and costs. However, after some significant tire recalls in the past several years, tire manufacturers have

Large tire manufacturers have facilities in different locations both in and outside of the United States. Training within a company may qualify you for international work.

become more focused on proving to consumers that their tires are safe, well designed, and thoroughly tested. Many tire companies are investing in new equipment, upgrading testing areas, and expanding research and development centers. As consumers and the government demand more consistent quality checks, the tire industry will likely rely on the skills of well-trained tire technicians. Those with degrees and computer skills will have the best opportunities.

How Do I Learn More?

PROFESSIONAL ORGANIZATIONS

The following organizations provide information on tire technician careers, schools, and employers:

American Society for Testing and Materials
100 Bar Harbor Drive
West Conshohocken, PA 19428
610-832-9585
http://www.astm.org

Rubber Manufacturers Association
1400 K Street, NW, Suite 900
Washington, DC 20005
202-682-4800
info@rma.org
http://www.rma.org

Tire Industry Association
1532 Pointer Ridge Place, Suite G
Bowie, MD 20716
800-876-8372
http://www.tireindustry.org

BIBLIOGRAPHY

The following is a sampling of materials relating to the professional concerns and development of tire technicians:

Crosby, Phillip B. *Quality is Still Free: Making Quality Certain in Uncertain Times*. New York: McGraw-Hill, 1995.

Haney, Paul. *Racing & High Performance Tire: Using Tires to Tune for Grip and Balance*. Warrendale, Pa.: SAE International, 2003.

Society of Automotive Engineers. *Tire and Wheel Technology*. Warrendale, Pa.: SAE International, 1999.

TITLE SEARCHERS AND EXAMINERS

At 3:00 P.M., Tom Przenieslo is finishing up his research on a piece of real estate property when he comes across a file with some confusing information. It shows the same property owner's name, but a different address than the one Tom has been researching all afternoon. With just a few hours to finish the title search, Tom knows he has to retrace his steps quickly to figure out which address is the right one.

Just after noon, he had received a rush order for a title search on property owned by Edward M. Harris. What Tom didn't know then was that Mr. Harris had requested that the county's tax bills for both of his properties be sent to his primary residence. Therefore, when Tom checked the public tax roll, he saw just one address for an Edward M. Harris and assumed that was the address in question.

For Tom, the afternoon has been a reminder of the title searchers' motto: "assume nothing." Even with his years of experience, Tom had inadvertently cut some corners by not checking another legal source to verify the property address. He glances at the clock now and rolls up his sleeves, thankful he's discovered the discrepancy in time to start the search process anew.

Definition
Title searchers and examiners conduct searches of public records to determine the legal chain of ownership for a piece of real estate.

Alternative Job Titles
Abstractors
Name searchers
Tax searchers
Title workers

High School Subjects
Business
English
Government

Personal Skills
Helping/teaching
Following instructions

Salary Range
$20,560 to $34,080 to $62,840+

Work Environment
Primarily indoors
Primarily one location

Minimum Educational Level
High school diploma

Certification or Licensing
Required in some states

Outlook
Decline

DOT
119, 209

GOE
04.02.02

NOC
4211

O*NET-SOC
23-2093.00, 23-2093.01, 23-2093.02

What Does a Title Searcher or Examiner Do?

Most house and land buyers are wrapped up in deciding whether their monthly payment will be affordable and whether they like the style and location of the house. One of the last things they think about is the property's history of ownership. However, if buyers aren't sure of a property's chain of ownership, they may later find out that the house didn't really belong to the seller in the first place or that the county is still owed a large amount of money on the property. Most buyers don't have this knowledge or the capability to do this type of research. This is where the title searcher and title examiner come in.

The *title searcher* examines public records to track the chain of ownership of the property. This ownership is known as the title to the property. From the moment the first nail is driven in to stake out the foundation, a house develops a chain of ownership. First, there is the bank loan needed to pay for the construction. Then the house is sold to the first owner, who probably takes out a loan to pay for the purchase. When he or she moves, the first owner sells the house to the second owner. The second owner also probably needs a bank loan to pay for the house. All of these transactions are recorded in records open to the public at the county recorder, clerk, or registrar. In recent years, most title companies have gained direct computer access to county records.

Lingo to Learn

Abstract A written history of ownership of a parcel of land that summarizes any occurrences that affect title of the land.

Deed A document used in a sale of land that passes the title to property from one person or entity to another.

Easement A right to the limited use or enjoyment of land held by another. Also, an interest in land to enable sewer or other utility lines to be laid or to allow access to a property.

Mortgage A formal document executed by an owner of property, pledging that property as security for payment of a debt.

Tract A parcel of land.

When this isn't possible, title companies send an employee (usually called a *runner* or *posting clerk*) to the county recorder's office each day to collect copies of the day's recorded documents. These are kept on file or on microfilm at the title company, eliminating the need for title searchers and examiners to leave the office for research.

Information from the county recorder on a specific property is referenced by the property's legal description and by the tax parcel or identification number. The title searcher must first determine that the legal description and tax parcel number given with the research request are accurate. This is done by comparing various legal records. The researcher then reviews chronologically all the deeds (transfers of title) and mortgages (loans) recorded against the property for correct spellings, proper signatures and notaries, and the proper sequence of events. While a misspelled name might seem like a harmless mistake to a layperson, it signals a red flag to an experienced title searcher or examiner. What appears to be a misspelling might actually turn out to be an heir to the deceased property owner. While most discrepancies are minor, they can make real estate transactions difficult if not corrected. Sometimes, mistakes made years ago make future transactions impossible.

In addition to the records from the county recorder, clerk, or registrar, the title searcher also looks at surveyors' maps and tax rolls and checks on street assessments, sewer taxes or assessments, county or city levies, easements, and liens. Taxes and assessments must be verified because they represent a possible claim on the property by the county or city. Easements need to be checked because they give another person or entity the right to use or access the property for a specific purpose. Liens are a charge or claim on the property toward payment of debt or obligation.

Using a standardized worksheet, the title searcher writes down the information found on the property, including the name of the records where the information was found, where the records are located, the dates of the transactions, and the names and addresses of the people involved.

Once the title searcher has completed his or her work, the information is passed on to the title examiner. The *title examiner* is usually more experienced in the legal issues of real estate transactions. He or she studies the legal documents and information compiled by the title searcher. The examiner will also review marriages, births, adoptions, divorces, and other legal transactions that can affect the chain of title. Sometimes examiners need to speak with lawyers, bankers, and brokers to gather more facts.

With this information, the examiner determines whether a title to a property is good and whether any claims against it are valid. The examiner then writes a report, sometimes called a "preliminary title report" or a "title commitment," outlining the information found. There will be a section describing the property; a section listing valid assessments, taxes, easements, and liens; and a section that lists steps that must be taken to enable clear title to be given. This report is used by lenders, attorneys, and others to determine whether the transaction is worth pursuing.

The job functions of title searchers and title examiners sometimes overlap and in some title companies, one person will do both jobs. Attorneys usually conduct the analysis if the title is complex. In addition to variations between companies, some states have different requirements and practices. Some states use an abstract instead of a title report. An abstract is a written summary of all that has transpired on a certain property. Once an abstract is written, it remains of public record. All future transactions are added to the existing abstract. The people who prepare these summaries are called *abstractors*.

What Is It Like to Be a Title Searcher or Examiner?

Tom Przenieslo has been employed as a title searcher/examiner for almost 20 years. He entered the field just after completing a nine-year stint in the Air Force and took the job until something else came along. He started out doing name searches, which involves tracking down information on the grantors and grantees involved in a real estate transaction. (A grantor is the party who is selling, and the grantee is the party who is buying.)

Tom would go to the office of the county recorder and "run an index and judgment book" on the specific names. In doing this, he would look through volumes of books that listed judgments and other legal transactions. The books were referenced by either the party's name or the legal description of the property. Tom found that he liked the work and decided to stay on when offered a permanent position. After working on name searches for a time, he was given more responsibility and began researching titles. Tom was in this position for a couple of years before being promoted to a title examiner, which he did for three years before becoming the office manager. Tom currently is an assistant vice president/operations manager for the Land Title Group.

Tom's day starts at 6:00 A.M., although he admits that he starts early to have quiet time for work before everyone else arrives. Most title searchers work typical office hours, Monday through Friday. Employers generally have a 40-hour week and pay time and a half for any additional hours.

On a typical day, an experienced title searcher can complete about 10 title searches. The demand for title searches fluctuates; Tom recalls having 150 new orders during one busy period. Currently, his staff receives about 30 new orders a day.

The title searcher has to do meticulous, detail-oriented work in an environment that is sometimes noisy and distracting. Tom finds it helps to keep his mind on one task and complete it before considering another order.

A title searcher's work begins when an order is received from a customer for a title insurance commitment. Customers include banks, mortgage lenders, real estate brokers, attorneys, and developers. The title searcher is usually given the property address and may also receive the legal description, the tax parcel number, and the grantor's name. The more information the searcher receives, the easier the task is.

Title searchers begin by verifying the tax parcel number, legal description, property address, and current owner. The next step is to research all grants and mortgages prior to when the current owner took title. In addition, title searchers have to determine what has transpired since the current owner took title.

There are basically two systems on which the needed information is recorded. One is the grantor/grantee system, in which everything is referenced by the party's name. Completing a search using this system of records is a little more difficult, Tom says, because each time the searcher comes across a new grantor, the searcher has to locate that name in the records. This can be very time consuming in a large metropolitan area with volumes of records.

The other system is the tract system, which is easier to use because the records are all based on the property. Each transaction that has ever taken place on a property is recorded in one record. Most counties utilize the grantor/grantee system; if the title searcher is lucky, the county also has the tract system.

Title searchers and examiners work in typical office environments. Office conditions can vary greatly from company to company. The work is not physically demanding, although it can be tiring to review the fine print of legal documents. Occasionally, the title searcher will need to travel to a property to verify lot lines and the placement of buildings and improvements.

Do I Have What It Takes to Be a Title Searcher or Examiner?

The most difficult part of being a title searcher, according to Tom, is knowing what details to look for when sifting through legal documents. To do this well, the title searcher must be methodical, thorough, and have a keen eye for detail. Some title searchers develop a personal checklist or system for reviewing documents. Conscientious title searchers and examiners learn not to make assumptions without verifying all the facts.

In some ways, a title searcher can be thought of as an investigator who uses logic and common

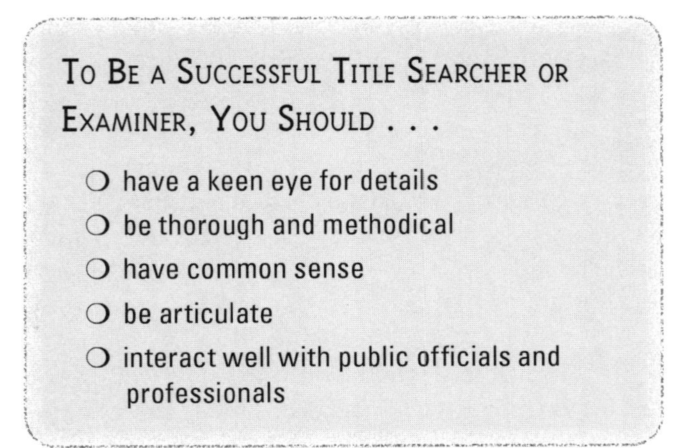

To Be a Successful Title Searcher or Examiner, You Should . . .

- have a keen eye for details
- be thorough and methodical
- have common sense
- be articulate
- interact well with public officials and professionals

sense to figure out what has really happened. A good title searcher must also be able to deal with work pressures without losing sight of the job. In addition, they must be able to relate well to other people, as the job requires the need to deal with public officials, attorneys, bankers, and real estate agents.

These same traits are also important for a title examiner. The examiner, however, must also be able to view the transaction as a whole, compiling each detail into a larger picture. The title examiner must also be able to write concisely and use correct English grammar to write clear reports.

How Do I Become a Title Searcher or Examiner?

A lot of title searchers enter the title insurance business just like Tom did: They hear of a job and take it to see if it suits them. A good place to start, says Tom, is a job as a file clerk or a name searcher (those who do basic research and office work). Once you get a job with the company, you can gain experience and get promoted or transferred into the title department.

EDUCATION

High School

Firms require their title searchers to have a high school diploma or its equivalent. Some employers offer entry-level positions to high school students in work-study programs. Tom reports that this has worked well and enables students interested in the field to gain the needed experience.

High school courses in typing, general business, math, data entry, and computer science are beneficial. In order to advance to a title examiner, you also need a good understanding of English grammar as well as the ability to write well. Therefore, take plenty of English classes.

Postsecondary Training

A title searcher or examiner is not required to have a college degree. Tom says, however, that a few college-level courses in real estate can give potential title searchers a good understanding of real estate transactions and related terms. He also believes that taking several computer classes that give you hands-on experience working with different software programs can be helpful in the office environment. These types of classes are usually offered by community colleges.

Tom received all of his training on the job, which is typical of most title searchers. Some companies have developed manuals to assist in training title searchers. In addition, once you are employed by a title company, bank, real estate company, or a related business, you can attend seminars sponsored by title insurance companies or professional associations. The American Land Title Association (ALTA, http://www.alta.org) and its affiliate state associations hold annual meetings and educational workshops.

CERTIFICATION OR LICENSING

There are a few states that require title searchers to be certified or licensed by an association or agency. Tom works in a state that does not require this. There are also locales that require title examiners to hold a law degree. The best way to find out the current requirements in your state is to contact a local title company or the state chapter of ALTA. In some instances, you can be hired by a company as a title searcher with the understanding that you will study for and pass any necessary certification exams within a specified time period. The Land Title Institute, which is the educational arm of ALTA, has compiled extensive information binders with sample questions to help you prepare for an exam. Even if you live in a state where certification is not required, you might think about using these study materials to accelerate your training.

Most title firms are members of ALTA and may also belong to state and regional associations. As an employee, you are granted automatic membership and are expected to uphold a code of ethics and standards of practice established by ALTA.

Who Will Hire Me?

Prospective employers are usually title insurance companies or abstractors. Large lending institutions may also have positions that are involved in title searches and examining. Local or state governments may also have a need for title searchers or examiners. In states that require title examiners to be attorneys, law firms may hire individuals to assist the attorneys in the searches.

A great number of title searchers and examiners find their first job in the title insurance business simply by answering a classified ad or by word of mouth. Look under the insurance or real estate sections in the classifieds. There are also several Web sites devoted exclusively to helping people find jobs in the real estate industry. As in many fields, personal contacts are excellent conduits for potential jobs.

To apply for a position with an employer of title searchers, be sure to send a cover letter with a resume. You should be open to the idea of accepting an entry-level position with a title company in order to familiarize yourself with the general nature of the work. There is frequent turnover in title companies as employees are promoted to positions of greater responsibilities. When a position opens up for a title searcher, you'll have already proven yourself as a dependable employee.

Where Can I Go from Here?

Tom is a good example of how far a title searcher can progress in a career. He started in an entry-level position and is now an assistant vice president for a major title insurance firm in a major metropolitan area. From here he could be promoted to the vice president level or to president.

Typically, a career as a title searcher or examiner begins in an entry-level position such as *file clerk*, *tax roll searcher*, or *receptionist* that involves general office work. A promising employee can advance to the position of title searcher and eventually title examiner. Title examiners can be promoted to team leaders, supervisors, or department managers, all of whom have supervising responsibilities.

Advancement in the title insurance business is not only a change in job function. Some firms have levels of responsibility within each position, such as assistant title searcher or senior title examiner. Increases in salary are another way that employers recognize their most experienced title searchers and examiners.

There are several factors that determine if an employee advances in the title insurance business. First is the employee's experience. Certain job skills can only be learned with time and firsthand experience. Aptitude and work ethic also play important roles. Other factors include the size of the company, the overall workload, and the employee's current position. It is much easier to move from name searcher to title searcher than it is to move from title examiner to department manager.

In-depth

The Reasoning behind Red Tape

Conditions for the sale and the transfer of property in colonial America were conducted by spoken word. A handful of dirt and a twig symbolized the transfer from seller to buyer. As a result, there was no permanent record of the transaction. This practice created an abundance of problems with ownership of a property.

A Virginia law passed in 1626 helped improve the situation by requiring that all land sales be recorded in the General Court at Jamestown within a year of the sale. By 1640, a deed without delivery of possession was fraudulent unless it was recorded in a local court.

What Are the Salary Ranges?

Salaries for title searchers and examiners vary between regions and companies. In rural and suburban areas, beginning title searchers may earn about $1,280 a month, which makes for a yearly income of $15,360. More experienced title searchers can earn around $1,600 a month. Salaries are generally higher in urban areas.

According to U.S. Department of Labor, median annual earnings of title examiners, abstractors, and searchers were $34,080 in 2003. Salaries ranged from less than $20,560 to more than $62,840. Title searchers and examiners may receive such fringe benefits as vacations, hospital and life insurance, profit sharing, and pensions, depending on their employers.

What Is the Job Outlook?

The demand for title searchers and examiners is directly related to the real estate market in the area. As the need for new financing of property or the construction of new houses increases, so does the need for title searches. Public utilities and construction companies also create demand because these companies need to make sure they have clear title to land where they are constructing new highways, power lines, and power plants.

According to the U.S. Department of Labor, employment of title searchers and examiners is expected to decline through 2012. With the Internet and other technology, title searches can be accomplished more efficiently, requiring fewer workers.

How Do I Learn More?

PROFESSIONAL ORGANIZATIONS

To learn about education opportunities available at the Land Title Institute, contact

American Land Title Association
1828 L Street, NW, Suite 705
Washington, DC 20036
800-787-2582
http://www.alta.org

To learn about education opportunities available through the ULI Real Estate School, contact

Urban Land Institute
1025 Thomas Jefferson Street, NW, Suite 500W
Washington, DC 20007-5201
800-321-5011
http://www.uli.org

BIBLIOGRAPHY

The following is a sampling of materials relating to the professional concerns and development of title searchers and examiners:

Evans, Marilyn. *Opportunities in Real Estate*. 2d ed. New York: McGraw-Hill, 2002.

Gaddy, Wade E., and Robert E. Hart. *Real Estate Fundamentals*. 5th ed. Chicago: Dearborn, 2000.

Hennin, S. *Real Estate Title Search Abstractor Basic Training*. Altoona, Pa.: Eiram Publishing, 2004.

Karp, James, and Elliot Klayman. *Real Estate Law*. 5th ed. Chicago, Dearborn, 2003.

Reilly, John. *Language of Real Estate*. 5th ed. Chicago, Dearborn, 2000.

VETERINARY TECHNICIANS

The first patient of the day has four white paws, a black tail, and whiskers. "Hey there, Blue," says Becky Karabinus, flipping through the medical chart on the counter. "It looks like Dr. Medler wants you to get a couple X rays."

Blue licks his paw, not looking too concerned. Blue's owner, Mrs. Nelvick, seems more nervous.

"He came in limping last night. He's an inside and outside cat, and I'm just afraid he got injured out there. He seems better today, but he still walks a little funny." Mrs. Nelvick bites her lip. "It's just that, I worry when he seems ill. I've had him for 14 years, you know."

"Oh, I understand," says Becky. "Blue has been our patient here for a long time. I'll take these X-rays and see if we can tell what the trouble is. We'll try to get Blue all fixed up—won't we Blue?" She gently picks up the cat and carries him to X ray.

Kate Larsen, another veterinary tech, rarely carries her patients into X ray. They're too big and unpredictable. When Kate works with bighorn sheep, elk, and deer, they're usually blindfolded and hobbled—gently tied around the forelegs—so they don't kick veterinary workers or themselves. "We drop net on as many animals as we can, usually baiting them with apple pulp," says Kate. "Then we draw blood, vaccinate them, ID them with a radio collar or ear tag, and let them go, real quick. These animals are wild, and they stress out easily. We have to move fast and we have to know what we're doing." Kate is a wildlife veterinary technician, and her animal world moves at a much different pace than Becky's.

Definition

Veterinary technicians perform a variety of duties to assist veterinarians in the care of animals. They may work in a variety of places including animal hospitals, zoos, kennels, and other settings.

Alternative Job Titles

Animal technicians
Veterinary assistants

High School Subjects

Biology
Chemistry
Mathematics

Personal Skills

Following instructions
Technical/scientific

Salary Range

$16,410 to $23,340 to $34,380+

Work Environment

Indoors and outdoors
One location with some travel

Minimum Educational Requirements

Associate's degree

Certification or Licensing

Required

Outlook

Much faster than the average

DOT

079

GOE

03.02.01

NOC

3213

O*NET-SOC

29-2056.00

What Does a Veterinary Technician Do?

Veterinary technicians work with veterinarians to assist with the health care of animals. They may work in such settings as animal hospitals, private veterinary clinics, zoos, kennels, horse farms, wildlife sanctuaries, shelters, and research laboratories. Although most veterinary technicians work with domestic animals, some work settings may involve treating exotic animals or endangered species. Veterinary technicians may work with small animals such as dogs and cats at a small animal hospital, or they may work with large animals such as horses, cows, pigs, and sheep at a clinic for farm animals. Often veterinary technicians who work with large farm animals are required to travel to the farm, as these animals are typically treated on site. Some veterinary technicians work in an environment that involves caring for both small and large animals.

During examinations, veterinary technicians often help to restrain the animal and perform routine visit procedures. They may administer injections,

Lingo to Learn

Companion animals Household pets, typically cats and dogs—as opposed to large animals such as farm animals, or exotics such as zoo animals.

Euthanize To kill an animal in a relatively painless way as an act of mercy. Typically done on terminally sick or injured animals.

Feline distemper (panleukopenia) An acute, usually fatal viral disease, especially of cats, characterized by extensive destruction of white blood cells.

Inpatient A patient who is lodged at the hospital or clinic due to surgery or illness.

Necropsy An examination done on a dead animal to determine cause of death.

Outpatient A patient who is treated and released directly after examination.

Parasitosis Infestation or disease caused by parasites. In animals this may include flea infestation, heart worm, lyme disease, tick fever, and many others.

Pathology The study of diseases and the changes produced by them.

clean wounds, apply and change dressings, and clean teeth. Veterinary technicians often talk with the animal's owner and write down information for the animal's file. In many clinics and private practices, it is the veterinary technician who explains treatment and animal care to the owner.

Veterinary technicians assist veterinarians in performing surgery. They prepare the animal for surgery and may be responsible for administering local, regional, or general anesthesia, and for monitoring the animal's vital signs. The veterinarian often asks the technician to provide specific supplies and instruments when needed. In addition, it is often the duty of technicians to monitor sick animals and animals recovering from surgery. In some cases, when an animal is very ill or injured without chance of survival, or in an overcrowded shelter, a veterinary technician may be required to euthanize the animal.

One of the main duties of veterinary technicians is to perform laboratory procedures. Laboratory work may compose up to 50 percent of a veterinary technician's job. This work involves taking samples from an animal's body to look for such problems as parasites, diseases, and infections. Laboratory work may also include assisting the veterinarian with necropsies to determine the cause of an animal's death, as well as taking and developing X rays.

Kate has been researching and studying chronic wasting disease in elk and deer since she began her job at the Colorado Division of Wildlife. The first documented case came in 1981, and since then there has been a serious spread of the disease in Larimer County, Colorado, and southern Wyoming. "We need to know what's causing it and what's spreading it," says Kate. "My goal is to get as much information about the disease as possible."

In some facilities, veterinary technicians are responsible for management and clerical duties. These duties may include recording, replenishing, and maintaining equipment, supply, and pharmaceutical inventories. Veterinary technicians can also schedule appointments, organize patient files, and keep books for billing and payment records.

Some veterinary technicians work in zoos or with wildlife. Because there are only a few zoos in each state and each zoo only employs a few technicians, zoo jobs are highly competitive and the field is difficult to break into. Like veterinary technicians at a clinic or hospital, a zoo or wildlife technician may be responsible for a great deal of laboratory work. However, these technicians typically will not have the duties of explaining treatments to owners, gathering information for the animal's file, or scheduling appointments. Instead, zoo and wildlife technicians may be asked to discuss cases with curators and other zoo professionals. Zoo and wildlife technicians often observe and work with animals in their "habitats," and this involves working outdoors.

Veterinary technicians work in other unexpected or less common settings. These include obedience schools, circuses, the military, and in information systems technology, where information on animals is compiled and provided by a veterinary technician via a computer network.

According to the North American Veterinary Technician Association (NAVTA), "In the past 20 years, veterinary medicine has grown rapidly in sophistication. Now, pet owners expect (and are entitled to) first-class nursing care and state-of-the-art diagnostic testing for household pets, as well as their large animals. To achieve this high level of health care, the veterinarian turns to a new professional—the veterinary technician."

What Is It Like to Be a Veterinary Technician?

Becky Karabinus has worked as a veterinarian technician for 18 years, and she's now head technician at Companion Animal Clinic in Tucson, Arizona. Her workweek runs Monday through Friday, 7:30 A.M. to 3:30 P.M., during which she performs a wide variety of tasks. "The way my day is organized depends partly on whether it's a heavy surgery day or a heavy appointment day. We can have anywhere from two to 15 inpatients and 20 to 25 outpatients a day," says Becky. "This determines whether I spend most of my day in surgery, in the lab, or with patients and their owners."

During a typical outpatient visit, Becky meets with the animal and its owner to discuss the reason for the visit, the owner's concerns, and, in the case of a new patient, the animal's health and history. Becky also performs routine procedures such as weighing animals, cleaning ears, taking temperatures, and clipping nails. Often, the technician is asked to draw blood or give injections. In the case of an injured animal, Becky cleans the wound and applies or changes the dressings. At the end of the visit, an important part of the technician's job is to review treatment instructions with the owner, making sure everything is understood. In addition, technicians at many veterinary clinics phone owners after a visit or a surgery to check on a patient's progress and see if the owners have any concerns.

If there's a surgery scheduled, Becky or another technician preps the animal by shaving and disinfecting the incision area and setting up the intravenous (IV) tube. Becky organizes the needed instruments, and, once in surgery, administers the anesthesia and monitors the animal's vital signs, keeping a close eye on heart rate, blood pressure, and breathing. After the operation, the technician makes certain the animal is coming out of the anesthesia properly. Becky works closely with sick inpatient animals and animals recovering from surgery. "I manage IV fluids and provide comfort and general patient care, such as feeding and medicating."

Two veterinary technicians calm a sheep as a veterinarian draws blood for a test. *(Stephen Ausmus / U.S. Department of Agriculture)*

Wildlife veterinary technicians experience a different kind of workday. Kate Larsen's job can begin as early as 2:00 A.M. "Right after sunrise is the best time to get with the animals," says Kate, "and sometimes we have to travel for hours to where they are. That makes for a pretty long day." The last time Kate went out into the field to work with animals, 80 volunteers accompanied her so they could vaccinate, tag, and draw blood from 13 bighorn sheep. "We're vaccinating against *Pasteurella haemolytica,* a bacteria found in bighorn sheep," says Kate. Once the animals are tagged, the wildlife division where Kate works "tracks them and follows them through the years, learning how they move, what the mortality rate of their lambs are, and how many lambs are born to each ewe."

Kate works with animals in research bins who were bred in captivity for research purposes. Part of

To Be a Successful Veterinary Technician, You Should . . .

- enjoy working with animals
- have a strong stomach
- stay calm and think clearly in emergency situations
- be a good listener
- follow orders well
- be careful, precise, and detail-oriented
- have good communication skills
- be patient
- be compassionate
- have a strong interest and aptitude in science and medicine

her job is to coordinate and manage the collecting, labeling, and handling of lab samples. Because the laboratory where Kate works is small, she sends all her samples out to a veterinary diagnostic lab at Colorado State University in Fort Collins, Colorado.

Like Kate, Becky also spends a large part of her day doing lab work. After collecting a sample, Becky looks at it under a microscope, checking for a variety of diseases, infections, or parasites that could be troubling an animal. Besides collecting and analyzing specimens, Becky X rays patients and develops and stores the radiographic films.

Doing variable research on wild animals and testing domestic animals for disease are two opposite tasks. Before getting a job as a wildlife veterinary technician, Kate worked in a small animal clinic for five years. "A clinic is a very controlled setting," says Kate. "Everything is available for you, people to help hold animals down, anesthesia, a muzzle if you need it. In the wild, you don't have any of that. It's all up to you to work with the animal."

Do I Have What It Takes to Be a Veterinary Technician?

"It may sound corny," Becky says, "but my favorite thing about my job is improving the quality of animals' lives and therefore improving the quality of their owners' lives, too. The bond between owner and patient is really important in veterinary medicine." It is clear that Becky has a great deal of compassion, both for animals and for people. This compassion and caring is vital to the job of veterinary technician.

The bond between owner and patient is really important in veterinary medicine.

However, Becky warns that someone who is simply interested in playing with animals may have a difficult time performing a veterinary technician's duties. "A common misconception is that we play with animals, but we don't do that too much," Becky says. "First, there isn't time, and most of the inpatients just aren't well enough for playing."

Veterinary technicians must be able to work with blood, hypodermic needles, and open wounds and incisions. In addition, the technician must be prepared for emergencies, many of which may be unpleasant and even gory. For this reason, anyone interested in becoming a veterinary technician should have a strong stomach and not wince at the sight of blood or panic in medical emergencies. Even if an animal is badly injured, a veterinary technician must be able to think on his or her feet and remain calm enough to perform the job well. Therefore, an aptitude for science and medicine, in addition to an interest in working with animals, is necessary for this job.

"The hardest part of my job is definitely performing euthanasia," Becky says. "Well," she adds, "it's not always the hardest. There are times when it's the absolute right decision. But it is the hardest in cases where the owners just can't afford the medical care. That's really difficult." Anyone who loves animals but cannot handle unpleasant medical situations will have a difficult time as a veterinary technician.

Veterinary technicians are an important part of a medical team. For example, the typical profile of a private veterinary practice consists of three veterinarians, two technicians, and three other assistants. Because of this, veterinary technicians should be good listeners and communicators, able to follow precise instructions from the veterinarian, and able to discuss cases with owners and other veterinary professionals.

How Do I Become a Veterinary Technician?

"I worked on a farm the entire time I was a teenager," says Becky. "That's how I first got interested in the field. In my work now, of course, and for most veterinary technicians, we come nowhere near cows, but I gained experience working with animals. It actually helped me a lot in college when we did study large animals."

Kate grew up in a small rural town in New Mexico. Her passion was horses, and she rode before she could walk. "When I was 17 years old, our family veterinarian, who I'd known most of my life, needed an assistant. I asked for the job and I got it," says Kate. "I was still in high school, and animals were my first love. I thought I'd end up as an equestrienne, but working with wildlife is my niche. I know that now."

EDUCATION

High School

Because postsecondary education is required for the job, it is important that students interested in becoming veterinary technicians complete high school. While still in high school, aspiring veterinary technicians need to begin building a strong foundation in the sciences, especially chemistry and biology. Not only will these courses provide students with the background needed for postsecondary training, but they will help high school students discover whether they have an aptitude for the field of medicine. For example, if you faint while dissecting a frog or feel woozy during a video on the cardiovascular system, you might want to reconsider your interest in the field of veterinary technology. In addition, health classes are important, as they introduce you to a variety of medical concepts.

It is also important to study mathematics in high school. In college and on the job, technicians use mathematics in a variety of ways, especially when working with pharmaceuticals to make sure an animal is receiving the correct dosage of medicine, and in determining radiation calculations and exposure time of X-rays. You may also want to get experience working with computers, as technicians at many clinics and hospitals use computers in data analysis when helping veterinarians make diagnoses on laboratory specimens.

Since veterinary technicians must communicate with animal owners and other members of the veterinary team and write information in patient charts, good communications skills are important to the job. While in high school, you should take college-preparatory courses in English or language arts.

Postsecondary Training

In 2004 there were 103 accredited veterinary technician education programs in the United States. These programs are accredited by the American Veterinary Medical Association (AVMA) Committee on Veterinary Technician Education and Activities and lead to an associate in applied science or other appropriate degree, with four-year degrees available at some programs. A list of programs is available at http://www.avma.org/navta. The programs can then be contacted directly for application information and entrance requirements. These programs exist in every region of the country. Becky received an associate's degree in veterinary science technology from the State University of New York in Delhi. Kate attended a two-year program at Colorado Mountain College, a community college in Glenwood Springs, Colorado.

Courses in veterinary technician programs are usually taught by veterinarians or veterinary technicians. The instructors in the program are aware of what employers expect technicians to know, and they teach toward these goals. According to the AVMA, "All programs are designed to provide background knowledge and basic skills upon which to build once you graduate, become employed, and begin to learn specific procedures."

The core curriculum of these programs includes fundamentals of chemistry, biological science, communication skills, humanities or liberal arts, and applied mathematics. Within these basics, there are over 20 required areas of study including ethics in veterinary medicine, animal nutrition and feeding, medical terminology, and surgical nursing and assisting, just to name a few. The programs involve reading, lecture, memorization, and test-taking, as well as laboratory sessions and hands-on work with live animals.

Advancement Possibilities

Veterinarians diagnose animal illnesses, treat diseased and injured animals medically and surgically, inoculate animals against diseases, and give advice on the care and breeding of animals.

Zookeepers provide day-to-day care for animals in zoological parks. They prepare diets, clean animal housing or enclosures, and monitor the behavior of the animals. They might also assist in research projects with the animals.

Some employees in veterinary hospitals and other animal care facilities have not completed a two-year AVMA program, but instead gained their experience on the job. These workers usually have the title of *veterinary assistant, animal health assistant, animal attendant,* or *animal caretaker,* among others. However, they are not considered to be veterinary technicians and their duties and salaries typically don't match those of a technician from an accredited program.

CERTIFICATION OR LICENSING

While state rules and regulations for certification of veterinary technicians vary, the AVMA defines a veterinary technician as "a graduate of an AVMA accredited program." Also, all states require veterinary technicians to pass a certification examination before they can practice.

Currently, veterinary technicians must be certified, registered, or licensed in every state except Delaware, Hawaii, Idaho, Montana, New Hampshire, Rhode Island, Utah, Vermont, and Wyoming. Usually, students in an accredited program will take the certification exam at the completion of their studies. However, if students miss the opportunity to take the exam with their class or if working technicians move to another state and must become recertified, it is up to those individuals to find out when and where they can take the test. To do this, individuals should contact the State Board of Veterinary Medical Examiners in the state in which they want to take the exam. When Becky moved to Arizona, she contacted the Arizona State Board of Veterinary Medical Examiners and learned that it administers a registration exam for veterinary technicians once a year. The North American Veterinary Technician Association (NAVTA) may also be contacted for further information on these exams. Depending on the state, the exam may be divided into oral, written, and practical application sections. Once a person has completed the two-year AVMA accredited program and passed the state exam, he or she is eligible to be hired as a veterinary technician.

INTERNSHIPS AND VOLUNTEERSHIPS

"Of course, the most obvious way to gain experience with animals while in high school is to have pets," says Becky. This is probably the easiest way to learn to care for and understand animals. But if a student can't or doesn't have any pets, there are still plenty of opportunities to work with animals before deciding whether or not to enter an AVMA program.

One way to get experience in animal care is through a job, internship, or volunteership. Students who have access to a farm might try getting work there, either in the summer or after school, as Becky did. This experience not only gave Becky an opportunity to work with animals, but it provided her with a headstart once she entered college. "4-H is also a good way to get to work with animals," says Becky. Students in 4-H raise, train, and care for a variety of animals, including farm animals and seeing-eye dogs or other helping dogs. In addition, private veterinary clinics, animal shelters, pet shops, and kennels often accept high school interns or even hire employees to help groom animals, clean cages, and walk boarders.

Who Will Hire Me?

After completing her associate's degree and passing the exam, Becky was hired for her first veterinary technician job, working as a manager on a cattle farm in upstate New York. "I was in charge of maintaining the general health of the animals," says Becky. Becky got this job the way she says that many jobs in her field are found—by word of mouth. "Someone told me about it, I interviewed, and I got the job. Since this job, though, I have worked only in small animal practices." Like Becky, Kate heard about the tech position at Colorado Wildlife Division through word of mouth. Kate worked for five years in a small animal clinic in Loveland, Colorado, before applying to be a wildlife veterinary technician. According to NAVTA, the first job for about 85 percent of graduate veterinary technicians is in private practice, with companion animal practice at the top of the list.

When her husband took a job in Tucson, Arizona, Becky began looking for a technician job there. Since she was new in town, she went through the yellow pages, looking for small animal clinics that were certified by the American Animal Hospital Association (AAHA), a certification that Becky believes reflects the type of clinic she wants to work for. She sent out a resume listing her education and work experience to many of the AAHA clinics in Tucson and received a phone call from Dr. Paula Medler at Companion Animal Clinic. Becky and Dr. Medler set up an interview appointment and shortly afterward, Becky was hired.

Besides finding job openings by word-of-mouth, or sending resumes out to a variety of places, Becky also recommends looking in newspaper classified ads for technician jobs at clinics. These ads may list openings under such categories as "Small Animals," "Animals," "Veterinary Technicians," "Animal Shelters," and others. When Becky moved to Tucson she learned that the Southern Arizona Veterinary Medical Association maintains a list of job openings in the area, and she says that other states and regions have organizations with similar listings. She suggests contacting NAVTA to find out about local technician associations that may list openings and calling state boards of veterinary medicine to find out if they maintain a list or if they know of an organization that does.

Often, college placement offices will assist recent graduates in securing positions as veterinary technicians. Technicians-in-training who have done internships in clinics or hospitals may get hired by these clinics, if space permits, once they have graduated from their program and passed the exam. For this reason, it is wise for student technicians to find summer employment or a school-year internship at a location where they would be interested in working once they graduate.

Technicians who are interested in working in zoos or research facilities should look in specialized publications of the field, such as *Veterinary Technician* and *Journal of Zoo & Wildlife Medicine*. People interested in zoo jobs may also want to contact the Association of Zoo Veterinary Technicians. Technician jobs in zoos, however, are highly competitive and relatively scarce.

Where Can I Go from Here?

Like Becky, who has been doing the job for 18 years, a veterinary technician may have such a love of her work that she chooses to remain in the position as a permanent career. In this case, advancement usually comes in the form of increases in salary and responsibilities. Because of her extensive experience, Becky holds the title of head technician at Companion and has extra responsibilities and benefits because of this. However, the job of veterinary technician also allows for a wide variety of other job advancement possibilities.

Going back to school to receive a bachelor of science degree, a technician can become a *veterinary technologist*. Or, a technician could even attend four years of veterinary school after receiving the B.S. degree to become a *doctor of veterinary medicine* (DVM).

Veterinary technicians may also make a variety of lateral career moves. Technicians may have to receive some supplemental training to make a lateral career move, but these usually do not entail extensive schooling. Lateral moves for a veterinary technician may include careers in veterinary pharmaceutical sales, obedience or assistance animal training, or kennel or pet supply store ownership or management. Veterinary technicians are also hired as instructors by colleges and universities that have veterinary

FYI

Through the 1950s, veterinarians trained their own employees on the job. These employees were often called veterinary assistants.

In the early 1960s, to meet the increasing technical demands of the veterinary field, colleges and universities developed formal academic programs to train veterinary technicians.

technician programs, as consultants with pet food manufacturers, and as agents or adjusters for large-animal insurance companies.

Some technicians may even choose to stay in the field of medicine but leave veterinary science. This move presents the opportunity of training for careers such as hospital laboratory technician, medical researcher, nurse, paramedic, or physician assistant. Through their jobs, veterinary technicians become well acquainted with both animal care and medical science and will find a variety of careers related to one or both of these fields.

What Are the Salary Ranges?

Earnings are generally low for veterinary technicians in private practices and clinics, but pay scales are steadily climbing due to the increasing demand. Better-paying jobs are in zoos and in research. Those fields of practice are very competitive (especially zoos) and only a small percentage of highly qualified veterinary technicians are employed in them.

Most veterinary technicians are employed in private or clinical practice and research. The U.S. Department of Labor reports that the median annual salary for veterinary technicians and technologists was $23,340 in 2003. The lowest paid 10 percent made less than $16,410 annually, and the highest paid 10 percent made more than $34,380 annually. Earnings vary depending on practice setting, geographic location, level of education, and years of experience. Benefits vary and depend on each employer's policies.

Kate's starting salary at the Colorado Division of Wildlife was $27,000 a year, and she was hired with five years of veterinary technician experience. "A wildlife tech is a very specialized field," says Kate. "If you're good, they're willing to pay you a lot to keep you around." In addition to salary, veterinary technicians may receive health benefits, free animal care and boarding, paid vacation, and sick leave, among other benefits. However, these benefits will vary depending upon the employer.

What Is the Job Outlook?

There are currently more than 54,000 veterinary technicians in the United States, and that number is expected to grow over the next decade, as the U.S. Department of Labor predicts much faster than average job growth for veterinary technicians through 2012.

The number of American households with one or more pets is on the rise, creating a need for more veterinary technicians in the companion animal field. An increased concern for animal welfare also means that more technicians will be hired by animal shelters and animal welfare societies. Veterinary medicine is a field that is not usually affected by the economy. In times of recession, people may postpone a large purchase or cut back on personal expenditures, but most people will continue to provide their animals with health care. For this reason, certified veterinary technicians can expect to find job stability.

Wildlife veterinary medicine is predicted to increase in scope and demand. This field used to be in the domain of ecologists. However, as the fields of wildlife and environmental studies grow, experts are discovering a need for veterinary professionals and paraprofessionals in this area.

How Do I Learn More?

PROFESSIONAL ORGANIZATIONS

The following organizations provide information on veterinary technician careers, accredited schools and scholarships, and possible employment:

American Veterinary Medical Association (AVMA)
1931 North Meacham Road, Suite 100
Schaumburg, IL 60173-4360
847-925-8070
avmainfo@avma.org
http://www.avma.org

American Veterinary Society of Animal Behavior
8119 Beechwood Lane
Clinton, MD 20735
drdvm@msn.com
http://www.avma.org/avsab

Association of Zoo Veterinary Technicians
http://www.azvt.org

North American Veterinary Technician Association Inc.
PO Box 224
Battle Ground, IN 47920
765-742-2216
http://www.navta.net

Canadian Veterinary Medical Association
339 Booth Street
Ottawa, Ontario K1R 7K1 Canada
613-236-1162
admin@cvma-acmv.org
http://www.canadianveterinarians.net

BIBLIOGRAPHY

The following is a sampling of materials relating to the professional concerns and development of veterinary technicians:

Battaglia, Andrea M. *Small Animal Emergency and Critical Care: A Manual for the Veterinary Technician*. Philadelphia: W. B. Saunders, 2001.

Jack, Candyce M., Patricia M. Watson, and Mark S. Donovan. *Veterinary Technician's Daily Reference Guide: Canine and Feline*. Philadelphia: Lippincott Williams & Wilkins, 2002.

McBride, Douglas F. *Learning Veterinary Terminology*. 2d ed. St. Louis: Mosby-Year-Book, 2001.

McCurnin, Dennis M., and Joanna M. Bassert, eds. *Clinical Textbook for Veterinary Technicians*. 5th ed. Philadelphia: W. S. Saunders, 2001.

Swope, Robert E., and Julie Rigby. *Opportunities in Veterinary Medicine Careers*. New York: McGraw-Hill, 2001.

WATER AND WASTEWATER TREATMENT PLANT OPERATORS

Definition
Water and wastewater treatment plant operators remove or make harmless the organisms, chemicals, and solid matter in wastewater (sewage). They monitor, operate, and maintain equipment at wastewater treatment plants.

Alternative Job Titles
Treatment operations and maintenance supervisor
Wastewater treatment plant technician

High School Subjects
Biology
Chemistry
Earth science

Personal Skills
Mechanical/manipulative
Technical/scientific

Salary Range
$21,080 to $34,180 to $52,880+

Work Environment
Indoors and outdoors
Primarily one location

Minimum Educational Level
Some postsecondary training

Certification or Licensing
Required by certain states

Outlook
About as fast as the average

DOT
955

GOE
08.06.01

NOC
9424

O*NET-SOC
51-8031.00

Rain had been soaking the California countryside for hours by the time Tim got the call in the night. The chief operator at the wastewater treatment plant was on vacation, the plant was in danger of flooding, and Tim Rhoades was needed immediately.

Tim rushed to the treatment plant inside a runoff dam operated by the U.S. Army Corps of Engineers. He left his car at the top of the dam, near a rowboat he could use to escape the flood if the waters rose much higher. "The flow was so high that our treatment system was backing up," he recalls.

Alone on the job, Tim hurried to begin shutting down the automated equipment, stopping the flow of chemicals, and trying to route the excess water out of the plant. He was relieved when an operator in training arrived to help him, and the two of them worked feverishly to get the situation under control.

A vortex skimmer had malfunctioned and was no longer removing debris from the water. The debris was taking up room, forcing the water to back up even more. Then the river broke its banks and flooded a surrounding area of about 40 acres. Tim and his helper started to take the treatment plant off line, which would allow the water to rush through the facility and continue downstream to the next treatment plant.

They worked through the night while the flood swept past. "The rains finally let up by morning. We were just about ready to finish turning off the flow when the waters receded, and we were able to turn it back on again," Tim says. If he had not been there, the plant would have overflowed, and wastewater would have run across the neighboring countryside.

What Does a Water and Wastewater Treatment Plant Operator Do?

Water from wells, rivers, and streams must be purified before people can drink it, and the water in sewers and other waste disposal systems must be treated before it can be released back into the environment. *Water and wastewater treatment plant operators* protect the environment and their communities by removing solid materials, chemical compounds, and micro-organisms from water or by taking other measures, such as adding chlorine, to render them harmless. They operate and maintain equipment at treatment plants, and they dispose of materials removed from the water. In a few facilities an operator might treat both water and wastewater, but in most plants an operator's duties are specialized.

Operators use meters and gauges to make sure the plant's equipment is operating properly, and they adjust controls or make minor repairs when necessary. They operate devices that feed chemicals into the treatment system, test and adjust the amount of chemicals being added, take samples of water or wastewater, and analyze samples in laboratories. They frequently use computers to monitor equipment, enter and analyze data, keep track of maintenance duties, and write reports.

Treatment plant operators sometimes work under stress to handle emergencies within the plant, such as chlorine gas leaks or oxygen deficiencies. They are trained to use safety equipment and techniques to protect the facility and the public.

The plant where Tim Rhoades now works in Missoula, Montana, processes seven and a half million gallons of water every day. It also treats sludge, sewage that has been processed. Unlike some small communities, which might have open sewage lagoons, Missoula has a fairly complex, automated treatment plant that routes wastewater through giant, enclosed tanks; the workers almost never come into contact with raw sewage. The sewage goes through a series of steps. Coarse materials are allowed to settle out of the wastewater, and material that floats, such as grease, is also removed. Bacteria are used to eat certain substances, and the operators at the plant expect that in the future they will be using more bacteria instead of chemicals to treat wastewater.

The plant operators at this facility cooperate with *maintenance mechanics*, who help keep the machinery running, and *laboratory technicians*, who analyze samples. There is a *pretreatment coordinator*, who oversees the materials that businesses may dispose of in the city sewer. There are also *collection system crew workers* who use high-powered jets of water to clean the city's 225 miles of sewer lines every two years. Treatment plant operators may also work with engineers, chemists, helpers, and supervisors.

Lingo to Learn

Gravity line A pipe elevated at the end farthest from the sewer, so gravity pulls the sewage downhill into the treatment plant.

Lagoon An open pond where sewage is treated and purified, often by natural processes.

Leach field A set of pipes protruding from a treatment system or septic system to distribute purified water into the ground.

Lift station A device with a pump that lifts sewage up from a low place in the sewer line to a higher line. The sewage then flows toward the treatment plant under the force of gravity.

Sludge Processed sewage that contains less water and a higher percentage of solids than raw sewage.

What Is It Like to Be a Water and Wastewater Treatment Plant Operator?

Tim Rhoades has worked as a water and wastewater treatment plant operator in Missoula for five years and has been in the trade since 1974. "I've enjoyed it all along," he says. "It's nice to be on a team, everybody working together and protecting the health of the community."

It's nice to be on a team, everybody working together and protecting the health of the community.

Tim's supervisor and chief wastewater treatment plant operator, Starr Sullivan, agrees: "One of the reasons I've stayed in this job is I'm doing something important. The better the job you do, the cleaner the water that goes in the river. I feel like a true environmentalist." He points out that legislators can pass laws to protect the environment and the community, but it's really the people at treatment plants who keep the water clean.

Starr supervises a crew of five other operators. The plant runs day and night, and usually two operators are on duty, but sometimes one of them works alone. Occasionally Tim works with the street crew that cleans clogged sewer lines throughout the city. Once, during a serious flood, he had to use pumps and a jet truck to clean culverts. Most of his time is spent at the treatment facility, however.

Tim arrives for work by 7:30 in the morning and begins each day by checking the oil levels on the equipment, noting any abnormal vibrations, and watching for any other indications of a malfunction. He takes flow meter readings and spends time mopping and waxing floors, hosing algae and other materials off the tanks, and cleaning his work area. "That's part of the job here, keeping things looking good," he says. In some plants the operators even mow the lawns.

Tim takes samples of the water and sludge; this must be done at the same time every day to ensure scientific stability, since temperature and other factors vary as the day goes on. He takes the samples to the plant's laboratory and performs various tests to determine how well the automated equipment is processing the wastewater. Some tests use gravity or a centrifuge to let solids settle out of the water so they can be measured and analyzed. Others involve using an oven to dry the sample, which is then analyzed. Laboratory analysis, like many of Tim's duties, requires mathematics to calculate quantities and other data.

Every day, Tim uses a sophisticated phase-contrast microscope to identify bacteria in the samples. Sometimes he places small samples on microscope slides and uses special stains to detect phosphorus and to identify the properties of the bacteria. He can tell what the condition of the sewage is by analyzing which types of bacteria are in it and in what quantities. This part of Tim's job requires a knowledge of microbiology and chemistry. At the Missoula plant, state-certified laboratory technicians perform chemical tests on the samples, but Tim has worked at smaller facilities where chemical tests were also part of his duties.

Beyond their routine duties, the plant's operators handle unusual situations that sometimes arise. If there is a flood, groundwater can overload the system, although that has not been a major problem yet. Sometimes Tim does receive an urgent call to handle a crisis at work, usually because of equipment failure or a power outage.

Sometimes the plant operators even help solve a mystery. A substance that is not supposed to be dumped into the city sewer might show up in the samples, and the operators work with the county health department to follow the substance upstream and discover who is pouring it down the drain. In that situation, Starr investigates businesses and often finds that a dry cleaning company is the culprit, although many industries generate wastes that can cause problems at the treatment plant.

"Dry cleaners use particularly nasty products. It can be a problem," Starr says. "Sometimes, once you discover it, it's already through. You try to educate people to clean their grease traps and their sand and oil interceptors. Most people are pretty cooperative."

Do I Have What It Takes to Be a Water and Wastewater Treatment Plant Operator?

To be a water and wastewater treatment plant operator, you need to be responsible, be able to work without much supervision, have mechanical ability, and be willing to work various shifts, since treatment plants operate around the clock. As a supervisor, Starr reads numerous trade magazines and other publications to keep up with changing regulations. In contrast, Tim does little reading, because the regulations that apply to his part of the job change less often.

Being a supervisor is Starr's least favorite part of the job. "I've never asked for it. It's always been given to me," he says.

"I like the technical aspects and the physical challenges," he adds. "You have to be physically able." For example, an operator might need to reach up and turn six-inch valves or carry heavy buckets up stairs. The job involves stooping, lifting, and climbing.

An operator also needs to be in good health, since there is danger of exposure to hepatitis and other diseases. "There's definitely a biohazard, but there are precautions we take," Starr says. "For people who are prone to illness or who have immune problems, this would probably not be a good choice of jobs. When I first got into this, I've never been so sick in my entire life." He says that operators who have been in the business fall into the habit of constantly washing their hands and taking other steps to avoid contracting diseases.

Workers can also fall off ladders, slip on wet floors, inhale toxic gases, and be injured by malfunctioning equipment. The collection system crews who clean the city sewer lines run a risk when they do a "confined-space entry," going into the sewer through a manhole. "In this business that's one of the leading causes of death, because of lack of oxygen and fumes," Starr notes. Treatment plant operators rarely participate in that type of duty, however.

How Do I Become a Water and Wastewater Treatment Plant Operator?

Tim Rhoades says you can work your way up in this field with a little schooling and a significant amount of on-the-job experience, or you can have more schooling and a little practical experience. Tim took the first route.

In high school he had a part-time job driving a flower delivery truck, and he decided to take some college courses in horticulture and become a florist. It was a difficult occupation. He comments, "You never knew what was going to happen from one day to the next. I wanted something with a little more stability." He tried working as a mechanic for a police department, then applied for an opening in a wastewater treatment plant in California when he was about 23 years old. He has been in the field more than 20 years.

Like Tim, Starr Sullivan did not plan to enter in the field but has been a plant operator for about 20 years. He holds a degree in graphic and fine arts. He knew someone who worked at a wastewater treatment plant, and he accepted a job there, thinking he would earn some money and move on. "I had no intention of staying," he recalls.

EDUCATION

High School

Starr notes, "Right now you absolutely have to have a high school diploma" or GED to become a water and wastewater treatment plant operator. He predicts that it will soon be necessary to hold at least an associate's degree to work in this field.

To prepare for a career as a plant operator, you should study chemistry, biology, mathematics, mechanics, and computers. Shop classes will help you assess your mechanical aptitude and learn how to work with tools and machines. Environmental studies are also beneficial.

To Be a Successful Water and Wastewater Treatment Plant Operator, You Should . . .

- be responsible
- be in good physical condition
- be in good health
- have mechanical ability
- be able to do mathematics
- be able to work with little supervision

Postsecondary Training

Tim studied horticulture at a junior college but did not earn a degree. Now he wishes he had taken more classes to help him prepare for a career in wastewater treatment. "I would have liked to have had an associate's degree in this field, but the circumstances wouldn't allow it," he says. Tim needs no degree for his job in Missoula, but he says an associate's degree is a prerequisite for obtaining certain licenses in some states, such as California and New York, and some employers even prefer to hire workers who hold engineering degrees.

During his first year of work at a wastewater treatment plant, Tim attended night classes at a technical college for about six months. "It wasn't bad," he says, but the classes were not easy. "This job is not easy. You have to know mathematics. You have to be able to read and write and keep logs and records."

Classes at community colleges, junior colleges, and vocational or technical schools typically cover water pollution control and other scientific and engineering subjects. Many of these schools offer two-year programs that lead to an associate's degree in water technology or wastewater technology and one-year programs that lead to certification in the field.

Many operators learn their trade through on-the-job training instead of college. They typically work under the supervision of experienced workers at first, learning to collect samples, record meter readings, and maintain electric motors, pumps, and other equipment. At larger plants they usually also complete classroom courses or independent studies.

FYI

Ground water, which fills in the pores in the soil beneath the earth's surface, is a valuable resource that is easily contaminated by such things as septic tanks systems, household chemicals, and salt from roads. The Water Environment Foundation offers the following tips you can follow to help preserve the quality of ground water:

- If you have a septic system, pump it out every one to three years.
- Apply the minimum pesticides and fertilizers when caring for your lawn.
- Replace any leaking underground storage tank on your property.
- If you have a well, test it for contaminants regularly.

Continuing education, which is mandatory to retain certification, is usually done at colleges or vocational or technical schools. In most states, agencies that control drinking water and water pollution offer training to help treatment plant operators improve their skills and broaden their knowledge. These programs cover topics such as treatment processes, laboratory procedures, safety, chlorination, sedimentation, biological treatment, sludge treatment and disposal, and management skills. Correspondence courses are also available.

CERTIFICATION AND LICENSING

The Safe Drinking Water Amendments of 1996, enforced by the Environmental Protection Agency, specify national minimum standards for certification and recertification of operators of water plants. Plant operators must therefore pass an examination to verify their competency. Most states also require that operators participate in continuing education to maintain their certification.

In most states there are various levels of certification, based on the operator's experience and training and on the size of the treatment plant. In Montana operators can obtain certification by accumulating two years of experience, or they can attend a technical school, for example, and receive operator-in-training certificates. Because the state awards only two levels of certification, Tim and Starr hold the same credential, although Tim is an operator and Starr is a chief operator.

In California, Tim says, there are five levels: attendant/trainee, operator, assistant chief operator, chief operator, and superintendent. To obtain an operator-in-training certification in California, you need only be working at a treatment plant. The certification is valid for one year, until you become eligible to take the more advanced certification examination. With most employers you have about two years to pass the examination, or you lose your job.

If you relocate, you might have to pass an examination to be recertified, but most states do accept certification from other states.

INTERNSHIPS AND VOLUNTEERSHIPS

High school students can sometimes find part-time or summer employment at wastewater treatment plants, but these positions are hard to find. It is not common to complete an internship or to volunteer in water and wastewater treatment. Experience in a machine shop would help you learn to work with tools and machinery.

LABOR UNIONS

Labor unions negotiate standard wages, raises, and benefits for their members. Many plant operators belong to unions for government employees. The workers at the Missoula treatment plant belong to the Montana Public Employees Association.

Who Will Hire Me?

Tim Rhoades entered the wastewater treatment profession by applying for an opening at a treatment plant in California. He took night classes while working at the attendant level for a year, then earned his operator's certification and has worked at that level ever since.

Starr Sullivan says it's probably easiest to find an entry-level job at a large treatment plant with a sizable team of workers who must know how to perform only specific tasks. At a small plant, there are fewer workers, and each of them must know how to perform a broad range of tasks.

Most treatment plant operators work for local governments. Some work for the federal government, utility companies, or independent contractors that perform sanitary work or provide water for local governments. (Many of these positions require that the applicant take the civil service examination.) Others are employed by industries, such as manufacturing, that generate wastewater. About half of the 99,000 treatment plant operators in the United States work in water treatment plants, and half work in wastewater treatment.

Starr says the demand for water and wastewater treatment plant operators does not vary much by geographic location: "I think the opportunities are pretty much the same anywhere." There are more opportunities in large cities, because urban areas generate more wastewater and require more drinking water. In small towns a plant operator is more likely to work part-time or be responsible for additional duties not related to water treatment.

Openings are listed on the Internet and in the classified advertisements in local newspapers. The Water Environment Federation (http://www.wef.org) posts job listings on its Web site.

Where Can I Go from Here?

Tim has been a plant operator for about 20 years and does not expect to advance in his job unless Starr leaves. That is not apt to happen, since the plant is one of the highest rated in the state. Advancement is difficult in a municipality, because the work force is relatively stable; an operator has to wait for someone to move or retire. Some positions do become available when new facilities are opened, however.

Starr worked for seven years without advancing beyond plant operator, although he did eventually become a supervisor. One reason he moved from Salt Lake City to Missoula, about nine years ago, was because the new job was a step up. After 19 years on the job, he is now the treatment operations and maintenance supervisor and chief wastewater treatment plant operator at a facility rated at the highest level of complexity.

The plant in Missoula was in a sorry state when Starr took over. Employees were filing grievances, the local newspaper kept writing negative articles because the facility was exceeding the pollution levels allowed on its permit, and some of the plant's employees were even having fist fights. "When I first got here, this was a nut house," Starr recalls. "I didn't know what I was going to do. It was management and process control problems. But this is a good place to work now."

Although Starr is not likely to leave his job, he does have several other options within the Missoula plant. He could become a maintenance mechanic, pretreatment coordinator, or laboratory technician. He could also join the collections system crew that cleans the city sewer lines.

To become a plant superintendent at a small facility, an operator needs experience and some postsecondary training. At a larger plant a bachelor's degree in science or engineering might be required.

Many plant operators return to school to study engineering. This makes them attractive to companies that are having communication problems between engineers and management. Starr says those two types of workers tend to speak almost in different languages, and companies are frequently willing to pay a substantial salary to someone who can communicate with and relate to both sides.

An operator also might be hired as a technician by a state drinking water or water pollution control agency. Technicians monitor and provide technical assistance to plants throughout the state. Training from a vocational-technical school or community college is usually required for technician jobs.

What Are the Salary Ranges?

Starr Sullivan makes about $35,000 a year and could earn much more if he worked in a large city. "Salaries are going up pretty rapidly. The money varies, depending on the unions and the size and complexity of the treatment plant," he says. Operators at the Missoula plant are unionized and start at about $14 an hour, or about $29,000 annually, with cost-of-living raises each year. "That's not bad for a blue-collar job," Starr comments.

Operators who return to school to study engineering can expect significantly higher salaries. "They earn a lot more money. I know one guy that probably makes more than the engineers he works with," Starr says.

Advancement Possibilities

Plant supervisors and superintendents oversee the general operation and administration of water and wastewater treatment plants. They supervise various employees, including plant operators.

Pretreatment coordinators enforce and administer regulations regarding what materials can be disposed of in sewer systems. They deal mostly with businesses, finding out which facilities are connected to the sewer system and what substances they are pouring down their drains. For example, a pretreatment coordinator might make sure a restaurant has a grease trap and that an automotive garage has a sand and oil interceptor.

Laboratory technicians test samples of water and sludge to measure suspended solids, bacteria such as E. coli, and nutrients such as phosphorus, nitrates, and ammonia. They monitor environmental concerns by determining how much oxygen the effluents use as they enter the river. They also conduct internal tests for quality control.

According to the U.S. Bureau of Labor Statistics, the median annual salary for water and wastewater treatment plant operators was $34,180 in 2003. The lowest 10 percent earned less than $21,080; the middle 50 percent earned about $26,520 to $43,040; and the top 10 percent earned more than $52,880. Salaries vary depending on the size of the facility and the number of employees the operator supervises.

At the Missoula plant, operators receive health insurance, a retirement plan, sick leave, and paid vacations. Life insurance and reimbursement for the cost of continuing education are also common benefits for workers in this field.

What Is the Job Outlook?

Opportunities in water and wastewater treatment are expected to increase about as fast as the average for all occupations through 2012. The population and economy will probably continue to grow, and so will the demand for water and wastewater treatment.

This is a stable occupation that is not affected much by economic ups and downs, since people always need drinking water, and the law mandates that cities must provide wastewater treatment. Workers in this field are rarely laid off, and competition for available jobs tends to be relatively low. "If you're good at your job, you're pretty much guaranteed a job," Starr notes.

"It's a good-paying job, steady work," Tim agrees. He adds that, even though the basic processes are the same, the field is changing as new technology and techniques are developed. In the near future, he says, treatment plants will be making more use of bacteria to break down the materials in wastewater. Operators will need to know biology and be able to comprehend new ideas as they come out. They will be part of a national effort to safeguard the environment.

"We're protecting the waterways. It's really important to the aquatic life," he notes. Starr recalls that, when he first entered this field, most people put it at the bottom of the list of what they would want to do for a living. Now, he says, it's much more technical and challenging, and it is perceived as an admirable occupation, a job many people would like to do.

Most treatment plants are operated by governmental or pseudo-governmental entities, such as city departments of public works. Many industries also generate wastewater, however, often as a by-product of a manufacturing process. Increasingly, these businesses are being required to purify their water before releasing it into the environment or into municipal sewer systems. This should create additional jobs for treatment plant operators. There will also be abundant job opportunities with private firms that operate and manage water and wastewater treatment facilities on a contract basis.

How Do I Learn More?

PROFESSIONAL ORGANIZATIONS

The following organizations provide information on water and wastewater treatment plant careers, accredited schools and scholarships, and possible employment:

American Water Works Association
6666 West Quincy Avenue
Denver, CO 80235
303-794-7711
http://www.awwa.org

Office of Ground Water and Drinking Water
Ariel Rios Building
1200 Pennsylvania Avenue, NW
Washington, DC 20460-0003
http://www.epa.gov/OGWDW

Water Environment Federation
601 Wythe Street
Alexandria, VA 22314-1994
800-666-0206
http://www.wef.org

BIBLIOGRAPHY

The following is a sampling of materials relating to the professional concerns and development of water and wastewater treatment plant operators:

Edwards, Joseph D. *Industrial Wastewater Treatment: A Guidebook*. Boca Raton, Fla.: CRC Press, 1995.

Letterman, Raymond D., and Larry W. Mays, eds. *Water Quality and Treatment Handbook,* 5th edition. Columbus, Ohio: McGraw-Hill, 1999.

Nathanson, Jerry A. *Basic Environmental Technology: Water Supply, Waste Management, and Pollution Control*. 3d ed. Upper Saddle River, N.J.: Prentice Hall, 1999.

Stephenson, Ralph L., and James B. Blackburn, eds. *The Industrial Wastewater Systems Handbook*. Boca Raton, Fla.: CRC Press, 1997.

WIRELESS SERVICE TECHNICIANS

"Ninety percent of my job is outside," says field technician Matthew Shaud. His company provides him with a 4x4 truck in order to gain access to some of the remote locations where cell sites are located. "During the winter months here in Pennsylvania, it can be really challenging to get to where your problem is. We have snowmobiles just for those types of situations."

Once Matthew arrives at his location, he still may be subjected to the elements. "You're basically going into a wood shack," he says. These sheds house the equipment Matthew must maintain to keep pager customers connected. "It's not heated too well. You've got the flipside in the summer—the heat, the bugs, the snakes." Contrasted with these settings are some of the multi-thousand-dollar tools Matthew uses, such as a communications systems analyzer that allows him to track signals.

Definition
Wireless service technicians maintain a specified group of cell sites, including the radio towers, cell site equipment, and often the building and grounds for the sites. Technicians routinely visit and monitor the functioning of the on-site equipment, performing preventive testing and maintenance. They are also responsible for troubleshooting and remedying problems that might arise with any of their sites.

Alternative Job Titles
Cell site technicians
Field technicians

High School Subjects
Computer science
Mathematics

Personal Skills
Mechanical/manipulative
Technical/scientific

Salary Range
$28,380 to $45,390 to $66,810+

Work Environment
Indoors and outdoors
Primarily multiple locations

Minimum Educational Level
Associate's degree

Certification or Licensing
Voluntary

Outlook
About as fast as the average

DOT
722

GOE
05.02.01

NOC
2147, 7246

O*NET-SOC
49-2022.00, 49-2022.03

What Does a Wireless Service Technician Do?

Wireless service technicians are sometimes also called *cell site technicians, field technicians,* or *cell site engineers.* These workers maintain cell sites—which consist of a radio tower and computerized equipment. Each cell site covers a geographic territory which varies in size. When a wireless call is made by someone within a particular cell site's geographic territory, radio waves are transmitted to that cell site's antenna. The antenna picks up the radio waves and transmits them through cables to computerized equipment that is typically located in a building adjacent to the antenna. This equipment then "reads" the radio waves, turns them into a computerized code, and sends the information on to a "switching center." At the switching center, the call is transferred to its destination—which might be another wireless phone or a traditional, wireline phone.

The equipment at each cell site—the antenna and computerized equipment—are important pieces of the wireless telecommunications network. If a cell site stops functioning for some reason, wireless users within that site's coverage area may not be able to use their mobile phones. Since many people rely heavily on these devices, a lapse in coverage can be very serious. Wireless service technicians are responsible for maintaining and troubleshooting the equipment and operations of the cell sites. The majority of cellular communication is currently voice transmissions. However, wireless service is increasingly being used to transmit data, such as Internet access. The data transmission equipment may be a separate, peripheral part of the cell site equipment, and the technician is responsible for maintaining it as well.

Wireless service technicians typically perform both routine, preventive maintenance and troubleshooting of equipment that has malfunctioned. Routine maintenance might include scheduled visits to each cell site to check power levels and computer functions. Technicians often carry laptop computers, which contain sophisticated testing software. By connecting their laptop computers to the cell site equipment, technicians can test to make sure the equipment is functioning as it should. Wireless carriers may also have backup equipment, such as generators and batteries, at their cell sites, to ensure that even if the primary system fails, wireless coverage is still maintained. Technicians may periodically check this backup equipment to make sure it is functional and ready to be used in case of emergency. In addition to maintaining the actual cell site computer equipment, wireless service technicians may be responsible for routine and preventive maintenance of the radio tower itself, and the building and grounds of the site. In many cases, technicians do not perform the actual physical maintenance on the tower and grounds themselves. Rather, they contract with other service providers to do so and are then responsible for ensuring that the work meets appropriate standards and is done when needed.

The frequency of the scheduled visits to individual cell sites depends upon the technician's employer and the number of sites the technician is responsible for. For example, a technician who is responsible for 10 to 15 sites might be required to visit each site monthly to perform routine, preventive maintenance. In some cases, these sites may be very near each other—perhaps within blocks of each other. In other cases, in less populated areas, the sites may be more than 20 miles apart.

When cell site equipment malfunctions, wireless service technicians are responsible for identifying the problem and making sure that it is repaired. The technicians must isolate the problem—it may be a service outage from the weather, an equipment failure, an antenna problem, or a security breach. Technicians run diagnostic tests on the equipment to determine where the malfunction is. If the problem is one that can be easily solved—for example, by replacing a piece of equipment—the technician handles it. If it is something more serious, such as a problem with the antenna or with the local wireline telecommunications system, the technician calls the appropriate service people to remedy the situation.

In addition to routine maintenance and troubleshooting responsibilities, wireless service technicians may have a range of other duties. They may test the wireless system by driving around the coverage area while using a mobile phone. They may work with technicians in the switching center to incorporate new cell sites into the network and make sure that the wireless calls are smoothly transmitted from one cell to another.

What Is It Like to Be a Wireless Service Technician?

Matthew Shaud is a field technician based in Harrisburg, Pennsylvania, and his work entails the installation and maintenance of paging transmitters and their related infrastructure. "I have a territory," he says. "It's about a 10-county area, of about 36 to 40 sites. You go up into the mountains and you'll see a radio tower with a building at the bottom of it. I'll have my equipment in one of those buildings. Each one has a phone line that has to work, so you can have dial-up communications with your equipment. That has to be maintained, as well as the electrical."

Sometimes accessing the sites can be the most difficult aspect of the job. Matthew has been assigned a company truck to handle the trek to some remote locations. "Basically I get paid to go four-wheeling," he says. He's been known to get stuck, get a flat tire, and has even had to leave the truck behind and use a snowmobile. "The company rents from site owners," he says. "We don't have any radio towers or anything like that, we just rent space on them. Sometimes the site is actually on the owner's property. We have a lease, and 24-hour access."

In addition to the truck, Matthew is assigned basic hand tools, as well as a personal computer that allows him to link directly to the company's transmitter. "I have a communications systems analyzer," he says, "which I use to determine the integrity of the square wave of my transmit signal. It's like a scanner with a TV screen on it, so you can look at your signal, see how it's going through the air, and the modulations." His company has also been experimenting with using two-way pagers. "I have a pager with a full keyboard. You can send and receive emails from the palm of your hand."

Most of the time, Matthew is on his own out in the field. He does have some help with installations,

Lingo to Learn

Cell site The base station antenna and other transmission and reception equipment that connects a wireless device (cell phone or pager) to the network.

Cellular Wireless communication used for mobile phones.

Decibel Measurement expressing the difference in power or intensity of sound.

Landline Traditional wired telephone service.

Paging A wireless device feature allowing for the reception of an alphanumeric message.

PCS Personal communication services. A wireless system generally using all digital technology and a different radio frequency than cell phones.

RF Radio frequency; a radio signal.

and he calls someone in if repair involves climbing the tower. Matthew starts his day by checking in at the office and dialing into monitoring sites to make sure all his transmitters are working. "But basically I hit the road," he says. "Some weeks I drive 1,500 miles, and that's in my own market." In some situations, such as in the event of a damaging storm, Matthew may be out in the field visiting multiple sites. "I'd be out there working to get them all fixed. I'm paid by the hour, so I don't mind that at all."

Matthew can't always plan what his workday will be like. "When I go into the office tomorrow, I don't know what I could be doing. My supervisor may say, 'I need you to drive here to look at this, the phone line's not working here,' or 'This site's off the air, I need you to go out and fix it.'"

Every time Matthew goes to a site to perform maintenance, he must fill out reports via the Internet. "You have to have a good grasp on RF theory and transmission," he says. "You have to know quite a bit about satellite communications as well, because these sites have a 1.2 meter downlink dish. It has a receiver and a dish, and you have to know how to align the dish. If you go to a site and, say, the dish has to be 228 degrees from North at a 33 degree elevation, and all you have is a compass, you have to know how to do it." In some cases, however, solving a problem may require simply making a phone call. "I'm on the phone with the phone companies all the time reporting lines down."

Do I Have What It Takes to Be a Wireless Service Technician?

The ability to work independently is one of the most important characteristics of a good wireless service technician. Most technicians work on their own, traveling from site to site and performing their duties with little or no supervision. They have to have the discipline and self-motivation to make their own schedules and set their own priorities. It is also important that technicians be highly reliable. They are often responsible for very expensive equipment at the cell sites.

"Time management is the key to keeping on top of things," Matthew says. "You have to learn to juggle things so that you're not sitting at home at night filling out reports." Matthew says that patience is also important, both for the various site owners you have to deal with, and for the waiting around that the work can require. "I had a phone call today that was 22 minutes, just to report a phone line that didn't work."

You have to learn to juggle things so that you're not sitting at home at night filling out reports

The willingness to learn and to adapt to change is another key personality trait of successful wireless service technicians. The job is a constant learning process, with technology that is frequently changing.

Finally, because so much of the job involves traveling between cell sites, it is vital that a technician have a valid driver's license and good driving record.

How Do I Become a Wireless Service Technician?

Matthew holds an associate's degree in electronics engineering technology from ITT Technical

Institute. His company also pays for him to attend ongoing training offered by the manufacturers of the radio equipment he services. To prepare for this line of work, Matthew advises students to develop strong math skills, and to learn what they can about electrical theory.

EDUCATION

High School

If you are interested in pursuing a career as a wireless service technician, you should take high school classes that will prepare you for further schooling in electronics. Physics classes will provide the background necessary to understand the theory of electronics. Because wireless service technicians jobs are so heavily computer-oriented, computer classes are also excellent choices. You should have a strong understanding of data communications, DOS, and Windows. Other important classes are those which will provide you with the basic abilities needed both in college and in the workplace—such as English, speech, and mathematics courses.

Postsecondary Training

A two-year associate's degree in a technical field is the minimum educational level needed to become a wireless service technician. Many technicians obtain degrees in electronics or electronic technology. For these degrees, coursework would likely include both classes and laboratory work in circuit theory, digital electronics, microprocessors, computer troubleshooting, telecommunications, and data communications technology. Other students might opt for degrees in telecommunications management or computer science. Students working toward a telecommunications degree might take classes on such subjects as local area networks, advanced networking technologies, network management, and programming. Computer science courses might include such topics as programming, operating systems, computer languages, and network architecture. Although most wireless service technicians have two-year degrees, some may have four-year degrees in computer science, telecommunications, electronic engineering, or other, similar subjects.

Other wireless service technicians may have military training in electronics or telecommunications.

To Be a Successful Wireless Service Technician, You Should . . .

- have the ability to work independently
- be highly reliable
- be able to set priorities and manage your time
- be willing to learn and adapt to change
- have a valid driver's license and a good driving record

No matter what sort of educational background new technicians have, they have to learn about the specific equipment used by their employers. Most wireless carriers send their technicians through formal education programs, which are typically offered by equipment manufacturers. In these programs, new technicians learn the operating specifics of the equipment they will be maintaining. A new technician is usually given a smaller number of cell sites to manage when he or she first begins and may be paired with a more experienced technician who can answer questions and conduct on-the-job training.

CERTIFICATION AND LICENSING

Though no standardized certification is required for wireless service technicians, a few organizations do offer some credentialing. The Electronics Technicians Association offers the title of Wireless Communication Electronics Technician to those who demonstrate knowledge of RF transmitting and receiving systems. The National Association of Radio and Telecommunications Engineers offers certification to technicians who design and install wireless systems that don't have to be licensed by the FCC (see "Sources of Additional Information").

Who Will Hire Me?

There are dozens of wireless service providers, both large and small, all over the United States. Anywhere that there is wireless service—that is, anywhere that you can use a cellular phone—there is a cell site, owned and maintained by a wireless provider.

Some of the largest wireless providers are T-Mobile, Nextel Communications, and Verizon Wireless. Many companies maintain a listing of available jobs on their Web site or provide a phone number you can call to find out about current openings.

In addition to these major players, there are smaller wireless carriers sprinkled throughout the United States in virtually every medium-sized and large community. You should be able to find a list of them by asking your local librarian for help or by doing a keyword search on "wireless service providers" on the Internet.

Another possibility is to browse through wireless industry publications, such as *RCR News* (Radio Communications Record), *Wireless Week, Telephony,* and *Wireless Review.*

Another way to find your first wireless technician's job is to look for and attend technical job fairs, expos, or exchanges. Because technically and technologically skilled employees are so much in demand, communities frequently have events to allow employers to network with and meet potential employees. Watch local newspapers for similar events in your community. Finally, an excellent source of job leads will be your college's placement office. Many wireless companies visit schools that offer the appropriate degree programs to recruit qualified students for employees. Some companies even offer a co-op program, in which they hire students on a part-time basis while they are still in school.

Where Can I Go from Here?

"I started out in this company working in pager repair," Matthew says, "an entry-level job. I made supervisor, then an opening came up in engineering."

In some companies, a natural path of advancement for a wireless service technician is becoming a *switch technician* or *switch engineer.* The switch technician works at the "switching center," which controls the routing of the wireless phone calls. The switching center is the brains of the operation, so a switch person needs to have a broader understanding of the system and may also have cell site experience.

Another avenue of advancement might be to move into system performance. *System performance workers* strive to maximize the performance of the wireless system. They run tests and make adjustments to ensure that the system is providing the best possible coverage in all areas and that signals from the different cell sites do not interfere with each other.

Advancement Possibilities

Switch technicians work at "switching centers," which control the routing of the wireless phone calls.

System performance workers run tests and make adjustments to ensure that the system is providing the best possible coverage in all areas and that signals from the different cell sites do not interfere with each other.

What Are the Salary Ranges?

According to the *Occupational Outlook Handbook,* electrical and electronics engineering technicians had median annual earnings of $45,390 in 2003. Those in the lowest 10 percent earned less than $28,380, while those in the highest 10 percent earned more than $66,810.

The job generally comes with other benefits as well. Many wireless companies provide their service technicians with company vehicles. Cellular phones and laptop computers, which technicians need to perform their work, are also common perks. Finally, most major wireless service providers offer a benefits package to their employees, which often includes health insurance, paid vacation, holidays, and sick days, and a pension or 401(k) plan.

What Is the Job Outlook?

Job opportunities for wireless service technicians are expected to grow about as fast as the average for all other occupations through 2012, despite a predicted slow-down of growth in the telecommunications industry overall. The main reason for the increase in jobs for wireless service technicians is the growth of the number of cellular service users. According to the Cellular Telecommunications Industry Association

(CTIA), the international association for the wireless telecommunications industry, in December 2004 there were more than 182 million wireless users worldwide—an increase of more than 23.4 million from 2003. And this growth is only expected to continue.

There are several reasons for this growth in wireless users. Perhaps the most significant is the steady decrease in prices for cellular service. Since 1988, the average monthly bill for wireless service has gone from approximately $100 to approximately $45, according to the Cellular Telecommunications Industry Association. A second reason for the growth in users is that coverage areas are increasingly broad and comprehensive. As more and more cell sites are added, more and more areas of the United States have cellular service. Areas that previously had no wireless service are being covered—and consequently, more people have access to and use for cellular phones and pagers.

A third factor in the growth is the continuous improvement in cellular phones and services due to technological advances. One recent innovation is a microwave-based digital communication technology called personal communications services (PCS). PCS is expected to increase wireless phone use by offering better quality and range. New technologies are also increasingly allowing people to transmit data as well as voice over wireless connections. Examples of wireless data communication include such applications as faxing and Internet access. Pagers and cell phones are also developing into handheld computers with more complex operations and even more usefulness.

In addition to the growing number of wireless customers, recent years have also seen an increase in wireless companies. This growth was spurred by the Federal Communications Commission's partial deregulation of the industry in 1993, which allowed for as many as nine carriers in a geographic market. This competition has added a large number of technicians' jobs, and is expected to continue to do so.

How Do I Learn More?

PROFESSIONAL ORGANIZATIONS

For information about certification, contact

Electronics Technicians Association International
5 Depot Street
Greencastle, IN 46135
800-288-3824
eta@eta-i.org
http://www.eta-i.org

For job postings, links to wireless industry recruiters, industry news, and training information, contact or visit the following Web site:

Cellular Telecommunications Industry Association
1400 16th Street, NW, Suite 600
Washington, DC 20036
202-785-0081
http://www.wow-com.com

For information on certification, contact

The National Association of Radio and Telecommunications Engineers
167 Village Street
Medway, MA 02053
508-533-8333
http://www.narte.org

For the latest on the wireless industry and job information, contact

Wireless Industry Association
9746 Tappenbeck Drive
Houston, TX 77055
800-624-6918
http://wirelessdealers.com

BIBLIOGRAPHY

The following is a sampling of materials relating to the professional concerns and development of wireless service technicians:

Dodd, Annabel Z. *The Essential Guide to Telecommunications*. 3d ed. Upper Saddle River, N.J.: Prentice Hall, 2001.

Gross, Lynne Schafer. *Telecommunications: An Introduction to Electronic Media*, 7th ed. Columbus, Ohio: McGraw Hill Higher Education, 1999.

Harte, Lawrence, Steve Kellogg, Richard Dreher, and Tom Schaffnit. *The Comprehensive Guide to Wireless Technologies*. Fuquay-Varina, N.C.: APDG Publishing, 2000.

Miceli, Andrew. *Wireless Technician's Handbook*. 2d ed. Norwood, Mass.: Artech House, 2003.

Miller, Gary M. *Modern Electronic Communication*, 6th ed. Paramus, NJ: Prentice Hall, 1998.

WOOD TECHNOLOGISTS

Fragments of veneer and core material sift onto Daren Purgill's desk as he runs his index finger along the broken piece of what was once a tabletop. Across from him sits the customer who owns the now useless tabletop.

"We just can't figure out what went wrong," the customer moans. "Our engineers swore that the table we built could support that entire computer system." He shakes his head. "But something went haywire and it cost my company a lot of money. Can you help?"

"Sure," Daren says, using his hand to sweep the dusty remains of the tabletop into a trash can. "We'll run some tests. We'll analyze the density and type of wood that you should be using and make suggestions. Don't worry. The next time you build that tabletop, it won't bow, it won't bend, and it sure won't break." After the man leaves, Daren begins assembling the support personnel he'll need to find a solution to the customer's problem. He contacts sawmill owners, machine operators, chemists, salespeople, and company presidents.

"It's my job to come up with a product that is cost effective and meets the customer's needs," he says. "I work in a very specialized field—wood technology. To do my job I need both a background in material science and the ability to work well with people."

Definition

Wood technologists determine the best type of wood for specific applications. Those involved with research may analyze the physical, chemical, and biological properties of wood. Others work in production and help evaluate and improve the effectiveness of industrial equipment and processes. Others deal with marketing and sales, management, or administration.

Alternative Job Title

Wood products technicians

High School Subjects

Biology
Chemistry
Mathematics

Personal Skills

Communication/ideas
Technical/scientific

Salary Range

$25,000 to $32,613 to $50,000+

Work Environment

Primarily indoors
Primarily one location

Minimum Educational Level

Bachelor's degree

Certification or Licensing

None available

Outlook

Faster than the average

DOT

040

GOE

N/A

NOC

2112

O*NET-SOC

N/A

What Does a Wood Technologist Do?

Prehistoric people tore branches from trees to create shelters and threw logs onto fires to keep warm. For thousands of years humans have used wood. Today it is the raw material in more than 5,000 different products and remains one of the world's most valuable resources. The job of wood technologists is to improve on wood's traditional uses while finding new ways to take advantage of wood's strength, endurance, and versatility.

Wood technologists understand the scientific properties of wood. Their job is to suggest the safest, most cost-efficient, least time-consuming, and most responsible way of working with this valuable resource. The day-to-day jobs wood technologists do vary a great deal, but they can be grouped into three broad categories: research, production, and marketing.

Research technologists work in labs. They investigate the anatomical, physical, chemical, and mechanical properties of wood. They research the best ways to dry, join, glue, machine, or finish lumber. Depending on the needs of their employers, they may be involved in new product research or in improving existing products. Because they have a thorough knowledge of wood's biological and physical properties, research technologists can test the behavior of wood under many circumstances. They suggest ways to put wood to the best possible use with the least amount of waste.

Other wood technologists are involved in production. This is the most diverse area of wood technology. From start to finish, these people oversee the manufacturing of wood products. Some begin their work right after the loggers cut the trees. They work in timber procurement or as production supervisors in sawmills. Others inventory the volume and quality of logs produced by the sawmills and then work with sales staff to match specific wood types to specific company needs. Other wood technologists, employed by the factories themselves, are more involved with the manufacture of specific products. For instance, they might oversee quality control at a paper mill or advise wooden ship builders on the best way to prevent insect damage. Others are design engineers for log-home builders or production supervisors at plywood mills. Still others help train factory workers in order to increase the value of the item manufactured and eliminate expensive mistakes of both time and material.

Another group of wood technologists specializes in marketing. The forest products industry is complex. Specific technical knowledge is necessary to buy and sell lumber, paper, and other wood products. These wood technologists combine scientific expertise about the physical characteristics of wood with an equal expertise about the business world. They handle customer service questions, make purchases for their companies, and sell wood or wood products to other businesses.

A secondary function of all wood technologists, no matter whether they work in labs, in production, or in sales, is to find ways to manage the resource of wood more efficiently. Wood is a renewable resource, but increasing concern for the environment means that wood technologists must ensure that wood is put to its best possible use. Care must be taken throughout the manufacturing process not to ruin material, let it degrade, or cause waste. For example, old saws used to take big bites out of wood and created lots of sawdust. Wood technologists helped to design a new saw that tears away much less material and creates less sawdust as well.

What Is It Like to Be a Wood Technologist?

Daren Purgill has worked in the product management branch of wood technology for almost seven years. "I work for a company that takes raw materials and manufactures component parts that go into other, similar products. There's a lot to watch out for. Today, for instance, we're making wooden lockers. Each locker has six components and each of those components has five parts. I have to keep them all in sequence so that the locker will go together correctly and meet the needs of the customer."

Daren's daily chores change each time he goes to work. Sometimes he's on the phone with a new customer, quoting manufacturing costs or discussing new products. Other times he handles customer service for regular clients, trying to find a better application for the products they're already using. For instance, a client who makes bridge timbers may call and report that the product decayed while in the field. The timber rotted and fell apart and the client wants to know why. "My job is to apply wood science to the problem and show the customer how to fix it."

My job is to apply wood science to the problem and show the customer how to fix it.

Sometimes he works on the computer, helping to install a new system that is tailored to the needs of his company. Or he might be on the shop floor, working with the crew and helping expedite orders. He constantly interacts with different people, from machine operators to corporate CEOs.

Daren spends a lot of time on the phone or in meetings. Once or twice a month he travels to meet with customers or suppliers. Other wood technologists, especially those involved in marketing, may travel even more frequently. Some may be gone for a week or more each month, while some salespeople (especially those working on a commission basis) may be on the road almost every day.

Chris Olson, another wood technologist, begins his day at the sawmill. Wearing boots and a heavy

Lingo to Learn

Dimensioned lumber Wood that has been measured and cut in three ways: by thickness, width, and length.

Grain The stratification of the wood fibers in a piece of wood.

Green sale Lumber purchased before its surface has been finished in any way.

Hardwood Heavy timber with compact texture, very desirable for use in the forest products industry.

Kiln Large furnace used to dry lumber.

Plywood laminate Different types of wood cut in very thin sheets and glued with opposing grains together. The resulting solid piece is stronger than a single sheet of wood. The higher-grade types are encased in a piece of veneer.

Pressed wood Wood chips, sawdust, and glue pressed together under heat to make a very strong, dense board.

Pulp A material prepared by chemical or mechanical means from various materials, such as wood or rags, for use in making paper and cellulose products.

Softwood Lighter, easily cut wood, but less desirable for use in the forest products industry.

Veneer Very thin, flexible piece of high quality wood, used as a finish to cover poorer quality wood.

Wood fiber Any of various fibers in xylem.

Xylem Complex tissue in the vascular system of higher plants, that along with vessels and wood fibers conducts water and dissolved minerals, stores food for the plant, and chiefly constitutes the woody element of the plant.

winter coat, he takes inventory of what types of logs are on hand. Later, back at the office, he schedules which logs should be cut, based on the volume of each species and on their quality. Logs are a perishable item, and Chris wants to use them while they are in prime condition. He consults with the sales department to see what wood their clients are asking for and adds that information to his scheduling plan.

Calculating profit and loss for each load of lumber is another of Chris's job functions. Every log has a certain value. Top grade is labeled number one value; lower grade is number five. Lumber values can be altered, depending on how smoothly production takes place. If people know what they're doing and do a good job, the company makes money on the operation. But if someone messes up, it costs the company. For instance, if wood is kiln-dried too quickly, the cell walls collapse; if the wood is not dried fast enough, it begins to mold. Either way the resource is lost. Thus another of Chris's functions is to set up training so that all company employees do the best job possible. That way, natural resources are conserved and company profits remain high.

Many wood technologists are involved with helping to manage forest resources wisely. "Sustaining biodiversity is important," Chris says. "Not just for the benefit of the trees and the wood industry, but for all living creatures." Part of his job is to oversee production so that his company maintains proper environmental standards. In the future there may be international standards of forest management to follow as well.

Do I Have What It Takes to Be a Wood Technologist?

"Wood technologists are like detectives," says Dr. Bob Rice, professor of Wood Science and Technology at the University of Maine. "Someone may come to you and say that there's a problem somewhere in the manufacturing plant. Something's not working right and you have to discover what it is." Part of a wood technologist's job is to uncover the mystery of how wood works. The other part of the job is to apply what they've learned.

Just like a good detective, good wood technologists are curious and persistent. They also like dealing with wood as a material. Perhaps they built shelves, refinished furniture, or worked construction when they were younger. One day, they wondered why one wooden house withstood a windstorm better than another or why one roof held the weight of a heavy snowstorm while another didn't. This type of hands-on experience and interest

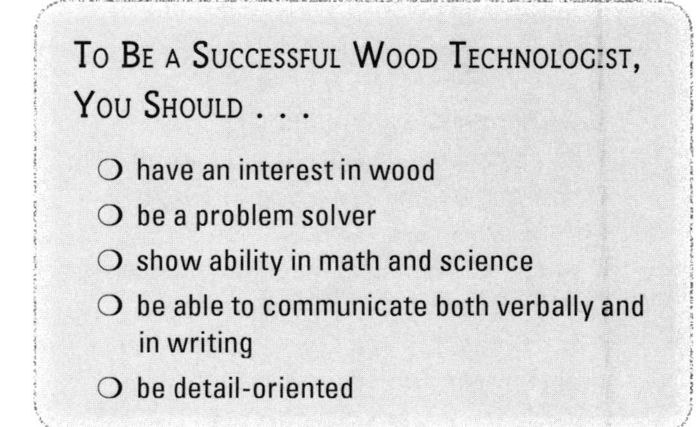

To Be a Successful Wood Technologist, You Should . . .

- have an interest in wood
- be a problem solver
- show ability in math and science
- be able to communicate both verbally and in writing
- be detail-oriented

in the physical properties of wood help make a good wood technologist.

"Wood technologists are not lab loners," Bob says. "They are outgoing and enjoy working with people. They communicate well, both in person and through writing. They enjoy working as part of a group, and as they advance, are able to direct the work of other people on their team."

"Since wood is a commodity," Daren adds, "that means that it's traded. Negotiation skills are essential for wood technologists involved in sales and production."

You need not be a mathematician to be a wood technologist, but you should enjoy the logic of math and be able to handle subjects such as calculus and physics. An aptitude for science, including chemistry and engineering, is also important.

Daren notes that wood technologists need an eye for detail. "You need to be thorough," he says. "If you miss one little technical specification, the product can fail and cost your company lots of money and employee effort."

Wood technologists are interested in conservation issues. Their job helps extend the life of the wood products already in use and designs additional products that will last a long time. By helping to make the best possible wood products, wood technologists save extra trees from being cut and help manage renewable natural resources.

"One thing to keep in mind about the field of wood technology," Daren cautions, "is that not every city has a wood manufacturing company. You may be limited to living in certain areas of the country. The job market also fluctuates according to the availability of timber and according to production costs.

"Still, what I like best about wood technology," Daren says, "is that I'm able to make decisions based on my judgments and knowledge. I'm able to say, 'I learned this and I'm using it.' There's a lot of decision-making freedom in my job. You're the paper signer; you're the one making the decision. You gain a lot of respect when you take charge like that."

How Do I Become a Wood Technologist?

Ever since he was seven years old, Chris Olson knew that he wanted to work in forestry. At first he thought he would like to be a forest ranger, but in college he discovered that those jobs were hard to come by and didn't pay much. "I knew I wanted to work with a renewable resource," he says, "and be with people who enjoyed nature." So he focused his bachelor's degree on urban forestry and forest management. Then he added a master's degree in finance. "Business and wood technology courses go together well," he says. "Now my job is to take the logs directly from the sawmill and deal with the specifics of production and timber quality. I use both my degrees every day."

EDUCATION

High School

High school classes in biology, chemistry, mathematics, drafting, physics, computers, and English are important. Three years of math, especially during the senior year, are essential. Be sure to fulfill the entrance requirements of the college or university you want to attend.

Postsecondary Training

Wood technologists must have a bachelor's degree. Many college and university programs are located within the agriculture, forestry, engineering, or natural resources departments.

Sometimes wood technologists combine their degree program with additional work in chemistry, biology, physics, mechanical engineering, materials science, and business administration. However, training for wood technologists is less concentrated on science and engineering than is training for wood scientists, a related profession. Course work for both wood technologists and wood scientists

Advancement Possibilities

Wood scientists explore the chemical, biological, and physical properties of different woods, searching for ways to grow, process, and use wood. Their goal is to make wood last longer and function better. They also experiment with new wood products and processing methods that increase wood's resistance to wear, fire, fungi, decay, and insects.

Lumber/forest products sales managers supervise other salespeople working for a lumber supply or forest products company. They develop pricing lists and marketing strategy and determine inventory, based on their analysis of market demand for particular wood or wood products.

Lumber/forest products manufacturers own and manage their lumber supply or forest products companies. Depending on the type of company—wood or forest products—manufacturers oversee every aspect of the company, including research, production, marketing, and sales, as well as the day-to-day operational concerns, such as accounting and employee benefits.

requires more science than does course work for foresters.

Wood technologists may obtain both a master's degree and a Ph.D., but these are not necessary to enter the field if one works in production or marketing. For wood technologists working in research and development, however, advanced degrees are usually required.

SCHOLARSHIPS AND GRANTS

Most colleges and universities offer general scholarships. Individual schools may have scholarships or grants reserved specifically for wood technology students. Contact the individual school for more information. In addition, the Forest Products Society offers student scholarships through their regional groups and various volunteer organizations (see "How Do I learn More?").

INTERNSHIPS AND VOLUNTEERSHIPS

Industry offers some internships for college students. These valuable hands-on experiences inform students about the day-to-day responsibilities of work as a wood technologist. A typical internship might be working for a lumber wholesaler. You learn how lumber is bundled, how wood is moved from one place to another, how scheduling is done, and what paperwork is involved. "By participating in routine work," Daren says, "interns learn about the industry from the ground up. When I went to work as a wood technologist, I understood the nature of the work involved because I'd interned. Right away I was able to accurately answer customer questions."

Wood technology students interested in research may have the opportunity to work as lab assistants for their college professors. Research assistants usually receive part or all of their tuition as well as a stipend in exchange for their help in the lab.

Who Will Hire Me?

Wood technology requires a narrowly focused education that is then applied to a broad job market. Like the majority of graduates, Chris found employment in the huge forest products industry, one of the nation's largest.

The lumber business—pulp and paper processors, furniture and cabinetry manufacturers, stain and coating finishers, and others—make up the forest products industry. Chris worked for a lumber company and then for a veneer producer before he landed his current job at Midwest Hardwood in Minnetonka, Minnesota. Graduates in this field have many opportunities. Depending on their area of specialization, they may work for business, government, or research institutions, such as universities.

Each spring, the Forest Products Society publishes a directory of graduating students that is made available to potential employers. While they have no job referral service, FPS does offer a free classified ad for each student in its newsletter (see "How Do I learn More?" for contact information).

Where Can I Go from Here?

"I want to move up to more and more managerial positions in both sales and customer service," Daren says. "Someday I'd like to be responsible for a complete product line and oversee an entire project like the manufacture of an X-ray table. From start to finish, I'd manage sales, the ups and downs of production, parts purchasing, and personnel. What a challenge!"

Because the field is so varied, there is no typical career path for wood technologists. Those who specialize in sales and marketing, like Daren, often start their careers as salespeople for lumber brokers. They know wood species and cargo loads, and they work on commission. They move up from salesperson or sales representative to sales manager.

While earning an advanced degree such as a master's or a Ph.D. may be useful for those working in research positions, wood technologists working in manufacturing find that adding a degree in business makes them more useful employees.

The dream of many wood technologists, whether they work in marketing, production, or research, is to someday own their own company. The success of wood technology graduates, especially those who decide to build their own business, depends not only on their technical skills but also on their ability to communicate with other people. "You have to be able to sell yourself," Daren says, "and work with other people from the machine operator on the plant floor to the president of another organization."

What Are the Salary Ranges?

Experience, level of education, employer, and work performed determine the salary ranges for wood technologists. Pay is similar to that of engineering graduates. According to the Web site Salary.com, wood technologists nationwide made an average salary of $32,613 in 2005. Salaries ranged from less than $25,000 at the entry level to more than $37,000 for wood technologists with more experience. With advanced education and years of experience in the field, wood technologists can earn more than $50,000 a year.

Generally, wood technologists receive standard benefits, including health insurance, pension plans, and paid vacations. Wood technologists who own their own companies must provide these benefits for themselves.

What Is the Job Outlook?

"Job opportunities are the biggest plus for this field," says Dr. Bob Rice of the University of Maine. "There are around four to six wood technology jobs available for every student with a bachelor's in wood science. Some companies call us and place a standing order for our students even before they graduate."

Employers will continue to ask for people who have mastery over a subject, combined with a broad-based, general education. As more and more companies decentralize their operations, the need for ever more skilled and specialized workers such as wood technologists increases. "Our program and many others are offering programs that combine the technical aspects of wood science with the business aspects," says Bob. "This prepares students who want to graduate and eventually run their own businesses."

Regardless of demand for their services, wood technologists who work directly in the timber industry are tied to its market fluctuations. When lumber costs go up too much, productivity drops. Plants may even be shut down immediately and jobs lost. Wood technology is a relatively new field, one in which product innovation and scientific breakthroughs occur fairly frequently. In addition, environmental concerns put pressure on industry to come up with more and better ways of using wood. This increases opportunities for wood technologists since they can help with research and development, product management, and resource conservation.

How Do I Learn More?

PROFESSIONAL ORGANIZATIONS

For information about student chapters and technical interest groups within this professional association:

Forest Products Society
2801 Marshall Court
Madison, WI 53705
608-231-1361
info@forestprod.org
http://www.forestprod.org

For industry information, contact

National Hardwood Lumber Association
6830 Raleigh-Lagrange Road
Memphis, TN 38184
901-377-1818
info2@nhla.org
http://www.natlhardwood.org

For career and education information, contact

Society of American Foresters
5400 Grosvenor Lane
Bethesda, MD 20814
301-897-8720
http://www.safnet.org

For information about careers in forest products, contact

Society of Wood Science and Technology
One Gifford Pinchot Drive
Madison, WI 53726
608-231-9347
http://www.swst.org

BIBLIOGRAPHY

The following is a sampling of materials relating to the professional concerns and development of wood technologists:

Bishop, Peter. *100 Woods: A Guide to Popular Timbers of the World*. Wiltshire, U.K.: Crowood Press, 1999.

Sjostrom, Ero. *Wood Chemistry: Fundamentals and Applications*. 2d ed. San Diego: Academic Press, 1993.

Walker, Aidan, Nick Gibbs, Lucinda Leech, Bill Lincoln, and Jane Marshall. *Encyclopedia of Wood*. Rev. ed. New York: Checkmark Books, 2005.

CHAPTER TITLES INDEXED BY THE *DICTIONARY OF OCCUPATIONAL TITLES (DOT)*

CHAPTER TITLES INDEXED BY THE *GUIDE FOR OCCUPATIONAL EXPLORATION* (GOE)

14: Medical and health services

14.02.01: Medicine and surgery

14.03.01: Dentistry

14.04.01: Health specialists

14.05.01: Medical technology

14.06.01: Medical therapy

14.07.01: Patient care and assistance

14.08.01: Health protection and promotion

CHAPTER TITLES INDEXED BY THE NATIONAL OCCUPATIONAL CLASSIFICATION SYSTEM (NOC)

CHAPTER TITLES INDEXED BY THE OCCUPATIONAL INFORMATION NETWORK (O*NET) - STANDARD OCCUPATIONAL CLASSIFICATION (SOC) SYSTEM

JOB TITLE INDEX

Page numbers in **bold** indicate major treatment of a topic.

A

D

E

F

G

H

Q

R

S

U

V

W

X

Y

Z